Studies in Art, Heritage, Law and the Market

Volume 9

The book series *Studies in Art, Heritage, Law and the Market* provides an international and interdisciplinary forum for volumes that

- investigate legal, economic, and policy developments related to arts, heritage, and intellectual property;
- critically assess how and for whom art and heritage values come about;
- promote novel forms of user engagement, participatory presentations, and digitalization of arts and heritage;
- examine the processes that transform cultural objects and practices into arts and heritage; and
- highlight new approaches in preservation and conservation science.

The series addresses a need for research and practice in the fields of art, culture, conservation, and heritage including a focus on legal and economic aspects. It deals with complex issues such as questions of authenticity and provenance; forgery and falsification; the illicit trade, restitution, and return of cultural objects; the changing roles of museums; the roles of experts and expertise; and the ethics of the art market.

Renée van de Vall • Vivian van Saaze
Editors

Conservation of Contemporary Art

Bridging the Gap Between Theory and Practice

Springer

Editors
Renée van de Vall
Faculty of Arts and Social Sciences
Maastricht University
Maastricht, The Netherlands

Vivian van Saaze
Faculty of Arts & Social Sciences
Maastricht University
Maastricht, The Netherlands

ISSN 2524-7425 ISSN 2524-7433 (electronic)
Studies in Art, Heritage, Law and the Market
ISBN 978-3-031-42356-7 ISBN 978-3-031-42357-4 (eBook)
https://doi.org/10.1007/978-3-031-42357-4

This work was supported by Maastricht University, Faculty of Arts and Social Sciences

This Springer imprint is published by the registered company Springer Nature Switzerland AG
The registered company address is: Gewerbestrasse 11, 6330 Cham, Switzerland

Paper in this product is recyclable.

Acknowledgements

This publication has been created within the project NACCA (2016–2019), which has received funding from the European Union's Horizon 2020 Research and Innovation Programme under the Marie Sklodowska-Curie grant agreement no 642892.

Contents

Introduction to the Volume

Renée van de Vall and Vivian van Saaze

For several decades, the conservation of contemporary art has constituted a dynamic field of research and reflection. At first, in the 1990s, this research field consisted primarily of conservation professionals working in or with museums and other heritage organizations. In those years, the condition of many experimental artworks dating from the 1960s and 1970s in museum collections became a concern, while conservators were often at a loss as to what to do with them. Organic materials used in sculptures or installations, like fat, chocolate or wax, were prone to decay; plastics became brittle or discoloured; media devices which grew technologically outdated would soon prove difficult to repair. Conservation of these works often meant intervening in the original materials to a degree that was difficult to justify in terms of prevalent conservation ethics. Conceptual, site specific and performance artworks complicated the focus of conservation efforts on the preservation of a material object in various ways. As a result, practical conservation problems called for technical and theoretical research and reflection, while, in turn, technical and theoretical research and reflection made it possible to frame practical problems of conservation in new ways.

In the Netherlands, the scandal around the restoration of Barnett Newman's *Who's Afraid of Red, Yellow and Blue III* and a discussion about the remaking of a Sol LeWitt *Wall Drawing* in the Kröller-Müller Museum served as important motivations for launching the *Modern Art: Who Cares?* research project (Hummelen and Sillé 1999, p. 14). As part of this project, a theoretical and a practical working group investigated ten non-traditional works of art, such as *Città Irreale* by Mario Merz, *Gismo* by Jean Tinguely and *Still Life of Watermelons* by Piero Gilardi. *Modern Art: Who Cares?* was not the only project, nor the first one, to address the difficulties of modern and contemporary art conservation. More or less at

R. van de Vall (✉) · V. van Saaze
Faculty of Arts and Social Sciences, Maastricht University, Maastricht, The Netherlands
e-mail: r.vandevall@maastrichtuniversity.nl; vivian.vansaaze@maastrichtuniversity.nl

R. van de Vall, V. van Saaze (eds.), *Conservation of Contemporary Art*, Studies in Art, Heritage, Law and the Market 9, https://doi.org/10.1007/978-3-031-42357-4_1

the same time, comparable projects were organized and many more were to follow, such as Tate's conference *From Marble to Chocolate* (1995), the Getty Conservation Institute's conference *Mortality Immortality* (1998) and the Variable Media Initiative's conference *Preserving the Immaterial* (2001).

Based on these initiatives, an international research field emerged, driven initially by a small group of dedicated researchers mainly affiliated with museums, heritage institutions, conservation studios, institutes for professional education and conservation curricula of universities of applied sciences. This group consisted largely of a community of practice (Amin and Roberts 2008) of conservation professionals, while involving fairly few academic scholars. Research was case-oriented, with a focus on individual artworks posing challenges as to their long-term conservation; researchers met in projects, working groups and conferences to exchange approaches, insights, and results. More general research work aimed at the development of models for registration, documentation, and decision-making.

Increasingly, however, more academic researchers and universities became involved as well. This is reflected for instance by the growing number of PhD dissertations devoted to challenges in the conservation of contemporary art, but also by more sustained research collaborations between academic and professional institutions. This development was facilitated by the establishment of national and international research projects initiated by consortia comprising both museums and universities (Laurenson et al. 2022). This volume is a result of one such project, the Marie Skłodowska-Curie Innovative Training Network *New Approaches in the Conservation of Contemporary Art* (*NACCA*).[1]

Central to *NACCA*'s research agenda was the conviction that given the current state of the field, the research already performed and the practical strategies being developed, it was time to take stock of and take a careful look at **conservation practices themselves** as a major factor in (co-) determining which works were being conserved and which were not, and, regarding the first category, what exactly it **is** about these works that is being conserved (cf. van Saaze 2013). The *NACCA* project, in other words, concentrated on the investigation and comparison of practices, defined by Schatzki (2001) as: "embodied, materially mediated arrays of human activity centrally organised around shared practical understanding" (Schatzki 2001, p. 11). The project's main question centred on how the identity, authenticity and values of modern and contemporary artworks are affected by the practices governing their conservation.

This volume consists of a selection of papers from *NACCA*'s final conference held at Maastricht University in March 2019 and several additional, commissioned

[1]The *NACCA* programme (2016-19) was coordinated by the Faculty of Arts and Social Sciences at Maastricht University. In total, fifteen PhD projects are part of the programme, each investigating underexplored aspects of contemporary art conservation. The Marie Skłodowska-Curie Innovative Training Network *NACCA* was funded by the European Union H2020 Programme (H2020-MSCA-ITN-2014) under Grant Agreement n°642892. https://nacca.eu.

chapters.[2] It investigates whether and how theoretical findings and insights can be translated into the daily work practices of conservators in the field, and, vice versa, whether and how the problems and dilemmas encountered in conservation practice find their way into broader research questions and projects. The volume is structured around five topics: (1) Theorizing conservation as a reflective practice; (2) The identity of the art object; (3) Professional roles and identities: Conservators, curators and artists; (4) Documentation and decision-making in theory and practice; and (5) The role of research in the art museum.

1 Theorizing Conservation as a Reflective Practice

The first part of this volume contains two reflections on what it means to study the conservation of works of contemporary art in museums through the lens of practice theory. As explained above, it is vital to examine actual conservation practices as a strategic research site for the identification of problems, strategies and solutions in contemporary art conservation. It is productive to conceive of conservation professionals as "experienced pioneers" (Mesman 2008), active in a scarcely mapped field requiring new kinds of decisions and interventions.

In the past twenty years, important contributions have been made to the development of conservation theory and ethics, including the formulation of practical protocols for modern and contemporary works of art. Many of these contributions emphasize the open, contextual and evolving nature of contemporary artworks and the situated character of conservation-ethical deliberation and decision-making, suggesting that it is in and through reflection on the day-to-day routines, the difficulties and dilemmas encountered on the work floor and the new directions tried out to solve problems, that adequate and shared approaches will eventually emerge. This raises the need for a deeper understanding of how to theorize practices and in particular of how to account for the interdependency of conservation's materiality and its reflexivity.

In a critical discussion with contributions inspired by Actor-Network Theory (Yaneva 2003; van Saaze 2013), Theodor Schatzki provides both a precise definition of what practices are and a fine-grained and differentiated account of the various ways material entities play a role in practices and contribute to social change. Here, Schatzki defines practices as activities "organised by rules, pools of understanding, and teleoaffective structures", thereby taking material entities (unlike ANT) not as part of practices but as intimately connected to them. Artworks and museums, then,

[2]The symposium aimed to strengthen the exchange between theory and practice in the conservation of contemporary art by exploring promising practices (and failures) and by critically questioning its conditions and drawbacks. The symposium was organized in collaboration with the Maastricht Centre for Arts and Culture, Conservation and Heritage (MACCH) and museum the Bonnefanten in Maastricht. In addition to presentations of the fifteen *NACCA* PhD projects, the symposium hosted several keynote lectures, panels, and round tables. https://nacca.eu/conference-2019/.

figure in his account as "components of material arrangements, constituting settings in which practices proceed." Schatzki distinguishes five types of relation between practices and material arrangements: causality, prefiguration, constitution, anchoring/institution and intelligibility. The second part of his chapter focuses on the contribution of artworks to social change. Distinguishing four main ways in which the material world can be responsible for change—bringing about, inducing, mediating and prefiguring—Schatzki argues (in contrast to Domínguez Rubio 2014) that works of art only make a very small *direct* contribution to social change, and that art is rather a conserving force in society. Their *indirect* contribution to social change, however, can be considerable, through changes in cultural forms and in people's perceptions, thoughts and motivations.

An important "gap" between conservation theory and ethics on the one hand and conservation practice on the other is that theory and ethics tend to generalize, whereas professional research into conservation questions tends to focus on individual case studies. The chapter by Renée van de Vall argues that the professional field has developed reflexive, "middle-ranging" practices of ethical deliberation that diminish the distance between the individual, empirical conservation case and the abstract and general guidelines or rules of conservation theory and ethics. She investigates a process of deliberation about the conservation of a contemporary artwork, Joost Conijn's *Hout Auto*, organized in the form of two "Platform meetings" by the Dutch Foundation for the Conservation of Contemporary Art (SBMK). Van de Vall's analysis of these discussions shows how this middle-ranging ethical work proceeds through a combination of various, theoretically contrasting deliberative techniques and suggests that the kind of ethics at work in the practice of conservation of contemporary artworks may be fruitfully understood in terms of posthumanist care ethics.

2 The Identity of the Art Object

Part 2 investigates the kind of "thing" conservators of contemporary art try hard to care for. From the start, the inadequacy of conventional ("scientific" or "modern") conservation guidelines to address contemporary works of art has been explained in terms of the latter's distinctive constitution. Although still thought of as objects, they were defined by conceptual or immaterial properties, rather than material ones. A gamechanger in the discussion about what made contemporary art different was Pip Laurenson's (2006) paper "Authenticity, Change and Loss in the Conservation of Time-Based Media Installations." Using Nelson Goodman's distinctions between autographic and allographic arts and between one-stage and two-stage arts, Laurenson proposed to think differently about the ontology of time-based media installations and installations in general: not primarily as a kind of object, like a sculpture, but more like a performed event, such as a theatre play or music. Rather than being tied to an authentic material entity which should be preserved in its original state, she defined installations by instructions stipulating their "work-defining properties", and they can therefore be re-executed time and again, in the same way as theatre plays and symphonies are being re-performed according to their scripts or scores, without losing their identity. Laurenson's proposal has been widely used, amended and criticized (e.g., Fiske 2009; Caianiello 2013; Phillips 2015; van de Vall 2015, 2022; Hölling 2017), and it also strongly resonates in the contributions to this part.

Brian Castriota's chapter aims to go a step further in decentring the artwork's ontology. Drawing on previous comments on Laurenson's paper and on poststructuralist/deconstructivist theorists in the wake of Derrida, Deleuze and Butler, Castriota challenges the idea of a single, fixed identity for works of contemporary art, whether secured by preserving an original, or preferred, material state or by a set of instructions. He questions the validity of the requirement for conservators to comply with a score by pointing at works that keep changing beyond the variability allowed by the score: works may continue to develop and be variously interpreted by different audiences and stakeholders. Instead, he conceives of works of art as potentially having multiple and evolving "centres", while the task of conservation is not to protect a singular identity but to safeguard the conditions that allow it to continue evolving and becoming.

Two contributions challenge the specificity of contemporary art. Cybele Tom's chapter argues that supposedly specific ontological characteristics of contemporary art, like variability and context-relatedness, can equally be ascribed to other heritage objects such as relics and religious statues. Rather than positing a fundamental difference between contemporary art and old art, she proposes to adopt an alternative, contemporizing care paradigm for both. Claudia Roeck shows how in spite of the seeming contrasts between the immateriality of internet-based artworks and the materiality of built heritage, the work-defining properties of both can be fruitfully compared. She uses this comparison to demonstrate how principles for the conservation of built heritage can be applied to conservation of internet art—including its preservation and presentation as a well-maintained ruin; but she also shows how built heritage conservation can benefit from notions like "reinterpretation", currently used in media art conservation.

Part 2 ends with a contribution by Marina Valle Noronha, who proposes to turn around the conventional notions of time that are foundational for museum collections and policies. Museums try to preserve artworks, in the present, as if they were in a supposedly initial (hence past) state in order to transmit them in an unaltered state to the future. But what do past, present and future mean? She uses Tristan Garcia's "flat ontology" as a frame to rethink these notions, which are constitutive for traditional museum collection and conservation practices, in terms of intensities of presence. In those terms, the present is a maximum of possible presence, the past is relatively present and the future is the maximum of absence. Rather than considering a presently disintegrated work of art (her example is *Two Cones* by Naum Gabo) as a total loss for an imagined but actually absent future (compared with its initial yet past state), the museum should accept its current presence together with its past yet still relatively present initial state and in combination with all other objects—replicas, re-interpretations—as a complex artwork family.

3 Professional Roles and Identities: Conservators, Curators and Artists

The care for and management of contemporary art as future European cultural heritage are in need of a fundamental rethinking of traditional professional expertise and roles. The traditional distinction between the professional roles of conservators, responsible for the material integrity and condition of artworks, and curators, responsible for the intellectual care for artworks, tends to become less relevant: conservators have to engage with art-historical and art-theoretical questions and curators with the future condition of the work. Both types of professionals need to be able to connect different kinds of scientific and technical expertise and relate conservation issues to the broader fields of art management, care and cultural policy. Moreover, there is an increasing awareness that museums need to adapt their infrastructures and go outside their institutions to collaborate with stakeholders—such as artists and their estates; technicians, programmers, and the public; and external experts—to care for works of art (Laurenson and Van Saaze 2014; van de Leemput and van Lente 2022; Goldie-Scot 2023). The challenge for conservators thus shifts from caring for the *material artwork* to maintaining the *ecologies* that support the perpetuation of the artwork. The contributions in this section investigate the challenges and opportunities of shifting boundaries between conservators, curators, artists and the broader "network of care" (Dekker 2018).

Rita Macedo addresses the professional identity of the contemporary art conservators in a museum context and analyses how practitioners think they are seen by their colleagues and audience members, and how they see themselves in their profession concerning their values, beliefs, the functions performed and the perceived relationships with colleagues. Drawing on a literature study and a large body of interviews, the chapter offers insight into the identity of the conservation professionals and their reported invisibility to colleagues and the public. Macedo argues that while some of the factors that negatively influence the conservator's self-perception come from beliefs and stereotypes formed along the construction of the professional identity, others are consolidated and perpetuated in the context of the museum, where these identities do not seem to have room for transformation or renegotiation through professional agency.

The following two contributions provide reflections from contemporary art conservators on their own working practices within the museum. Sanneke Stigter advocates that such an autoethnographic approach helps conservators to gain a better understanding of the shaping of an artwork's physical form, while also laying bare the conservator's personal bias as revealing traits of the profession. To illustrate the value of such an approach for conservation, she reflects on her own personal testimonies of encounters with artworks from the 1960s through the 1980s. Scrutinizing the histories of these artworks, she furthermore demonstrates that although conceptual artists set out to dematerialize the object in art, the importance of the materials and techniques used should not be underestimated. This insight, according to Stigter, has repercussions for the way conservators and curators should engage with conceptual artworks.

Maike Grün reflects on her own conservation practice by investigating her role and decision-making in the reinstallation of Thomas Hirschhorn's room installation *Doppelgarage* (2002) in the Pinakothek der Moderne, Munich, Germany. The decision to work from documentation of previous iterations, rather than involving the artist in the reinstallation process, had several consequences that provide insight into potential tensions between curators, conservators and artists. In this instance, the artist reacted adversely to the reinstallation, and this led to unexpected changes in the roles of the actors involved.

In the last section of this chapter, Anna Schäffler reflects on her experience of working for the estate of German conceptual artist Anna Oppermann. The chapter argues that the care for the legacy of contemporary artists requires new structural models for conservation and preservation and may lead to a radical shift of western memory culture. Schäffler sketches a future of decentralized memory organization in which both private actors and civil society become significant stake- and memory holders for contemporary art.

4 Documentation and Decision-Making in Theory and Practice

In contemporary art, the idea that an artwork is a finished and self-sustaining end product made by the artist alone has given way to a more open-ended and dynamic conception of the work's modes of existence. As we have seen in the previous sections of this volume, installation, multi-media and performance artworks may vary considerably from one iteration to the next, depending on the context of their execution, the practitioners involved and their reception by different audiences. We already mentioned the importance of Pip Laurenson's proposal (Laurenson 2006) to conceive the ontology of time-based installations, and installation art in general, as defined by a score or script that can be performed in various ways rather than by their original materiality. Subsequent responses to Laurenson's article (for an overview see Brian Castriota's contribution to this volume), including work by Laurenson herself (e.g., Laurenson 2016), commented on and further developed this notion, pointing to the changeability of not only "performances" but also "scores", and foregrounding the open-endedness of artworks' "unfolding" as epistemic objects.

These theoretical developments put a lot of emphasis on the gathering, documenting, and archiving of information about the processes of production and reproduction constituting contemporary artworks. Taking care of these works depends on taking care of the various kinds of knowledge involved in these processes, to such a degree that it has become difficult, and perhaps no longer productive, to draw sharp distinctions between the work proper and the information about it. This has been argued for instance by Hanna Hölling, who proposes to think about works of art *as* archives, an archive being "not only a physical repository of documents, files and leftovers, but also an intangible, non-physical realm of tacit knowledge and memory in an ever-enduring state of organization and expansion," a dynamic entity from which artworks are actualized and to which they contribute (Hölling 2017, p. 260).

If Hölling's proposal may be radical, the recognition that documentation constitutes the core of the identity of works of contemporary art is widespread. What is emphasized in theory, however, is not always easy to implement in practice, due to a lack of institutional resources, appropriate infrastructures, adequate procedures and working routines. The contributions of this section all scrutinize recent practices developed by museums and other institutions that have experimented with the organization of their collections and archives, with the engagement of networks of collaborators and audiences, and with sharing experience and knowledge within and across institutions. The final chapter demonstrates how the changed understanding of the identity of the work has not only led to a changed understanding of the role of documentation, but also of conservation decision-making, necessitating a revision of the well-known SBMK Decision-Making Model Contemporary Art.[3]

Gabriella Giannachi addresses the role of the audience in the design, experience and documentation of contemporary art. Her contribution reflects a change in the theoretical understanding of contemporary art, from an *ontological* conception of artworks as objects or events to an *epistemic* conception of artworks as sets of knowledge-producing processes and practices. It is important, she emphasizes, to document not only the canonical, but also the participants' accounts of the trajectories of such processes and practices. Four case studies of mixed media artworks—Blast Theory's *Day of the Figurines* (2006) and *Rider Spoke* (2007), a research project, *Performance at Tate* (2014–2016), and a prototype platform, *The Cartography Project* (2016)—illustrate the importance and the challenges of capturing, organizing and keeping audience-generated documentations updated.

Dušan Barok addresses the changing conditions for sharing knowledge and documentation across institutions. By investigating why the contributions to the once widely used INCCA database for conservation documentation decreased dramatically after 2011, he is able to sort out some of the main factors responsible for both its success and its decline. Part of the explanation lies in the tabular structure of the database and the availability of metadata only where information needs to remain confidential. There were also external developments, however, that made an inter-institutional, over-all reference catalogue less relevant, such as diversification of the field into specializations, changing EU funding policies, and a shift in orientation of dissemination formats, from distributing data among practitioner-researchers towards more narrative-based scholarly research published in academic journals.

Aga Wielocha's chapter in this section challenges the separation of museum collections, which comprise art objects, from museum archives, which contain documents. Drawing on concepts from information science, Wielocha proposes to

[3] https://www.sbmk.nl/en/tool/decision-makingmodel.

afford equal importance to art objects and documents in a museum's collection. She illustrates the feasibility of her proposal by two examples of institutions that have revised the traditional separation of collection and archive and the interrelated classification principles: the Museu d'Art Contemporani de Barcelona and the Van Abbemuseum in Eindhoven. In her conclusion, Wielocha rephrases Hölling's concept of the artwork as an archive by referring to the artwork as an "anarchive", adding the freedom to adjust its organization according to the needs of a particular artwork.

In the last chapter of this section, Julia Giebeler, Gunnar Heydenreich and Andrea Sartorius present their 2019 revision of the SBMK Decision-Making Model Contemporary Art (1999) and test it for conservation and presentation of the political environment *Thermoelectronic Chewing Gum* (1970) by Wolf Vostell. The 1999 SBMK model still assumed the possibility to stipulate an original or ideal state of an artwork, which could be used as a benchmark to identify discrepancies between the current state and its meaning. Since then, the recognition of the complex trajectory and evolving character of many contemporary artworks and the diverging perspectives of different stakeholders involved in their reiteration has led to a more dynamic understanding of the decision-making process. The 2019 revision of the Decision-Making Model aims to incorporate this understanding. The authors describe the step-by-step use of the revised model on Vostell's environment, and they conclude that the model indeed serves to structure complex decision-making processes, to document the various opinions held by the stakeholders and to contextualize and add transparency to their interpretations.

5 The Role of Research in the Art Museum

In the 2022 approved new ICOM definition, the term "research" figures prominently as the first museum function mentioned, presenting research as a primary responsibility of today's museum. At the same time, what constitutes research in the art museum and what is considered appropriate research continues to be subject to heated debate as well as to be in transition (Pringle 2019). As mentioned in the first section, in this volume we consider reflection on practices an innovative theoretical way to understand the conservation challenges presented by contemporary art. In line with Emily Pringle's influential *Rethinking Research in the Art Museum* (2019), museum practices may be considered forms of research in their own right. "Locating museum professionals' practice as research gives space for practitioners to ask questions, which are explored through a process of enquiry, and generate new insights that go out into the world. It provides a framework that allows for experimentation, but also promotes thoughtful programming and embedded reflection." (Pringle 2019, p. 70).

In the wake of these emerging reflective practices, conservators are increasingly drawing on ethnographic research methods to study actual, day-to-day, conservation practices entangled in larger networks of care. In the same vein, we see an increase in academic researchers from backgrounds as diverse as sociology, museum studies, philosophy and conservation theory, engaging with conservation practices through ethnographic research. Methodologically, this research in, of and with museums ranges from interviews to auto-ethnography, embedded research, participant observation and "immersed participation", to use a term of Puig de la Bellacasa (2017). Besides an interest in conducting and reflecting on research in the museum, the contributors to this section share an understanding of research as a potential avenue for revisiting existing care practices and forging institutional change.

In the first contribution to this section, Louise Lawson, Duncan Harvey, Ana Ribeiro and Hélia Marçal trace the research process and development of Tate's *Strategy for the Documentation and Conservation of Performance Art*. After discussing the history of how since 2005 performance art has entered museum collections, they discuss the collaborative work processes in Tate's Conservation Department and analyse the documentation and conservation of performance-based art as knowledge-making activities. The aim of the chapter is twofold: first it explores the intertwinement of theory and practice in the development of the *Strategy*, and, second, it demonstrates how the acquisition and display of performance-based art in the museum also prompts revision of conservation processes and procedures.

If Caitlin Spangler-Bickell also discusses the relations between conservation and display practices, her investigations focus on the importance of the exhibition period for collection care. Because conservators need to turn their skills and energy to preparations for the next exhibition soon after completing work on an installation, Spangler-Bickell puts forward that the exhibition period is an underrepresented biographical phase in conservation—an especially urgent deficiency for works that are fully "activated" only when on display. She therefore argues for expanding the collections care remit to integrate the "front-of-house" with behind-the-scenes conservation practice by making use of "ethnography *for* conservation" during the exhibition life phase. A participant observation study in the gallery space of the interactive exhibition *Take Me (I'm Yours)* at Pirelli Hangar Bicocca illustrates how this methodology may improve practices of collection care.

The contribution by Anke Moerland and Zoë Miller draws on literature from the fields of sociology, art and law to assess the conflicts that occur in relation to the conditions of ownership, access, display and integrity of the artwork. The chapter explores the relationship between artists and museums in terms of trust and control and considers the role that contracts can play to manage expectations of artists and museums, as well as to regulate aspects of the conservation of contemporary artworks currently not addressed by copyright law. Their research in and of the museum shows how legal doctrinal methods may help to explain how copyright law applies to aspects of the conservation of contemporary art, and which provisions contracts could include to address parties' expectations.

The final contribution of this volume provides an encouraging outlook on conservation as reflective care practice. Drawing on Tate's research project on *Reshaping the Collectible: When Artworks Live in the Museum*, Pip Laurenson demonstrates how externally funded research might afford thicker care time to enable an engagement with works that challenge the structures, systems and temporalities of the museum. She introduces the idea of a "timescape" (Adam 1998, 2008) and explores the different temporalities of the contemporary art museum, of works of art and of care practices. With Maria Puig de la Ballacasa, Laurenson argues for the importance of attending to this multitude of temporalities and demonstrates how "making time" has the potential to adjust modes of museum care that are potentially more just and attuned to artistic practices.

To conclude, we would like to reiterate that in this volume we set out to bridge the "gap" between the daily work practices of conservators of contemporary art on the one hand and conservation theory and ethics on the other. Through single and comparative case studies and theoretical reflections, these various contributions together provide fruitful insights on how the identities, authenticities and values of modern and contemporary artworks are affected by the practices governing their conservation, and how we might improve these practices and the institutional contexts in which they are embedded. Our gratitude goes out to the authors of the chapters, for their valuable theoretical insights into the working practices of contemporary art conservation, and for their patience in bringing this book to its readers. We would also like to thank the following people for their invaluable contributions to this volume as production assistant, reviewers, and editors: Talitha Wilmsen, Martha Buskirk, Gunnar Heydenreich, Ysbrand Hummelen, Tatja Scholte, Glenn Wharton, Linnea Semmerling, Hanna Hölling, Ton Brouwers and Laura Hofmann. Last but not least, a special thank you to all who participated in the Marie Sklodowska-Curie Innovative Training Network on *New Approaches in the Conservation of Contemporary Art* (*NACCA*), in particular the former early career researchers (in alphabetical order): Dušan Barok, Brian Castriota, Martha Celma, Iona Goldie Scot, Panda de Haan, Joanna Kiliszek, Sophie Lei, Thomas Markevicius, Zoë Miller, Nina Quabeck, Claudia Roeck, Artemis Rüstau, Caitlin Spangler-Bickell, Maria Theodoraki and Aga Wielocha. What an amazing journey it has been.

References

Adam B (1998) Timescapes of modernity: The environment and invisible hazards. Routledge, London

Adam B (2008) Of timescapes, futurescapes, and timeprints. Paper presented at Lüneburg University, 17 June 2008. https://citeseerx.ist.psu.edu/document?repid=rep1&type=pdf&doi=57c02886201ab5de160be7461638b9c39cb66781. Accessed 29 Jan 2023

Amin A, Roberts J (2008) Knowing in action: beyond communities of practice. Res Policy 37(2): 353–369

Caianiello T (2013) Materializing the Ephemeral. The preservation and presentation of media art installations. In: Buschmann R, Caianiello T (eds) Medienkunst Installationen Erhaltung und Präsentation/Media art installations preservation and presentation. Dieter Reimer Verlag, Berlin & Stiftung imai, Düsseldorf, pp 207–229

Dekker A (2018) Collecting and conserving net art. Moving beyond conventional methods. Routledge, London and New York

Fiske T (2009) White walls: installations, absence, iteration and difference. In: Richmond A, Bracker A (eds) Conservation: principles, dilemmas and uncomfortable truths. Butterworth-Heinemann, Amsterdam, pp 229–240
Goldie-Scot I (forthcoming 2023) An experimental acquisition: Ralph Lemon's *Scaffold Room* (2014) at the Walker. In Hölling HB, Pelta Feldman J, Magnin E (eds) Performance: the ethics and the politics of conservation and care. Vol. 1. Routledge
Hölling HB (2017) Paik's virtual archive. Time, change, and materiality in media art. University of California Press, Oakland
Hummelen Y, Sillé D (eds) (1999) Modern art: who cares? The foundation for the conservation of modern art and The Netherlands Institute for Cultural Heritage, Amsterdam
Laurenson P (2006) Authenticity, Change and Loss in the Conservation of Time-Based Media Installations, Tate Papers, 6 (Autumn 2006). https://www.tate.org.uk/research/tate-papers/06/authenticity-change-and-loss-conservation-of-time-based-media-installations
Laurenson P (2016) Practice as research: Unfolding the objects of contemporary art conservation. Inaugural lecture delivered at Maastricht University, 18 March 2016. Available via YouTube. https://www.youtube.com/watch?v=rEZzsg3OzJg
Laurenson P, van Saaze V (2014) Collecting performance-based art: new challenges and shifting perspectives. In: Remes O, MacCulloch L, Leino M (eds) Performativity in the gallery: staging interactive encounters. Peter Lang, Oxford, pp 27–41
Laurenson P, van Saaze V, van de Vall R (2022) Bridging the gaps between theory and practice through cross-institutional collaboration in the conservation of contemporary art. In: Swinnen A, Kluveld A, van de Vall R (eds) Engaged humanities: rethinking art, culture, and public life. Amsterdam University Press, Amsterdam, pp 271–304
Mesman J (2008) Uncertainty in medical innovation. Experienced pioneers in neonatal care. Palgrave Macmillan
Phillips J (2015) Reporting iterations: a documentation model for time-based media art. Revista de História da Arte 04:168–179
Pringle E (2019) Rethinking research in the art museum. Routledge, London etc
Puig de la Bellacasa M (2017) Matters of care: speculative ethics in more than human worlds. University of Minnesota Press
Schatzki TR (2001) Practice theory. In: Schatzki TR, Knorr Cetina K, von Savigny E (eds) The practice turn in contemporary theory. Routledge, London etc, pp 1–14
Sillé D (1999) Introduction to the project. In: Hummelen IJ, Sillé D (eds) Modern art: who cares? The Foundation for the Conservation of Modern Art and the Netherlands Institute for Cultural Heritage, Amsterdam, pp 14–19
van de Leemput D, van Lente H (2022) Caring for decline: the case of 16mm film artworks of Tacita Dean. In: Koretsky Z, Stegmaier P, Turnheim B, van Lente H (eds) Technologies in decline. Socio-technical approaches to discontinuation and destabilisation. Routledge, London etc, pp 185–199
van de Vall R (2015) The devil and the details: the ontology of contemporary art in conservation theory and practice. Br J Aesthet 55(3):1–18
van de Vall R (2022) Theories of time-based media conservation: from ontologies to ecologies. In: Engel D, Phillips J (eds) Conservation of time-based media art. Routledge, London etc, pp 13–27
van Saaze V (2013) Installation art and the museum. Presentation and conservation of changing artworks. Amsterdam University Press, Amsterdam
Yaneva A (2003) Chalk steps on the museum floor. The "Pulses" of objects in an art installation. J Mater Cult 8(2):169–188

Renée van de Vall is emeritus professor of Art & Media at Maastricht University. Her research focuses on the phenomenology of spectatorship in contemporary art, on processes of globalization of contemporary art and media, and on conservation theory and ethics in the context of contemporary art. She was project leader of various research projects, most recently (2016-2019) of the Marie Sklodowska-Curie Innovative Training Network on *New Approaches in the Conservation of Contemporary Art* (*NACCA*).

Vivian van Saaze is associate professor of Conservation Theory and Museum Studies at Maastricht University and senior specialist in Modern and Contemporary Art at the Cultural Heritage Agency of the Netherlands (RCE). She is involved in several collaborative research projects and acted as interim project leader of the Marie Sklodowska-Curie Innovative Training Network on *New Approaches in the Conservation of Contemporary Art* (*NACCA*).

Part I
Theorizing Conservation as a Reflective Practice

Artworks in Art Museums

Theodore Schatzki

Abstract This essay gives an overview of what is involved in using practices to analyze art in art museums. It begins by discussing the general use of theories of practices in this context, drawing a contrast with actor-network theory. The essay then conceptualizes art and art museums as parts of material arrangements, which people encounter as they carry on certain practices. Topics considered include the polysemy of art works, their contributions to spatiality, the multiple relations that link practices and art works, and the materiality of the works (including the contribution this materiality makes to their identity). A final section examines art works in relation to social change. It argues that, although art works of the sorts found in museums only rarely are directly responsible for social change—art in this regard is a conserving force—, they can importantly contribute indirectly to social change by altering minds.

Keywords Artworks · Museums · Practices · Artworks as material objects · Identity and authenticity of artworks · Artworks and social change

The topic of the present essay is what is involved in approaching contemporary art in art museums through practices. This topic is ultimately motivated by the now pervasive recognition that many features of artworks—like of other entities—depend on the contexts in which artworks occur. The more specific motivation is that in recent years more and more scholars have treated practices as central to the contexts that are pertinent to understanding objects of this or that type. This practice has found its way into studies of contemporary art, art conservation and art museums. For example, van Saaze (2013) claims that objects such as artworks are "constructed" in social practices, but she rues the fact that scholars of art typically overlook practices. Asking what is involved in using practices to analyze art in art museums aims to further this development.

T. Schatzki (✉)
Department of Philosophy, College of Arts and Sciences, University of Kentucky, Lexington, KY, USA
e-mail: schatzki@uky.edu

R. van de Vall, V. van Saaze (eds.), *Conservation of Contemporary Art*, Studies in Art, Heritage, Law and the Market 9, https://doi.org/10.1007/978-3-031-42357-4_2

1 Theories of Practices and Art

Vivian van Saaze advocates a performative approach to artworks and art conservation. According to her approach, conservation is a performance and artworks participate as much as people do in the practices of making and conserving art. Van Saaze draws on Bruno Latour's Actor-Network Theory (ANT), especially its concept of an actant, to conceptualize two things. The first is the participation of artworks in museum practices of collecting and conserving. These artworks and practices mutually shape one another. The second is the practices themselves. Elsewhere I have (e.g., 2002) discussed problems with blanket attributions of agency to nonhumans and noted the absence of any notion of practices in ANT. The closest actor-network theory comes to conceptualizing practices is in highlighting the doings of humans and nonhumans; an ANT practice approach to art and art museums involves following human and nonhuman actors and their doings. This is, however, a rather thin notion of practices. A charitable interpretation is that ANT simply leaves practices unconceptualized. A less charitable reading is that it treats "practices" as just another word for actions or doings, thus with no distinct meaning.

So-called "theories of practices" develop much richer accounts of practices as organized actions. According to this family of accounts, actions are inherently part of larger collections of actions that reflect or realize a common organization. It is this common organization, and the resulting ordering of actions into collections, that differentiates theories of practices from ANT (and from so-called practice-based studies, e.g., Gherardi 2019). Of course, theories of practices differ among themselves about what organizes actions. Bourdieu, for instance, drew together such phenomena as social space, habitus, stakes, strategies and the layouts of settings in conceptualizing what organizes practices. Shove et al. (2012), by contrast, take off from Reckwitz (2002) in holding that blocks of meanings, competences and materials organize practices. My own account claims that practices are organized by rules, pools of understanding and teleoaffective structures.

Another point on which theories of practices diverge is the relationship of material entities to practices. All practice theories recognize the presence of material entities in social life and attend to them both conceptually and in the empirical studies they inform. But a major division among such theories concerns whether material entities are part of practices or instead intimately connected to them. As indicated, for example, Shove et al. treat material entities as one type of element that organizes practices. By contrast, the theories of Bourdieu and myself treat arrangements of material entities as distinct from but intimately connected to practices, constituting settings in which practices proceed.

I will not dwell on these differences in the present context. However, both axes of difference—practice organization and the relationship of materiality to practices—help define what it means to approach art in art museums through practices. Doing this requires recognizing that whatever activities are studied are part of wider arrays of activity organized by common structures: grasping these activities thus requires attention to what organizes them. Approaching art through practices also entails appreciating the material entities involved with them. Works of art—including musical compositions, videos and time media installations—are material entities (see below). They are, as a result, assimilated into theories of practice according to how such theories conceptualize such entities. On my own account, for example, artworks are treated as components of material arrangements. I hasten to add that the fact that artworks are material entities does not entail that that is *all* they are.

To my knowledge, very little has been written in a practice theoretical vein about works of art. Bourdieu (e.g., 1990, 1993, 1996) is the only author who has dedicated substantial pages to the subject (see also Schatzki (2014) on art bundles). The below account of analysing contemporary artworks in art museums through practices uses my own ideas about practices. Doing this means, inter alia, that the actions and practices that need to be taken into account are performed exclusively by human beings and that artworks are part of wider arrangements of material entities that are closely interwoven with practices. As a result, attention must be paid to relations that hold between artwork-embracing arrangements and relevant practices.

2 Approaching Artworks in Art Museums Through Practices

I indicated above that artworks, as material entities, are part of arrangements, amid which practices proceed. An arrangement of entities is simply a set of interrelated material entities as interrelated. Works of art, as material entities, are inevitably components of arrangements. In a museum, for instance, any artwork is part of an arrangement embracing walls, floors, benches, mountings, bases, air, AC and heating systems, people, clothing, grime on shoes, circulating dust and the like. In the museum courtyard, moreover, a work, often a sculpture, might be part of an arrangement embracing trees, grass, gravel walkways, benches, bushes, bugs and people etc. And in the square facing the museum a work could be linked to expanses of pavement, fountains, stone bases, trees, horses, street vendors and musicians, and the like.

All these arrangements constitute settings in which people act. Artworks are no different from other material entities in this regard. Another way they are no different from many other material entities is that they tend to be parts of arrangements of particular sorts. Hung on walls with accessible spaces in front of them is one such type of arrangement. Standing in a room or erected in an enclosed or semi-enclosed outdoors space with places for sitting and paths for moving are two more. Benches, gravel paths, chairs, lights, information plates, people and animals etc. complete the arrangements.

Museal arrangements that include works of art are entwined with particular practices. Museums, for example, evince practices of curation, conservation and security, which hang together with those of management. These practices link with still others that are relevant to examining art in art museums, for example, practices of publicity, art appreciation and cleaning. Sometimes, moreover, artworks are created in museums (e.g., the copy of Bruegel's *Beekeepers* chalked on the floor of the Musée d'art moderne de la ville de Paris described in Yaneva 2003), in which case practices overtly concerned with the making of artworks come into view. Additional practices carried on in a museum include those of parenting, gossiping, planning and, at least in movies, espionage. Every practice just mentioned is or can be important to approaching artworks in art museums through practices. Then, there are all the practices focused on art carried on outside art museums in galleries, in public squares, in living rooms, in offices, on sidewalks, in vacant lots and the like. The focus of the present essay, however, is museums alone. In any event, a researcher must have a capacious sense of the range of practices that might be taken account of when approaching art in art museums through practices. This is true even if one's topic is a conceptual issue about the meaning or identity of a work of art (see below).

When they encounter entities, people, generally speaking, are acting. Entities might be gazed at, observed, watched, looked over, listened to, smelled, felt, touched, thought about, imagined and so on. They can also be used, manipulated, held, tossed up and down, passed to others and the like. Activities of these types are also components of practices: in performing them people carry on particular practices. Many such activities, perceptual ones included, also occur as part of multiple practices. Someone, for instance, might look at or watch something while cooking, while carrying on a conversation, while taking a break from work, while thinking absentmindedly, while taking in art, while guarding a museum room, while wondering whether the works in the room were rightly placed and so on. Finally, these acts, in happening as part of particular practices, are subject to the organizations of these practices. These organizations differ. That for the sake of which watching something is acceptable or prescribed differs among surveillance practices at prisons, surveillance practices at museums, flirting practices among co-workers, spectator practices at sporting events and practices of appreciating art in museums.

The practices, in the enactment of which works of art are encountered, are many. People can look at or bump into artworks in art appreciation practices, brush and vacuum them in cleaning practices, appeal to them in parenting practices, notice them during conversations or when engaged in espionage, and so on. What an artwork is encountered as varies among practices and often is tied to the organizations of these practices or the sorts of activities that compose them. A work of art, moreover, is not always encountered *as* a work of art. This typically occurs, of course, when people are appreciating or installing art; in fact, if someone espies a work of art when carrying out some other practice—say, holding a conversation—and begins to consider it as a work of art, she has likely switched (or is wavering) between appreciating art and conversing. Finally, the range of activities in which artworks are encountered as art depends on the particular works involved and can include activities as varied as studying, looking over, walking around, contemplating, picking up, lifting, moving, dusting, drawing, painting, listening, watching and taking in.

A work of art can have many meanings. Something's meaning is what it is encountered *as* (in a wide sense of encountering that includes making, understanding, and thinking about something). A work of art can have many meanings because the meanings of material entities, artworks included, depend on the activities and practices in which they are encountered. A particular artwork can be something to identify a museum with in publicity, something to conserve, something to draw, something to gaze and marvel at, something that can keep the kids' attention occupied and so on. An artwork does not cease being an artwork when it assumes these other meanings. What's more, it remains one and the same object regardless of how many things it is encountered as—one and the same work of art regardless of how many (additional) meanings it assumes. It is not the case, as Annemarie Mol (2002) claims about tuberculosis, that a given work of art is as many entities—let alone as many artworks—as there are practices in which it is encountered. Rather, it is one entity with multiple meanings, one of which, i.e., artwork, it retains in at least most practices in which it assumes other meanings. The entity's origin and location help explain how this retention works. Note that a similar structure of core plus additional meanings characterizes entities other than art works, for instance, use objects and even sometimes people.

Like other material entities, furthermore, artworks establish spatialities, as part of material arrangements and in conjunction with practices and what people are up to in carrying the practices on. Spatialities are arrays of places and paths through which people move. A place is a place to X, whereas a path is a way from one place to another. A place from which to view art is an obvious example. Another is the paths people take through museum rooms and courtyards, walking, chatting and looking (cf. Ingold 2000). In helping to establish arrays of places and paths, artworks also help institute locales in the sense of Martin Heidegger's (1971) *Orte*: regions where certain activities and patterns of activity are coordinated with arrangements of material entities and happen at places and along paths that these arrangements help establish. Locales are often given names such as street corner, subway car, boardroom, public square, museum gallery, meeting room; the presence of art in them is sometimes enshrined in their names, e.g., the Botticelli Room. Locales also constitute delimited or relatively delimited settings for action. Note that art is typically found in locales and rarely in landscapes, which are expansive visual portions of the world falling away from people (see Schatzki 2010).

Artworks tend to be components of locales of particular types, for example, museums (galleries, offices, function rooms, vacant lots, private homes etc.). Specific constellations of practices and arrangements mark these locales. Yaneva (2003, p. 117) distinguishes between the museum as site and as setting. I am not sure what she means by this distinction in the context of her actor-network analysis of the museum as "a messy world composed of heterogeneous actors with a variable ontology" (*ibid*). I will appropriate, however, the distinction as follows: the museum as site is a constellation of interrelated practices and arrangements as part of which particular events and processes pertaining to art occur, for example, appreciation, curation and conservation. The museum as setting denotes the material arrangements that compose this constellation and the fact that these arrangements constitute settings in which people act and carry on practices. All social formations but the simplest, including museums, are both site and setting: the constellation of practices and arrangements that composes a social formation encompasses social processes, and its constituent material arrangements form settings in which participants enact these practices. Note, incidentally, that Latour and Yaneva's (2008, p. 88) conception of the museum as an ecology in effect treats the museum as just a setting (though it construes the components of this setting as actants).

I mentioned above that practices interweave with arrangements. Exploring this interweaving reveals several notable features of artworks in museums. My comments will concentrate on five types of relation between practices and arrangements: causality, prefiguration, constitution, anchoring/institution and intelligibility.

Causal relations go from practices and the activities that compose them to arrangements and the material entities that compose them—and vice versa. People, for instance, *intervene* into the world, effecting changes there. They set up art installations, clean them, damage them, steal them, cordon them off, build structures that house them and so on. Conversely, material objects, events and processes *induce* people to perform actions. Artworks induce activities such as scrutinizing, looking at, looking over, listening, touching, sighing, admiring, whispering, criticizing, shouting, pausing, hurrying and pondering. Indeed, museums are set up so that these reactions, which modern educated people must consider valuable, can occur; this is why museums typically incorporate generous spaces, spread artworks out, and make them easily accessible experientially. To be sure, intervening in the world and inducing action are different forms of causality. Nonetheless, they are both ways in which entities bear responsibility (see Heidegger 1977) for events and changes in the world.

A second relation between practices and arrangements is prefiguration. Prefiguration is the difference that the present makes to the future. This difference is often conceptualized as enablement and constraint, or the delimitation of possibilities. It actually embraces more. For the present does not just circumscribe what, going forward, is and is not possible, that is, feasible or infeasible. It also qualifies possible ways of continuing as easier or harder, shorter or longer, cheaper or more expensive, more or less time consuming, conforming or daring, permitted or proscribed, and so on in registers that matter or are relevant to people. How feasible actions stack up on these registers differentiates them and determines what people are likely to do. It is clear that material arrangements prefigure people's activities and the practices they carry on. A cell phone, for instance, radically affects the saliencies of different ways of catching up with friends and, as a result, how people likely do so. Similarly, exhibitions of artworks prefigure what teachers, conservators and lovers of art etc. do. Contemporary installation art illustrates this idea well. Art conservators who are responsible for installation pieces today face an array of salient ways of acting different from the one facing conservators who are responsible for old masters. The differences are tied to differences in the artworks involved and in the dilemmas they raise relative to the ends of art conservation practices. Thrown into and projecting different, differently qualified possible actions, what these conservators do can easily differ from what their more traditional colleagues do.

The third type of relation between practices and arrangements is constitution. What I mean by "constitution" is particular material entities or arrangements thereof being essential to particular practices or, vice versa, particular practices being essential to particular entities or arrangements. Horses and horseshoes, for instance, are essential to horseshoeing, just as metal forging practices are essential to horseshoes. As this example suggests, essentiality is not necessity in any strong sense of the term, for example, "required in all possible worlds." It instead amounts to something like "required in the historical circumstances" or "required as things stand or for the time being." In this sense, artworks are essential to practices of art appreciation or art conservation. Note that this proposition, possibly despite appearances, is not a matter of definition. People *could* scrutinize, look over, watch, stroll around, maintain and repair, say, refrigerators in the ways they do works of art. Indeed, they do some of these things when purchasing a fridge. But vis-à-vis artworks these activities compose regular practices, whereas vis-à-vis appliances they are more sporadic and fragmented. Note, further, that this difference between artworks and appliances might not arise from features of these entities taken by themselves. It could instead reflect the arrangements and bundles that these entities are components of. If a refrigerator is put in a museum gallery, visitors, or at least many visitors, will act towards it as they more unthinkingly do towards artworks and even have accompanying "aesthetic experiences." Of course, the arrangements of museums, galleries and homes are not needed for art appreciation practices to occur; an artwork installed on the side of a building or on a busy sidewalk is also likely to induce acts of appreciation. At the same time, I wonder whether artworks can exist in the absence of practices of art appreciation. In any event, a museum constellation evinces a variety of constitutional relations, though some of its bundles—for example, those involving parenting practices—probably lack these.

A fourth relation is anchoring and instituting. I have already discussed this phenomenon. It is material entities and arrangements, in conjunction with practices, anchoring places, and paths for activity and instituting locales. Museum constellations provide clairvoyant examples of this relation. The Botticelli and *One Candle* galleries, the sculpture garden, the gift shop, the entrance and the café—these are all locales, encompassing arrays of places and paths established by the material arrangements that compose them in conjunction with the practices interwoven with these arrangements.

The final relation I will discuss is intelligibility. This relation concerns how entities acquire meaning through bundles. As discussed, a material entity can be many things. A shell, for instance, can be a paperweight. It acquires this meaning, moreover, in certain bundles, for instance, those of curio production or those carried on in home offices, and it can retain this meaning in further bundles, including those of gifting and selling/buying. A shell can also be a weapon or an object of great monetary worth, again, in, or on the background of, certain practices. Of course, a shell's meaning as shell likewise ultimately derives from certain practices, namely, those of biology or those pursued on visits to seashores. Even its meaning as material entity depends on practices, in this case, on the broad range of practices in which it is or can be encountered and dealt with as such an entity. Similarly, an artwork acquires the meaning, artwork, in certain practices, for instance, those of art production, art appreciation, criticism, and the selling and purchasing of art. And once acquired, this meaning can stay with the object as it enters different bundles, for example, those located at corporate offices. Parallel remarks can be made about art museums. A particular built edifice is an art museum, or a museum building, by virtue of practices in which it is encountered and dealt with as a structure that houses or is supposed to house art. Such practices include those of construction, city planning, municipal or state policy-making and budget appropriation, publicity, art curation and management, art appreciation, and so on. The meaning is mobile, too, in the sense that if, say, a city resident taking a visitor on a tour of the city points and says, "That's the museum," the use of the word "museum" in the practices the resident and guests are carrying on picks out the place that houses art, that was approved, planned and constructed, that people visit to see art, and whose staff members diligently display and maintain artworks.

I emphasize that the approach to artworks in art museums outlined here treats these entities as material entities. A material entity is something with a physical-chemical composition. Like museums, artworks—even graphical works and virtual collections available only online—are material objects. In fact, artworks and museums are encountered and dealt with *as* material entities in a wide range of practices—of appreciation, installation, cleaning, conservation, perambulation and the like. However, being material does not make everything about something material. What I mean is that events and processes of nonmaterial sorts can and do befall material entities. Events and processes are material when they occur to entities due to these entities' physical-chemical composition. An example is gravitational attraction and falling, which happen to material entities, including artworks, due to their physical-chemical composition. Many events and processes are not material in this sense. If I pick up a shell off my desk and give it to someone as a gift, the event of gifting is social, not material, even though it involves material objects and states of affairs, for example, the shell and its movement in space. A wide range of nonmaterial events and processes, including performances of actions, befall the material arrangements—including the human bodies and art works—amid which practices are plied. This fact, however, does not impugn the material character of these arrangements. Indeed, materiality lends solidity and stability to bundles and social states of affairs (see Olsen 2010), and chances are that the vast bulk of nonmaterial events and processes would not occur if arrangements were not material. This is true, for example, of most performances of action. If artworks and museums (as well as humans) were not material entities, it would be hard to appreciate, visit, clean, display or maintain them, or even to be concerned with the nature of their identity or authenticity.

Materiality is also intimately connected to the identity (and authenticity) of artworks (cf. Laurenson 2006). Identity is not the same as meaning. Whereas meaning is what something is encountered as, identity is an entity, say, a work of art, being the same entity over time. Identity establishes that there is a single, selfsame entity, which can have multiple meanings. As a general proposition, the identity of any material entity lies in its material persistence. For centuries, moreover, the material persistence of works of art filled out how people understood the identities of these works. Since, however, the beginning of what Walter Benjamin (1968) called the age of technical, or material, reproduction, criticisms of this idea have mounted. It is even sometimes said that the reproducibility of written works such as musical compositions, poems and plays, like the eventual character of musical and theatrical performances, should have problematized the idea earlier. In any event, today certain installation pieces again put pressure on the idea (see, e.g., Laurenson 2006 and van Saaze 2013). In my opinion, however, these developments do not challenge the basic idea that the identity of a work of art is tied to materiality. They simply broaden the range of material states of affairs relevant to identity beyond persistence to include derivability. The production of an artwork still involves a material Ur-work of some sort that is central to the identity (and authenticity) of the work. This holds not just of paintings and sculptures, but also of photographs, movies, videos and poems as well as works of music, theatre and dance. Even the advent of digital production has not fundamentally altered the situation since the initial production of a work on a particular digital device or network of devices can be taken as the original work that other versions copy or reproduce. In short, the identity of a material entity, including a work of art, lies in its material heritage—regardless of the arrangements the entity is part of, the practices in which it is encountered, and the chains of activity and material events and processes that arise from it.

This way of looking at the identity of artworks is temporal and causal in character. It ties the identity of an artwork to either the persistence of or the causal derivation of copies, versions, and descendants from an original product. The derivation can be effected through different processes, including writing by hand, making copies with a printing press, taking pictures, seeing and subsequently recreating, mechanically reproducing, digitally proliferating, or replacing worn, broken or missing parts. The questions that arise concern such matters as the fidelity of copies or processes of reproduction, the ease of producing copies or versions, and the extent of replacement as well as the significance of replaced components: if *One Candle* (see van Saaze 2013) could not have been easily, and in principle more or less perfectly, duplicated, the issue of how many One Candles there are would not have arisen. For the same reasons, the question of whether a copy of the *Mona Lisa* drawn by an artist visiting the Louvre is the *Mona Lisa* does not arise. The materiality of the original work—the first *One Candle* or the *Mona Lisa*—is essential to its being an entity that can be the starting point of subsequent series of events and processes. Indeed, materiality is crucial to identity regardless of how conceptual a work of art is or how much its identity seems to lie in something other than material heritage. Consider, for instance, the digital copying of a movie in the form of DVDs. The original product—ultimately, a gigantic series of 1s and 0s realized as a distribution of atoms—is subject to a causal copying process that results in further distributions of atoms realizing the same series. It is (1) the material distinctness of each of the multiple molecular arrangements that ensures that there are different DVDs and (2) the convertibility of these arrangements into perceptually the same images and sounds that qualifies them as copies of the same movie.

3 Artworks and Social Change

A recent book of mine (Schatzki 2019) explores the contribution of the material world to social change. This contribution is substantial, far greater than is sometimes supposed. In fact, I argue, material entities events and processes constitute one of two major dynamos in social life; the other is chains of activity. The remainder of this essay explores the contributions that artworks make to social change. Their *direct* contribution, I aver, is miniscule. Indeed, art is in this regard a conserving force in society. At the same time, works of art make important *indirect* contributions to change.

Before explaining this, I should state that by "change" I mean significant difference. Some theorists equate change with difference simpliciter. This equation implies that because any event, and even more any process, introduces infinitely many differences into the world, any event or process is responsible for infinitely many changes there. This way of thinking makes it hard to see how anything persists, a dilemma similar to the one Heraclitus created in claiming that no one can step in the same river twice. Persistence, furthermore, is not the absence of difference: nothing persists—remains the same entity—over time without evincing differences (necessarily with earlier states of itself). In particular, all artworks become different over time: paint deteriorates and discolours, hewn stone deteriorates, equipment breaks down and is repaired or replaced, and objects are dropped or knocked over and damaged. But an artwork, despite becoming different, can remain the same work. This suggests that difference cannot simply be equated with change. My intuition is that differences amount to changes only when they are significant, and that whether or not differences are significant depends on what follows from them, what they are juxtaposed with, and who is judging the matter. Incidentally, it follows from the proposition that an artwork can persist despite becoming different that the identity of any work—like that of any material entity—encompasses material differences. Indeed, identity is always identity through difference. This proposition holds equally of a singular work like the *Mona Lisa*, a time media installation or installation piece such as Nam June Paik's *Untitled* (see Domínguez Rubio 2014), and a work such as *One Candle*, copies or versions of which proliferate. The idea of identity over difference also dovetails well with the idea that artworks can have trajectories (van de Vall et al. 2011) or careers (van Saaze 2013). For the idea of a trajectory or career presumes that the same entity exists over time: the fact that an entity has a trajectory or a career indicates that *it* has become different.

I should also say a word about what *social* changes are. Social changes are by definition changes in social phenomena. Social phenomena, moreover, consist in slices and aspects of bundled practices and material arrangements, including constellations thereof (see Schatzki 2002). This analysis implies that social changes, changes in social phenomena, consist in changes to (slices and aspects of) bundles and constellations. Changes in art conservation, for example, consist in changes to the practice-arrangement bundles that art conservation practices are part of, thus, changes in these practices, including in the activities, ends, understandings, tasks and emotions that compose them; changes in the material arrangements to which these practices are bundled, including in the artworks that compose them; and changes in relations between these practices and material arrangements and among these practice-arrangement bundles. Any social change likely embraces a myriad of changes of these sorts.

There are four basic ways the material world can bear responsibility for differences in social life and, thus, for social changes. To begin with, material events and processes can bring about differences and changes, that is, make them happen. Earthquakes, for instance, can wreak destruction on human lives and abodes: they bring about these destructive changes. Wind and rain, moreover, can wear down built structures, just as solar flares can interrupt communications. And infection can spread through a body and cause, that is, bring about disease or even death, just as contamination can ruin stored grain in a barn or granary. Being responsible for changes by bringing them about tallies with what many people think of as causality: states of affairs being made to happen independent of human activity. When the material world makes things happen in social life, the results can be destructive or worse. This is why human beings are forever constructing material structures to block or mitigate such effects.

The second sort of responsibility that the material world can bear for differences and changes in social life is to induce changes in activity, and thus in practices and bundles. Material entities, events and processes can induce all sorts of changes in activity. For example, earthquakes, infection, contamination, weathering and solar flares do not simply bring about changes; they also induce people to change how they act, including which material entities and arrangements thereof they fashion. More generally, over the course of any day almost anyone responds to numerous material events and processes. When a whistling tea kettle induces someone to pick up the kettle and fill her mug with hot water, a material process has led to performances of particular actions. Similarly, when a monumental art installation causes someone to open his eyes wide in amazement, the installation has induced a particular behaviour. In this way, the material world bears massive responsibility for social changes. All sorts of significant differences in social life arise from people's reactions to material entities, events and processes.

The third sort of responsibility that the material world can bear for social differences and changes is mediating the chains of activity that, in criss-crossing bundles and constellations, constitute and lead to social changes. I mentioned above that chains of activity constitute the second chief dynamo in social life. A chain of activities is series of activities, each of which responds to the previous member or to a change that the previous member brought about. Material entities, events and processes regularly mediate such chains. If someone switches on a monitor and others gather to watch something on Apple TV, chains that envelop the activities of turning on the monitor and watching it are mediated by the flow of electricity and the functioning of the monitor, together with the flow of text and images across it. Monitors and screens likewise mediate chains encompassing people verbally reacting to one another when they converse over Zoom. Similarly, when an artwork in a museum gallery induces a wide-eyed response, a chain encompassing the installation of the work and the reaction is mediated by, among other things, the work itself. A little imagination quickly reveals just how extensively the material world mediates chains of action. Given the immense responsibility that such chains bear for social changes, this is a very significant contribution that the material world makes to social change.

The final way in which the material world bears responsibility for social differences and changes is by prefiguring activities that constitute, bring about or lead to changes. For present purposes, the overall difference that prefiguration makes to activity can be specified as the making more or making less likely of possible actions, through the synthesis of the multiple saliencies that possible actions bear given (aspects of) the present state of the world. This type of responsibility for events and processes differs greatly from the other types discussed. It is neither a bringing about, an inducing, nor a facilitation of actions and material events/processes. It is more like a labile medium in which these actions and occurrences happen and form series, thereby shifting the medium. In a museum, for example, works of art prefigure people's paths through the building and, thus, where they act and what their activities bring about or induce.

Works of art do not bring about much social change. Although they might be dynamic in the sense of self-moving or -energizing (though maybe only after being plugged in), they do not, like humans, intervene in practices and bundles and alter them. Nor do they befall, infiltrate or irrupt into social life. At the same time, artworks clearly bear responsibility for differences and, possibly thus for changes, in the other three ways described: they induce actions, mediate chains of action and prefigure what people do. How much they accomplish these depends on circumstances and varies from case to case. Generally speaking, however, the differences that artworks bear responsibility for are small and insignificant. Not much real social change directly results from the presence of art in our lives.

In a most interesting article, Fernando Domínguez Rubio describes what he claims is "the active and causally-effective" role that artworks play "in the production and sustenance of cultural forms and meanings" (Domínguez Rubio 2014, p. 620). He observes that the introduction of certain installation or media works in museums has undercut standardized ways museum employees deal with works of art (e.g., classify, maintain, install and view them). Thereby, it has shifted the relative positions of curators and conservators in museum divisions of labour and, in this sense, been responsible for an "unfolding of different institutional and organization forms" (2014, p. 620). In resisting standard practices, boundaries and meanings, these works qualify as what Domínguez Rubio calls "unruly objects." He opposes unruly objects to docile ones: objects, including artworks, that because they can be handled in standard ways do not lead to changed practices and changed institutional or organizational forms.

The differences Domínguez Rubio describes clearly amount to changes in the lives of museum employees. They are not likely, however, to qualify as changes in any other regard. It is not clear, consequently, that the particular MoMA case Domínguez Rubio describes (involving Nam June Paik's *Untitled*) instances social change or simply certain practices becoming different. Even though the altered division of labour spread to museum bundles beyond MoMA, it is not obvious that museal institutional and organizational forms before and after the spread were much different and that the differences therefore qualify as social change. Artworks are certainly responsible for all sorts of difference: how, for instance, curators, conservators or consumers of art act towards artworks differs according to the type of artwork involved. What's more, limited differences, or differences confined to smallish constellations such as museums, can accumulate and eventuate in change. But the truth is that artworks rarely lead to significant changes in bundles and constellations. Only to a limited extend do the "physical properties of artworks…shape the ways in which organizational and institutional dynamics within the museum unfolds over time…" (ibid.).

Similarly, Yaneva (2003) goes too far in saying that each installation or creation of a work of art in a museum changes the museum (and those installing or creating it). It is true that whenever a work of art is installed or produced in a museum the museum, strictly speaking, becomes different. In most cases, however, the difference is miniscule. In these cases, it is pedantic and not even true to claim that the installation or creation of a work of art changes the museum or those installing or creating it. Change occurs only if, say, the monumentality of an artwork secures the museum's fame for years or if an installation requires a large-scale rearrangement of works in the museum. A museum changes with the installation or creation of an artwork only if there is something unusual, monumental, or lasting about the work involved or its repercussions for the museum and its public. The acquisition of the *No Ghost Just a Shell* collection by the van Abbemuseum in the Netherlands is probably an example (see van Saaze 2013).

Material entities regularly bear partial responsibility for changes in a host of ways that works of art generally do not. Food, biological agents, weapons, fire and the like effect changes by acting on human bodies. Artworks, by contrast, do not generally achieve this; an exception might be some works that incorporate human bodies, for example, via tattoos. Similarly, artworks do not often contribute to changes by connecting arrangements in the ways that electricity, communication systems, bridges, mountain passes and rivers do. And, as suggested, artworks do not intervene into and destroy bundles as earthquakes, storms, invading armies, fire, gas leaks and the like do. Nor do artworks mimic bodies and technological set-ups in opening bundles to material or biological flows; indeed, in this regard works of art are relatively inert. Technology, too, alters practices and bundles in ways unmatched by works of art. Phones, computers, cars, planes, atomic bombs and the like have instigated social changes that affect most lives, and not just in the more developed world. Nothing like this can be said about works of art. Nor do artworks pose logistical issues of the magnitude that coping with material space raises (e.g., distance) or exert the lasting impacts on bundles and constellations that material spaces exert (e.g., the locations of cities). In being incorporated into museums and private collections, finally, works of art end up being much less mobile than such material entities as money, documents, bodies, cars, skateboards and organisms. As a result, they fail to effect the sort of dispersed connectivity that such entities can achieve.

These matters are obvious. What they indicate, however, is that works of art bear relatively little responsibility for changes in social life. Maybe, however, no one has ever claimed that they do. Still, it is striking that this could be true of such a prominent category of material object. This situation suggests that art is largely a conserving force in society (I do not write "conservative" for reasons that will be soon be clear). That is, bundles that include artworks among their components are relatively stable and are not the source of chains of action or material events and processes that are responsible for change. Consequently, I affirm Domínguez Rubio's characterization of museums as "objectification machines" (2014, p. 620) that seek to stabilize artworks materially and conceptually. Indeed, the success of museums in this regard might be part of the story about why artworks bear relatively little responsibility for social changes.

At the same time, works of art do bear responsibility for changes of two sorts, both of which can or do bear indirect responsibility for social changes (i.e., changes in bundles and constellations). The first is changes in cultural forms. Works of art undoubtedly bear significant responsibility for cultural changes, for instance, evolutions in art. In this regard, Domínguez Rubio is right that works of art play a causally-effective role in the production and maintenance of *cultural* forms and meanings—it is just that they do not play this role vis-à-vis social forms. Changes in cultural forms, however, only occasionally bear responsibility for social changes.

Works of art, moreover, can affect people's thoughts, perceptions and motivations and in this way indirectly bear responsibility for social changes. Artworks can have this effect in many ways. They portray, reveal, and thereby call attention to social states of affair; they make people realize things or become pensive, contemplative or angry; they hold up people's lives and induce them to confront themselves; they articulate and instigate thought; they teach people to look at things more closely; they overtly protest particular states of affairs; and in their inventiveness and capacity to shock they can make people understand that difference and change are real and viable. As Adorno (1998) suggested, artworks raise the utopian possibility of the end of suffering. In these and other ways, works of art make people more open to and interested in social change and even point towards the directions it should take. As a result, artworks join other artistic forms such as literature, cinema, drama, poetry, dance and even musical composition in indirectly bearing responsibility for social change. I hasten to add that indirect responsibility for social changes does not imply insignificant responsibility. On the contrary: shaping thought and action can be the start of significant change. Not surprisingly, consequently, repressive governments have long suppressed art.

Curators and conservators are keepers of objectification and stability. Curators organize the objectified forms that contribute to stabilization, while conservators maintain them. Their efforts thereby secure museums as sites of objectification and social persistence. At the same time, curators and conservators organize as well as preserve past cultural upheavals and stand watch over intellectual and personal shock, provocation, mirroring, attention-focusing and protest. They can concentrate, however, on their jobs. Artworks, together with practices of art appreciation, take care of the rest.

References

Adorno, T (1998) Aesthetic theory (trans: Hullot-Kentor R). University of Minnesota Press, Minneapolis

Benjamin W (1968 [1936]) The work of art in the age of mechanical reproduction. In: Arendt H (ed) Illuminations: essays and reflections (trans: Zohn H). Schocken Books, New York

Bourdieu P (1990 [1965, 1970]) Photography: a middlebrow art (trans: Whiteside S). Polity Press, Cambridge

Bourdieu P (1993) The field of cultural production. Essays on art and literature. Johnson R (ed) Polity, Cambridge

Bourdieu P (1996 [1992]) Rules of art. (trans: Emanuel S). Polity, Cambridge

Domínguez Rubio FD (2014) Preserving the unpreservable: docile and unruly objects at MoMA. Theory Soc 43:617–645

Gherardi S (2019) How to conduct a practice-based study. Problems and methods, 2nd edn. Edward Elgar, Cheltenham

Heidegger M (1971 [1954]) Building, dwelling, thinking. In: Heidegger M (1971 [1954]) Poetry, language, thought (trans: Hofstadter A). Harper, New York, pp 143–162

Heidegger M (1977 [1954]) The question concerning technology. In: Heidegger M (1977 [1954]) The question concerning technology and other essays (trans: Lovitt W). Harper, New York, pp 3–35

Ingold T (2000) To journey along a way of life. Maps, wayfinding, and navigation. In: Ingold T (2002) The perception of the environment. Essays in livelihood, dwelling and skill. Routledge, London, pp 219–242

Latour B, Yaneva A (2008) "Give Me a Gun and I Will Make All Buildings Move": an ANT's view of architecture. In: Yaneva A, Latour B, Geiser R (eds) Explorations in architecture: teaching, design, research. Birkhäuser, Basel, pp 80–89

Laurenson P (2006) Authenticity, change, and loss in the conservation of time-based media installations: a conceptual framework for traditional fine art conservation. Tate Papers 6 (Autumn), https://www.tate.org.uk/research/publications/tate-papers/06/authenticity-change-and-loss-conservation-of-time-based-media-installations. Accessed 5 Oct 2018

Mol A (2002) The body multiple: ontology in medical practice. Duke University Press, Durham

Olsen B (2010) In defense of objects. Archaeology and the ontology of objects. AltaMira Press, Lanham

Reckwitz A (2002) Toward a theory of social practices. A development in culturalist theorizing. European. J Soc Theory 5(2):243–263

Schatzki T (2002) The site of the social. A philosophical exploration of the constitution of social life and change. The Pennsylvania State University Press, University Park

Schatzki T (2010) The timespace of activity. Performance, society, and history as indeterminate teleological events. Lexington Books, Lanham, MD

Schatzki T (2014) Art bundles. In: Zembylas T (ed) Artistic practices. Social interactions and cultural dynamics. Routledge, London, pp 17–31

Schatzki T (2019) Social change in a material world. Routledge, Abingdon

Shove E, Pantzar M, Wilson M (2012) The dynamics of social practice. Everyday life and how it changes. SAGE, London

van de Vall R, Hölling HB, Scholte T, Stigter S (2011) Reflections on a biographical approach to contemporary art conservation. In: Bridgland J (ed) ICOM-CC: 16th Triennial Conference, Lisbon, 19-23 September 2011. Critério, Lisbon, pp 1–8. http://hdl.handle.net/11245/1.344546

van Saaze V (2013) Installation art and the museum. Presentation and conservation of changing artworks. Amsterdam University Press, Amsterdam

Yaneva A (2003) Chalk steps on the museum floor. The "pulses" of objects in an art installation. J Mater Cult 8(2):169–188

Theodore Schatzki is Professor of Geography and Philosophy at the University of Kentucky and Professor of Sociology at Lancaster University. He is interested in a wide variety of theoretical issues about social life, which he approaches through the theoretical stream known as "practice theory." Among his books are *Social Practices* (1996), *The Site of the Social* (2002) and *Social Change in a Material World* (2019).

Doing Ethics in Practice: SBMK Platform Meetings

Renée van de Vall

Abstract This chapter investigates a process of deliberation about the conservation of a contemporary artwork, organised in the form of two "Platform meetings" by the Dutch Foundation for the Conservation of Contemporary Art (SBMK). It argues that: 1. SBMK Platform meetings help to bridge gaps between conservation theory and practice by constituting "middle-ranging" practices of ethical deliberation; 2. this middle-ranging ethical work proceeds through a combination of various, theoretically contrasting deliberative techniques; 3. investigation of the values implicitly articulated in the deliberation process suggests that the kind of ethics at work in the practice of conservation of contemporary artworks may be fruitfully understood in terms of posthumanist care ethics. By articulating the role, dynamics and values of the Platform meetings, the chapter aims to clarify why and how such meetings can contribute to both professional conservation practice and the development of theoretical conservation ethics.

Keywords Contemporary art conservation · Middle-ranging practices · Ethical deliberation · Situated ethicality · Posthumanist care ethics

1 SBMK Platform Meetings

This chapter investigates a process of deliberation about the conservation of a contemporary artwork, organised in the form of two "Platform meetings" by the Dutch Foundation for the Conservation of Contemporary Art (SBMK).[1] SBMK is an organisation supported and financed by a great number of Dutch art museums, established in the mid-1990s. Ever since its landmark project and symposium on *Modern Art: Who Cares?* (1997/1999), it has become a major stimulator for the development of research in the field of contemporary art conservation in the

[1] Stichting Behoud Moderne Kunst.

R. van de Vall (✉)
Faculty of Art and Social Sciences, Maastricht University, Maastricht, The Netherlands
e-mail: r.vandevall@maastrichtuniversity.nl

R. van de Vall, V. van Saaze (eds.), *Conservation of Contemporary Art*, Studies in Art, Heritage, Law and the Market 9, https://doi.org/10.1007/978-3-031-42357-4_3

Table 1 SBMK Platform meeting protocol. *Structuur casusbespreking werkgroep Balans* (SBMK June 2008); translation and references to the steps of the Decision-Making Model (DMM) by author with assistance from Lydia Beerkens

Meeting I (DMM steps 1-4)
1. Presentation artwork
2. Explanation case
3. Summary problem statement
4. Response and reflection working group
5. Rephrasing problem statement
In between the meetings
6. Follow up research
Meeting II (DMM steps 5-7)
7. Re-presentation to working group
8. Weighing alternative options by working group
After meeting II (back to "problem owner")
9. Reporting
10. Giving feedback to the working group

Netherlands. Among the many types of activities undertaken by the SBMK are Platform meetings and special thematic days and research projects. Usually, Platform meetings are organised when a member of the SBMK, for instance a conservator of one of the associated museums, proposes to discuss a difficult case from the museum's collection. The SBMK coordinator and core Platform members propose to invite experts, as well as participants from the network, like conservators from other museums with comparable works in the collection. At least two meetings are held, following a protocol rooted in the SBMK (1999) decision-making model (Table 1 and Fig. 1).[2]

My interest in SBMK's practice was fuelled by two considerations.[3] First, the oft-voiced concern that conservation of contemporary works of art defied existing conservation-ethical guidelines and would benefit from systematic investigation of the way conservation professionals deal with ethical dilemmas on the work floor. Secondly, the growing theoretical interest in how everyday problems and routines shape ethical awareness and commitment, articulated in the "turn to practice" or "practice theory" in philosophy and social sciences.[4]

[2] A revision of the model was initiated by the Cologne Institute of Conservation Sciences (2018; also available on the SBMK website; for a thorough discussion see the chapter by Julia Giebeler, Gunnar Heydenreich and Andrea Sartorius in this volume); as the platform meetings analysed took place before 2018, I refer to the old model.

[3] I have been involved in SBMK activities since the research project *Modern Art: Who Cares?* (see van de Vall 1999), and over the years I have occasionally participated in, or been present at SBMK meetings and projects, such as the project and symposium *Serra on the Move* (2014), about the relocation of sculptures by Richard Serra (https://www.sbmk.nl/nl/projecten/project-serra). I was invited by Paulien't Hoen to observe the Platform meetings. Participants were asked beforehand for their permission to tape and use the meetings for my research, while the resulting article was sent around for their consent before publication.

[4] For a full explanation of these considerations see the Introduction to this volume.

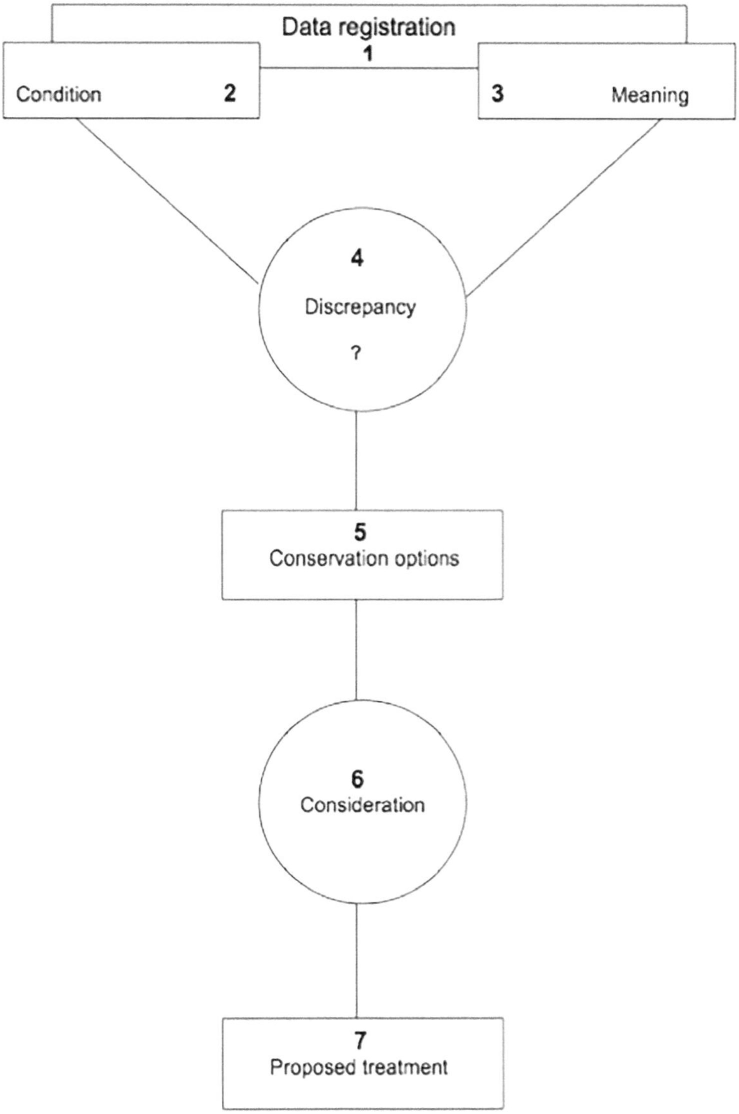

Fig 1 SBMK Decision-Making Model for the Conservation and Restoration of Modern and Contemporary Art (1999) (https://www.sbmk.nl/en/tool/decision-makingmodel)

2 *Hout Auto*

The object discussed in the Platform meetings that I participated in was Joost Conijn's *Hout Auto* (Wood Car), which is in the collection of Central Museum Utrecht. *Hout Auto* is twice what the name says it is. It is a car made (partly) of wood, but it also runs on wood, that is on the gas that is produced when wood is burnt in the metal burner at the back of the car. With this car, Joost Conijn travelled around in Central and Eastern Europe in 2001 and 2002. There is a video film made of the journey, which always needs to be shown together with the car and vice versa.[5] The car is a complete and original Citroën DS, but its original body was replaced by wood panels and it runs on a wood burning fuelling system, added by the artist. The traditional DS engine engineering determines part of the conservation problem.

Hout Auto differs from most other objects in the museum's collections, because it is a car and has to function like a car.[6] The main reason why it has to be able to function is that the car cannot be moved without the engine running: like all Citroën DS cars, the coachwork is lifted by a hydraulic system when the engine starts and only then the wheels will move. So the engine has to be switched on when the car is to be moved—it cannot just be pushed for instance—in and out of the transportation truck when it is on loan, and in and out of the exhibition venue. The artist wants the car to be exhibited in the lifted driving position. When the engine is turned off, wooden blocks keep the car's body at the right height. The wood burner added by Joost Conijn is no longer used; the car still runs on the gasoline tank, which makes the car easier to operate. The car has to be driven around at least twice a year to keep the engine in proper condition. Exhaust fumes are a problem, in particular when the car leaves an enclosed space and the exhaust will flow towards the interior space, rather than the open air. A solution for the exhaust fumes is to attach a hose to the exhaust pipe that will dispose of the fumes in the outdoors. The chassis is in a problematic condition. Moreover, storage is a problem, because it is not advisable to keep inflammatory fluids in a museum depot. The car is often asked for loans, but moving it around is a risky and unpredictable affair and the receiving institution needs to be aware of what is coming.

Given this context, a main question for the SBMK platform discussions was: should future conservation of *Hout Auto* include its functioning as a car? Two meetings were organised, one on November 20, 2015 in the external storage rooms of the Central Museum and a second on August 30, 2016 in De Hallen,[7] Haarlem, where *Hout Auto* was then exhibited. Present were: the SBMK coordinator Paulien 't Hoen (only at the first meeting); Lydia Beerkens, SBMK board member

[5] Part of this film is accessible on Joost Conijn's website: http://www.joostconijn.org/film/houtauto/index.php. Accessed 13 April 2020.

[6] The following description was derived from the case presentation by Arthur van Mourik and Marije Verduijn on November 20, 2015 and from van Mourik (2017, 2018).

[7] De Hallen is a part of Frans Hals Museum; since 2018 the venue is called Frans Hals Museum, location Hal.

and chair of the meetings; Marije Verduijn, head of collections, and Arthur van Mourik, conservator at the Central Museum; photographer and film maker Rob Jansen, involved in the maintenance of the *Hout Auto*; Danielle Laudy, collection manager of the Rabo Art Collection; Christel van Hees, head conservation and restoration at Museum Boijmans van Beuningen, Nicole Delissen, SBMK board member and independent museum professional, and, at the second meeting only, Susanna Koenig, head of exhibition organisation at Frans Hals Museum/De Hallen. Apart from one question at the end of the second meeting, I did not participate in the discussions. The questions I asked for the analysis of the discussions were:

- Are the Platform discussions a form of ethical deliberation?
- If the answer to the question is positive, what forms/techniques of ethical deliberation do participants in the Platform meetings use?
- How can we best understand the kind of conservation ethics articulated in these discussions?

In the following I will argue that: 1. SBMK Platform meetings help to bridge gaps between conservation theory and practice by constituting "middle-ranging" practices of ethical deliberation; 2. this middle-ranging ethical work proceeds through a combination of various, theoretically contrasting deliberative techniques; 3. investigation of the values implicitly articulated in the deliberation process suggests that the kind of ethics at work in the practice of conservation of contemporary artworks may be fruitfully understood in terms of posthumanist care ethics.

3 The Platform Meetings as a Form of Ethical Deliberation

The meetings roughly followed the SBMK protocol. Most time in the meetings was taken up by the explanation of the specific characteristics of the case and the technical and procedural complexities involved in handling *Hout Auto*, which might lead to the question of the extent to which the discussions were indeed "ethical." The term "ethics" was referred to only once: in response to the question whether the future maintenance of *Hout Auto* was or was not taken into account with the acquisition, the answer was "well, this brings us to ethics. . .," accompanied with laughter. This mentioning of ethics could also be because of my presence: I had explained shortly before that I was interested as a researcher in how in SBMK meetings ethics was being done in practice. It struck me, however, that there was actually much ethics implied in the various technical and procedural details, as continuously the car's physical integrity or "well-being" was at stake, and this had to be balanced against interests of other actors or objects, such as the other objects in the museum depot or the safety of the public. Moreover, a contrast emerged between the proper condition of *Hout Auto* as a car and its status of an artwork, which added an ethical dimension to the technical details as well.

An example of such implied ethicality can be found in the following conversation about the fact that the car should be exhibited on driving height and how to do this without relying on the hydraulic system, which only works with the engine turned on:

Marije: What Joost [Conijn] told me on the telephone, he said you could screw off this sphere [part of the hydraulic system, RvdV] and put a [wooden] stick in [the system] . . . Rob: Never do this! What happens, this stick takes up all the oil, and the stick will start rotting at a certain point.

Marije: So if you put it "on height," you do not use the hydraulic system any more but you put it on height by default. Rob: Yes. The disadvantage is you can no longer put it in a higher position, you either have to put it in the highest position or you have to take with you all different sizes of sticks. What I do myself, I have a DS in my garage which doesn't ride [anymore], and then I fetch a broomstick, which I saw into different sizes . . . Lydia: Then you stick them in the spheres. Rob: Yes, you first have to lift the car, then you put the sticks in, then you screw the spring sphere onto it and you leave it sit in that position. And then it will not bounce anymore. Paulien: So you say: never do this, but you actually do it yourself. Rob: Well, it is a car I use for its parts, [after which] it will go to the scrapyard. That is not what you should do with an artwork.

The conversation highlights the close connection of technical with ethical considerations: a specific potential solution, putting sticks in the hydraulic system to keep the car on height, has a particular disadvantage, namely that the sticks will rot, which is acceptable in one specific case, namely when a car is used for its parts, but never in another, namely when a car is an *artwork*.

In this close connection between technical and ethical deliberation, conservation typically resembles clinical medicine. Like reasoning about clinical cases in medicine, the deliberation aiming at conservation decisions could be called a form of "practical wisdom" or *phronesis* (van de Vall 1999). It has been argued (Waring 2000) that clinical medicine is not an example of *phronesis* because considering it as such (as for instance Jonson and Toulmin (1988) have done) would conflate technical practice with morality, which is (at least in Aristoteles' use of the term *phronesis*) always concerned with an exercise of virtue. Virtuous actions are their own, unconditional ends: acting well is done for its own sake, whereas actions performed in medical practice have a goal which is different from the action itself: health. This argument presupposes that one can exercise technical skills and knowledge in a purely instrumental way, which might be the case when both the end (for instance: "health") and the way to reach that end are known and undisputed. However, both in medical practice and in conservation, this is often not the case. What the equivalent of "health" would be for the *Hout Auto* in its specific life stage is a topic of debate, and therefore a deliberation about which technical solutions are morally acceptable or not demands more than purely technical insight: the sense of what is morally appropriate to "do with an artwork." Conversely, morally "acting well" in conservation involves acting knowingly with an eye to the possible consequences of an intervention, like the expectation that a wooden stick will rot when taking up oil.[8]

Another distinction that this snippet of conversation questions is that between ethics and morality. Wildes (2000) distinguishes between morality and ethics in terms of first and second order discourse:

> Morality is the level of first order discourse in which we live and make moral decisions. Morality is the moral world that we simply assume and take for granted in our everyday life. Ethics is the level of second order discourse which steps back from our everyday assumptions and practices to examine the basic assumptions about the moral world, such as why we regard consequences or duty as the definitive mark of morality. This second order discourse is not only the realm of philosophers or ethicists. Conflicts, at the level of morality, often lead people to this second level discussion. (Wildes 2000, p. 3, quoted in Wildes 2007, pp. 47-48 (n))

Boenink (2013) makes a comparable distinction, but diversifies "doing ethics" to include a range of deliberative activities:

> Whereas morality is the set of norms and values current in a certain community, ethics is the reflection on morality. Such reflection is not limited to ethicists with a specific academic training; most human beings engage in it from time to time. Moreover [. . .] doing ethics is not identical with passing judgment on the moral desirability of an act or a way of doing. It encompasses a broad set of activities, including recognising and interpreting the values at stake in a specific situation, imagining how the meaning of these values might shift because of the changes of the situation at hand, imagining alternatives for action as well as the consequences of these actions for the stakeholders involved. (Boenink 2013, p. 59)

In terms of both Wildes' and Boenink's definitions, what the participants in the Platform meetings did was without doubt a form of doing ethics: stepping back from the everyday working procedures "to examine the basic assumptions about the moral world" (Wildes 2007, pp. 47–48 (n)). What I noticed, however, is that this examination is often very implicit and only seldom takes the shape of a discussion of these assumptions as such. This is partly because of the form these deliberations take, as I will explain Sect. 4, which is only seldom an explicit application of principles. What I would like to question, moreover, is that Platform participants were doing ethics during the Platform meetings **only**. The opposition suggested by Wildes and Boenink is one between a taken-for-granted morality of daily life routines and the critical ethical reflection that is made possible by a stepping aside from these routines—a stepping aside solicited for instance by a situation of moral conflict. I do not question the affordances of a separate deliberative situation as provided by the Platform meetings. These meetings work so well because they allow participants to detect similarities and differences between the case at hand and other cases and as such allow for the development of "middle-range" theories operating in "the space between the theoretical imagination and the richly empirical textures of lived experience" (Wyatt and Balmer 2007, p. 622).[9] What the participants' stories

---

[8] Aristoteles' is a virtue ethics, but there are also ethical schools that start from consequences or duties (cf. Brody 2003).

[9] As proposed by Robert Merton, middle range theories operate between "the minor but necessary working hypotheses that evolve in abundance during day-to-day research and the all-inclusive systematic efforts to develop a unified theory that will explain all the observed uniformities of social behaviour, social organization and social change" (quoted in Wyatt and Balmer 2007, p. 621).

revealed, however, is that critical reflection and ethical deliberation are at the heart of their daily work and permeate work-floor routines, even if it is not always made explicit verbally. The opposition between a taken-for-granted morality and critical ethical questioning flounders, because the problems encountered in the handling of contemporary artworks are so often unprecedented (how often do conservators have to drive around in their artworks?). In other words, there is very little that can be taken for granted. This is why I would like to point to the continuity, rather than the distinction, between the moral and the ethical: not only are ethical reflection and deliberation implicitly at work in everyday practice; more explicit and specialized deliberations about ethical dilemmas are steeped in the supposedly merely instrumental practical and technical considerations of conservation work. The Platform meetings act as middle-ranging instances, active mediators between general considerations and individual problems, allowing for a more explicit and systematic articulation and confrontation of values at stake in practice, without becoming a full-fledged, theoretical meta-discourse that reflects on these values for their own sake.

4 Techniques of Deliberation

In discussions on moral reasoning[10] in bioethics various forms and styles of deliberation have been discerned, often placed in critical opposition to each other. Claims about the adequacy or inadequacy of such forms and styles can be normative (this is how moral reasoning *should* proceed) or descriptive (this is how moral reasoning *does* in fact proceed), or a combination of both. My aim here is not to decide what is right or wrong,[11] but to compile a list of deliberative techniques, not only in order to articulate how the discussion in the Platform meetings evolved, but also to be able to recognise moral reasoning in forms that are not at *prime facie* recognisable as "morality" or "ethics."

An "applied ethics" approach to moral reasoning that is particularly dominant in ethical committees sees moral reasoning as a form of deductive reasoning from, as well as specification of, general ethical principles that themselves are rationally determined. Examples of such principles are (in the case of bioethics): promoting autonomy (to respect individual freedom); pursuing non-maleficence (to do no harm); beneficence (to do good) and justice (to be fair) (in The Belmont Report of the National Commission for the Protection of Human Subjects of Biomedical and

---

[10]In these discussions the distinction between moral sphere and ethical sphere is not always made; in fact, deliberation is often called "moral" where I would rather call it ethical (I follow here the terms used in the literature I quote).

[11]For instance: casuists tend to oppose adherents of applied ethics approaches, and De Marco & Ford propose balancing as a method that is better able to support moral decision-making than applied ethics specification or casuist case comparison.

Behavioral Research (Hoffmeister 1994, p. 1155));[12] or the respect of human dignity, the best interest of the child, the non-commoditization of the human body and its corollaries, and the gratuity and anonymity of donation of human organs and products (in the case of the French National Ethics Advisory Committee (Spranzi 2013, p. 93)). The challenge is to specify these general principles in such a way that they adequately cover to the peculiarities of individual cases.

For comparable principles for conservation ethics we can look at the guidelines stipulated in Article 5, 6, 8 and 9 of ECCO's 2002 Ethical Code,[13] for instance Article 5: "The conservator-restorer shall respect the aesthetic, historic and spiritual significance and the physical integrity of the cultural heritage entrusted to her/his care." This requirement might be challenged by Article 6: "The conservator-restorer, in collaboration with other professional colleagues involved with cultural heritage, shall take into account the requirements of its social use while preserving the cultural heritage." There are many forms of social use that may damage an object's physical integrity, and the question is how to match the requirements of its social use with its preservation, which remains the overriding aim. Article 8 outlines the requirement of minimal intervention: "The conservator-restorer should take into account all aspects of preventive conservation before carrying out physical work on the cultural heritage and should limit the treatment to only that which is necessary." Whereas Article 9 points to the reversibility of treatment: "The conservator-restorer shall strive to use only products, materials and procedures, which, according to the current level of knowledge, will not harm the cultural heritage, the environment or people. The action itself and the materials used should not interfere, if at all possible, with any future examination, treatment or analysis. They should also be compatible with the materials of the cultural heritage and be as easily and completely reversible as possible."

Where the applied ethics approach starts from general, rational reflection on values and principles and subsequently applies them "top down" to individual cases, a contrasting approach, moral casuistry, starts from the specificities of individual cases, and reasons "bottom up" to find applicable general rules with the help of comparison and reasoning by analogy:

> Faced with a moral quandary or decision the casuist will reflect on the nonmoral and moral features of the case at hand and compare these features to a paradigm case, one where there is stable social consensus about the right course of action. General ethical norms emerge from families of cases to guide moral reasoning over new or more ambiguous cases. Trained reflection on the features of new cases may then lead us to adjust, refine, or better specify the general norms via the mechanism of a reflective equilibrium, seeking the appropriate balance between general moral norms and concrete cases or decisions [. . . .]. (Kelley 2007, p. 65)

---

[12] Interestingly, this same committee is used by Jonsen and Toulmin (1989, pp. 16–19) to argue the merits of a casuist approach.

[13] http://www.ecco-eu.org/fileadmin/user_upload/ECCO_professional_guidelines_II.pdf.

Casuists claim that casuistry comes more closely to moral deliberation in everyday practice than an "applied ethics" approach. For conservation ethics this has been argued as well (van de Vall 1999, 2015; Wharton 2018).

Critics of moral casuistry contend that moral deliberation in practice cannot do without general rules, guidelines or principles and can be best understood as a back and forth between individual case and general principles (Arras 1991); or in terms of the creation and adaptation of values, which are more practice-bound and flexible than norms or principles (Spranzi 2013); and that rather than by explicit comparison with paradigm cases and reasoning by analogy, moral deliberation proceeds by a more implicit comparison with anecdotal evidence and storytelling about like cases (Braunack-Mayer 2001; cf. Hoffmeister 1994); or that the balancing of pros and cons of conflicting values in particular cases leads to better decision-making (DeMarco and Ford 2006). Casuistry, moreover, is seen as producing conformity to existing norms and confirm the ethical status quo as it would not able to address issues that require ways of thinking beyond those provided by the analogical reasoning of casuistry (Hoffmeister 1994, p. 1160). It would not account for the normativity of morality "because it claims only to be elucidating the values and principles that are immanent in cases or in the social and cultural traditions within these cases are compared." (Hoffmeister 1994, p. 1159)

In Sect. 5 of this chapter I will return to these last two criticisms, as I will agree that casuistry is primarily a method or a procedure and therefore does not help to guide reflections on the particular content or relative importance of values referred to in case comparisons. In the following section I will analyse the discussions in the Platform meeting to identify the kind of deliberative techniques employed, sometimes in combination: the application of general principles; storytelling; case comparison by analogical reasoning and case comparison by storytelling; and balancing. Rather than seeing them, and the ethical approaches they are connected to, as excluding each other, I consider them to be complementary, each of them contributing to a fuller and more detailed articulation of the dilemmas at stake.

It was interesting that general principles, like the traditional conservation guidelines mentioned above, did pop up in the discussion, but in a way that rather stretched their meanings. The guideline that the integrity of the work should be respected was present throughout the discussion. But it was, in particular in the second meeting, connected to the work's current biographical stage (although not consistently): yes, driving the car *had been* an essential part of *Hout Auto* functioning as a work of art, but was so no longer in this phase of the artwork's career; perhaps it could become relevant again in the future. In between the two SBMK meetings two of the participants attended a conference on kinetic art, which proved very enlightening for their understanding of *Hout Auto* (conferences also do lot of middle-ranging work). This conference solidified an insight that already was present in the first meeting: that you cannot expect the same things of an artwork in all its life-stages.[14] Here a comparison was helpful:

[14] Cf. van de Vall et al. (2011).

> Lydia: When do you put in a new engine and when do you let it go? The idea of a work of art "in retirement" comes from the Tinguely Museum; some works have been retired; they may be presented without moving; for other works a movie is made to be shown next to the non-moving work; there are all kinds of forms in between still living and being written off.

The question of what exactly constitutes the work's identity and whether this identity might change when a work is "retired" was the most telling example of "recognising and interpreting the values at stake in a specific situation, imagining how the meaning of these values might shift because of the changes of the situation at hand" (Boenink 2013, p. 59). This did not, however, entail an explicit mentioning of the value of the work's physical integrity and significance or the principle of respecting it.

The guideline of minimal intervention came up at the end of the second meeting, but more as an attitude than as a principle. When I asked why no one in the meeting pleaded for taking out the engine altogether, the answer referred to the professional reticence of conservators and their preference for step-by-step changes. The guideline of the reversibility of treatments appeared as well, but in the guise of keeping options open for the future: maybe in a hundred years it might be desirable that *Hout Auto* could drive again and would that be possible? This indicates that these guidelines are very much alive, but not in the form of general principles that are explicitly referred to and subsequently specified in their application to a particular problem, but rather as incorporated in a professional *ethos*, a disposition or "spirit" in which members of the conservation community work, to use a term from care ethics—an ethos that will thoroughly form their perception of the possibilities and constraints of a situation, but cannot *a priori* determine what is the best way to proceed.[15] It was also interesting that there was a lot of storytelling in the discussions. This confirms a conclusion drawn by Braunack-Mayer (2001), who interviewed fifteen general practitioners about how they dealt with ethical problems and analysed the forms of moral reasoning they used for their answers. One of her conclusions is that GPs use a case-by-case approach, grounded in the telling of stories and anecdotes derived from their experiences. She distinguishes three ways in which stories function: as purely *descriptive* accounts to illustrate the nature of their work; and as "moral trumps," either in a *deontological* fashion, illustrating a moral maxim or rule-of-the thumb, or in a *consequentialist* fashion to focus on outcomes.

> The GPs tended to use their stories as trumps on moral talk, in other words, to provide empirical authorization for why things should be done in certain ways [...]. Their moral trumps worked in two ways: in deontological fashion to illustrate a maxim or rule-of-thumb or in consequentialist fashion to focus on outcomes. [...] a small group of stories [...] were descriptive, told to illustrate the nature of work in general practice. (Braunack-Mayer 2001, p. 76).

Likewise, some stories in the Platform meetings were mainly descriptive, in that they served to highlight the special character of *Hout Auto*, like the story about what happened in the context of an exhibition in Assen:

---

[15] For an insightful articulation of the conservator's ethos, see Stigter (2016).

Marije: What also happened is that we were called by the police. The ambassador of Israel would visit this room and the secret service had examined the car and found it far too suspicious; they thought that perhaps all kinds of bombs were hidden in the tank. If that would certainly be possible, it was not the case of course. They asked us whether we could fully account for it, and, yes, even though the car was always in a secure setting, someone could have sneaked in at some unguarded moment ... yet finally they felt assured and decided not to cut it open.

Other stories served as a "moral trump"; these were often not about *Hout Auto* itself but about comparable cases, the "trump" supposedly also being applicable to *Hout Auto*. Generally speaking, deliberation was informed by comparison: often featuring stories or anecdotes of experiences with real objects like DS old-timers, but also marked by a more speculative use of fictional cases, which cannot be called a story. Such fictional speculations went like: what if we treated *Hout Auto* as if it were a bronze sculpture? DS old-timers and bronze sculptures featured as extremes of a continuum of objects, while all kinds of other objects between these extremes passed in review: design objects with motors, such as hair dryers, lamps, other car-like artworks, kinetic artworks or pianos. Some of these comparisons were embedded in stories, others were not. During the introduction round for instance, Rabo Art collection manager Danielle Laudy explained why she was interested in the case, by telling how they work with artworks containing engines, which led to a comparison of how such works function in corporate collections and in museums. This comparison did not contain a story or anecdote but rather a more generalizing account:

Danielle: This work [a lightwork by Rob Birza] is continuous, there is a bar at the back in the auditorium, and when there is an event this lightwork is turned on and is moving. Because it is on often, it needs a lot of attention and small repairs, [such as] bulbs that have to be replaced, which is a returning cost factor [...]. Lydia: Most important for you is that a corporate collection exhibits most of its works almost permanently, whereas a museum will keep many of its works in long-term storage until they are exhibited. In a corporate collection the works are permanently in use. Danielle: Yes, yes. Rob: Which means that there is much more wear and tear. Lydia: Yes, unless you take it into account and have a regular overhaul.

Other comparisons were indeed more story-like. In the kind of moral trump stories, sometimes the trump was consequential, as when the possibility was discussed whether it would be possible to take the engine out and put another one in later:

Rob: Well I know this [car] restorer, a DS builder; he lives in France now but he used to live in Ouderkerk aan de Amstel for a long time and I have had conversations with him because every Thursday night we would meet there with all kinds of people from the DS world to tinker with these cars and so on. We had a discussion once because there is so much [that will break down]. When I put in a new dynamo, a week later something else will break down in that car and then there is the high voltage again ... Arthur: Everything works upon everything. Rob: Because everything wears out on everything in a classic car. And everybody said, hey, you are right! It is like that because I had this and those *garagistes* know this all too well, and they don't mind changing something because they know the car will be back after a few weeks with another problem, so they will have a new job again [...] So if you think we take out the engine and put it back after a hundred years and then it will drive again, you're bound to have to do one repair job after another.

In this account, *Hout Auto* was compared with old-timers to explain the *similarities* between them: what goes for an old DS also goes for *Hout Auto*. Other stories were meant to highlight *differences* between *Hout Auto* as an artwork and other old-timers, like in the following part of the earlier quoted story about the broomsticks, in which the moral trump was deontological:

> What I do myself, I have a DS in my garage which doesn't ride. I fetch a broomstick, which I saw into different sizes . . . Lydia: Then you stick them in the spheres. Rob: Yes, you first have to lift the car, then you put the sticks in, then you screw the spring sphere onto it and you leave it sit in that position. And then it will not bounce anymore. Paulien: So you say: never do this, but you actually do it yourself. Rob: Well, it is a car I use for its parts, after which it will go to the scrapyard. That is not what you should do with an artwork.

Some stories finally articulated the hybrid nature of *Hout Auto*:

> Arthur: Here we see 2007 Boijmans . . . Paulien: That is Joost himself. Arthur: You see that plastic was wrapped around the car . . . Paulien: When again did you buy it? Arthur and Marije: 2003. Arthur: The last time . . . It has also been to Ahoy in Rotterdam for two days, and the last time in 2014 to Assen; here it is placed in the exhibition room and here it was covered because the lux was too high. Paulien: Because the lux was too high, this is terrific. Arthur: Yes, because you don't want the wood to discolour . . .

Here the situation was seen as rather paradoxical: like an old-timer, *Hout Auto* has to be driven around in full daylight, but in the exhibition space it is heavily protected against that same light, because it is not an ordinary old-timer but a work of art.

The Platform discussions partly confirm another conclusion by Braunack-Mayer about moral deliberations of GPs: that although their stories represent "a form of homespun casuistry," this form "underplays one of the central elements of casuistic reasoning—the paradigm case," when understood in the strict sense of being "public cases with a long history of debate, discussion and correction" (Braunack-Mayer 2001, p. 73). General practitioners never alluded to publicly debated cases, but only to cases from their own practice. The same was true for the participants of the Platform discussions. However, in the deliberation, *Hout Auto* was consistently compared with two kinds of objects—old-timers and bronze sculptures—that in a general sense might fit Albert R. Jonsen's stipulation of presenting unambiguous maxims:

> A case in which the circumstances were clear, the relevant maxim unambiguous and the rebuttals weak, in the minds of almost any observer. The claim that this action is wrong (or right) is widely persuasive. There is little need to present arguments for the rightness (or wrongness) of the case and it is very hard to argue against its rightness (wrongness). (Quoted in Braunack-Mayer, op. cit. 73.)

Throughout the discussion balancing of values and options took place—which is not surprising as balancing is at the heart of the decision-making model (and the core members of the Platform meetings were formerly called the "Balans" (balance) group). DeMarco and Ford define balancing as

> a metaphor for the attempt to determine the relative importance of conflicting values in particular cases or classes of cases in order to come to a conclusion mainly about moral obligations. Balancing may be intuitive or deliberative, or a hybrid of the two. In *intuitive balancing*, reasons are not offered to support the decision that one value is of greater

importance than another involved in a particular conflict. *Deliberative balancing* provides reasons for believing that one value has greater importance than another. (DeMarco and Ford 2006, pp. 490–491)

In the Platform discussion, balancing was less about conflicting values than about the relative possibilities and risks of conflicting options for conservation, which implicitly referred to background values such as the work's authenticity and manageability within the collection. What aspects of *Hout Auto* were most important in the current situation and how would it be possible to safeguard the most important aspects, but leave open the possibility to maintain other aspects too?

Christel: So in terms of care and maintenance you should go back to the question: why do you actually have this? And then you could also decide that it should be able to drive once in a while to render visible the essence of the work as such, if that's what it is. Marije: It has never been the idea to show the car driving while it was in the collection. The car has become a stage prop. It has become a sculpture illustrating the story told in the film. That is how it has always been part of the collection. Christel: If that is the case, things are far easier; then we can say that we simply removed its function, its functionality. But then I would advocate doing it in such a way that eventually it can drive again. Paulien: You can always bring this function back, isn't it? Rob: To let it run on gas? Paulien: Or on wood! Rob: Yes.

According to DeMarco and Ford, the practice of balancing "is attentive to the fact that the issues involved in many cases form a potential continuum. For example, risk can involve any percent, harm avoided can vary from the almost inconsequential to death, and a parent's reasons may vary from simple convenience to deeply held religious conviction supported by extensive involvement in a religion" (DeMarco and Ford 2006, p. 491). This continuum-character of moral deliberation became very apparent after the crucial step made in the first meeting that driving was no longer an essential part of the *Hout Auto* as a work of art, but only served its transportation. From then on the discussion was no longer about how best to keep up the engine or what loan protocols to write, but: how to move the car when it no longer drives and: what to do with the engine, its fluids, and how to store it? The option most seriously discussed was to treat it as a very heavy sculpture and design a custom-made platform on wheels for its transportation. This actually opened the opportunity to formulate comparisons with pianos or bronze sculptures.

Lydia: Look, when you say it will go on loan for over a year and you in fact decided already that this is a bronze sculpture measuring some 1.80 metre by 5 metres and [weighing] some 1200 kilos, you can come up with a perfectly fitting position, one which does not only support it at particular points but serves as a comprehensive support, so as to prevent it from sagging, and—just like a piano—with wheels you can fold out and [make it] electronically manoeuvrable so you can ride it carefully in and out, and once you set it up [in its permanent position], you fold the last pieces inward so that optically it sits in its lifted position. In this way, you have it on display.

However, the objection was made that the car's entire underside had to be renewed, for otherwise the car will not be able to rest on its display place. And wouldn't that be a bridge too far in terms of tampering with a work of art?

Rob: But this plate will touch the car at particular points. And the bottom of the car is awfully bad. The chassis of the bottom is, uh, Swiss cheese. Lydia: What do you need to improve it? It is a matter of doing new welding underneath once, and then it will be fine, am I right? Rob:

Yes and probably also the bars alongside . . . Lydia: yes, so what will it cost if I bring the car to you? Rob: Well, I won't do it myself; I still have two cars myself that need repairing, well what will it be, 7000 [euros] . . . Lydia: For 7000 you have an underside and I suppose that you have a very fancy electronically manoeuvrable platform construction with wheels in and out . . . Rob: This last option is a good plan, that other plan, well then you have to deal with an artwork that the artist has made—we just talked about a bronze sculpture but suppose that the sculpture is a bit too thin and you want to make something underneath and it appears that the sculpture is too weak and you make another sculpture—it comes down to making another car. That's no longer the work of art made by Joost.

But if the engine would not need to function any longer, why keep it in the car? And just keep the gas tank? Or go back to the artist's version with the wood burner?

Nicole: I would say that you should keep the engine; just to have as much as possible of the original object. So that when, for whatever reason, a movement would arise [at some point], that you want to be able to go back to that wooden stove; that this is possible then. Paulien: You can see under the hood that it has worked. [various voices] Yes. Lydia: That is also the case with design objects that have everything still within as well, even if with the hair dryer or toaster of the '60s you could take out the engine if you only put it in the case. Danielle: But what do you do with the jerrycan then? That wasn't in it originally. Marije: That is how it is bought, that is what Conijn put inside. Lydia: Tinkered inside. Paulien: It is very much Joost Conijn, to put in an engine and that then it works; that is very much his style. Nicole: I can imagine that you really document this with him, also retrospectively: what was his reason to go for this gasoline story at the time?

5 Towards an Ethics of Care

Taken together, the application of principles, case comparison, storytelling and balancing allow for a rich array of considerations and concerns to be articulated and taken into account. But they merely constitute procedures or techniques for deliberation; they do not help us to decide which values are more important than others and why. I've tried to discover what were important values for the platform members. I venture the conclusion that although more traditionally acknowledged values like the work's integrity—with the concomitant guidelines of its protection through minimal intervention and reversibility—do play an important role, they do so more as ingredients of an attitude or ethos than as explicit rules; they have become part of a more complex web of values and concerns that are highly situation-dependent, include emotional attachments and human relations involved in the process of working with the object, as well as an attachment to the object itself.

Compared with the logic of the decision-making model, where the starting point is identifying discrepancies between current and the original condition and meaning, the deliberations were more focused on identifying possible identities for *Hout Auto*, and placing them in biographical stages and contexts of practice. Where the decision making model proceeds by weighing the pros and cons of various *conservation options*, the deliberations seemed more engaged with weighing the pros and cons of various *scenarios for desirable futures*, considering these futures in terms of the practices needed to sustain them, each practice encompassing specific networks of objects, activities, people, tools, skills, understandings and emotions.[16] Against the scenario of prolonging the current practice in which the car itself drives into and out of the exhibition space, a scenario was proposed in which the car would be transported on a movable platform, either with the engine still in the car or with the engine removed altogether. Each scenario required a different constellation of equipment, skills and people. Where the current scenario included for instance Rob's coming over to drive the car, trucks for the car's transport, hoses for the exhaust fumes and wooden blocks to exhibit it on the right height, for the alternative scenario mention was made of a movable platform with wheels folding in and out, trucks large enough to contain the car in its upward driving position, mechanical height adjustors to keep the car on height, auto-movers, and drivers with the strength to steer the car the last few meters without power steering or brakes.

The original object was an important consideration, but the deliberations changed after the acknowledgement that driving was perhaps essential in an earlier stage but was no longer part of the functioning of *Hout Auto* as a work of art; the car had become a prop or illustration for the film. Yet, it was also striking, that the second identity of the work, *Hout Auto* as a darling of DS old-timer enthusiasts, kept coming up in the discussion, if in terms of a possible future that shouldn't be excluded.

> Rob: I can imagine that in twenty years another car organisation comes around, saying: now we are going to let all cars that are artworks worldwide drive again one way or another on a circuit. . . . Lydia: Panamarenko. Rob: And then that wouldn't be possible with this car. Arthur: It would if we do it in such a way that it can drive again. Rob: Yes and, as you say, with everything new inside . . . In this sense it is important that that is possible again. Paulien: And then we will call you [laughter].

But the movement from one scenario to another was not so easily made. It was not only a rational decision, and one of the reasons for this was that maintaining the "old" *Hout Auto* required an array of practices and people, which had a more than instrumental dimension, or even an emotional one. The head of collections actually remarked that she found it a very big step to take leave of the *Hout Auto*'s identity as a car because it seemed a terribly cold thing to do; it also implied taking leave of the technician's regularly coming over to drive the car and all the energy and carefulness going into its maintenance.

Marije: No, I find I was very much along the line that we already have shared, but I found it a very big step or what, and I notice that I find it comfortable to notice that you all share in the direction . . .

Lydia: The big step is to realize that it doesn't function anymore.

Marije: That has a terrible coldness to it. And that you [Rob] come twice each year that is also just . . . Paulien: You'll just come twice a year [laughter]. Here I am, it's in the contract!

Marije: But I was also very much yes, and you know, and it is no longer original and nobody ever sees it, so you experience it as a sculpture with a film . . .

[16] For an exploration of the notion of "networks of care" in the context of contemporary art conservation, in particular net art, see Dekker (2018). Cf. also Scholte's (2022) notion of a "social space of perpetuation and care."

So well I found it a very big step, as you know, I mean how much energy and carefulness and I don't know what, that for me was also a reason to hear how you think about this more broadly. It assures me that all of you do not find it so very strange to follow this idea.

Similar emotional dimensions came up about other aspects of the maintenance practice as well: the adventure of driving around, the excitement of the public looking at the car driving. But also the anxiety and annoyance about the risks and unpredictability of its transport.

Arthur: I find it [the car] an unreliable thing; it is a laborious object to work with for loans, we carry responsibility for the whole . . . [Other voices, mixed:] It is also full of risks: the car may explode, burn down . . . Arthur: It is quite a happening, the parties who take part in the loan should know that. It must be very clear to them what they are dealing with. Every time it is quite labour intensive to make that clear. Paulien: A happening it remains, that is the nice thing; you keep the happening. [Various voices:] Sure enough, but it becomes less risky. Rob: If you talk about a happening that is the driving and that the engine runs and there is a lot of smoke coming out and crowds of people in the streets – in Nantes it was gigantic: the whole street was packed and in Ahoy Hall we had the Shell marathon, which was also big, with many from the public running alongside the car . . . Paulien: What you indicate as the happening is, as far as the public is concerned, that it drives. Arthur: Yes, but Rob that is nice what you say but that is exactly, that part exactly is like a boy's adventure book, but I also find that difficult . . . It is my task to ensure control and that part feels a bit difficult.

The loan to Museum De Hallen provided a good opportunity to go through all the movements of transporting *Hout Auto* again. Getting it into the museum was a problem, as a pillar barred the entrance through the front doors on the ground floor. An alternative was to move it in through a window, but in that case the windowsill had to be replaced and the municipality's property department did not approve the replacement. The next option was to lift the car and move it in through large windows at the front side on the first floor, as had been done before with large works by Joseph Beuys and Thomas Hirschhorn; only now a temporary wall impeded its passage, which could not be removed as it was needed for the exhibition. So finally the car was put in a container and hoisted to the level of a smaller window in the building's sidewall; the car had to drive over a bridge connecting the container with the museum room. Rob made a film of the whole, very precarious procedure.[17]

Susanna: We did have the problem that the axle[18] started to scrape the floor when it came in.
Rob: When driving in, yes, that happened because there was a small bridge [. . .].
Arthur: The engine is in the front so the weight goes to the nose.

[17] The film "REISKOORTS - HOUT AUTO - De Hallen / WANDERLUST - WOODEN CAR" by STUDIO XLM can be watched on Vimeo: https://vimeo.com/studioxlm/wanderlust.

[18] In Dutch: "as"; unclear whether this referred to a wheel axle or driving shaft.

Rob: Because in the front there is a heavy part, but there is one at the back as well; and at a certain moment the whole thing started to tilt over, you see in the film that at a certain point the container started to lean over backwards. And I was in the car and couldn't get out because those doors at the side couldn't open; that was a very suspenseful moment.

The whole operation took a lot of preliminary research, consultation and collaboration. An important factor in getting the loan to succeed was the determination and experience of the responsible curator and the trust between the loan giver and the loan taker.

> Susanna: This has been very laborious and at one point I thought: I just want this car to come; this was just a matter of honour that it should succeed. We did cancel it one time because we didn't see any possibility, due to the building, to move it inside. A lot of measuring was needed; Arthur came by another time to look at everything again ... The *Hout Auto* is yours, you wanted it as much to succeed as we did. Arthur: Yes. Susanna: That made it very pleasant; if you have a loan giver who seems hesitant ... Marije: I think it was also your experience; you had already managed to get in more big objects here; if you had just started out, you probably would not have dared to do it.

Finances played a role and permissions; access and safety were issues, as the window looked onto a shopping street where other trucks would be loading and unloading in the morning and people would be shopping later on. The safety of the public was another reason not to let the car drive:

> Arthur: A reason for not driving it is this: when people see it, they run to look at it and see what happens, and they want to touch the car; but if there is an accident there is the issue of insurance. Is the Frans Hals Museum accountable or the Central Museum? [...] During the loan in Assen, I noticed there were visitors who didn't know what happened and when they see the car they think let's go there and have a look underneath it. This gives rise to situations in which you don't know what people will do and what the car will do.

The proposition I would like to make is, rather than understanding conservation ethics in practice as primarily geared to *protecting* works, to see it as an ethics of *care* for the mutual flourishing of the work and its surrounding ecosystem. Again, the comparison of conservation ethics with bioethics is fruitful. In their work on synthetic biology, Rabinow and Bennett (2009) explain that in the 1970s the predominant form of bioethics was focused on protection; it was designed to prevent abuse of vulnerable subjects by medical researchers. For example, in the Tuskegee experiments, in which patients with latent syphilis were not given proper treatment,

> bioethical equipment was designed to protect human subjects of research, understood as autonomous persons. Hence its protocols and principles were limited to establishing and enforcing moral bright lines indicating which areas of scientific research were forbidden. (2009, p. 218)

Protection is still an important issue, but has become part of a more comprehensive approach principally concerned with "the care of others, the world, things and ourselves. Such care is pursued through practices, relationships, and experiences that contribute to and constitute a flourishing existence" (Ibid).

This new bioethical emphasis on flourishing has a parallel in recent theory of contemporary art conservation, where for instance notions of artworks' *unfolding* (Laurenson 2016) or *becoming* (Castriota 2019) have been proposed. The distinction between the two types of ethics is not further elaborated by Rabinow and Bennett (2012). However, care ethics is nowadays a thriving field, both as a specialisation within ethics—the branch of ethics concerned with a specific aspect of human activities and attitudes—and an approach to ethics in general (Gardiner 2009; Brouwer and van Tuinen 2019). Taken in this latter sense, care ethics tends to distance itself from both the utilitarian type of ethics that considers moral good in terms of the greatest happiness of the greatest number and the Kantian (deontological) type of ethics that is oriented to the rational determination of the rights and obligations of individuals. Because in this alternative sense life is conceived as ontologically relational, care is seen as a natural inclination of human (and in posthumanist strands also non-human) beings, rather than as something that an inherently isolated and egoistic individual needs to be forced to do through considerations of self-interest or duty. In the words of Tronto and Fisher:

> On the most general level, we suggest that caring be viewed as *a species activity that includes everything that we do to maintain, continue and repair our 'world' so that we can live in it as well as possible*. That world includes our bodies, our selves, and our environment, all of which we seek to interweave in a complex, life-sustaining web. (Quoted in Tronto 1993, p. 103)

Central concepts of care ethics are responsibility, trust, commitment and attentiveness, rather than justice, rights, duties or obligations. Care ethics can be directed to both private and public life and institutions, but tends to start from the former—or to question the distinction. It is often close to strands of virtue ethics, communitarianism and feminism; it frames moral situations as specific situated, and practice-related.

> Care is perhaps best thought of as a practice. The notion of a practice is complex: it is an alternative to conceiving of care as a principle or an emotion. To call care a practice implies that it involves both thought and action, that thought and action are interrelated, and that they are directed toward some end. The activity, and its end, set the boundaries as to what appears reasonable within the framework of the practice. (Tronto, op. cit., p. 108)

This focus on practice is very important. Joan Tronto particularly emphasized that the ethics of care does not only include that a need for care is recognised and a responsibility assigned; that care is *given* and *how* it is given and whether and how it is *received* are just as important aspects of care-ethical consideration. Initially Tronto (1993) distinguished four aspects of care, each with its concomitant value:

- *Caring about*, noticing the need to care in the first place, which requires *attentiveness*.
- *Taking care of*, assuming responsibility for care, which requires *responsibility*.
- *Care-giving*, the actual work of care, which requires *competence*.
- *Care-receiving*, the response of that which is cared for, which requires *responsiveness*.

In 2013 she added a fifth aspect:

- *Caring with*, aligning care with democratic commitments to justice, equality, and freedom for all, which requires *plurality, communication, trust and respect, solidarity*. (Tronto 2013, p. 23; 35)

Although this fifth aspect ultimately addresses care on the level of society as a whole, which may not always be an explicit issue in individual conservation cases, the fact that she sees care as a conglomerate of nested practices allows us to use the relevant values for discussing the relational dimensions of care also on a more restricted level.

Tronto stresses that the phases of the care process must fit together into a whole; hence I found it interesting to note that in the Platform discussions they were always intermingled. The discussions identified *Hout Auto*'s needs for care in a very detailed way; based on the participants' long experience of care giving—to the work and to similar objects—its responses could be recognised and predicted. In a care approach to ethics, the mixing of ethical and technical considerations, as I discussed in the first section of this chapter, does not detract from the ethical nature of the deliberation. Quite the opposite: experience with the technical aspects is included in the values of competence of care-giving and responsiveness of care-receiving. Finally, the relational aspects of care came up in the conversation when the long-lasting relationship between the museum and Rob in his role of technical expert, or the trust Arthur and Marije had in Susanna's experience during the loan arrangements with De Hallen, were mentioned: ultimately these factors were perhaps even more important than the technical details.

In this case, however, the principal care receiver was an object, not a human being. In this context, Maria Puig de la Bellacasa (2017), taking Tronto's (1993) work as a starting point, extended the notion of care to a "more than human only" matter, to cover both techno-scientific assemblages and nature-cultures.[19] In Puig de la Bellacasa's posthumanist ethics, the work of caring implies a material engagement with a world that touches as much as it is touched and therefore transforms the caregiver; the emotional attachments participants formed over time with *Hout Auto* and its maintenance, both positive and negative, are examples of such mutual transformation. The way she conceives of a non-normative, *situated ethicality* or *ethos* guiding caregivers, rather than in terms of pre-existing rules or guidelines, is also fruitful for the appreciation of the tentative, open-ended attitude of the deliberations, which mirrored the unprecedented aspect of the ethical questions at stake. She tries to formulate ethics in a way that avoids normative stances but still recognizes obligations—not as moral principles but as intensities and gradations of ethicality: "Ethical obligations of care have a contingent necessity that emerges from material and affective constraints [of a specific situation] rather than moral orders"

[19] See also Pols (2015) for an outline of an empirical ethics, and Power (2019) for a repurposing of Tronto's "caring with" as "caring-with." Both Pols and Power exchange Tronto's normative approach with an empirical-analytical one, while both include socio-material/human-technology relations.

(op. cit., p. 152). It is ethos that grounds ethical principles rather than following them (ibid., p. 127), in a process of world-making that creates new possibilities and constraints when it responds to existing ones. "Practices create a relational ethos with a world, a process through which material constraints are co-created [. . .]. In turn, constraints recreate relational, situated possibilities and impossibilities" (Ibid., p. 153). In other words: a new scenario for *Hout Auto*, designed to respond to the constraints of the current problematic situation, will create new care-giving practices, new webs of care, new constellations of equipment, skills and people. This will in turn create new possibilities for the unfolding of the work and, without doubt, new constraints and problems.

As a practice in its own right, we could conclude that the specific role of the SBMK Platform meetings could be phrased in terms of their contribution to the aspect of *caring with*: in creating a culture of *plurality, communication, trust and respect,* and *solidarity*. This makes the middle-ranging work of the SBMK Platform meetings more than procedural. Although they work with a specific protocol, the Decision-Making Model, their impact is more pervasive. They set the stage for an open discussion in an atmosphere of respect, trust and solidarity in which all aspects of care can be addressed from a plurality of perspectives. The analysis of the Platform deliberations has shown that the meetings proceed through a variety of forms of moral deliberation, which facilitates the articulation of a broad range of concerns: not only technical and ethical dilemmas come to the fore, but also emotional ones. General ethical guidelines and principles are not absent in the moral reasoning surrounding the care for the work, neither on the work floor nor in the middle-range deliberations developed in the meetings, but take the form of incorporated professional attitudes, an ethos giving a general direction to rather than imposing specific ways of dealing with the work. The variety of deliberative techniques enables the mapping of the complex relational web that *Hout Auto* is part of and the alterations it will go through within a changed practice of care-giving. It is by enabling the articulation of a wide range of considerations that the SBMK fosters an ethos of attentiveness, responsibility, competence, responsiveness, respect and trust that supports the continued flourishing of works of contemporary art.

Acknowledgements The research for this chapter has been made possible by two publicly funded research projects: *New Strategies in the Conservation of Contemporary Art* (NWO, 2009-2013) and *New Approaches in the Conservation of Contemporary Art* (Marie Sklodowska-Curie Innovative Training Network 2016-2019). I thank the members of both research communities for their continuous inspiration and support. I also thank the participants of the Platform meetings for their consent to include me in the meetings, to use their words and for their feedback on previous drafts of this text. Special thanks go to Paulien 't Hoen, Lydia Beerkens, Marije Verduijn and Arthur van Mourik.

References

Arras JD (1991) The revival of casuistry in bioethics. J Med Philos 16:29–51

Boenink M (2013) The multiple practices of doing 'ethics in the laboratory': a mid-level perspective. In: van der Burg S, Swierstra T (eds) Ethics on the laboratory floor. Palgrave Macmillan, New York, pp 57–78
Braunack-Mayer A (2001) Casuistry as bioethical method: an empirical perspective. Soc Sci Med 53:71–81
Brody BA (2003) Taking issue: pluralism and casuistry in bioethics. Georgetown University Press, Washington DC
Brouwer J, van Tuinen S (2019) To mind is to care. V2 Publishing, Rotterdam
Castriota B (2019) Authenticity, identity, and essentialism: Reframing conservation practice. In: Mairesse F, Peters RF (eds) What is the essence of conservation. Materials for a discussion. Papers from the ICOM-CC and ICOFOM session at the 25th General Conference held in Kyoto, 4 September 2019, pp 39–48
Dekker A (2018) Collecting and conserving net art. Moving beyond conventional methods. Routledge, London
DeMarco JP, Ford PJ (2006) Balancing in ethical deliberation: Superior to specification and casuistry. J Med Philos 31:438–497
Gardiner K (2009) Why care? On motivation in care ethics. PhD thesis University of Groningen
Hoffmeister B (1994) The forms and limits of medical ethics. Soc Sci Med 39(9):1155–1164
Jonson AR, Toulmin S (1988) The abuse of casuistry. A history of moral reasoning. University of California Press, Berkeley
Jonsen AR, Toulmin S (1989) The abuse of casuistry. A history of moral reasoning. University of California Press, Berkeley, Los Angeles, London
Kelley M (2007) Casuistry naturalized. In: Cherry MJ, Iltis AS (eds) Pluralistic casuistry. Balancing moral arguments, economic realities, and political theory. Springer, Dordrecht, pp 65–82
Laurenson P (2016) Practice as research: unfolding the objects of contemporary art conservation. Maastricht University, Maastricht (inaugural speech)
Pols J (2015) Towards an empirical ethics in care: relations with technologies in health care. Med Health Care Philos 18:81–90
Power ER (2019) Assembling the capacity to care: caring-with precarious housing. Trans Inst Br Geogr 44:763–777
Puig de la Bellacasa M (2017) Matters of care. Speculative ethics in more than human worlds. University of Minnesota Press. Minneapolis
Rabinow P, Bennett G (2009) Human practices: Interfacing three modes of collaboration. In: Parke EC, Bedau M (eds) The Ethics of protocells: moral and social implications of creating life in a laboratory. The MIT Press, Cambridge, pp 263–290
Rabinow P, Bennett G (2012) Designing human practices. An experiment with synthetic biology. The University of Chicago Press, Chicago
Scholte T (2022) The perpetuation of site-specific installation artworks in museums. Staging contemporary art. Amsterdam University Press, Amsterdam
Spranzi M (2013) Clinical ethics and values: how do norms evolve from practice? Med Health Care Philos 16:93–103
Stigter S (2016) Between concept and material. Working with conceptual art: a conservator's testimony. PhD thesis University of Amsterdam
Tronto JC (1993) Moral boundaries. A political argument for an ethics of care. Routledge, New York
Tronto JC (2013) Caring democracy: markets, equality and justice. New York University Press, New York
van de Vall R (1999) Painful decisions. Philosophical considerations on a decision making model. In: Hummelen Y, Sillé D (eds) Modern art: who cares? Foundation for the Conservation of Modern Art and the Netherlands Institute for Cultural Heritage, pp 196–200
van de Vall R (2015) Documenting dilemmas: on the relevance of ethically ambiguous cases. In: Matos LA, Macedo R, Heydenreich G (eds) Revista de História da Arte 4:7–17. http://revistaharte.fcsh.unl.pt/rhaw4/RHAw4.pdf

van de Vall R, Hölling H, Scholte T, Stigter S (2011) Reflections on a biographical approach to contemporary art conservation. In ICOM-CC: 16th Triennial Conference, Lisbon, 19-23 September 2011: preprints [cd-rom] by J. Bridgland (ISBN 9789899752207). https://doi.org/10.1177/1745691612459060

van Mourik A (2017) The conservation ethics of and strategies for preserving and exhibiting an operational car: The motion and standstill of Joost Conijn's *Hout Auto* (Wood Car). In: Rivenc R, Bek R (eds) Keep it moving. Conserving kinetic art. Proceedings from the meeting organized by the Getty Conservation Institute, the ICOM-CC Modern Materials and Contemporary Art Working Group, and Museo del Novecento Palazzo Reale, Milan, Italy, June 30–July 2, 2016. The Getty Conservation Institute, Los Angeles, pp 146–147 https://www.getty.edu/publications/resources/virtuallibrary/9781606065365.pdf. Accessed 24 Apr 2022

van Mourik A (2018) Documenting three complex installation artworks: Ways of securing knowledge and information for museum practice in the future. 26th annual CIDOC - ICOM Conference 2018, Heraklion, Crete, Greece. http://network.icom.museum/fileadmin/user_upload/minisites/cidoc/ConferencePapers/2018/CIDOC2018_paper_131.pdf. Accessed 24 Apr 2022

Waring D (2000) Why the practice of medicine is not a phronetic activity. Theor Med Bioeth 21: 139–151

Wharton G (2018) Bespoke ethics and moral casuistry in the conservation of contemporary art. J Inst Conserv 41(1):58–70

Wildes K (2000) Moral acquaintances: methodology in bioethics. University of Notre Dame Press, Notre Dame

Wildes K (2007) Ethics and deep moral ambiguity. In: Cherry M, Iltis AS (eds) Pluralistic casuistry: moral arguments, economic realities, and political theory. Springer, Dordrecht, pp 37–48

Wyatt S, Balmer B (2007) Home on the range: what and where is the middle in science and technology studies? Sci Technol Human Values 32(6):619–626

Renée van de Vall is emeritus professor in Art & Media at Maastricht University. Her research focuses on the phenomenology of spectatorship in contemporary art; on processes of globalisation of contemporary art and media; and on conservation theory and ethics in the context of contemporary art. She was project leader of various research projects, most recently (2016–2019) of the Marie Sklodowska-Curie Innovative Training Network *New Approaches in the Conservation of Contemporary Art (NACCA)*.

Part II
The Identity of the Art Object

The Enfolding Object of Conservation: Artwork Identity, Authenticity, and Documentation

Brian Castriota

Abstract Conservation approaches for contemporary artworks have increasingly turned to a work's identity as the object of conservation and perpetuation. Within the "performance paradigm" of conservation (van de Vall, Revista de História Da Arte 4, 7–17, 2015a) authenticity is often predicated on a manifestation's compliance with an artist's explicit directives. In practice, this paradigm is challenged by works of art that unfold in protracted states of creation and accrue new modes of presentation. This chapter reads notions of artwork identity, authenticity, and documentation for conservation purposes through poststructuralist, feminist, queer, and agential realist discourses. It troubles the assumption that conservators have access to a "view from above" (Haraway, Feminist Studies 14(3), 575–599, 1988) and that the boundaries or properties of an entity are determinate prior to and separate from our observation and description. Within Karen Barad's agential realist framework, the documentation of artwork identity is reframed as a perspectival and partial representation of significances, which are made determinate through—and therefore entangled with—the specifics of our measurement or observation. This chapter shows how, through both our investigations and the documentation we create and leave behind, conservators and conservation researchers are enfolded with the entities we seek to know and care for, and how their boundaries and properties are continually enacted and reconfigured through these material-discursive practices. The objective referent of conservation documentation is therefore refocused as and around the *phenomena* produced through conservation research and practice.

Keywords Significant properties · Identity · Authenticity · Documentation · Time-based media · Agential realism

B. Castriota (✉)
National Galleries Scotland, Edinburgh, UK
e-mail: bcastriota@nationalgalleries.org

R. van de Vall, V. van Saaze (eds.), *Conservation of Contemporary Art*, Studies in Art, Heritage, Law and the Market 9, https://doi.org/10.1007/978-3-031-42357-4_4

1 Introduction

Becoming is not an unfolding in time but the inexhaustible dynamism of the enfolding of mattering. —Karen Barad (2007, p. 180)

In classical theories of conservation that emerged in Europe in the nineteenth and twentieth centuries, both the physical integrity and authenticity of works of art were thought to rely on the endurance of a particular physical object and its various aesthetic potentials. Within this paradigm, conservation activities were centred largely around mitigating changes perceived as loss to a physical object through minimal and ideally reversable material interventions. With many works of art produced today and in recent decades, the perpetuation of an artwork's presence is not contingent solely on the physical persistence of a discrete, spatiotemporal artefact nor is a work's authenticity guaranteed only by maintaining the continuity of original material fabric. Many artworks that incorporate ephemeral or consumable materials, audio-visual technologies, liveness, and other conceptual practices that challenge traditional, Western paradigms of art making do not persist as experienced entities by simply maintaining a finite and unchanging material assemblage. In many cases, these works recur in multiple "equally genuine instances" (Goodman 1968, p. 113) as physical objects, events, and experiences made present in time and space through the episodic recombination of replenished or new materials and media, equipment, and/or human interactions.

Against the backdrop of the wider "communicative turn" of the 1990s wherein heritage frameworks and conservation theories in the Global North began to recognise the cultural contingency and mutability of perceptions of authenticity (Villers 2004; Muñoz Viñas 2005; van Saaze 2013, p. 75), frameworks for fine art conservation began to be reconceived to accommodate the particularities of modern and contemporary artworks. As with many non-Western objects of cultural heritage and new, born-digital archival objects and records, the classical conservation frameworks—with their prioritisation of material fixity—were also no longer sufficient for the diversity of modern and contemporary artworks in and entering museum collections around the world. Entrenched understandings of authenticity—predicated on the continuity of historic material substance—necessitated a reformulation.

New theoretical frameworks and practical approaches have emerged in the last two decades wherein the focus of conservation has expanded away from material fixity towards a fixity of artwork identity, essence, or experience. At the heart of these frameworks is a recognition of the artwork as an abstract entity, manifested or instantiated in time and space by one or more concrete objects or events (Castriota 2021a; Irvin 2013). In time-based media conservation in particular, authenticity is often framed as a quality that can be guaranteed by ensuring a work's various manifestations remain compliant with the artist's explicit directives or the properties singled out as constitutive of the artwork's identity. In this "performance paradigm" of conservation—as Renée van de Vall (2015a) has termed it—this is typically achieved by discerning an artwork's "score."[1] Recognising the inevitable absence of the artist and the insufficiency of a paper certificate alone to confer authenticity on an instantiation, these efforts are motivated by the belief that fidelity to some definitive set of material or relational conditions or parameters defined by or in consultation with the artist will allow the work to recur with authenticity and mitigate perceived losses to its integrity. This has led to a pervasive supposition that conservators or other collection care staff may reveal and protect an artwork's identity or essence by extracting the rules for its display or activation through artist questionnaires, interviews, and other empirical methods. Within the performance paradigm of conservation, *score compliance* has emerged as one of the implicit, post-material metrics for gauging authenticity in the conservation of time-based media, installation, and performance artworks.[2]

Although some works may appear to be more amenable to what Hanna Hölling characterises as "textual stabilisation" (2016, p. 18), both score reduction and the enforcement of score compliance can be difficult or infeasible for some works. Material and contextual circumstances are liable to change and, as a result, an artist may make certain declarations about how a work should be enacted or manifested that contradict previous declarations or sanctions.[3] The fact that many contemporary artworks are editioned—existing in multiple collections with the artist often retaining an AP or "artist's proof"—leaves open the opportunity for artists to continue editing, revising, and updating their works. Directives may therefore become thinned or multiplied over time as new versions, edits, and presentation modes arise. There may also not always be clear or unanimous agreement between an artist, their representatives, collection caretakers, and audiences about what constitutes a work's significant properties; different perspectives on a work's significant properties may arise, and these may be at odds with those of an artist or a caretaker at one point in time. Whether a manifestation is score-compliant may, in these cases, become a matter of perspective.

In this chapter, I provide an overview of the prevailing conservation discourse around artwork identity and authenticity for time-based media, installation, and performance artworks. I outline the primary shortcomings of approaches wherein authenticity is seen to be derived through score-compliant enactment and identity is framed as the object of fixity. I challenge the premise that an artwork's identity is a latent quality or singular and wholly knowable entity that may serve as the object of conservation, and I argue that it instead be recognised as a continuously (re)produced

---

[1]Notable discussions include Viola (1999), van Wegen (1999), Rinehart (2004), Laurenson (2004, 2006), MacDonald (2009), Noël de Tilly (2011), Caianiello (2013), van de Vall (2015b), and Phillips (2015).

[2]The notion of "score compliance" with respect to the authenticity of contemporary artworks is discussed explicitly by van de Vall (2015b), although the term originates in Nelson Goodman's *Languages of Art* (1968, p. 117; pp. 186–187) and is not common parlance in conservation literature.

[3]Here I adopt Sherri Irivin's (2005) phraseology around implicit and explicit sanctions. See also Wharton (2015).

representation of significances made determinate through and as part of our practices. Although the distinction is frequently collapsed, I show how artwork identity is fundamentally distinct from the verbal or textualized directives solicited from or created in collaboration with artists to guide decision-making around a work's materialisation(s); whilst these may serve as a quasi-score and may inform perspectives on a work's identity, they are not one in the same. I also reframe the oft-invoked concept of authenticity as the degree to which an encountered object, event, or experience is regarded by an individual as an instance of the artwork it is purported to be, a judgement that is modulated by both empirical evidence, context, as well as the evaluator's experiences, memories, and values.[4]

This chapter builds upon Pip Laurenson's (2016) discussion of contemporary artworks as "epistemic objects" which are open, incomplete, and whose significances continually emerge through their indefinite "unfolding." I also extend Hélia Marçal's body of scholarship applying Donna Haraway's (1988) writing around "situated knowledges" and Karen Barad's (2007) agential realist framework to conservation theory and practice.[5] By thinking notions of artwork identity and its documentation with Barad's theory of agential realism—developed out of their work as a theoretical particle physicist—I propose that our textual documentation of artworks-as-conservation-objects be understood not as scores to aid in the enforcement of score compliance, but as representations of Baradian *phenomena*, where phenomena are defined as the specific *intra-actions* between objects and *agencies of observation* (which, in this context, include conservation researchers), both of which "emerge from, rather than precede" the intra-actions that produce them (2007, p. 128). In this text I adopt Barad's term *intra-action*, which recognises the "ontological inseparability" and mutual, co-constitutive entanglement between measuring agencies and objects (i.e., knower and known), in contrast to *interaction*, which relies on the assumed "prior existence of separately determinate entities" (ibid.).[6] Within this agential realist framework I argue that the objective referent of conservation documentation is not an artwork or object of conservation separate and apart from our observation or measurement, but rather the phenomena that are constituted by our intra-actions with and around the works we are investigating and seeking to secure a futurity for.

Using a case study of a radio-transmitted sound installation by artist Susan Philipsz (b. 1965, Glasgow, Scotland), I show how one artwork's perceived identity is (re)configured through specific material-discursive intra-actions, rather than something pre-existent that is revealed and exposed through empirical inquiry. Conservation practices for contemporary art are imagined within a "processual paradigm" (van de Vall 2015a) not as a rote process of score reduction and policing of score

[4] I derive this definition of authenticity from the Consultative Committee for Space Data Systems' *Reference Model for Open Archival Information Systems* where authenticity is defined as: "The degree to which a person (or a system) regards an object as what it is purported to be. Authenticity is judged on the basis of evidence" (CCSDS 2012, p. 9).

[5] See in particular Marçal (2018, 2019, 2021a, 2021b, 2022) and Castriota and Marçal (2021).

[6] See also Marçal (2021b, p. 2).

compliance, but instead as part of a continuous enfolding and (re)configuring of intra-acting agencies, which include both the objects of conservation practices and those observing, representing, and providing care, and through which such distinctions and boundaries are enacted and made determinate. In this way I argue contemporary artworks—like all parts of the world—are not simply becoming in their unfolding but through their *en*folding.

2 Beyond Score Compliance Authenticity

In much of the discourse around modern and contemporary art conservation from the late 1990s an artwork's authenticity is framed as a singular quality that can be guaranteed by soliciting the artist's approval (Beerkens 1999, p. 71), or through the conservator's careful excavation of a work's "essence" (Guldemond 1999, pp. 79–81).[7] Since the turn of the millennium, the objective of conservation has moved away from achieving material stability towards the identification and perpetuation of properties deemed constitutive of the work's "identity" or "essence," which may or may not include original materials.[8] This thinking was propelled by the writing of Pip Laurenson (2004, 2006), who extended to time-based media artworks several philosophical concepts from Nelson Goodman (1968) and Stephen Davies (2001), recognising the many parallels between time-based media installations and musical works. This included the notion of a "two-stage" model of a work's creation, where the properties identified as essential or "work-defining" may serve as a kind of score that may be used to guide decision-making around a work's manifestations.[9] Rebecca Gordon proceeded along similar lines as Laurenson with her notion of an

---

[7] In her discussion of authenticity around the re-fabrication of neon tubes used in a work by Mario Merz, Lydia Beerkens—noting an uneasiness with employing replacement tubes—ultimately concludes that "authenticity may be guaranteed by requesting the artist's approval" (1999, p. 71). Jaap Guldemond suggests that an artwork's "essence" is not just established by the artist's voice, but also by the curator and conservator's "careful analyses of the visual aspects and the content of the work" (1999, p. 81).

[8] Artwork "identity" as the object of conservation is a common feature of the literature, popularised in part through the *Inside Installations* project (2004–2007). Notable discussions include van Wegen (1999), Laurenson (2004, 2006), Jones and Muller (2008), Fiske (2009), van Saaze (2009, 2013), Brokerhof et al. (2011), van de Vall et al. (2011), Jadzińska (2011, 2012); Phillips (2012, 2015), Ensom (2019). References to an artwork's "essence" are also common; see Guldemond (1999, p. 81), Stringari (1999), Mancusi-Ungaro (1999, p. 392), Coddington (1999, p. 24), Bek (2011, p. 207), Rinehart and Ippolito (2014, p. 178).

[9] Goodman refers to a work's "constitutive properties" (1968, p. 116) whilst Davies (2001) uses the terms "work-defining properties" (p. 27), "work-defining features" (p. 166), "work-defining directives" (p. 153), and "work-determinative instructions," (p. 112) which inspired Laurenson's writing. This concept of constitutive, significant, and essential properties and "faithful instances" (Laurenson 2004, p. 49) is inherited from a wider discourse in aesthetics where artworks are conceptualised as abstract objects, or *types*, manifested in one or more token instances; for an overview of this discourse see Castriota (2021a). For discussions of "significant properties" in the

artwork's "critical mass" (2011, 2014), defined as "the optimum choice and grouping of factors or attributes that demonstrate the core identity of the work of art" (2014, p. 97).

The framework put forward by Laurenson has since become foundational to practical models and approaches employed in time-based media art conservation. At the heart of Joanna Phillips' (2015) Documentation Model for Time Based-Media Art is a Goodmanian ontology that distinguishes between a work's score and its manifestations, produced in two distinct stages. In this model, the work's significant or essential properties are synthesised by conservators from the artist's explicit directives as well as the implicit sanctioning of properties or formal features in a work's previous manifestations. These processes of what Tina Fiske has termed "tethering" (2009) are aimed at achieving some degree of durability for artworks that do not persist through a fixed material substance. Through this kind of essentialisation or score reduction it is thought that such works may be made into discrete, coherent, "durable and repeatable" (Laurenson and van Saaze 2014, p. 34) museum objects that can be enacted and manifested in perpetuity, thereby securing their presence. Implicit here is a belief that the conservator can minimise the "erosion of identity between instances of the work" (Fiske 2009, p. 234) and prevent any unauthorised deviation that might be viewed as losses to its integrity. This is seen to be achieved by soliciting and collecting verbal instructions and directives from artists at the point of acquisition, and ensuring—through conservation oversight—that manifestations thereafter remain compliant by embodying the properties, attributes, behaviours, and relations identified as significant, essential, or work-defining. In the application of these frameworks and models there is often a presumption that compliance translates into a guarantee of authenticity and that what constitutes an artwork's essence is both knowable and consensual.

Although often overlooked, Laurenson importantly cautioned against drawing direct analogies between musical works and time-based media artworks,[10] and noted that that an artwork's identity may be difficult to pin down: "Making decisions about what is important to preserve means deciding what is essential in identifying a particular installation as a faithful instance of that work. However, what is important to the identity of these works is often uncertain" (Laurenson 2004, p. 49). She also added that a work's identity may be labile even after entering a museum collection.[11] More recently, Laurenson (2016) has drawn upon the writing of sociologist Karen

context of digital objects and records see Holdsworth and Sergeant (2000), Hedstrom and Lee (2002), Yeo (2010), and Ensom (2019). See also the discussion of "character-defining features" of built heritage and historic landscapes by Jester and Park (1993), Birnbaum (1994), and Birnbaum and Capella Peters (1996).

[10]Laurenson (2004, p. 49) comments, "...it is not possible to draw a direct analogy to musical works—time-based media installations are not specified by a score, and media elements are decoded without the interpretative role of a performer."

[11]"Early in the relationship with a new work, the museum often accommodates the exploration and development of the identity of the work, only later acting more conservatively to contain the work in its established form" (Laurenson 2004, p. 51).

Knorr Cetina (2001) to consider how contemporary artworks may be understood as indefinitely "unfolding" epistemic objects, that is, as abstract objects of knowledge whose significances may accrue and vary over time.[12]

Several other influential texts on the conservation of contemporary art have also highlighted how the differences introduced in the course of a work's iteration may alter the work's perceived identity, fracturing the perception of a singular, immutable essence. Van de Vall et al. (2011, p. 3) comment that a "work does not necessarily stop changing when it enters a museum collection" and add to this observation that not every artwork exists as "an organic or functional whole possessing a singular identity." Phillips (2012, p. 140) writes that a work's identity is not always fully formed close to the work's initial manifestation; she cautions conservators against prematurely determining a "young" artwork's work-defining properties as it may enter a collection while in a "state of 'infancy'" and in the process of "forming its identity." In the documentation model she developed, Phillips (2015, p. 175) also notes how each manifestation of a work "may inform" its identity or score. In her writing on the multiple nature of Nam June Paik's video installation *One Candle*, Vivian van Saaze similarly observes that "what was considered to be the core of the work varied from one person to the next" (2013, p. 77), leading her to conclude that this work is "more than one, less than many" (2009, pp. 196–197). More recently, Caitlin Spangler-Bickell (2021) has noted how many contemporary artworks exist in a state of multiplicity with a "dividual" and "partible" objecthood, in a challenge to theoretical frameworks and essentialising approaches to artwork documentation predicated on the assumption that every artwork retains a singular, monolithic identity or essence. Accordingly, we might ask: Is it part of the caretaker's remit to police score compliance and protect an artwork's identity from erosion or deviation? Is the authenticity of a work predicated purely on score-compliant display or enactment? And if a work's identity or essence is something plural or in flux, what exactly is the role of conservation?

3 The "View from Nowhere": Essentialism, Centring, and Representation

Although there is a growing acceptance of this processual understanding of artwork identity and a recognition that it may evolve through time, both conservation theory and practice continue to fall back on the essentialist assumption that an artwork retains a singular identity or a "true nature" (Muñoz Viñas 2005, p. 92) at any given

[12] Knorr Cetina (2001, p. 181) explains, "Objects of knowledge appear to have the capacity to unfold indefinitely. They are more like open drawers filled with folders extending indefinitely into the depth of a dark closet. Since epistemic objects are always in the process of being materially defined, they continually acquire new properties and change the ones they have. But this also means that objects of knowledge can never be fully attained, that they are, if you wish, never quite themselves."

moment that can be totally known through empirical methods or simply by asking the artist. The role of the conservator is still often framed as the excavator and protector of an original, or, at the very least, *singular* identity or essence. Such thinking can be traced to post-Enlightenment, materialist theories of authenticity—with an "emphasis on entities and their origins and essences" (Jones 2010, p. 181)—where the conservator is compelled by an ethical directive to uncover, recover, and protect.

The notion that things are defined or determined by an abstract and eternal essence has been a recurring subject of Western philosophy. Feminist theorist Diana Fuss characterises essentialism as "a belief in the real, true essence of things, the invariable and fixed properties which define the 'whatness' of a given entity" (1989, p. xi). Following deconstructionist philosophical discourse in the late 1960s and 1970s, many social constructionist frameworks in cultural studies began to challenge the idea that national, racial, ethnic, gender, or sexual identities are identified "on the basis of transhistorical, eternal, immutable essences" (ibid.).

According to essentialist and structuralist conceptualisations of identity, the manifestations of every entity are determined and constrained by a static and immutable essence, that is, bounded by a seemingly stable ground or centre that limits deviation and permutation. In his 1966 lecture 'Structure, Sign and Play in the Discourse of the Human Sciences,' Jacques Derrida put forward a critique of what he called "centred structure." He argued that classical thought presumed every structure was ruled or governed by a *centre*, which above all served to "limit what we might call the *play* of structure. By orienting and organizing the coherence of the system, the centre of a structure permits the play of its elements inside the total form" (2001, p. 352). In the classical model, the centre constituted the structure's core but was importantly seen as free from what Derrida called the "play of difference" or the substitution of meanings that might occur within the structure. He explained,

> The concept of centred structure is in fact the concept of a play based on a fundamental ground, a play constituted on the basis of a fundamental immobility and a reassuring certitude, which is itself beyond the reach of play. (ibid.)

This notion of play is what allows for variation or permutation, but only up to a certain point: in the structuralist linguistic model, the centre establishes a tolerance for deviation by effectively marking off a boundary, beyond which "the substitution of contents, elements or terms is no longer possible" (ibid.).

This model remains at the heart of the way we tend to think about an artwork and its identity. Essentialising approaches employed in contemporary art conservation that trace boundaries around an artwork's essential properties might be characterised in Derridean terms as processes of *centring*. As a work of art is transfigured into an object of cultural heritage or *musealium* within the museum (Stránský 1985), an institutional centre is often constructed through the musealisation process. A centre is effectively traced by delineating the rules and parameters about how a work may be activated, exhibited, and interacted with, or the physical matter or features that must endure for the work to be perceived as "whole." Properties endowed with a greater significance—lying closer to or within this centre—are those that might be considered essential, work-defining, or constitutive of its critical mass. If these properties are not maintained or embodied in a work's future manifestations, it is thought that concerns around authenticity may arise. However, as we will see, the essentiality of some properties and the insignificant or incidental nature of others are not binary or eternal statuses, nor can they always be determined conclusively.

Judith Butler notes in *Gender Trouble* that what we take to be an "internal essence" is in fact "manufactured through a sustained set of acts" (1990, p. xv) and that "identity is 'performatively' constituted by the very expressions that are said to be its results" (1990, p. 34). The concrete objects and/or events presented as instances of a particular work—understood as an abstract object or entity—may be thought of along similar lines as J. L. Austin's performative utterances or *performatives*, which Butler extends to non-verbal bodily acts around gender expression. These formal manifestations—that is, particular physical objects or episodes of enactment/installation—are typically conceived of as the products of a score-based enactment or materialisation, like cakes made by following a recipe. However, identity is not the same thing as a recipe or score. Although certain directives communicated by an artist may be used to guide how a work is manifested or enacted, it is an artist's directives and a work's manifestations (experienced by audiences) that *performatively* affirm an individual's sense of the work's identity through repetition, or rupture that sense of continuity or self-sameness through difference or deviation.[13] This is to say that a work's manifestations are not the *results* of its identity so much as they help constitute our sense of what that identity might be, alongside the various other ways works of art or heritage objects may be actualised in time and space.[14] This may, nevertheless, lead to the creation of representations in the form of conservation reports that can also have a causal effect on how a work or entity is materialised, resulting in a kind of "iterative intra-activity" (Barad 2007, p. 208) between these various performatives.

As we can see identity is not only processual but also perspectival and representational, which is to say that representations of an entity cannot be detached from the individuals doing the representation. Prevailing conservation theories and documentation practices remain built upon a scientific view that our "observations reveal pre-existing properties of an observation-independent reality" and which "take observation to be the benign facilitator of discovery, a transparent and undistorting lens passively gazing at the world" as Barad (2007, p. 195) puts it. Building on the ideas of physicist and philosopher of science Niels Bohr, as well as Haraway's (1988) feminist critique of classical notions of scientific objectivity, Barad explains how this view of the world is based in Newtonian physics and a "Cartesian presupposition that there is an inherent boundary between observer and observed, between knower and known" (2007, p. 154). According to metaphysical individualism, the world is made up of separate entities with "individually determinate

[13] For a lengthier discussion of Butler's notion of performativity in relationship to the construction of artwork identity, see Castriota (2021c).

[14] For a discussion of the various ways works of art are actualised beyond formal gallery manifestations, see Castriota (2021b).

boundaries and properties whose well-defined values can be represented by abstract universal concepts that have determinate meanings independent of the specifics of the experimental practice" (p. 195).[15] By contrast, Barad explains that Bohr's indeterminacy principle—understood as "a quantitative statement of complementarity" (p. 302) evidenced by wave-particle duality and the double-slit experiment—highlights the "ontological inseparability or entanglement of objects and agencies of observation" (p. 309), that is, how the "determinateness of the properties and boundaries of the 'object'" depends on the "specific nature of the experimental arrangement" (p. 302) or measuring apparatus.[16] In Barad's posthumanist elaboration—which also draws upon experiments in quantum physics that have further corroborated Bohr's interpretations—measurements do not reveal the properties of independently existing objects. Rather, measurements are "the intra-active marking of one part of a phenomenon by another" (p. 338), where the boundaries and properties of its entangled, component parts "become determinate only in the enactment of an agential cut delineating the 'measured object' from the 'measuring agent'" (p. 337).[17] It is therefore *phenomena* that are the "objective referent of measured properties" (p. 309).

Nevertheless, a Newtonian-Cartesian view of the world continues to underpin prevailing conservation theories and practices. This is characterised by an "epistemological assumption that experiments reveal the pre-existing determinate nature of the entity being measured" (p. 106), and—as Haraway (1988) puts it—the idea that we occupy a "view from above, from nowhere" (p. 589), impartially "representing while escaping representation" (p. 581). We see this reflected in the assumption of inherent divisions or cuts separating the conservator or conservation researcher (the observer/knower) from the object of conservation (the observed/known). We may connect it with the prevalent self-image of the conservator or conservation researcher as an impartial observer gazing from above, discerning the "properties of observation-independent objects" (Barad 2007, p. 114), which are assumed to be determinate prior to and seperate from their inquiry. It is also forms the basis of documentation

[15] Barad (2007, p. 106) writes, "Objects are assumed to possess individually deterministic attributes, and it is the job of the scientist to cleverly discern these inherent characteristics by obtaining the values of the corresponding observation-independent variables through some benignly invasive measurement procedure."

[16] For Barad, apparatuses—such as an experimental set-up—are material-discursive practices that enact boundaries and "produce differences that matter" (2007, p. 106). In so doing, they are also phenomena ("constituted and dynamically reconstituted as part of the ongoing intra-activity of the world") that are "formative of matter and meaning, productive of, and part, of, the phenomena they produce" (ibid.). For an explanation of the double-slit experiment and its onto-epistemological implications, see Barad (2007, pp. 97–106; 247–352).

[17] Barad derives their notion of *agential cuts* from Bohr, who challenged the assumed inherent separation between the measuring apparatus (which includes the observer) and what is measured or observed. Cuts, according to Barad, are "agentially enacted not by wilful individuals but by the larger material arrangement of which 'we' are a 'part'...'they' and 'we' are co-constituted and entangled through the very cuts 'we' help enact." (p. 178).

Fig. 1 Susan Philipsz, *You Are Not Alone*, 2009. Installed at the Radcliffe Observatory, Oxford in 2009 (Photo: Andy Keate, © Susan Philipsz)

practices focused around establishing boundaries and marking off—in no uncertain terms—the properties deemed inherently constitutive of the object of conservation.

An ongoing challenge to frameworks for authenticity rooted in the performance paradigm of conservation are those works whose boundaries appear to "shift from within" (Haraway 1988, p. 595), that is, when empirical inquiry around a work's significant properties fails to reveal a singular, consensual centre, or a "true" essence or core of the work's identity. In what follows I present a case study of such a work that troubles the supposition that an artwork or heritage object has "determinate properties that are independent of our experimental investigations of them" (Barad 2007, p. 106). I will show how the assessed significances of particular artwork properties are inseparable from the conditions of our observation, and I will consider how conservation documentation at the level of identity is therefore less an objective representation of the entity being studied or conserved so much as it as a perspectival and partial representation of the phenomena produced by our measurement and of which we are an entangled part.

4 Case Study: Susan Philipsz's *You Are Not Alone*

Susan Philipsz's radio-transmitted sound installation *You Are Not Alone* is a work that has developed into a multiplicity of variants or versions since it was first realised in 2009. The work was initially conceived as a commission for Modern Art Oxford in 2009, installed in the nearby, late eighteenth-century Radcliffe Observatory

Fig. 2 Transmission equipment installed in the upstairs offices of Modern Art Oxford (Photo: Andy Keate, © Susan Philipsz)

(Fig. 1). Inspired by Guglielmo Marconi's radio telegraphy experiments at the turn of the twentieth century, Philipsz took the commission as an opportunity to thematise distance and connection through the history of the astronomical observatory and the poetics of how sound waves and other signals persist in their infinite reverberations.

For the commission, Philipsz began collecting recordings of radio interval signals from radio stations around the globe, some still operational and some defunct. Developed in the 1920s and 30s, these brief musical sequences functioned as sonic fingerprints for listeners to identify a particular station between broadcasts. Like a nineteenth-century naturalist, Philipsz collected sixty-seven of these endangered or extinct radio interval signals and worked with musician Julius Heise to re-record them on a vibraphone. Two stereo tracks (four channels) containing the vibraphone renditions were created, with each musical sequence played three times in a row. In accordance with telecommunication regulations in the United Kingdom, a Programme Making and Special Events Licence was obtained from Ofcom authorising the use of two UHF bandwidths for the duration of the work's installation in Oxford. The two half-hour audio tracks, played on loop, were broadcast at 856.8 and 860.6 MHz by two SBS TX400 transmitters and aerials located in the upstairs offices of Modern Art Oxford (Fig. 2) to aerials (Fig. 3), two RX400 receivers (Fig. 4), amplifiers, and four speakers installed at the Radcliffe Observatory over a mile away for the duration of the work's exhibition.

For its reinstallation at Haus des Rundfunks in Berlin in 2012 (Fig. 5), Philipsz reconfigured the four-channel work into a two-channel, stereo format as a response

Fig. 3 Detail of the aerials installed at the Radcliffe Observatory, Oxford in 2009 (Photo: Eoghan McTigue, © Susan Philipsz)

Fig. 4 Detail of receivers and amplifiers installed at the Radcliffe Observatory, Oxford in 2009 (Photo: Eoghan McTigue, © Susan Philipsz)

to the building's historical connection with the development of stereophonic sound and broadcast technology. There, the audio component was transmitted on UHF radio frequencies across the central hall of the building. It was also re-edited in response to the work's context; several radio interval signals were added, with the

Fig. 5 Susan Philipsz, *You Are Not Alone*, 2009. Stereo version installed at Haus des Rundfunks, Berlin, 2012 (Photo: Nick Ash, © Susan Philipsz)

sequence beginning with Radio Berlin International and ending with Sender Freies Berlin (Connolly 2014).

During the course of my doctoral research secondment with the National Galleries Scotland in 2017—as part of the *NACCA* project—a number of recent works by Philipsz were featured in their NOW exhibition series, including *You Are Not Alone*. Although not a collection work, I was immediately drawn to this installation as a possible test case to consider how a work's significant properties are established and maintained despite material and contextual variation. On the occasion of its re-installation in Edinburgh, Philipsz decided to create a regionally specific version of the work by adding several newly recorded interval signals from stations around the North Atlantic in order to draw a connection with the installation's geographic context. As a loan from the artist—effectively a display of the artist's AP or "artist's proof"—the logistics and equipment sourcing for the work's re-installation were organised by Senior Curator Julie-Ann Delaney who communicated closely with the Philipsz studio in the run up to the opening. There were no written display specifications supplied by the studio; Philipsz and her studio assistant and partner Eoghan McTigue instead pointed Delaney to images and published accounts of the Oxford and Berlin manifestations as a reference, and Delaney worked with a local AV company to procure UHF transceivers and the necessary radio broadcast licence from Ofcom. However, due to the short lead-in time and other logistical challenges, an alternate AV company and relay system using digital, encrypted 5 GHz wireless transmitters and receivers had to be used.

Fig. 6 Playback equipment for *You Are Not Alone*, installed in Gallery 10 of Modern One in 2017 (Photo: Brian Castriota)

With Delaney liaising between the Philipsz studio and the AV company Zisys Events, the final installation consisted of an equipment rack containing a channel mixer, a compressor and gate unit, an LED level visualiser, and a media player, displayed on a pedestal in the middle of Gallery 10 in Modern One (Fig. 6). An XLR cable ran out the back of this unit to the wall, up the side of Modern One to a Xirium Pro transmitter (Fig. 7) mounted on the roof. From there, the signal was broadcast wirelessly across Belford Road to the Xirium Pro receiver mounted on the weathervane on the roof of Modern Two (Fig. 8). The audio was relayed through an XLR cable to an amplifier and speaker perched on the windowsill at the top of the east stairwell (Fig. 9).

Delaney gave the installation a double date of 2009/2017 on the wall label to reflect the changes both to the re-edited audio component and transmission technology (Delaney 2017), although the medium line asserted the work was a "radio-transmitted sound installation." During and following the work's display in 2017 I returned—or *re-turned*[18]—again and again to the question of whether this manifestation was a fully "authentic" instance of *You Are Not Alone* without a true, analogue RF transmission of the audio component. Was this property a "core" part of its identity, and had its identity been "eroded" as a consequence of this deviation? Had the lack of a conservator's active involvement or intervention failed the work in

[18]For Barad (2014) *re-turning* is not a return to a point of origin or departure but a diffractive methodological turning over and over (like soil) to iteratively and intra-actively produce new insights and diffraction patterns.

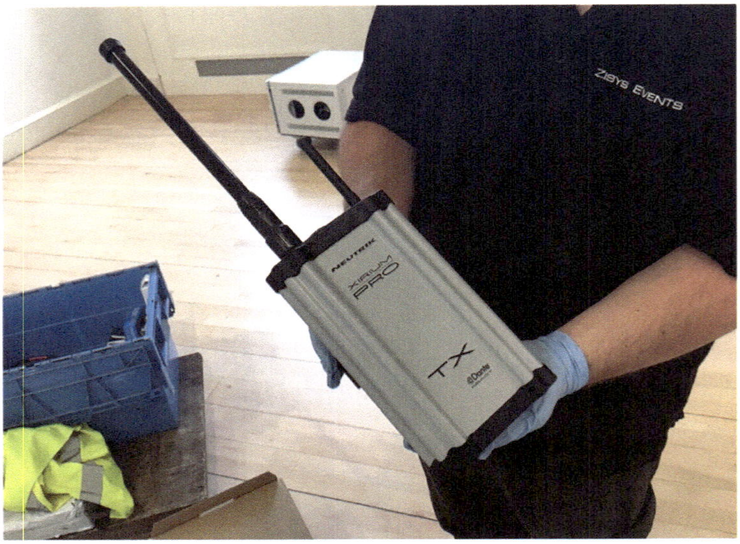

Fig. 7 Euan Kerr from Zisys Events holding the Xirium Pro transmitter prior to installation on the roof of Modern One (Photo: Brian Castriota)

Fig. 8 Xirium Pro receiver installed on the roof of Modern Two (Photo: Brian Castriota)

some way? What, ultimately, is the significance of the wireless, audio relay technology employed in the work? Where might we mark the boundary between the work's essential and incidental proprieties? These were some of the questions that

Fig. 9 *You Are Not Alone* installed in the East Stairwell of Modern Two (Photo: Brian Castriota)

guided my subsequent inquiry and are the kinds of questions conservators of contemporary artworks often ask both of themselves and artists.

Delaney worked in tandem with Philipsz and McTigue for the months leading up to the opening, and the final product of that collaboration—including the equipment employed and audio relay system—was signed off by Philipsz, who was present for final audio adjustments in the days before the exhibition opened and pleased with the outcome. The 2017 installation of *You Are Not Alone* at the National Galleries Scotland was therefore in all practical terms authorised. Were we to predicate the installation's authenticity not only on the basis of it being authorised by the artist, but also in terms of its "precision of resemblance" to the work's initial instantiations (see Innocenti 2013, pp. 225–226), many arguably essential aspects that featured in Oxford and Berlin were retained: pre-recorded vibraphone renditions of radio interval signals were wirelessly transmitted from one location to another and made audible to visitors in the galleries.

However, several features were present that were notable differences compared with the Oxford and Berlin manifestations, most notably the fact that the work was transmitted not using modulated analogue radio frequencies in the UHF range (300 MHz–3 GHz), but rather, by using an encrypted, 5 GHz digital audio transmission system. It could be argued that the Xirium Pro transmission is a "radio transmission" insofar as it is carried on electromagnetic waves with frequencies within the SHF (Super High Frequency) band of the electromagnetic spectrum; the SHF band is technically considered the upper end of radio frequencies, although SHF and EHF (Extra High Frequency) bands are often classed as microwave. This detail—which I discussed with Delaney at the time—was a factor in her decision to describe the work as a "radio-transmitted sound installation" on the wall label's medium line and in publicity materials, even if the medium line conjured other analogue associations.

Even if we can make the case that the installation in Edinburgh retained the significant, *conceptual* property of wireless transmission using radio frequencies, an important *aesthetic* feature of the work was arguably missing. With the 5 GHz digital transmitter and receiver the audio fidelity was greatly improved, allowing for studio-quality audio to be transmitted. The work no longer retained the static and crackle of the analogue radio transmissions perceptible in Oxford and Berlin, a feature that has been commented on positively by both Philipsz and reviewers. In his essay "Lullabies for Strangers"—published by Modern Art Oxford to accompany the 2009 commission—Joerg Heiser (2010, p. 25) wrote:

> But just as a lullaby can become unsettling, the vibraphone sounds—especially as they are emitted here with the soft crackling of radio—make you think of a total stranger trying to communicate with you as if you were his closest friend; or of a message from a once close friend reaching you out of the blue, after you thought they had disappeared forever.

In a public lecture at the National Galleries of Scotland following the opening, Philipsz (2017) remarked:

> I find analogue radio fascinating, there's something quite magical about analogue radio transmission. . .And it's really interesting that it's so variable as well. Whereas now it's digital radio, everyone uses digital radio, but there's something—I mean you can really tell that it's analogue when you first hear it, there's something in the sound.

That said, when asked directly in an interview I conducted with her and McTigue in 2018 if anything were "lost" by not maintaining the analogue radio transmission in Edinburgh, Philipsz responded:

> No, not really, not really. I think if it is being projected over a long distance you get the sense of the distance. When you use an analogue radio, you sort of feel that it emphasises the distance, you know? But when it was going from [Modern] One to [Modern] Two then I think it was okay. Yeah, that was fine. I didn't think it lost anything.

Philipsz and McTigue (2018) went on to explain to me how *You Are Not Alone* was in fact installed twice in 2014—at Fundació Tàpies in Barcelona and at Bielefeld Contemporary—not with analogue, UHF transmitters but with wireless, digital transmission systems similar to what was used in Edinburgh in 2017. McTigue noted that this "digital version" was also a viable option that made the work easier to install and more reliable. Digital wireless relay of the audio component was therefore implicitly sanctioned by Philipsz back in 2014, explicitly sanctioned in emails and personal communication between Delaney and the studio in 2017 authorising its use, and even more explicitly in the interview I conducted with her and McTigue in 2018. Nevertheless, the history of the work's display as a UHF transmission, Philipsz's published description of the work's medium as "radio transmission" (2014, p. 62, 72), and her fondness for the aesthetic qualities afforded by analogue radio broadcast all lend weight to the view that analogue transmission of the vibraphone melodies *is* significant and not incidental. All may be understood as performatives that reify certain perspectives on the work's identity, and in this case we can see how multiple centres—that is, representations of significance—may be traced when these performatives are contradictory.

In its various presentation formats, transmission technologies, and re-edits of its audio content, the work *You Are Not Alone* is both singular—with each installation bearing the same title or nominal identity—and multiple—with each being instances of multiple subtypes or versions of the work. We can say that the 2017 manifestation was another instance of the digital version as well as the prime instance of the Scottish version with its re-edited audio. In this way, although we speak about one artwork-as-type, it also exists in a state of multiplicity through each of these subtypes of the artwork *You Are Not Alone* and their token instantiations in time and space.[19] The question of authenticity in this context thus concerns the degree to which the 2017 manifestation should be regarded as an instance of the abstract entity *You Are Not Alone* more generally, rather than an instance of just one or more of these versions or subtypes of the work.

Based on a certain selection of statements and other evidence of past display, one could make the case—or mark the boundary—that analogue RF broadcast of the audio is a highly significant feature of the work that should be maintained in order to achieve a full—or fully authentic—instance or occurrence of the work. Conversely, one could also point to an alternate selection of evidence to argue that it is simply wireless relay of the audio using any technology that is required to manifest a legitimate, authentic instance of the work. Although Philipsz explicitly sanctioned the use of digital wireless relay, it may become a matter of perspective as to whether this was a fully authentic instance of *You Are Not Alone*, contingent on whether we—based on the evidence collected—attribute significance to analogue RF broadcast of the audio component and regard it as a significant or essential property of the overall work. In effect, this property is at once significant and incidental, resolved as only one or the other depending on how we observe or assess it. Prevailing theories and practices of conservation assume an entity's properties or attributes to be something quantifiable and determinate outside of any inquiry on our part. Even if we employ autoethnographic methodologies that recognise how "things are disturbed when we measure them" (Barad 2007, p. 107), they rely on a Newtonian assumption that we can subtract out our disturbances through reflective approaches and thereby come to a more objective account of the object of our investigation.[20] Particularly for artworks that accrue multiple versions or subtypes, we can see how their constitutive properties may exhibit a kind of quantum indeterminacy in that they do not have inherently determinate, measurement-independent values separable from the specific conditions of our observation or experimental arrangement.

---

[19] For further discussion of the type-token ontology in the context of contemporary artworks and their multiple version and variants see Castriota (2021a).

[20] Barad (2007, pp. 108–115), following Bohr, explains that this assumption is untenable given what quantum mechanics tells us about the nature of measurement.

5 The View from Within: Rethinking Documentation Practices

Although there is a growing acceptance of the processual paradigm of conservation, there remains an entrenched presupposition—both in conservation theory and practice—that an artwork might have a single, authoritative constellation of essential or work-defining properties at any given moment. This assumption stands in stark contrast to the practical reality that many artworks retain neither a fixed nor a singular constellation of significant properties, as both judgments of significance and a manifestation's authenticity are relational, that is, socially and contextually situated and continually (re)configured, including through conservation research.[21] Haraway (1988, p. 595) comments, "Boundaries of objects of knowledge materialize in social interaction. Boundaries are drawn by mapping practices; 'objects' do not preexist as such."

As the example of Philipsz's *You Are Not Alone* demonstrates, rigorous empirical inquiry at the level of identity does not uncover an artwork's objective essence so much as it reveals how significances are (re)configured in part through the material-discursive practices of exhibition and conservation research activities. In our investigations "we do not uncover preexisting facts about independently existing things as they exist frozen in time like little statues positioned in the world. Rather, we learn about phenomena—about specific material configurations of the world's becoming," as Barad (2007, p. 91) puts it. They explain

> The point is not simply to put the observer or knower back *in* the world (as if the world were a container and we needed merely to acknowledge our situatedness in it) but to understand and take account of the fact that we too are part of the world's differential becoming. (ibid.)

From an agential realist perspective, an artwork's identity is not something latent awaiting our discovery—it is our perspectival representation of properties that matter, whose significances become determinate through and as part of the measurement apparatus and the cuts we help enact in the process of our investigation. There are no "observation-independent objects" (Barad 2007, p. 198) for us to know that pre-exist or exist separate from our measurement or inquiry. What is generated are phenomena constituted through specific intra-actions, that is, the effects of "boundary drawing practices that make some identities or attributes intelligible (determinate) to the exclusion of others" (p. 208). In this way significant properties are emergent, that is, they are made to matter—in both senses of the word—by the unceasing, reconfiguring intra-actions that come with our being not *in* but *of* the world.

Barad notes how "the objective referent for identities or attributes are the phenomena constituted through the intra-action of multiple apparatuses" (p. 208; see

[21] See Villers (2004), Muñoz Viñas (2005), Yeo (2010, pp. 97–98), Jones (2010), Jones and Yarrow (2013), van Saaze (2013, p. 75), Marçal (2021b).

also p. 202).[22] Conservation research activities—read as Baradian apparatuses—can be understood as open-ended, boundary-drawing, material-discursive practices that "come to matter" (p. 206). They are "productive of (and part of) phenomena" (p. 142) and the "boundaries and properties of 'components' of phenomena become determinate" (p. 148) through the agential cuts enacted as part of these practices. The objective referent in our documentation is therefore not the work or its identity as such, but the phenomena created by the intra-actions between the measurement apparatus (which includes us) and the objects of our inquiry, with the understanding that such a distinction is an agential cut, that is, a "cutting together-apart" (Barad 2014) enacted within phenomena where the two are differentiated and entangled. Prevailing documentation methods and formats often perpetuate what Haraway (1988) terms the "god trick of seeing everything from nowhere" (1988, p. 581); the reports or textual documentation produced by conservators characterising an artwork's identity are often full of authoritative, declarative statements about a work's essence and ontological perimeters, and clinical passive-voice descriptions that efface the conservator or conservation researcher's role in processes of knowledge production.[23] But as we can see, there is no pre-existing object to know or represent "outside" of our inquiry—any notion of a determinately bounded or propertied object is a distinction or cutting together-apart we enact *within* and as part of phenomena. Accordingly, our documentation must account for the phenomena produced through and as part of our investigations and which, crucially, include us as intra-acting agencies.

Objectivity, within an agential realist framework, is not a matter of detachment or "producing undistorted representations from afar; rather, objectivity is about being accountable to the specific materializations of which we are a part" (Barad 2007, p. 91). Any representation we might create to mark a work's anatomy, dependencies, significances, and edges—however rigorously investigated—can only ever be a partial and schematic picture because we are part of the phenomena. But, as Haraway notes, "only partial perspective promises objective vision" (1988, p. 583). Being accountable in our documentation practices requires us to resist "unlocatable knowledge claims" (ibid.) by taking account of our partial view from within and—as Hélia Marçal (2017, 2021a) has advocated—explicitly recognising the situatedness of our perspective in our documentation.[24] Accountability also requires us to understand

[22]For a discussion of the objective referent see Barad (2007, pp. 338–340). For a discussion of measurement and objectivity, see Barad (2007, pp. 342–350).

[23]Zoë Miller (2021, p. 202) describes the entrenched "tradition of epistemic invisibility of the conservator" in conservation reports, where passive voice constructions work to "conceal the subjective, discursive role the conservators may play in the shaping of the knowledge and information contained within these documents."

[24]In her application of Haraway's (1988) notion of *account-ability* to conservation practice, Marçal (2021a, p. 60) emphasises the need for conservators to "account for their own actions and identities, and to critically analyse how power dynamics were destabilised and re-framed through practices of relocation." Marçal (2017, pp. 102–103; 2021a, p. 59) has also recommended including in conservation reports an "Aim of Documentation" and a "Documentation of Absence" field.

how the cuts we help enact in our marking off and *mattering* of significant properties and boundaries—at the exclusion of others—causal structures are generated. The documentation created for conservation purposes is not inert—it carries a causal potential as it is often used to generate display or activation specifications and guide decision-making around the properties of a work that are (re)materialised or perpetuated. In so doing it may further reinforce certain perspectives on what the work is whilst precluding others. Through our documentation, we are propagators of certain perspectives—inevitably privileging some properties over others—and we play an active role not only in identifying which properties matter in our documentation, but also how they come to matter in an artwork or heritage object's ongoing materialisation(s). In this way, through our documentation, we remain causally entangled with that which we seek to represent. Accountable practice is therefore predicated on our accounting for the phenomena we are co-constituting through both our research and the documentation we create. Accountable practice also entails a reframing of our documentation as perspectival and partial representations of phenomena produced through and as part of our inquiry, of which we are an entangled and agential part, and which can never be known or represented fully.

6 Conclusion

According to agential realism, our marking of the boundaries and significant properties of an object or entity is not an objective accounting of a reality that pre-exists our observation or measurement. Both our investigations and representations contribute to a reconfiguring of a part of the world that makes certain properties momentarily determinate within a particular context, with the understanding that this "indeterminacy is never resolved once and for all" (Barad 2007, p. 179). Because "different agential cuts materialize different phenomena," we are responsible for how our intra-actions "contribute to the differential mattering of the world" (Barad 2007, p. 178).[25] In the context of conservation, this is not only true for more obviously material interventions like cleaning or refabrication, but also preventive conservation methods like documentation, as all our material-discursive practices may contribute to the materialisation—or mattering—of that which is thought to matter whilst excluding and foreclosing other possibilities.[26] In this way we are entangled—cut together-apart—with that which we seek to know and care for.

This stands in stark contrast to what we might call Newtonian-Cartesian frameworks for conservation where the evaluator or documentation author is still very

[25] For a discussion of our ethical responsibility to the cuts we enact in conservation practices, see Marçal (2021b) and Castriota and Marçal (2021).

[26] "Intra-actions," Barad (2007, p. 393) explains, "do not simply transmit a vector of influence among separate events. It is through specific intra-actions that a causal structure is enacted. Intra-actions effect what's real and what's possible, as some things come to matter and others are excluded, as possibilities are opened up and others are foreclosed."

often positioned outside and separate from the object of conservation and its representation. If we accept both the processual dimensionality of the entities we seek to care for and the ways in which our practices of custodianship are inevitably entangled and enfolded with them, it becomes untenable that we have access to a view from nowhere, outside and *inherently* separate from the objects of our conservation practices. The agential realist critique of an intrinsic knower-known or subject-object distinction does not imply that there is no distinction or that an objective referent is inaccessible. On the contrary, it implies that that distinction is continually enacted over and over, we are responsible for our parts in these enactments, and that what we come to know is not the "true" work or heritage object and its essential properties but rather phenomena generated through specific agential intra-actions. Within such a framework the objective referents are the phenomena produced by multiple, entangled, intra-actively (re)configuring boundary-drawing practices, which include us as agencies of observation. It is through our measurement that "the boundaries and properties of 'components' of phenomena become determinate" and "particular material articulations of the world become meaningful" (Barad 2007, p. 333). This is to say I am not discovering boundaries and properties of an "object" that pre-exist my observation; I am—as part of both my inquiry and representation—marking off components of phenomena and making determinate properties that matter at the exclusion of others. What is made determinate is partially a trace of my selection of research methods, my decisions about who or what to consider as relevant to or part of the object of conservation, my framing of the evidence collected, and the form and format of my representation. These actions and choices are not simply made by a wilful me, but rather are entangled with inherited practices and other political forces that must also be considered and accounted for.

The reports and documentation we create should therefore not be construed as authoritative accounts of observed entities and their constitutive properties separate and apart from our investigations. Our representations are made not from a position of absolute externality, but rather with a view from within. They are diffracted by our partial perspectives, the cuts we help enact both in our research and our representation, and the larger material-discursive practices of which we are a part. We are productive of and part of the phenomena produced through our inquiry, and through our representations—by virtue of their causal potential—we become further enfolded with that which we seek to know and safeguard.[27] "Representations," Barad writes, "are not snapshots or depictions of what awaits us but rather condensations of traces of multiple practices of engagement" (2007, p. 53). Representations have and will continue to have a utility in conservation practices: they allow us to abstract, momentarily make sense of, and communicate knowledge pertaining to a

[27] In an agential realist framework, intra-actions also reconfigure us: "Our (intra)actions matter—each one reconfigures the world in its becoming—and yet they never leave us; they are sedimented into our becoming, they become us" (Barad 2007, p. 394). Marçal (2021b, p. 4) extends this to conservation practices, commenting that "every intra-action with an artwork changes the conservator."

particular entity with the view towards securing a futurity for the properties that matter and that may come to matter. But approaches that frame an entity's identity as something pre-existing or separable from those representing it are *mis*representing the nature of the phenomena we are part of and co-constituting through our practices. This is not to say that we are seating ourselves at a table to which we were not invited. Rather, we were there all along.

Acknowledgments I wish to extend my gratitude to Susan Philipsz, Eoghan McTigue, and Julie-Ann Delaney for their participation in this research, my thesis supervisors—Dominic Paterson and Erma Hermens—for their support throughout my doctoral studies, as well as the entire *NACCA* network of supervisors and ESRs. I also wish to extend particular thanks to Hélia Marçal and Rebecca Gordon whose thinking, scholarship, and friendship have been instrumental to my own personal becoming, and that of the ideas presented here.

Some of these ideas have taken published form previously (see Castriota 2019, 2021c), however they have since been substantially re-turned in preparing this text and they will undoubtedly continue to be reworked and reconfigured in the future. This research received funding from the European Union's Horizon 2020 research and innovation programme under the Marie Skłowdoska-Curie grant agreement No. 642892.

References

Barad K (2007) Meeting the universe halfway: quantum physics and the entanglement of matter and meaning. Duke University Press, Durham, North Carolina

Barad K (2014) Diffracting diffraction: cutting together-apart. Parallax 20(3):168–187. https://doi.org/10.1080/13534645.2014.927623

Beerkens L (1999) The preservation of a city of light. In: Hummelen Y, Sillé D (eds) Modern art: who cares? An interdisciplinary research project and an international symposium on the conservation of modern and contemporary art. The Foundation for the Conservation of Modern Art and the Netherlands Institute for Cultural Heritage, Amsterdam, pp 67–73

Birnbaum CA (1994) Protecting cultural landscapes: planning, treatment and management of historic landscapes. Preserv Briefs 36:1–16

Birnbaum CA, Capella Peters C (eds) (1996) The Secretary of the Interior's standards for the treatment of historic properties with guidelines for the treatment of cultural landscapes. U.-S. Department of Interior, National Park Service, Cultural Resource Stewardship and Partnerships, Heritage Preservation Services, Historic Landscape Initiative, Washington, DC

Butler J (1990) Gender trouble: feminism and the subversion of identity. Routledge, New York

Caianiello T (2013) Materializing the ephemeral: the preservation and presentation of media art installations. In: Buschmann R, Caianiello T (eds) Media art installations preservation and presentation: materializing the ephemeral. Dietrich Reimer Verlag, Berlin, pp 207–229

Castriota B (2019) Authenticity, identity, and essentialism: reframing conservation practice. In: Mairesse F, Peters RF (eds) What is the essence of conservation? Materials for a discussion. Papers from the ICOM-CC and ICOFOM session at the 25th General Conference held in Kyoto, 4 September 2019. ICOFOM, Paris, p 39–48

Castriota B (2021a) Variants of concern: authenticity, conservation, and the type-token distinction. Stud Conserv 67(1–2):72–83. https://doi.org/10.1080/00393630.2021.1974237

Castriota B (2021b) Instantiation, actualization, and absence: the continuation and safeguarding of Katie Paterson's *Future Library* (2014–2114). J Am Inst Conserv 60(2–3):145–160. https://doi.org/10.1080/01971360.2021.1977058

Castriota B (2021c) Object trouble: constructing and performing artwork identity in the museum. Art Matters Int J Technical Art Hist (Special Issue 1):12–22
Castriota B, Marçal H (2021) Always already fragment: integrity, deferral, and possibility in the conservation of cultural heritage. In: Schädler-Saub U, Weyer A (eds) Das fragment im digitalen zeitalter: möglichkeiten und grenzen neuer techniken in der restaurierung. Hendrik Baßler Verlag, Berlin, pp 63–78
Connolly M (2014) Reverberations in time and space. In: Franzen B, Lingwood J (eds) Susan Philipsz: You Are Not Alone. Verlag der Buchhandlung Walther König, Cologne, pp 82–84
Davies S (2001) Musical works and performances: a philosophical exploration. Oxford University Press, Oxford
Delaney J (2017, December 8) Personal interview
Derrida J (2001) Structure, sign and play in the discourse of the human sciences. In: Writing and difference. Routledge, London, pp 351–370
Ensom T (2019) Technical narratives: analysis, description and representation in the conservation of software-based art. PhD dissertation, Kings College London
Fiske T (2009) White walls: installations, absence, iteration and difference. In: Richmond A, Bracker A (eds) Conservation principles, dilemmas and uncomfortable truths. Butterworth Heinemann, Oxford, pp 229–240
Goodman N (1968) Languages of art: an approach to a theory of symbols. Bobbs-Merrill Company Inc, Indianapolis Ind
Gordon R (2011) Rethinking material significance and authenticity in contemporary art. PhD dissertation, University of Glasgow
Gordon R (2014) Identifying and pursuing authenticity in contemporary art. In: Hermens E, Lennard F (eds) Authenticity and replication: the "real thing" in art and conservation. Archetype Publications, London, pp 95–107
Guldemond J (1999) Artificial respiration. In: Hummelen Y, Sillé D (eds) Modern art: who cares? An interdisciplinary research project and an international symposium on the conservation of modern and contemporary art. The Foundation for the Conservation of Modern Art and the Netherlands Institute for Cultural Heritage, Amsterdam, pp 79–81
Haraway DJ (1988) Situated knowledges: the science question in feminism and the privilege of partial perspective. Fem Stud 14(3):575–599
Hedstrom M, Lee CA (2002) Significant properties of digital objects: definitions, applications, implications. In: Proceedings of the DLM-Forum. Available via Semantic Scholar.
Heiser J (2010) Lullabies for strangers. In: You are not alone. Modern Art Oxford, Oxford, pp 11–33
Holdsworth D, Sergeant DM (2000) A blueprint for representation information in the OAIS model. In: 8th NASA Goddard Conference on Mass Storage Systems and Technologies. http://storageconference.us/2000/papers/D02PA.PDF
Hölling HB (2016) The aesthetics of change: on the relative durations of the impermanent and critical thinking in conservation. In: Hermens E, Robertson F (eds) Authenticity in transition: changing practices in art making and conservation. Archetype Publications, London, pp 13–24
Innocenti P (2013) Keeping the bits alive: authenticity and longevity for digital art. In: Serexhe B (ed) Preservation of digital art: theory and practice. Ambra V, Viena, pp 217–230
Irivin S (2005) The artist's sanction in contemporary art. J Aesthetics Art Crit 63(4):315–326. https://doi.org/10.1111/j.0021-8529.2005.00214.x
Irvin S (2013) Installation art and performance: a shared ontology. In: Mag Uidhir C (ed) Art and abstract objects. Oxford, Oxford University Press, pp 242–262. https://doi.org/10.1093/acprof:oso/9780199691494.003.0012
Jester TC, Park SC (1993) Making historic properties accessible. Preserv Briefs 32:1–14
Jones S (2010) Negotiating authentic objects and authentic selves. J Mater Cult 15(2):181–203. https://doi.org/10.1177/1359183510364074
Jones S, Yarrow T (2013) Crafting authenticity: an ethnography of conservation practice. J Mater Cult 18(1):3–26. https://doi.org/10.1177/1359183512474383

Knorr Cetina K (2001) Objectual practice. In: Schatzki TR, Knorr Cetina K, von Savigny E (eds) The practice turn in contemporary theory. Routledge, London, pp 175–188

Laurenson P (2004) The management of display equipment in time-based media installations. In: Roy A, Smith P (eds) Modern art, new museums: contributions to the Bilbao Congress, 13–-17 September 2004. International Institute for Conservation of Historic and Artistic Works, London, pp 49–53

Laurenson P (2006) Authenticity, change and loss in the conservation of time-based media installations: a conceptual framework for traditional fine art conservation. Tate Papers 6. https://www.tate.org.uk/research/tate-papers/06/authenticity-change-and-loss-conservation-of-time-based-media-installations

Laurenson P (2016) Practice as research: unfolding the objects of contemporary art conservation. Inaugural lecture delivered at Maastricht University, 18 March 2016. Available via YouTube. https://youtu.be/rEZzsg3OzJg

Marçal H (2017) Conservation in an era of participation. J Inst Conserv 40(2):97–104. https://doi.org/10.1080/19455224.2017.1319872

Marçal H (2018) From intangibility to materiality and back again: preserving Portuguese performance artworks from the 1970s. PhD dissertation, Universidade Nova de Lisboa

Marçal H (2019) Contemporary art conservation. Published as part of the research project Reshaping the Collectible: when Artworks Live in the Museum, Tate. https://www.tate.org.uk/research/reshaping-the-collectible/research-approach-conservation

Marçal H (2021a) Situated knowledges and materiality in the conservation of performance art. Art Matters Int J Technical Art Hist (Special Issue 1):55–62

Marçal H (2021b) Towards a relational ontology of conservation. In: Bridgland J (ed) Transcending boundaries: integrated approaches to conservation, ICOM-CC 19th Triennial Conference Preprints, Beijing, 17–21 May 2021. International Council of Museums, Paris, pp 1–9

Marçal H (2022) Becoming difference: on the ethics of conserving the in-between. Stud Conserv 67(1–2):30–37. https://doi.org/10.1080/00393630.2021.1947074

Miller Z (2021) Practitioner (in)visibility in the conservation of contemporary art. J Am Inst Conserv 60(2–3):197–209. https://doi.org/10.1080/01971360.2021.1951550

Muñoz Viñas S (2005) Contemporary theory of conservation. Routledge, London

Noël de Tilly A (2011) Scripting artworks: studying the socialization of editioned video and film installations. PhD dissertation, University of Amsterdam

Phillips J (2012) Shifting equipment significance in time-based media art. Electr Media Rev 1:139–154

Phillips J (2015) Reporting iterations: a documentation model for time-based media art. In: Matos LA, Macedo R, Heydenreich G (eds) Revista de História Da Arte 4:168–179. http://revistaharte.fcsh.unl.pt/rhaw4/RHAw4.pdf

Philipsz S (2014) *You Are Not Alone*. In: Franzen B, Lingwood L (eds) Susan Philipsz: You Are Not Alone. Verlag der Buchhandlung Walther König, Cologne, pp 61–81

Philipsz S (2017) Public lecture at the National Galleries of Scotland, Edinburgh, October 25, 2017

Philipsz S, McTigue E (2018, August 31) Personal interview

Rinehart R, Ippolito J (2014). Re-collection: art, new media, and social memory. Leonardo. The MIT Press, Cambridge

Spangler-Bickell C (2021) Dividuality, partibility, individuation: a paradigm for the care of expanding artworks. ArtMatters Int J Technical Art Hist (Special Issue 1):98–105

Stránský Z (1985) Originals versus substitutes. ICOFOM Study Series Originals 9:95–102

van de Vall R (2015a) Documenting dilemmas: on the relevance of ethically ambiguous cases. In: Matos LA, Macedo R, Heydenreich G (eds) Revista de História Da Arte 4:7–17. http://revistaharte.fcsh.unl.pt/rhaw4/RHAw4.pdf

van de Vall R (2015b) The devil and the details: the ontology of contemporary art in conservation theory and practice. Br J Aesthetics 55(3):285–302

van de Vall R, Hölling HB, Scholte T, Stigter S (2011) Reflections on a biographical approach to contemporary art conservation. In: Bridgland J (ed) ICOM-CC: 16th Triennial Conference,

Lisbon, 19–23 September 2011. Preprints. Critério, Lisbon, pp 1–8. http://hdl.handle.net/11245/1.344546
van Saaze V (2009) Authenticity in practice: an ethnographic study into the preservation of *One Candle* by Nam June Paik. In: Hermens E, Fiske T (eds) Art conservation and authenticities: material, concept, context. Archetype, London, pp 190–198
van Saaze V (2013) Installation art and the museum: presentation and conservation of changing artworks. Amsterdam University Press, Amsterdam
van Wegen DH (1999) Between fetish and score: the position of the curator of contemporary art. In: Hummelen Y, Sillé D (eds) Modern art: who cares? An interdisciplinary research project and an international symposium on the conservation of modern and contemporary art. The Foundation for the Conservation of Modern Art and the Netherlands Institute for Cultural Heritage, Amsterdam, pp 201–209
Villers C (2004) Post minimal intervention. The Conservator 28(1):3–10. https://doi.org/10.1080/01410096.2004.9995197
Viola B (1999) Permanent impermanence. In: Corzo MA (ed) Mortality immortality?: the legacy of 20th-century art. Getty Conservation Institute, Los Angeles, pp 85–94
Wharton G (2015) Artist intention and the conservation of contemporary art. AIC Objects Specialty Group Postprints 22:1–12
Yeo G (2010) 'Nothing is the same as something else': significant properties and notions of identity and originality. Arch Sci 10:85–116. https://doi.org/10.1007/S10502-010-9119-9
Bek R (2011) Between ephemeral and material: documentation and preservation of technology-based works of art. In: Scholte T, Wharton G (eds) Inside installations: theory and practice in the care of complex artworks. Amsterdam University Press, Amsterdam, pp 205–15
Brokerhof AW, Scholte T, Ankersmit B, Wijers G, Vermaat, S (2011) Installation art subjected to risk assessment: Jeffrey Shaw's Revolution as case study. In: Scholte T, Wharton G (eds) Inside installations: theory and practice in the care of complex artworks. Amsterdam University Press, Amsterdam, pp 91–101
Coddington, J (1999) The case against amnesia. In Corzo MA (ed) Mortality immortality? The legacy of 20th-century art. The Getty Conservation Institute, Los Angeles, pp 18–24
Consultative Committee for Space Data Systems (CCSDS) (2012) Reference model for an Open Archival Information System (OAIS): recommendation for space data system practices. CCSDS Secretariat, Washington, DC. https:// public.ccsds.org/pubs/650x0m2.pdf
Jadzińska M (2011) The lifespan of installation art. In: Scholte T, Wharton G (eds) Inside installations: theory and practice in the care of complex artworks. Amsterdam University Press, Amsterdam, pp 21–31
Jadzińska M (2012) Back to the future: authenticity and its influence on the conservation of modern art. In: Szmelter I (ed) Innovative approaches to the complex care of contemporary art. Academy of Fine Arts, Archetype Publications: Warsaw, London, pp 82–99
Jones C, Muller L (2008) Between real and ideal: documenting media art. Leonardo 41(4):418–419. https://doi.org/10.1162/leon.2008.41.4.418
Laurenson P, van Saaze V (2014) Collecting performance-based art: new challenges and shifting perspectives. In: Remes O, MacCulloch L, Leino M (eds) Performativity in the gallery: staging interactive encounters. Peter Lang, Oxford, pp 27–41
MacDonald C (2009) Scoring the work: documenting practice and performance in variable media art. Leonardo 42(1):59–63. https://doi.org/10.1162/leon.2009.42.1.59
Mancusi-Ungaro, C (1999) Original intent: the artist's voice. In: Hummelen Y, Sillé D (eds) Modern art: who cares? An interdisciplinary research project and an international symposium on the conservation of modern and contemporary art. The Foundation for the Conservation of Modern Art and the Netherlands Institute for Cultural Heritage, Amsterdam, pp 392–393
Rinehart, R (2004) A system of formal notation for scoring works of digital and variable media art. Paper presented at the Electronic Media Group Specialty Session of the Annual Meeting of the American Institute for Conservation of Historic and Artistic Works, Portland, OR, 14 June 2004. http://archive.bampfa.berkeley.edu/about/formalnotation.pdf

Stringari, C (1999) Installations and problems of preservation. In: Hummelen Y, Sillé D (eds) Modern art: who cares? An interdisciplinary research project and an international symposium on the conservation of modern and contemporary art. The Foundation for the Conservation of Modern Art and the Netherlands Institute for Cultural Heritage, Amsterdam, pp 272–281
Jones C, Muller L (2008) Between real and ideal: documenting media art. Leonardo 41(4):418–419. https://doi.org/10.1162/leon.2008.41.4.418
Laurenson P, van Saaze V (2014) Collecting performance-based art: new challenges and shifting perspectives. In: Remes O,MacCulloch L, Leino M (eds) Performativity in the gallery: staging interactive encounters. Peter Lang, Oxford, pp 27–41.

Brian Castriota is Time-Based Media Conservator at the National Galleries Scotland, Freelance Conservator for Time-Based Media and Contemporary Art at the Irish Museum of Modern Art, and Lecturer in Conservation of Contemporary Art and Media at University College London's History of Art Department. He has previously held lecturer positions at the University of Glasgow and the Institute of Fine Arts, New York University. He completed graduate-level training in conservation at the IFA-NYU (2014), he was a Samuel H. Kress Fellow in Time-Based Media Conservation at the Solomon R. Guggenheim Museum (2014–2016), and he received a PhD in History of Art from the University of Glasgow (2019). As part of the Marie Skłowdoska-Curie ITN *New Approaches in the Conservation of Contemporary Art* (*NACCA*) his doctoral research examined notions of artwork identity and authenticity commonly invoked in conservation theory and practice, and he has published various articles and book chapters on these topics.

When Old Was New: Rethinking Traditional and Contemporary Art and Their Paradigms of Care

Cybele Tom

Abstract The widespread belief that old and contemporary works of art are fundamentally different from each other, warranting distinct and separate conservation approaches, needs examination. Immateriality and mutability, two qualities considered to be unique to contemporary artworks of unconventional object ontology, are also features of old objects and artefacts, especially when considered in their original contexts. The chapter argues that the perceived differences between old and contemporary are neither inherent nor fundamental, but arise from an under-examined tendency to identify a traditional work with a more or less fixed material character, while ignoring its functionality and complex multivalency. Once we recognize that both old and new artworks have intangible and variable essential characteristics, the theories and paradigms of care that have hitherto been considered exclusive to each are at the disposal of all conservators no matter their field of specialty: a traditional paradigm that focuses on material preservation and, what will be called here, a contemporizing paradigm that allows the perpetuation of essential immaterial aspects. The chapter urges a reconsideration of old artworks when they were new, aimed at increased relevance of contemporary art conservation theory to the care of old, "traditional" artworks, and in turn, innovative research of old art that may contribute to theories of contemporary art conservation.

Keywords Conservation theory · Contemporary art · Treatment paradigm · Decision making · Object biography · Authenticity

1 Introduction

What is a reversible treatment in the context of Urs Fischer's large wax candle sculptures which melt, combust and disintegrate over the course of their display? What action would qualify as minimally invasive for Victor Grippo's *Analogía, I* in

C. Tom (✉)
Department of Art History, University of Chicago, Chicago, IL, USA
e-mail: cybtom@uchicago.edu

R. van de Vall, V. van Saaze (eds.), *Conservation of Contemporary Art*, Studies in Art, Heritage, Law and the Market 9, https://doi.org/10.1007/978-3-031-42357-4_5

which raw and perishable potatoes connected to electrodes generate electricity measured by a nearby voltmeter? And what does conservation documentation entail for a performance work by Tino Sehgal for which all forms of record-keeping is prohibited? (van Saaze 2015).

Such perplexing questions as these have prompted the widely held belief that some contemporary artworks are fundamentally different from old or so-called traditional artworks, necessitating conservation approaches beyond the traditional ethical framework of care.[1] This chapter challenges that belief, arguing instead that old and contemporary works of art have more in common than commonly held, in order to explore the relevance of contemporary art conservation theory to the care of old, "traditional" artworks, and in turn, how the study of old art may still contribute to theories of contemporary art conservation. After first identifying two qualities of contemporary artworks that signal an unconventional or non-traditional object ontology—immateriality and mutability— the chapter then points to several old works that share the same traits. The crux of the argument is that the perceived differences between old and contemporary artworks are neither inherent nor fundamental to those categories, but arise from an under-examined tendency to identify the essence of a traditional work with a more or less fixed material character. In other words, the contrast between old and new works lies in how conservators (and others who interpret cultural objects) approach them. Due to advances in the theory and practice of the conservation of contemporary art, there are now at least two accepted paradigms of care theoretically at the disposal of all conservators no matter their field of specialty—a traditional paradigm that focuses on material preservation and, what will be called here, a "contemporizing" paradigm that allows the perpetuation of essential immaterial, intangible characteristics.

2 Divergent Paths

The care and conservation of contemporary art has been on a separate path from that of the so-called traditional media like sculpture, painting and photography.[2] Early concerns tended to focus on the practical problem of experimental materials and technique in modern works (Cranmer 1987; Domergue et al. 1987). The discourse later turned to issues of artist intent, meaning and authenticity (Coddington et al. 2002; Graham and Sterrett 1997; Hummelen 1999). Artworks were increasingly multivalent and complex, often with essential but elusive characteristics. What aspects made the artwork authentically itself? Which were to be conserved? Such

[1] The traditional ethical framework is delineated in several western prescriptive documents such as the American Institute for Conservation's Code of Ethics and the European Confederation of Conservator-Restorers' Organisations' Code of Ethics, as well as in overviews by (Appelbaum 2007) and (Muñoz Viñas 2005).

[2] An important early pioneer of this separate path is the research initiative *Modern Art: Who Cares?* which produced the seminal book, (Hummelen and Sillé 1999).

questions were elucidated through Laurenson's concept of "work-defining properties" (Laurenson 2006).

As a response to insufficient or irrelevant guidance from the standard sources of ethical and practical guidance in the care of cultural heritage—e.g., codes of ethics, charter documents, treatment case studies—disjunction from the traditional treatment path has led to a robust infrastructure for the advancement of understanding and care of contemporary art. Networks of professionals, conferences, treatment protocols and terminology, paradigms of documentation and decision-making, and venues for training and education have been dedicated in its service because of the perceived unconventional nature of the contemporary.[3] Time-based media art (Engel and Phillips 2019; Laurenson 2004; Phillips 2012), installation art (Pugliese and Ferriani 2009; Wharton and Molotch 2009), performance art (Cone 2017; Marçal 2017; Phillips and Hinkson 2018) and otherwise variable media art—what makes them so problematic?

In the next sections, I describe two characteristics, often mentioned in case studies of problematic contemporary works, that seem to fundamentally distinguish contemporary art from old art. However, as counter-argument, I raise several examples of old art which also possess these seemingly unconventional qualities, re-opening the possibility for fruitful collaboration and exchange between the sub-fields.

3 No Longer Material

The first proposition is that having essential properties that are immaterial is a sufficient condition for a contemporary artwork to be fundamentally different from an old work.

According to the traditional conservation framework, the authenticity of an object depends on the persistence of its unique physical identity. The object may have immaterial properties but these are secondary to or dependent on its work-defining, or essential, properties, which are all material. Thus, with the goal to minimize further physical change, conservators would endeavour not to replace the wood planks of the Ship of Theseus, instead leaving lacunae where possible and, when structurally necessary, consolidating rotten boards in order to retain as much original material as possible. The Ship is an "autographic" object: anything that imitates its physical nature would be a forgery since it would not be *the* unique object that Theseus sailed upon.[4]

[3]INCCA, NACCA, VOCA, NeCCAR, Variable Media Network, CAN Working Group, ICOM-CC's Modern and Contemporary Working Group are just a few of many groups dedicated to issues in contemporary art conservation.

[4]The distinction between autographic and allographic works was first proposed in (Goodman 1976) and further discussed in (Laurenson 2006).

In contrast, many contemporary works are no longer *only* material, but have work-defining properties that are immaterial, aspects that confound the traditional conservation framework. Sol LeWitt's *Wall Drawings* are well-known examples, existing beyond the physicality of the drawings themselves (Hogan and Snow 2015; van de Vall 2015). Able to be re-executed in any setting by following a set of artist-authorized instructions given on a piece of paper, they all share the key work-defining property of being the result of his written instructions. A LeWitt wall drawing inheres neither entirely in the executed wall drawing, nor entirely in the certificates of authenticity and instruction. Rather, its identity rests somewhere between those things and its processual concept. Hence, the confusion and differences of opinion among conservators when asked what measures should be taken to preserve a particular instantiation of one: if the work was only material, the primacy of its preservation would have been uncontested (van de Vall 2015). In fact, when an instantiation of a wall drawing is destroyed, the authenticity of the work is unaffected; but if an image (that visually conforms to the instructions) is printed on the wall rather than drawn according to the artist's instructions, it would not be an authentic instantiation.

Similarly, Felix Gonzalez-Torres's candy installations are guided by loose concepts of candy type, ideal mass of candy and visitor participation (Buskirk 2000; Spector 2003). The material, candy, does not constitute the artwork, but serves to instantiate the interactive aspect of the work and convey a coded meaning. It is crucial that viewers are able to take candy away; preserving the original candy pile would in fact go against the authenticity of the artwork. Instead, the candy should be replenished when depleted by visitors.

In both examples, perpetuation of an immaterial work-defining property—for example, conceptual, processual, interactive and so forth— is more important to the work's authenticity than preservation of its original material character. In contrast to these contemporary examples, removal of discoloured paint from a surface -- darkened chrome yellow from Van Gogh's *Sunflowers*, say -- to expose unoxidized paint below, is unacceptable because original material is removed and the surface texture of the brushstroke skinned (Kendriks 2016). The difference seems stark indeed.

A glimpse into the medieval concept of object identity or object "origin" offers an alternate perspective to the primacy of material in old artworks (Nagel and Wood 2005, p. 404). Richard Krautheimer famously demonstrated in his 1942 paper that historical imitations of the Holy Sepulcher in Jerusalem had many more differences than similarities when it came to physical form: some were circular, some polygonal, some with single nave, others an ambulatory, some with eight columns, others with 12, and so forth (Krautheimer 1942). The essence "copied" from the original building prototype seems to have little to do with its optical likeness, either in plan or elevation, rather a symbolic association based on medieval numerology (e.g., sides and columns adding up to a divine number), a spiritual concept, or gestured form (curved rather than precisely circular). Some pre-modern makers and viewers, it seems, found the identity of the Holy Sepulchre to inhere in something other than its visual appearance per se, such that its legitimate copies embodied a shared immaterial idea that instantiated the original. (Smith 1992).

Alexander Nagel has observed that depositing soil from the site of the Crucifixion "soaked with the blood of Christ" in a chapel in Rome entitled that secondary site to be known as Jerusalem (Nagel 2012, p. 100). A site double was generated, he writes, but "rather than a visual replica, the constellation/installation initiates a process of activation" (Ibid.). In both architectural examples, it is the transfer of an immaterial aspect—a concept, an arrangement, a referenced event—that perpetuates the original work. Material plays a role, but a secondary one.

Talk of activation leads quite naturally to relics, another class of objects that transcend their material nature. On the one hand, a relic depends on its unique physical history, for instance that it is *the* shroud that wrapped the body of Jesus, or that it is *the* staff that Moses used. A relic is therefore a unique object, where something that merely resembles it carries no meaning since it does not have the revered history of the relic. In this sense, a relic seems like a totally autographic work dependent on its physical history. However, the primary *function* of relics was to serve as a source of sacred power. Their physical history may be unique, but they function through replication. Medieval accounts of pilgrim worship tell us explicitly that relics have the ability to *transfer* their power. The relic of the cross at Golgotha was "offered. . .to the pilgrims to kiss—just once a year. . .Little ampullae filled with oil from lamps that burned at the Sepulchre were presented to the relic. In a miracle that mimicked the pilgrim's own sanctification. . .the fluid in the ampullae *once touched to the cross* bubbled up and would have overflowed if not quickly capped and preserved. Such fluid had the capability of holding "the blessings received from many martyrs" (Hahn 1997, p. 1086). On the sides of the ampulla is a moulded depiction of kneeling pilgrims at the foot of the cross (Sever 2016). The image documents the source *and* the process by which the liquid inside is made holy, much like LeWitt's certificate and diagram for a wall drawing. That which makes a relic is something supra-material: its holy power to bless, heal, save and so on.

One might object that a relic functions through physical contact, and thus is dependent on its material nature after all. But the stuff of a relic is often nothing much to look at. Consistently referred to by early Christians as "dust," a relic was usually hidden inside a reliquary, covered in layers of material like fabric, parchment, and precious metals adorned with gems (Nagel and Wood 2010, p. 298). It was rarely even visible to the worshipper or pilgrim. The reliquary, the rich framing, promotes the relic within, and yet the reliquary is nothing without the relic; its costly material is substantive as long as the relic is known to be within. And because the relic alone may not be believable, *authentics* (certificates of authentication), and *inventio* (narratives of finding) accompany the relic to prove its unique lineage (Hahn 2017, p. 7). In the end, whether it is *actually* the bones of so-and-so or constructed to be the bones of so-and-so through sanctioned mechanisms, is quite literally immaterial. A relic's substance is secondary, a replaceable instantiation of the socio-religious narrative erected around it.

In considering old, and in particular religious objects when they were contemporary, we are reminded of the immaterial power and spiritual functionality they carried when embedded in their ritual contexts. Moreover, it becomes clear that they have lost their immaterial characteristics because they are out of context within the modern secular museum ecosystem (inclusive of conservation, registration, exhibition) which defines them by their physical properties and condition. *The Annunciation of the Rosary* by Veit Stoss, still set within the dazzling architecture of St Lorenz Church in Nuremberg, makes the point dramatically. Painted in the eyeball of its Angel Gabriel are accurate reflections of the church's surrounding windows (Taubert and Taubert 2015, p. 70). This tiny detail marks the sculptural group as a part of a much larger complex that is the church itself. The whole is a site-specific installation. The sculptural group has physical features that directly refer to and depend on its architectural setting for subtle meaning. Historical records also indicate that the Annunciation was intentionally lowered for high-ranking visitors throughout the 17th and 18th centuries, arguably itself a form of ritual or performance (Ibid., p. 73). Out of original context, the sculpture would lose its relational, dialogic quality with its suprastructure and surroundings—an important immaterial aspect— becoming a different kind of thing altogether. Imagine extracting one of the paintings from the Rothko Chapel, or displaying only one reel of slides from Robert Smithson's *Hotel Palenque*: the isolated part can still be appreciated, but a viewer ignorant of its origin experiences either a fraction of its meaning or a disparate one.

Some contemporary works are unconventional because their material identity is secondary to their functionality. Similarly, many old works possessed a functional character essential to their meaning. Stripped over time of their affective powers, old objects become disproportionately reliant on their material character. But this common aging trajectory does not imply their ontological status is somehow different from that of a contemporary work. Both old and new works have immaterial work-defining properties.

4 No Longer Fixed in Time

A common traditional conservation goal is to stabilize the artwork, to arrest or minimize further physical change. Underlying this goal is the presumption that the pristine artwork—the state against which its authenticity should be measured—is sometime shortly after it has left the maker's workshop, and that subsequent physical alteration, whether natural or interventive, subtractive or additive, is more or less undesirable.[5] Traditional artworks depend on a relatively static physicality. The more they deviate from their original physicality the less authentic they become.

By contrast, some contemporary artworks are considered unconventional because they are no longer fixed in time. Rather than having a single ideal state, they have dynamic trajectories because they are meant to be ephemeral, variable or in

[5] For the sake of brevity, "more or less" is meant to gloss over—inadequately—the fact that some change is valued more favourably than others. For example, a fine paint craquelure is a favourable result of physical change, while fatty bloom is not. Arguably, both are forms of material deterioration.

transition. Zoe Leonards's *Strange Fruit* involves real pieces of fruit that have been hand-stitched and embellished by the artist, scattered on a floor, and allowed to decompose in real time (Temkin 1999). The decay of the fruit, intimate and made unique by the artist's hand, is intentional and essential, a work-defining property. Unlike Gonzalez-Torres's candy, the fruit cannot be replaced. Rather, the sense of loss compounds with each subsequent iteration of the artwork until, presumably, the fruit disintegrates. (Its trajectory is remarkably similar to a relic: as more pilgrims visit and participate in the ritual of the relic, its power grows.) The Whitney Museum of American Art's 2018 exhibition *Zoe Leonard: Survey*, which included *Strange Fruit*, about thirty years after an early iteration in Philadelphia, advanced this trajectory (Cotter 2018). Though not typically categorized as a time-based media artwork, Leonard's installation is certainly one which has duration.

Another contemporary work, Sharon Hayes's *In the Near Future*, exemplifies multiple ways in which an artwork is no longer fixed.[6] First, the work exists in two phases, as a performance and an installation. In the first phase, performances were staged in several cities where the artist held up anachronistic signs of protest on the street. In the second phase, the artwork transitioned to a museum installation involving 35 mm slide images taken of phase one that are projected onto walls with self-advancing slide carousel projectors, themselves a technological anachronism. Although it seems the first phase is firmly of the past, its place in generating the content of phase two continues to be essential to the artwork. It is not clear whether phase one could be re-performed, generating additional or alternative content for the installation and contributing more possibility for change. Second, the installation is dimensionally variable, meaning that the size of the room and arrangement of the projectors can change. Important to note is that its variability in this regard doesn't only mean that it can be displayed differently in many contexts, but also that the artwork will morph with each successive iteration. As more details are put to the test in different settings, the set of its work-defining properties may grow and change, eventually describing an artwork quite different from its first iteration. Its physical variability opens the door to fluidity of identity and authenticity.

Compared with a sculpture or painting that has rigid dimensionality and form, such contemporary artworks seem unconventional indeed. But if we probe further, we encounter many old objects that were variable as well, with mutable meaning. A polychrome wood sculpture of St John the Baptist by Juan de Mesa is hollow and fully carved-in-the-round, made to participate in religious processions. A deposition crucifix has jointed limbs, built to be taken down from the cross in re-enactments of Christ's Passion. Such objects were first and foremost performative, (another immaterial property), needing at the very least, ritual, right timing and interaction with viewers to be fully activated. For full meaning to unfurl, they also required duration.

[6] Details here related about Sharon Hayes's work were gleaned from a private interview conducted by the author with the conservators in charge of the work at that time, Joanna Phillips and Jeffrey Warda, as part of a research assignment in a Spring 2012 graduate seminar at NYU Department of Museum Studies, entitled *Topics in Museum Studies: The Museum Life of Contemporary Art* (MSMS-GA 3330), taught by Glenn Wharton.

Winged altarpieces remained closed until high holy days when they were opened to reveal a rich paint and sculptural program within—an old and slower kind of time-based medium unfolding over the liturgical year (Taubert and Taubert 2015, p. 11). Their comparatively static existence today only means they have transitioned to a different phase from their performative or kinetic one, which is now dormant. One scholar writes that the "modern museum presents images in stasis. But in earlier periods, instability was a fundamental part of their being" (Jasienski 2020, p. 25).

There were also ephemera, objects intended to die, or prohibited from surviving.[7] Wax votives, lit and placed in devotion at a shrine, would burn down just like one of Urs Fischer's *Untitled* wax candle sculptures. The circulation of the Eucharistic wafer was closely guarded; any not consumed during liturgy was properly disposed of (Kumler 2015, 2011). Today, only documentation of their existence—press moulds, illustrations and of course the ritual itself—survive.

Finally, it should be noted that most old objects have also had dynamic trajectories, sometimes changing dramatically because of human intervention. Archival photographs of one medieval sculpture show that it had changed from the centre image as Saint Alexis in 1864, to Saint Louis under art dealer Joseph Demotte in 1934, and to a figure of a king in 1952 in the collection of the Metropolitan Museum of Art in New York (Kargère and Marincola 2014, p. 17). Such examples, in which the very identity or subject matter of an object changes, are ubiquitous. Replaced hands on Hindu sculpture may unintentionally signify through their mudras a different deity than originally intended. An oil overpaint on a Renaissance bas-relief subtly changed the subject matter from the sacred intimacy between mother and baby Jesus where the figures gaze intently at each other, to an outward facing Christ Child that beholds the viewer (Tom and Sutherland 2017). Spolia ensconced in a new setting take on political significance that didn't exist in their original contexts. While these old works were not initially intended to morph in the ways they did, their ready mutability and the popularity of their afterlives suggest these old artworks can be continually made and remade as the evolving products of "many hands" rather than a fixed object by a single hand (Kemp 2020).

5 "Things not Necessarily Meant to be Viewed as Art"

So far, this chapter has considered several old objects that share similar ontological qualities with "unconventional" contemporary artworks in that they are—or at least *were*—not only material, and not fixed in time. The examples have borrowed heavily from medieval Europe where the widely ranging and associative ways in which objects signified is well-known (Kumler and Lakey 2012). But other kinds of old objects bear these qualities as well. Pushing against the conservator's emphasis on

[7]The author thanks the Research in Art & Visual Evidence (RAVE) community at University of Chicago and Aden Kumler for raising this point.

original material, stakeholders of indigenous collections have vocalized numerous other complex ways in which so-called ethnographic objects derive meaning from their network of human users (Peters 2016). For instance, a West African power association mask has jealously guarded secrets of making and restrictive codes of viewing that may be transgressed in a modern research museum context (Molina 2019; O'Hern et al. 2016). With clear performative and ritualistic aspects, exactly how or when it is activated is largely unknown to those who stand outside its circle of makers. Out of context, it loses its immaterial characteristics and is increasingly perceived as a fixed aesthetic or historical object. Design objects such as lamps may have their electrical cords cut in order to satisfy white box museum aesthetics, effectively denying its function (Delidow et al. 2009). Musical instruments that cannot be played, armour that cannot be worn, chairs that cannot be sat upon—the list goes on. Essentially, what these examples indicate is a category of objects that are not intended as art. Jeffrey Weiss has called them "things not necessarily meant to be viewed as art" (Weiss 2013). Claudia Brittenham, arguing that carved Mayan lintels would have been hard to see, in distinct contrast to the close, privileged view we have of them in the museum context, writes that museums are "utterly foreign to the moment of the works we now construe as 'art'" (Brittenham 2019, p. 25). When brought under the conventions of the art museum, all objects not necessarily meant to be viewed as art become potentially alienated from their immaterial character.

It might be argued that such non-art objects *automatically* become fixed in materiality once they leave their original context: when comparing old objects with contemporary works, then, we should compare them *in the museum setting*; compared thus, old and contemporary works *are* fundamentally different. To this criticism, I argue there is a crucial distinction between a *necessary* alienation and one that is tacitly accepted without resistance. For old objects, the latter is true. But for many contemporary works, curators and conservators act as willing co-conspirators in breaking down the walls and norms of their institutions to accommodate the artworks and ensure no essential aspect of them is left out. The Guggenheim's massive and costly manifestation of Doug Wheeler's *PSAD Synthetic Desert III* from the artist's drawings in the Panza Collection is one recent instance of how eager institutions are to do this.

Additionally, the work of the Salvage Art Institute (http://salvageartinstitute.org/), a travelling display of artworks that have been declared a total loss by insurance criteria and therefore no longer suitable for exhibition or participation in the art market, demonstrates how quickly the conventions of a museum can be upended to accommodate the needs—in this case, the legal requirements— of a (legally, economically) unconventional object: the legal restriction against displaying a shattered *Balloon Dog* by Jeff Koons dissolves as soon as we stipulate that the object is no longer the artwork it was, that *Balloon Dog* is now *Balloon Dog**, where "*" signifies that it is no longer art.

The perceived fundamental differences between contemporary artworks and so-called traditional artworks appear to be misplaced. Old objects, particularly those not originally intended as art, are also unconventional *if they are allowed to be so*.

6 A Contemporizing Paradigm

Rather than posit a fundamental difference between contemporary art and old art, it seems more accurate to acknowledge that the unconventional aspects of many contemporary artworks have engendered an alternate care paradigm to the traditional framework that privileges material integrity above all else. This alternate approach might be called the contemporizing paradigm because it seeks to perpetuate the functionality and mutability of new works by privileging its immaterial aspects and capacity to change. It resists the urge to freeze and preserve a work in time, instead embracing a conceptualization of the artwork as continually evolving.

The proposition, then, is that the disjunction between contemporary and "traditional" lies not with the ontological nature of artworks or objects themselves, but external to them as differences of approach that can result in markedly divergent work-defining properties over time. The 2007 display of Joseph Kosuth's *Glass (One and Three)* at the Stedelijk Museum demonstrates the point well (Stigter 2011; van de Vall et al. 2011). Consisting of a pane of glass resting against the wall on the floor, a photograph of the pane of glass on the floor, and a printed dictionary definition of "glass", the work presents a cheeky self-reflexive pun on the concept of "glass," showing three distinct representations of glass that all have the same referent. After researching the short history of the artwork, conservators decided to replace the photograph of the glass against the wall with a new image that accurately represented the pane of glass in its new setting against a different floor and wall in the museum. Encouraged by the artist's certificate of instructions for the work, it can be said that stakeholders, in this case, applied the contemporizing paradigm, thereby inviting the possibility of other modifications in the future to keep visual parity within the work. But they just as well may have applied a traditional paradigm, choosing to keep and preserve the original components. The result of the latter counterfactual decision would have set the artwork on a different trajectory, one that affirms the identity of the work's dependence on the original materials and first instantiation.

Locating the difference in the approach rather than the object itself does not in any way undermine the work of conservators of contemporary art in recent decades: it does *not* imply that the separate path taken by contemporary art conservation has been in vain or founded on a false dichotomy. On the contrary, the astute sensitivity to and concern for the multivalent nature of contemporary works have enabled this alternate contemporizing paradigm of care. Now quite established, the contemporizing paradigm can be applied to a new work, setting it on a certain dynamic trajectory, but might also be applied, contrary to current custom, to an old work in order to reactivate an important characteristic, function, power, etc. that it possessed when it was itself contemporary. In the case of the proverbial Ship of Theseus, conservators might opt instead to closely document the ship's course and maintain the ship's ability to make legendary sea voyages, replacing boards and re-making parts as necessary. This ship would be more performance than relic. On the flip side, stakeholders are free not to apply the contemporizing paradigm to a new work. In this regard, close investigation of the trajectories of old artworks, specifically with an eye to identifying moments or phases when a new direction was taken, may be useful to conservators wondering about the long-term effects of certain kinds of decisions, and in which cases it is desirable to let an older-than-new artwork age. In examining very long trajectories, one might start with the following questions: is the need to update, redo, overpaint or re-refashion an object an indication that it has ceased to feel contemporary for viewers of that place-time? What factors contribute to the need to update? What are the mechanisms by which aging objects become documents of their own past? How have maker-communities in the past defined and responded to notions of obsolescence? Answering these questions with contemporary challenges in mind may help us understand and evaluate the future trajectories of contemporary artworks.

7 Conclusion

Things not necessarily intended to be viewed as art show themselves to be as unconventional as the most problematic works of contemporary art: not only material in their identity and no longer fixed in time. Thus, perceived differences between old works and contemporary works may be more accurately and usefully explained by the existence of two valid paradigms of care, one that privileges the unique material integrity of a work, another that honours the multivalent and often immaterial significance of objects. Liberated from the notion that old and contemporary works are fundamentally different, stakeholders are free to apply, or not, the contemporizing paradigm to old and new works alike. With regard to a contemporary artwork, the option not to use the paradigm may allow it to gradually age as its identity becomes increasingly determined by a particular instantiation of itself. With regard to an older artwork, the option to adopt the paradigm may lead to innovative approaches for conservation, interpretation and display.

References

Appelbaum B (2007) Conservation treatment methodology. Elsevier Butterworth-Heinemann, Oxford

Brittenham C (2019) Architecture, vision, and ritual: seeing Maya lintels at Yaxchilan structure 23. Art Bull 101:8–36. https://doi.org/10.1080/00043079.2019.1564175

Buskirk M (2000) Planning for impermanence: art works containing materials that decay or become obsolete. Art Am 88:112–119, 167

Coddington J, Mancusi-Ungaro C, Varnedoe K, Levin J (2002) Time and change: a discussion about the conservation of modern and contemporary art. Conserv GCI Newsl 17:11–17

Cone LN (2017) The variable and changing status of performance art relics and artifacts in museum collections. Beitr. Zur Erhalt. Von Kunst-Kult. 106–112
Cotter H (2018) Zoe Leonard's messages strike hard — and cast a spell. N.Y. Times
Cranmer D (1987) Ephemeral paintings on "permanent view": the accelerated ageing of Mark Rothko's paintings. In: Grimstad K (ed) ICOM Committee for Conservation 8th triennial meeting: Sydney, Australia, 6–11 September 1987: preprints. Getty Conservation Institute, Los Angeles, pp 283–285
Delidow M et al (2009) Turn it on—turn it off. Lighting in MoMA's Collection of Architecture and Design. Presented at the Future Talks 09: Technology and Conservation of Modern Materials, Design Pinakothek der Moderne, Munich, Germany
Domergue D, Lowinger R, Menveg D (1987) Change the art or change the artist: a question of ethics in the conservation of contemporary art. In: Preprints of papers presented at the Fifteenth Annual Meeting: Vancouver, British Columbia, Canada, May 20–24, 1987. American Institute for Conservation of Historic and Artistic Works, Washington DC, p 34–42
Engel D, Phillips J (2019) Applying conservation ethics to the examination and treatment of software- and computer-based art. J Am Inst Conserv 58:180–195. https://doi.org/10.1080/01971360.2019.1598124
Goodman N (1976) Languages of art: an approach to a theory of symbols. Hackett Publishing, Indianapolis
Graham J, Sterrett J (1997) An institutional approach to collections care of electronic art. Newsl West Assoc Art Conserv 19:26–28
Hahn C (1997) Seeing and believing: the construction of sanctity in early-medieval saints' shrines. Speculum 72:1079–1106. https://doi.org/10.2307/2865959
Hahn CJ (2017) The reliquary effect: enshrining the sacred object. Reaktion Books, London
Hogan J, Snow C (2015) Sol Lewitt's wall drawings: conservation of an ephemeral art practice. Objects Spec. Group Postprints Am Inst Conserv Hist Artist Works Objects Spec Group 22:37–45
Hummelen Y (1999) The conservation of contemporary art: new methods and strategies? In: Corzo MA (ed) Mortality immortality? The legacy of 20th-century art. Getty Conservation Institute, Los Angeles, pp 171–174
Hummelen Y, Sillé D (1999) Modern art: who cares? An interdisciplinary research project and an international symposium on the conservation of modern and contemporary art. Foundation for the Conservation of Modern Art and the Netherlands Institute for Cultural Heritage, Amsterdam
Jasienski A (2020) Converting portraits: repainting as art making in the early modern Hispanic world. Art Bull 102:7–30. https://doi.org/10.1080/00043079.2019.1638674
Kargère L, Marincola MD (2014) Conservation in context: the examination and treatment of medieval polychrome wood sculpture in the United States. Metrop Mus Stud Art Sci Technol 2:11–50
Kemp J (2020) Book review of Paik's virtual archive: time, change, and materiality in media art. J Am Inst Conserv 59:79–83. https://doi.org/10.1080/01971360.2019.1676902
Kendriks E (2016) "Paintings fade like flowers": color change in paintings by Vincent van Gogh. In: Clarricoates R, Dowding H, Gent A (eds) Colour change in paintings. Archetype Publications Ltd, London, pp 39–51
Krautheimer R (1942) Introduction to an "Iconography of Mediaeval Architecture." J Warbg Court Inst 5:1–33. https://doi.org/10.2307/750446
Kumler A (2011) The multiplication of the species: Eucharistic morphology in the middle ages. Res Anthropol Aesthet 59–60:179–191. https://doi.org/10.1086/RESvn1ms23647789
Kumler A (2015) Sacrament to street food: the troubled history of the waffle. Cabinet Q. Art Cult:63–71
Kumler A, Lakey CR (2012) Res et significatio: the material sense of things in the middle ages. Gesta 51:1–17. https://doi.org/10.1086/669944
Laurenson P (2004) The management of display equipment in time-based media installations. In: Roy A, Smith P (eds) Modern Art, New Museums, Contributions to the Bilbao Congress,

13–17 September 2004, vol 49. International Institute for Conservation of Historic and Artistic Works, London, pp 49–53

Laurenson P (2006) Authenticity, change and loss in the conservation of time-based media installations. A conceptual framework for traditional fine art conservation. Tate Papers 6. https://www.tate.org.uk/research/tate-papers/06/authenticity-change-and-loss-conservation-of-time-based-media-installations

Marçal HP (2017) Conservation in an era of participation. J Inst Conserv 40:97–104. https://doi.org/10.1080/19455224.2017.1319872

Molina S (2019) Sustaining the lives of art objects. AMA J Ethics 21:450–454. https://doi.org/10.1001/amajethics.2019.450

Muñoz Viñas S (2005) Contemporary theory of conservation. Elsevier Butterworth-Heinemann, Oxford

Nagel A (2012) Medieval modern: art out of time. Thames & Hudson, New York

Nagel A, Wood CS (2005) Toward a new model of renaissance anachronism. Art Bull 87:403–415

Nagel A, Wood CS (2010) Anachronic renaissance. Zone Books, Distributed by MIT Press, New York, Cambridge

O'Hern R, Pearlstein E, Gagliardi SE (2016) Beyond the surface: where cultural contexts and scientific analyses meet in museum conservation of West African power association helmet masks. Mus Anthropol 39:70–86. https://doi.org/10.1111/muan.12102

Peters RF (2016) The parallel paths of conservation of contemporary art and indigenous collections. Stud Conserv 61:183–187. https://doi.org/10.1080/00393630.2016.1200839

Phillips J (2012) Shifting equipment significance in time-based media art. Electron Media Rev 1: 139–154

Phillips J, Hinkson L (2018) New practices of collecting and conserving live performance art at the Guggenheim museum. Beitr Zur Erhalt Von Kunst-Kult 124–132

Pugliese M, Ferriani B (2009) Preserving installation art: hypothesis for the future of a medium in evolution

Sever D (2016) A pilgrim's self-identification: sixth-and seventh-century lead pilgrim flasks from the Holy Land. Diogenes 4:35–48

Smith JZ (1992) To take place: toward theory in ritual. University of Chicago Press

Spector N (2003) Felix Gonzalez-Torres, *Untitled (Public Opinion)*, 1991. In: Depocas A, Ippolito J, Jones C (eds) Permanence through change: the variable media approach. Daniel Langlois Foundation for Art, Science and Technology, Montreal, pp 92–99

Stigter S (2011) How material is conceptual art? From certificate to materialization: installation practices of Joseph Kosuth's *Glass (one and three)*. In: Scholte T, Wharton G (eds) Inside installations: theory and practice in the care of complex artworks. Amsterdam University Press, pp 69–80

Taubert J, Taubert J (2015) Polychrome sculpture: meaning, form, conservation. Getty Conservation Institute, Los Angeles

Temkin A (1999) Strange fruit. In: Corzo MA (ed) Mortality immortality? The legacy of 20th century art. Getty Conservation Institute, Los Angeles, pp 45–50

Tom C, Sutherland K (2017) Overpaint removal from a quattrocento polychrome bas-relief: challenges in interpreting painted sculpture. In: Bridgland J (ed) ICOM-CC 18th triennial conference preprints, Copenhagen, 4–8 September 2017. ICOM Committee for Conservation, Paris

van de Vall R (2015) The devil and the details: the ontology of contemporary art in conservation theory and practice. Br J Aesthet 55:285–302. https://doi.org/10.1093/aesthj/ayv036

van de Vall R, Hölling HB, Scholte T, Stigter S (2011) Reflections on a biographical approach to contemporary art conservation. In: Bridgland J (ed) ICOM-CC 16th triennial conference Lisbon 19–23 September 2011: preprints. Critério, Lisbon, pp 1–8. http://hdl.handle.net/11245/1.344546

van Saaze V (2015) In the absence of documentation. Remembering Tino Sehgal's constructed situations. Rev História Arte Spec Issue Perform Doc 4:55–63
Weiss J (2013) Things not necessarily meant to be viewed as art. Artforum 51:221–229
Wharton G, Molotch H (2009) The challenge of installation art. In: Richmond A, Bracker A (eds) Conservation: principles, dilemmas, and uncomfortable truths. Elsevier, London, pp 210–222

Cybele Tom is a doctoral candidate in the Department of Art History at the University of Chicago. Her research interests concern the ritual culture of early- and high-medieval Europe, its material objects and issues in their life, aging, and obsolescence. Previously a conservator at the Art Institute of Chicago, Tom specialized in the technical examination and care of polychrome sculpture. Recent publications in that area include a paper on the visual effects of the paint and overpaint of a fifteenth century Sienese bas-relief of the Madonna and Child (*ICOM-CC Preprints,* 2017) and the shifting material identity of a painted wood sculpture of the bodhisattva Guanyin (*Perspectives,* 2022). She holds an MA in Art History and Conservation from the Institute of Fine Arts, New York University. Since 2015, she has served on the editorial board of the *Journal of the American Institute for Conservation*.

Languages of Conservation: A Comparison Between Internet-Based Art and Built Heritage

Claudia Roeck

Abstract As relational, social practices in a changing environment, internet-based art and built heritage require a substantial effort to maintain functionality. This chapter explores the hypothesis that architecture conservation and conservation of internet-based art encounter the same challenges and follow the same principles. The comparison allows one to articulate the materiality of internet-based art, which may not be obvious at first glance. Most important, it suggests that conservation approaches for built heritage may expand the conservation options for internet-based art. To substantiate the hypothesis, I analyse the significant properties of an internet-based artwork, *TraceNoizer* (2001–2004) by LAN, according to the same criteria used in built heritage conservation. After demonstrating that I can describe internet-based art using categories from built heritage, I apply conservation strategies for built heritage to internet-based art to discover new conservation approaches. The pursuit of a common language for the conservation of built heritage and software-based art is another goal of this comparison.

Keywords Conservation strategies · Built heritage · Digital heritage · Conservation · Preservation · Internet-based art · Net art

1 Introduction

The sheer mass of a building suggests its permanence and stability. However, appearances are deceptive. When built in 1889, the Eiffel Tower was intended to last for only 20 years.[1] Since then, every seven years, 60 tons of paint have been applied to prevent the Eiffel Tower from rusting. Apart from the ravages of time, buildings undergo reoccurring changes of use and expansions of space and functions. The website of the Eiffel Tower gives an impression of this kind of changes: improvement of accessibility for visitors of the Eiffel Tower by adding handrails and

[1] https://www.toureiffel.paris/en/the-monument/key-figures. Accessed 29 Jan 2022.

C. Roeck (✉)
University of Amsterdam, Amsterdam, The Netherlands

R. van de Vall, V. van Saaze (eds.), *Conservation of Contemporary Art*, Studies in Art, Heritage, Law and the Market 9, https://doi.org/10.1007/978-3-031-42357-4_6

ramps, renovation of elevators and restaurants, surrounding the Eiffel Tower with a glass wall to improve security, etc.[2] These ongoing changes enable the touristic exploitation of the Tower and the funding of its maintenance. Not only the building, but also its surroundings are protected. The gardens, as well as the view on the Eiffel Tower, are listed heritage. Although the building is massive and has been a landmark for many decades, it is undergoing constant change.

In contrast, internet-based art seems to be immaterial. One just opens a laptop with a browser and an internet connection in order to see the work (nowadays even a smartphone can be good enough). It is not necessary to have the source code of the work on one's own computer. The navigation does not require any physical effort. However, internet-based artworks are not as immaterial as they look at first sight.

To visualise the materiality of internet-based art and to expand its conservation options, I compare the conservation of internet-based art with the conservation of built heritage. After looking for communalities between these very different conservation objects, I will research whether conservation strategies for built heritage can be applied to internet-based art and whether they can contribute to solve the conservation dilemmas between historical accuracy and aesthetical and functional requirements.

Comparison of internet structures with built structures is not new. The internet platform The Digital City,[3] founded in 1994, facilitated access to internet and email and thus the communication among the residents of Amsterdam. The metaphor of the World Wide Web as a city and the homepages as houses was also used for the geocities.org[4] platform, whose users were called homesteaders. Both platforms are not online anymore. Many colloquial terms for the World Wide Web still refer to buildings or built structures such as "web address" for "uniform resource locator (URL),"[5] "under construction" with a corresponding image for a website that is not finished.

In conservation of software-based and internet-based art, the building metaphor has mainly been used to express the obsolescence of the digital technology by using the term "ruin" for abandoned, anachronistic, only partially or non-functional digital objects (Magagnoli 2016, p. 2), (Laforet 2009, p. 22). Magagnoli did not discuss the consequences of this metaphor for the conservation of digital objects in depth, and Laforet focussed on the archaeological conservation approach without referring to architectural conservation. She called it "the museum of internet art as a living archive" (Laforet 2009, p. 186). This living archive hosts digital artworks that consist of fragments and provides contextual information. She bases her theory on media archaeology and the variable media approach. It will be interesting to see, how

[2] https://www.toureiffel.paris/en/news/works. Accessed 29 Jan 2022.

[3] De digitale Stad (DDS), https://nl.wikipedia.org/wiki/De_Digitale_Stad. The digital city was subject of an archaeological excavation in 2017/18 (S. Alberts et al. (2017).

[4] https://en.wikipedia.org/wiki/Yahoo!_GeoCities The geocities platform was archived by the internet activists "Archive Team" (Lurk et al. 2012, p. 247).

[5] https://en.wikipedia.org/wiki/URL. Accessed 29 Jan 2022.

this comparison with conservation strategies for built heritage resonates with Anne Laforet's archaeological conservation approach.

2 Method

To extend the conservation options for internet-based art, I compare conservation of built heritage with conservation of internet-based art in two steps. The hypothesis I explore in a first step is that the conservation objects "built heritage" and "internet-based art" have several similar characteristics relevant for their conservation. Having argued for their similarity, I will examine, the applicability of three conservation strategies for built heritage to internet-based art.

For the comparison of the conservation objects in Sect. 4, I will use *TraceNoizer*, an internet-based artwork, as an example and compare its significant properties to the ones of the Eiffel Tower. The categories applied to describe both objects, *TraceNoizer* and the Eiffel Tower, are based on the method that built heritage specialists Kuipers and Jonge developed to analyse and describe built heritage. Their description is based on building layers (Kuipers and Jonge 2017, p. 87) as well as on an analysis of the construction history of the building (Kuipers and Jonge 2017, p. 73). Their final goal is to find an "adaptive reuse" of the building.

Afterwards I will apply conservation strategies used in built heritage to internet-based artworks in Sect. 5 and draw conclusions about their applicability in Sect. 6. As *TraceNoizer* and the Eiffel Tower cannot cover all the cases, I will also use other artworks and buildings as examples.

3 Characteristics of TraceNoizer (2001–2004) and the Eiffel Tower (1887–1889)

The following paragraphs will analyse the characteristics of *TraceNoizer* (2001–2004) and of the Eiffel Tower (1887–1889) according to the abovementioned building layers-spirit of place, surroundings, site, skin, structure, space plan, interior surfaces, services, and stuff—used by Kuipers and Jonge (2017, p. 87) to analyse built heritage. In addition to the layer analysis, they also map the construction history of the building. I will add a paragraph about the construction history of both examples after the layer description. To facilitate the reading, I begin with a short introduction of the Eiffel Tower and *TraceNoizer*.

The Eiffel Tower was built from 1887 to 1889 as the entrance to the 1889 World's Fair.[6] The tallest building in Paris was designed by the engineers Maurice Koechlin and Émile Nouguier. Originally, it was designed as a temporary structure. But due to

[6]Information from https://en.wikipedia.org/wiki/Eiffel_Tower. Accessed 29 Jan 2022.

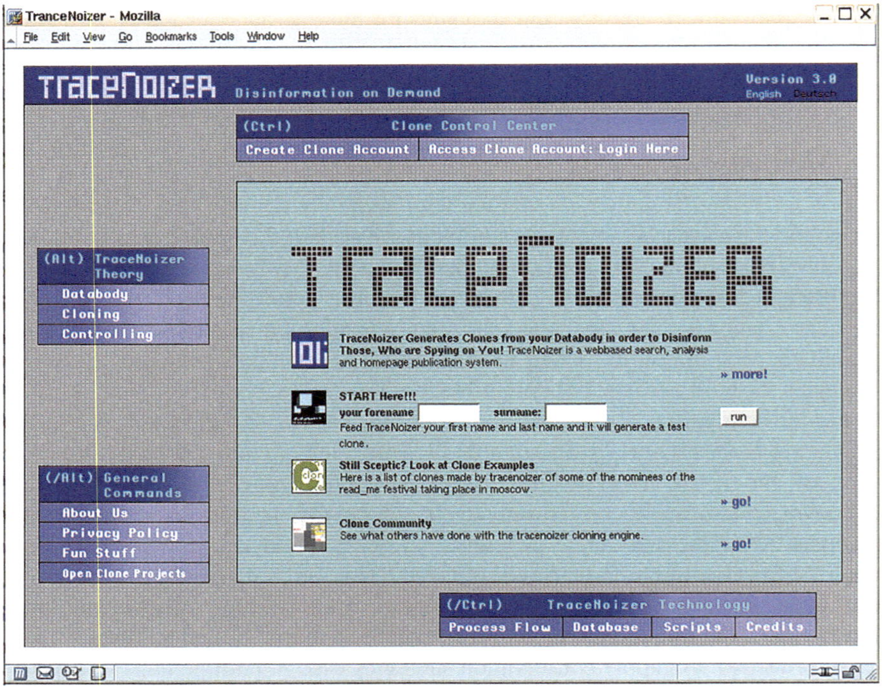

Fig. 1 Screenshot of *TraceNoizer* homepage as conserved on a Linux Live CD by Fabian Thommen

its use for radio transmissions, the city of Paris extended its permit. It also served scientific experiments. The Tower quickly became the landmark of Paris and an important tourist attraction.

TraceNoizer is an internet-based artwork created by the artists group LAN[7] between 2001 and 2004 (Fig. 1). The House of Electronic Arts acquired this website in 2017. TraceNoizer addresses the concern of internet users about the control of their data. Thus, *TraceNoize*r aims to obfuscate the traces a user left behind in the Web. On the *TraceNoizer* website, one could enter one's name and *TraceNoizer* would search the internet for websites containing that name by using Google Search. It would then randomly assemble new websites out of the search results. The more new websites were produced, the less likely it was that the original websites would be found by the search engine. The original traces, in other words, would disappear in the background noise of the newly produced websites. The artists call the part of *TraceNoizer* that produces the fake websites "clone engine."

The following paragraphs characterise the Eiffel Tower and *TraceNoizer* according to the layers used by Kuipers and Jonge (2017, p. 87):

[7] Annina Rüst, Fabian Thommen, Roman Abt, Silvan Zurbruegg and Marc Lee.

Spirit of Place The Tower's location at the banks of the river Seine and its surroundings of the Champ de Mars and Jardins du Trocadero underline its importance as a landmark, as an icon of iron architecture, symbol of development (paired with nostalgia from today's point of view) and of romance. For an internet-based artwork the spirit of place could be translated with aura.[8] The aura of *TraceNoizer* consists of its charisma of an early internet-based artwork made by pioneering artists and of a touch of resistance to consumer internet culture and authority. From today's point of view, it evokes nostalgic feelings.

Surroundings (Wider Environment) The Eiffel Tower is a landmark of Paris. As such, Paris can be seen as its wider environment. Because the city needed radio towers, and later because the Eiffel Tower became an important tourist attraction, the Tower was not taken apart again, as originally intended.[9] The Eiffel Tower still transmits radio and television frequencies and is as such part of a communication infrastructure. As a tourist attraction, it is based on a touristic infrastructure consisting of a transportation and accommodation network. As such, the Eiffel Tower is embedded in a sociotechnical environment. The Web in general is the wider environment of *TraceNoizer*. As *TraceNoizer* processes websites, the web environment is crucial for *TraceNoizer*. Since the creation of *TraceNoizer*, Web 1.0 was succeeded by Web 2.0, while social media became much more important than personal websites, and this negatively affected the functionality and interpretation of *TraceNoizer*. Both, *TraceNoizer* and the Eiffel Tower, are part of a sociotechnical system that undergoes constant changes. They are not isolated objects, but narrowly bonded to their changing surroundings.

Site (Closer Environment) The closer environment of the Eiffel Tower consists of the park surrounding it. It allows high numbers of tourists to enjoy the Tower from up close in a beautiful environment. Furthermore, metro stations in the vicinity facilitate the transport of visitors to the Tower. *TraceNoizer*'s close environment consists of links to external websites.[10] These links lead to two artworks that are the result of the use of the clone engine of *TraceNoizer* by other artists. In the meantime, these links became obsolete.

Skin (Aesthetics of the Building) The Eiffel Tower is a bit untypical in this respect, as its aesthetics are a direct consequence of the technical construction. The arrangement of the girders and the struts produces the aesthetics and the stability of the Tower at the same time. Both the construction and the aesthetics were cutting edge at the time of its construction, as well as an expression of its modernity. The graphical design of a website can be analysed from a technical point of view or from an

---

[8]The term "aura" of an artwork is coined by Walter Benjamin (Benjamin 1936, p. 5). According to him, unique artworks have an aura which means they are embedded in a certain time and space related context such as traditions or rituals.

[9]https://www.toureiffel.paris/en/the-monument/eiffel-tower-and-science.

[10]Tracenoizer.net → clone community "Illegal immigrants dis.information" (2002) by Darko Firtz and "Eventmodul::anonymous.databody.muttering" (2001) by Knowbotic Research etc.

aesthetic point of view. *TraceNoizer* based its graphics on frames. This was typically a method used in the 2000s to position content within a website. From the aesthetic point of view, *TraceNoizer* was designed without the flashy colours, blinking symbols and moving gifs that were common at the time. However, from its design (colours, font, font size and resolution, use of side bars) it is clearly visible that the website was designed at least 10 years ago.

Structure (Including Construction Materials) The technical construction of the Eiffel Tower is wrought-iron lattice while the website *TraceNoizer* is a server-side dynamic website. This means that the dynamic part, the clone engine and its database, is executed on the webserver and not in the browser (the client). This website construction has consequences for the conservation: crawlers such as the Internet archive uses cannot crawl the software, database or logic that is executed on the webserver. Crawlers can only harvest responses of the webserver to its requests. In order to preserve the logic of such a website, access to the webserver or source code and database is necessary.

While the material of the Eiffel Tower is mainly wrought-iron, the material of *TraceNoizer* are the programming languages HTML, PERL and PHP. PERL and PHP are the languages used to program the clone engine. Like wrought iron that enables the lattice construction, PERL and PHP enable the generation of new clone-websites for *TraceNoizer*. PERL is a language that is particularly apt to manipulate text. As the clone engine searches and parses websites consisting of HTML text, the artist chose PERL to program the clone engine. Engel and Phillips confirm this point of view: "Similar to other areas of art technology, these choices of medium [for instance programming language] can be deliberate (artist-intended), or contingent. In both cases, the source code may be integral to an artwork's identity, even if it is typically hidden from the audience and rarely part of the audiovisual or interactive experience." (Engel and Phillips 2019, p. 181).

Space Plan In the case of Eiffel Tower, a map gives the position of the different floors and restaurants and how they can be reached by lifts and staircases. *TraceNoizer* has several pages that can be visualised with a site map. The site map shows how each page of *TraceNoizer* is linked to the other pages of *TraceNoizer*, a kind of navigational map.

Interior Surfaces This layer is difficult to interpret for internet-based art and for the specific case of the Eiffel Tower. It is therefore not considered here.

Services (Infrastructure) The Eiffel Tower's service layer consists of the electric power system, the communication system and the water supply system within the Tower. The infrastructure of an artwork is usually invisible, although it has a vital function: it runs the background processes that enable the artwork. For *TraceNoizer* such infrastructure consists of internet ports, the internet protocol suite, protocols such as http and https, webserver software, and the markup language html. Naturally, this is based on a wider infrastructure of the whole internet, such as fiber-optic cables, routing equipment, domain name system etc.

Stuff (Mobile Parts) All mobile parts, such as for instance restaurant and ticket office furniture at the Eiffel Tower, are "stuff." For *TraceNoizer*, that is more difficult to define. It could be the *TraceNoize*r screensaver, which one could download, or a *TraceNoizer* T-Shirt, which one could order on the website.

Kuipers and Jonge recommend visualising the construction and conservation history in a map ("Chrono-mapping," 73). For the Eiffel Tower and *TraceNoizer*, this is summarised in the following paragraph.

Construction and Conservation History The Eiffel Tower does not feature single restoration moments, but it is regularly maintained, and its amenities are permanently upgraded and adapted to the needs of visitors. Many changes of the Eiffel Tower have replaced older versions, fragmenting or demolishing certain layers. For instance, the lifts were upgraded and replaced by newer systems many times.[11] From 2008 to 2014, the lift from 1899 was restored, adapted to current requirements. In other words, the Eiffel Tower is a conglomerate of old and new pieces and historical layers are not discernible at first sight.

TraceNoizer was created from 2001 to 2004 during which the artists further developed the artwork and added more features. According to the folder structure in the source code, there is one new version each year until 2004. This can also be retraced in the Internet Archive.[12] The conservation history of *TraceNoizer* started with a conservation measure undertaken by one of the artists. In 2004, Fabian Thommen created a Linux live CD. It contained the webserver including operating system and internet browser. *TraceNoizer* went offline in 2011 but had not been fully functional several years before that. While the graphical surface is still intact, the clone engine is no longer able to produce fake websites. The subsequent conservation measures were undertaken by the House of Electronic Art in 2018 in order to make the work accessible online again.

It can be concluded from the above comparison that Internet-based artworks and buildings can both be described based on layers. These layers described above are receptacles and can be layered themselves. Internet-based art and buildings have environments (term used for software) and surroundings (term rather used for buildings) and often their boundaries (between what is part of the work and what not) are difficult to define. As long as the building and the Internet-based artwork are in use, they are both changing continuously, as they need to be adapted to current needs of their users as well as to external infrastructures. All these characteristics are relevant for conservation and some of them a challenge. In this respect, it will be interesting to compare the conservation ethics and strategies of both fields.

Another conclusion from the comparison is that Kuipers and Jonge's concept of building layers and mapping of construction history does not provide sufficient information to analyse the building: despite its goal to find adaptive uses there is no category that describes the use history of the building. Use is only represented in

[11] https://www.toureiffel.paris/en/the-monument/lifts. Accessed 29 Jan 2022.

[12] https://web.archive.org/web/2019*/www.tracenoizer.net. Accessed 29 Jan 2022.

Riegl's value matrix (Kuipers and Jonge 2017, p. 87) as use value, but not as a separate topic for investigation. Furthermore, researching the reasons for changes and their connection to sociotechnical developments could help to evaluate the significance of certain technologies and materials and explain or expose external dependencies. I recommend adding some of Laurenson's "areas of focus" for significant properties of software-based art,"[13] such as "external dependencies," "processes" and "context." On the other hand, Laurenson's areas of focus could profit from a layered approach regarding the "structural elements," while "context" could be expanded with sociotechnical context and conservation history. If the suggestion to include socio-technical context in the artwork documentation is not new (Lurk et al. 2012, p. 250), it is not yet practised in museums. As Annet Dekker states in her dissertation about the conservation of internet-based art, "conservation tends to discard the importance of the social space" (Dekker 2014, p. 18).

It is now clear that internet-based art and built heritage can be described in the same terms that are relevant for conservation decisions. The following section will discuss, how conservation strategies for built heritage can be applied to internet-based art.

4 Conservation Strategies for Built Heritage Applied to Internet-Based Art

In 2004, the Variable Media Network defined four conservation strategies for the conservation of variable contemporary art: storage, migration, emulation and re-interpretation.[14] Almost the same terms are used in digital preservation, although their definitions[15] differ from those of the Variable Media Network. In contrast, built heritage conservation does not use such a categorization. The conservation strategies for built heritage I investigate originate from different sources. I chose the strategies "adaptive reuse," "re-interpretation based on the combination of old and new materials" and "reconstruction" as they are different from the contemporary art strategies mentioned above. Sections 4.1 to 4.3 describe these conservation strategies for built heritage conservation and assess whether they can be applied to conservation of internet-based artworks.

[13] Areas of focus for significant properties of software-based art according to Laurenson (2014): content, appearance, context, other versions, formal and structural elements, behaviour, durations of processes, spatial or environmental parameters, external dependencies, function, processes, artist's documentation, rules of engagement, visitor experience and legal frameworks.

[14] https://www.variablemedia.net/e/index.html → terms → strategies. "To emulate a work is to devise a way of imitating the original look of the piece by completely different means". "To migrate a work involves upgrading equipment and source material."

[15] Thibodeau (2002, pp. 18–19): "Emulation strives to maintain the ability to execute the software needed to process data stored in its "original" encodings, whereas migration changes the encodings over time so that we can access the preserved objects using state-of-the-art software in the future."

4.1 *Adaptive Reuse—"Function Follows Form"*[16]

The trigger for restorations of built heritage is often not the building quality or the aging of its material. Most buildings undergo major changes because their original function cannot be sustained, and a new use must be found for the building. Such changes of use are a consequence of the evolution of the sociotechnical environment (layers "surrounding" and "site" in Sect. 4). Industrial technologies change, production is farmed out abroad, the living standard changes, transportation and communication infrastructures are renewed, and energy and safety requirements evolve.

However, as argued by the architect Jan Duiker (1890–1935), one of the spokesmen of the Modern Movement, "whenever a building's purpose had to change, the form would lose its raison d'être. In such cases, the building should either be adapted or demolished altogether" (Kuipers and Jonge 2017, p. 99). This point of view does not include a third possibility: the adaptation of the use to the building in order to preserve it: "Function follows form"[17] instead of "form follows function," as Kuipers and Jonge put it. Kuipers and Jonge, both working in and researching the field of built heritage in the Netherlands describe the procedure for a building's adaptive reuse.[18] Besides a technical and historical analysis of the building layers, they recommend a value-based analysis based on Riegl[19] by mapping building parts and layers with different values. Based on this analysis, they determine the most important building elements and characteristics before they negotiate an adapted use and the necessary building changes with the building owners. Depending on these negotiations, the required changes of the building can range from minimal to substantial.

The ruin Santa Catalina de Badaya in Spain (Fig. 2) can be seen as an example of minimal intervention. The adaptive reuse of Santa Catalina de Badaya as a botanic garden does not require too many changes of the original buildings. Nor does it afford large scale reconstructions. The conservation focussed on the material remains of the buildings and brought them to the foreground. On the flipside, its original functions as a residence or monastery cannot be reinstated. While the restoration of Santa Catalina de Badaya is obvious to the visitor due to the contrasting materials used, other measures such as the stabilisation of the castle walls are not visible.

---

[16] Term used by Kuipers and Jonge (2017, p. 114).

[17] Dito.

[18] In Dutch "adaptive reuse" is "herbestemming". Wikipedia (accessed 29 Jan 2022) describes "herbestemming" slightly different than "adaptive reuse". The Dutch Wikipedia definition describes "herbestemming" as assigning a new use to a building in order to preserve cultural, historical, architectural and other values. In the English Wikipedia definition, "adaptive reuse refers to the process of reusing an existing building for a purpose other than which it was originally built or designed for. It is also known as recycling and conversion. Adaptive reuse is an effective strategy for optimizing the operational and commercial performance of built assets."

[19] Riegl (1903).

Fig. 2 Santa Catalina de Badaya (SP) restored by isuuru architects (Source: http://isuuru.com/pat_consolidacion.html. Accessed 29 Jan 2022): Restored ruin with clearly contrasted wooden additions and less visible consolidations (Photo: © isuuruarquitectos)

The mechanism of why internet-based art becomes dysfunctional after only a few years is similar to the context of built heritage: its sociotechnical environment changes: protocols, programming languages and webservices evolve, browser plugins become obsolete, the way how people use the internet changes. Internet-based artworks often end up as ruins before they are acquired by a collector or museum for the reasons mentioned above. The custodians have to decide between the preservation of the original material and the restoration of the original functions and aesthetics.

In contrast to built heritage, adaptive reuse applied to art is not about repurposing the artwork. The artwork's purpose should not change, as conservation should not change the meaning of the artwork. In the short- and mid-term, it is not the purpose, but the functionality of the artwork that is impeded through obsolescence. In addition, the user knowledge how to interact with internet-based art evolves and the interaction with an old artwork might not come natural to a young user. In that sense adaptive reuse can mean that a user needs to be shown how to interact with the artwork instead of updating the interface of the artwork to current technology. Hence, adaptive reuse for internet-based artworks can mean compromises on the level of functionality in favour of less invasive changes and on the level of usability (use no longer self-explanatory) by having to explain more about the artwork.

TraceNoizer (2001–2004) can figure as an example of an internet-based artwork that was restored with minimal interventions and whose functionality was not fully restored. For the restoration of full functionality, an external library not maintained since 2002 would have needed to be substantially adapted without a guarantee that these changes would improve the result much.[20] Furthermore, there was reason to assume,[21] that the work did not function perfectly before, either. For this reason, the work was restored so that the users can create the clones, but it was accepted that the clones are faulty, and that the users cannot save and access them later. To give the user the opportunity to see what a clone looked like in 2002, the *TraceNoizer* clone project archive was restored.

For both the conservation of the former monastery Santa Catalina de Badaya and the website *TraceNoizer* "migration"[22] was employed by applying many small interventions that changed the building and artwork substance. However, in combination with adaptive reuse, other strategies such as adding a building layer or encapsulation can be applied. Kuipers and Jonge mention the example of the Van Nelle factory where a second skin was added on the inside of the building envelope to improve the building climate for reuse as office spaces (2017, pp. 118–119). The former commanders house of the Holocaust memorial in Westerbork, the Netherlands, was encapsulated with a glasshouse for protection from the weather. Such layer-based strategies also exist for internet-based art. An emulator[23] encapsulates software. For instance, a client computer is emulated to enable the use of obsolete internet browsers. This adds the emulator as a layer to the client computer. A digital interface-layer functions as a translator between old technology and new technology. An example for this would be a library-layer that translates an old protocol to a new one. To summarise, adaptive reuse only aims to reduce the impact on the building or artwork substance, but it does not prescribe how to achieve that goal.

Returning to the two cases, the former monastery Santa Catalina de Badaya and the *TraceNoizer* website, both lost either their former use and/or their former functionality. I would even go so far to claim that if a building changes its use there will always be building parts that lose their function even if these parts are preserved. For *TraceNoizer*, this is similar. Although the code is still there, certain parts of the code do not function any longer. However, as the artwork is not assigned

[20]The work was based on the fact, that users had their own homepages hosted by free hosting services such as geocities, whereas today users have social media instead of homepages. The "rainbow" library parses the text of the websites provided by the search engine. However, as most websites found today are not websites with manually written HTML code, as was the case in 2001, but rather are composed by content management systems (used in social media and blog posts), the parsing code needs adaptations.

[21]According to the Jury of the *READ_ME Festival 1.2* http://readme.runme.org/1.2/adden.htm (accessed Jan 2021): "*(...), TraceNoizer is not literally effective at introducing noise into our data identities; after several weeks we still couldn't find our data clones in search engines at all. TraceNoizer's interest to the jury, however, was its use of algorithmic processes as critique.*"

[22]Migration is a term used in digital preservation. It is used here in a more general way as the sum of many small changes applied directly to an artwork or building, slowly changing it if repeated for many times. Changes can encompass stabilisation measures, retouching or completing, or adaptations to new use.

[23]Emulation is a term used in digital preservation. Computer hardware is represented as software (the emulator). It is a common strategy for the preservation of video games. The old video games can be played within the emulator.

a new purpose, the reduced functionality makes it more difficult to understand the artwork. For both, the former monastery Santa Catalina de Badaya and the *TraceNoizer* website additional explanations and documentation are needed to compensate for this loss of functionality and change of use. Today, due to the minimal interventions and the publicly available explanations, the buildings and the website are solutions in between a ruin and a fully functional monument or object.

4.1.1 Visibility of Conservation Interventions

The visibility of changes is a returning topic in conservation ethics.[24] In contrast to Santa Catalina de Badaya, the user will not notice changes made in *TraceNoizer* immediately, because the changes only influenced the functionality of the website and not its design. These changes were made on the source code level and can be visualised in a version control system. Version control systems are used in software development but are also very useful in preservation of software-based art (Engel and Phillips 2019, p. 191). The programmer can bundle and describe changes in so called commits (Fig. 3). Each commit comprises source code changes of multiple files. These changes can be viewed line by line (see Fig. 4) as archaeological software layers. Depending on the copyright of the source code, the code in a cloud-based versioning control system can be made publicly accessible.

Interestingly, built heritage conservators are also starting to consider version control systems to manage and visualise building changes. For instance, Chaturvedi et al. (2017) describe a concept for the use of version control for planning alternatives.

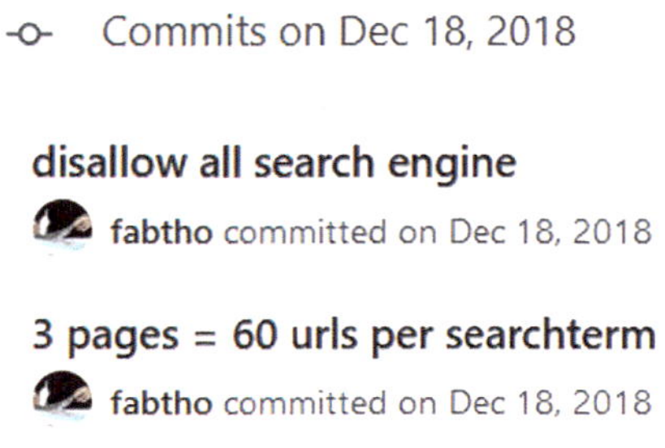

Fig. 3 *TraceNoizer* (2001–2004). Changes of source code bundled in commits on the versioning control platform "github." A commit can be related to many different files. By clicking on such a commit, each single change of code line can be seen as in the following figure:

[24] For instance, Art. 12 of the Venice Charter (1964). Or the Athens Charter (1931).

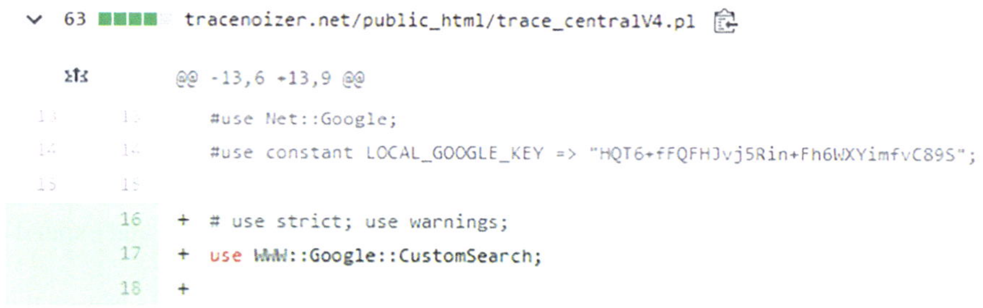

Fig. 4 *TraceNoizer* (2001–2004) Additions on code level, line by line: Replacement of non-functional Google API with a current one. The changes are visualised with github (https://github.com/fabtho/tracenoizer. Accessed 29 Jan 2022) versioning control

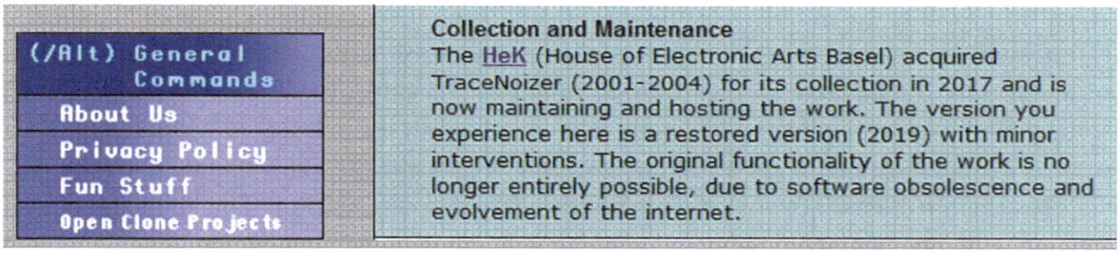

Fig. 5 Imprint of TraceNoizer.net, menu "About us." Text added by the House of Electronic Arts Basel

Another option of making the user aware of the changes of *TraceNoizer* is to mention the restoration in the imprint or credits of the website. On the *TraceNoizer* website (menu "about us", Fig. 5), the House of Electronic Arts added a paragraph on "Collection and Maintenance" to give the user some minimal information about the restoration and maintenance of the work. The user can contact the House of Electronic Arts if desired.

4.2 Re-Arch Approach or Reinterpretation Based on the Combination of Old and New Materials

Architects often have a view on the conservation of built heritage that differs from the one of built heritage specialists. Their creative handling of building conversions and reconstructions can have a huge impact on the original building and on its use. *Re-Arch* (Stimuleringsfonds voor Architectuur 1995), a book written by architects, discusses the architectural design for built heritage from the architect's perspective. The authors claim that there are two main approaches to design for built heritage. The first approach is to design a new building or an extension as a continuation of the existing building without contrasting it. The new building (part) is supposed to intensify and visualise the important traits of the old building. In the second approach, the new building actually contrasts with the old building and highlights the differences. Furthermore, as Provoost, one of the authors of *Re-Arch* states: "It is precisely layering and juxtaposition that can be linked to the idea of the historical experience. By coldly juxtaposing objects or by wrapping them with translucent materials, unpredictable frictions and paradoxes can arise. They do not need to be dissolved or synthesized, but offer, as they are, a new form of harmony and proximity. The aim of Re-Arch is to create something that transcends the old and the new" (Provoost 1995, p. 35).[25] Their approach to preserve, convert and expand a building is not only conservation-based but also design-based.

This double purpose can be recognised in the restoration of the Neues Museum in Berlin. The representatives of the Prussian Cultural Heritage Foundation and the architect tried to preserve as much original material as possible (Fig. 7) and to outline the previous staircase (Fig. 8). However, they did not reconstruct the former room decorations as seen in Fig. 6. Chipperfield formulated this double purpose as follows: "Desiring neither to imitate nor invalidate the remaining complex of ruined fabric, a Piranesian structure of bricks and architectural fragments, our concern has been motivated by the desire to protect and to repair the remains, to create a comprehensible setting, and to reconnect the parts back into an architectural whole" (Chipperfield 2009, p. 56). The result (Fig. 8) is a reinterpretation of the old museum depicted in Fig. 6.

This design-based approach is rather rare in art conservation. The reinterpretation strategy of the Variable Media Approach[26] might be closest to this approach. Because of the uneasiness of conservators to use reinterpretation, LIMA, a research and conservation institution for media art in Amsterdam, advocates reinterpretation of media artworks in order to "ensure that media art remains understandable" (Wijers and UNFOLD network 2017, p. 1), but also to foster discussion between artists, audience, curators and conservators about the interpretation of the artwork.

The reinterpretation of the internet-based artwork *TraceNoizer* came up in an artist's interview[27] about the conservation of *TraceNoizer*. Its creators mentioned the idea of a contemporary reinterpretation. Instead of cloning "fake" websites, the cloning and remixing of Facebook accounts would have been a possible answer to current internet practices. After a discussion they concluded that this reinterpretation of *TraceNoizer* would result in a new work. As they did not intend to create a new work, but to preserve the existing one, they did not pursue this idea.

This hypothetical example of *TraceNoizer*'s reinterpretation is based on a new platform with new technology. Neither design nor substance (source code) would remain. This differs from the Re-Arch approach, which combines old elements with the design of new elements in order to form a new whole and trigger a historical experience, as for instance in Neues Museum in Fig. 8. The difference between

[25] "Historical experience" is a term coined by the Dutch history theorist Frank Ankersmit (1993, p. 14 ff). It describes the personal experience when seeing traces from the past (as an example he uses a painting from the 18th century depicting a scene from that period).

[26] http://www.variablemedia.net/e/welcome.html. Accessed 29 Jan 2022.

[27] Artist's interview on 22 June 2017 with the artists of *TraceNoizer*: Fabian Thommen, Marc Lee and Annina Ruest. Interviewed by Claudia Roeck.

Fig. 6 Water colour of the main museum staircase by Hedwig Schultz-Voelcker (ca. 1910) (© bpk/Kupferstichkabinett, SMB/Jörg P. Anders)

reinterpretation and conversion/migration is blurred in this case, as conversions with prominent new design elements are at the same time reinterpretations.

The reinterpretations of the internet-based artwork *TV Bot* (2004) by Marc Lee come closest to the Re-Arch approach. The artist himself updated and reinterpreted the work twice, once in 2010 and once in 2016. He keeps only the most recent version online, while the older versions are still accessible as screencasts (TV Bot 1.0, see Fig. 9).

TV Bot took pride in being the most current news channel in the world with news not older than one hour. In an interview,[28] Marc Lee mentioned that he wanted to

[28] Serexhe (2013), p. 427.

Fig. 7 Museum Island, Ruin of the Neues Museum Berlin 1985 (© bpk/Zentralarchiv, SMB/Schreiber)

Fig. 8 Neues Museum Berlin, built by Friedrich August Stüler 1843, restored by David Chipperfield, staircase with historical plaster casts, 2009 (© bpk/Achim Kleuker)

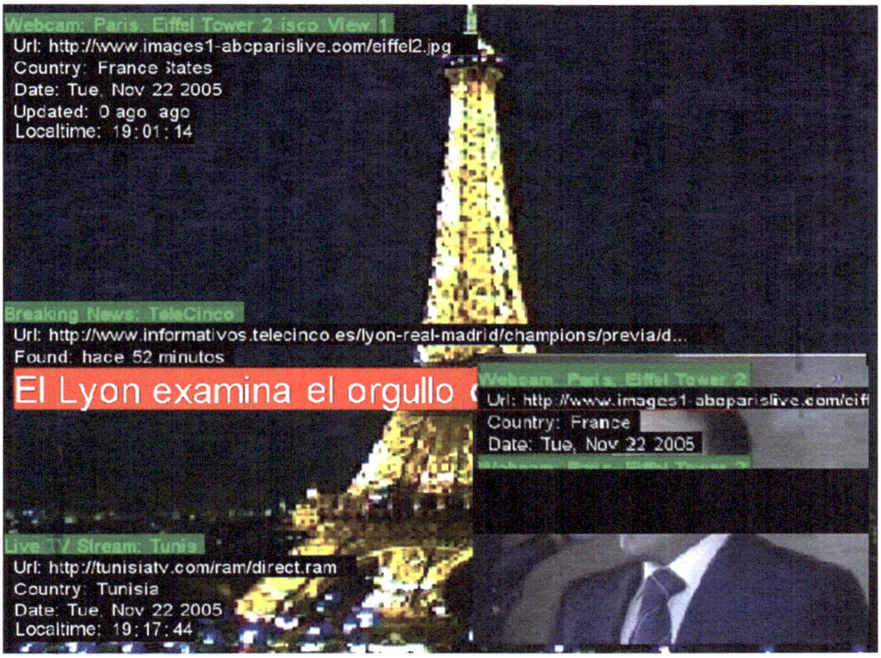

Fig. 9 Screenshot of *TV Bot 1.0* (2004). Red/black/green colour scheme for headlines

show, how simple it is to imitate a news channel by replacing the news editors with software. A good description of the first and second *TV Bot* version can be found in (Serexhe 2013).

When Marc Lee created *TV Bot*, social media did not exist yet. *TV Bot 1.0* used a list of more than 1000 web sources such as webcams, news platforms and radio streams. A RealPlayer browser plugin was necessary to view the website.

In 2010, the artist had to adapt the website to Flash technology, as the news platforms started to stream their news in Flash. He also introduced the social media platform Twitter as a news channel. The look and feel of the website did not change much (TV Bot 2.0, see Fig. 10).

The artist reused code of *TV Bot 1.0* and adapted it. In this sense, the code changes could be compared to the changes of the Neues Museum mentioned above. In contrast to the Neues Museum, however, the visitor or user is not aware of these changes and cannot perceive the layering and juxtaposition of old and new material mentioned by Provoost above.

In 2016 the artist had to revise the work for a third time as the streaming technology Flash became obsolete. *TV Bot 3*.0 does not look like a "serious" news channel, but rather like a candy-coloured blog of a social media influencer (TV Bot 3.0, see Fig. 11).

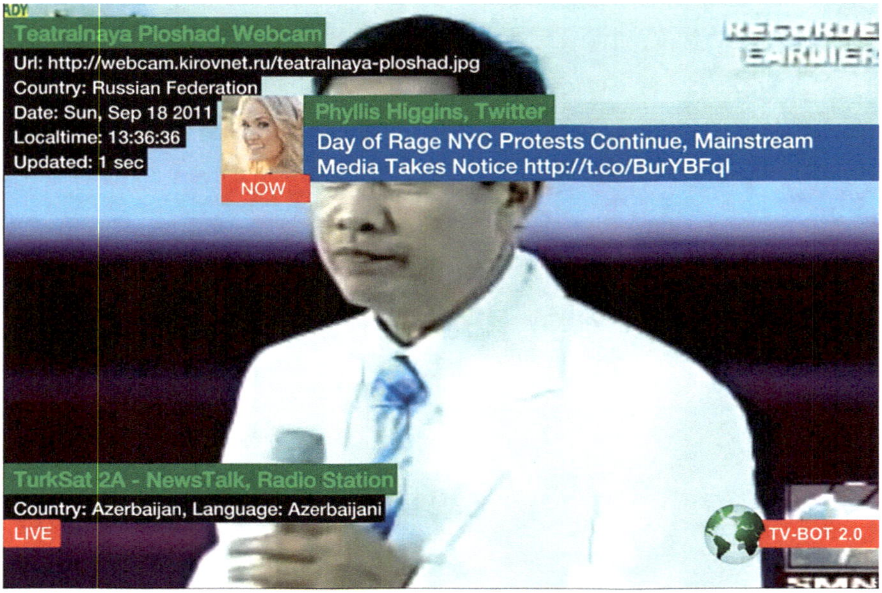

Fig. 10 Screenshot of *TV Bot 2.0*. Twitter was added (blue headline). Red/black/green/blue colour scheme for headlines

Fig. 11 *TV Bot 3.0*. Pink colour scheme. About 1000 news- and webcam channels replaced by 5 to 6 social media platforms

According to an interview with the artist in January 2021, the artist adapted the work to the postfactual period. Due to the emergence of social media the artist replaced the more than one thousand webcam, radio, and news sources with five to six social media platforms. Although the artist could not reuse the code, *TV Bot 3.0* is still a website programmed in almost the same programming languages (HTML, JavaScript, CSS and PHP) as the previous versions of TV Bot.

The reinterpretation history of *TV Bot* brings out three characteristics of web-based art that do not feature in the case of built heritage:

- Skin layer: the major changes on the webserver (backend) are not visible on the website (frontend), as is in the case of built heritage where a different material can indicate the filling of lacunae.
- Structure/material layer: it is not possible to understand what is happening on the webserver (backend) without having access to it. For this reason, the user does not know the information sources accessed by the work and the logic/algorithms it applies.
- Site (close environment): Following from the first two points it is not possible to understand the changes made between the versions of the work. The sociotechnical environment's level of change and its impact on the artwork is therefore difficult to grasp.

As a response to the first point, the artist placed the links to the three artwork versions on his website[29] next to each other. With respect to the two other points, more background information about the sociotechnical context and the restoration of the work would contribute to a better understanding of the work. The idea of *TV Bot* was revolutionary in 2004. It was probably the first bot that showed such current news while social media did not exist yet. Nowadays, the topicality of the news stream does not cause the same surprise as back in 2004. It could even be argued that the idea of the work changed slightly with *TV Bot 3.0* by highlighting the postfactual period more than previous TV Bot versions. Knowing the work's history of changes and its environment helps to value and position the idea and originality of the work. Together with the parallel display of two or more versions, this enables the historical experience of "layering and juxtaposition" mentioned by Provoost.

4.3 *Reconstruction*

Reconstructions of built heritage are common if sometimes contested. A prominent example is the Berlin Palace, a baroque palace whose façade was reconstructed in 2020. Due to heavy damages during WWII, the East German government demolished the Berlin Palace in 1950 and replaced it by a modernist building, hosting the parliament of the GDR, called Palace of the Republic. After the German

[29] https://marclee.io/en/tv-bot-world-news-as-soon-as-it-happens/. Accessed 29 Jan 2022.

reunification, the Palace of the Republic became obsolete. After twenty years of public debate[30] about the fate of the modernist Palace of the Republic, it was decided to demolish it and replace it with a reconstruction of the former baroque Berlin Palace. The reconstruction is a modern building of the same external dimensions as the former baroque Berlin Palace, comprising three reconstructed façades and a courtyard of the former structure. The use of the new building as a museum and cultural centre for the public is very different from its former use as an administrative building, which is why the interior building layout and structural design differ completely. One argument for the reconstruction of the façades was closing the aesthetical gap of the historical cityscape of the Museum Island (Fig. 12).

Such a reconstruction strategy can also be applied to internet-based art. Fig. 13 sets an example for a digital reconstruction of an internet-based artwork. The artwork, a YouTube video, played with the expectations of the YouTube users. The artist tagged the video with frequently used "spam" keywords that did not match the video content. Due to the "abuse" of these keywords YouTube took down the artist's video. Rhizome still had the video, but without the YouTube platform, it would not be understandable. Rhizome reconstructed the look of the YouTube

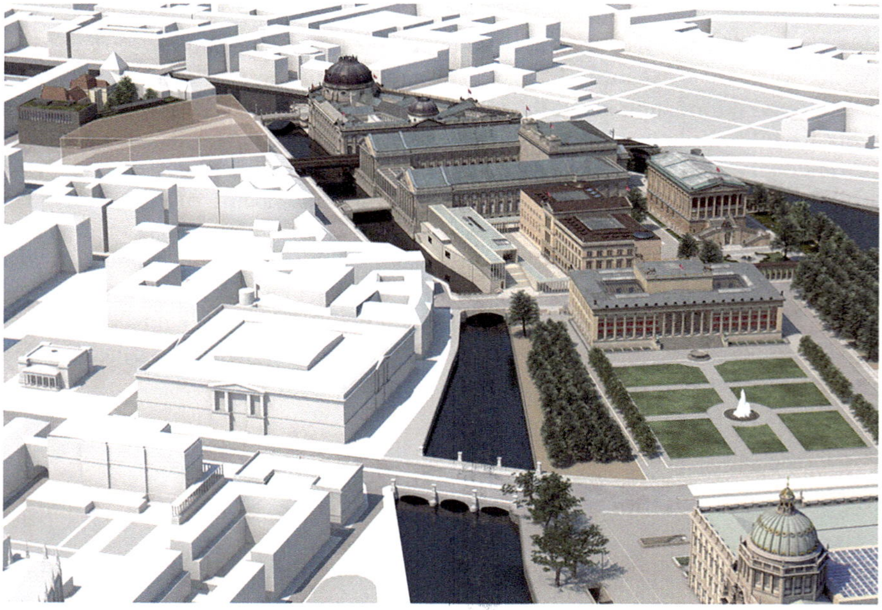

Fig. 12 3D-model of the future Museum Island Berlin, view from the south (in the lower right hand corner the Humboldtforum) (© bpk/Stiftung Preußischer Kulturbesitz, ART+COM)

[30] Summary of the debate: https://en.wikipedia.org/wiki/Berlin_Palace. Accessed 29 Jan 2022.

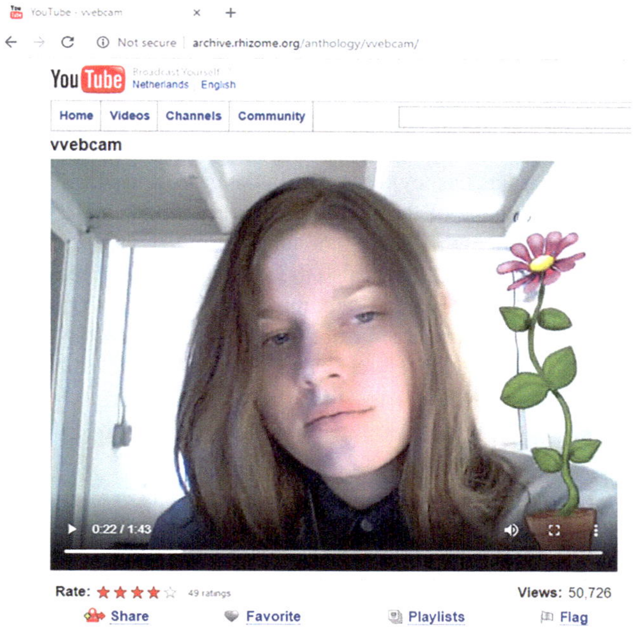

Fig. 13 *VVebcam* (2007) by Petra Cortright. Reconstruction of a YouTube channel by Rhizome: http://archive.rhizome.org/anthology/vvebcam/The reconstruction is recognizable in the URL of the website (it is not a YouTube domain)

platform so the user can understand the context of the video, but the YouTube platform as such does not function. The "fake" is immediately visible in the URL: http://archive.rhizome.org/anthology/vvebcam/ is not a YouTube domain. Rhizome chose this URL very carefully to make clear who hosts the website and that it must have been altered in some way. This reconstruction of YouTube can be compared to the reconstruction in Fig. 12, where just the façades (skin) of the Berlin Palace were reconstructed, while the building's interior was completely changed. The reconstruction of the skin allows one to have a more complete idea of the work.

Disappearing web-services and linked websites are a major problem for many internet-based artworks. For certain artworks, it can be a solution to reconstruct these services partly to simulate their output and freeze the environment.[31] The artwork *VVebcam* by Petra Cortright is now, after the reconstruction or simulation of the YouTube-service, independent from the YouTube platform and therefore more stable in the long term. In the example of the Berlin Palace, the reconstruction of

[31] Miksa et al. (2015, p. 78) refer to this reconstruction or simulation of a web service as "web service mock up."

the façades only had an aesthetical function (on the level of the cityscape and of the building), while it did not reduce the dependencies and the maintenance.

Prior to the reconstruction of the Berlin Palace there was a broad discussion in Germany about the justification of reconstruction and what requirements it has to meet to be authentic.[32] Often, reconstructions are reconstructions of the skin layer (façade), while all the other layers inside are adapted to current uses or tastes, a practice often criticized as Disneyfication.[33] In the case of the Berlin City Palace, the outer dimensions and shape of the buildings had to be preserved, in addition to the skin. "Structure," "services," "space plan" and "stuff" were not reconstructed. For the internet-based artwork VVebcam also the skin was reconstructed. Neither "space plan" (other videos) nor "services" (communication with YouTube users) nor "structure" (inner working/architecture of YouTube) were reconstructed. The criticism of "Disneyfication" did not present itself in this case, as the (partial) reconstruction was necessary to understand the artwork.

5 Conclusions

By starting from a comparison of built heritage with internet-based art, similar characteristics were found in both. They are both relational, social practices in permanently changing environments with visible and invisible layers. Often the need for conservation is caused by a change of the sociotechnical environment, rather than by material breakdown. This motivated me to explore the viability of conservation strategies used for built heritage and apply them to internet-based art.

In contrast to the definitions of the variable media network or digital preservation, the conservation strategies for built heritage are not divided into fixed categories or concepts. Rather, a procedure to achieve a sustainable conservation project or an individual concept is applied.

The adaptive reuse approach of Kuipers and Jonge is a process-based strategy used in built heritage conservation. As its application to internet-based art established, any conservation goal in between a "ruin" and a fully functional work can be a valid option. The use or function of the object is adapted so that the necessary changes in the artwork material can be minimised. The artwork is stabilised, well maintained and documented but certain functions are not restored if this requires big interventions. This resonates with Ann Laforet's "museum of internet art as a living archive" (Laforet 2009, p. 186), an archaeological museum that hosts digital fragments of net art. The documentation of the artwork context, such as pertaining to restoration goals, original functionality, the work's idea and change of the socio-technical environment, is crucial for this approach.

[32] Bundesinstitut für Bau-, Stadt- und Raumforschung, Bonn (2010) contains an extensive overview of discussions about reconstruction in Germany.

[33] Bundesinstitut für Bau-, Stadt- und Raumforschung, Bonn (2010), p. 74, p. 134.

The adaptive reuse approach does not prescribe how the minimal interventions are implemented. Layers are not only a category for description, but they can be a point of departure for preservation measures. Layers can be added to adapt and protect the building or artwork. They are placed between or on top of already existing layers. As such they can create a transition to the old substance without having to change it. Encapsulation, which corresponds to emulation in digital preservation, has a similar protective effect. In contrast, migration is a strategy independent from the concept of layers that changes the substance of the object by introducing many small changes.[34] It is applied not only in digital preservation, but also, quite frequently, in the restoration of built heritage.

The design-based Re-Arch-approach creates a historical experience by combining old building parts with newly designed parts. The work is fully functional, but the functions are adapted to the new reinterpretation, even if this asks for big interventions. The architects handle the "conservation design" creatively. With this approach, the most important difference between internet-based art and built heritage becomes apparent: the user cannot differentiate old from new web page parts. The historical experience is not possible, and the juxtaposition of different layers is not visible. The materiality of the pixels stays the same, no matter what software they are made of. The changes can only be seen on the web server layer, where the user does not have access. Therefore, it is important to document the work logic (algorithms), the web sources (services), the tools (programming languages and libraries) and changes in a way that it is accessible to the public. Furthermore, the visualisation of changes in internet-based artworks calls for creative solutions. There is a potential for more solutions than the ones given in this article.

The third strategy tested on internet-based art involved reconstruction. It is used to rebuild and imitate historical buildings that do not exist any longer. In internet-based art, this strategy can be employed to replace external dependencies, such as web services that changed or do not exist any longer. The Internet Archive can be interpreted as a partial reconstruction of the historical internet. Web archives can be used to recreate the surroundings of a website (using the building layer terminology), providing context to the artwork. Although such reconstructions possibly do not restore the whole functionality of the artwork, they make the artwork better readable and more independent from external infrastructure such as web services.

Sociotechnical developments are a frequent cause of changes of built heritage and of internet-based art, but they are not documented routinely. Their documentation would help to recognise external dependencies and the value of the material of the conservation object, as well as serve as an important input for selecting preservation strategies.

[34]This definition of migration in the field of digital preservation as the sum of many small changes differs from the definition of the "variable media network" (migration = updating to a new medium/ technology); still, it is adopted here, as it better fits internet-based artworks and can be separated more easily from the reinterpretation strategy.

In museums only conservators and curators usually have access to the full documentation of artworks. With a publicly accessible documentation anybody could broaden their knowledge about a work and shape their opinion about a reinterpretation. The documentation can become part of the work, as Aga Wielocha concludes in her dissertation. She promotes to conceive of an artwork as an "anarchive" (Wielocha 2020, p. 232), an anarchive that grows with each artwork version. This is particularly relevant for Internet-based art where the layers and conservation interventions are not visible.

Despite the obvious differences between built heritage and Internet-based art, there are surprisingly many communalities that make it possible to analyse them in similar terms and derive conservation strategies from built heritage conservation, which can enrich the conservation of internet-based art. This comparison could be even extended to software-based art or contemporary art in general, increasing the cross-sections between the various languages of conservation.

Acknowledgements This research was funded as part of *NACCA* (*New Approaches in the Conservation of Contemporary Art*, www.nacca.eu), a Marie Skłodowska-Curie Innovative Training Network of the European Union. The House of Electronic Arts provided the case study *TraceNoizer* (2001-2004), the artists information about the work. Marc Lee was available for an interview about TV Bot. Dr. Julia Noordegraaf, Dr. Renée van de Vall and anonymous reviewers supported me with feedback for this article.

References

Alberts G, Went M, Jansma R (2017) Archaeology of the Amsterdam digital city: why digital data are dynamic and should be treated accordingly. Inter Hist 1–14

Ankersmit FR (1993) De historische ervaring. Historische Uitgeverij, Groningen

Bundesinstitut für Bau-, Stadt- und Raumforschung, Bonn (2010) Positionen zum Wiederaufbau verlorener Bauten und Räume. Forschungen 143

Chaturvedi K, Smyth CS, Gesquière G, Kutzner T, Kolbe TH (2017) Managing versions and history within semantic 3D city models for the next generation of CityGML. In: Rahman AA, Abdul-Rahman A (eds) Advances in 3D Geoinformation // Advances in 3D geoinformation. Springer, Switzerland, pp 1–16

Chipperfield D (2009) The Neues Museum architectural concept. In: Hamm OG (ed) Das Neue Museum Berlin: Konservieren, Restaurieren, Weiterbauen im Welterbe. Seemann, Leipzig

Dekker A (2014) Enabling the future, or how to survive forever: A study of networks, processes and ambiguity in net art and the need for an expanded practice of conservation. Doctoral Thesis, Goldsmiths, University of London

Engel D, Phillips J (2019) Applying conservation ethics to the examination and treatment of software- and computer-based art. Journal of the American Institute for Conservation 58

Kuipers M, Jonge WD (2017) Designing from heritage.: Strategies for conservation and conversion. TU Delft, Delft, Netherlands

Laforet A (2009) La conservation du net art au musée: les stratégies á l'oeuvre. PhD, l'Université d'Avignon

Laurenson P (2014) Old media, new media? Significant difference and the conservation of software-based art. In: Graham B (ed) New collecting: Exhibiting and audiences after new media art. Ashgate Publishing Limited, Surrey (UK) /Burlington (USA), p 73–96

Lurk T, Espenschied D, Enge J (2012) Emulation in the context of digital art and cultural heritage preservation. PIK - Praxis der Informationsverarbeitung und Kommunikation 35. https://doi.org/10.1515/pik-2012-0048

Magagnoli P (2016) The internet as ruin: Nostalgia for the early World Wide Web in contemporary art. transformations. J Media Cult

Miksa T, Mayer R, Rauber A (2015) Ensuring sustainability of web services dependent processes. IJCSE 10:70. https://doi.org/10.1504/IJCSE.2015.067058

Provoost M (1995) Re-Arch: Nieuwe Ontwerpen Voor Oude Gebouwen. In: Stimuleeringsfonds VA (ed) Re-Arch: Nieuwe Ontwerpen Voor Oude Gebouwen. Rotterdam: Uitgeverij 010, pp 9–37

Riegl A (1903) Der moderne Denkmalkultus, sein Wesen und seine Entstehung. W. Braumüller, Vienna and Leipzig

Serexhe B (ed) (2013) Digital art conservation: Preservation of digital art. Theory and practice, 1st edn. Ambra V, Wien, Karlsruhe

Thibodeau K (2002) Overview of technological approaches to digital preservation and challenges in coming years, Kenneth Thibodeau. In: The state of digital preservation: An international perspective. Conference proceedings. Council on Library and Information Resources, Washington DC, pp 4–31

Wielocha A (2020) Collecting archives of objects and stories: On the lives and futures of contemporary art at the museum. PhD thesis University of Amsterdam

Claudia Roeck is affiliated to the University of Amsterdam, where she pursues a PhD about preservation strategies for software-based artworks. This PhD position is part of the EU funded project *New Approaches in the Conservation of Contemporary Art* (*NACCA*). She worked as an assistant time-based media conservator at Tate, and participated in conservation projects at LIMA, an archive and research platform for media art in Amsterdam, at the Netherlands Institute of Sound and Vision and is currently conservator at the House of Electronic Arts, Basel.

No Longer Artwork

Marina Valle Noronha

Abstract In this conceptual chapter I explore, from a curatorial perspective, a new approach to the lifespan of artworks in museum collections. At a time when the managing of collections is under pressure because of new theories on the conservation of contemporary art, the conventional understanding of collection management might no longer hold. I speculate on how philosopher's Tristan Garcia's non-linear notion of time, in which the future does not exist and time is marked by intensities of presence, makes us re-think the engagement with objects perceived as deviant in collections. I investigate further implications of recent attempts in contemporary conservation theory that account for the temporal nature of artworks and explore what it means for artworks that, despite attempts to progressive thinking, they are still perceived as no longer suitable for display because of their material degradation. Through this, I aim at offering ways of engaging with objects whose changing artwork properties have been, for different reasons, regarded as impaired by their hosting institutions. I focus on what I call a "complex object family" formed by different entities of artist Naum Gabo's *Construction in Space: Two Cones*, 1927–1937. As part of this complex object family formation, I also discuss versions of artist Marianne Vierø's work *Great Transformation* (2015).

Keywords Contemporary curating · Collection management · Artworks' lifespan · Changing objects · Speculative time

1 Introduction

More than alarming, the current situation faced by many museums in terms of finance and storage opens up the ground for new approaches to conservation and curating. A shift is needed on how museum professionals think of and engage with

M. Valle Noronha (✉)
Department of Art and Media, Aalto University, Espoo, Finland
e-mail: marina.vallenoronha@aalto.fi

R. van de Vall, V. van Saaze (eds.), *Conservation of Contemporary Art*, Studies in Art, Heritage, Law and the Market 9, https://doi.org/10.1007/978-3-031-42357-4_7

changing objects.[1] In the paradigm proposed in this chapter artworks are less and less seen as "eternal," while also the idea of individual object is becoming obsolete. The understanding that artworks undergo constant changes challenges the characterization of museums as places where objects go to rest.[2] Fernando Domínguez Rubio (2020) speaks of the museum as creating "some working fiction of permanence and durability" (p. 253), which would require "that in order for some-thing to be eternal in this particular way, it would need to exist in time while being unaffected by time" (p. 157). In the storage room, the modern idea of art that is based on an illusion of stability, or on the idea that an artwork is permanent, no longer holds.

A move from preserving artworks' initial state to incorporating artworks' lifespan takes us to a notion of collecting that is based on presence and includes absence. A space where objects are understood as temporal entities. I believe curating can proactively learn from discussions and theories on the conservation of contemporary art that account for change, ways to re-assess the current, often conventional engagement with objects in collections. With this in mind, this exploratory chapter refers to both traditional and contemporary artworks. I expand Hanna Hölling's account of traditional works, as long durational and subjected to change, beyond conservation and into the curatorial realm. To advance the discourse on changing objects, I present a notion of presence that collecting institutions might not be aware of. This approach, introduced by Tristan Garcia, could contribute to a progressive re-thinking of collection management and conservation practices.

In short, Garcia's perspective introduces a reality of things that, regardless of what they are, participate in a flat-ontology system where things are equal in the world. Their temporality should be understood in terms of intensities of presence, which shifts around the conventional progression of time modalities (from left to right, see Fig. 1). In terms of presence, the timeline progresses from the future, which, contrary to conventional understanding of time, is rearranged here and comes before the past. Because the future has no presence, it comes first. It is followed by the past with its fading presence, which in turn is followed by the constantly evolving *now* (or the present, the very moment you read this chapter). The present will always lead the timeline because of its maximum presence. These two commitments—to an equality of things (in thought) and to intensities of presence—form the structural thinking in this chapter.

---

[1] A first draft of this introduction was presented at the conference *Museums as Agents of Memory and Change* in Tartu and Tallinn, Estonia, 24–26 April 2019. I elaborate on the paths to wider access to artworks in collections in the context of the research for my doctoral dissertation at Aalto University, Finland.

[2] The official definition of museum varies slightly according to authoritative institutions such as the International Council of Museums (ICOM), the American Alliance of Museums (AAM), Association of Art Museum Directors (AAMD) and Museums Association (MA), to mention a few. However, a recent controversy during the ICOM meeting in Kyoto, 2019, on what defines a museum in the 21st century in terms of sustainability, community decision-making and ethics triggered increasing public debate. If this has not yet given rise to concrete changes, prevailing museum definitions are more and more being questioned; as also exemplified by the fact that the MA hosted a conference on the issue in 2019.

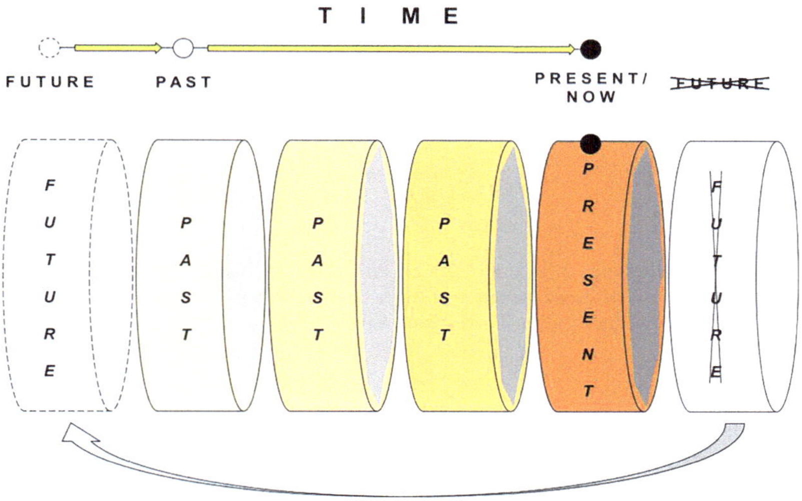

Fig. 1 This study is based on Tristan Garcia's non-linear approach to time that is defined by intensities of presence: the present, or now, has the maximum presence; the past has a fading presence; and the future (on the left), which has no presence, comes before the past. In this perspective, the future (on the right) does not exist, which is why it is crossed out and, instead, moved to the left

In what follows, I propose an enquiry into how museums may re-think their relationship with objects perceived as deviant by collecting institutions. To illustrate this thinking and analyse the changes artworks undergo, I will discuss a "complex object family" formed by different entities of artist Naum Gabo's *Construction in space: Two Cones*, made somewhere in the years between 1927 and 1937.[3] *Two Cones*, which has gone through a metamorphosis, has intrigued me for some time now. Iconic, the work is notorious for its material degradation. Due to it being extensively discussed in the conservation field, the work prompts questioning of the status, materiality, and temporality of artworks. Made out of cellulose acetate, *Two Cones* "rested undisturbed in an airtight display case" until 1960, when the Philadelphia Museum of Art (PMA), the institution that hosts it to this day, decided to open it (Siegl 1966, p. 151). Within less than 24 hours the work started to crumble apart. It became evident to the PMA that *Two Cones* was beyond repair, after which the work was classified as no-longer-suitable for display. Together with other versions of *Two Cones*, which are hosted by the PMA and Tate and also considered unsuitable for display, these objects form a "complex object family." This "complex

[3]The 1927 date is debatable as potentially the work was made as late as 1937. See Colin Sanderson and Christina Lodder, 'Catalogue Raisonné, Constructions and Sculptures of Naum Gabo' in *Naum Gabo: Sixty Years of Constructivism*, eds. Steven Nash and Jörn Merkert (Munich: Prestel Verlag, 1985), p. 215.

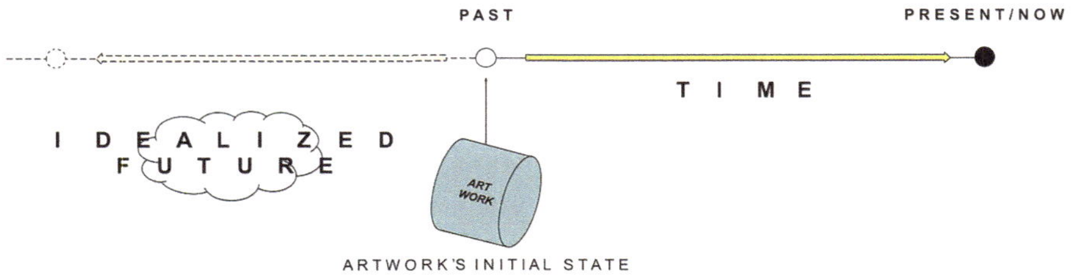

Fig. 2 The idealized future, which does not exist, is often envisioned by collecting institutions (in replacement of the now) as an attempt to preserve objects in the initial state in which they entered a collection. Instead, institutions could investigate ways of engaging with the past through artworks' present state

object family," I juxtapose with versions of Marianne Vierø's work *Great Transformation* (2015), which in turn addresses *Two Cones*' evolving state.

Contrary to the view of the PMA and Tate, I will argue that the disintegrated state of *Two Cones* did not cause it to stop being an artwork, nor that it is unsuitable for display today. First, I make the case, following Garcia's flat-ontology, that all objects in a collection are equally relevant. Next, I explain how, according to contemporary conservation theory, the incorporation of *change* and the notion of time extend also to "traditional" artworks, implying that *Two Cones* should be considered an artwork suitable for display, regardless of its state. Finally, I suggest that, adding to the last point and following Garcia's notion of objects and time, that *Two Cones*, in its current (disintegrated) state, represents the maximum presence possible in the here and now.

More in general, I argue that a revised notion of collecting which accounts for change contradicts the traditional idea of accumulating artworks to be preserved for eternity. In my view, collecting institutions usually work towards an idealized future, which according to Garcia's thinking does not exist. In other words, traditional thinking ordinarily refers to the conservation goal as something determinate that would happen in the future but would reinstate the past: the indefinite preservation of the initial state of an artwork. Such state, obviously, can only *be* in the past, as it belongs to the "already happened." Moreover, the presence of an artwork's initial state necessarily involves a fading presence, as it moves away from the present as time passes. It is impossible for conservation to hold on to the fading presence of something that already took place. Instead, it can help to navigate the evolving presence of an artwork (Fig. 2).

While choosing to preserve for a future that does not exist or in trying to hold on to artworks' initial state, museums might work against the presence of the artworks in their collections and, consequentially, against themselves. When museums neglect change, one might argue that artworks in a collection cease to be present. How can museum professionals envision (and advocate) a more interesting life for objects than that of being stored or crated?

In other words, I advocate that collecting institutions, through the agency of museum professionals and their practices, promote the present, always evolving state of an artwork. By concentrating on some idealized future, one will neglect the present, short-circuiting the idea of collecting (and preserving) for what is to come—the present again (albeit in a new guise).

The infographics (figures) featured in this chapter reflect my interpretation of Garcia's extended notion of time and presence regarding artworks in collections.

2 Managing Change

The traditional understanding in conservation practice and theory that objects should be preserved in the same condition in which they entered a museum collection has been questioned for some time now. Studies in the conservation of contemporary art such as by Laurenson (2006), Renée van de Vall et al. (2011), van Saaze (2013), Hölling (2016), and Annet Dekker (2018)—all accounting for the temporal nature of contemporary artworks—have contributed to new perspectives in conservation. Countering traditional thinking, these scholars understand that processes of *change* and *loss* that artworks go through across time are essential to the notion of conservation of contemporary art. Instead of focussing on the material or visual form of artworks, contemporary practice builds upon the idea that objects are subjected to transformations, changes and indeterminacy.

Not surprisingly, much of traditional conservation judgement is based on the "physical integrity" of a work. But "the notion of art as a 'fixed' material object has become highly problematic," prompting expansion in the vocabulary of contemporary conservation (van Saaze 2013, p. 36). Terms such as flexible, fluid, variable and medium-independent appear to have replaced fixed, stable, material authenticity and medium-specific (van Saaze 2013, p. 56). The Electronic Media Group of American Institute of Conservation (EMGAIC) applies time-based-media as a term to "any artwork that has both physical and temporal dimensions." [4] Positionings as such shifted the discussion away from the idea of a single object to a complex object that is subjected to change. The main point here is that, because of the temporal nature of art in general, all artworks, regardless of their medium specificity or current state, incorporate time.

To tackle the variability of works, critical thinking was brought to conservation through professionals working on heritage and ethnographic collections (Laurenson 2006). van de Vall et al. (2011, p. 3) have introduced the concept of a biographical approach, where "the meaning of an object and the effects it has on beings and events may shift during its existence, due to changes in its physical state, use, and social, cultural, and historical context". To leave the studio or to enter a collection does not mean the beginning or end of a biographical trajectory—they are two of the many reference points in an artwork's biography (Fig. 3).

[4] See http://www.conservation-wiki.com/wiki/Electronic_Media.

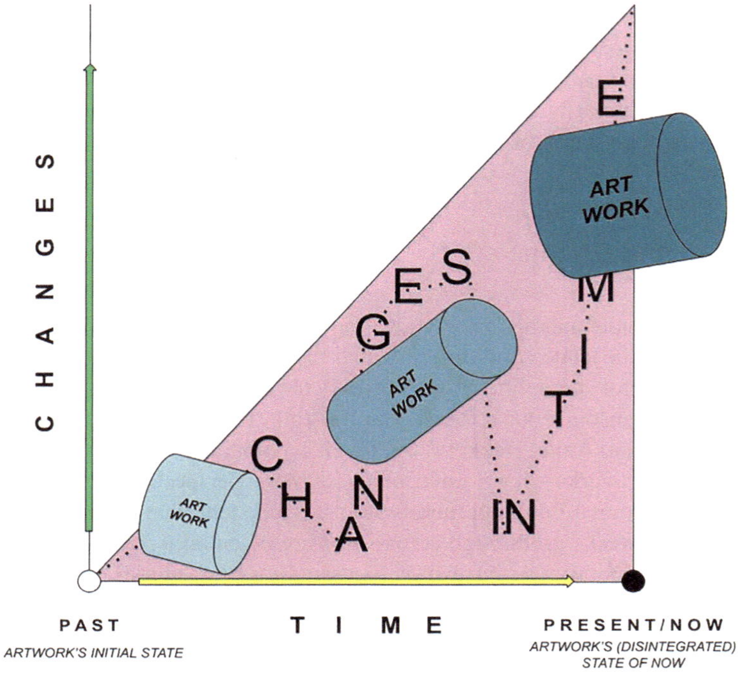

Fig. 3 An artwork's evolving identity and changes over time

Instead of a "truth-enforcement operation" (Muñoz-Viñas 2005, p. 65), contemporary conservation has learned from social process approaches in anthropology studies. Rather than operating under a single value, as noticed by van Saaze (2013), contemporary conservation theory puts forward negotiation, equilibrium, discussion and consensus (p. 76). In this more inclusive scenario, objects are influenced (and affected) by the changing environment and the other way around.

The traditional perspective that seeks stability and rejects change is commonly believed to follow a linear progression of time. In turn, the notion of time—often associated with change—is seen in a negative light by traditional conservation. However, Dekker (2018) explains that "[a]s a practice, conservation has always changed the 'authentic' state of a work" (p. 7). Interestingly, what traditional conservation seeks, at least in theory, is a constant return to the previous condition of an artwork. But in always trying to escape change, traditional conservation ends up as well subverting the linear conception of time, as pointed out by Hölling (2013, p. 157). Regardless of the tradition one follows, time is an intrinsic component of artworks.

In order to challenge the conventional conservation and curatorial practice, Hölling enquires whether all artworks should be conceived as temporal entities, including traditional paintings and sculptures. In this context she uses the notion of "long-durational artworks" (Hölling 2016, p. 19). To re-think traditional objects through the lens of the new means to re-think the conventional thinking in museum, conservation and curatorial practices. This prompts an opportunity to engage with (traditional) artworks as durational objects, or in Hölling's words, to "think of artworks of all kinds as everchanging and evolving entities that continually undergo physical alteration and transition" (Hölling 2016, p. 22). Before presenting a new reading of artworks that currently do not conform to the conventional norms of museum collections as a means to create conditions for their survival, I will first explain the theoretical framework for this chapter, Garcia's flat ontology, followed by a discussion of notions of time and presence.

3 Flat-ontology System, Time, and Presence

Garcia (2013) explains his philosophy as "thought-experiments on the 'equality' of all things" (p. 15). In a flat-ontology system,[5] the point is not that things are ontologically equal or that everything is equivalent. Instead, to enter this system is to be open to the idea that all objects (imagined or not) are equally significant, existing in "equal ontological dignity to each individuated thing" (Garcia 2014a, p. 4). A flat-ontology "[refuses] to presuppose an ontological difference between two kinds of objects (humans and non-humans, for example)" (Garcia 2013, p. 17). This perspective helps to re-think the notion of managing collections because it not only confers equal importance to objects, but also establishes non-hierarchical relationships between objects themselves and between objects, practitioners, and hosting institutions.

This way of thinking creates a parallel to artworks in collections, offering potential ways of understanding artworks as engaged in relationships with others, as well as with the changes they go through. Overall, this theoretical background might also help revise what museums do to artworks no longer considered suitable for presentation.

To advance this perspective, it is worth having a deeper look at Garcia's approach to time modalities. As for Garcia, the relationship between artworks in a collection and between an artwork and time is of the same type. The importance of the present state of an object is equal to that of its previous states in the past.

Moreover, a different understanding of time calls for a serious consideration of other timelines in museums and collections than human ones. To claim that something lasts forever is to limit a thing to a temporal dimension narrowly understood in human terms. As Hölling argues, "the problem of the understanding of artworks as being *in time, in duration*, . . . has something to do with the understanding of time in terms of endurance as cut to the human dimension" (Hölling 2016, p. 17). Because

[5] This system, also called object-oriented ontology (OOO), shares similarities with those proposed by more well-known philosophers, e.g., Graham Harman and Quentin Meillassoux, with references to the notion of a flat-ontology having existed since Alexius Meinong (1853–1920). See Graham Harman, preface to *Form and Object* by Tristan Garcia (Edinburgh: Edinburgh University Press, 2014): xxiv.

the human-centric approach is currently highly questioned, we know that this understanding is limited; yet museums seem to cling to it and thereby neglect possibilities to creatively develop a combination of conserving, curating and collecting.

In a search for a philosophical model that concerns "*only* time, yet *completely* time" (2014b, p. 1), Garcia takes as a starting point Saint Augustine's conception of time. Augustine states that the three tenses of time are "the present of past things, the present of present things, and the present of future things" (as cited in Garcia 2014b, p. 2), while we tend to refer to these, inaccurately, as past, present, and future. According to Garcia (2014b), there are three philosophical traditions concerned with Augustine's conception. Briefly put, the first tradition, associated with presentism and phenomenology, is further developed by Husserl, Heidegger, Sartre, and others. The second tradition is dialectical and associated with eternalism, and reflects on contradictions of being and non-being— represented by thinkers such as Hegel, Marx, Bloch, Benjamin. Less known is the third, analytical tradition, which explores the redistribution of time modalities and eternity, as reflected primarily in the work of Charlie Dunbar Broad, who in turn was influenced by Bergson and Whitehead and who criticizes McTaggart's dialectical view. In 1923 Broad formulated the so-called Growing Block Universe Theory (GBUT),[6] in which modalities of time are replaced by intensities of presence. Garcia further developed this conception and he arrived at the solution that time should be arranged in terms of presence.

4 Intensities of Time and Presence

The understanding of time in this chapter, or another order of time as introduced by Garcia, presents a rupture with the Cartesian perspective in which time flows from past to present and to future. Garcia argues that presence, instead of time modalities, is the guiding force in this *intensive* order of time, where:

> the present is first, as maximal intensity of presence; the past, which is a second order in the very interior of the order of time, is the classification of events by the relative weakening of their presence; the future, finally, which is the ground rather than the horizon of time, corresponds to the greatest possible absence. (Garcia 2014b, p. 11)

This explains why, for Garcia, the future—which has no presence, and is only absence—does not exist. This subtlety is crucial here when discussing the assessment of objects and acknowledging the importance of the numerous changes objects (regardless of the will of their hosting institution) go through in collections.

[6]GBUT is based on a dynamic conception of the universe that sees the universe as a block, continuously expanding itself in terms of presence. The past and present *are*, while the future, which has no presence, does not exist. Because of the continuous character of the present, the universe is constantly increasing in size, as more things are added all the time. GBUT's downside is that it treats the present of now and that of yesterday (or 1937) as one and the same.

Although conservation tends to reinforce an eternal present, "it is more interesting to follow the variability of the work and thereby accept the idea that time is not neutral or objective," as argued by Dekker (2018, p. 9). Similarly, Domínguez Rubio (2020, p. 4) claims "that objects are not given once and for all but are fragile and temporal realities." If we cease thinking of time in terms of modalities (past, present, future), according to Garcia (2014b, pp. 7–9), we envision time instead as variations of intensities of presence. "Temporal order is *both* the increase of presence and the decrease of indeterminacy" (Cogburn 2017, p. 179). Time is nothing other than the accumulation of presence.

Moreover,

> Contrary to the past, [the future] is not an ordered process. [It] is a fixed point of reference—without extension and in minimal intensity—which progressively detaches itself from the present, which is an irrevocable increase in the determinations of the universe. We therefore do not get closer to future as time passes: in reality, we move away from it. (Garcia 2014b, p. 9)

If this model puts museum practices on shaky ground, it also offers new possibilities to them. To re-think the temporality of objects in terms of intensity of presence is to question not only the approach to objects in collections but also the discourse on the management of changes in collections. By understanding the present as *maximal presence*, one realises that being present is paramount for existence. The presence of an object in a collection is directly related to its ability to survive in spite of change. This is, however, contrary to the conventional understanding of how collections manage changes, unwanted or not. In most cases, objects are assumed to behave according to expectations; and if they do not, their artwork status is removed from them.

An artwork, as a temporal object, "runs forward as it is in the present, and runs backwards as it is in the past" (Garcia 2014b, p. 11). Needless to say, this applies to artworks in collections—we think of them as becoming more and more present as they enter a collection. In the order of time, as argued by Garcia, "the past, a given state. . . passes and moves away from the present; it finds itself progressively buried under more and more ulterior states of itself" (2014b, p. 11). One might think of the changes that an object undergoes—the initial state of an object moves more and more away from the present (now) state of that object; the original state of an object becomes less and less present. Time, in other words, "both intensifies [an object's] presence and orders the different states of [an object's] presence—that is to say, [its] past—by degrading them" (Garcia 2014b, p. 11). Not surprisingly, this is exactly the distinctive legacy of *Two Cones*.

5 Constructions in Space

The decision to make *Two Cones* inaccessible followed conservation guidelines from the 1960s. Would the fate of *Two Cones* be different if the work's purported disintegration had occurred today, given the new perspectives in conservation? An approach that is not narrowly based on the materiality of the object can open us to a creative approach to the development/biography of an artwork, as emphasised by Dekker (2018, p. 8). Even under contemporary conservation's critical progress against traditional thinking and its openness to change, it is likely that this would not have (yet) been the case. In a thought experiment, would the crumbling apart of *Two Cones* today be understood as another point in the trajectory of the artwork—like leaving Gabo's studio or entering the PMA collection? What is necessary for its disintegration to be understood as a continuation of its being an artwork instead of its ceasing to be artwork?

After entering a museum collection, as we know from *Two Cones*, artworks keep changing—as they might lose or acquire properties—throughout their loan journey, exhibition history, or storage room stay. From a discussion in 2009, van de Vall et al. recall that "rather than 'preserving objects' conservators are 'managing change'—sometimes with the artists around, but very often without them."[7] This new perspective guides us to re-thinking not only objects, but also collecting and curating, in relation to the under-constant-change-understanding of time. Rather than perceiving artworks as having a single preferred state, museum professionals could fully embrace artworks as having *evolving identities*—and, in turn, understand objects as time entities.

Writing about the conditions of net art, Dekker (2018, p. 5) reports that museum professionals avoid discussing the conservation of artworks where change is imminent because of their fear of the new (it is known that because of its dependency on technology, time-based media can quickly become obsolete). When dealing with this art form, museum professionals have to come to terms with change in a more radical way. An artwork "is a complex document with kinks, folds, hiccups and slippages, which twist and bend in various directions, creating uncertainty and unpredictable behaviour," argues Dekker (2018, p. 16). With that in mind, one can conclude that Gabo, when experimenting with plastic's new technology in the first half of the 1900s, unknowingly added obsolescence to his work while at the same time preparing the ground for something new—in a manner quite similar to the fast pace in which new technology might confer obsolescence to net art works.

How could museums actively collaborate with time instead of dismissing it? On the meaning of the word "contemporary," Boris Groys (2009) writes that "[t]o be con-temporary means to be 'with time' rather than 'in time'" (p. 6). In this view, time

[7] van de Vall et al. recalls the statement made in the round table discussion *Ethical Dilemmas in the Conservation of Modern and Contemporary Art* at the Getty Conservation Institute on 29 April 2009. See https://www.getty.edu/conservation/publications_resources/videos/public_lecture_videos_audio/ethical_dilemmas.html.

can get some help from time-based art. An artwork becomes "a comrade of time—because time-based art is, in fact, art-based time" (p. 7). For the management of collections, it is important to witness the presence of objects in time. Moreover, "to be con-temporary ... can thus be understood as being a 'comrade of time'—as collaborating with time, helping time when it has problems, when it has difficulties" (p. 6). Artworks' evolving states are a reminder for collecting institutions that they can help facilitate the troubled understanding of time that often idealizes a non-existent future. When addressing issues of time, the changeable character of objects in a museum collection enables us to re-think them in their current condition (regardless of when they were created) as contemporary. By acknowledging and accepting that artworks change over time, it becomes possible to collaborate with time, so to speak, within the context of a museum collection.

6 Appearance of Other Objects: A Complex Object Family

To exhibit works like *Two Cones*, as argued by Hölling (2016), is to ask more profound questions concerning their nature and functioning. In dealing with instability, there is always the inevitable element of chance. It is far from easy, after all, to imagine how a work will look like at different moments in time. Almost any work of art may and ultimately will undergo major changes across time.

As the deterioration of *Two Cones* unfolded, it gave rise to the emergence of other objects. Since its deterioration, this work started to proliferate its features through different objects, listed here chronologically: (1) a scaled model (made out of celluloid), 1927–1937; (2) the original artwork (made out of cellulose acetate), 1927–1937; (3) a study copy (using Plexiglas), 1968 (Price et al. 2009); and (4) an artist replication of the original (again in celluloid), 1968. Given the deteriorated state of the original work and following unsuccessful discussions between the PMA and Gabo, the museum commissioned an artist (Arturo Cuetara) to make the study copy, which is at the PMA together with the original. Gabo donated the scaled model and the artist replication to Tate in 1977; both have faced deterioration.

These objects that proliferated after the work crumbled apart added something new to *Two Cones*. As pointed out by van Saaze (2013), "in the passage of an object through time things are also created; the outcome is something new" (p. 25). *Two Cones*' disintegrated, "new" state prompted the emergence of new objects. While engaging with such indeterminate object-multiples, collection conservators are faced with new questions, which potentially allow for the formulation of new strategies (van Saaze 2013, p. 146).

Treated as commodities, artworks' trajectories in museums are usually guided by market economies and reinforced by the traditional conservation approach. Hölling (2016) argues also that "the process of musealisation counters disappearance" (p. 19). But if *Two Cones* is denied the status of artwork, what kind of disappearance does the process of musealisation exactly counter here? Since its deterioration, the work no longer conforms to conventional museum collecting norms. Artworks that present (signs of) impairment in relation to their initial state are usually excluded from or segregated within collections. *Two Cones* can be seen as representative of many artworks in a similar condition within museum collections.

By understanding a family of artworks together—as collective—argues van Saaze (2013), one "opens up possibilities for creating and exploring new relationships and directions... that... were unthinkable or considered unsuitable for a museum" (p. 180). In groups, artworks might be understood as equal entities that establish a bilateral relationship amongst each other. Since artworks keep changing, museums then no longer store whole or complete works, but parts of works, as stressed by van de Vall et al. In being together, parts of objects form collections. A family of (parts of) artworks form a conceptual collection that questions the conventional approach of museums towards objects. As such, *Two Cones* can no longer be reduced to a single artwork.

To add to this already peculiar object-multiples biography, a few other objects based on *Two Cones* were made by artist Marianne Vierø. Her work, called *Great Transformation* (2015), [8] consists of an edition of two, in addition to an archive copy of a 3D rapid prototype 1:1 reproduction in recently developed plastics of the original version of *Two Cones* as of its decomposed state in 2014. *Great Transformation* adds again to the artwork family of *Two Cones*, now consisting of (at least) seven objects. So, in addition to the four items listed at the beginning of this section, there are three more: (5) one of *Great Transformation*'s editions is at the PMA; (6) an artist edition is with Vierø herself; and (7), an archive copy, presented as a gift to Gabo's estate. The natural degradation of Vierø's work is part of its original conception. In fact, Vierø chose materials for *Great Transformation* that will visibly degrade over time.

Vierø's work brings contemporaneity to Gabo's, and, in turn, *Two Cones* is the reason why *Great Transformation* exists. As noted by the PMA, they are all subjected to the same warps, bends, and cracks. *Great Transformation* contains *Two Cones* and the other way around. Vierø's work makes *Two Cones* visible as it is in its current condition. As argued by Hölling, "One could focus attention on the aesthetics and qualities of change, accepting change as a positive value with regard to both short-durational and long-durational works" (Hölling 2016, p. 18). Singularity can be obtained by keeping things connected, even if apart in spacetime, as illustrated by the case of *Two Cones*.

Two Cones and its object-multiples constitute a complex object family: seven individual evolving biographies, timelines, and ageing processes blend into each other as an intriguing whole. They continue to develop, resisting storage rules and challenging museum conventions. The complex artwork family in this case is conditioned by each of the individual works and by how they interact with each

[8] Marianne Vierø's work was commissioned by the Philadelphia Museum of Art and first shown there in 2016 as part of the exhibition *Into Dust: Traces of the Fragile in Contemporary Art*, June 6 - October 25, 2015, curated by Amanda Sroka. The work was then acquired by the museum in 2015 with acquisition funds and proceeds from deaccessioned works. See https://www.philamuseum.org/collections/permanent/333811.html.

other, together—without necessarily being in the same space or sharing the same time. How to account for the presence of objects like *Two Cones*—becoming—and understand them as an active part of a collection? When assessed in terms of presence, the complex artwork family of *Two Cones* presents itself as the maximum of presence to collections that might still be insisting on neglecting change.

7 Objects, Changes, Absence, Presence

The situation of *Two Cones* is contradictory in terms of presence because even though various versions of the work are comprised in the PMA and Tate's respective collections—they have accession numbers, have not been deaccessioned—they are not recognised as artworks suitable for display. By acknowledging *Two Cones'* trajectory as part of its biography, these museums would proactively address this work's contemporary presence in their collections. This would confer relevance to the artwork, instead of increased absence (the refusal of its present state). If being contemporary is the acceptance of the current state of an artwork, museums, when denying change, automatically deny contemporaneity as well. By not acknowledging the changes objects undergo, museums, as a result, seem to accept absence in the form of artworks which are denied their present state (Fig. 4).

Objects that do not conform to the norm are denied existence because of a conflict between their initial and current state. But if we understand artworks as being present, the significance of the "disintegrated state," meaning the result of their accumulated presence, has to be acknowledged as equally valid. Even though parts of *Two Cones*' instances have, for the collections that host them, lost their artwork qualities, the complex object's evolving (despite disintegrating state) presence of now is the maximum of its possible presence. Every past state of *Two Cones* can only have a fading presence/increased absence. To attempt to preserve an artwork in its initial state it is to deprive it from its presence.

The disintegrated version of *Two Cones* has gathered perhaps more interest than the initial state of the work. As pointed out by Dekker (2018), "meaning is constituted *through* the object and is not necessarily or solely held *within* the object" (p. 4). The meaning of the disintegrated state became more interesting than the illusion of a stable *Two Cones*. As discussed by van Saaze (2013), the authenticity of works can be discovered through context (p. 87). Even if not initially intended, the disintegration has become familiar, intrinsic to the work. Similarly, one can claim that the authenticity of *Two Cones* of now can be discovered over time, through conservation research, by familiarity with the evolving state of the work, by seeing, hearing, or reading (about) it over and over again (Fig. 5).

As art historian Altshuler (2005) claims, "works exhibited in museums are placed in the future, identified as playing a role in an anticipated history" (p. 2). By trying to grant presence to the past through projecting itself into the future, museums, through conventional conservation approaches, might in turn skip the present state of artworks altogether. The "ideally preserved" version of the artwork, which does

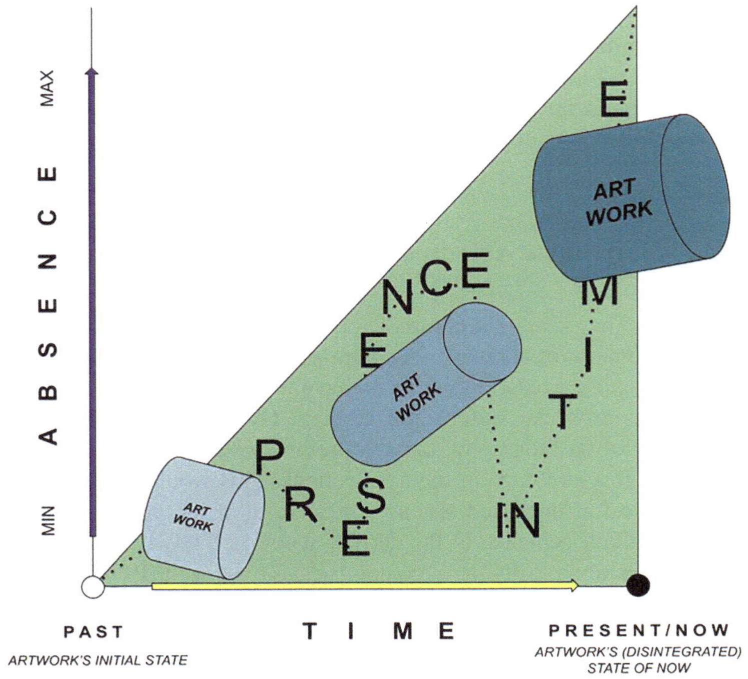

Fig. 4 Presence is directly related to the changes that objects undergo. To understand objects as being present in a collection, one must acknowledge and accept their changes as part of their evolving identities

not exist and can only be seen as an idea, refers to an equally idealized version of the future, which, in turn, cannot exist either. Instead of a fading past or non-existent future, museums need to focus on what artworks hold—through presence and change—to promote access and usage.

By challenging the conventional approach to presence and change, *Great Transformation* highlights the presence of *Two Cones* in its current state. It approaches the disintegration of an artwork as a relevant fact in its biography. The fact that they both disintegrate draws attention to their constant evolving state. However, while *Great Transformation* is free to pursue its natural disintegration,[9] *Two Cones* is still confined in its no-longer-suitability as an artwork by the museum. Garcia (2014a) claims that "by affecting the form of our representation through some new representation of the world, an interesting work creates its own interest" (p. 276). As a complex object that continuously "misbehaves," *Two Cones*' disintegrated state opens up possibilities for becoming a contemporary object. Together, the complex artwork family transforms the form in which its members appear. And still, as time

[9] As mentioned, inspired by *Two Cones*, *Great Transformation* is made of materials that are meant to degrade over time.

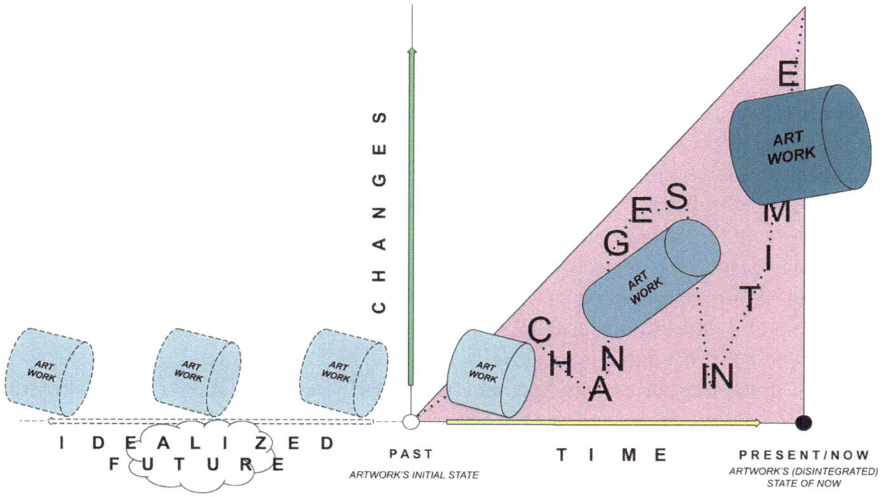

Fig. 5 The future, which does not exist, is instead imagined as in its idealized state by conventional collection management. When an artwork's state is preserved for the idealized future, it represents absence and in turn has no presence

passes, they continue to look different again, individually, following the deterioration of their own material temporalities. Together, these objects are in flux; they are time-based.

8 Conclusion

Although contemporary conservation theory puts forward progressive thinking, museums still face challenges in understanding change when it comes to "traditional" artworks. Artworks can actually move in and out of states because their (flexible) status is not solely connected to the way they look or how they "shape." But can collecting institutions also approach with flexibility what it means to collect presence and change? It is key to comprehend that the initial state of artworks is merely temporary. *Two Cones* demonstrates that objects shape their own times. Changing artworks can point to artistic understandings beyond the "original ones." Garcia's flat-ontology system highlights the contradictory position museums take, where in trying to preserve the past, museums eventually lose presence, and in turn, contemporaneity.

When museums make the disintegrated status of a work inaccessible, we may question the ways of collecting they promote. Museums need to start accepting artworks' changing, evolving states more often. Otherwise, a museum's understanding of art is conditioned to a time that has fading presence (past), or that has never been present (future). Contemporary conservation does not 'secure' the permanence of an ideal condition in the future. Museums need to involve a combined (conservation, curatorial, legal, museological) approach to objects in collection.

Museum professionals must think of scenarios where different understandings coexist. What one specific museum defends might be (and usually is) only part of the whole truth. In this speculative scenario, there is room for creativity and experimentation, both of which are much needed today. Collaborations between museums could take a step further and think in terms beyond acquisition or display. Different museums, under shared ethics, could potentially promote different ways of collecting, managing collections, and learning from objects they host instead of declaring them inaccessible. This perspective prompts new discussions around ownership and understands artworks beyond their materiality—to collect something does not necessarily mean to materially own it.

To re-think the current engagement with works, as van Saaze (2013) stresses, encourages us to "reformulate the existing protocols of exhibition against the constraints of fixed time-space, that prevent artworks and exhibitions to expand beyond temporal boundaries" (p. 157). Objects in a collection are space-time-bound. They are entitled to their own logics that build their trajectories, forming a more layered and more intriguing collecting environment. If the notion of collecting is freed from a restrictive understanding of time, artworks in museums positively add to each other, and contemporary artworks add to the understanding of "old" works.

A collection that would only carry artworks in their initial state of acquisition short-circuits the idea of collecting. Small shifts over time lead to shifts in the presence (and history) of things, including ways of managing collections (Appadurai 1986, p. 36). Museums should safeguard not only objects but also change, instead of safeguarding objects from change. Through the everchanging objects they hold, museums can choose to *highlight* presence instead of attempting to *hide* it. This approach would move us towards a contemporary notion of artworks and, by collaborating with changing objects and time, collecting institutions will move towards a contemporary approach to collecting itself.

Acknowledgments This chapter is based on research funded by the Finnish Cultural Foundation.

References

Altshuler B (2005) Collecting the new: museums and contemporary art. Princeton University Press

Appadurai A (1986) Introduction: Commodities and the politics of value. In: Appadurai A (ed) The social life of things. Cambridge University Press, Cambridge, pp 3–63

Cogburn J (2017) Garcian meditations: the dialectics of persistence in form and object. Edinburgh University Press, Edinburgh

Dekker A (2018) Collecting and conserving net art: Moving beyond conventional methods. Routledge

Domínguez Rubio F (2020) Still life: ecologies of the modern imagination at the art museum. University of Chicago Press

Garcia T (2013) Crossing ways of thinking: on Graham Harman's system and my own. Parrhesia 16:14–25
Garcia T (2014a) Form and object: a treatise on things (trans: Ohm MA, Cogburn J). Edinburgh University Press, Edinburgh
Garcia T (2014b) Another order of time: towards a variable intensity of the now. Parrhesia 19:1–13
Groys B (2009) Comrades of time. E-Flux Journal 11:1–11
Hölling HB (2013) Re:Paik. On Time, changeability and identity in the conservation of Nam June Paik's multimedia installations. Ph.D. thesis, University of Amsterdam
Hölling HB (2016) The aesthetics of change: on the relative durations of the impermanent and critical thinking in conservation. In: Hermens E, Robertson F (eds) Authenticity in translation: changing practices in contemporary art making and conservation. Archetype Books, London, pp 13–24
Laurenson P (2006) Authenticity, change and loss in the conservation of time-based media installations. A conceptual framework for traditional fine art conservation. Tate Papers 6. https://www.tate.org.uk/research/publications/tate-papers/06/authenticity-change-and-loss-conservation-of-time-based-media-installations
Muñoz-Viñas S (2005) Contemporary theory of conservation. Elsevier, Burlington
Price BA, Heuman J, Pullen D, Robson S (2009) Naum Gabo's *Construction in Space: Two Cones*: history and materials. In: Keneghan B, Egan L (eds) Naum Gabo's *Construction in Space: Two Cones*: history and materials. Archetype Publications, London, pp 81–88
Siegl T (1966) Conservation. Philadelphia Museum of Art. Bulletin 62(291):129–156
van de Vall R, Hölling HB, Scholte T, Stigter S (2011) Reflections on a biographical approach to contemporary art conservation. In: Bridgland J (ed) ICOM-CC: 16th Triennial Conference: Lisbon, 19-23 September 2011. Preprints, p 1–8. http://hdl.handle.net/11245/1.344546
van Saaze V (2013) Installation art and the museum: presentation and conservation of changing artworks. Amsterdam University Press, Amsterdam

Marina Valle Noronha is a curator and doctoral researcher at Aalto University, Finland, where she investigates curatorial theory, ethics of care, and the commons within museum collections. In her work, Valle Noronha puts forward forms of public engagement with objects that promote transparency and participation in decision-making. She holds an MA in curatorial studies from CCS Bard, US, a BA (Hons) in architecture from UFMG, Brazil, and was a Brooks International Fellow at Tate, UK.

Part III
Professional Roles and Identities: Conservators, Curators, and Artists

Visible Issues. Insights Into the Professional Identity of the Conservator

Rita Macedo

Abstract This chapter addresses the professional identity of the contemporary art museum conservator. It departs from a general review of the literature about the professional role of the conservator to focus on how practitioners see themselves in their profession when it comes to their values, beliefs, the functions performed and perceived relationships with colleagues. I also discuss how conservators think they are seen by others (colleagues or the anonymous public). Aware of the complexity of relationships that shape the contemporary art museum, this chapter focuses specifically on the identity of conservation professionals and their reported invisibility to colleagues and the public. I argue that while some of the factors that negatively influence a conservator's self-perception come from beliefs and stereotypes formed along with the construction of professional identity, others are consolidated and perpetuated in the context of the museum, where these identities do not seem to have room for transformation or renegotiation, through professional agency.

Keywords Professional identity · Conservators · Invisibility · Museums · Contemporary art conservation

1 Introduction

Opening the website of ICOM—International Council of Museums—we can read in big letters, concerning its mission and objectives, that ICOM is an "organisation of museums and museum professionals which is committed to the research, conservation, continuation and communication to society of the world's natural and cultural heritage, present and future, tangible and intangible."[1] Research, conservation and communication are thus the three domains of museum activity. If this chapter focuses on conservation performed in the contemporary art museum, I also argue

[1] https://icom.museum/en/about-us/missions-and-objectives. Accessed 22 Oct 2020.

R. Macedo (✉)
NOVA School of Science and Technology, Lisbon, Portugal
e-mail: ritamacedo@fct.unl.pt

R. van de Vall, V. van Saaze (eds.), *Conservation of Contemporary Art*, Studies in Art, Heritage, Law and the Market 9, https://doi.org/10.1007/978-3-031-42357-4_8

that the identified factors influencing conservators' professional identity may exceed this precise context. While the realities at play may vary across different museum contexts, and the factors influencing the professional identity of conservators may not be limited exclusively to those working in contemporary art museums, the primary aim of this chapter is exploratory.

Over the last twenty years, a vast array of studies appeared around conservation and its numerous specialisms, including conservation of contemporary art.[2] The field has grown immensely, both from within the practices involved and through the input of academic training and research. Although several publications have addressed the emergence and development of the profession, very few address the way conservators see themselves in their social-professional contexts.[3]

This chapter is grounded in a set of semi-structured interviews with conservation professionals. They were asked to respond to questions on how they see themselves as professionals, on the main challenges of being a conservator in the field of contemporary art, on the principal constraints and obstacles of the profession, and on how they feel about their jobs and perceive the status of their profession.[4] The interviewees unanimously highlighted the relative invisibility of the profession in general, and of the conservator in particular. Departing from their testimonies and the literature regarding the development of the conservation profession, I will elaborate on the contexts of what may explain this invisibility and how it influences the conservator's professional identity.

The chapter argues that identity issues are shaped by a set of factors related to identity construction aspects, embodied by stereotypes, that are linked up directly with the origins of the profession. These aspects seem mainly related to the prevalence of science and the privileging of explicit knowledge (over tacit knowledge), as well as to the lack of a more reflective approach. Other contextual aspects, associated with the functioning of the museum are also considered as contributing factors to the reported invisibility. The structure of contemporary art museums and how they are tied to hierarchies, dualities in knowledge cultures, issues of collaboration and agency seem to impact conservators' professional identity while also impeding its renegotiation.

After explaining the research methodology and clarifying professional identity and professional agency as concepts, I discuss the findings in a preliminary fashion, by sketching the main problems identified in the empirical research. The next sections provide an overview of the emergence and development of the conservation

---

[2] Hundreds of articles, conference papers, book chapters and books on this subject were published in the last two decades. Given the impossibility of referencing all of them, a selection of these appears in the literature of this chapter.

[3] Several studies about the role of the conservator touch on its social dimension. See D'haenens (2019), Ashley-Smith (2009, 2017, 2018), Brown (2017), Brajer (2009), Casanova (2011).

[4] This paper reflects on research carried out in the context of the *New Approaches in Contemporary Art Conservation* (*NACCA*) project on 'Contemporary Art Conservators and Curators: Roles, Collaboration, Training and Ethics'. In so doing, I mainly focus on the point of view of conservators, which featured as a minor aspect of the research performed for this project.

profession, followed by a brief description of the context of the art museum and how it evolved in theory and practice over time. The final section returns to the empirical data and expands on the identified negative factors linked to the construction of the conservation profession and the context of the art museum, where opportunities for renegotiation of this professional identity may present themselves.

2 Methodology

The empirical findings include interviews with 35 conservators across 7 countries (5 in Europe and 2 in the United States of America), representing a mix of professional museum conservators, private conservators working for museums, and former conservators that presently have managing positions.[5] In agreement with the participants, the collected information was kept confidential and anonymous. Many of the insights from these interviews were confirmed by participants in the *IIC Student & Emerging Conservator Conference*, held at the Cologne Institute of Conservation Sciences in September 2019. This meeting in part focused on questions like "How do we see ourselves as conservation professionals? Also, however, how are we seen by others, both by colleagues in institutions and by the general public?"[6] In a panel session titled 'Conservator Meets Institutions', the situation of the conservation profession within museums and the ways to promote the profession were discussed by a group of conservation managers who previously worked as conservators and who approached issues related to the conservator's self-identity as professional, providing important information about professional identity factors. The questions matched some of those we considered throughout the research. Even if the scope of the conference exceeded the context of contemporary art museum conservators, it helped us to corroborate the data we gathered and to consider that although contemporary art conservation in the museum raises different issues, many of the difficulties mentioned by the interviewers were felt by conservators to be present in other areas as well.

[5]The empirical research is based on interviews conducted by the author and two co-researchers supervised by the author, Maria Theodoraki, early-stage researcher in the *NACCA* project (Marie Sklodowska-Curie Innovative Training Network (2016–2019), and Rute Rebocho, master's researcher from Nova Universiade de Lisboa (2019–2020). Maria Theodoraki's research process also involved direct observation in two museums, one in Europe and one in the United States. Rute Rebocho's thesis focuses on interviews with the staff of five museums who perform conservation tasks (even though not all of them were trained as conservators) in contemporary museums/collections in Portugal. All interviews took place in-person. The interviewees were chosen to form a sample composed of conservators and curators working for or with contemporary art museums of different sizes, public and private, in Europe and the US. All the interviews revolved around functions performed, values and beliefs associated with the profession, perceived relationships with colleagues, as well as how the interviewees experienced being perceived by others and the public. The interviews were audio-recorded, transcribed, coded and analyzed.

[6]Questions in the announcement of the conference (IIC, 2019).

3 Professional Identity, a Complex Concept

To delineate the concept of professional identity, we have reviewed literature from the fields of sociology and psychology, most of it focusing on institutional and organizational theory. A high percentage of these studies concentrated on two groups of professionals: teachers and nurses. Most of the authors agree that the concept of professional identity is complex, mainly associated with discourse, narrative, ethical standards, structure and agency. They also stress that identity cannot be fixed because it is of a dynamic, relational and situational nature (Akkerman and Meijer 2011; Enyedy et al. 2006; Cardoso et al. 2014; Eteläpelto et al. 2014).

Eteläpelto et al. sum up four theoretical frameworks of identity: humanist theories, which see the individual self as autonomous and separated from the social structures; structural theories, which emphasize the material conditions and social structures, where identities are subjugated to the structures; the notion of the "enterprising self", who maintains identity and sense of self within structures and can transform those structures; and, finally, the post-structural approach, which considers the individual determined yet "negotiating actively and relationally within social conditions" (Eteläpelto et al. 2014, p. 649). The authors also emphasize that the post-structural self is seen as "practicing agency through resisting, outmaneuvering, and avoiding strong social suggestions while creating a social position which is consistent with individual subjectivity and identity" (2014, p. 649). These four historical approaches are still subject to debate. For example, scholars will put different emphasis on the roles of context and agency, and thus on how strongly social and material conditions are seen as determining the nature of individual identities sense of self.

Kaplan & Garner, in *Developmental Psychology* (2017) underline that "professional identities are tied up not only to personal identities but also to specific and structural situations that need be analyzed case by case," while also highlighting that the concept is complex and dynamic and is related to "doing and being in practice" (Kaplan and Garner 2017, p. 2039). Recent discussions adopt the foundations of the socio-cultural approach, highlighting the importance of the social and material conditions and the workplace context, but they also hold that individuals are not neutral mediators within structures. They have a degree of agency that allows for change in their practices and work communities (Eteläpelto et al. 2014, p. 650).

In this chapter, I adopt the view of Eteläpelto et al. about personal identity as being "constituted by subjects' conceptions of themselves as professional actors," including "subjects' professional commitments, ideals, interests, beliefs and values, ethical standards, and moral obligations" (2014, p. 650). Likewise, I also stress that professional identity can be renegotiated in work contexts and aim at an understanding, in the case of the professional identity of the contemporary art museum conservator's professional identity, of where the obstacles and constraints of this renegotiation may reside.

Professional agency is a key concept because, according to researchers in the field, it is mainly through agency that professionals transform the realities of their jobs. Eteläpelto et al. (2013, p. 61) argue that professional agency "is practiced when professional subjects and/or communities exert influence, make choices and take stances in ways that affect their work and/or their professional identities." It can manifest itself in different ways, "not merely as entering into and suggesting new work practices, but also as maintaining existing practices, or struggling against suggested changes. Such agency is realized within socio-cultural constraints and bounded by the resources available, all of which encompass subjects' temporally-formed discursive, practical, and embodied relations to their work contexts" (2013, p. 61). Most importantly, agency is necessary for the reshaping or renegotiation of professional identities (2013, p. 48).

4 Conservators' Professional Identity—A First Look

The interviewed conservators unanimously expressed the feeling that their work is invisible to the public in general and not recognized or acknowledged by many of their colleagues in museums, especially the curators. The most salient aspects of the conservators' self-narratives are related to issues of subordination, vertical hierarchies, lack of authority in the decision-making process and social importance of the performed work. These factors all seem to be intertwined and negatively influence the conservator's professional identity. Most of the interviewees mentioned a subordinated relationship with curators, which they associate with negative aspects of the conservators' self-image and with their invisibility to others. In the 2019 *IIC Student & Emerging Conservator Conference – The Conservator's Reflection*, conservator Joanna Phillips,[7] when discussing the different conservator's pay scales in European and US museums, argued that conservators cannot collaborate with other disciplines and professionals if they are not regarded as equal players. Phillips, now director of the Conservation Centre in Düsseldorf (Germany), addressed the hierarchies between museum conservators and curators regarding agency, decision-making and remuneration, asserting that "These hierarchy legacies, where conservators are situated lower than curators do not only affect our day to day lives with low salaries and much frustration, they affect professional practices and research areas that are based on interdisciplinarity" (Phillips, IIC 2019, p. 35:15).

Literature on professional identity construction was particularly useful to reflect on the conservator's situation regarding hierarchies, visibility, and subordination. As a very high percentage of studies about professional identity focus on nurses and their hierarchical relationship with physicians, we could not avoid to notice

[7] See biographical note in https://joanna-phillips.tumblr.com/CV. Accessed 29 Sep 2019.

similarities between nurses and conservators. For example, the issue of visibility and subordination is mentioned quite often and seems to be associated with stereotypes.[8] Studies about nurses' professional identities establish that the role of the nurse is mainly associated with that of being the "doctor's handmaiden" (Bridges 1990; Ten Hoeve et al. 2013, p. 296) Their roles are linked to other professions (for example physicians) and they are subordinated to them. Like conservators, nurses are also related to a practical knowledge that is orally transferred. According to Heldal et al., "Traditionally, nurses have had an oral tradition regarding the transfer of skills and knowledge, while doctors have also relied on codified knowledge developed through extensive programmes to provide evidence" (Heldal et al. 2019, p. 4).[9]

5 From the Hand to the Mind: The Dominance of Science and the Emergence of a Professional Identity

This section intends to review some crucial aspects regarding the origins, consolidation and beliefs manifested in the history of the conservation profession. This summary resorts to the work of researchers who reviewed the history of the profession (Philippot 1996; Clavir 1998, 2002; Caple 2000; Villers 2004; Munõz Viñas 2005; Van Saaze 2013).

The various negative factors influencing the way conservators view their profession, in particular invisibility, seem to be rooted in part in an asymmetrical understanding of how knowledge is seen and used in conservation. The disconnection between body and mind, nature and culture, and objects and humans contribute to this situation (Hummelen et al. 2008),[10] and this might be at the root of stereotypes that are still incorporated in some professional values and beliefs.

Historically, restorers were craftsmen or artists with no training in science, history or ethics, who repaired or reconstructed the aesthetic appearance of an object according to their taste or the taste of those hiring them. The emancipation of conservation from restoration comes with science and its competence to focus on the object's nature and the condition of the materials. Miriam Clavir calls attention to the dominance of science, arguing that its methodology, knowledge and values are significant regarding the distinction between conservation and traditional restoration.

---

[8] With respect to the self-concept of nurses, we rely on the definition of Takase et al.: "'nurses' self-concept can be defined as information and beliefs that nurses have about their roles, values and behaviors" (2002, p. 197).

[9] See also (Richardson and Storr 2010). According to Summers and Summers (2009), historically nurses were subordinated by physicians for reasons that include the disparity of power between genders. In the case of conservators, the gender situation seems evident, because most of the professionals are women. The relation between gender and professional agency deserves further investigation in the field of conservation.

[10] For more on this asymmetry in the field of conservation, see Hummelen et al. (2008).

She adds that the legitimacy afforded by science grew in association with the large and powerful public museums, and that through science—within the framework, objectives and policy of the museum—conservation solidified as a profession (Clavir 2000, p. 24). Accordingly, the first conservation professionals were either scientists (chemists or physicists) or people with good manual skills (restorers).

Science continued to maintain its importance for the development of conservation as a practice and a body of knowledge without major questioning throughout the twentieth century. After World War II, however, the cleaning controversies involving the London National Gallery paintings revealed that a kind of rivalry had emerged, pitting a techno-science party, led by natural scientists, against an historical-humanist party, led mainly by art historians. The historical-humanist party argued for a decision-making process not only based on scientific, analytical methods but also influenced by values and contexts. Still, this party has been responsible for the development of principles and ideas (like minimal intervention, reversibility) that continue to be centred on physical integrity and material authenticity. As argued by Villers, these concepts "derive from a positivist paradigm of understanding and a belief in objectivity" (Villers 2004, p. 3). Muñoz Vinãs, who defines contemporary theory of conservation against classical theories, stresses that so-called "scientific" conservation "exemplifies many of the principles common to all classical theories" (Muñoz Viñas 2005, p. 75), and that the belief in objectivity of scientific conservation (its focus on facts and materials rather than ideas) has contributed to the notion that no philosophical foundation is necessary for it to work. In his view, scientific conservation deals with materials, not ideas, and in doing so, it employs its tools to apprehend the material world as hard sciences do (Muñoz Viñas 2005, pp. 79–80).

Contrary to classical theories, the so-called contemporary theory of conservation assumes that objects are conserved not only because of their physical materials, but also because of the cultural knowledge they embody. That knowledge is complex, multifaceted and related to different stakeholders. Therefore, it is important also to understand the meanings attributed to the object and to decide about the necessary measures to preserve its materials, appearance, function, information and so on.

6 Contemporary Art Conservation

The belief in the fundamental necessity to protect the integrity of the physical object and the confidence in science as the foundation for ethical preservation began to be challenged in contemporary art conservation when museums began to acquire artworks that were not meant to be collected. Installation art, happenings, performance art and other time-based media works contributed to creating an awareness of the fragile and complex nature of these artworks. Various aspects account for a significant challenge to conservation practices (Wharton and Molotch 2010), such as their variability in terms of space, time and values attributed; the absence of specific borders; and the instability of materials, equipment and status.

Consequently, the idea of managing change became more important than the attempt to freeze an object in time. As argued by van de Vall et al., "rather than preserving original objects, conservation of contemporary art should be thought of as managing change" (2011, p. 1). In the same vein, Wharton (2016, p. 34) argued that the increasing acceptance that an object is not a fixed thing but a "slow event,"[11] as well as the more active collaboration with curators and artists, prepared conservators—trained to preserve the original—for their new roles as collaborators in managing change of contemporary variable works.[12] The complexity of contemporary art also comes with the constant state of incompleteness of many artworks and their unfolding possibilities within the museum, which according to Laurenson brings valuable research opportunities. Leaning on sociologist Knorr Cetina's development of the concept of epistemic cultures, Laurenson proposes that artworks can be seen as epistemic objects of research for different people (artists, conservators, curators), while she also understands conservation as a knowledge-producing practice, stressing that the practice is impacted by the possibilities and nature of the artwork (Cetina 2007; Laurenson 2016).

According to Van Saaze, contemporary art conservation involves a distributed decision-making process, in which a vast and diverse number of people collaborate, ranging from the living artist or their heirs, personal assistants, former curators, present curators and gallerists to registrars, art historians, architects, exhibition designers, acquisition and loan managers and technology experts. This opens different ways of interacting, and a need to rethink crucial notions in conservation,[13] including the role of the conservator. Van Saaze described contemporary art conservation as part of a network of objects and subjects, where different kinds of knowledge collaborate to ensure the care and sustaining of this heritage. Building on Actor-Network Theory (ANT) that focuses on the practices enacted and produced by networks of humans and non-humans,[14] Van Saaze argues that the contemporary art conservator (like the curator) can be considered "an interpreter, mediator or even a (co-) producer of what is designated as the 'artist's intention'" (2013, p. 33).

[11] Wharton (2016, p. 34) attributes the description of an object as a "slow event" to Stanley Eveling (University of Edinburgh) in an unpublished paper.

[12] For the purposes of this chapter, the idea of "managing change" is only addressed from the point of view of contemporary art conservation. It should be mentioned, however, that researchers from other areas, particularly those related to ethnographic objects, archeology and historic sites or landscapes were the ones who started to challenge the "freezing paradigm" eliciting the idea of conservation as a managing change activity (see for example Avrami et al. 2000; Muñoz Viñas 2005; Clavir 2002; Villers 2004; Sully 2013).

[13] "The developments in artistic practices therefore ask for a rethinking of certain concepts and established principles that belong to traditional conservation strategies, such as the notions of 'original', 'copy', 'minimal intervention', 'authenticity', 'reversibility', and 'artist's intention'" (Van Saaze 2013, p. 23).

[14] Originally developed by Bruno Latour and Michel Callon (Callon 1986; Latour 1987), ANT has many ramifications and relations with other theories and research contexts. Vivian van Saaze was the first to use it in the context of conservation in art museums.

The discussions that over the last two decades have arisen from the nature of the objects, and the necessity to find solutions, have contributed to a transformation of the practice of conservation, whereby it is not so much seen anymore as an objectivity-based practice but as rather a systemic and relational one. The role of the conservator has followed this orientation. In contemporary art conservation theory and practice, the professional role of the conservator has shifted away from earlier concepts and towards the role of reflective practitioner and knowledge producer, involved in networks that change the artworks along with museum processes.

In the following section, I briefly address the context of the art museum to assess whether there is room for positive factors that may affect and encourage renegotiation of the conservator's professional identity.

7 The Contemporary Art Museum: Knowledge, Collaboration and Communication

New museology recognized the fundamental role of the museum and opened a critical debate about its authoritative and informative character. In this vein, Hooper-Greenhill (2000) reminds us how museums are creations of the Enlightenment, when the importance of reason and rationality increased to displace the superstitions and subjective knowledges of earlier periods. Drawing on Lyotard's thoughts about the "grand narratives" or "metaprescriptions" developed with a universal determination, the author argues that museums were set up and developed to disseminate such more reason-based, objective picture of the world. She stresses that the Enlightenment inherited the dream of Descartes to base all knowledge on what could be deduced from reason alone. In other words, reason became the new authority, meant to ground a 'true' worldview. And it was this way of thinking and doing that produced the split between mind and body and the predominance of the mind over the body in Western society (Hooper-Greenhill 2000, p. 13).

New museology also advocated a critical examination of the museum practices and the structures that inform and sustain them, calling attention to the behind-the-scenes relationships between professionals, artworks and audiences and encouraging new ways of communication and expression. Despite its solid criticism, focusing on the social and the political inside and outside of museums, practices seem to not have significatively changed (McCall and Gray 2014, p. 20). New museology, however, called attention to many important aspects, particularly the transmission model used by museums, centred on the exhibition, where "the curator as scholar, expert on the collections and knowledgeable about the relevant discipline, leads the project, chooses the objects for display and decides what to say in the text panels and labels" (Hooper-Greenhill 2000, p. 25).

Post-critical museology, a term coined by Dewdney et al. (2013) and informed by Latourian thought and anchored in practice theory, goes beyond new museology arguments by claiming that "theory is meaningless if not related to real practice."[15] As the authors argue, there will not be a change in the museum without a relational approach, and they point out that contexts in which the academy and the museum function as separate entities, whereby one (the academy) is detached from the everyday practices of the other, will not contribute to transforming its traditional structure.

For this reason, post-critical museology proposes that museums be centred on the audience. This will involve a hybrid or "distributed museum" where all those who operate in and across the organizations and communication networks contribute to a reconfiguration of the traditional museum conception (Dewdney et al. 2013, p. 239).[16] The authors emphasize the importance of all actors being part of the networks of humans and objects, including the professionals who work behind the scenes. In the distributed or post-critical museum, all is interrelated, the various roles, elements and activities cannot be separated and only take on meaning in the performative action involved.

Post-critical museology rejects representational models of society, individuals and action, while also abandoning the traditional concepts of labour, class and community, and, instead, seeking "to network the agency of group formation and point to new ecologies of belonging" (Dewdney et al. 2013, p. 241). This framework has the potential for radical transformation of the art museum and therefore may help overcome the negative factors related to the conservation profession. With its focus on the relational and performative nature of the networks of objects and humans, it questions hierarchies and challenges the old model of the curator-centred museum, proposing a distribution of knowledge and agency across the network. In the following section, I apply this post-critical approach to the empirical research, while also providing some hints as to how this approach can be transformative for the conservation profession in the museum context.

8 Roles, Visibility, Agency

Returning to the empirical information it is quite clear that the data collected from the research does not conform to this collaborative, transdisciplinary and reflexive view of the art museum. In fact, conservators reported that they rarely seem to feel part of a network, where they are regarded as equals. Both in our interviews with conservators and in the presentations at the conference *Emerging Conservators*, the

[15] Post-critical museology is a term coined by the authors of the book with the same name. The publication is one of the outcomes of *Tate Encounters: Britishness and Visual Culture*, a three-year collaborative research project carried out at Tate Britain in London and geared to a reconfiguration of the relationship between art and audiences, including exploration of issues of global migration and the new media ecologies.

[16] Just as museum professionals become the audience, those previously conceived as the audience of the museum become producers of the distributed museum (Dewdney et al. 2013, p. 240).

professional boundary between conservators and curators was easy to notice. Conservators portray curators as a group of professionals who generally do not understand or value the tasks conservators perform. The notion that curators do intellectual work and conservators manual work persists in the conservator's narratives.

The professional boundary between conservators and curators and the association of both professional roles to body (conservator) and mind (curator) is hardly new. In 2007 Leslie Carlyle, then Head of Conservation at Tate, said at the opening of the conference *Shifting Practice, Shifting Roles*: "historically conservators, curators and art historians are stuck in a rut made by centuries-old debate about the value of the hand versus the mind" (Carlyle 2007). As nurses, who depend on doctors to make decisions (Ten Hoeve et al. 2013, p. 296) conservators also depend on curators, meaning that they are not seen as autonomous professionals. Throughout our research, conservators often affirmed that they do not feel entitled to make decisions. In the contemporary art museum, where the principal functions are related to exhibitions and artworks' acquisition, most conservators say that, although they might be consulted, they do not decide about the final appearance of artworks in exhibitions, not even in installations in which they interviewed the artist and accompanied the whole process. In these cases, the final decision is in the hands of the curator. A small fraction of the respondents, mainly working in large-scale museums, reported that they are involved in interdisciplinary and interprofessional team meetings, but very few feel they are heard.

Concerning acquisitions, a high percentage of the interviewees reported that they are not given a seat at the table of final decisions. They are consulted—asked to give a formal, written or informal opinion—but their statements are often ignored. According to conservators, curators make the final decision on the artworks to propose to the owner, museum director or board of trustees for acquisition. Conservators are the mediators. Moreover, they describe themselves as the professionals equipped with the knowledge to evaluate the cost of maintaining or replacing components of a work of art. But they are not present in meetings with those who make the decisions about acquiring a work of art or not.

Lack of agency and autonomy in decision-making are critical issues in how conservators see themselves and how they feel to be seen by others. Concerning this subject, in the panel 'Conservators Meet the Institutions' at the conference *Emerging Conservators*, Joanna Phillips mentioned a brochure on a website of the German Museum Association (*Deutscher Museumsbund*), which includes a specific definition of the roles of the conservator and the curator: "the curator plans and controls the archiving and inventory programs and oversees the conservation and restoration of the collections including their documentation."[17] The conservator "develops, with the curator's agreement, all the activities that serve the preservation and preventive conservation and restoration of the museum's collections." Where applicable, the conservator executes the previously predetermined restoration work. These descriptions underscore the limited professional agency assigned to

[17]Deutscher Museumsbund e.V. 2008, 20-3 (Phillips IIC, 2019).

conservators.[18] The curator needs to give permission to all activities developed by the conservator, while the curator "plans", "controls" and "oversees", even including "restoration work."

As mentioned, this lack of agency and decision-making power seems to be connected to the type of knowledge involved and has much influence on professional identity. Conservators are always associated with manual work and 'knowing-how', rather than with 'knowing that', with tacit or embodied knowledge.[19] On the other hand, conservation emancipated from restoration through expertise derived from the natural sciences. Science helped conservation to move away from subjective restoration to a more objective-based practice (Clavir 2002).

Despite the theoretical criticism led by the new museology and post-critical museology, my research established that conservators in their narratives largely feel to inhabit a curator-led and hierarchized museum, where the curator's knowledge represents the respected and privileged expertise. The importance of knowledge has been studied in organizations, as professionals operate and interact according to their knowledge and "knowing". Cook and Brown (1999) discuss the relation between explicit and tacit knowledge (and also knowing and knowledge). They remind us that for the last three centuries Western culture has been profoundly influenced by the Cartesian epistemology that privileges explicit rather than tacit knowledge. Cook and Brown recall that we are taught to "best minimize or 'control for' the clouding influences of our senses and subjective impressions through analytical reasoning, and thus acquire our most reliable knowledge about the world." Tacit knowledge and knowing how seem to be overlooked.[20]

My aim here is not so much to reflect on the nature of conservation or the role of the conservator as such, however. The concerns are all interrelated and the fact that the art museum professions of care deal with the same epistemic objects from

[18] Joanna Phillips claims that there are several differences between the way conservators are seen in Europe and in the United States. In 2008, Phillips, originally trained as a conservator in Germany, moved to the Guggenheim Museum in New York, where she launched the first media conservation lab in a US museum. According to her testimony, not only the Guggenheim but generally in the US, museums place great importance on interdisciplinarity and cross-departmental teamwork. She explains that curators and conservators, exhibition designers, technicians and registrars all work closely together, particularly in exhibitions, acquisitions and loans. "The different disciplines respect each other's areas of competence and decisions are made together as a group" (Phillips IIC 2019).

[19] In his book *Conservation Skills: Judgment, Method and Decision Making*, Caple identifies the "technician" as the first stereotype. He states that "where others decide (curators, archeologists, museum directors) the conservator implements the decision." Caple identifies other stereotypes (scientist, parent/mother/nurse, naysayer, frustrated curator) and the "artist/craftsman/restorer". In fact, both technicians and craftsmen have a direct connection with the manual labor that science overrides. This kind of labor, according to Caple, is associated with a lack of decision-making power (Caple 2000, p. 184).

[20] According to Poliany, tacit knowledge is tied to the human body. His famous example about riding a bicycle says that when riding a bicycle, we don't use any analytical tools. Through practice and training we make it possible for our neural and muscular system to do it. But we cannot really explain to anyone how we do it. See (Cook and Brown 1999, p. 384).

different epistemic cultures should be stressed for the sake of the objects, the professionals, and the underlying social dynamics.

In *We Have Never Been Modern* (1993), Bruno Latour claims that the seventeenth century created these dichotomies, separating sciences and politics, nature and culture, humans and non-humans, thus creating a series of subsequent dichotomies that are still entrenched in many discourses and practices. His work has informed important studies in conservation and museum studies research, some of them cited in this chapter. The relationships between artworks, people involved in their care, the market, organizations, and institutions that purchase, store, conserve and exhibit them are part of complex networks that, as well argued by Van Saaze, keep transforming these objects (van Saaze 2013).

The construction and renegotiation of conservator's professional identity should be seen in this light, as conservators are part of these relational and hybrid networks of professionals and objects where different kinds of knowledge converge in everyday practices, according to different scenarios.

9 Conclusion

In this chapter I focused on the professional identity of the conservator in the contemporary art museum, by considering the emergence and development of the conservation profession, the complexity and relational functions performed by contemporary art conservators and the social-professional dynamics of the art museum and its potential to accommodate change. Most of the conservator respondents identified the invisibility of the conservator, as confirmed by participants in the conference *Emerging Conservators*. As my research revealed, lack of agency or effective participation in decision-making and subordination feature as both cause and consequence of this "invisibility". Manual labour and the type of knowledge (tacit) associated with the conservator, as linked in particular to the origins of the profession, seem to be responsible for stereotypes that negatively influence the conservator's professional identity. On the other hand, according to the information collected in the interviews, we may confirm that the radical transformations proposed by both new museology and post-critical museology have not yet taken place, which compromises the renegotiation of the conservator's professional identity.

The politics behind apparent hierarchies and social relationships are strongly influenced by more complex structures derived from both social, political and economic powers. The purpose of this chapter was to address a *status quo* fed by different actants/actors. The unfolding of these other causes may be pursued in a subsequent situated study developed in a wider range of institutions.

References

Akkerman SF, Meijer PC (2011) A dialogical approach to conceptualizing teacher identity. Teach Educ 27(2):308–319

Ashley-Smith J (2009) The adolescence of the profession. Paper presented at the symposium Conservation, principles, dilemmas and uncomfortable truths, The Royal Academy of Arts, London, September 2009

Ashley-Smith J (2017) A role for bespoke codes of ethics. In: Bridgland J (ed) Preprints ICOM-CC 18th Triennial Conference, 4-8 September 2017. International Council of Museums, Paris

Ashley-Smith J (2018) The ethics of doing nothing. J Inst Conserv 41(1):6–15. https://doi.org/10.1080/19455224.2017.1416650

Avrami EC, Mason R, de la Torre M (2000) Values and Heritage Conservation: Research Report. Getty Conservation Institute. Los Angeles, CA http://hdl.handle.net/10020/gci_pubs/values_heritage_research_report. Accessed 20 May 2020

Brajer I (2009) Taking the wrong path: learning from oversights, misconceptions, failures and mistakes in conservation. CeROArt, http://journals.openedition.org/ceroart/1127. Accessed 23 May 2020

Bridges JM (1990) Literature review on the images of the nurse and nursing in the media. J Adv Nurs 15:850–854

Brown JAE (2017) Conservation now. J Inst Conserv 40(2):133–151. https://doi.org/10.1080/19455224.2017.1321560

Callon M (1986) Some elements of a sociology of translation: Domestication of the scallops and the fishermen of St Brieuc Bay. In: Law J (ed) Power, action and belief: a new sociology of knowledge. Routledge & Kegan Paul, London, pp 196–233

Caple C (2000) Conservation skills: judgement, method and decision making. Routledge, London

Cardoso I, Batista P, Graça A (2014) Professional identity in analysis: a systematic review of the literature. Open Sports Sci J 7:83–97

Carlyle L (2007) Shifting practices, shifting roles, Tate, London, 22 March 2007 https://www.tate.org.uk/context-comment/video/shifting-practice-shifting-roles. Accessed 25 May 2020

Casanova MDCL (2011) De artífice a cientista: Evolução da conservação e do estatuto profissional do conservador- restaurador de documentos gráficos no AHU (1926-2006). Faculdade de Ciências e Tecnologias, Universidade Nova de Lisboa

Clavir M (1998) The social and historic construction of professional values in conservation. Stud Conserv 43(1):1–8. https://doi.org/10.1080/00393630.1998.12068815

Clavir M (2002) Preserving what is valued. Museums, conservation, and First Nations. UBC Press, Vancouver

Cook SDN, Brown J (1999) Bridging epistemologies: the generative dance between organizational knowledge and organizational knowing. Organ Sci 10:381–400. https://doi.org/10.1287/orsc.10.4.381

D'haenens M (2019) The role of conservators: an international survey on conservation within contemporary art collections. Int J Young Conserv Restor Works Art 3:33–45

Dewdney A, Dibosa D, Walsh V (2013) Post-critical museology: theory and practice in the art museum. Routledge, Oxon

Enyedy N, Goldberg J, Welsh KM (2006) Complex dilemmas of identity and practice. Sci Educ 90(1):68–93

Eteläpelto A, Vähäsantanen K, Hökkä P, Paloniemi S (2013) What is agency? Conceptualizing professional agency at work. Educ Res Rev 10:45–65

Eteläpelto A, Vähäsantanen K, Hökkä P, Paloniemi S (2014) Identity and agency in professional learning. In: Billett S, Harteis C, Gruber H (eds) International handbook of research in professional and practice-based learning. Springer, London, pp 645–672

Heldal F, Kongsvik T, Håland E (2019) Advancing the status of nursing: reconstructing professional nursing identity through patient safety work. BMC Health Serv Res 19(1):418. https://doi.org/10.1186/s12913-019-4222-y

Hooper-Greenhill E (2000) Changing values in the art museum: rethinking communication and learning. Int J Herit Stud 6(1):9–31. https://doi.org/10.1080/135272500363715
Hummelen Y, van Saaze V, Versteegh MM (2008) Towards a symmetrical approach in conservation? Preprints ICOM-CC Triennial Meeting, New Delhi, India pp 1041–1047
Kaplan A, Garner JK (2017) A complex dynamic systems perspective on identity and its development: the dynamic systems model of role identity. Dev Psychol 53(11):2036–2051. https://doi.org/10.1037/dev0000339
Knorr Cetina K (2007) Culture in global knowledge societies: knowledge cultures and epistemic cultures. Interdiscip Sci Rev 32(4):361–375. https://doi.org/10.1179/030801807X163571
Latour B (1987) Science in action: how to follow scientists and engineers through society. Open University Press, Milton Keynes
Latour B (1993) We have never been modern. Harvard University Press, Cambridge
Laurenson P (2016) Practice as research: Unfolding the objects of contemporary art conservation. Inaugural lecture delivered at Maastricht University, 18 March 2016. Available via YouTube. https://www.youtube.com/watch?v=rEZzsg3OzJg
McCall V, Gray C (2014) Museums and the 'new museology': theory, practice and organizational change. Museum Manage Curatorship 29(1):19–35. https://doi.org/10.1080/09647775.2013.869852. Accessed 3 May 2020
Muñoz Viñas S (2005) Contemporary theory of conservation. Butterworth-Heinemann, Oxford
Philippot P (1996) Restoration from the perspective of humanities. In: Historical and philosophical issues in the conservation of cultural heritage. Getty, Los Angeles, pp 216–228
Phillips J (2019) The conservator's reflection: IIC 2019 Student & Emerging Conservator Conference, Panel 'Conservators Meet Institutions', Cologne, CICS, 12–14 September 2019, https://www.youtube.com/watch?v=uzKBbA3TsBk, Accessed 21 Sept 2022
Richardson A, Storr J (2010) Patient safety: a literature review on the impact of nursing empowerment, leadership and collaboration. Int Nurs Rev 57:12–21
Sully D (2013) Conservation theory and practice: Materials, values, and people in heritage conservation. In: Macdonald S, Rees Leahy H (eds) The international handbooks of museum studies. Wiley & Sons Ltd, Chichester, pp 293–314
Summers S, Summers HJ (2009) Saving lives: Why the media's portrayal of nurses puts us all at risks. Kaplan Publishing, New York
Takase MKE, Burt L (2002) Does public image of nurses matter? J Prof Nurs 18(4):196–205
Ten Hoeve Y, Jansen G, Roodbol P (2013) The nursing profession: public image, self concept and professional identity. A discussion paper. J Adv Nurs 70(2):295–309. https://doi.org/10.1111/jan.12177
van de Vall R, Hölling HB, Scholte T, Stigter S (2011) Reflections on a biographical approach to contemporary art conservation. In: Bridgland J (ed) ICOM-CC: 16th Triennial Conference, Lisbon, 19-23 September 2011. Critério, Lisbon, pp 1–8. http://hdl.handle.net/11245/1.344546
van Saaze V (2013) Installation art and the museum. Presentation and conservation of changing artworks. Amsterdam University Press, Amsterdam
Villers C (2004) Post minimal intervention. The Conservator 28(1):3–10. https://doi.org/10.1080/01410096.2004.9995197
Wharton G (2016) Reconfiguring contemporary art in the museum. In: Hermens E, Robertson F (eds) Authenticity in transition: changing practices in art making and conservation. Archetype Publications, London, pp 27–36
Wharton G, Molotch H (2010) The challenge of installation art. In: Bracker A, Richmond A (eds) Conservation: principles, dilemmas, and uncomfortable truths. Elsevier, London, pp 210–222

Rita Macedo is an Associate Professor at the Department of Conservation and Restoration at NOVA, School of Science and Technology (Portugal). She trained in Art History and has worked in the field of Conservation and Restoration of Cultural Heritage since her PhD in Conservation. Macedo has coordinated the first research project on *Documentation of Contemporary Art in Portugal* (2011–2014). This collaborative project involved major Portuguese contemporary art museums and aimed to gather and produce documentation to conserve complex contemporary artworks that were critically endangered. Between 2011 and 2019, she was part of *NeCCAR* (Netherlands Organization for Scientific Research) and *NACCA* (Marie Sklodowska-Curie Innovative Training Network 2016–2019). As part of *NACCA*, she coordinated a research project titled 'Contemporary Art Conservators and Curators: Roles, Collaboration, Training, and Ethics', focusing on the perspective of conservators. More recently, Macedo has focused on the intersection of living heritage and the concept of the museum. In 2020, she joined the European project *T-Factor* (Horizon 2020), which aims to promote social regeneration in cities through temporary uses. She is conducting research to create a bottom-up museum that aims to foster community development, a sense of belonging, as well as learning environments. Throughout her career, Macedo has developed a variety of national and international collaborations that resulted in the establishment of research teams and projects. She has built an innovative and dynamic team of young researchers who have successfully tackled a variety of challenges in heritage conservation.

Conceptual Art and Conservation

Sanneke Stigter

Abstract This chapter addresses the function of a "conservation research approach" in the study of conceptual art in combination with the role of the curator's expertise, advocating an autoethnographic approach in relation to contemporary art conservation as a function of museum practice. This approach is exemplified by means of the author's personal testimonies of encounters with artworks by John Baldessari and Ger van Elk. These accounts help to provide a better understanding of the shaping of an artwork's physical form in various contexts, while also laying bare the conservator's personal bias as revealing traits of the profession. In addition, histories of works by Joseph Kosuth, Lawrence Weiner and Sol LeWitt are used to develop the argument that although conceptual artists set out to dematerialize the object in art, they chose their materials and techniques carefully to underline their ideas.

Keywords Conceptual art · Conservation theory · Conservation research · Cultural biography · Autoethnography · John Baldessari · Ger van Elk · Sol LeWitt

1 Introduction

While some conceptual works of art are made anew every time they are put on display, others are taken from storage and assembled on site, depending on the work's requirements and on the way in which they are managed. Aimed at negating the unique material object in art, conceptual artworks frequently confront the conservator with difficult dilemmas. This chapter explores a "conservation research approach" aimed at assessing conceptual art practices by tracing artwork biographies with a responsibility towards the future of the involved works. To read this angle, the chapter proposes autoethnography as a methodological approach to assess the influence of museum professionals on these artworks and to raise their sensibility of the role of personal input with respect to the lives of artworks in the museum. This

S. Stigter (✉)
Department of Conservation and Restoration of Cultural Heritage, Faculty of Humanities, University of Amsterdam, Amsterdam, The Netherlands
e-mail: s.stigter@uva.nl

R. van de Vall, V. van Saaze (eds.), *Conservation of Contemporary Art*, Studies in Art, Heritage, Law and the Market 9, https://doi.org/10.1007/978-3-031-42357-4_9

in turn highlights the significance of contemporary art conservation research, and reveals the values and principles that underlie this approach (Stigter 2016a).[1]

While conservation theorist Salvador Muñoz-Viñas has suggested that conservators have little to do with the management of conceptual art, explaining that "conservation is technically prepared to deal only with material objects" (2010, p. 15), this study aims to illustrate the value of a conservator's point of view in both the conservation and the study of conceptual art, suggesting that their materialised manifestations can be of greater significance than is generally thought. Although the focus of this chapter is on work from the classical conceptual art period, from the mid-1960s to the late 1970s, its argument applies to all works of art of which it is claimed that their material make-up is of secondary importance and hence vulnerable to inattentiveness.

The general tendency to marginalise the material side of conceptual art follows from the dictum that "the idea or concept is most important aspect of the work" (LeWitt 1967, p. 80), something that conceptual artists proclaimed themselves right from the start, demonstrating and democratizing their art in manifesto writings and statements (see below). Although these artists were keen on explaining their work in statements and publications, most critics agree that conceptual art is difficult to pin down. Conceptual art is "all over the place" (Lippard 1973, p. vii), "an art of questions" (Osborne 2002, p. 14), and "a loose collection of related practices" (Corris 2004, p. i). Some critics simply refrain from giving a definition altogether (Newman and Bird 1999), or prefer "conceptualism" as an overarching term (Smith and Bailey 2017).

Art critic and curator Lucy Lippard's description of conceptual art at the time is particularly relevant in this context: "Conceptual art, for me, means work in which the idea is paramount and the material form is secondary, lightweight, ephemeral, cheap, unpretentious, and/or 'dematerialized'" (1973, p. 18). By characterising conceptual art's material form as ephemeral and cheap, one suggests that the materials used are quite specific in their ability to downplay the artwork as a precious object. In addition to being unpretentious and physically irrelevant, language and photography often served as media of choice, and these were interpreted as immaterial and reproducible, respectively, while many works are conceived as self-referential through the use of context and site. It is a question, however, to what extent the use of language is "immaterial" in the visual arts (Miller 2012), and how reproducible the medium of photography is when considering the materiality of photographs (Stigter 2016b; Marchesi 2017), and whether the use of site allows for variability without changing a work's content (Scholte 2021).

The fact that the artists themselves emphasised their ideas rather than the materiality of their work could lead one to think that conservation has little to do with conceptual art. However, contemporary art conservation is not just about safeguarding the artwork's material condition; it is also about preserving immaterial features, ephemeral properties and the way of making a conceptual work manifest,

[1] This chapter is based on my PhD thesis, defended 29 June 2016.

depending on how the identified work-defining properties are valued (e.g., Laurenson 2006; van Saaze 2013; Stigter 2017; Marçal 2019; Giebeler et al. 2021). A conservation research approach, then, involves in-depth analysis of an artwork's various properties over time, both material and conceptual ones, down to the minutest detail and, importantly, with the aim of passing the work on to the future to the best of knowledge. This last aspect is pivotal in distinguishing a conservation research approach from a material culture studies approach, whereas the approach in itself merges well with studies into the materiality of art, as part of a broadening of the conservation discipline today (Hölling 2017a). I mention this distinction specifically because of the conservator's inherent responsibility towards the future life of artworks, and their perhaps common anxiety to do something wrong in this respect, because of their intimate proximity to the work of art when engaging in a conservation treatment or installation process. This makes that conservators have an extra sense for materiality, or a "material consciousness," as it has been called by conservator Hanna Hölling, borrowing from the work of Richard Sennett (2017b, p. 88). Materiality is not only understood here as a technical feature, but also as including social and historical connotations, in addition to signs of use and wear, properties and traces that conservators are keen to explain in terms of such sociocultural background.

As a conceptual lens, a conservation research approach entails a heightened sense of awareness during scrutiny, triggered by the responsibility for the inevitable translation into practice, e.g., during conservation treatment, re-installation or remaking of the work, which will inevitably include the conservator's influence. As personal input is generally kept to a minimum by principle, indicated in various codes of ethics and guidelines for conservation (AIC 1994; Sease 1998; CAC/CAPC 2000; AICCM 2002), the inherent reluctance on the part of the conservator to interference is profound. While already difficult to adhere to in the practice of conservation, minimal intervention is impossible with artworks that require re-interpretation every time they are put on display, and this is even undesirable for artworks that require change. However, acting restraint is still key in the conservator's critical understanding of their own behaviour in relation to the works of art that they take responsibility for.

To put this strong emphasis on conservation into perspective, this chapter proposes self-study and autoethnography as a methodological tool. Autoethnography is an established qualitative research method from the social sciences that is helpful to expose personal bias in a critical observation of oneself, for instance when having to take decisions on intervening with an artwork to guarantee its future. From the definitions listed by sociologist Norman Denzin, it becomes clear that they vary, but that the common denominator is self-study (Denzin 2014, pp. 19–20). Autoethnography involves both a method and a written account that is evocative and, therefore, functional to others (Ellis and Bochner 2006). This is why I consider the use of autoethnography in conservation a form of conceptual reversibility (Stigter 2016c). The account is always a first-person narrative and constructed in such a way that it invites the reader to engage with the problem and think along. In the case of a conservator's testimony, the reader will take on the same sense of responsibility steering the train of thoughts during analysis or practice. This also implies that the line of reasoning can be mentally undone in anticipation of a next step or different options eliciting similar care and critical analysis.

2 Autoethnographic Encounter

London, 8 January 2010. I'm looking at John Baldessari's calendar-shaped book *Ingres and Other Parables* (1972), displayed in a vitrine at Tate Modern.[2] It was opened at the pages with the title story. Here is what I read:

INGRES

This is the story of a little known painting by Ingres. Its first owner took good care of it, but as things go, he eventually had to sell it. Succeeding owners were not so cautious about its welfare and did not take as good care of it as the first owner. That is, the second owner let the painting's condition slip a bit. Maybe it all began by letting it hang crookedly on the wall, not dusting it, maybe it fell to the floor a few times when somebody slammed the door too hard. Anyway the third owner received the Ingres with some scratches (not really tears), and the canvas buckled in one corner–paint fading here and there. Owners that followed had it retouched and so on, but the repairs never matched and the decline had begun. The painting looked pretty sad. But what was important was the documentation–the idea of Ingres; not the substance. And the records were always well kept. A clear lineage, a good genealogy. It was an Ingres certainly, even though the painting by this time was not much.

The other day it was auctioned off. Time had not been kind to the Ingres. All that was left was one nail. Maybe the nail was of the original, maybe it was used in the repairs, or maybe Ingres himself had used it to hang the painting. It was all of the Ingres that remained. In fact, it was believed to be the only Ingres nail ever offered in public sale.

Moral: If you have the idea in your head, the work is as good as done.

I was intrigued. Not because of the way the artist book was exhibited, in a closed vitrine instead of hanging on the wall, as the hole-punched pages would suggest. This detail came to my attention only later. Being an art conservator myself, it was the content of the story that first drew my attention.

In a playful and witty manner, Baldessari's text narrates the story that had caused a drastic change in the painting's material life, surprisingly in line with what anthropologist Igor Kopytoff has termed a "cultural biography of things" in his

[2]This work is known as Baldessari's first artist book, edition unknown. The work was exhibited during the exhibition *John Baldessari: Pure Beauty*, 13 October 2009-10 January 2010.

eponymous essay, which has greatly influenced material culture studies in tracing how an object changes, acquiring new meanings in different contexts (Kopytoff 1986). Baldessari lets an early modern painting by Jean-Auguste-Dominique Ingres change from a painted canvas into a nail that once supported its presentation. This is, of course, an original way to ridicule the adoration of the physical object in art. Expressing critique of the object in art is one of the most important aspects that conceptual artists aimed for (Newman and Bird 1999, p. 19).

At the same time, the Ingres story makes clear that once an artwork enters the art world, many factors come into play that will shape its life, conservation being one of them. Time and social interaction—or neglect—alter the artwork's form and can impose a shift in meaning; the nail changed from support to icon. It is this trajectory, a material journey, notably caused by the lack of conservation that had sparked my attention.

Only later it occurred to me that something similar was happening to this work of Baldessari. The clean presentation of *Ingres and other Parables* in a closed vitrine compromised the work's intended function. The calendar format suggests a display on the wall to allow the audience to actively select a story by flipping the pages. I did not realise this at first, almost oblivious as I was towards these immaterial features that equally belong to the artwork and that are clearly just as vulnerable as the thin paper support of the offset-printed publication. Integrating the viewer's perspective and being able to interact with the work as implied by the informal style of the calendar book format can be seen as typical features of conceptual art. The vitrine, on the other hand, was closed.

3 Autoethnography and Object Biography

The autoethnographic account of my encounter with Baldessari's *Ingres and other Parables* above reveals my professional bias as contemporary art conservator. Careful protection of the physical object to prevent material decay is vital from an art conservator's perspective, which is why I accepted this as normal presentation, not aware of other options. Yet for Baldessari, at the time, the mass-produced calendar book was designed to undermine precisely the object-based approach and the museum's hands-off policy. *Ingres* is made as a commodity item that is to be hung from a nail so that one can choose a story to read after browsing through it. Due to good care, or different use rather, the holes in the pages to hang the book are still intact, intimating its intended form of presentation and use. These seemingly minor details illustrate the critical balance between conceptual message and material form, expressed not only in the way the artwork has been made or produced, but also in how it has been managed over time and is being presented to an audience, framed by a certain context, in this case a Baldessari retrospective in a major museum.

It goes without saying that it is essential to fully understand the relation between the work's conceptual message and how this relates to its material condition to inform decision-making for conservation, as is most clearly expressed in the

Decision-Making Model for the Conservation of Modern and Contemporary Art (Hummelen and Sillé 1999) and its revised version in 2019, updated in 2021, to accommodate newer artforms and theoretical approaches in contemporary art conservation (CICS 2021). While the first model was designed for object-based work and revolving around balancing a work's history, intention and materiality, the revised model incorporates process-based art and is accepting the notion that artworks can be in flux and change over time. This has become clear with time-based artworks, which differ with each instantiation (e.g., Laurenson 2006; Scholte and Wharton 2011; Laurenson and van Saaze 2014; Philips 2015). Conceptual art tried to free-up the artwork from its material form altogether, comment on it or resist a fixed material form. In *Ingres*, Baldessari seems to provokingly indicate this by illustrating his story with a photograph of a nail to represent the Ingres painting (see Fig. 1).

The Ingres story, in my view, points to the question whether we should try to resolve the relation between concept and material by a better understanding of the influence of an artwork's biography on what the artwork entails? Baldessari's parable seems to suggest that the idea of the artwork could remain in information, provided that the work is documented well enough and can be traced back by close reading of the object as presented. Evidence of the work's life is left behind in all sorts of tracks and traces, hidden in archives, in people's minds and, importantly, enclosed in the work's physical manifestations.

Triangulating these various sources and combining research methods is typical of a conservation research approach when assessing a work's condition, including the information derived from practice-led research, conducted during conservation treatment or reinstallation. Kopytoff's model of object biography has meanwhile been adopted in conservation research, after philosopher Renée van de Vall had proposed it, exemplified by using the work of Hanna Hölling, Tatja Scholte and myself (2011). This model should allow conservators not only to trace the work's changes over time but also to better understand the changes in relation to the different socio-political frameworks in which it has functioned. This can explain a different weighing of values around artworks for decisions made in the past and raise sensitivity for different viewpoints today.

Adopting a biographical approach aims to understand the influence of the artwork's social life on its appearance as part of its identity, transcending the traditional conservation paradigm that ideally looks for an artwork's initial form and appearance from around the moment of its origin. The biographical model, on the other hand, recognizes that artworks change, allowing for a more dynamic view than is traditionally the case in conservation. It should be noted, however, that compiling an artwork's biography is also shaping the work, as it is reconstructing the work's identity for a specific reason or from a particular point of view. This notion is important when such a biography becomes part of the work's archive, especially when considering the archive to communicate the artwork altogether (Hölling 2017b; Wielocha 2021). It is important to be transparent about who is compiling the artwork biography and for what reason and for which purpose, when it comes to putting the narrative into perspective.

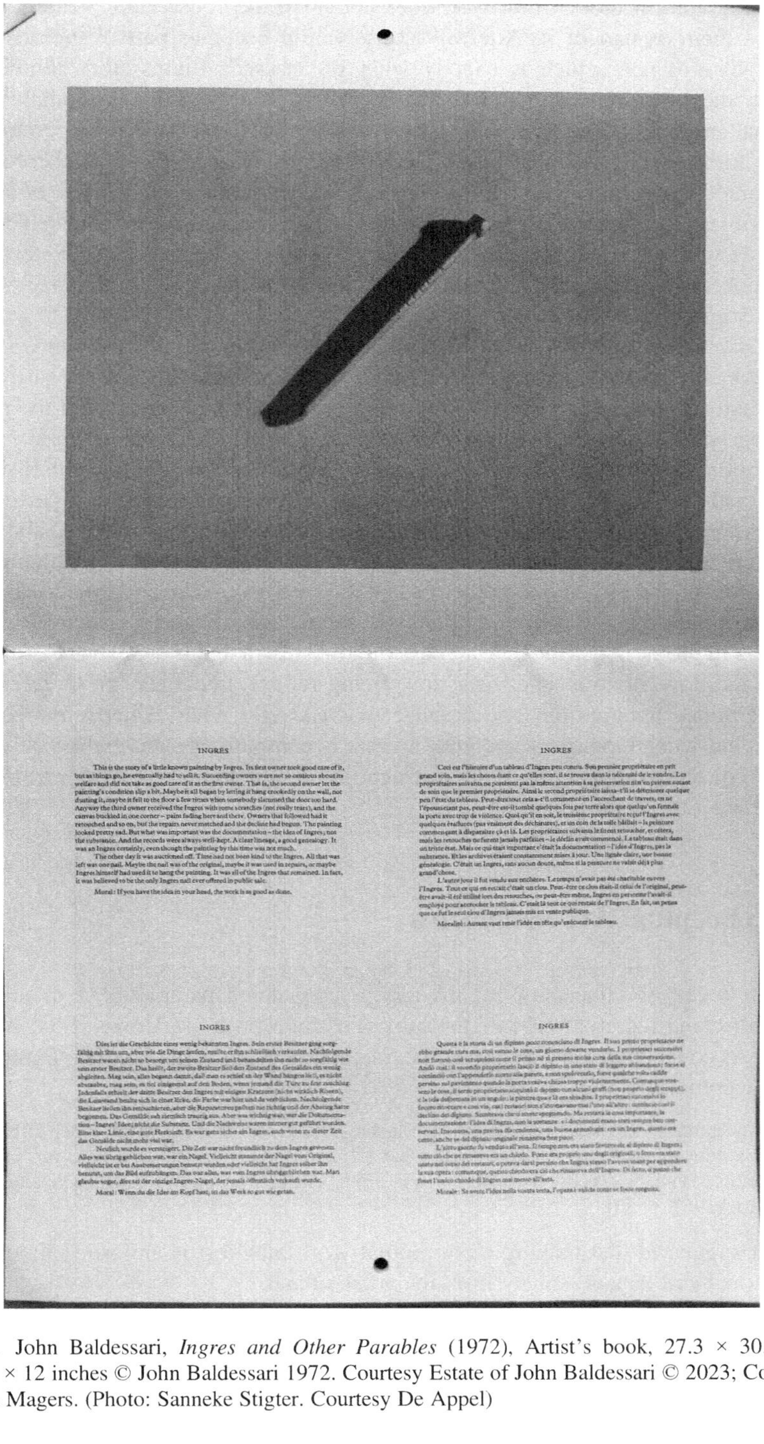

Fig. 1 John Baldessari, *Ingres and Other Parables* (1972), Artist's book, 27.3 × 30.5 cm; 10 3/4 × 12 inches © John Baldessari 1972. Courtesy Estate of John Baldessari © 2023; Courtesy Sprüth Magers. (Photo: Sanneke Stigter. Courtesy De Appel)

A biographical model, however, does not solve the conservator's dilemmas. It absorbs them as part of it. After all, conservation becomes part of the artwork's biography—or not, which is exactly what Baldessari's Ingres story illuminates. Indeed, the biographical model is not normative and excludes accountability of personal input when orchestrating an artwork's manifestation. While curators are aiming to convey a particular message in exhibitions, framing the work accordingly, traditionally conservators are taking care to avoid personal input. This is, of course, impossible with contemporary art that needs to be reconstructed and reinstalled, which is why acknowledging personal input is something that conservators have become keen to incorporate in their accounts to distinguish their part from that of the artist (Stigter 2011, 2015, 2016c; Marçal 2012; Cotte et al. 2016; Ashley-Smith 2017; Sweetnam and Henderson 2021). An artwork biography can, and perhaps should, include some notion of oneself to make clear who is the narrator constructing it. An autoethnographic approach could serve well to render transparent the role of the biographer, researcher, conservator or curator in the life of the artwork.

Adopting an autoethnographic approach enables one to take personal, professional and cultural bias into account when conducting research and performing conservation practice. This not only helps to reflect on decision-making; above all, it solicits a reflexive stance from the researcher and practitioner, heightening the sense of responsibility at the moment when this is both critical and functional to the outcome. Although reflexivity is often used interchangeably with critical reflection, it differs in promoting critical awareness of how knowledge is created (D'Cruz et al. 2007) and how this translates to action. Being reflexive enables one to defer from predetermined assumptions and manage practice right when it happens, which is convenient when having to deal with art that is contradicting the traditional principles of conservation and providing instructions on how to make a work manifest, or stating what the work is.

4 Conceptual Art Statements

As introduced, in conceptual art the idea is considered paramount, a dictum that almost became synonymous with the subject of conceptual art (Corris 2004; Alberro 2009). As conceptual artist Sol LeWitt explained early on in his seminal 'Paragraphs on Conceptual Art':

> In conceptual art the idea or concept is the most important aspect of the work. When an artist uses a conceptual form of art, it means that all of the planning and decisions are made beforehand and the execution is a perfunctory affair. The idea becomes a machine that makes the art. (1967, p. 80)

LeWitt suggested that making a conceptual work manifest is almost a clinical act, impersonal and factual—away from the artist's hand.

Conceptual artists distanced themselves from artistic crafts and instructed third parties to produce their work, preferably in reproducible form to demonstrate that this can be completely outsourced. Advances in communication systems greatly facilitated the organisation of conceptual work. Instructions by mail, telephone or telefax sufficed. In 1971, after having installed a work according to instructions in their Cologne gallery, Paul Maenz wrote to conceptual artist Joseph Kosuth: "We hope you are satisfied with the interpretation of your instructions" (Galerie Paul Maenz).[3]

According to LeWitt, a conceptual artwork *may* be executed, but does not have to be materialised in order to exist as a work of art, as specified in line number 10 of his 'Sentences on Conceptual Art' (1968) (1999, p. 107). Conceptual artist Lawrence Weiner expressed this idea around the same time in his 'Declaration of Intent' (1968), initially only published in the catalogue of the exhibition at Seth Siegelaub's gallery, *January 5-31, 1969* (Barry et al. 1969):

1. The artist may construct the piece.
2. The piece may be fabricated.
3. The piece need not be built.
   Each being equal and consistent with the intent of the artist the decision as to condition rests with the receiver upon the occasion of receivership.

Later, Weiner's 'Declaration of Intent' became known in painted form, in typical Weiner lettering, on long term display at Dia Beacon in New York State, high on the walls of the entrance hall ever since its opening in 2003. As with most contemporary work, it is indeed "a fantasy" to think that conceptual artworks solely exist as ideas, as art critic Camiel van Winkel calls it, for "without a material medium, nobody can become aware of any concept" (2005, p. 28). Van Winkel quotes conceptual artist Mel Bochner to illustrate his point: "Outside the spoken word, no thought can exist without a sustaining support" (2005, p. 28). Indeed, a catalogue page already does the trick, while Weiner's statement in silver lettering on museum walls makes the work accessible to a much wider audience.

Baldessari, too, made his work manifest in a format that could be widely distributed in the case of *Ingres and Other Parables*. The materiality of the calendar book adheres to some of the main principles in conceptual art; it is a reproducible and cheap commodity item, expressed through the work's fabrication and its calendar form respectively. This makes the physical artwork a carrier of information just as much as the content in undermining the worship of the unique material object in the visual arts. The calendar has a flimsy character typical of a throwaway product that has served its purpose at the end of the year. These associations are evoked by the chosen materials and techniques as well as its form, all supporting the work's conceptual message. This line of reasoning is indicative of the conservator's perspective, focussing on material connotations that serve the work's narrative.

The examples of Baldessari's calendar, LeWitt's manifesto writings and Weiner's 'Declaration of Intent' include the role of the viewer to complete the work as art, turning the artmaking process into an intellectual endeavour of the spectator. Weiner

[3]Unsigned carbon of a letter to Joseph Kosuth, 16 February 1971.

calls upon the imagination even, placing the choice for the way of completion of the work with the viewer. This idea echoes the spirit of Roland Barthes' famous essay from that time, 'The Death of the Author' (1968), which states that the reading of a text, or any artwork, is not determined by the author's intention, but by the individual's reception of the work (2006). The creation of the artwork in the eye of the beholder is in line with mitigating the artist's authority and the unequivocal idea of artist's intention. After all, anyone may perceive the artwork and, therefore, make the work, anywhere at any time.

While the idea of distributed authorship, acknowledging personal input when seeing and interpreting artworks, is valid from the viewpoint of the spectator, such open interpretation can hardly form the foundation on which those entrusted with the care for artworks can take decisions. This becomes especially clear in the case of conceptual art that needs to be remade every time it is being put on display. This shift in authority towards the viewer seems of little use to conservators who are seeking evidence in the artwork itself, its history and artist statements to guide their decisions on whether or not to intervene, a general starting point in conservation (Price et al. 1999; Clavir 2002; Muñoz-Viñas 2005; Stigter 2011). Conservators are concerned about whether the physical manifestation of a work is in such condition that it enables the artwork to function as intended or deemed in order. Once a work of art is released from the artist's studio, or from the artist's mind in the case of conceptual art, their execution may be delegated to third parties. Museum professionals may take over once such work has been acquired, engaging in a commitment to care for it.

5 Conceptual Art and Museum Practices

The aim of conceptual art to have the idea prevail over its material execution led to many new forms of expression, influenced by the social and technological developments of the time. Artists came to think more in terms of networks and relations rather than objects. A good example is Ger van Elk's *La Pièce* (1971). It seems a simple wooden block painted white, but this has been done on the most dust free part of the world on both poles of the Atlantic Ocean, reached on board of an icebreaker. The result was minimal in material and size, but large in gesture and geographical scope. Van Elk documented the art-making process in photographs and film and plotted the exact locations of the art-making process on a nautical map. Finally, the object, *La Pièce*, was displayed on red velvet in a vitrine during the exhibition for which it was made, *Sonsbeek: Buiten de Perken* (1971). Although this took place in Park Sonsbeek in Arnhem, *La Pièce* was exhibited in the Royal Tropical Institute in Amsterdam, in reaction to the exhibition's subtitle, which translates as *Beyond Borders*. The wooden block was exhibited together with the photographs and the map, while the film was part of the film programme at the heart of the exhibition in Park Sonsbeek under a distinct title, *La Pièce–A piece for Sonsbeek* (Cherix 2009, pp. 86–87). After the work's inaugural exhibition, the map was never displayed again, while the wooden block has been part of many exhibitions, as has the film in separate exhibition programmes. Such museum practices demonstrate the museum's arbitrary attitude towards associated documentation and what it is that makes up the artwork, being focussed on the object rather than the process.

Indeed, I realized that the nautical map was never discussed during the sale when it entered the Kröller-Müller Museum in 2009.[4] This is where I worked at the time, and I had been engaged in the conservation of the artist's work before. I was amazed when I saw *La Piece* mounted to the wall in Van Elk's studio in Amsterdam one day, for this was an icon of conceptual art in the Netherlands. Moreover, it had been made for a seminal edition of the Sonsbeek exhibition.[5] I knew that the Kröller-Müller Museum would be a great context for the work because of its collection of Sonsbeek works, as well as its conceptual art collection, including early work by Van Elk. Directly after my visit, I called the museum director, Evert van Straaten, to inform him that *La Pièce* was still in the artist's possession. This was something I had never done before. Initiating acquisitions is beyond the conservator's remit. However, as I expected, the museum director was interested and managed to find the funding to acquire *La Pièce*. It was only upon receiving the object and the two photographs in the museum that I enquired with Van Elk whether the map still existed. This alerted the artist, and he found it much later, after moving his studio, and handed it to the museum.

This miniature story of how a conceptual work of art enters a collection shows that the way in which it has been exhibited over time is detrimental to what is being conveyed and remembered. Art historians Deborah Cherry and Fintan Cullen importantly point to the other side of display: "that which is hidden or removed from view" and yet renders significance to the displayed (2007, p. 476). By omitting the documentary material, paradoxically *La Pièce* had gained the object status it aimed to ridicule, so nicely underpinned by its presentation on an especially made red velvet cushion (see Fig. 2). Van Elk explained its use as follows: "I always do this with style, the cushion, that is part of it. It is a bit ironical" (Depondt 1996).[6] Van Elk used the visual language of precious object display with this choice of materials for *La Pièce*, exploiting the connotation of red plush, contrasting it with the immaculate little white block, which he mockingly called a "piece of soap" to devalue its object status once again (S. Stigter 2012, p. 107).

[4]Inventory number KM 131.538.

[5]*Sonsbeek: Buiten de Perken* was curated by Wim Beeren, later director of the Stedelijk Museum Amsterdam and assisted by, among others, Evert van Straaten, later director of the Kröller-Müller Museum.

[6]Translated from Dutch: "Dat doe ik altijd met stijl, dat kussentje, dat hoort erbij. Het is een beetje ironisch."

Fig. 2 Curator Toos van Kooten and Ger van Elk unpacking his work *La Piece* (1971) in the conservation studio of the Kröller-Müller Museum, 15 May 2009. Painted wooden block on velvet cushion, 1.5 × 7.15 × 9 cm (without cushion). Collection Kröller-Müller Museum, KM 131.538 (Photo: Sanneke Stigter/Kröller-Müller Museum)

6 Certificate and Paradox

Once conceptual art entered the art market, ironically this led to a reinforcement of exactly the system that the artists had attempted to undermine. Their work turned into marketable goods and became valued in the monetary system of economics, which is measured by scarcity. A curious paradox. The red cushion for *La Pièce* cunningly accentuates this ambiguity.

Curator and art-dealer Seth Siegelaub ingeniously managed the practice of conceptual art (Alberro 2003). In 1971 he had a lawyer draw up 'The Artist's Contract' to lay down the artists' rights about their work once it was sold.[7] The agreement included a clause on "repairs," suggesting that this could be necessary for conceptual artworks, or desired (Siegelaub 1973, p. 349). In practice, the artist's contract has rarely been used (Buskirk 2011, p. 100). Lawrence Weiner even pointed to the perversity of the agreement, as it was based on the system that they were trying to undermine (Eichhorn 2009, p. 84).

Siegelaub's business strategy to protect the right of executing a conceptual artwork, based on instructions provided, means that the potential physical existence of the work is being controlled by sales. This proceeds through the exchange of a document that became known as the certificate, which includes the title of the work, or statement, and sometimes instructions. However, such a certificate is not

[7]The Artist's Contract is officially called The Artist's Reserved Rights Transfer and Sale Agreement.

necessarily a license to refabricate a work, as became strikingly clear when the Italian collector Giuseppe Panza had copies of his works by Carl Andre and Donald Judd made for an overseas exhibition in 1989. Andre and Judd publicly distanced themselves from these copies in an advertisement in *Arts in America* (Scheidemann 1999, p. 242). Although this incident relates to minimal art rather than conceptual work, it shows that the relation between a work defined on paper and its material execution is a precarious one.

On the art market, certificates are also used to certify a work's authenticity, and to provide the semblance of protection against fraud. It was for this reason that van Elk has made a certificate for *La Pièce* nearly forty years after it was made. His concern was raised when MoMA curator Christoph Cherix had also seen *La Pièce* in his studio and asked him whether he had made a second version, as he could not believe that no museum ever bought it (B. Stigter 2012).[8] This is when van Elk realised that there is no way to prove the work's material authenticity. It was not signed, and the idea of the ultimate white piece of art did not allow for that. To overcome this, van Elk suggested signing a highly detailed photograph of the painted wooden block by way of securing the work's physical identity as part of the sale transaction. This signed document would then function as a "displaced signature," in the words of art historian Martha Buskirk for certificate (2011, p. 99).

Being the responsible conservator at the time, I made those detailed photographs for this purpose, some in raking light showing the wood grain of the block and the paint texture. I brought them to the studio, and the artist selected two of the photographs, which he printed-out in order to sign. At that moment, a telling situation occurred. Right after he had added the work's title to the prints and placed his autograph, he suddenly said, "But this cannot be exhibited," realising that with this gesture he normally authorises new work. Upon my suggestion to add this for clarity, he added *This print is not for display* (see Fig. 3).[9] A remarkable consequence of this whole course of action is that while the concept of *La Pièce* reflects fierce criticism of the art world's object-based focus, the newly made certificate emphasises the work's status as a unique object, stressed by its specific material characteristics now specified in a certificate. In 2004, only a few years before, van Elk had called it a "trick question" when I informed about the significance of the sloppy brushstrokes as a reference to the art making process at sea (2012, p. 107). Perhaps this interaction had contributed to the development of the idea for a certificate based on these brushstrokes, which would illustrate that every action around and artwork, even discussing it, can inform its future.

While Baldessari and van Elk were wittingly mocking the celebration of the physical object in art in their work, they did use specific materials and techniques to

[8] Also conveyed in personal communication, Amsterdam, 29 January 2009.

[9] In Dutch: "Deze afdruk is niet voor exposeren." Personal notes, 9 July 2009, conservation archive Kröller-Müller Museum. The certificate was made in Van Elk's Amsterdam studio in the Palmdwarsstraat at the time, 17 June 2009. It is catalogued with a separate inventory number, KM 131.541 and related to *La Pièce*.

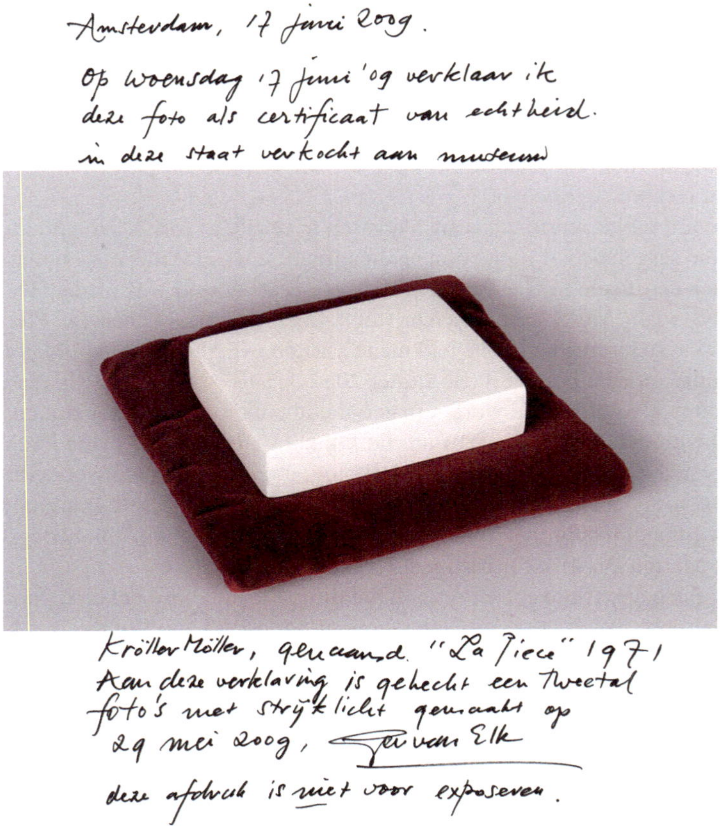
Amsterdam, 17 juni 2009.
Op woensdag 17 juni '09 verklaar ik
deze foto als certificaat van echtheid.
in deze staat verkocht aan museum
Kröller Möller, genaamd "La Piece" 1971
Aan deze verklaring is gehecht een tweetal
foto's met strijklicht gemaakt op
29 mei 2009, Ger van Elk
deze afdruk is niet voor exposeren.

Fig. 3 Ger van Elk, *Certificate for La Piece (1971)* (2009), inkjet print, 29.7 × 21.5 cm, one of three sheets. Collection Kröller-Müller Museum, KM 131.541 (Photo on certificate: Sanneke Stigter; scan of certificate: Kröller-Müller Museum)

express their ideas. A contemporary art conservation research approach makes this connection apparent and underlines the significance of certain material features for the works of art, illuminating a different side of conceptual art, valuing their physical manifestations as carriers of meaning. These "carriers" have entered collections, meaning that they are cared for when stored, installed and put on display. For the artists, however, the work might have been concluded with the idea, recalling Baldessari's motto of the Ingres parable: "If you have the idea in your head, the work could be considered as good as done," LeWitt's notion of execution as a "perfunctory affair" and Weiner's statement that the work "need not be built."

7 Conservator and Curator

As the story of *La Pièce* illustrates, acquisition is a pivotal moment in an artwork's life at which time the work is redefined for various purposes, starting with the museum's collection inventory. The work's properties are articulated by the professionals responsible, the curator, museum director or registrar and perhaps mediated by the conservator when assessing the work's material condition or requirements, predicting future behaviour or impossibilities, exploring possible alternatives even when the work includes immaterial and ephemeral features. It is precisely at this moment that the work of the contemporary art conservator ideally begins; in a critical stance to observe what is happening to the work during this phase, including a reflection of one's own part in this process.

The question is, however, whether conceptual artworks require the attention of a conservator at all when they exist primarily in idea. This is an often-heard claim, and it was also Ger van Elk's reaction when I explained about my research.[10] Whereas in theory conceptual art challenges the idea of conservation as part of the museum mechanisms it opposes, in practice conceptual art has become part of this system, which calls for an assessment of the conservator's role in relation to this art form.

Conservators always relate an artwork's manifestation to its alleged content and history. Similar to technical art historians, they pose questions about the way a work was first made, possibly intended, and how this has evolved over time. Close reading of an artwork's material specificities is necessary to interpret their condition in relation to its function. This requires not only in-depth knowledge of materials and techniques, but also a thorough understanding of the artist's ideas, those of the art movement and the socio-cultural context in which they have originated, which is crucial to make good judgements as basis for well-informed decisions on conservation and presentation of a work.[11] The process of decision-making is a valuable process that includes weighing various stakeholder opinions and treatment options. It will illuminate the artwork's various characteristics from different angles, enriching their significance to the artwork, which is potentially insightful from an art historical perspective as well.

As many conceptual artworks become visible only when being installed or materialised, this moment of installation can be seen as an act of conservation in its own right. Therefore, both the conservator's role and the curator's involvement are vital to the way conceptual artworks evolve over time. Curators generally do not interfere with an artwork's material form but may ask others to do so based on their ideas about the work's appearance in a given context. However, their role in decisions for the artwork's materialisation and display is seldom found in documentation in museum archives and can only be traced afterwards through research in exhibition archives, photographic evidence and oral histories.

---

[10] Personal communication, Amsterdam, 8 November 2013.

[11] All of these aspects are considered in the Decision-Making Model for Modern and Contemporary Art.

Conservators, on the other hand, are trained to meticulously document change throughout an artwork's life, be it caused by accidents during handling, storage and exhibition, or by their own interventions during a conservation treatment. As indicated, they are overly aware of intervening with an artwork given their restrained attitude imposed by their professional codes of ethics. This is different for curators, who generally focus on an artwork's overall function and appearance as part of an exhibition or collection. If conservators are not involved in the care for conceptual works of art, which is often the case, significance of a work's materiality can be easily overlooked precisely because of the proclaimed secondary status of a conceptual work's physical form. To prevent unnecessary loss of information and to facilitate optimal presentation possibilities, a conservator's input is helpful with every new instalment of a conceptual artwork to ensure its careful perpetuation in time.

The dual identity of materialised conceptual artworks is why it is so valuable to have both a curator and a conservator involved when managing the practices that may influence their future. This is not just because curators and conservators supplement each other in knowledge, as conservator Lydia Beerkens suggests, attributing desired appearance to the curator and material feasibility to the conservator (2012, p. 41). Ideally their insight overlaps, so that both professionals provide insight on content as well as form to make well-informed decisions about the work's prefered state in a given context. Both specialists can read the same source with a different understanding, thereby enlarging their mutual insight. It is not a matter of dividing tasks, but of joining forces in the conservation and presentation of conceptual art. A dialogue is required precisely because of the complex intertwinement of concept and material in conceptual art, in which idea and form function in unison. If conceptual art is about content and form, contemporary art conservation is about works of art and collaboration.

8 Contemporary Art Conservation

The conservator's role in preservation and the presentation of conceptual art, however, is not always self-evident. Conservation theorist Salvador Muñoz-Viñas has referred to an artwork's intangible and performative qualities as a "slippery path," suggesting this should not be taken on by conservators. He takes conceptual art as an example to illustrate his point, quoting LeWitt and Kosuth to demonstrate their detachment from the material object in art, as if this were reason to exclude their work from the conservator's domain. Muñoz-Viñas claims that "since the material aspects have become secondary, it is the *process* of creation that is considered important" (2010, 14). I argue, however, that it is not the process *of* creation, but the process *as* creation that is important in conceptual art. Not the act of creating, but the processes set in motion by conceptual artists in institutions and through viewer participation. A conceptual work of art is often a critical reflection on these processes, as seen in Weiner's 'Declaration of Intent', and more metaphorically in Baldessari's *Ingres and Other Parables*, both of which are undermining the idea of the creative act as being related solely to the artist's genius.

Attempting to strengthen his argument, Muñoz-Viñas elaborates: "Most notably for conceptual artists, it is indeed the creation of the idea within the artist's mind that is considered to be relevant" (2010, p. 14). He sees this confirmed in author and journalist Tom Wolfe's satirical essay *The Painted Word* (1975), in that "Conceptualists" consider "genius and process of creation" as the only two things at the heart of art (2010, p. 15). This is an odd explanation of conceptual art, since conceptual artists set out to make art democratic, precisely in opposition to "genius" painters, such as the abstract expressionists.

The physical artwork as a symbol of the artist's persona is something that conceptual artists highly criticised. Conceptual artists started leaving their studios to enter the public domain and engage with the public. Kosuth, for instance, used the newspaper as a platform, while van Elk employed the public pavement and Baldessari invoked the notarial sector for an affidavit to declare that he had burned all of his paintings.[12] It was the politics of their work that was important to these artists, not how they came up with ideas. As art historian Alexander Alberro explained: "the conceptual in art means an expanded critique of the cohesiveness and materiality of the art object, a growing wariness toward definitions of artistic practice as purely visual [...] and an increased emphasis on the possibilities of publicness and distribution" (1999, p. xxvii). In other words, conceptual art attempted to move away from the artist genius and the process of creation rather than the other way round.

It is undoubtedly in a polemical way that Muñoz-Viñas claims that conceptual artists "unashamedly show a complete ignorance or disregard for the technical matters of art" (2010, p. 15). However, apart from the fact that this is not completely true, judging from the case studies on van Elk and Baldessari, in addition to examples for LeWitt (see below), Muñoz-Viñas omits to address what happens with conceptual artworks in museums, possibly following his own assumption that their preservation is not the conservator's task. In fact, this merely illustrates the vulnerability of seemingly informally produced artworks that can be remade time and again.

Because of the low-cost and inferior materials used, the material make-up of conceptual art is prone to be neglected or discarded, whether or not intentional, but bound to happen precisely when conservators are not involved. Admittedly, it could be the case that original materials have been kept in use by mistake, using initial parts instead of making new ones, as has happened with many of Kosuth's *Proto-*

---

[12] I am referring to Joseph Kosuth's *I. Space (Art as Idea as Idea)* (1968); Ger van Elk's ***Luxurious Street Corner* (1969) and his *Replacement Piece*** (1969); and John Baldessari's *Cremation Project* (1970).

Investigations (Stigter 2011). If original materials are kept, their fragility and subsequent material failure may cause problems later on, which could then still lead to heedless replacement or renewal, discarding the work's material history and potentially meaningful details. On the other hand, there is also a chance that intentional change of specific parts could be mistaken for a licence to pursue additional changes that might be too radical. Ultimately, incomprehension of the function of specific materials or parts in a conceptual artwork could lead to careless alterations and even shifts in meaning as a result, making the work drift away from the initial idea, incorporating new ones instead.

It is not without reason that fierce discussions arose when the Gemeentemuseum in The Hague, the Netherlands, destroyed a wall drawing of Sol LeWitt during refurbishments in 1998. It upset the artist, who had not been consulted. When asked whether it makes a difference for a conceptual work if its execution disappears, LeWitt fiercely replied, "Of course! The representation of the idea is essential" (Sütö 1998).[13] LeWitt had personally approved of the wall painting's final form, which, moreover, had been made for permanent display. This account suggests that conceptual artworks are generalised too easily as existing independent of their materialised form, leading to the destruction of authorised executions as a result. LeWitt's wall drawings require craftsmanship, as "each execution is unique according to the specific site and the interpretation of the drafter(s)" (van de Vall 2015, p. 292).

If Muñoz-Viñas suggests that it is not the task of conservators to treat intangible heritage, but that they can help by "directly acting on tools" (2005, p. 41), I argue that artworks always consist of both idea and manifestation in one, and that these cannot be considered in isolation. A conceptual artwork is expressed by its physical manifestation, which is in turn communicating its immaterial features. Therefore, conservators cannot treat one aspect of a work of art without considering the other and vice versa. One can only consider an artwork's physical manifestation *in relation* to its function, content and context, which may be interdependent and thus to be considered and treated as a whole. By looking beyond the idea of conservation as restricted to material aspects only, the question as to whether conceptual art should be conserved is not put aside but taken as a challenge, and turned into the question of *how* this can be done best.

A clear advantage of having a specialized conservator involved when dealing with conceptual artworks pertains to their ability to interpret the way in which visual information is communicated through physical matter and in relation to time and place. These less obvious lines of information may remain unnoticed when they are not brought together in the mind of a specialist who is able to combine various sources in relation to an artwork's material specificities in order to interpret the work as a whole, relating material condition to the conceptual idea or content and vice versa. Many conservators of contemporary art are also fully trained art historians and focus on precisely the difficult dilemmas that Muñoz-Viñas calls "inconvenient"

[13] Original quote in Dutch: "Natuurlijk is de verbeelding van het idee essentieel."

(2010, p. 15). Conflicting viewpoints present a challenge that needs to be addressed, preferably in an effort that combines both research and practice, and ideally involving all stakeholders, e.g., the artist, owner, curator and conservator.

It must be emphasised that intangible features, such as the idea of renewal, change and interaction, can be just as vulnerable as the supposedly insignificant materiality of conceptual artworks, and may be readily overlooked in a museum context. Hence my own failure in taking a critical stance when I first saw Baldessari's *Ingres and Other Parables* presented in a closed display case, preventing people from flipping the pages. It was only later that I realized that the display had turned the work into a museum object, revisiting my experience from an autoethnographic point of view. This is something to consider when deciding on a form of presentation as to whether it allows the work to be fully functional. Once the specific materiality of a work's manifestation or a specific immaterial feature is neglected, this can trigger a chain of reactions misleading other professionals who may continue to work with flawed artworks as a consequence, without knowing even. Presenting Baldessari's Ingres nail as a work of the French neoclassical painter would be a telling result.

9 Conclusion

Using examples of John Baldessari, Ger van Elk and Sol LeWitt, among others, this chapter has illuminated how a "conservation research approach" can reveal a generally underexposed side of conceptual art, placing the work's identity and history in a different light. The practice of remaking instructed artworks has caused clashes with artists before, demonstrating that the relation between concept and material is a delicate one, and suggesting a change in the idea of conceptual art's alleged independence of its material form, or at least a different perspective, which flags the importance to be careful about the materiality of conceptual art, in whichever form the work is being communicated. The chapter has furthermore demonstrated that it is useful to analyse museum practices through the lens of conservation to expose the influence of museum practice on the way a work proceeds in time, using a biographical model and autoethnography as methodological tools. This methodological approach serves not only as an additional lens on conservation research and practice but also as a mirror, raising a critical eye to professional bias when having to take decisions about conservation strategies that will shape an artwork's biography, pinpointing potential personal interest. The awareness raised by the autoethnographic approach elicits a reflexive stance and a heightened sense of responsibility on the part of the professional during practice when this is functional to the outcome, something that is important to both conservators and curators. In addition, the use of storytelling in autoethnography can also be valuable to engage a larger audience interested in the workings of the behind the scenes of the museum and a closer look at artworks. Therefore, to preserve and enjoy conceptual artworks, the critical eye of both the curator and the conservator are welcome to interrelate their capacity to focus on content, materiality and immaterial features, regardless of whether or not the material form is considered to be of secondary importance. In the end it is the presentation of an artwork's manifestation that should allow the work to function, on the wall, in a vitrine or on a red velvet cushion.

Acknowledgements I sincerely thank the technical committee of this volume and the anonymous peer-reviewers for their valuable feedback. This contribution is partly based on my PhD for which I thank my advisors Deborah Cherry, Julia Noordegraaf, Ella Hendriks and Glenn Wharton for guidance and support. In addition, a special thanks to the initiators and dear colleagues of the *New Strategies in the Conservation of Contemporary Art* research group, Renée van de Vall, Vivian van Saaze, Deborah Cherry, Tatja Scholte and Ysbrand Hummelen, as well as fellow researchers in this consortium Annet Dekker, Hanna Hölling, Paolo Martore, Angela Matyssek and Panda de Haan for valuable discussions and inspiration. Last but not least, I thank my former colleagues at the Kröller-Müller Museum and Ger van Elk in memoriam

References

AIC (1994) AIC Code of ethics and guidelines for practice. http://www.nps.gov/training/tel/guides/hps1022_aic_code_of_ethics.pdf. Accessed 28 Apr 2020

AICCM (2002) Code of ethics and code of practice. https://aiccm.org.au/about/code-ethics-and-practice. Accessed 28 Apr 2020

Alberro A (1999) Reconsidering conceptual art, 1966-1977. In: Alberro A, Stimson B (eds) Conceptual art: A critical anthology. MIT Press, Cambridge, MA, pp xvi–xxxvi

Alberro A (2003) Conceptual art and the politics of publicity. MIT Press, Cambridge, MA

Alberro A (2009) Institutions, critique, and institutional critique. In: Alberro A, Stimson B (eds) Institutional critique: an anthology of artists' writings. MIT Press, Cambridge, pp 2–19

Ashley-Smith J (2017) A role for bespoke codes of ethics. In: Bridgland J (ed) ICOM-CC 18th Triennial Conference preprints. International Council of Museums, Paris, p art. 1901

Baldessari J (1972) Ingres and other parables. Studio International Publications Ltd, London

Barry R, Huebler D, Kosuth J, Weiner L (1969) January 5–31, 1969. Seth Siegelaub, New York

Barthes R (2006) The death of the author. In: Bishop C (ed) Participation. MIT Press and Whitechapel, Cambrige and London, pp 41–45

Beerkens LGM (2012) Restauratie van moderne kunst: een nieuwe specialisatie binnen het restauratievakgebied. PhD thesis, Radboud Universiteit Nijmegen

Buskirk M (2011) Certifiable. In: Hapgood S, Lauf C (eds) In deed: Certificates of authenticity in art. Roma Publications, Amsterdam, pp 97–102

CAC/CAPC (2000) Code of Ethics and Guidance for Practice of the Canadian Association for Conservation of Cultural Property and of the Canadian Association of Professional Conservators. https://capc-acrp.ca/en/what-is-conservation/publications. Accessed 28 Apr 2020

Cherix C (2009) In & out of Amsterdam: Travels in conceptual Art, 1960-1976. The Museum of Modern Art, New York

Cherry D, Cullen F (2007) Spectacle and display: setting the terms. Art Hist 30:475–480

CICS (2021) The decision-making model for contemporary art conservation and presentation, 2019, updated version: 1.2. pp 1–30

Clavir M (2002) Preserving what is valued: museums, conservation, and First Nations. UBC Press, Vancouver

Corris M (ed) (2004) Conceptual art: theory, myth, and practice. Cambridge University Press, New York

Cotte S, Tse N, Inglis A (2016) Artists' interviews and their use in conservation: reflections on issues and practices. AICCM Bull 37:107–118. https://doi.org/10.1080/10344233.2016.1251669

D'Cruz H, Gillingham P, Melendez S (2007) Reflexivity, its meanings and relevance for social work: a critical review of the literature. Br J Soc Work 37:73–90
Denzin NK (2014) Interpretive autoethnography, 2nd edn. SAGE Publications, Los Angeles, London, New Delhi, Singapore, Washington DC
Depondt P (1996) "Dat is angst voor kunst." Ger van Elk is nergens lid van en het met niemand eens. In: de Volkskrant. https://www.volkskrant.nl/nieuws-achtergrond/dat-is-angst-voor-kunst-ger-van-elk-is-nergens-lid-van-en-het-met-niemand-eens~b1e4588b3/. Accessed 28 Apr 2020
Eichhorn M (2009) The artist's contract: Interviews with Carl Andre, Daniel Buren, Paula Cooper, Hans Haacke, Jenny Holzer, Adrian Piper, Robert Projansky, Robert Ryman, Seth Siegelaub, John Weber, Lawrence Weiner, Jackie Winsor. Verlag der Buchhandlung Wahlter König, Cologne
Ellis C, Bochner A (2006) Analyzing analytic autoethnography: an autopsy. J Contemp Ethnogr 35: 429–449. https://doi.org/10.1177/0891241606286979
Galerie Paul Maenz Galerie Paul Maenz records, 1956-1991 (bulk 1970-90). Research Library, Getty Research Institute (Unpublished), Los Angeles
Giebeler J, Sartorius A, Heydenreich G, Fischer A (2021) A revised model for decision-making in contemporary art conservation and presentation. J Am Inst Conserv 60:225–235. https://doi.org/10.1080/01971360.2020.1858619
Hölling HB (2017a) The technique of conservation: on realms of theory and cultures of practice. J Inst Conserv 40:87–96. https://doi.org/10.1080/19455224.2017.1322114
Hölling HB (2017b) Paik's virtual archive: time, change, and materiality in media art. University of California Press, Oakland
Hummelen Y, Sillé D (eds) (1999) Modern art: Who cares? An interdisciplinary research project and an international symposium on the conservation of modern and contemporary art. In: Foundation for the Conservation of Modern Art and Netherlands Institute for Cultural Heritage, Amsterdam
Kopytoff I (1986) The cultural biography of things: Commoditization as process. In: Appadurai A (ed) The social life of things: commodities in cultural perspective. Cambridge University Press, Cambridge, pp 64–91
Laurenson P (2006) Authenticity, change and loss in the conservation of time-based media installations A conceptual framework for traditional fine art conservation. Tate Papers 6. https://www.tate.org.uk/research/publications/tate-papers/06/authenticity-change-and-loss-conservation-of-time-based-media-installations
Laurenson P, van Saaze V (2014) Collecting performance-based art: New challenges and shifting perspectives. In: Remes O, MacCulloch L, Leino M (eds) Performativity in the gallery: staging interactive encounters. Peter Lang, Bern, pp 27–41
LeWitt S (1967) Paragraphs on conceptual art. Artforum 5:79–83
LeWitt S (1968) Sentences on conceptual art. In: Alberro A, Stimson B (eds) (1999) Conceptual art: a critical anthology. MIT Press, Cambridge and London, pp 106–108
Lippard LR (1973) Six years: The dematerialization of the art object from 1966 to 1972. University of California Press, Oakland
Marçal H (2019) Contemporary art conservation. In: Tate Research Reshaping the collectible: When artworks live in the mueum. https://www.tate.org.uk/research/reshaping-the-collectible/research-approach-conservation. Accessed 8 June 2020
Marçal HP (2012) Embracing transience and subjectivity in the conservation of complex contemporary artworks: contributions from ethnographic and psychological paradigms. PhD thesis, Universidade Nova de Lisboa
Marchesi M (2017) Forever young. The reproduction of photographic artworks as a conservation strategy. PhD thesis, University of Leiden
Miller S (2012) As long as it lasts. Art value – Positionen zum Wert der Kunst 6:32–35
Muñoz-Viñas S (2005) Contemporary theory of conservation. Elsevier Butterworth-Heinemann, Oxford

Muñoz-Viñas S (2010) The artwork that became a symbol of itself: reflections on the conservation of modern art. In: Schädler-Saub U, Weyer A (eds) Theory and practice in the conservation of modern and contemporary art. Reflections on the roots and the perspectives. Archetype Publications, London, pp 9–20
Newman M, Bird J (eds) (1999) Rewriting conceptual art. Reaktion Books Ltd., London
Osborne P (ed) (2002) Conceptual art. Phaidon, London
Philips J (2015) Reporting iterations: A documentation model for time-based media art. In: Matos LA, Macedo R, Heydenreich G (eds) Revista de História da Arte Série W, pp 168–179. http://revistaharte.fcsh.unl.pt/rhaw4/RHAw4.pdf
Price NS Jr. MKT, Vaccaro AM (eds) (1999) Historical and philosophical issues in the conservation of cultural heritage. the Getty Conservation Institute, Los Angeles
Scheidemann C (1999) Men at work: The significance of material in the collaboration between artist and fabricator in the 1960s and 1970s. In: Hummelen Y, Sillé D (eds) Modern art: Who cares? An interdisciplinary research project and an international symposium on the conservation of modern and contemporary art. Foundation for the Conservation of Modern Art; Netherlands Institute for Cultural Heritage, Amsterdam, pp 242–246
Scholte T (2021) The perpetuation of site-specific installation artworks in museums: staging contemporary art. Amsterdam University Press, Amsterdam
Scholte T, Wharton G (eds) (2011) Inside installations: Theory and practice in the care of complex artworks. Amsterdam University Press, Amsterdam
Sease C (1998) Codes of ethics for conservation. Int J Cult Prop 7:98–115
Siegelaub S (1973) The artist's reserved rights transfer and sale agreement. Leonardo 6:347–350
Smith T, Bailey R (2017) One and five ideas on conceptual art and conceptualism. Duke University Press, Durham
Stigter B (2012) Mijn standaardtarief voor oud werk is twee ton. In: NRC Handelsblad. https://www.nrc.nl/nieuws/2012/09/15/mijn-standaardtarief-voor-oud-werk-is-twee-ton-1150969-a492310. Accessed 28 Apr 2020
Stigter S (2011) How material is conceptual art? From certificate to materialisation: Installation practices of Joseph Kosuth's *Glass (One and Three)*. In: Scholte T, Wharton G (eds) Inside installations. Theory and practice in the care of complex artworks. Amsterdam University Press, Amsterdam, pp 69–80
Stigter S (2012) Reflections on the artist interview and the conservator's point of view by example of Ger van Elk. In: Beerkens L, 't Hoen P, Scholte T et al (eds) The artist interview. For conservation and presentation of contemporary art. Guidelines and practice. Jap Sam Books, Heijningen, pp 102–111
Stigter S (2015) Co-producing conceptual art: a conservator's testimony. In: Matos LA, Macedo R, Heydenreich G (eds) Revista de História da Arte 4:103–114. http://revistaharte.fcsh.unl.pt/rhaw4/RHAw4.pdf
Stigter S (2016a) Between concept and material. Working with conceptual art: A conservator's testimony. PhD thesis, University of Amsterdam
Stigter S (2016b) Through the conservator's lens: from analogue photowork to digital printout. How is authenticity served? In: Hermens E, Robertson F (eds) Authenticity in transition: changing practices in contemporary art making and conservation. Archetype Publications, London, pp 169–178
Stigter S (2016c) Autoethnography as a new approach in conservation. Studies in Conservation: IIC 2016 LA Congress: Saving the Now 61:227–232. https://doi.org/10.1080/00393630.2016.1183104
Stigter S (2017) A behaviour index for complex artworks: A conceptual tool for contemporary art conservation. In: Bridgland J (ed) ICOM-CC 18th Triennial Conference Preprints, Copenhagen: 4–8 September 2017. ICOM, Paris, p art. 0910
Sütö W (1998) Conceptuele werken sneuvelen bij renovatie van Haags Gemeentemuseum LeWitt wist niets van verwijderen kunst. In: de Volkskrant. https://www.volkskrant.nl/nieuws-

achtergrond/conceptuele-werken-sneuvelen-bij-renovatie-van-haags-gemeentemuseum-lewitt-wist-niets-van-verwijderen-kunst~b0d3c3f3/. Accessed 28 Apr 2020
Sweetnam E, Henderson J (2021) Disruptive conservation: challenging conservation orthodoxy. Stud Conserv. https://doi.org/10.1080/00393630.2021.1947073
van de Vall R (2015) The devil and the details: the ontology of contemporary art in conservation theory and practice. Br J Aesthet 55:285–302. https://doi.org/10.1093/aesthj/ayv036
van de Vall R, Hölling HB, Scholte T, Stigter S (2011) Reflections on a biographical approach to contemporary art conservation. In: Bridgland J (ed) ICOM-CC 16th Triennial Conference Preprints, Lisbon 19–23 September 2011. Critério-Produção Grafica, Lda, Almada, pp 1–8. http://hdl.handle.net/11245/1.344546
van Saaze V (2013) Installation art and the museum: Presentation and conservation of changing artworks. Amsterdam University Press, Amsterdam
van Winkel C (2005) The obsession with a pure idea. In: Héman S, Poot J, Visser H (eds) Conceptual art in the Netherlands and Belgium 1965-1975: artists, collectors, galleries, documents, exhibitions, events. Stedelijk Museum Amsterdam and NAi Publishers, Amsterdam, pp 28–47
Wielocha AB (2021) Collecting archives of objects and stories: on the lives and futures of contemporary art at the museum Collecting Archives of Objects and Stories. PhD thesis, University of Amsterdam

Sanneke Stigter is Assistant Professor Conservation and Restoration at the University of Amsterdam specialized in Contemporary Art and PI of several research projects on Oral History, directing the *Interviews in Conservation Initiative*. Both art historian and conservator, her focus is on museum practice, artist involvement and conservation strategies, using her previous experience as museum professional, including as Head of Conservation of Contemporary Art and Modern Sculpture at the Kröller-Müller Museum. She has been involved in many international research projects, such as *Inside Installations*, *NeCCAR* and *NACCA*, is on steering committees of INCCA and SBMK, and is teaching in art conservation, curatorial studies and artistic research.

Reinstalling Thomas Hirschhorn's *Doppelgarage* (2002): Bridging Gaps Between Theory, Practice and Emotion in the Preservation of Installation Artworks

Maike Grün

Abstract The focus of this chapter is the reinstallation of Thomas Hirschhorn's room installation *Doppelgarage* (2002) in the Pinakothek der Moderne, Munich, Germany, in 2016. Those responsible (curator and conservator) decided on a reconstruction using only conservation documentation—without the artist's participation. This decision had several immediate consequences: the artist reacted adversely to it, while it also exposed an apparent contradiction in current conservation theory, including the risk of losing "knowing-how" (as distinct from "knowing-that") about the reconstruction process, and led to unexpected changes in the roles of the actors involved. As the one who served as conservator managing the reconstruction in 2016, I use this opportunity to examine my actions and to embed them in the current theoretical discussion on conserving installation art. If the conservator's feelings do not tend to be an object of professional contemplation, I explore and describe them here as indicators of potential problems in the reconstruction Hirschhorn's work. Specifically, I argue that reflection on those issues contributes to bridging important gaps between theoretical frameworks of conservation and the methods selected for this project.

Keywords Documentation · Artist's participation · Decision-making · Autoethnography · Minimal intervention · Autographicity

1 Introduction

With its footprint of 120 square metres and more than 400 parts, *Doppelgarage* ("*Double Garage*") by Swiss artist Thomas Hirschhorn (b. 1957) is one of the largest and most complex artworks in the modern art collection of Pinakothek der Moderne,

M. Grün (✉)
Bayerische Staatsgemäldesammlungen, Doerner Institut, Munich, Germany
e-mail: maike.gruen@doernerinstitut.pinakothek.de

R. van de Vall, V. van Saaze (eds.), *Conservation of Contemporary Art*, Studies in Art, Heritage, Law and the Market 9, https://doi.org/10.1007/978-3-031-42357-4_10

Munich, Germany.[1] The walk-in environment, consisting of two rooms connected by a passage, is completely furnished with PVC flooring, cardboard wall covering and garish fluorescent light, and it is filled with huge objects, books, tools and oversize mushroom landscapes with circulating model trains. Everything is held together by brown and transparent packaging tape. The artist himself has in fact compared his work to an oversized collage (Grün 2011b, p. 223).

The intensive and eye-catching use of adhesive tape is probably the reason why chances were slight from the outset that *Doppelgarage* would materially survive undamaged. Packaging tape, after all, will commonly turn into a crumbly mass and no longer stick after some years.

After its first installation at Pinakothek der Moderne in 2005, and its dismantling in 2006, *Doppelgarage* was to be reinstalled after a ten-year hiatus in 2016. This intervening period of ten years, during which this work of art was in a state of slumber, provides us with an opportunity to reflect on its life in the museum and on theoretical discussions in the conservation community. Much would basically remain the same during that ten-year interval: the museum and its facilities, the curator, the conservator (the author of this chapter), as well as most of the art handlers employed by the museum. The artist is still active and approachable. But there is also much that has changed. Although the museum streamlined some of its activities which resulted in more closely defined responsibilities, those pertaining to curators and conservators (as well as artists) appear to have entered in a state of flux. Moreover, there has been a change of paradigms within the research community, involving a shift from the principles of fine art conservation to new conceptual frameworks, as well as from attention to the "freezing" of artworks to a focus on their "unfolding." The term allographicity—in contrast to autographicity—was introduced, as was the difference between "slow art" and "fast art."

Because the reconstruction of *Doppelgarage* was carried out in strict accordance with the conservation documentation, without consulting the artist, I ran into several uncomfortable situations during the process. If feelings or emotions rarely feature explicitly on a professional level,[2] in this case they are important because they revealed gaps in our reconstruction process. These gaps were varied in nature. One of them, for example, related to my concerns of having implemented particular measures in relation to *Doppelgarage* contrary to current conservation theory—despite my professional good intentions. In this chapter I will revisit our actions in 2016 while reinstalling *Doppelgarage* and study them from an autoethnographic

---

[1]The Doerner Institut, represented by the author, was partner in the EU-funded projects *Inside Installations* and *PRACTICS*, 2004–2010, for which *Doppelgarage* served as a case study. For photos and information, see Grün (2011a, b); see also the Inside-Installations-Website: http://www.arienneboelens.nl/_inside-installations/artworks/artwork.215.research01.html. Accessed 4 May 2020.

[2]Regarding conservation strategies, van de Vall (2017, p. 85) recommends describing perceived dilemmas as follows: "Documentation best serves the conservation of contemporary art when it does not only collect and record information about the work and its history, but also the dilemmas conservators have felt themselves confronted with when deciding their conservation strategy."

perspective, marked by self-reflection and close observation of one's own practice.[3] As such I situate this effort in the current theoretical discussion and aspire to bridge perceived gaps between theory and practice. I will argue that the principles of fine art conservation are still relevant to contemporary installation art. This step "backwards in time," so to speak, may prove to be necessary in a quite unexpected way and underlines the value of solid documentation.

2 Doppelgarage at Pinakothek der Moderne: A Chronology

2.1 The Artwork

Upon entering *Doppelgarage*, you find yourself in an unusual environment. The glaring light of the neon tubes, the presence of larger than life-sized objects resting on a roughly-laid grey PVC floor and the rattling of ever-circling model trains immediately capture your attention. Countless pictures cut from news magazines showing scenes from the First Gulf War, demolished Arab houses and the collapsed World Trade Centre are attached to the walls and the objects. Curator Bernhart Schwenk writes, that in *Doppelgarage*

> a kind of workshop or hobby cellar, fundamental categories of human feeling and action are negotiated: violence and counterviolence, revenge and reconciliation. The point of departure for the creation of the work is the events of September 11, 2001. Like scarcely any other work of contemporary art, the *Doppelgarage* reflects political, economic, and social dependencies and contradictions at the beginning of the 21st century in their confusing complexity. (Pinakotheken 2016)

The packaging tape is everywhere: as a construction element invisible to the viewer, it holds together the cardboard elements that form the sculptures. It is a visual link where segments of the wall cladding are joined, or the PVC sheets overlap. Numerous objects, for example the nest-like sculptures, are completely covered with it. "Flypapers" hanging on each lamp are made of 1.5-metre suspended single and loosely fluttering strips of brown tape to which magazine pictures are stuck.

Before *Doppelgarage* became part of the museum's collection, it had been shown twice: in an exhibition at Arndt & Partner Gallery in Berlin in 2002, for which it was created, and again at Schirn Kunsthalle in Frankfurt/Main in 2003. It was acquired for our collection in 2004, and subsequently reinstalled in 2005. Prior to that point, it was the artist and his assistants who had, in each case, constructed and reinstalled it. The initial installation across two rooms in Berlin was the model for the rebuilds in Frankfurt and Munich. The *Doppelgarage* was tailor-made for the Berlin spaces,

---

[3] "Autoethnography is a form of qualitative research in which an author uses self-reflection and writing to explore anecdotal and personal experience and connect this autobiographical story to wider cultural, political, and social meanings and understandings" (https://en.wikipedia.org/wiki/Autoethnography, accessed 12 Feb 2022). I thank the unknown peer reviewer for bringing this term to my attention.

which were arranged in a straight line, accessible from the front, and having a combined length of 21 metres. The Frankfurt and Munich rebuilds were supervised by the artist and adapted as necessary. In Munich, these changes were extensive. A length of 21 metres could not be provided, so the rear room was shortened by one metre. To accommodate this change, parts of the wall cladding were variously cut, pushed over each other or removed, while the large, golden cigar-shaped object was shortened by roughly 80 cm. The entrance in the front room was moved to the side, and an emergency exit was added at the back.

2.2 *Transfer of Knowledge to the Museum Professionals*

During the reconstruction in 2005, the transfer of knowledge from Hirschhorn and his assistants to the conservators and museum technicians began. The technicians provided hands-on assistance, along with tools, electricity and light. The conservators observed and documented the entire process.

Once the reconstruction was complete, the documentation continued.[4] The components of the work were inventoried, and this list was supplemented by a number of additional resources. These included photographs and textual descriptions of the installation process, the finished work, its dismantling in 2006, tachymetric floor and elevation plans, and photogrammetric plans, which produce views of the walls.

In 2010, I prepared a preservation strategy (Grün 2011b, p. 232), which covered the following points: I initially proposed "preventative measures," like covering the neon tubes with UV film. I then suggested "conservation of the work's basic features," where necessary, focussing on the elements and objects essential for its completeness and readability. I argued, thirdly, for the "acceptance of systematic ageing," such as the fading of the magazine clippings. Finally, I urged for acceptance of the "limits of conservation intervention," starting from the assumption that one day a point will be reached when the artwork's material disintegration will have progressed to the extent that conservation is no longer possible or serves no useful purpose.

Two examples of damage to "basic features" had become apparent by 2010, when some of the crates in the storage were opened to carry out spot checks: one of the giant mushroom-like objects had bent over, and a "nest" had collapsed because the tape that bound it had come apart.[5] The discovery of such serious damage was appropriate to the apocalyptic picture that had been predicted for the future of the *Doppelgarage* from the outset. A Bavarian radio program broadcast in 2005 on the occasion of the first presentation in the Pinakothek der Moderne cut straight to the heart of these concerns:

[4] For a detailed description and photographs, see Grün (2011a).

[5] See photographs of the collapsed nest in Grün (2011b, p. 229).

> Hirschhorn's *Doppelgarage* is thought-provoking art in the best sense of the word. In a few years, problem-solving thinking will also be required of conservators at the Pinakothek der Moderne. How brown adhesive tape behaves after a few years, how this *Doppelgarage* can be stored without falling apart are issues facing the happy owners of a genuine Hirschhorn. (Grün 2011b, p. 221)

2.3 Decision-Making 2016

In 2016, the "happy owners," represented by our curator and head of contemporary art, Bernhart Schwenk, decided to put the *Doppelgarage* on display again. The space was to be the same as in 2005 meaning that, for the first time, no adaptions needed to be made. In line with my abovementioned preservation strategy, the central questions on this occasion were: what is the condition of the *Doppelgarage*? Have the "limits of conservation intervention" already been reached?

At the time, the *Doppelgarage* was in a hard-to-reach external warehouse and had not been checked for up to ten years.[6] The entire artwork was packed in a total of 25 crates, some of which were large. Upon opening them I expected the worst, but much to my surprise—apart from the damage already known—there was nothing new to note and the general condition of the work was good. The tape, in particular, was doing its job just fine.[7] The explanation for this lies in the material diversity of packaging tape, as there are various supports and adhesives available. The best tape, from the point of view of the packaging industry, has a rubber adhesive layer that allows it to withstand extreme temperature fluctuations while travelling the globe. But this adhesive wears off within a few years. There is also a less high-quality tape with an acrylic adhesive layer that isn't as temperature-resistant but is more durable in a stable museum climate. When Hirschhorn and his assistants opted for the cheaper version, in keeping with his claim to produce non-elitist art, they inadvertently increased the durability of *Doppelgarage*.

The decision on how to rebuild the work was made by Bernhart Schwenk and myself. If its condition had been poor, we would have installed it as best we could with unforeseen consequences:

> We would have called in the artist. After all, there would have been several questions that should have been answered "at discretion"—whose discretion?—for example: Is it at all possible to assemble the work in a bad condition? Which parts should be left out? What is being reproduced?[8]

[6]For lack of space, parts of our collection are stored in external art depots operated by private providers. The provision of individual crates—which in this case had to be lowered from an upper level by a forklift truck—is invoiced separately. In this context, "hard-to-reach" means associated with a high expenditure of time and money.

[7]For more information on Hirschhorn's use of adhesive tape, see Grün (2011b, pp. 223–226).

[8]Personal communication from Bernhart Schwenk, 19 Feb 2019.

But this was not the case, so we followed our original construction procedure using our documentation and without consulting the artist. The idea was to keep full control over the result which was to come as close as possible to the 2005 condition, including the restoration of the mushroom and the nest.[9] We submitted to a self-test: would the documentation be sufficient to achieve this goal?

2.4 *Reinstallation 2016*

For the reinstallation, the 2005/2006 documentation was available for the entire construction team. The documents were placed on two large worktables, in analogue (printed) form for easier access and mobility.

What struck me as missing, despite all the photos, lists and plans, was the muscle-memory or "finger knowledge" (tacit knowledge) of someone familiar with Hirschhorn's unique technique of applying the adhesive tape, since it was all about reuniting many individual parts into a collage. But with the experience of Frank Maier, who had been on the art handling team of Galerie Arndt und Partner, as well at the Pinakothek, we managed to obtain this know-how, a valuable supplement to the paper documentation. Maier had acquired extensive knowledge of several constructions and dismantlings of the *Doppelgarage*, even though he was not one of Hirschhorn's assistants.

In a first step, the temporary fixtures, i.e., the walls and ceilings, were constructed according to geodetic plans drawn up in 2006. After that, *Doppelgarage* was put together piece by piece and opened to visitors on the 26th of June 2016. The response to the reconstruction we received from insiders who knew the *Doppelgarage* from 2005, was unanimous. Everyone thought it had been reconstructed just as they remembered it, as if it had never been dismantled. On the occasion of the reinstallation, Bernhart Schwenk invited Hirschhorn for an evening talk, organised a subsequent panel discussion with the three of us in October 2016, as well as a guided tour by the artist for the sponsors. As Hirschhorn's train that day was two hours late, Bernhart and I had little time to walk with him through the *Doppelgarage*. After Hirschhorn's initial and spontaneous enthusiasm upon seeing the new installation, his tone became increasingly terse. He expressed his annoyance to me pointing to several details, which apparently we "had not understood." He explained that the cables between the lamps were hanging too far down, that we had obscured important text sheets with a shelf and had partially

[9]The restoration of the mushroom and the nest was carried out under the principle of minimal intervention: based on the photographic documentation from 2005, the elements were returned to their original position. Where possible, the existing adhesive tape was used and partially made sticky again by inserting an acrylic adhesive. Only in exceptional cases (especially with the nest, as tensile forces act on the tape here) new acrylic tape was applied, the colour of which was chosen beforehand. For this reason, the work's previous condition could not be matched to the last detail, but the "completeness and readability" of the *Doppelgarage* was nevertheless maintained.

pasted over other text elements with brown tape. Since I could not refute his criticisms on the spot, I simply listened to him and took notes.

While the artist carried out the tour for the sponsors, I went to the Conservation Lab and searched for the covered areas in the photo documentation of 2005. Much to my relief everything was as it had been built in 2005 by Thomas Hirschhorn and his assistants. I showed Hirschhorn the photos in question just before the evening event began. He looked closely at everything and asked, "How many [photos] do you have?" "Two thick folders," I answered. He said nothing, and the event began. To Bernhart's question as to what his feelings had been like when entering *Doppelgarage* after not having seen it for ten years, Hirschhorn answered:

> It was great, as I said, great, that was my first impression, it was how I left it. [...] For me as an artist who enters his own work that he did not set up himself, but you have rebuilt it here! I found the spirit just as I left it, I was happy. A moment of happiness. [...] I found it again as I wanted it. As I had built it myself three times, I found it the fourth time.[10]

In November 2017, after nineteen months of being on display, *Doppelgarage* was dismantled and put back into storage.

3 Bridging Gaps

3.1 In the Grey Zone of Theoretical Frameworks

When *Doppelgarage* became part of our collection, the overwhelming challenges that installation art offered as an emerging genre in museum collections needed to be addressed. Extensive documentation and research "to develop guidelines for future conservation and re-installation" (Scholte 2011, p. 13) was considered state of the art to ensure the continued existence of installation artworks. The detailed documentation that we prepared in 2005/2006 can be understood in this spirit. One can say that our perspective implied a focus on the present in its relation to the future. In the subsequent years, however, the paradigm began to shift towards highlighting a focus on the present—a change prompted by developments in time-based media conservation. A new conceptual framework was developed that considers the temporary and ephemeral nature of this genre (Laurenson 2006). Here, the focus is inevitably directed to the here-and-now, because "change materializes periodically rather than continuously, and usually occurs on the occasion of the artwork's display" (Phillips 2015, p. 171).

Much has been written about the need for a paradigm shift in the field of contemporary art conservation and especially in the areas of time-based media, performance and installation art. Brian Castriota (2019, pp. 39–40) summarizes the

[10] A video of this event can be seen on https://vimeo.com/229969035. Accessed 23 Feb 2019. Translation by Michael Scuffil.

process of "reframing conservation practice" under the programmatic heading "From material fixity to fixity of essence":

> In absence of an abiding material substance, novel theoretical frameworks and practical approaches have emerged in the last twenty years wherein the focus of conservation activities has been reoriented towards the identification of a work's significant, essential or constitutive properties. [...] This paradigmatic shift was propelled by the writing of Pip Laurenson [...] recognising the many parallels between time-based media installations and musical works [...]. Fundamental to this framework is the notion of an artwork's 'two-stage' mode of execution and implementation, where a work's essential properties—defined and recorded in a score—may serve as the basis for enacting its manifestations in multiplicity.

Castriota identifies the "absence of an abiding material substance" as the reason for the new frameworks—a circumstance that does not necessarily affect installation art.

It is possible that this observation from Pip Laurenson has led to installation art being mentioned in the same breath as time-based media installations and performances because of its "two-stage mode":

> As we shall see, the fact that these works [time-based media installations] are installations has perhaps a greater impact on the development of a conceptual framework for their conservation than the fact that they involve time-based media. (Laurenson 2006, p. 1)

Van de Vall (2017, [84], p. 92) discerns three distinct paradigms: the scientific, the performance and the processual. As she explains, there is

> a generally accepted but nowadays relatively less relevant paradigm of scientific conservation [for which the preservation of the material integrity of the work as a physical is the central aim of conservation], an increasingly acknowledged performance paradigm [in which the core of the work is considered to consist in its concept, which should be realized through the faithful performance of a set of instructions stipulating the features defining the work's identity] and a still very experimental processual paradigm [in which not the correspondence of an eventual result with a pre-existing concept, but the process is assumed to be the core of the work and the main aim of conservation is support of the work's continuation through transmission of the required information, skills and procedures to the designated participants or stakeholders].

Although van de Vall describes traditional, or "scientific conservation," as still "accepted but less relevant," it is often fraught with negative connotations in the context of preserving installations. The "traditional view of conservation" is associated with a wish to "to freeze artworks in a single state" (Macedo et al. 2012, p. 5). Yet "[i]nstallations are—by nature—designed to change" (Goldie-Scott and Lei 2019). The impact of this misalignment is significant, as Hölling has explained: "[T]he traditional paradigm of conservation which presumes to fix objects in time by arresting change (intrinsic or extrinsic to them) resonates in the prevalent concept of a museum tied to a concept of safeguarding physical, static artifacts" (Hölling 2016, pp. 4–5). Her summary is unflattering: "Such concept of a museum is often compared to a tomb, crypt or mausoleum" (Hölling 2016, p. 20).

On the strength of these descriptions one can get the impression that traditional "scientific conservation" is not appropriate to preserving installations. From this perspective, the procedure of restoring *Doppelgarage* in a minimally invasive manner and rebuilding it as faithfully as possible based on exact documentation seems downright absurd.[11] I need not mention that we did just that, however—with the best of intentions. Have we thereby made ourselves the keepers of a mausoleum, with *Doppelgarage* as its corpse?

To resolve this dilemma, I would like to assess *Doppelgarage* and our actions in relation to its reinstallation and how this artwork can be classified within the current theoretical discussion. In this, I follow the basic consideration that if there are different conservation paradigms, the converse should be true as well, i.e., there should be criteria by which every work to be conserved can be assigned to an appropriate paradigm. After all, it is the work of art with its special and unique characteristics that should serve as starting point for linking it to a particular paradigm. Below I will present several writings that deal with the classification of works of art.

Hölling (2016, p. 10) discerns "slow" and "fast" art, considering the relativity of temporal duration:

> Unlike traditional artworks such as paintings or sculpture, which are subject to entropy and decay and which might be defined as "slow art" due to the pace of their decline, performance, installation, and digital artworks might be classified as a sort of "fast art" because they are typically created to be experienced for only very short durations of time before they "end". [...] Slow art stands at the center of a traditional concept of the museum as a harbour of physical artifacts.

According to this definition, the *Doppelgarage* would be both—slow *and* fast art—because it consists of sculptures ("physical artifacts") but is also defined by the finiteness of its respective presentations.

The notions of autographicity and allographicity can also be of help in this matter. In analysing authenticity and authorship, Laurenson (2006), following Nelson Goodman, introduced a distinction between autographic and allographic artworks:

> Autographic arts, like painting and sculpture may depict the hand of the artist and paradigmatically leave the studio as a complete work. Allographic arts, like music and performance, are installed or performed each time they are displayed in a second moment of creation. (Laurenson 2016, p. 34:19)

Once again, according to these definitions, *Doppelgarage* would correspond to both categories. On the one hand it was produced exclusively in the artist's studio, with the help of assistants, but under Hirschhorn's strict instructions. On the other hand, it can only be experienced when it is on display, which means it must be (re)installed. This again would imply that *Doppelgarage* is of "dual nature." In regard to slide-based artworks, Francesco Leonelli (2019, pp. 151–153) points in his chapter "Are slide-based artworks simultaneously allographic as well as autographic art forms?" to the "dual nature" of this genre: "how, actually, should one approach the problem that slides are simultaneously finished artworks as well as modifiable forms when being reproduced?"

But perhaps Laurenson's phrase "in a second moment of creation" is the solution—in my opinion, the exact reconstruction according to precise plans has

[11] I am indebted to Gunnar Heydenreich, who helped me detect this gap.

nothing in common with a "second moment of creation," but is rather to be understood as bridging the exhibition break of a "first moment of creation." According to this understanding, *Doppelgarage* (so far!) would be an autographic work of art. The circumstances that (1) the state of preservation is (still) good, (2) no spatial alterations are necessary, and (3) comprehensive documentation is available, play an essential role in this sorting.

And which conservation paradigm is now valid? Laurenson (2006, p. 4) suggests "that the concept of authenticity operating in the traditional conceptual framework of conservation is appropriate for a framework in which the objects of conservation are the autographic arts [. . .]."[12] This assessment goes hand in hand with an understanding of the preservation strategy mentioned above, which is deeply committed to traditional principles. The surprisingly good general condition and the possibility of restoring existing damage according to the principles of "scientific conservation," using minimally invasive and restorative methods, made it possible to show *Doppelgarage* exactly as it had been ten years earlier. One could argue that the "frozen" installation with its 9/11 theme was a memorable experience precisely because its "own world," as it were, had stood still for over ten years while the outside world had continued to turn. But would that, in fact, be correct? Even though I reported on the good general condition of *Doppelgarage*, traces of its "systematic aging" were unmistakable: the magazine photos were slightly faded, transparent adhesive tape had yellowed, the cardboard boxes of some of the sculptures had given way slightly under their own weight and had lost some of their tension. Analogous to the viewers, who may have gained some grey hair and a few extras wrinkles in the intervening decade, *Doppelgarage* had also gotten on in years—but this was exactly what made the reunion so appealing. In this respect, the word "frozen" is incorrect, as it may have applied to the "completeness and readability" of the work, but not to the micro-processes that had occurred imperceptibly, but which nevertheless had had a decisive effect.[13]

But what would have happened if, in 2016, during the condition check, we had found that the "limits of conservation intervention" had been reached? At this point, I can only make guesses—a conceivable scenario would be that the tape had worn off, the "collage" had then fallen apart and larger over mouldings would have been necessary, which could not have been reconciled with "minimal intervention":

> As soon as one or more of an artwork's components are replaceable and any degree of interpretation is required to re-configure the piece for installation, the notion of

[12] Her sentence ends: "but inadequate for works which are not."

[13] I regard the verb "to freeze," as used in relation to the traditional conservation paradigm, to be ambiguous. It purports to provide information about the (supposedly unchanged) condition of the artwork but is rather an interpretation and conceals processes of change and aging inherent in all matter. I propose to replace the term with "to be considered as contained": an artwork is "contained" when "its expression lies within its own material form, as in traditional paintings or sculptures. This category generally requires a conservation strategy based on preserving the original materials" (Stigter 2017, p. 2).

allographicity provides a useful conceptual framework for conservation and documentation. (Phillips 2015, p. 174)[14]

The abovementioned changes would have resulted in the transition of *Doppelgarage* to an allographic work of art.

3.2 Finger Memory and Documentation—"Knowing How" and "Knowing That"

If you put the work in storage and don't display it for ten years, you've diminished your ability to keep it because you might not be able to install it properly. (Jill Sterrett in: Getty Conservation Institute 2009)

This quotation expresses my concerns shortly before the installation of *Doppelgarage* very well because a correct installation is an important part of the conservation of complex artworks (Stigter 2017, p. 6). The decision was taken to carry out the reconstruction in strict compliance with the documentation—without the artist. In 2016, we already had considerable experience in the successful reconstruction of multi-part and installational works.[15] And yet I had reservations in this case. What made me doubt that we could do it without the artist? What was the difference between this and other artworks, where I felt no doubts at all? With the engagement of Frank Maier these doubts were dispelled. With his "tacit knowledge" of the technique of joining the individual parts of *Doppelgarage*, he filled the gap that was still missing in order to install the work "properly," because even the seemingly careless application of the adhesive tape in its various functions demands skill. This was the missing link, which was not covered by the documentation. Frank Maier, himself a visual artist, replied as follows to my question about what he could do better than others who were involved in the construction of the *Doppelgarage*:

The feeling for the handling of "special materials" in the art context, i.e., the adhesive tape and how to use it, is difficult to communicate through photographic material if you have no experience. The reconstruction true to the original, through quasi spontaneous sticking together of the individual elements, the "simple" stapling [of the wall claddings] and yet remaining precise, [...] the implementation [...] in a Hirschhorn habitus [..., in that] I was able to do much more than those who had never before had anything to do with Hirschhorn's works.[16]

Following Gilbert Ryle, van Saaze (2013, p. 140) has described two different concepts of knowing: "knowing how" and "knowing that." As she explains:

"Knowing how" refers to the kind of knowledge involved in action and movement whereas "knowing that" is a knowledge of facts and information. [...] Ryle argues that "know how" is shown in the things that people do: in the physical movement and overt behaviour.

[14] Phillips claimed the same thing regarding time-based media artworks.

[15] E.g., Roman Ondák *Passage* (2004), Mark Manders *Silent Factory* (2000).

[16] Frank Maier in response to a questionnaire by Maike Grün, 21 Nov 2017.

> "Knowing how," in other words, is concerned with practical reason and doing, and is related to tacit, practical knowledge, and skill as distinct from theoretical knowledge and reasoning.

Transferred to the assembly of *Doppelgarage*, Frank Maier's knowledge embodies "knowing how," the documentation exemplifies "knowing that." Both fields of knowledge were essential.[17] It is, therefore, helpful when purchasing or first setting up the artwork to be clear about what types of knowledge will be required for a reinstallation in the future and how this can be ensured in the long term.

3.3 The Conservator's Changing Role

The scene in which Thomas Hirschhorn poured out his criticism upon me in the middle of the well-attended *Doppelgarage* is one of the most unpleasant things I have experienced in my professional life to date. It hit me completely unexpectedly. How could it come to this? The following is relevant here:

> In contrast to a great number of traditional artworks, which rely on their physical presence in their original materials [...] iterant artworks exist only on the basis of an instruction or a score that must be installed, projected, performed. This questions the traditional functionality of a museum as an institution harbouring artworks as objects. (Hölling 2016, p. 11)

This quotation contains two aspects which I consider essential to answer my question: "Iterant artworks exist only on the basis of an instruction or a score" and "Traditional functionality of a museum as an institution." Generally, the creation of instructions or scores is associated with the artist and are his part of the job. Hirschhorn summed it up above: "As I had built it myself three times, I found it the fourth time." The first three set-ups had been carried out by Hirschhorn and his assistants. The latter had their own "score" in the form of drawings and photos on a laptop and Hirschhorn, of course, had his memories of those efforts. For the fourth set-up, the conservation documentation served as a "score," thus replacing the presence of the artist. The conservator's role here was that of score-writer.

Bernhart Schwenk answered my question and justified the decision to do the reconstruction in the absence of the artist: "I had confidence in your conservatorial feel, based on the entire documentation you have created. Through the documentation, the work has entered our mental inventory."[18] Bernhart's observation points to who in this case was the central stakeholder in this installation and had the greatest impact on the work's appearance: the conservator. Usually the curator and/or the artist make decisions in matters of presentation. In this instance, the role shifting, whereby these responsibilities ended up in my hands as conservator, evolved out of

[17] Frank Maier describes the various documentation documents as "helpful" (photogrammetric plans; photo documentation of the dismantling 2006), "very helpful" (list of components) and "indispensable" (geodetic layout plans and views; photo documentation of the installation on display 2005). He did not consider any of these elements to be expendable. Ibid.

[18] Personal communication from Bernhart Schwenk, 19 Feb 2019.

the entire process and happened more or less by accident, unplanned. The same redistribution of roles occurred in the context of the reinstallation of several other artworks under strict observance of conservation documentation. Interestingly, it was Hirschhorn's harsh criticism that made me think of it. And because of this, it was me who was the focus of his criticism, since I had entered his territory through my "score-writing" and—so he thought—had made my own interpretation of his work.[19]

How a museum conservator defines his/her role depends on many factors, such as individual training, the structure of the museum, the specialisation of colleagues in other departments and the staffing level in general. These overriding factors are subject to change over time. Regarding specific and time-limited projects, personal experience can lead to a temporary redistribution of roles. To ensure that this does not happen unconsciously, it makes sense to break the project down into tasks and to create an agenda for the individual participants—possibly outside the usual distribution of roles. The more aware we are of our role, the more easily we will communicate and collaborate with artists.

4 Conclusion

As a conservator trained in the traditional conservation model, I see the development of new conceptual frameworks as a great opportunity necessary to professionally preserve works of art that the old framework cannot accommodate. I can well remember my perplexity at the start of my career when faced with conservation problems that seemed to require magic to solve. In this respect, the development of new models that recognise change and transformation as a fundamental possibility is a tremendous relief and an indispensable aid for practising conservators in their daily decisions. Nevertheless, I have the impression that in this new approach, which began in the disciplines of time-based media and performance where the need was most obvious, other contemporary genres (e.g., installation art) were hastily taken on board. It is easier to find theoretical literature on installation art works that do *not* fit into the traditional conservation paradigm than on those that do. The group comprising the latter, however, is currently the majority in our collection. In my opinion, research into the grey zone in which a work of art fluctuates between its classification and paradigms is still pending. In the case of *Doppelgarage* I put forward the following aspects as further criteria for classification: the (good) state of preservation, the (lack of) need to make (spatial) changes and the availability of sufficient

[19] The extended role of the conservator, e.g., as "interpreter, mediator, co-producer" (Van Saaze 2013, p. 115) or "performer" (Macedo et al. 2012) was widely discussed. Whether and to what extent these activities might also be relevant within the traditional conservation model needs to be investigated.

documentation. I am sure that regarding other works of art an even wider list of criteria could be elaborated.

As I hope to have shown, the theoretical discussion of conservation issues is important and helpful for the practitioner to sort out decisions made or situations that have arisen in practice and to learn from perceived "gaps." At the same time, it is necessary to test the theoretical concepts in practice. In mutual conversation, gaps between theory and practice can be bridged.

I would like to suggest that the achievement of new frameworks should not be seen as a paradigm shift, but rather as a paradigm diversification, where all models—traditional and new—are on an equal footing, in the knowledge that perhaps each will be applied at a particular time. Herewith I see the best possibility to preserve works of art in their change and in the course of time.[20]

Here are my findings in brief:

- Talk about your tasks. They can deviate from the usual role allocation in your professional structure.
- Discern between "knowing that" and "knowing how." Make sure that neither is missing.
- Classify the artwork you are working on. This will be the starting point for paradigm assignment.
- All paradigms matter. The principles of "scientific conservation" can and should be applied to installation art—if and as long as this is possible.
- And finally: listen to your feelings and welcome them as potential whistle-blowers on a professional basis. They can help to point out structural inconsistencies and thus lead to more clarity.

I am curious about the next reinstallation of *Doppelgarage*.

Acknowledgements I would like to express my deep gratitude to Nina Quabeck, Gunnar Heydenreich, Bianca Albrecht and Martina Pfenninger Lepage for their valuable input. Special thanks go to Barbara Sommermeyer for her wise and precise feedback on my manuscript. Thanks also to the anonymous peer reviewer and the editors of this volume, who sharpened my text with their valuable comments. Luke Smythe took on the mammoth task of turning my German English into British English and improved the text beyond that, for which I am indebted to him. I thank Thomas Hirschhorn, Bernhart Schwenk and Frank Maier for productive and lively cooperation. Finally, I would like to thank my colleagues at the Doerner Institut, including (but not limited to) Heide Skowranek, Florian Schwemer, Irene Glanzer, Eva Müller-Artelt, Wolfgang Wastian and Ilona Koroma for the many fruitful discussions we have had together and will no doubt continue having in future.

[20] See also Stigter (2017, p. 2): "An artwork's behaviour may vary over time and even shift between 'contained,' 'installed' and 'performed,' indicating potential fundamental changes."

References

Castriota B (2019) Authenticity, identity, and essentialism: Reframing conservation practice. In: Mairesse F, Peters RF (eds) What is the essence of conservation? Materials for a discussion, Papers from the ICOM-CC and ICOFOM session at the 25th General Conference held in Kyoto, 4 Sep 2019, pp 39–48. http://network.icom.museum/fileadmin/user_upload/minisites/icofom/images/Icofom-EssenceofConservation-FINAL.pdf. Accessed 24 May 2020

Getty Conservation Studio (2009) Competing commitments: a discussion about ethical dilemmas in the conservation of modern and contemporary art. Newsletter 24.2 (Fall). https://www.getty.edu/conservation/publications_resources/newsletters/24_2/dialogue.html. Accessed 9 June 2020

Goldie-Scott I, Lei S (2019) Instruction, notation, score. In: Cologne Institute of Conservation Sciences / TH Köln (ed) The decision-making model for contemporary art conservation and presentation, Version 1.1, May 2019, Glossary, pp 24–25. https://www.th-koeln.de/mam/downloads/deutsch/hochschule/fakultaeten/kulturwissenschaften/f02_cics_gsm_fp__dmmcacp_190613-1.pdf. Accessed 26 Sept 2019

Grün M (2011a) Coordinates and plans: geodetic measurement of room installations. Methods and experience gained at the Pinakothek der Moderne, Munich. In: Scholte T, Wharton G (eds) Inside installations. Theory and practice in the care of complex artworks. Amsterdam University Press, Amsterdam, pp 185–194

Grün M (2011b) 'My work isn't ephemeral, it's precarious'. Discussion of a 'conservation' strategy for *Doppelgarage* by Thomas Hirschhorn. In: Scholte T, Wharton G (eds) Inside installations. Theory and practice in the care of complex artworks. Amsterdam University Press, Amsterdam, pp 221–234

Hölling HB (2016) Lost to museums? Changing media, their Worlds, and performance. In: Lubar S et al (eds) Museum History Journal, special issue devoted to the Lost Museums Colloquium, Brown University, pp 1–15. https://www.academia.edu/30706773/Lost_to_Museums_Changing_Media_Their_Worlds_and_Performance. Accessed 7 June 2020

Laurenson P (2006) Authenticity, change and loss in the conservation of time-based media installations: A conceptual framework for traditional fine art conservation. In: Tate Papers 6, Autumn 2006, https://www.tate.org.uk/research/publications/tate-papers/06/authenticity-change-and-loss-conservation-of-time-based-media-installations. Accessed 22 Feb 2019

Laurenson P (2016) Can artworks live in a museums collection? Talk at MoMA, New York City, 19.09.2016, https://vimeo.com/184868009. Accessed 28 May 2020

Leonelli F (2019) Slide duplicates and the 'critique of variants'. Points of contact between media conservation, philology and art theory. In: Sommermeyer B, Haaften C (eds) Back to the future. Riding the slide carousel, Kerber Bielefeld/Berlin, pp 139–155

Macedo R, Nogueira A et al (2012) The Conservator as a performer. ATINER'S Conference Paper Series, No: ART2012-0087. https://www.academia.edu/37973138/The_Conservator_as_a_performer. Accessed 3 May 2020

Phillips J (2015) Reporting iterations: A documentation model for time-based media art. In: Matos LA, Macedo R et al (eds) Revisita de História Da Arte 4:168–179. http://revistaharte.fcsh.unl.pt/rhaw4/RHAw4.pdf. Accessed 19 May 2020

Pinakotheken (2016) Reset. Thomas Hirschhorn – *Doppelgarage*. https://www.pinakothek.de/ausstellungen/reset-thomas-hirschhorn-doppelgarage. Accessed 4 June 2020

Scholte T (2011) Introduction. In: Scholte T, Wharton G (eds) Inside installations. Theory and practice in the care of complex artworks. Amsterdam University Press, Amsterdam, pp 11–20

Stigter S (2017) A behaviour index for complex artworks. A conceptual tool for contemporary art conservation. In: ICOM-CC 18th Triennial Conference 2017 Copenhagen. https://www.icom-cc-publications-online.org/PublicationDetail.aspx?cid=66ddfe9a-c4fc-46d4-8f99-d63a9f86c4b1. Accessed 11 Sept 2019 van de Vall R (2017) Documenting dilemmas. On the relevance of ethically ambiguous cases. In: Matos LA, Macedo R et al (eds) Revisita de História Da Arte 4:7–17. http://harte.fcsh.unl.pt/rhaw4/RHAw4.pdf. Accessed 19 May 2020

van Saaze V (2013) Installation art and the museum. Presentation and conservation of changing artworks, Amsterdam University Press, Amsterdam

Maike Grün has been working as a conservator at the Doerner Institut, Bayerische Staatsgemäldesammlungen, in Munich, Germany, since 2001. She is in charge of the Sammlung Moderne Kunst at the Pinakothek der Moderne. Her writings focus on art technology and conservation of the modern and contemporary works kept there, for example, paintings by Max Beckmann or installation art works such as *Das Ende des 20. Jahrhunderts* by Joseph Beuys and *Doppelgarage* by Thomas Hirschhorn.

The Increasing Role of Artists' Estates in the Preservation of Contemporary Art

Anna Schäffler

Abstract Today's challenges in dealing with the legacy of contemporary artists require new structural models for conservation and preservation and are leading to a radical shift of our western memory culture. The growing importance and discussion of artist estates in recent years is one of the results of this development. Based on my experience of working for the estate of German conceptual artist Anna Oppermann (1943–1992), I argue not only that artist estates become important sites of knowledge for the preservation and contextualization of contemporary art, but also that this major change and dissolution can be understood as a decentralized memory organization in which both private actors and civil society become significant stakeholders for contemporary art. In elevating preservation to a condition of contemporary art, the instituent potential of contemporary art preservation becomes apparent through these emerging so-called "networks of care."

Keywords Estate · Legacy · Networks of care · Posthumous · Instituent potential · Knowledge site

1 Introduction

Based on my work with the Estate of German conceptual artist Anna Oppermann (1940–1993), I focus in this contribution on the increasing responsibility of artists' estates as legal entities in the preservation of contemporary art and the consequences this has for institutions.[1] Being an art historian, I write from the perspective of the second generation of caretakers of this Estate. Since 2010 I have been working on and with the Estate both in my scholarly research and in my curatorial practice, and I have been responsible for setting up the artist's installations in several museums over

[1] In recent years there has been a growing number of publications concerning the topic of artists' estates and legacy planning, e.g., Battista and Faller (2020); McClean (2018).

A. Schäffler (✉)
Preservation as a Service, Munich/Berlin, Germany
e-mail: mail@annaschaeffler.info

R. van de Vall, V. van Saaze (eds.), *Conservation of Contemporary Art*, Studies in Art, Heritage, Law and the Market 9, https://doi.org/10.1007/978-3-031-42357-4_11

the past years.[2] By starting from a description of the conditions and genesis of an estate, using that of Oppermann as an example, I identify generally emerging challenges in the posthumous dealing with artistic legacies that feature at the intersection of art history, conservation and curatorial practice.

The term "artist's estate" does not only refer to a variety of concepts, but it also differs from one country to the next, and therefore it cannot be pinned down to one meaning. In a legal sense, an estate includes all assets and liabilities of a natural person that are transferred to their heirs:

> In the context of succession, the law does not differentiate between art and other assets of an estate nor between the estate of an artist and that of another person. For the law, the only relevant question is organizing the restructuring of financial assets-including corresponding rights and obligations-that becomes necessary due to the death of an individual.[3] (Würtenberger 2016, pp. 14–15)

In archive terminology the term "estate" describes all unofficial documents of a natural person stemming from their private, artistic or official activities.[4] Depending on the definition, an artist's estate will thus comprise more than the artistic work itself; it may also consist of written documents, publications, documentation and correspondence that contextualize the work and can provide important information for research. In this article I use "Estate" (with a capital "E") for the legally authorized group of caretakers in terms of administration and rights, and "estate" (with a lower case "e") as referring not only to the physical materials left behind by the deceased artist and posthumously added through processes of preservation, but also to the immaterial dimensions as well as interrelated intangible knowledge and practices. Finally, these two areas are of course not separate but deeply interconnected—e.g., in decision-making during the process of preservation.

2 Anna Oppermann's Estate: The Early Phase

From the end of the 1960s onwards, the German conceptual artist Anna Oppermann developed extensive processual arrangements that she called "ensembles." Each presentation of an installation was a unique iteration of the artwork. The installations continued to change over the years in a process of loops and recursive modifications, condensations, divisions and multiplications. Despite numerous solo and group exhibitions, including *documenta 6* (1977) and *8* (1987) in Kassel and the Venice Biennale in 1980 (curated by Harald Szeemann), the ensembles were not collected by museums during Oppermann's lifetime, nor was she successful on the art market,

---

[2] See my publication on preserving Anna Oppermann's ensembles, which is based on my practical experience of installing these works (Schäffler 2021a, b).

[3] Würtenberger also gives a short overview of different jurisdications in Anglo-Saxon and continental European common law and expiration periods of estates (2016, pp. 15–17).

[4] See also Fayet and Favre (2014, p. 6).

with the exception of a few private collectors who acquired smaller reductions of ensembles or individual canvases directly from Oppermann. By the time of her early death in 1993, she had created about seventy ensembles of different sizes, which were stored in her private residences and a rented storage. As indicated by Herbert Hossmann, her partner of many years:

> Anna Oppermann had made no provision for the time after her death; only a few items were sorted and archived. She had also not bequeathed to me how to deal with the ensembles after her death. What should be preserved, what should remain hidden, what should be destroyed? Is it possible to show the ensembles stored in the depot again, without the situational additions, extensions? Is it possible to reconstruct the last publicly presented condition—usually 10 to 15 years ago? Do I (or who?) have the right to develop the ensembles further and reinstall them? Or can the work be shown only in its individual parts, the canvases isolated on the wall, the drawings under passe-partout in a frame?[5] (Hossmann 1994, p. 3)

These were the questions Hossmann had to address after Oppermann's death. She in fact left neither a will on how to proceed with the installation of the ensembles after her death, nor any information as to who should actually take on this task. In their common living spaces, an apartment in Hamburg and a house in Celle, where Oppermann spent her last years, she left behind numerous ensembles in various stages of development. Hossmann decided not to convert one of the locations into a kind of artist's house and open it to the public. This would have been one way of preserving the last structures created by Oppermann. According to Hossmann, however, the domestic environment was hardly a suitable setting for making her oeuvre accessible to the public. Recalling his thinking at the time, he often refers to the bewilderment he experienced when entering the house of the late writer Arno Schmidt, located in a village near Celle. While looking at the walking stick in the corner, the pair of glasses on the desk and the jars with homemade jam on the shelf he decided not to stage his partner's life as if she just had gone out and would return any moment. Apart from that, Hossmann wanted to keep on living in the house in which he himself grew up. Although Oppermann's ensembles are closely interrelated with her personal environment, this early division between private and public realms set the tone for the subsequent dealing with her oeuvre. Another decision of Hossmann was not to set up a foundation and keep the estate together, but rather to work towards the insertion of the ensembles in public and private collections in order to keep them contextualized with other artworks.

On Hossmann's initiative, in the year of Oppermann's death a publicly funded working group for the processing of the estate was formed, which included Hossmann himself as well as Ute Vorkoeper and Karolina Breindl, who both did research on Oppermann's ensembles at the time.[6] Moreover, he tried to establish a broader advisory group of custodians, art historians, linguists and computer scientists with university and museum affiliations, but this endeavour failed. In his view,

[5] Preliminary remark by Herbert Hossmann on the 1994 interim working reports, 'Anna Oppermanns un-endliche Bildwerkarchive. Zum Umgang mit dem Nachlaß,' Hamburg, Brussels 1994, p 3.

[6] See also Vorkoeper (2006).

the primary task of securing Oppermann's estate involved initially examining all ensembles and cataloguing them. At first the working group divided the existing materials into object areas, such as photo archives, lost individual parts, individual works after 1967, diaries and sketchbooks, general written analyses, comments, and reflections on her method, technical accessories and variable architectural elements, as well as correspondence and biographical documents. Based on the first catalogue raisonée published jointly by Oppermann and Hossmann in 1984, a review of the estate furnished a total of 66 ensembles in various stages of development. In accordance with the last public presentation in each case, the components of individual ensembles had been kept by the artist in boxes and sometimes in plastic bags. However, these boxes were often incomplete because the same materials were used in different ensembles, thus spanning a network of references between them. Clearly, this artistic self-archiving according to a individual systematic arrangement and based on Oppermann's artistic output and occasional presentations of her works does not follow any institutional archival logic or standardized methods. Although she handled the materials more cautiously in later years, her self-archiving conforms to the image of the active artist who knows that in the event of loss or damage new material can always be added, redrawn, photographed, collected—an attitude that posthumously can turn into quite a challenge. After she died, the various materials left behind took on an additional meaning of uniqueness, of unrepeatability.

The examination of the materials also confronted the working group with the difficulty of deciding which parts should be assigned to which ensemble—a controversial undertaking since potentially everything could be part of an ensemble, including photographic documentation, common decoration elements or newspaper clippings, children's toys or pendants, furniture and tablecloths. With the private and artistic estates merged, in the case of the ensembles these secondary sources and contextual pieces form part of the artwork. Furthermore, the ensembles' logic of interwovenness subverts any clear allocation of some of the materials. And above all there always existed more materials than had ever been used in the installations as such, for example photo prints and duplicates of installation shots. Over the course of several months, the working group attributed the existing materials and classified them as so-called active or passive ensemble elements, i.e., work or archive components. From today's perspective, this decision-making process was the first and crucial phase of structuring Oppermann's work for posterity. The challenge of this systematization was and still is the fixity and homeostasis of a single posthumous order, which in fact hardly reflects the artist's quite flexible attitude during her lifetime. This needs to be taken into consideration in today's analysis of the ensembles as well. My own starting point as a member of the second generation of posthumous installers of her works differs from that of the first generation. My examination of the ensembles is based on a meanwhile largely catalogued body of work and established installation practices.

3 Artist's Estates as Sites of Knowledge

Without Herbert Hossmann's private commitment over many years and his long-term administration of her estate, Anna Oppermann's ensembles would simply no longer exist today. Because large ensembles were not collected by museums during her lifetime, the Estate alone took care of their preservation for over twenty-five years. Hossmann and Oppermann lived together since the late 1970s, and from this time onwards he assisted in nearly all installations of her ensembles. It was fortunate for the estate that a competent person took on this task, even though Hossmann was not her legal heir (Oppermann's son Alexander is). Hossmann and Oppermann never married, and, as indicated, she left no will. Apart from legal responsibility, then, what is also at stake in this case is moral and artistic responsibility: is there anyone who feels the need to pass on an artist's estate to later generations and does this person feel capable of doing so? It was only recently, after dedicating a lifetime to the care of her work, that he has begun to address the fact that he was never asked if he wanted to take on this burden.

That Hossmann was an administrative lawyer, had contacts with public funding institutions and was thus able to organize partial financing of the processing of the estate was a relief. Apart from this, he had already taken on the task of systematizing the photographic documentation (contact prints and slide frames, for example) during Oppermann's lifetime. However, such an initial situation with a committed partner dedicated to the administration of the estate represents an exceptional ideal case. After all, works of art are legally indistinguishable from other objects bequeathed after death. This means decision-making power about art estates might devolve to private heirs who lack the necessary experience or knowledge for dealing with them. An Estate's excessive demands can challenge heirs so fundamentally and overwhelmingly that due to a lack of knowledge artists' legacies can be entirely lost.[7] In retrospect, the posthumous handling of the Oppermann Estate is unusual because of its non-institutional preservation lasting for almost three decades.

Generally speaking, we see here an effect on the location of knowledge associated with conservation, which is no longer found primarily within museums but within an artist's estate. Such estates become increasingly important as knowledge sites while they pass on practices, retain contextual information, and take on preservation tasks. The functions for a decentralized organization of the memory of the artists' estates could be extended beyond the classical functions of the museum to include documentation, transmission and contextualization. Everything hinges, however, on the long-term nature of this task, which is why time and money become two basic factors. Managing estates is a considerable economic factor: long-term renting of storage space, continuous checking of the material condition and, if necessary, hiring

[7] Frank Michael Zeidler from Deutscher Künstlerbund (Association of German Artists) therefore demands that artists already start dealing with these questions concerning their estate during their lifetime with the aim of (a) preserving their art and (b) lifting the burden off the heirs' shoulders, see Zeidler (2015).

a conservator to secure the material, ensuring the objects, continuously updating digital formats, and so on. Particularly if digitization is part of the conservation concept, an ongoing and continuous examination becomes inevitable.

The Estate of Anna Oppermann is proof of how a private administration and care can ultimately lead to the public recognition of an artistic oeuvre. But in fact, it was only quite recently, when Galerie Barbara Thumm started to create a market, that public and private collections began acquiring Oppermann's ensembles. Today, when an institution wants to show one of her ensembles, they mostly contact the gallery, which has been administering the estate since 2010. The current strategy of the Estate is to place as many ensembles as possible in public and private collections. So, in contrast to a foundation, which would keep the works and lend them for exhibitions, the ultimate aim in this case is to dissolve the depository of her works. Still, the Estate continues to be the point of reference not only for sales, but also through building an archive of the trajectory of each ensemble, even for those sold already, fostering academic research on her work, continuing to inventory the materials and editing a new catalogue raisonée, including her early works from before the ensemble method.

Oppermann's incompatibility with the market and museums while she was alive in retrospect turns out to be an advantage: it enabled her, and later the Estate, to develop an informal kind of self-preservation. Without institutional interference the Estate established a unique practice that was not formalized institutionally from the beginning. In 2010 I assisted Ute Vorkoeper for the first time at Temporary Kunsthalle Berlin where I was curatorial assistant and where I became acquainted with the approach of "Interpretierende Neuinstallierung" ("Interpretive new installation") that the Estate had been developing since the 1990s, allowing a posthumous installation practice open for interpretation, change and process based on Oppermann's artistic method.[8]

This strategy works insofar as more of Oppermann's ensembles were acquired by private and public collections in recent years. Nevertheless, as mentioned, the Estate is still sought after by museums for the realization of the ensembles. As of yet there is no precedent of an ensemble that was installed independently by conservators. Reinstallations of Oppermann's ensembles in a museum—regardless of whether the work is in the collection or on loan from the Estate—have so far been carried out mainly by members of the Estate. In recent years, as first-generation caretakers Herbert Hossmann and Ute Vorkoeper have retired, this has changed again. All decisions regarding the installing and reprocessing of works by Oppermann in a gallery will today be taken in consultation with the legal heir, Alexander Oppermann, and me. In retrospect, the knowledge transfer from first to second generation caretakers involved a smooth trajectory, through joint practice and accompaniment of installations and discussions over a time span of ten years. Looking to the future, it is now important again to redistribute the responsibilities

---

[8] About the challenges of preserving Oppermann's ensembles and the Estate's own specific installation practice, I have written in detail (Schäffler 2019).

of this practice so that it can be carried on independently of me. On the one hand, the goal is to involve even more people in the Estate, but, on the other hand, it is also important to encourage curators and conservators of museums who now own works by Oppermann to undertake the next installation themselves.

So far, however, elaborate realizations of Oppermann's works tend to be delegated to external experts. Often the necessary preparatory work cannot be carried out in the everyday hamster wheel of an accelerated exhibition system, also given the scarcity of personnel, time and financial resources in public institutions—familiar subjects for conservators to complain about. In addition to the intensive preparation phase, i.e., researching the artistic position, contextualizing an artwork and conceptualizing a presentation, the installation of a larger ensemble will take several days and is a full-time task. And there is a further aspect: in order to ensure the preservation of a processual and installative work, an ongoing commitment is necessary, one that extends beyond the individual exhibition over a longer period of time and that requires constant engagement with the work. Who assumes this responsibility and develops such a long-standing passion?

This example also underscores that the larger political issue here pertains to the resources of museums in the preservation of contemporary art. In this context, however, one could also consider whether there might not be a need for a third space in which these kinds of expertise converge and in which synergy effects are created across different institutions. For example, in media art: since not every museum can afford a media conservator, or even needs one due to the small number of works in the collection, several museums could share such expertise in a network, which would also be at the cutting edge of technological development. A similar approach could be thought of for complex installations like Oppermann's: a public centre of expertise specialized in passing on and exploring such practices and being the point of contact for these cases. Such a publicly funded structure would have another important advantage: after all, for as long as knowledge remains solely within the private structures of Artists' Estates, it will not be publicly accessible.

Of course, representatives from artists' estates are only one of many negotiation process actors in a network of experts, who fill in, as it were, for the artist posthumously, such as conservators, curators, exhibition designers, technicians and insurance company staff. For this reason, there is the need to take a closer look at these networks when examining the preservation of installation art.[9] This in turn requires an additional methodology from anthropology, which helps reveal these negotiation processes within the network, for example the construction of authenticity during preservation (van Saaze 2013). The diffusion of preservation tasks will engender "networks of care" *outside* the museum, causing expertise no longer to lie solely with museum staff (Dekker 2014).[10] As a consequence, the institution has to

[9] On the notion of understanding the artwork as a process of negotiation, see for example Yaneva (2003).

[10] Also see the volume *Networks of Care. Politics of Preserving and Discarding* (Schäffler et al. 2022).

establish and maintain lasting connections with people outside the institution. The fundamental shift in conservation practice towards a multidisciplinary network involving different stakeholders in the handling of artworks has also caused a shift in the understanding of preservation from material objects to the organization and control of a network of various actors. The museum itself is restructured, and conservation becomes the mediator of these collaborative processes:

> We are now less inclined to discuss registration, conservation, and curatorial functions as separate activities. Rather, we mutually discuss collection care, collection management, and stewardship. Preservation efforts are often the result of collaborative efforts among conservators, curators, educators, archivists, and technicians.[11]

Consequently, what will move to the fore next is the question of hierarchy: who decides? But also: whose values are considered relevant and who's not? Who can and may receive valuable works of art? Which memory is preserved, whose history is told or not? The selective view of an institution can led to the exclusion of other value concepts. This is the case when, for instance, the conservation perspective prevails due to standardized protocols, excluding other aspects, or if the institutional formalization cannot do justice to these other aspects. Dean Sully has described this problematic hierarchical relationship between various participants in the conservation process as follows:

> The authority to decide what is valued is largely the domain of heritage specialists as "insider" stakeholders. "Outsider" groups of other specialists, non-specialists and the public are likely to express values that diverge from those of the heritage specialists. These views may remain hidden to the conservation process, and excluded from it because of lack of opportunity, language, or incentive to participate. Obviously, this has implications for how decisions are made and ultimately how to conserve. (Sully 2015, p. 306)

As one approach in dealing with this dilemma, Sully suggests a self-reflective attitude towards one's own role in the process.[12] He also proposes a reversal of the relations of authority and adaptation of the conservators to their environment:

> Here the idea is that a community's traditional systems, skills, and knowledge are privileged over universalized concepts of heritage. Consequently, the conservation specialist works within the custom, practice, and protocol of the communities involved, necessitating a reflexive approach in which the agency of all the participants, including the conservation specialist, are [sic!] acknowledged [...]. (Sully 2015, p. 306)

This is in line with my own experience of collaborating with the staff of various museums on the installation of ensembles. The objects to be preserved structure the

[11] 'Susan Lake in a conversation with Matthew Gale, Tom Learner, Jeffrey Levin and Jill Sterrett. Competing Commitments: A Discussion about Ethical Dilemmas in the Conservation of Modern and Contemporary Art.' In: *Getty Conservation Institute Newsletter* 24.2., Autumn 2009, http://www.get-ty.edu/conservation/publications_resources/ newsletters/24_2/ dialogue.html. Accessed 31 July 2022.

[12] On the growing importance of applying auto-ethnographic methods during preservation processes, see also Stigter (2019), as well as Schäffler (2019).

relationship between museum and public. In an unexpected way, this could in turn lead to a redemption of art and life, as demanded by artists in the 1960s.

4 Instituent Potential

The examination of the relationships of authorship and power between artists and institutions is in fact part and parcel of installation art itself. In examining these relationships, artistic practice shifted from the production of a single work to a broader reflection on the conditions of art production and reception itself. As argued by Boris Groys: "One might then say that installation practice reveals the act of unconditional, sovereign violence that initially installs any democratic order" (Groys 2009). By establishing a place outside the usual order, the artistic installation opens a vista onto the conditions of this very order. By subjecting the installation to its own conditions, installation art and the practice of installation therefore always include the emancipatory potential of the artistic assumption of control and self-empowerment over the context.[13] Reflecting the contextual conditionality is now, posthumously, up for debate in a completely new way. As far as the preservation of Oppermann's works is concerned, but also of other processual art practices of Paul Thek, Jason Rhodes or Dieter Roth, one could speak here of a certain compulsion to which preservation is subject.

Processual works generate preservation practices and processes themselves, for instance by being site-specific and thus enforcing a change of installation in new contexts. They also do so by implementing plants that need to be watered and taken care of beyond the exhibition periods —in the case of one of Oppermann's grass lilies the museum's registrar took the plant into his office. If one follows Von Hantelmann and Lüthy, a changed relationship between art and action arose in two respects with the concept of the integration of art into social processes, surfacing in the 1960s at the latest: "On the one hand, 'action' advances to become a medium of art, on the other hand, art becomes a medium of (social) action in a new way" (von Hantelmann and Lüthy 2010, p. 7). This ambiguity also underlies the present study. On the one hand, Oppermann takes her own procedure as the starting point for her artistic work while also explicitly making it the subject of her ensembles. On the other hand, the potential of her work's preservation, according to this thesis, lies precisely in the social effectiveness—in creating and altering the social reality—of these preservation practices carried out on the basis of works of art. And what is more, it is only in the posthumous situation that the possibility of art practices as

[13] In this context, Oskar Bätschmann has described the emergence of a new type of exhibition artist, see Bätschmann (1997). The tension between artist and exhibition curator regarding authorship and power relations was addressed by Daniel Buren in 1972 in his "exposition d'une exposition" exhibition (see catalogue: *documenta 5, Befragung der Realität, Bildwelten heute,* Kassel 1972). The exhibition appears to be an invention of the curator but is at the same time an artistic work. The installation can only oppose this by organising itself and setting up its own regulations.

commons becomes explicit, as the actions are no longer carried out by the artist, but by various actors in the preservation process.

The institutional-critical potential of these works no longer lies solely in a commentary function, but rather requires institutional action to take a position and become visible itself. Domínguez Rubio calls them "unruly objects": "They are active elements playing a key structuring role in the production of classifications by actively shaping how categories are drawn and redrawn and how different meanings and forms of value are produced and distributed within the museum" (2014, p. 13). Posthumously, these art practices gain an additional relevance because they not only demonstrate institutional critique, but also force the institution to undergo a profound change by demanding new forms of preservation, such as establishing relations outside institutional confines. Mastering these tasks leads to the transgression of existing institutional boundaries and at the same time allows new structures to emerge. The museum becomes visible as a system of relationships rather than an institution with universal interpretative sovereignty.

Redirected at the institutions, these artistic practices might even have a binding effect and call for a scaling down of institutional commodities through "instituent practices," a concept that Stefan Nowotny and Gerald Raunig developed as a third phase of institutional critique after the canonized institutional critique of art practices of the 1970s and 1990s. The concept greatly helps us in understanding the challenges contemporary art poses for institutional structures. The revelation of structure is consequently "'transforming the arts of governing' not only in relation to the institutions of the art field or the institution art as the art field, but rather as participation in processes of instituting and in political practices that traverse the fields, the structures, the institutions" (Nowotny and Raunig 2016, p. 59). And it is only today, i.e., with a certain time delay, that the institution is really affected by these critical approaches. And this institutional effectiveness of institutional critique takes place not least in the preservation processes and practices transgressing traditional conventions.

Here an alternative form to institutionalized memory is emerging, namely collective memory as a place of preservation. Private artists' estates, as the example of Anna Oppermann shows, become central carriers of knowledge and actors within the preservation of contemporary art. Is a new form of civil society memory organization emerging here? For the present context, I would like to propose the concept of memory organizations, since these are precisely non-institutionalized forms. Instead of the preservation of institutional memory we are dealing with cultural and collective forms of memory and their transmission of knowledge. As a result, artists' estates are increasingly becoming the subject of the history of knowledge themselves—just as the institutional history of museums is used today to write the history of knowledge. The question of artists' estates is not only about the advantages and disadvantages of digitalization or storage, but the estates themselves must be understood as places of tradition and knowledge transfer.

This shift can be seen in connection with concepts of the collaborative common good, as has also been observed in economic structures in recent years. Matthias Munkwitz speaks of the collaborative common good regarding artists' estates:

> The discussion now also in matters of recording and looking after artists' estates and estates takes note of the economic changes in society in the first two decades of the 21st century from the point of view of "production abundance" and draws the appropriate conclusions from this. The demands—and the involvement—are an expression of civic commitment, i.e., social capital in the sense of collaborate commons. [. . .] This means that important activities for the maintenance of the community must be regulated even more than before through civil society, i.e., civic engagement. (Munkwitz 2016, pp. 49–50)

Under the rubric "creative commons," this issue is also about the democratization of cultural goods and, above all, about making them accessible to the public. In the long run, this socialization of preservation tasks could prove to be the central upheaval that in the future will also change the understanding of art per se: as a collaborative public good.[14]

References

Bätschmann O (1997) Exhibition artist. Cult and career in the modern art system. Cologne

Battista K, Faller B (eds) (2020) Creative legacies: critical issues for artists' estates. Lund Humphries Publishers

Dekker A (2014) Assembling traces, or the conservation of net art. In: NECSUS, Spring 2014. http://www.necsus-ejms.org/assembling-traces-conservation-net-art/. Accessed 31 July 2022

Domínguez Rubio F (2014) Preserving the unpreservable: docile and unruly objects at MoMA. Theory and Society 43(6):617–645. https://escholarship.org/uc/item/9qr4d9qx

Fayet R, Favre D (2014) Umgang mit Künstlernachlässen in der Schweiz, study commissioned by the Presidential Department of the City of Zurich, Department of Culture, Visual Arts Department. Zurich

Groys B (2009) Politics of installation. In: e-flux journal, #2, January 2009. https://www.e-flux.com/journal/02/68504/politics-of-installation/. Accessed 31 July 2022

McClean D (ed) (2018) Artist, authorship and legacy: a reader. Ridinghouse

Munkwitz M (2016) Betrachtungen zum Aufbau eines Zentrums für künstlerische Vor- und Nachlässe in Sachen. Künstlernachlässe, Jahresmagazin des Landesverbandes Bildende Kunst Sachsen 4:49–51. https://www.lbk-sachsen.de/files/downloads/pdf/lbk_Jahresmagazin_2016.pdf. Accessed 31 July 2022

Nowotny S, Raunig G (2016) Instituierende Praxen. Bruchlinien der Institutionskritik. Turia & Kant, Vienna (also published online http://transform.eipcp.net/transversal/0106/raunig/en.html)

Schäffler A (2019) Out of the box. Preservation on display. In: Hölling HB, Bewer F, Ammann K (eds) The explicit material. Material and object inquiries on the intersection of academic, curatorial and conservation studies. Brill, Leiden, pp 167–185

Schäffler A (2021a) Die Kunst der Erhaltung. Anna Oppermanns Ensembles, zeitgenössische Restaurierung und Nachlasspraxis im Wandel. Edition Metzel, Munich

Schäffler A (2021b) Reorienting custody through common care for artists' estates. In: Artists' legacies. Preservation, study, dissemination, institutionalisation, Fundação Arpad Szenes Vieira da Silva, Lisbon, pp 23–33

[14] Based on this, compare my reflections on the concept of post-custodianship and the consequences for the memory landscape: Schäffler (2022).

Schäffler A (2022) Preservation after the dissolution of boundaries in the arts: Distribution and instituent practices. In Schäffler A, Schäfer F, Buurman N (eds) Networks of care. Politics of preserving and discarding. Berlin, pp 86–88
Schäffler A, Schäfer F, Buurman N (eds) (2022) Networks of care. Politics of preserving and discarding. Berlin
Stigter S (2019) Autoethnography as a new approach in conservation. Stud Conserv 61(2):227–232
Sully D (2015) Conservation theory and practice. Materials, values, and people in heritage conservation. In: McCarthy C, Macdonald S, Leahy HR (eds) Museum practice. International handbooks of museum studies, Vol. 2. Wiley Oxford, Malden, p 293–314
van Saaze V (2013) Installation art and the museum. Presentation and conservation of changing artworks. Amsterdam University Press, Amsterdam
von Hantelmann D, Lüthy M (2010) Handeln als Kunst und Kunst als Handeln. Zur Einführung. In: Gludovatz K, von Hantelmann D, Lüthy M, Schieder B (eds) Kunsthandeln. Zurich, pp 7–12
Vorkoeper U (2006) After the death of the author. On re-installing Anna Oppermann's processual and open ensembles. Conference contribution at Inside installations, S.M.A.K. Ghent. Published online: http://www.deponat.de/data/gent-vortrag_11_2006.pdf. Accessed 31 July 2022
Würtenberger L (2016) The artist's estate. A handbook for artists, executors, and heirs. Berlin
Yaneva A (2003) When a bus met a museum: following artists, curators and workers in art installation. Museum Soc 1(3):116–131
Zeidler FM (2015) Begrüßung und Einführung. In: Künstlernachlässe—Wohin mit der Kunst?, Documentation of the conference by Deutscher Künstlerbund in cooperation with Berlinischen Galerie, Berlin, pp 17–25

Anna Schäffler is an art historian and curator based in Berlin. Her research on the contemporary preservation of art and cultural assets includes theory and practice at the intersection of art history, conservation and curating. Her projects, lectures and publications focus on emerging practices of contemporary art preservation and artistic autonomous strategies for archiving. Beyond her academic research and curatorial work, Anna advises artists, private and public institutions on strategies for long-term preservation. She is the curator of Anna Oppermann's retrospective at Bundeskunsthalle Bonn in 2023.

Part IV
Documentation and Decision-Making in Theory and Practice

Documenting Hybrid Mixed Media Art Forms: The Role of the Audience

Gabriella Giannachi

Abstract Documentation plays a key role in the conservation of art, yet a key factor in documentation, the role played by the audience in the design, experience and documentation of art, is generally overlooked. In complex hybrid artworks the role of the audience is key to understand how an artwork is conceived and received. While researchers and museums have started to address this gap, it remains to be seen how best to include both documentations about the role of the audience and documentations by the audience in museum documentation. The chapter looks into a number of case studies which illustrate the significance of the role of the audience in documenting contemporary art and discusses the responsibilities of researchers and museum professionals in facilitating the conservation of materials produced by and about the audience in their archives and/or collections.

Keywords Documentation · Mixed reality · Audience participation · Mapping

1 Introduction

New approaches are needed to bridge the gap between the theory and practice of documentation and archiving of hybrid works, especially mixed media artworks. The gap is produced by the discrepancy between a work considered ontologically as an object, and a work considered from an epistemic point of view as a set of knowledge-producing processes and practices. The new approaches should not only focus on the documentation of the artists' intention, or on the work of researching, producing, designing and curating art, but also on the work of interpreting art carried out by various audiences including the press as well as participants, spectators and bystanders. These new approaches, to be effective, would ideally become part of museum documentation practice.

G. Giannachi (✉)
Centre for Intermedia and Creative Technologies, University of Exeter, Exeter, UK
e-mail: G.Giannachi@exeter.ac.uk

R. van de Vall, V. van Saaze (eds.), *Conservation of Contemporary Art*, Studies in Art, Heritage, Law and the Market 9, https://doi.org/10.1007/978-3-031-42357-4_12

We know that documentation plays a major role in the conservation of art, yet a key factor in documentation, the role played by the audience in the design, experience and interpretation of art, is generally overlooked. As I argue, the role of the audience is crucial in relation to hybrid mixed media artworks, not only to understand how an artwork is conceived and received, but also in relation to how it changes over time. While researchers and museums have started to look into what kinds of knowledges works produce, it remains to be seen how best to include documentations about the role of the audience and documentations by the audience in museum documentation. Specifically, I discuss four case studies which illustrate the significance of the role of the audience in documenting contemporary art and indicate the responsibilities of researchers and museum professionals in facilitating the conservation of materials produced by and about the audience. I hope to show how a shift in focus from the ontology of a work (what the work is) to its epistemic capacity or potential (what knowledges it produces) may begin to address the widening gap in the field of complex hybrid art documentation.

It has been established that artworks, especially those that entail a hybrid, technological and performative dimension, should no longer be conceived of purely as objects or even solely as time-based events, but rather they should be considered as processes and practices. These start before the artworks exist as material objects or events, and continue after their assumed "completion." Most artworks, after all, adopting Umberto Eco's (1979) well-known expression, are *opere aperte*, open works, whose lives go on evolving over time. Considering artworks as processes and practices within the context of documentation gives an insight into why invaluable information about the aesthetics, creativity and legacy of these works ought to be preserved, not only about the artworks as artistic products, be it objects or events, but also about their conception, design, co-production, exhibition, reception and, as shown by recent research by the Unfold network led by the curator and museum director Gaby Wijers at LiMA, their reinterpretation by other artists or practitioners over the years (Wijers et al. 2017).

In the context of the documentation and conservation of art, a seminal study by the philosopher Renée van de Vall, and conservation professionals Hanna Hölling, Tatja Scholte and Sanneke Stigter suggested that since "the meaning of an object and the effects it has on people and events may change during its existence", we should construct the 'lives' of artworks "as individual trajectories" (2011, p. 3). The study draws from Bruno Latour and Adam Lowe's use of the term "trajectories" to describe how an artwork does not behave like an "isolated locus" but as a "river's catchment, complete with its estuaries, its many tributaries, its dramatic rapids, its many meanders and of course with its several hidden sources" (2008, p. 3). Computer scientist Steve Benford and I also used the same term "trajectories" in the context of the design and orchestration of spaces, times, roles and interfaces in complex mixed reality artworks (2011). This study intended to create a distinction between canonical and participant trajectories to express the constant tension between the artists' design of and the participants' actual journeys through these works. Here, I suggest that when creating a documentation of hybrid mixed media artworks, it is crucial that both canonical and participant trajectories are documented and preserved if a rich future understanding of what it means to be a participant in such a work, or to experience such a work, is to be arrived at. I also show in this context the importance of understanding not only what a work is, but also what it did and could still do from an epistemic point of view.

When documenting artworks, especially hybrid mixed media works, we should attempt to capture their life histories, by which I mean their conception, design, co-production, exhibition, reception and re-interpretation, not only in the words of the artists but also in those of the producers, performers, designers, curators, and audiences that took part in them. While in theory there is no question that these research strategies are crucial in terms of building an understanding of the behaviour of hybrid mixed media works over time, in practice the draw on resources to carry out such documentations has so far rendered this an impractical proposition. Whereas research into the life histories of works therefore plays a crucial role in telling us about what these works are, and how they may be preserved, it can be impactful within the museum context if the capture and archiving of audience documentations become part of museum documentations. The four case studies discussed below, consisting of three artworks and a project prototype, are meant to illustrate the value of documentation for the field of hybrid mixed media art, but they also reveal the complexity of its applicability within the museum context.

2 Blast Theory, *Day of the Figurines* (2006)

The first case study is a documentation of Blast Theory's *Day of the Figurines* (2006), which was a massively multiplayer board-game for up to a thousand participants who could interact with the game and each other remotely via SMS through their mobile phones from anywhere in the world. The game took place over a period of 24 days in a digital setting based on an imaginary British town where players could visit a number of destinations, be allocated missions and dilemmas, and interact "live" with other players. The piece, developed in collaboration with Nottingham University's Mixed Reality Lab, was part of a larger research project, *IPerG*, funded by the European Commission's IST Programme. The world premiere took place in Berlin at Hebbel am Ufer, where 165 players joined in the game.

To participate in *Day of the Figurines*, audiences visited Hebbel am Ufer where they found a large-scale white metal model of an imaginary town at table height. On the board there were fifty cut-up destinations based on a typical British town including, for instance, a 24-Hour Garage, a Boarded up Shop, a Hospital, an Internet Café and the Rat Research Institute. Each of the destinations was cut out of the table surface and bent up vertically to form a white silhouette. Two video projectors beneath the surface of the board shone through holes in the table and reflected off mirrors mounted above it, enabling the surface of the table to be augmented with projections of live information from the game.

As part of their game registration, audiences selected a figurine from a display of one hundred figurines arranged on a second, smaller square table. Assisted by an operator, they gave their figurine a name, and answered a few questions about him or her which were designed to facilitate the construction of a minor role play. Before leaving the space, audiences, who had by now become players in *Day of the Figurines,* were given some basic instructions about the game, which explained how to move, speak, pick up and use objects, find other players, receive help, and leave the game.

The first SMS was received soon after registering. If the player chose a destination, orchestrators would move the figurine within it. Here the figurine was likely to encounter other players with whom they could exchange SMS in real time (or live, as in a live performance). Players might have also encountered objects, and be presented with dilemmas and missions in the form of multiple-choice questions and open questions, some formulated in real time by the game operators. As time went by, with each day corresponding to one hour of game time, the town went through a series of transformations and as events started to occur, players soon learnt that by eating and drinking certain foods, or advising others on how to do so, their health could improve or, if in poor health, be restored. Once players had registered, they could leave and continue to engage in the game wherever they were. Some players remained very active, others behaved more like spectators, and a few quit the game or died, and so were cut off from the game. As in most other works by Blast Theory, the experience of the game was therefore highly subjective.

I documented the work as part of the AHRC-funded *Performing Presence* project (2006–2009), which aimed to explore the construction of individual and social presence in live, mediated and simulated performance. The aim of the documentation, in this case, was to evidence how a sense of social co-presence featured in this work. I therefore decided to document the work by conducting a 24-day-long auto-ethnography describing what was happening in my life as well as in the game. Crucially, the documentation also traced the initial research and design phase, reflecting also about the project's initial evaluation by the artists and the computer scientists at the Mixed Reality Lab. Documenting the game for 24 days generated interesting evidence of how *Day of the Figurines* affected my personal life, about how players interacted with each other, and about the level of orchestration necessary to keep the game *live,* and so for the audience to feel present within it. While presenting some preliminary findings about this at the Mixed Reality Lab in Nottingham, I realized that despite my sustained engagement I had only partially documented the work because the Lab held in-game data to which the public had no access. When juxtaposed against my documentation, however, this offered a much richer picture of what I and other participants had experienced during the game. As part of this richer picture, design and orchestration decisions became apparent, and these are crucial towards building an understanding of how to orchestrate engagement and facilitate presence and social co-presence within mixed reality artworks. Findings produced by this project led to the development of the trajectories framework, distinguishing between canonic and participant trajectories, to which I referred above. This was subsequently used in a wide range of publications in both humanities and human computer interaction journals (Benford and Giannachi 2011).

The framework, capturing the importance of tracking the audience experience, is also useful in the context of the documentation of hybrid mixed media works.

In the UK, Research Councils usually have an obligation to preserve data generated by research for a period of five years. There is no guarantee, then, that after this period any of the data and associated unpublished documentations would be preserved. Moreover, there were a couple of other researchers and some members of the public documenting the work. Because the work was highly subjective it would have been advisable to capture some of these participant trajectories. Finally, while the platform was analysed by the staff in the lab in a number of papers, it was not part of the overall project documentation largely because of the difficulty of documenting human computer interaction *in the wild*. This means that the overall documentation of *Day of the Figurines* is scattered between two universities, the artists, and the blogs of a number of participants. Despite the significance of this work in new media history, as well as in human computer interaction, the wider documentation of this work, offering important insight into the role of the audience in documenting art, might therefore be only in part available to future audiences. This suggests that museums should perhaps take a more pro-active approach at archiving documentations of works that may not form part of their collections but may still be of critical significance to specific artistic fields, so that future researchers, artists, curators and audiences could still have access to these documentations in years to come.

3 Blast Theory, *Rider Spoke* (2007)

Documenting *Day of the Figurines* inspired me to do a documentation of Blast Theory's subsequent work, *Rider Spoke* (2007-), in collaboration with documentation expert and art historian Katja Kwastek, then working at the Ludwig Boltzman Media Art Research in Linz. *Rider Spoke*, a location-based game for cyclists, was developed by Blast Theory in partnership with the Mixed Reality Lab as part of the European research project *IPerG*. The work encouraged participants to cycle around a city in order to record personal memories and make statements about their past, present and future that were associated with particular locations in the city and/or find and listen to the responses of preceding players. The recordings built over time as each day's best recordings were loaded into the system overnight to appear in the performance the following day. The experience of the piece, then, was systematically counter-pointed by its historicity—the present moment being torn between past and future game trajectories.

Participants, who arrived at the hosting venue, usually in the early evening, either on their own bicycle or to borrow one, were registered at the reception, where they were briefed about the work by Blast Theory staff and informed about how to use the interface and cycle safely. Riders then left the venue individually and had about one hour to complete the experience. After the first few minutes, a narrator asked them to find a place they liked, choose a name and describe themselves. While proceeding on their bikes, participants listened to further questions and were prompted to look for hiding places in which to record their answers or listen to the stories of others. The questions asked them to reflect on significant moments of their life while engaging with the city through which they cycled. While these kinds of instructions encouraged them to use details from the physical world around them to start reflecting about themselves, others turned them into voyeurs, required to transform everyday life occurrences into spectacles. Towards the end, riders were given one final task, to make a promise for the future. After the promise, they were asked to return to the hosting venue where the device was dismounted from their bike and their deposit returned. Over time, Blast Theory was able to select the best answers and so the work revealed a map formed by the rich history of engagement from each of the participant trajectories through the work. The life of the work, in this case, consisted of the summation of each participant's trajectory, an overlay of participants' recordings into a kind of diachronic map that could be described as a living archive.

The documentation was carried out in September 2009 by staff from the Universities of Exeter and ethnographers from the Mixed Reality Lab, as well as personnel from the Ludwig Boltzmann Institute Media.Art.Research in Linz, as part of Horizon. As the aim was to capture multiple aspects of the work, as well as their juxtaposition, a range of equipment was utilised to make the recordings of the participants' experience. The riders' location was recorded using a GPS device. In-game audio was recorded along with the participants' responses and any environmental sounds. Following advice from Henry Lowood, an expert in the documentation of virtual game worlds at Stanford University, videos were taken of the riders from two key vantage points (a "chase cam" followed the bike, creating a third-person perspective, and an upwardly mounted "face cam" mounted on the handlebars of the participant's bike, creating a first-person perspective). An original requirement was to allow data to be immediately re-played to participants during a post-trial interview. To this end, all data was recorded to memory cards so that these could be immediately downloaded into a laptop for data review.

Each documentation started at the *Rider Spoke* registration desk to capture the induction process habitually carried out by Blast Theory—often neglected by documentors—and terminated with a semi-structured interview conducted straight after the experience in a studio space within the Ludwig Boltzman Institute Media. Art.Research to compare the data captured by the ride, the GPS and in-game data, with the riders' memories of what they experienced. Two riders were fully documented (first- and third-person documentation plus GPS and interview); six riders were partially documented (third-person documentation plus GPS and interview); and one rider was very partially documented (GPS and interview). The documentation revealed that participants had highly subjective experiences and that their memories of these experiences were not always aligned with the in-game records of these experiences.

The use of a documentation platform, CloudPad, which was subsequently devised to annotate these documentations, revealed that documentations can operate as memory prompts not just for the audiences but also for the artists, who were inspired by CloudPad to add personal detail to the documented materials. However, while these findings were invaluable from a research perspective, the data were not subsequently turned into a documentation that could be used by museums or the public at large. As in the case of *Day of the Figurines,* the documentation remained scattered between two universities, the Ludwig Boltzman Institute Media.Art. Research, which has since closed, and the artists. This means that important insights into a work may have been systematically collected, but that no long-term preservation strategy was put in place to curate this documentation into a public-facing set of documents and no agreement with museums was made to provide access to these documentations in years to come. Still, the documentation underscored the importance of the introduction of ethnomethodological methods into the field of performance documentation, after which I decided to expand on them more systematically in a subsequent project, *Performance at Tate*.

4 Musée de la Danse, *If Tate Modern was Musée de la Danse?* (2015)

My third case study was an investigation into the rich history of performance at Tate from the 1960s to the present day. For this project, I decided to adopt some of the findings from my work with Blast Theory and the Mixed Reality Lab and investigate the role of the audience and participants in documenting the work, looking also at the value of documenting salient phases in the curatorial process, by which I mean the conversations between artists and curators at the time when the planning of the work had started in relation to the host venue, Tate Modern. The idea behind this was to look at the work as a set of processes and practices rather than as an event or object. The work selected for documentation was Musée de la Danse's *If Tate Modern was Musée de la Danse?* (2015). The choice of this work was made on the basis of the Musée de la Dance's recurrent inclusion of audiences in processes of transmission, and the documentation challenges caused by the fact that the work involved ninety dancers, lasted twenty hours over a period of two days, was streamed live and was simultaneously staged across several locations at Tate Modern. The aim of this documentation was to understand how Tate's documentation practices could be augmented by involving the audience in the process and by capturing the work both before and after it took place.

Conceptually, for the choreographer Boris Charmatz, who since 2009 had been leading the Musée de la Danse, a choreographic centre based in Rennes, dance is akin to "wearing 'glasses'" with a "corrective function" (Wood 2014). This means that one kind of institution (e.g., Tate) could be seen through the lens provided by the other (e.g., Musée de la Danse), an aspect Tate Curator Catherine Wood wanted us to capture. For this reason, we decided to employ the Mixed Reality Lab ethnographer Peter Tolmie to document how the Musée de la Danse's inhabitation of a number of spaces in the museum challenged "the viewing behaviour of visitors", turning Tate into a more fluid space, one, in Wood's words, "filled with potential" (Wood 2015).

The documentation had started well before the piece was staged at Tate Modern, so as to capture the conversations between and decisions made by Charmatz and the Tate curators Wood and Capucine Perrot, especially those pertaining to the significance of the juxtaposition of the permanent collection at Tate and the Musée de la Danse's history of work. As Tate had created an appetite for the piece in advance of the scheduled event by sharing a question via social media, asking audiences to imagine what a dancing museum would look like and to think about where it might take place, we decided to prompt social media use through a twitter Q&A, which was held with Charmatz in the lead up to the performance. The responses revealed that the audience was keen on the idea of "curating" Tate as a fluid space.

Tate's standard photography and live broadcast were used to capture the event itself, while photographer Louise Schiefer was employed to capture what visitors looked at, so as to document the work literally from the point of view of the audience. Members of the team, their families and staff at Tate were also encouraged to record their own experience of the piece via social media through the twitter hashtag #dancingmuseum created at the time of the Q&A with Charmatz. Finally, a video documentation was produced, both of the work showcased in the Turbine Hall, and of the work that took place in the Galleries, while smart-phone photography was shared using Facebook, Instagram and Twitter. The marketing photographs were shot by photographer Hugo Glendinning, prior to the opening of the piece, and influenced early responses by those members of the public who had engaged through social media.

From the documentation of the exchanges between Wood and Charmatz, it transpired that the former had envisaged for the work to be "an evolving model of the Museum," in which one place was super-imposed with another, something that is already, at least metaphorically, explicit in Glendinning's image. Wood indicated, "[i]t could be as much the planting of a conceptual perspective as a demarcated space." In particular Wood suggested, "[t]o try an astronomical metaphor, if the majority of the museum behaves according to a framework of certain space-time co-ordinates, how would the placement of the 'musee de la danse' open up an alteration of those co-ordinates, where such laws do not apply, or are 'curved'?." In other words, Wood was interested in drawing attention "to the human activity existing within all the 'found' spaces of the museum," those "'readymade' dances that are already happening there [. . .] set this in conversation with the event-dance that is programmed" (Wood 2013). So, in commissioning an ethnomethodological study and the photographers, it was decided to pay particular attention to the way audiences worked at responding to the transformation of spaces that curators had anticipated would occur during *If Tate Modern was Musée de la Danse?*

The ethnomethodological study, which covered a wide demographic, including individuals as well as families, was carried out over two visits: one set took place the weekend before the performance and the other during the days of the performance. Tolmie found that there was a constant flow throughout the galleries on non-performance days and that, generally speaking, the dwell time was short, a few seconds, maximum two minutes per work, slightly longer for video works. However, this changed significantly on performance days when dwell time in a single place could be ten minutes or more. There were also multiple choke points, that is, points where people stopped, especially at the entrances to galleries. Once performance spaces were created, people, except for children, were reluctant to cross them. Group cohesion also changed in the sense that people would usually tolerate some degree of separation in museums, but during this performance they stayed tightly together.

In response to the transformation, visitors organised themselves as audiences and started looking at the central spaces, where the performances were taking place, rather than the walls, where the Tate collection tends to be located. Visitors commented on how things were being set up and organised themselves in much the same way for both the rehearsals and the actual performances. Moreover, while visitors do not tend to look at each other much during gallery visits, they were notably looking at one another much more during the performances. In particular, the ethnomethodological study found that about 90% of visitors stopped for at least a few moments, 50% stayed for up to five minutes, and around 10% stayed across multiple performances, while less than 1% tried to walk around the gallery as though nothing was happening around them. Interestingly, while some visitors became audiences, or even participants, some amongst them also became "documentalists" by literally documenting the work photographically through social media.[1] Most visitors switched between these modes during the course of their visit. This suggests that during *If Tate Modern was Musée de la Danse?* visitors were particularly active in designing their visiting experience, which, in turn, indicates that performance may constitute a powerful mechanism in shaping museum visits as experiences.

This extensive documentation of both the expectations and reactions to the work led to the publication of a report, a thesis and numerous articles and book chapters. However, once the research was completed the documentation was not made available to the public. Nevertheless, the project did lead to a development on what is known as the Tate Live List. In addition to this, alongside Head of Collection Care Research at Tate Pip Laurenson's and the performance studies and documentation theorist Vivian van Saaze's 'Collecting Performance-based Art: New Challenges and Shifting Perspectives', this list was an outcome of the Collecting the Performative Network funded by the AHRC between 2012–14. The Live List, one of the most comprehensive frameworks about the conservation of live art that is available to the public on the Tate website, intends to produce prompts for those thinking about acquiring or displaying live works. As a consequence of findings by the *Performance at Tate* project, performance studies researcher Acatia Finbow was able to work with the conservation department at Tate to further develop this list so as to consider documentation and produce what is now known as the Live Art Documentation Template. Crucially the template looks at the life of a work in the museum and prior to its point of entrance in the museum, producing also "iteration reports" based on the model of the Guggenheim iteration reports initiated by Senior

[1] I am indebted to Annet Dekker for introducing me to this term, which is used here loosely to describe members of the public who take on the role of document creators in a systematic way.

Conservator, Time-based Media Joanna Phillips in 2015. Interestingly, the latter both includes feedback on public reception and actual visitor feedback, even though this does not tend to be in the format of documentation unless we may assume that the heading "other" could be used for this purpose. The template actually does include feedback by curators, exhibition designers, media technicians, conservators and external contractors indicating that in tracking these individuals' reasoning behind their aesthetic, conceptual, practical or economic decisions, iteration reports help generate a deeper understanding of the behaviours of an artwork under different circumstances (Time-Based Media). So, by taking the curators' point of view into account, this template could be documenting not only the artistic intention, but also, in the words of van Saaze, a work's interpretation or co-production (2013, p. 115).

These templates begin to address the fact that a work may have different iterations and that it is important to document the audience's reception of a work. However, they still only partially address the fact that some works are the result of a collaboration or even, as in the case of the two Blast Theory examples, a research collaboration. For example, in the case of the two Blast Theory works the human computer interaction design and orchestration elements are not fully captured in the documentation. This shows that it is important to include a wider range of contributors in the documentation of an artwork; that not only works belonging in museum collections are worth documenting; and that documentation constitutes a fascinating practice that museums might wish to engage with more broadly for works that have been hosted but not necessarily acquired by them. In particular, the documentation of *If Tate Modern was Musée de la Danse?* also showed the value of utilising ethnomethodological methods in documentation so as to unpack the reasons behind audience's behaviours more systematically. At the same time, the extensive documentation by and of audiences also raised interesting ethical questions as to the rights of museums to preserve such documentations without prior agreement.

5 The Cartography Project Prototype (2016–17)

The fourth case study is about a prototype platform that I developed with researchers at the University of Nottingham and Tate as part of Horizon, the EPSRC-funded *Cartography Project*. The platform, developed in 2016, consists of two parts: a web application responsible for enabling participants to input data and generate visualizations, and an associated server that is meant to store all the relevant data and allow for collaboration among users. By utilising an online interface, these may facilitate the entering of data—including text, image, video and audio commentary—pertaining to artworks, artists, participants, spectators, institutions, festivals and installations in the field of participatory art practice in museums and art galleries.

The primary purpose of the platform was to visualize the rich and burgeoning history of the field of participatory art, comprising participatory events developed by artists, practitioners and associates within and beyond the arts sector forming part of Tate Exchange. This is a new civic space in the Tate Modern Switch House, offering a site for collaborative and innovative projects, attempting to realise museum studies expert Richard Sandell's vision of a museum as an agent for social inclusion and change (2010). Initiatives like Tate Exchange suggest that museums may pursue not only the facilitation of or participation in such participatory practices, as shown by the curator and experience designer Nina Simon in her 2010 *The Participatory Museum*, but also their documentation or even co-curation.

To ensure that the platform was developed so as to generate a Cartography that would empower artists but also other practitioners and participants to document their work, a set of workshops was conducted at Tate Britain and Tate Liverpool in 2016 and 2017, in which leading practitioners from the field of participatory arts were asked to contribute their ideas to the design of the platform as well as their response to and critique of the original proposition. This iterative way of researching and developing the platform made it possible for us to consider a number of cartographic models and finally select, following the first workshop in 2016, a relational model based on the Graph Commons platform, an existing open source platform created by the artist Burak Arikan, so as to make visible the range of processes and practices that operate in this field.

A few characteristics of the field of participatory art practices played a significant role in our way of thinking about documentation in this context. As art historian Claire Bishop indicated, participatory artists often produce situations rather than objects; works of art tend to be conceived of as projects, rather than performances or artefacts; and the audience is reconceived as co-producer or participant (2012, p. 2). For this reason, we decided that it was important that the platform should support multiple perspectives and contested viewpoints; that the visualization of lineage would show long-term projects by association across countries and organizations; and that practitioners in this field be brought in the research stage already and they should also be enabled to generate entries even when they were not associated with any existing element in the Cartography. The participants in the first workshop considered the latter as particularly significant for those artists whose work may not be in a museum or gallery collection as of yet.

The participants in our first workshop also quickly identified potential difficulties, summed up by the comment: "This project needs ambassadors and community leaders to broker the information gathering." This comment suggests that the production of documentation should perhaps not happen purely online, which is confirmed by Tate's work on the five-year HLF-funded *Archives and Access* project, and that, instead, facilitated participation is essential for many audiences new to the material or the online format when it comes to their actual participation. To document participation, then, one needs to facilitate the conditions for participation in the first place.

Our second engagement workshop took place at Tate Liverpool in 2017. Liverpool has a rich history of this practice, and therefore we asked participants, who were members of three major participatory art projects in Liverpool (*OK The Musical*, *Homebaked* and *The Welsh Streets*), to feed back to us by focussing in particular on the importance of place in their work. In presenting their work to us, a number of factors became apparent. All three groups used social media (Instagram, Facebook,

Vimeo, YouTube) to illustrate their practice to us. Worryingly, this suggests that the documentation of these artists' works is currently located in third party-owned platforms in the hands of commercial providers which tend to have no basic archiving standards—which merely justified our impression that our project in itself was timely. All groups, however, indicated that at that point in time the Cartography looked like a history of art, placing artists at the centre, if in a practice that was not quite artist-centric. Moreover, some groups pointed out that the Cartography, at that stage of its development, did not visualise different versions of a work, was too static, and unable to show a whole range of materials that might be submitted, including, as in the case of *The Welsh Streets* project, letters from residents, images and photos, a play, a film, amateur responses, interviews, learning materials and even a gardening project. Finally, participants in *Homebaked* indicated that the visualisation did not communicate any sense of urgency, thus raising the concern as to why people would want to participate in such a project. Additionally, they specifically mentioned that the motivations or issues that drove their initiative—such as gentrification, housing justice—should be an option for organising or searching the platform instead of the artists' names.

The feedback from the Liverpool workshop significantly impacted on the subsequent iteration of the platform but also revealed a number of factors that in the documentation of our encounters with heritage are often forgotten. First, documentation does have an urgency as people's memories will not last forever, but we also know that not all artists are actually interested in documentation. Secondly, documentation is ethically charged, which implies that apart from participation one should also take into consideration the ethics, ownership and authority over the documentation of participation. Thirdly, in most forms of art we tend to prioritise individual artists over their collaborators, and this may go at the expense of losing significant information about a work. Finally, art should also be documented through its reception—especially in the case of hybrid, ephemeral, non-object based or subjective art—but the available means for capturing reception, as this study may have shown, tend to be extremely time-consuming and therefore unsustainable within the museum context.

While all forms of documentation are at some level hierarchical, the co-habitation of different hierarchies may be what a digital platform like that created by the *Cartography Project* can visualise in a range of ways. It is this emergent practiced space, then, this relational form of documentation, that may show us how the "History" of this particular art can be rewritten as an intersection of a whole range of "histories" of collaboration that may inspire generations in years to come. While this research identified an interesting possibility for rendering documentation a more social or even shared practice, the proposition remained at the level of theory as no further funding was made available to develop the prototype. Again, it would be interesting to see museums adopt more participatory models of documentation, so as to capture not only the ontology of a work, and the artist's intention in relation to it, but also the epistemic qualities or capabilities of a work—that is, knowledge about the contexts in which a work was co-curated, performed or even just engaged with by audiences.

6 Towards an Audience Documentation Framework

The first two case studies, *Day of the Figurines* and *Rider Spoke*, revealed the importance of capturing audience-generated documentations to understand the audience's often subjective experience of a work. In a sector which is increasingly dominated by the production of experiences, it is clearly a desirable outcome that at least some of these experiences are documented by the public as well as by professional documentalists. These two documentations also underlined the importance of capturing interdisciplinary research, design, curation and, accordingly, more general practices and processes. The case studies raised the question, however, as to who will preserve these documentations in the long run and as to whether all documentations are in fact equally valid, suggesting that the intent behind a documentation is a contextual factor that also needs to be documented.

The third case study, *If Tate Modern was Musée de la Danse?*, made it clear that even when a work is thoroughly documented by both documentalists and the public it is only when these documentations are organised (in other words curated and archived for public use) that they will remain accessible in the long run. This case study also showed that while the public has an appetite to document and to contribute documentations to museums, most museums do not have the financial means or the time to preserve these audience-generated documentations for public use. Moreover, there are various ethical considerations to be taken into account when preserving documentations created outside of the museum.

Audience-generated or audience-facing documentations tell us more about the life or trajectory of a work—to use the terms introduced by van de Vall, Hölling, Scholte and Stigter—than conventional forms of documentation. This raises a complex question in relation to an artwork's ontology (what the work is) and its epistemic potential (what knowledge it could produce), including the question as to whether the life of a work, and so the knowledge it produces, is actually part of the work. As Laurenson suggested in *Histories of Performance Documentation* (Giannachi and Westerman 2018, pp. 34–35), the two should in fact be viewed as interrelated, and artworks should be seen in their capacity to "unfold" when re-engaged with (p. 35), a term also chosen by Wijers at LiMA to describe her network which explored reinterpretation as a strategy for preservation (Wijers et al. 2017). This suggests that when documenting we need to make a work's epistemic potential more explicit, rather than focus, as we tend to do, on its ontology. In other words, we need to see the work as changing over time rather than just capture it at a specific moment in time. This also suggests that documentation is not a closed but rather an open practice, by which I mean that documentations should be periodically revisited and updated not only by curators but also by different audiences to consider new documents and their interrelationship with each other.

Finally, the last case study, the *Cartography Project*, shows that by focussing only on the artists' intention, as is traditionally common in documentation, we miss out on findings about the input of other stakeholders in the work, which, especially in the case of participatory art but also of art produced through research processes in collaboration with universities or commercial providers, as in Blast Theory's work, means that we only have one perspective about a work that is in fact often produced by a team with a wide range of competencies. Museums and other cultural organisations may wish to trace these groups of participants or researchers to build a richer history of documentation of participatory art forms. Museums may also wish to help companies to preserve their histories which are currently often shared with the public on third-party platforms, which from the angle of archival interests involve increasingly unreliable, commercial media.

In some ways it should not surprise us that, despite all this research into documentation, there is still a gap between the theory and the practice of documentation of complex hybrid artworks. In a 2001 interview published in *A Brief History of Curating New Media Art* (Cook et al. 2010), Barbara London, then curator of Media Art at MoMA, pointed out that in 1995 MoMA did not have a website and that, unlike at other museums, their website had emerged from a curatorial initiative (pp. 59–60). In other words, art museums have acknowledged websites as strategies for curation, documentation, and archiving only in the last two decades or so. This was the case for Artport, for example, launched on the Whitney Museum website in 2001 as a documentation portal dedicated to netart and digital art for which artists created splash pages on a monthly basis with links to their work as a way to document their own art (Paul in Cook et al. 2010, p. 96). The site subsequently started to commission work like Martin Wattenberg's *Apartment* (2000–2004), showing that a documentation or archival site could become both a commissioning and an exhibition site. There has not been a strong link between documentation, curation, preservation and replay or re-interpretation yet. What is more, the lack of investments in documentation, which is crucial to the other practices, means that in the future we will have only partial information about complex digital artworks at best.

While Artport only documented work at the Whitney, other websites, like Rhizome, documented across museums, raising the question as to whose responsibility it is to document and what our collective responsibility is to preserve existing documentations and their platforms. It is known that the question of what to document and archive is accelerated by new technologies. It is also known that, in the words of new media theorists Beryl Graham and Sarah Cook, "a useful thing about new media is that in some cases the media can document itself 'as it happens' because materials placed on the Internet by users are to a certain extent stored there" (2010, p. 200). However, as Katie Lips commented regarding the social media *Bold Street Project,* which uses a combination of a Website, a blog and Flickr sites to gather materials by many participants, these documentations tend to be "messy" (Lips 2007) and, therefore—as we have also seen in almost all the examples I cited—difficult to preserve and re-use in years to come. Of course, art or documents placed on third party-owned internet platforms are hardly safe, as is true of the web as a medium of preservation. Finally, audience generated documentations are rarely preserved, despite the fact that in some cases these are the only surviving records of these works.

So, we must devise more systematic ways of documenting and archiving a wider range of complex hybrid art works. We should probably now mistrust the web, where many artists and audiences deposit their documentations, for it is unclear how best to preserve and even outsource web-based documentations in the long run. Not only do we need to think of what we document but also about who should document and where we should preserve documentations. Documentations should enter museum collections alongside the artworks they are associated with. Moreover, museums may wish to archive also documentations of works that were hosted, rather than acquired, so that they too would remain accessible to the public. We know now, having traced the history of performance art documentation, that many documentations in this field turned into artworks themselves over time. So, we should learn from performance studies and start thinking about preserving documentations of all complex hybrid art more systematically, for today's documentations may be tomorrow's iterations of the work. These documentations should include materials generated by audiences at different points in time and should cross-refer to how the same work is situated in documentations produced by different museums.

In her essay 'Towards an Oral History of New Media Art,' written in 2008, new media theorist and documentation expert Lizzie Muller imagines that "it is the year 2032" and the reader is "a 25-year-old artist living in London writing a doctoral thesis on the explosion of interactive installation art at the turn of the century." The Tate, in her prediction, is hosting a "permanent exhibition devoted to computer-based interactive art from the 1970s to the present day," and while there are numerous books about the topic, there is very little available, says Muller, about how audiences at the time experienced these works (2008, p. 2). Among the works that Muller suggests do have an audience-generated record you find, she says, Blast Theory's *Day of the Figurines,* which may well be in reference to the documentation I mentioned earlier in this study. Next, Muller reminds the reader that both the Variable Media Network and the Capturing Unstable Media initiative had stated that the audience experience is important (2005). For her, a way to capture oral histories was through the video-cued recall interview technique, a proposal adapted from ethnographic methods using semi-structured interviews and exit interviews (2008, p. 4), which we adopted in the documentation of *Rider Spoke* and which indeed did generate a wealth of useful data but which, nevertheless, remained an academic exercise since the interviews were not finally integrated into a public-facing resource. Moreover, these documentations were all generated by experts, and so, in a way, shared a common objective. However, in neither case were documentations initiated by the public preserved alongside these more formal documentations. This could lead to, in the long run, the loss of the point of view of the non-expert viewer.

In her essay 'Old Media, New Media?,' Laurenson identifies "areas of focus for significant properties for software-based art that are distinct in a significant way from traditional time-based media works," and among a range of parameters she identifies visitor experience, suggesting that museums should look into "how are people intended to interact with the work? How do people interact with the work?" (in Graham 2014, p. 94). This distinction between a canonical understanding of how visitors might interact with a given work produced by artists or curators and how participants may *actually* interact with it seems to provide an interesting field of study for documentation, illustrating also how the ultimate success of creativity not only resides in the artistic intention but also in its interpretation by the audiences.

Unless we start to document artworks not only in relation to their ontology (what the work is) but also in relation to their epistemic capacity or potential (what knowledges it produces), we will only preserve part of the history of the work. This implies that a researcher in the year 2044, writing their thesis on complex digital art, will not be able to trace the history of this field any better than in 2008, or even at present, in 2019, 11 years after Lizzie Muller wrote her insightful study. Hopefully museums will continue to bring together curators and researchers to shift the field and narrow the gap between theory and practice in the intricate and yet fascinating field of hybrid mixed media art documentation.

Acknowledgements I gratefully acknowledge the following grants: 'Performance at Tate' (AH/M004228/1), Horizon (EP/G065802/1), and 'Documenting digital art: re-thinking histories and practices of documentation in the museum and beyond' (AH/S00663X/1) which funded the research underpinning this study.

References

Benford S, Giannachi G (2011) Performing mixed reality. The MIT Press, Cambridge

Bishop C (2012) Artificial hells: participatory art and the politics of spectatorship. Verso, London and New York

Cook S, Graham B, Gfader V, Lapp A (eds) (2010) A brief history of curating new media art. The Green Box, Berlin

Eco U (1979) 'Il ruolo del lettore'. In: Lector in Fabula, La cooperazione interpretative dei testi narrative. Bompiani, Milano

Giannachi G, Westerman J (eds) (2018) Histories of performance documentation. Routledge, London and New York

Graham B (ed) (2014) New collecting: exhibiting and audiences after new media art. Ashgate, Franham

Graham B, Cook S (2010) Rethinking curating: art after new media. The MIT Press, Cambridge

Latour B, Lowe A (2008) The migration of the aura, or how to explore the original through its fac similes. In: Bartscherer T, Coover R (eds) Switching codes. University of Chicago Press, Chicago, pp 1–18

Laurenson P, van Saaze V (2014) Collecting performance-based art: new challenges and shifting perspectives. In: Leino M, MacCulloch L, Remes O (eds) Performativity in the gallery: staging interactive encounters. Peter Lang, Frankfurt-am-Main, pp 27–41

Lips K (2007) Bold Street project. Paper presented at the "Had to be there symposium" Foundation for Creative Art and Technology (FACT), Liverpool, 16 Oct 2007

Muller L (2008) Towards an oral history of new media art. http://www.fondation-langlois.org/html/e/page.php?NumPage=2096. Accessed 16 June 2022

Sandell R (2000) Museums as agents of social change. Mus Manag Curatorship 17(4):401–418

Simon N (2010) The participatory museum. http://www.participatorymuseum.org. Accessed 16 June 2022

Thompson S (2002) Re: Curating critically. New Media Curating Discussion List, 12 Feb

Time-Based Media (n.d.). https://www.guggenheim.org/conservation/time-based-media. Accessed 16 June 2022

van de Vall R, Hölling HB, Scholte T, Stigter S (2011) Reflections on a biographical approach to contemporary art conservation. In: Bridgland J (ed) ICOM-CC: 16th Triennial Conference, Lisbon, 19–23 September 2011. Preprints. Critério, Lisbon, pp 1–8. http://hdl.handle.net/11245/1.344546
van Saaze V (2013) Installation art and the museum. Amsterdam University Press, Amsterdam
Wijers G, Garcia Diaz L, Sancto C (eds) (2017) Unfold: mediation by re-interpretation. https://www.li-ma.nl/lima/sites/default/files/Unfold_verslag_excl.pdf. Accessed 16 June 2022
Wood C (2013) Personal email to Boris Charmatz, Performance at Tate archive
Wood C (2014) Personal email to Boris Charmatz and Martina Hochmuth by Catherine Wood, Performance at Tate archive
Wood C (2015) 'If Tate Modern was the Musée de la Danse?', programme notes

Gabriella Giannachi is Professor in Performance and New Media at the University of Exeter. She has published *Virtual Theatres* (2004); *The Politics of New Media Theatre* (2007); *Performing Nature: Explorations in Ecology and the Arts*, ed. with Nigel Stewart (2005); *Archive Everything* (2016 and, in Italian, 2021); *Histories of Performance Documentation,* co-edited with Jonah Westerman (2017); *Documentation as Art,* co-edited with Annet Dekker (2022) and *Technologies of the Self-Portrait* (2022 and, in Italian, 2023).

Sharing Knowledge in Art Conservation: From Repository Building to Research Publishing

Dušan Barok

Abstract As contemporary art makes its way into museum collections, knowledge sharing between organisations is important for developing a common frame of reference and identifying best practices in an evolving field, but is hampered by ethical, legal and technical complexities. In this article, I ask how constraints to knowledge and documentation sharing between institutions can be overcome. Over the past decades, there have been a number of initiatives for the inter-institutional exchange of documentation and research materials on the conservation of contemporary art. I focus on an online database project created by the International Network for the Conservation of Contemporary Art (INCCA) to share conservation documentation among practitioners in a semi-public setting. The main success of the INCCA database appears to have been to provide access to templates of forms and reports used in emerging practice, and to enable networking and increased exchange between members. I further identify the network as a research-based initiative and recognise its role in consolidating the conservation of contemporary art as a discipline. I conclude that this shift has precipitated the movement of knowledge exchange away from the circulation of data in the network to publicly oriented knowledge production.

Keywords Art conservation · Contemporary art · Documentation · Database · Network · Research · Publishing

1 Introduction

Contemporary art challenges standard notions and conduct in museums. Artworks such as installations, performances and media art appear in changing iterations and their meaning is often conveyed through their intangible aspects, their biography and tacit knowledge of the artist and the museum (Hummelen and Scholte 2004, p. 208).

D. Barok (✉)
Oslo, Norway
e-mail: db@societyofalgorithm.org

R. van de Vall, V. van Saaze (eds.), *Conservation of Contemporary Art*, Studies in Art, Heritage, Law and the Market 9, https://doi.org/10.1007/978-3-031-42357-4_13

Although collecting institutions have embraced contemporary art, they often lack adequate expertise and resources to care for it. The non-object-based nature of this art creates requirements on laborious testing of new methodologies and increased emphasis on documentation (Heydenreich 2011; van de Vall 2015; Phillips 2015). Meeting the special requirements for its preservation and presentation (van Saaze 2013) is further hindered by its generally secondary position to the more widely recognised older works. One remedy for organisations has been the pooling of resources for the development of new working methods and the co-production of documentation. Here, however, they face another obstacle. Collecting institutions as a whole are reluctant to convey practical knowledge about works of art. This is mainly for their commitment to confidentiality set out in the museum code of ethics, but also for their prevailing attitude of concealment in preservation matters (ICOM 2017, p. 42; Frasco 2009, pp. 85–92; van Saaze 2011, pp. 250–251; van Saaze 2013, pp. 20–24, 43; Scheidemann 2016). As contemporary art enters collections, knowledge sharing between organisations is important for the development of a common frame of reference and the identification of best practices in an evolving field, but is hampered by ethical, legal and technical complexity. How to solve this problem? Is it possible to overcome the constraints on the distribution of knowledge and documentation between institutions? And if so, how to organise this exchange so that it is beneficial for preservation practice?

To answer these questions, in this article I study initiatives for the interinstitutional exchange of documentation and research materials on the conservation of contemporary art. I focus on an online database project set up by the International Network for the Conservation of Contemporary Art (INCCA) in a pioneering effort to share conservation documentation among experts in a semi-public setting. I place it in a historical context and identify a set of motifs that shaped its mission and form. My analysis of its use over time reveals a combination of factors that contributed to its eventual decline. The main success of the INCCA database appears to have been to provide access to the templates of forms and reports used in emerging practice and enable networking and intensify exchanges between members. My examination of INCCA's further efforts leads me to identify the network as a research-based initiative and recognise its role in consolidating the conservation of contemporary art as a field. I conclude that this shift has precipitated the diversion of knowledge exchange from the circulation of data in the network towards public oriented knowledge production.

2 Setting Ground for Sharing Knowledge in Contemporary Art Conservation

Issues in modern and contemporary art conservation have been discussed among collecting institutions for several decades. An early, significant undertaking to establish a framework for cross-institutional collaboration was an international symposium organised by Heinz Althöfer in Düsseldorf in 1977. For fifteen years prior to the event, he worked as conservator at Kunstmuseum Düsseldorf that during that time acquired works by contemporary local artists such as Zero Group and representatives of *Objektkunst* (Althöfer 1977, p. 13). Althöfer organised the symposium shortly after his appointment as head of a newly established municipal scientific conservation laboratory, notable for its access to an x-ray machine allowing for more nuanced investigation of objects.[1] The aim was to align its working agenda with the needs of art museum collections in the wider geographical area and establish a research programme on the restoration of modern and contemporary art (Caianiello 2005, p. 41).[2] The idea was to discuss the questions of modern art conservation in a small working group. The group eventually grew to 58 individuals who gathered at the symposium entitled *Restaurierung moderner Kunst* (1977), coming primarily from museums and organisations in West Germany, but also in Brussels, Amsterdam and Copenhagen and including the coordinator of ICOM's Working Group on 20th Century Paintings.[3]

Althöfer's 'Working Programme' written after the symposium as the opening essay for proceedings does not deal with issues of painting exclusively, even though they are in majority. Attention is paid to other media and materials, as well as to the conservator's judgment (decay intervention, replaceability/fixability of engines). Althöfer concluded the essay by listing seven problematic subjects in the conservation of modern and contemporary art. Four points relate to heavily crackled, detached, multi-layered paintings, large format paintings, monochromatic painting and coloured canvas. The fifth highlights the use of non-traditional materials in collage and combine painting as well as paper, photography, plastics, and plexiglas. The sixth adheres to the "ideological" question of interference in the natural decay of materials such as chocolate and fat. The last one discusses the repairability of engines. All in all, the 1977 manifesto formulated theoretical issues of the originality and authenticity of modern art as conservation questions. At the closing of the symposium, a working group was set up to follow upon the programme, albeit for the next two decades the activity of the Düsseldorf laboratory remained largely local.[4] The symposium, however, directed the attention of conservators to changing artworks and to the necessity of interpretative judgment.

Another legacy of this early initiative was the recognition of the necessity of contact and collaboration between conservators and other professions, as well as an outline of the path towards it. In his Düsseldorf manifesto, Heinz Althöfer called for

[1]The institution continues to exist today as the Restaurierungszentrums der Landeshauptstadt Düsseldorf/Schenkung Henkel. Since 2019, the centre is led by Joanna Phillips, formerly head of media conservation at Guggenheim Museum, New York.

[2]"Restaurierung moderner und zeitgenössischer Kunstobjekte" in the original German. Author's translation.

[3]The group was renamed the Modern and Contemporary Art Working Group by 1981 (Weiss and Stoner 1981, 81/6/1-9).

[4]Notably, between 1978–1981, the Restaurierungszentrum conducted a survey of 442 objects and between 1979–1983 it collected 39 questionnairies from artists (Weyer and Heydenreich 1999).

the intensification of contacts with artists, manufacturers, art historians, museum professionals, scientists and collectors (1977, p. 8). Following the symposium discussions, Althöfer concluded that in order for this to happen, "first, a collection of facts [about materials and methods] is required, followed by an exchange of facts," and emphasized that "materials and methods should be investigated scientifically" (1977, p. 8).[5]

While collecting institutions continued to develop strategies for preserving changing artworks, significant cross-institutional partnerships began to emerge only much later. Among the most influential were Variable Media Network (2001–2004) and Matters in Media Art (2003–2015). Both were designed as consortia of museums and archives aiming to develop best practice protocols for the collection and preservation of media art.[6] If their efforts resulted in models and guidelines for the care of time-based media, they did not establish means for documentation interchange. The Variable Media Network published several brief case studies, intended to illustrate the hypotheses of documentation model rather than serve as a platform for exchange (Depocas et al. 2003, pp. 70–114).

Efforts for both the development of new preservation strategies and establishing a platform for sustained distribution of knowledge and data found common ground in another large-scale initiative, entitled International Network for the Conservation of Contemporary Art (INCCA). The network is active to this day and offers a compelling example of how contemporary art conservation has sought to reconcile collaboration and sharing with conservation ethics.

3 International Network for the Conservation of Contemporary Art

INCCA has played a key role in catalysing cooperation among institutions collecting contemporary art. Since its foundation in 1999, the initiative organised three multi-annual projects, two large conferences, a number of seminars, workshops and exhibitions, published two books, realised dozens of case studies and initiated interest- and regional networks. Today it counts over two thousand institutional and individual members worldwide. On an ongoing basis, members publish announcements on the INCCA's online platform, which has become a go-to source for professional news from the field. For the purpose of this essay, I will focus on one section of the platform, a database for conservation documentation. I will investigate

[5] Author's translation.

[6] The Variable Media Network was founded by Guggenheim Museum and Daniel Langlois Foundation, Montreal. Its members included Berkeley Art Museum/Pacific Film Archives (Berkeley), Franklin Furnace (New York), Performance Art Festival+Archives (Cleveland), Rhizome.org (New York) and Walker Art Center (Minneapolis). Matters in Media Art was a consortium of three major museums: MoMA, SFMOMA and Tate. See the projects' websites at http://web.archive.org/web/20190209014527/http://www.variablemedia.net/e/welcome.html and mattersinmediaart.org.

motivations behind establishing this resource as a platform for circulating knowledge and data among organisations, how did it resolve confidentiality concerns and to what extent has it contributed to improving the care of contemporary art.

The emergence of INCCA is firmly linked with a defining moment in the area of contemporary art conservation. In the 1990s, many museums began to see that their acquisition, registration and decision-making needs to be adapted to meet the demands of new art, but it was not clear how. With this in mind, the international symposium *Modern Art: Who Cares?* was organised in Amsterdam in 1997. It was hoped that the programme leading up to the event would help collecting institutions build confidence and bolster legitimacy to deal with "non-traditional objects of modern art" (Sillé 1999, p. 14). This was to be achieved by creating new models for registration and decision-making, and developing new terminology and workflows along the way (Sillé 1999; Berndes 1999). The symposium was attended by 450 professionals (Marontate 1997). In terms of scale, it was the largest gathering on the conservation of art of living artists, comparable to general conferences of learned societies in well-established disciplines.[7] Representatives from key museums such as Tate, V&A, Guggenheim, National Gallery of Art, Stedelijk Museum, Van Abbemuseum, Pompidou and MUMOK were present.[8]

One aim of the event was to design a common pool of resources and expertise among collecting institutions. A seminar was dedicated to establishing an international electronic network (Schinzel and Hummelen 1999). The rapidly growing World Wide Web could improve communication and access to much needed information on artists' materials and techniques. The participants began outlining a website which would accommodate this exchange. In addition, it would host discussions, profiles of professionals and other resources (Schinzel and Hummelen 1999, p. 340).

The symposium organiser, the Netherlands Institute for Cultural Heritage (ICN), followed upon these objectives and together with Tate and nine other museums and organisations prepared a multi-annual project which received funding from the European Commission.[9] The newly established International Network for the

[7] Six months after the *Modern Art: Who Cares?* symposium, the Getty Conservation Institute organised a conference explicitly dedicated to contemporary art. The three-day long *Mortality Immortality? The Legacy of 20th-Century Art* attracted over 350 participants (Constantine 1998). It brought together "professionals from a range of disciplines—artists, museum directors, curators, conservators, art historians, dealers, collectors, and scientists, as well as a philosopher and a lawyer—to offer their individual perspectives on the intent of the artist, the effect of the art market, ways to cope with rapidly evolving media technologies, and fine art as popular culture" (GCI 1998).

[8] Aside from museums, there were participants from research centres and universities such as Restaurierungszentrum Düsseldorf, Konservatorskolen Copenhagen, University of Ghent and Academy of Fine Arts in Warsaw. Alongside conservators, the interdisciplinary setting gave voice to academics and researchers, curators, scientists, museum directors and artists.

[9] The founding consortium also included Guggenheim Museum, SMAK Ghent, MUMOK Vienna, SBMK (Netherlands), Restaurierungszentrum der Landeshauptstadt Düsseldorf, Konservatorskolen Copenhagen, La Caixa Foundation (Barcelona), Galeria d'Arte Moderna in Turin and Academy of Fine Arts in Warsaw.

Conservation of Contemporary Art created a website as the backbone of the initiative. When it went online in the early 2000s, it was a cutting-edge resource for the new field. It featured announcements, a bibliography, member profiles and, notably, a database of artists' archives designed to handle documentation, supported by a custom thesaurus (Wharton 2005, pp. 174–175).

For the remaining decade, INCCA's core activity was a series of European projects. They represented a pioneering example of coordinated action among dozens of collecting institutions. The questions pertained to the practical issues of restaging works but also more general issues such as methodologies.[10] Results were made accessible to members in the form of metadata in the INCCA database, dossiers on dedicated websites, and articles. There was no journal devoted to this area of study, and there still isn't one.[11] But INCCA's cooperative, practice-oriented and organised approach to studying works and issues helped to professionalise conservation research and contributed to establishing this domain in academia as well. The scholarly aspect of INCCA was supported by the continuous presence of universities and research organisations among partners.[12]

Today, INCCA continues to operate as a key agent in contemporary art conservation. Technically, it does not have a legal body; rather, it is a long-term activity of the Dutch governmental agency for cultural heritage (Rijksdienst voor het Cultureel Erfgoed, RCE).[13] It has a steering committee, bylaws and counts a steadily growing number of members worldwide (exceeding 2200 as of 2019, see Fig. 1).

[10] The network organised numerous case studies, two large conferences, a number of seminars, workshops and exhibitions, published two books, initiated interest and regional networks and accumulated hundreds of documents in its database.

[11] Art conservation journals include *Studies in Conservation* published by the International Institute for Conservation of Historic and Artistic Works (IIC) in London since 1952; *Journal of the American Institute for Conservation* published by the American Institute for Conservation of Historic and Artistic Works (AIC) since 1960; *Journal of the Institute of Conservation* published by ICON in London since 1977; *Conservation Journal* published by V&A Museum in London since 1991; *Technè* published in Paris since 1994; and *Journal of Conservation and Museum Studies* published by Institute of Archaeology of UCL London since 1996.

[12] On average, they made up one third of its 16 to 30 partners per project.

[13] The INCCA initiator ICN became part of RCE in 2011. Between 2007–2021, the network coordinator Karen te Brake-Baldock occupied the post of "(inter)nationale kennisnetwerken" in the department "Rijkserfgoedlaboratorium" (National Laboratory). See RCE (n.d.). Ilka van Steen and Paula Chang successively took on the role of INCCA coordinator. Previously, Tatja Scholte served in the role from 1999–2007 (Learner 2014).

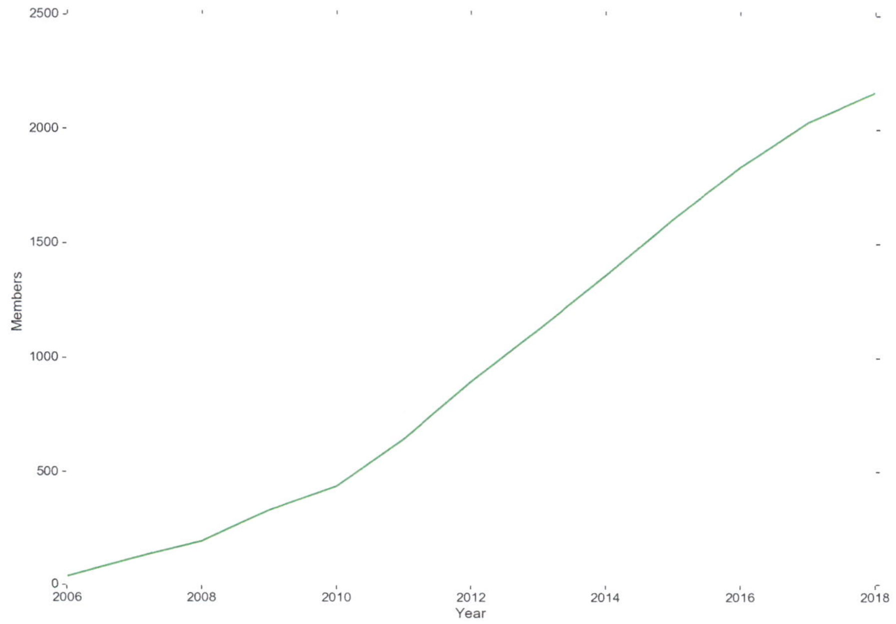

Fig. 1 Number of members of INCCA (This and all graphs included in this chapter result from my analysis of the snapshot of members and documents data from the website incca.org taken on 15 October 2018. The snapshots were created by scraping the website as data could not be exported directly)

4 INCCA Database

Today, the INCCA database makes up the 'Member documents' section of the more extensive INCCA's online platform (Fig. 2). The main section of the platform today is also populated by member contributions, which are publicly accessible and include event and publication announcements and diverse news from the field.

The database contains references to 1100 documents situated in more than 90 organisations. An analysis of the entries according to document type shows that artist interviews now make up the bulk of content, roughly one third (Fig. 3). This is despite the fact that they are just one form of recorded exchange with artists. Other forms are marginal. For example, questionnaires, make up only 4%, artists' statements 2%, and correspondence less than 1%. One reason for this could be that their inclusion has not been explicitly encouraged. In the case of correspondence, it is also much less portable and more ephemeral type of documentation. Interviews in the INCCA database also outcount other, more traditional forms of museum records such as conservation reports, condition reports, installation guidelines and treatment reports. How can this preference for sharing interviews be explained? Why was it perceived as beneficial for preservation practice?

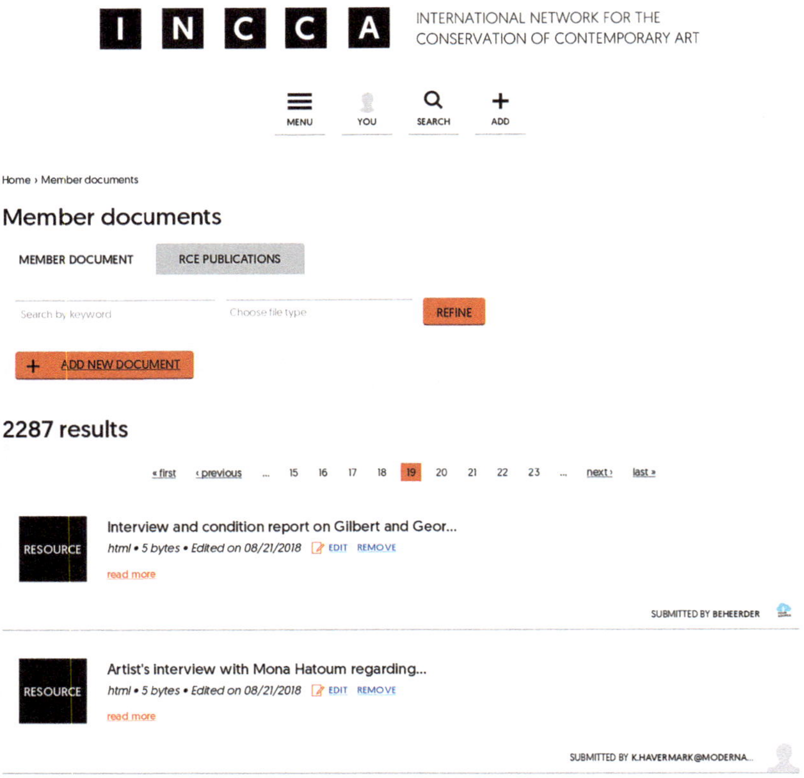

Fig. 2 The INCCA database section of INCCA online platform, 2019 (Screenshot taken from https://www.incca.org/search?search_api_multi_fulltext=&node_field_free_tagging[0]=6344&page=19)

In its mission of advancing art conservation through research and documentation, INCCA echoed calls for researching and exchanging information about materials and methods issued at the Düsseldorf conference two decades earlier (Althöfer 1977, p. 8).[14] As I will argue, Althöfer's emphasis on scientific investigation has been taken up in INCCA through increasing association with academia. But what is more important now, rather than *facts* per se: the founders of INCCA put *the artist* into the centre of attention. The artist's opinion was considered relevant not only for weighing options for material treatment, but came to be recognised as crucial for preserving (conceptual) *identity* as opposed to state of the artwork.

Pip Laurenson (2006) defines the concept of the identity of the work as what "describes everything that must be preserved in order to avoid the loss of something

[14] Author's translation.

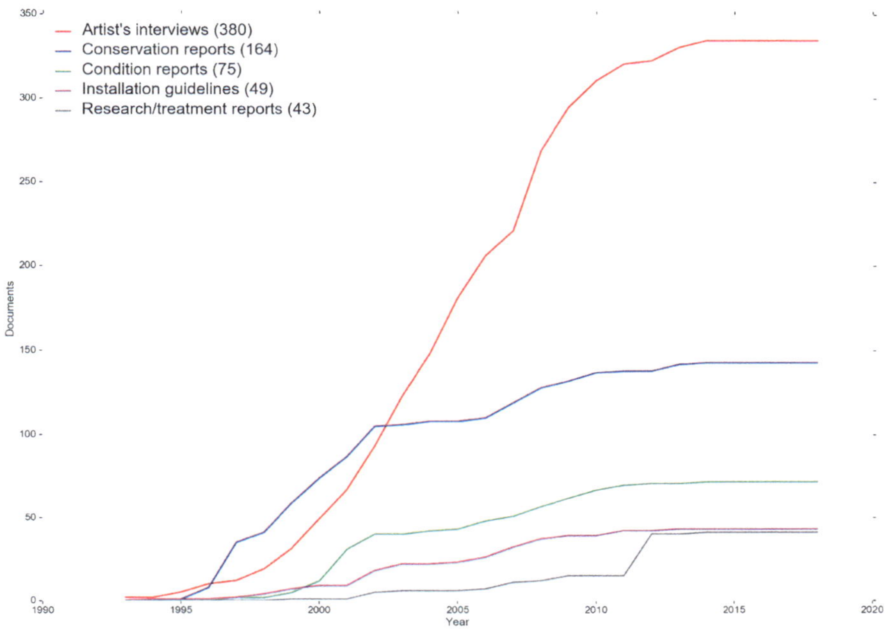

Fig. 3 Number of documents in the INCCA database per type (five largest shown) (This graph does not represent the time when the respective documents were entered into the database; this information was not available for the analysis. Rather, it represents the moment when the documents were originally created)

of value in the work of art." This shift in focus reflected the changing direction of conversations in the domain of art conservation in the 1990s with respect to the iterativity of the artwork. Artist interviews would record the opinion of the artist and the process of weighing possible options together with the conservator, gradually articulating the artist's intent. Before then, artists were rarely involved in conservation. In fact, museums seldom followed a systematic approach, nor did they build registries for future reference (Weiss and Stoner 1981). This is why the INCCA network prioritised interviews as the principal research material right from its inception when it specified in more detail its priorities as to set up "the relevant joint international guidelines" for artist interviews, conduct them in order to "collect information direct[ly] from the artist" and build for them a shared registry (Hummelen 2000; Scholte et al. 2001).[15]

However, museums collect information from artists under the condition of confidentiality, which is one of the guiding principles in museum practice and conservation. In its code of ethics, the International Council of Museums (ICOM)

[15] Later, its twofold aim was reframed more broadly as to "collect primary source information from artists' archives or artists and their representatives" and to share knowledge and (especially unpublished) information for conservation purposes (Hummelen and Scholte 2012).

prescribes museum professionals to "protect confidential information obtained during their work" and remember that "information about items brought to the museum for identification is confidential and should not be published or passed to any other institution or person without specific authorisation from the owner" (ICOM 2017, p. 42).[16] Collecting institutions are therefore bound to shield documentation from the public as it contains sensitive details. In order to balance professional ethical standards and demand for a cross-institutional resource, INCCA founding members settled on limiting the database content to metadata rather than full documents, in addition to restricting access to members (Tatja Scholte, personal communication, 23 April 2019). As a result, the database provides members a catalogue of records for materials they can request from their individual contributors.[17] This is in contrast to the rest of its online platform which is public without restrictions. First limited to the network's initiators, membership had been soon expanded to professionals and researchers from across the field. While it offered benefits such as creating public profiles, the most important factor in the expansion of member base was to gain direct access to unpublished research and information in the database, according to a user survey (Brake-Baldock 2009).[18] More specifically, over two thirds of respondents stated that they search the content several times a year to make use of existing interviews and questionnaires for research and as aids for their own organisations (Brake-Baldock 2009). This confirms that artist interviews were indeed the driving force behind the operation of INCCA database.

Despite the increasing relevance of documentation for preserving art, contributions have decreased sharply, however (Fig. 4). How can this be explained? In what follows, I suggest several factors responsible. I will also address the question of whether this also implies that improving the care of contemporary art by maintaining a cross-institutional resource for documentation is no longer viable.

5 The Impact of Cultural Policies on INCCA's Changing Forms of Collaboration

The analysis of annual contributions to INCCA database reveals that the vast majority of documents were created between 1999–2011. This period corresponds to the duration of INCCA's main research undertakings. While INCCA's pilot project (1999–2002) concentrated on conducting artist interviews, producing

[16]The principle has been also adopted by national conservation institutes. For example, see the code of ethics of the American Institute for Conservation (AIC), point 7, https://www.culturalheritage.org/about-conservation/code-of-ethics.

[17]Currently, INCCA steering committee is considering merging the database with its platform and opening up collected metadata records to public, with an opt-out option for contributors (Karen te Brake-Baldock, personal communication, 16 April 2019).

[18]In 2009 survey, 29 out of 40 respondents considered it important, unlike 5 who thought otherwise.

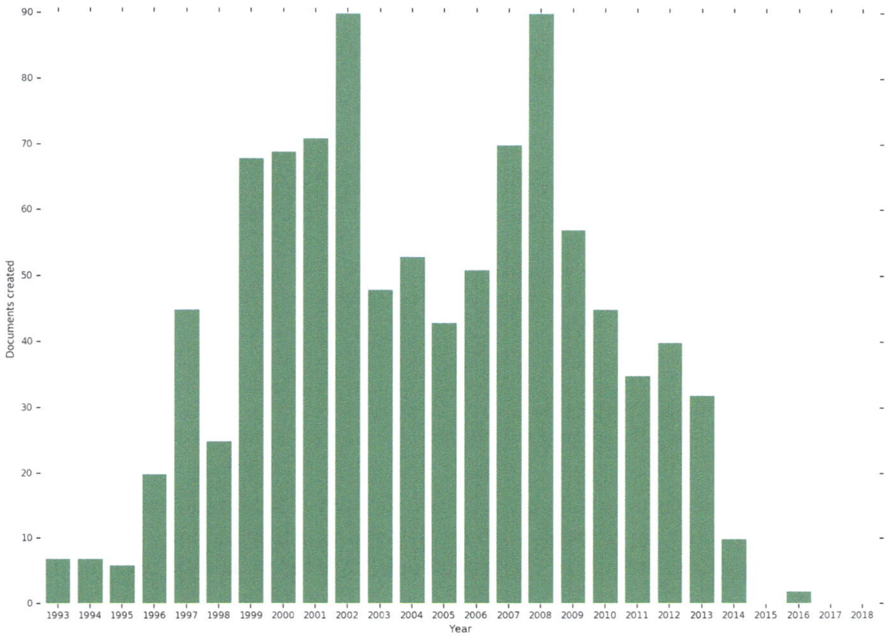

Fig. 4 Number of records in the INCCA database per year of creation

guidelines as well as developing an online database for their registration along with other documentation (Hummelen et al. 1999; INCCA 2002; Hummelen and Scholte 2004, pp. 210–212), it was followed by *Inside Installations* (2004–2007) that kept focus on the artist as a primary source of information but narrowed it down from studying intent across each oeuvre to case studies of selected works. Here, the participating organisations investigated and documented over thirty complex installations from their collections, the process of which was presented and analysed in three exhibitions, a scholarly online publication and a book published through an academic press (Hummelen and Scholte 2006, pp. 8–9; Scholte and 't Hoen 2007; Scholte et al. 2007; Scholte and Wharton 2011).[19] The third, and to this day, last major research initiative of INCCA was entitled *PRACTICs* (short for *Practices, Research, Access, Collaboration, Teaching In Conservation of Contemporary Art*, 2009–2011). Here, the attention leaned towards the profession of conservation itself and explored ways how it can be taught and communicated to the public. Rather than documenting artworks, participants produced a documentary film, seminars and two major symposia, and initiated long-term working groups for education and selected geographic regions (INCCA 2011; McCoy 2010). Taking the three projects together, across the span of a decade we can observe a gradual transition of emphasis from

[19]The *Inside Installations* book was eventually published in 2011, as part of the next project *PRACTICs*.

Table 1 Focus shift in INCCA projects

Project	Duration	Main focus	Key method	Documentation sharing	Main outcomes
INCCA	1999–2002	Artist	Interview	Metadata (members only database)	Online platform, Database
Inside Installations	2004–2007	Artwork (Installation art)	Case study	Articles, Documents	Online knowledge base, Exhibitions
PRACTICs, Access2CA	2009–2011	Conservation community, Public	Dialogue, Discussion	–	Symposia, Book,[a] Film, Working groups

[a] The main symposium, *Contemporary Art: Who Cares?*, as well as the book produced in the framework of *PRACTICs* feature results of the previous project, Inside Installations

building professional information commons, through collaborative knowledge production and publishing to public-facing dialogue and discussion (Table 1). With these developments, the role of non-public databases faded into the background.

Does this mean that museums no longer needed to exchange data and insight as a means to improve the care of contemporary art? I will argue that the answer to this question is deeply conditioned by changing conditions of international cooperation in cultural heritage in Europe where the majority of INCCA members operate. The relevance of studying the impact of funding on contemporary art conservation has been recognised earlier (van Saaze 2011, p. 251) and the following analysis takes a step in this direction.

INCCA's core activities were made possible through cultural funding from the European Union (EU). In fact, INCCA's foundation in the late 1990s coincided with an extension of the domain of cultural policy of the EU to movable heritage. The Union identified its mandate for action in this area primarily as the promotion of networking and partnerships. The repositioning of cultural heritage funding not only made it possible for INCCA to facilitate international programme but had a direct impact on its methods of knowledge production and sharing.

The EU's predecessor, European Communities (EC), first introduced funding for cultural heritage in the early 1980s. Scholars in critical heritage studies identified several factors responsible for it. In the period of energy crises and unfolding economic recession, the EC entered a crisis of political legitimacy. This context prepared a ground for "the idea that monuments and sites could act as a remedy, tying citizens together" (Niklasson 2017, p. 142). By then, it was accepted that social integration will not come about merely as a by-product of economic integration (Shore 2000, p. 18). Other reasons included Italy's continuous call for funds for its cultural heritage, the accession of Greece into the EC, the will to counterbalance American and Japanese cultural authority, and the desire to participate in the international movement for heritage protection (Niklasson 2016). The European Historical Monuments and Sites Fund (EHMF) was established to support the reconstruction of monumental heritage sites linked to national states. In practice, the scheme sponsored primarily restorations of the archaeological sites of "European significance" with Parthenon and Acropolis as flagship projects (Niklasson 2016, pp. 18, 90–91).[20]

In the next decade, in the wake of the Maastricht Treaty (EC 1992), the political climate was different. First of all, the fall of the Berlin Wall activated the process of enlargement to the east. The end of the Warsaw Pact marked the emergence of a multipolar world, in which the role of new Europe was uncertain. In the EU, identity politics took precedence, as was soon manifested in the introduction of the EU flag, an anthem and exchange study programmes. This corresponded to a change in its stance on cultural heritage. The economic value of culture had always been essential to the Commission where heritage sites were seen as drivers for tourism. But the policies prioritising monumental sites that emblematise origin myths of nation states were sidelined in the climate of integration. They could no longer be trusted to convey the testimony of European past on their own (Niklasson 2017, pp. 146–147).

In 1997 the European Commission launched a union-wide action programme in the area of cultural heritage, Raphael.[21] The Commission set networking and partnerships as one of its main domains of funding.[22] Projects with participants from multiple countries were more likely to get support. As it happened, both *Modern Art: Who Cares?* and INCCA were part of the first generation of international heritage actions financed through this scheme. It was natural to seek funds for an international initiative in contemporary art conservation from EU's new cultural heritage programme, as it had no precedent or comparable alternative. The flagship of the nascent INCCA became an online database pioneering novel means of collaboration in cultural heritage.

The subsequent framework, Culture 2000, merged together EU's three cultural financing programmes and in terms of heritage it prioritised the so-called "Cultural Heritage Laboratories." Here, rather than an instrument of integration, cultural heritage became a "vehicle of cultural identity." It was against this context that the INCCA network received financial support for more scholarly oriented, case-based research into preserving installation art under *Inside Installations* (2004–2007). Consequently, the priority in cultural funding in the Culture 2007 scheme shifted

---

[20] While EHMF distributed 42.7 million ECU to restoration action in 459 projects, financial support for Parthenon and Acropolis alone amounted to 5.5 million ECU (Niklasson 2016, pp. 90–91).

[21] Along with the programmes for "contemporary creation" and books and reading, called Kaleidoscope 2000 and Ariane, respectively (GRRP4 2015, p. 8).

[22] The program was divided into five areas, with international networking and partnerships spanning all of them. The areas were "Networks and partnerships" (roughly: thematic networks, collaboration of museums and research institutes, research publications), "Cooperation with third countries and international organizations" (World Heritage List sites preservation, comparative research), "Development and promotion of the cultural heritage in Europe" (preservation and management of sites, laboratory research), "Access to heritage" (memorial events, multilingualism, digital points of access), and "Innovation, further training and professional mobility" (research, conferences, exchange programmes, ICT training). See European Community (1995, p. 4).

Table 2 The impact of European cultural policy on INCCA research design (based on European Commission (2017) and Niklasson (2017))

Programme	Period	Priority	Goal	Supported project
Raphael	1997–1999	Professional networks & partnerships	European integration	INCCA
Culture 2000	2000–2006	Research projects, "laboratories"	European identity	Inside Installations
Culture 2007	2007–2013	Circulation (of workers & works), dialogue	European citizenship	PRACTICs/ Access2CA
Creative Europe	2014–2020	Networks & platforms	Creative innovation	

in favour of fostering the development of European citizenship, encouraging cross-border mobility of cultural operators and works of art as well as intercultural dialogue. The public-oriented *PRACTICs* was supported through this scheme.

In retrospect, it is apparent that European Union's changing cultural policy shaped the objectives and methods of INCCA projects (Table 1), as can be observed in the network's transition of emphasis from collecting information through producing knowledge to presentation (Table 2). The support scheme was revised several times in the past twenty years, largely in line with changes to how culture was instrumentalised to meet the political and economic priorities of EU. While in the 1990s, the EU viewed culture as a vessel of integration, the current Creative Europe scheme (2014–2020) frames culture as a catalyst for creativity, growth and employment, perceiving it as an engine of competitiveness on the world stage. In effect, EU's support of cultural heritage gradually shifted from professional networks to creative platforms. By then, however, INCCA stopped seeking financial support as a cultural heritage project and instead aligned itself with academic initiatives funded through the EU's research and development programme.

The structural reliance of INCCA's focal activities on EU's changing policies explains why maintaining an online catalogue of documentation was seen as a viable way to share expertise only in its early stage, resulting in its eventual retreat. This is not the sole factor, however.

6 From Building Repository to Research Publishing

The process of setting up the INCCA database involved extensive discussions of the project group on whether to include full documents or merely metadata, what should be their structure and which system to adopt (Tatja Scholte, personal communication, 6 July 2017). It was clear, though, that regardless of what information would be shared, access should be restricted to members. Within several years the situation somewhat changed. The sensitivity of conservation information about art objects had been allowed more nuance when it was agreed that documentation of case studies in the Inside Installations project would be published online without restrictions. However, instead of creating a new, public section in the existing INCCA database, the project group decided to build a new website for this purpose. One reason for this was that its structure proved too restrictive. For example, information did not always come from an artist but often from other stakeholders, including artist's studios, foundations and galleries. More importantly, rather than restricted to self-contained individual files, documentation of contemporary artworks typically includes multi-layered and interdependent items such as interview recordings, transcriptions and notes, threads of e-mail communication and data and multimedia supporting condition reports.

This can be illustrated by Pierre Huyghe and Philippe Parreno's processual work *No Ghost Just a Shell* (1999–2002), selected for a case study in *Inside Installations*. The work revolves around a virtual manga figure brought to life by 18 different invited artists who featured it in paintings, videos, wallpaper, music and various objects. The works were shown separately on various occasions and eventually drawn together in a travelling exhibition that ended at the Van Abbemuseum, where it was acquired for the collection in its entirety (van Saaze 2013). The exhibition was stage-managed by Huyghe and Parreno and later shown in a different version at other locations. The museum, however, was still not prepared to display the work without assistance of the artists.[23] For that reason, as part of INCCA's project, the museum's curator and head of collections, Christiane Berndes, decided to set up the exhibition anew but in different formats and to ask Huyghe and Parreno for their reaction. The process involved a series of new "instalments" at different locations. On this occasion, the researcher conducted meetings and exchanged e-mails with the work's stakeholders. The case study's dossier on the *Inside Installations* website provides a narrative account of staging each iteration and contextual documentation, including the section 'Artists interviews' featuring an inventory of five meeting reports and e-mail correspondence with artists' assistants and three artist contributors (Fig. 5).[24] Like other dossiers on the website, its layout had to be adjusted to document this specific artwork.

The database format may be suitable for the description of documents according to complex categories, which facilitates their identification, especially if the content of the documents itself is not included. This was the case of the INCCA database (Fig. 6). Nevertheless, even in contemporary database systems, it would be difficult to extract this complex descriptive information automatically and instead need to be entered manually, which is a lengthy process. In addition, it is hard to comprehensively record the layered relationships between documents in tabular form. The database is not flexible enough to accommodate descriptive nuances and relations

[23] http://web.archive.org/web/20071021093447/http://www.inside-installations.org/artworks/detail.php?r_id=378&ct=research.

[24] http://inside-installations.sbmk.nl/artworks/artwork.356.interview.html. In addition, the dossier contains a bibliography of writings by and about Parreno, including those related to the work. http://inside-installations.sbmk.nl/OCMT/mydocs/pp%20hov%20bibliography.pdf. For a detailed analysis of the work's "career" in the museum, see Van Saaze (2013, pp. 143–180).

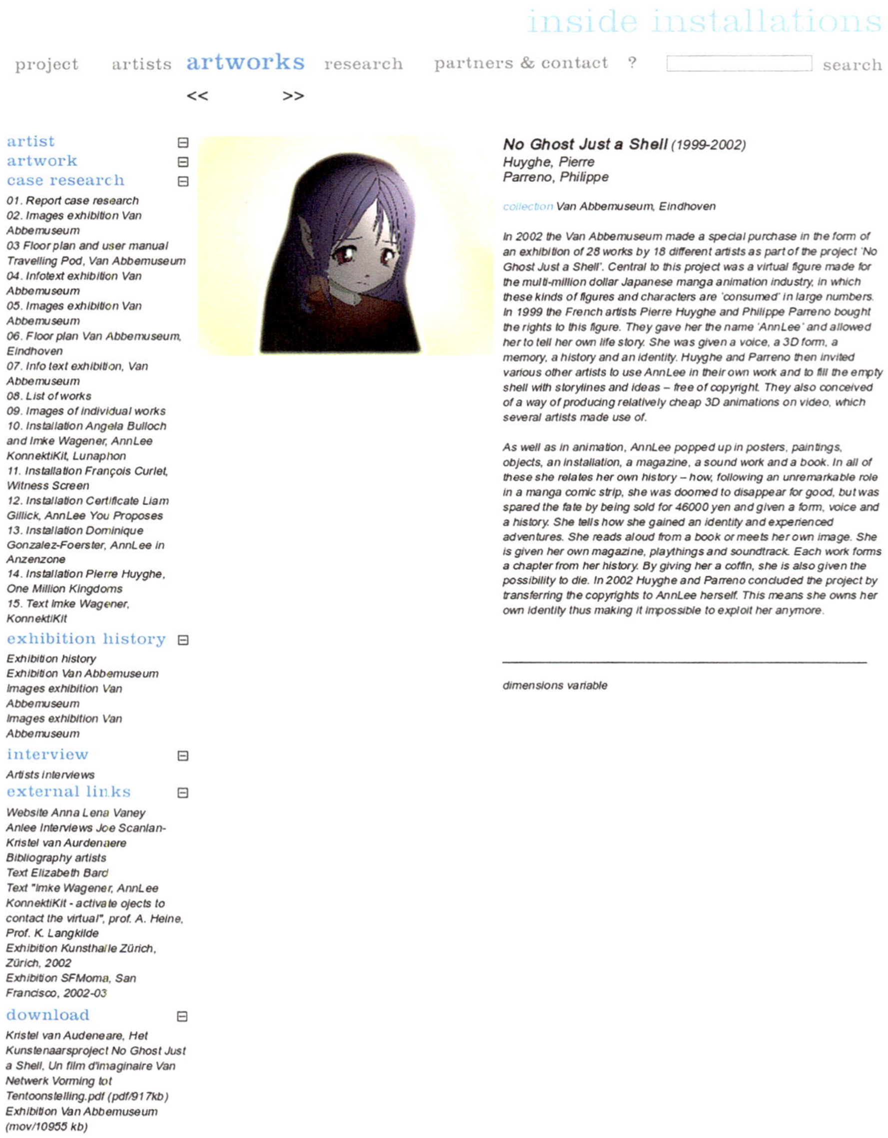

Fig. 5 *No Ghost Just a Shell* on the *Inside Installations* website (Screenshot taken from http://inside-installations.sbmk.nl/artworks/artwork.356.html)

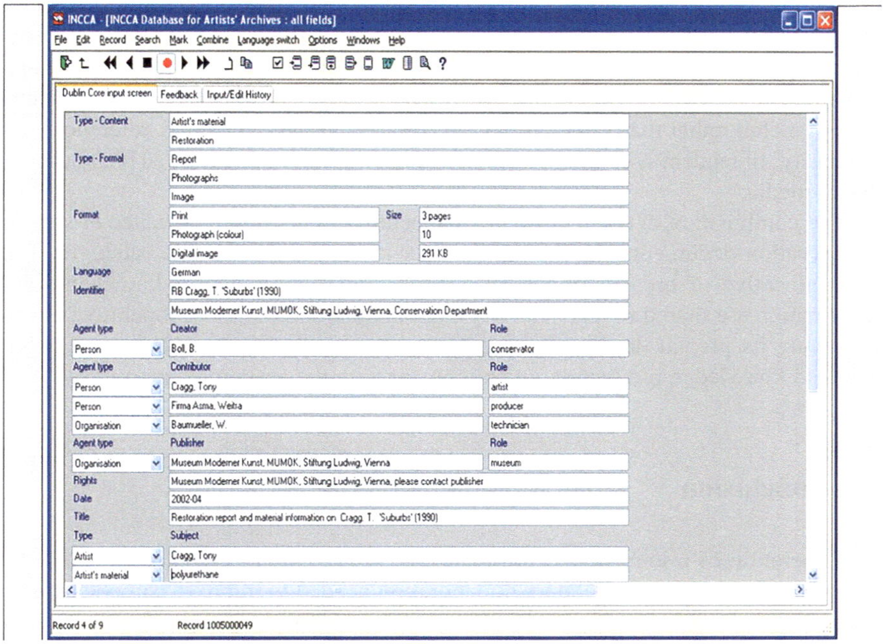

Fig. 6 Section of INCCA database editor, 2004

between documents. Similar challenges are well known from operating collections management systems that are designed to handle object-based works (van Saaze 2013). A more common practice is to store the breadth of documentation in intricate folder structures on an intranet. This informed the way *No Ghost Just a Shell* and other works are presented on the Inside Installation website.

Another factor in INCCA's database decline is that reports and other documents are structured and use language particular to an institution, as they are not intended for outside use. Substantial effort is needed to make the content and structure of conservation records legible to third parties. This was confirmed in the INCCA user survey that identified the main reason preventing members from contributing as "the documentation [not being] organised enough for distribution to colleagues" (Brake-Baldock 2009). In addition, some documents have since become inaccessible due to changes in staff, confidentiality levels or technical reasons.

We may also observe that over the years, the domain of contemporary art conservation has changed significantly. Specialisations have emerged in time-based media, software-based art, performance, biological materials, plastics and other sub-areas. Document and material types have diversified rapidly, and the metadata sharing approach may prove insufficient for works of art consisting of time-based media and datasets. These areas need to identify and develop their contact points in different ways, rather than a universal registry.

Not less importantly, it appears that the network has established itself as a field. With the growing demand for contemporary art conservators, specialised educational opportunities continue to expand, while professional and academic events have mushroomed.[25] Practitioners and researchers might not feel exactly as members of a club rather than colleagues with common sense of practice, references and solidarity. In tandem with this, much exchange has moved to informal channels and social media.

The combination of these factors explains the decline of the relevance of sharing conservation documentation through an inter-institutional reference catalogue. It is also indicative of broader transformations in the ways in which knowledge and information are shared in this field. My examination of INCCA's cooperative efforts following its pivotal database project shows that central to this shift were public oriented knowledge production and alignment with the academic community.

7 Conclusion

The operation of a joint digital infrastructure is one way of creating the space for international and interdisciplinary collaboration needed to improve competencies in the preservation of contemporary art. In the late 1990s, a group of conservators, curators and researchers representing a number of collecting institutions joined forces to establish a network, INCCA, to meet these needs. Their starting point was the realisation that in order to preserve works of art, it is necessary to bring artists and stakeholders to the table, together with conservators and curators. The new initiative designed goal-oriented and practise-based research that brought together practitioners (museum professionals) and researchers (research centres, universities). They set up a database to collect references to research materials and documentation and make them available to participants and others in need. After several large-scale projects, however, sharing activity declined sharply and the relevance of the model could no longer be taken for granted.

I identified a range of phenomena that hinder the further relevance of online record repositories for sharing knowledge in art conservation. In practical terms, the content and structure of conservation documentation is rarely legible to third parties and the tabular database is often not flexible enough to accommodate descriptive nuances and relations between documents. At the structural level, the primary focus of EU policies on cultural funding have shifted from supporting networking to creative industries, where competitiveness rather than care has been promoted. In addition, in recent decades, contemporary art conservation has established itself as a field, became collegial and much of the exchange is taking place through informal

[25] See https://monoskop.org/Art/Conservation#Events for an overview of contemporary art conservation symposia, conferences, workshops and seminars.

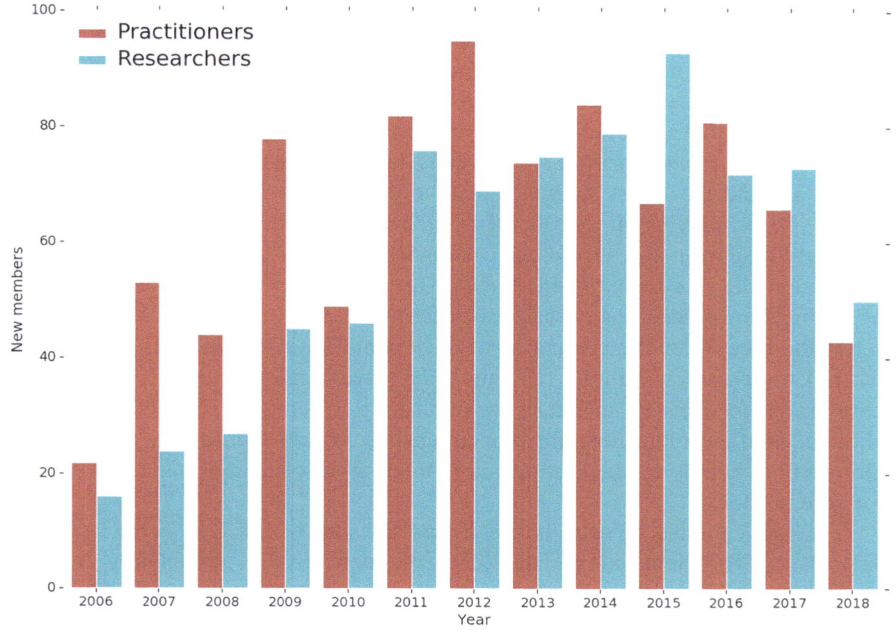

Fig. 7 Professional affiliations of new members of INCCA annually

channels and social media. And as it becomes ever more diverse and specialised, the need for a single resource for the whole field is not as strong.

The key here is INCCA's identity as a research-based initiative. What had been once a progressive approach to tackling practical issues through conducting research and distributing results has now become a norm. Institutions no longer need to rely on an umbrella organisation to initiate collaborative research, nor do they depend solely on a central platform to amplify research results. Rather, its potential lies in facilitating communication and contacts in what can be called networked scholarship. Quan-Haase, Suarez, and Brown note that "networked scholarship can entail exchange of information, insights, and advice across geographic and disciplinary boundaries within connected networks focused on thematic research questions" (2014, p. 14). The 'News & Events' section featured on the frontpage of the INCCA platform could provide a basis for network development in this direction. Further support is offered by the changing structure of the INCCA membership base, but also in the wider field of art conservation. As my analysis shows, while the base was originally made up mainly of practitioners, by 2010 professional researchers matched their annual number of new members (Fig. 7). In a broader sense, the proliferation of scholarly research has led to the professionalisation of conservation research, as is evident from the number of major academic-led research initiatives in recent years.[26] I have argued that this has reduced the relevance and appeal of providing access to conservation documentation as a way of sharing knowledge in favour of scholarly and research publishing.

Publications are not limited to articles, proceedings and monographs but extend to knowledge bases and research catalogues, the example for which was set with the website for INCCA's *Inside Installations* discussed above. More recent examples include the *Rauschenberg Research Project* of SFMOMA and the Rauschenberg Foundation and the Artist Archive Initiative of the New York University, which started, interestingly, from the side of an archive rather than museum collection.[27] Although these open access research catalogues contain a large amount of data and information, they are primarily article-based and provide a narrative interpretation of the findings on a case-by-case basis for each work of art included. This approach moves the focus from the circulation of documents as such to their use as archival material to support narration. This not only solves legibility problems, but also leaves room for clearing materials for publishing in terms of sensitive details. In addition, it offers more flexibility in organising content than a tabular database. Ultimately, scholarly research brings more funding opportunities than the construction of repositories.

This shift can also be seen in the recent redesign of INCCA website (Brake-Baldock 2014). Launched in late 2016, the new layout prominently features announcements of new books, articles, conference videos and other publications, many of which are available in open access.[28]

As museums are currently adopting a policy of open access to collection information, they herald openness as a means of ensuring their social function (Bailey 2019). The trajectory of INCCA can be read in parallel with this call. Starting by sharing documentation metadata through a common protected online resource, the participating museums eventually embraced openness by other means: publishing.

Acknowledgements I would like to thank Karen te Brake-Baldock for her contributions and support during my internship at INCCA's hosting organisation, the Cultural Heritage Agency of the Netherlands. I would also like to express my gratitude to Julia Noordegraaf, Tatja Scholte, Renée van de Vall, Sylvia van Schaik, Ron Kievits, Yuri van den Linden, Kris Roderburg, Frank Bergevoet, Cor Mulders and Daphne Nieuwenhuijse, as well as the anonymous reviewers, for their contributions. Earlier versions of this essay were presented as talks at the NACCA | MACCH Conference at the Jan van Eyck Academie in Maastricht and the ICOM 25th General Conference/CIDOC Annual Conference in Kyoto, both in 2019. The research was realised as part of the Marie Skłodowska-Curie Innovative Training Network *New Approaches in the Conservation of*

[26]For example *New Strategies in the Conservation of Contemporary Art* (*NewS*, 2009–2013), *Network for Conservation of Contemporary Art Research* (*NeCCAR*, 2012–2015), *New Approaches in the Conservation of Contemporary Art* (*NACCA*, 2015–2019), *Cultures of Conservation* (2017–2022), *Conservation of Art in Public Spaces* (*CAPuS*, 2018–2020) and *Documenting Digital Art* (2019–2022).

[27]See http://inside-installations.sbmk.nl/, https://www.sfmoma.org/rauschenberg-research-project/ and http://artistarchives.hosting.nyu.edu/Initiative/, respectively. The Artist Archives is currently dedicated to the work of David Wojnarowicz and Joan Jonas.

[28]https://incca.org/updates.

Contemporary Art (*NACCA*), funded by the European Union H2020 Programme (H2020-MSCA-ITN-2014) under Grant Agreement no 642892.

References

Althöfer H (1977) Arbeitsprogramm für die Restaurierung moderner und zeitgenössischer Kunst. In: Althöfer H (ed) Restaurierung moderner Kunst. Restaurierungszentrum Düsseldorf, Düsseldorf, pp 6–8

Bailey J (2019) Solving art's data problem – Part one, Museums. Artnome. https://www.artnome.com/news/2019/4/29/solving-arts-data-problem-part-one-museums. Accessed 29 Jan 2022

Berndes C, Working Group Registration and Documentation (1999) New registration models suited to modern and contemporary art. In: Hummelen Y, Sillé D (eds) Modern art: who cares? An interdisciplinary research project and an international symposium on the conservation of modern and contemporary art. Foundation for the Conservation of Modern Art and Netherlands Institute for Cultural Heritage, Amsterdam, pp 173–177

Brake-Baldock K (2009) INCCA survey summary. ICN, Amsterdam

Brake-Baldock K (2014) The new INCCA website: giving context to curated information on the conservation of contemporary art. In: ICOM-CC 17th Triennial Conference 2014 Melbourne. https://www.icom-cc-publications-online.org/PublicationDetail.aspx?cid=2dda0cee-e806-45e1-b75b-0e64e76df257. Accessed 29 Jan 2022

Caianiello T (2005) Der "Lichtraum (Hommage à Fontana)" und das "Creamcheese" im museum kunst palast. transcript, Bielefeld

Constantine M (1998) Preserving the legacy of 20th-century art. The GCI Newsletter 13.2. http://www.getty.edu/conservation/publications_resources/newsletters/13_2/feature1.html. Accessed 29 Jan 2022

Depocas A, Ippolito J, Jones C (eds) (2003) Permanence through change: the variable media approach. Solomon R. Guggenheim Museum, Daniel Langlois Foundation, New York, Montreal

European Commission (2017) Mapping of cultural heritage actions in European Union policies, programmes and activities. European Commission-Culture, Brussels

European Community (1992) Treaty on European Union. Official Journal of the European Communities 35.C191

European Community (1995) European Community action in support of culture. Brussels

Frasco L (2009) The contingency of conservation: changing methodology and theoretical issues in conserving ephemeral contemporary artworks with special reference to installation art. University of Pennsylvania, Philadelphia

Getty Conservation Institute (1998) Mortality immortality? The legacy of 20th-century art (1998). In: The Getty Conservation Institute. http://www.getty.edu/conservation/publications_resources/public_programs/conferences/20thart.html. Accessed 29 Jan 2022

GRRP4 (2015) The evolution of EU cultural policy in the post-Maastricht period. https://cultureactioneurope.org/files/2015/12/The-Evolution-of-EU-Cultural-Policy-in-the-Post-Maastricht-Period.pdf. Accessed 29 Jan 2022

Heydenreich G (2011) Documentation of change – change of documentation. In: Scholte T, Wharton G (eds) Inside installations: theory and practice in the care of complex artworks. Amsterdam University Press, Amsterdam, pp 155–171

Hummelen Y (2000) International Network for the Conservation of Contemporary Art (INCCA). In: Newsletter of ICOM CC – Working Group Paintings. ICOM Committee for Conservation. http://web.archive.org/web/20010427223513/http://cecor.eba.ufmg.br/icom-cc/index/organiz/HPAGEWG/newsletters/NEWSLEtter_p1_2.htm. Accessed 29 Jan 2022

Hummelen Y, Scholte T (2004) Sharing knowledge for the conservation of contemporary art: changing roles in a museum without walls. Stud Conserv 49(2):208–212. https://doi.org/10.1179/sic.2004.49.s2.045
Hummelen Y, Scholte T (2006) Capturing the ephemeral and unfinished: archiving and documentation as conservation strategies of transient (as transfinite) contemporary art. Technè 24:5–11
Hummelen Y, Scholte T (2012) Collecting and archiving information from living artists. In: Stoner JH, Rushfield R (eds) Conservation of easel paintings. Routledge, London
Hummelen Y et al (1999) Pilot project "Artists' interviews". Netherlands Institute for Cultural Heritage, Amsterdam. http://web.archive.org/web/20010726072849/http://www.icn.nl/engels/6.4.3.html. Accessed 29 Jan 2022
ICOM (2017) ICOM Code of ethics for museums. International Council of Museums, Paris. https://icom.museum/wp-content/uploads/2018/07/ICOM-code-En-web.pdf. Accessed 29 Jan 2022
INCCA (2002) Guide to good practice: artists' interviews. INCCA, Amsterdam. https://www.incca.org/articles/incca-guide-good-practice-artists-interviews-2002. Accessed 29 Jan 2022
INCCA (2011) PRACTICs. http://web.archive.org/web/20140721035055/http://www.incca.org/practics. Accessed 29 Jan 2022
Laurenson P (2006) Authenticity, change and loss in the conservation of time-based media installations: a conceptual framework for traditional fine art conservation. In: Tate Papers, no.6, Autumn 2006. https://www.tate.org.uk/research/publications/tate-papers/06/authenticity-change-and-loss-conservation-of-time-based-media-installations. Accessed 3 Feb 2022
Learner T (2014) Karen te Brake-Baldock on INCCA's past, present and future. Modern Materials and Contemporary Art Newsletter 3:16–20. http://www.icom-cc.org/54/document/mmca-newsletter-april-2014/?action=Site_Downloads_Downloadfile&id=1311. Accessed 29 Jan 2022
Marontate J (1997) Modern art: who cares? Boekmancahier 9(34):407–418
McCoy R (2010) Contemporary art: who cares? A discussion with Karen te Brake-Baldock. Art21. http://magazine.art21.org/2010/07/20/contemporary-art-who-cares-a-discussion-with-karen-te-brake-baldock/. Accessed 29 Jan 2022
Niklasson E (2016) Funding matters: archaeology and the political economy of the past in the EU. Stockholm University, Stockholm
Niklasson E (2017) The Janus-face of European heritage: revisiting the rhetoric of Europe-making in EU cultural politics. J Soc Archaeol 17(2):138–162. https://doi.org/10.1177/1469605317712122
Phillips J (2015) Matos LA, Macedo R, Heydenreich G (eds) Reporting iterations: a documentation model for time-based media art. Revista de História da Arte 4:168–179. http://revistaharte.fcsh.unl.pt/rhaw4/RHAw4.pdf
Quan-Haase A, Suarez JL, Brown DM (2014) Collaborating, connecting, and clustering in the humanities: a case study of networked scholarship in an interdisciplinary, dispersed team. Am Behav Sci 59(5):565–581. https://doi.org/10.1177/0002764214556806
Rijksdienst voor het Cultureel Erfgoed (n.d.) K.E. (Karen) te Brake-Baldock. https://erfgoedmodernetijd.nl/gebruikers/karen-te-brake-baldock. Accessed 29 Jan 2022
Scheidemann C (2016) Why not ask the artist? VoCA J. https://journal.voca.network/why-not-ask-the-artist/. Accessed 29 Jan 2022
Schinzel B, Hummelen Y (1999) An international computer network for the exchange of information on artists' materials and techniques. In: Hummelen Y, Sillé D (eds) Modern art: who cares? An interdisciplinary research project and an international symposium on the conservation of modern and contemporary art. Foundation for the Conservation of Modern Art and Netherlands Institute for Cultural Heritage, Amsterdam, pp 336–340
Scholte T, 't Hoen P (eds) (2007). www.inside-installations.org. Project Presentation and preservation of installation art. ICN/SBMK, Amsterdam. https://www.sbmk.nl/source/documents/inside-installations-kl.pdf. Accessed 29 Jan 2022

Scholte T, Wharton G (eds) (2011) Inside installations: theory and practice in the care of complex artworks. Amsterdam University Press, Amsterdam. https://library.oapen.org/handle/20.500.12657/33489. Accessed 29 Jan 2022
Scholte T et al (2001) The INCCA Project. http://web.archive.org/web/20010715045257/http://www.icn.nl:80/engels/6.2.html. Accessed 29 Jan 2022
Scholte T et al (2007) Inside installations. https://inside-installations.sbmk.nl. Accessed 29 Jan 2022
Shore C (2000) Building Europe: the cultural politics of European integration. Routledge, London
Sillé D (1999) Introduction to the project. In: Hummelen Y, Sillé D (eds) Modern art: who cares? An interdisciplinary research project and an international symposium on the conservation of modern and contemporary art. Foundation for the Conservation of Modern Art and Netherlands Institute for Cultural Heritage, Amsterdam, pp 14–19
van de Vall R (2015) Documenting dilemmas: on the relevance of ethically ambiguous cases. Matos LA, Macedo R, Heydenreich G (eds) Revista de História da Arte 4:7–17. http://revistaharte.fcsh.unl.pt/rhaw4/RHAw4.pdf
van Saaze V (2011) Acknowledging differences: a manifold of museum practices. In: Scholte T, Wharton G (eds) Inside installations: theory and practice in the care of complex artworks. Amsterdam University Press, Amsterdam, pp 249–255
van Saaze V (2013) Installation art and the museum. Amsterdam University Press, Amsterdam
Weiss K, Stoner JH (1981) Documenting contemporary art collections: a survey. In: Preprints: ICOM Committee for Conservation, 6th triennial meeting, Ottawa, 21–25 September 1981. ICOM Committee for Conservation, 81/6/1-1-12
Weyer C, Heydenreich G (1999) From questionnaires to a checklist for dialogues. In: Hummelen Y, Sillé D (eds) Modern art: Who cares? An interdisciplinary research project and an international symposium on the conservation of modern and contemporary art. Foundation for the Conservation of Modern Art and Netherlands Institute for Cultural Heritage, Amsterdam, pp 385–388
Wharton G (2005) The challenges of conserving contemporary art. In: Altshuler B (ed) Collecting the new: museums and contemporary art. Princeton University Press, pp 163–178

Dušan Barok is an artist, researcher, and organizer whose work is concerned with digital culture, memory, and activism. He studied information technology at the University of Economics in Bratislava, networked media at the Piet Zwart Institute in Rotterdam, and media and memory studies at the University of Amsterdam. He is founding editor of a research platform for the arts and humanities, Monoskop, and has been involved in collectives including 3/4, Burundi.sk, Multiplace and La Société Anonyme. In 2020, he initiated New Media Museums, a project aimed at improving the care of time-based media art in public collections in Central Europe.

Collections of (An)archives: Towards a New Perspective on Institutional Collecting of Contemporary Art and the Object of Conservation

Aga Wielocha

Abstract The immanent features of contemporary art, understood as a new paradigm of artistic practice, call for new approaches to the institutional collecting and all interrelated practices, including conservation. The identity of a contemporary artwork is distributed between physical objects and processes, and concepts and contexts, which shape an artwork throughout its career. These intangible agents often exist in, and thus might be transmitted only through, various kinds of documents. The resulting documentation does not only contain information about an artwork's provenance, history, meanings and character but it hosts an important part of the artwork itself. As decisions about the future presentations of artworks, and hence their interpretations, are made on the basis of documentation, the latter not only shapes but also determines the future of contemporary artworks. Still, in today's museum practice the documentation is often secondary when compared to physical objects and undervalued within the hierarchy of museum priorities. This essay traces emergent institutional attempts to link, both conceptually and practically, museum collections and collection-related documentation. Its aim is to demonstrate that these approaches, while initially developed to address needs differing from traditional conservation, can serve as sources of inspiration for the development of long-term preservation strategies for contemporary art.

Keywords Contemporary art museums · Conservation · Documentation · Artworks as archives · Collection management systems · Museum databases · Cataloguing of contemporary art

---

This chapter presents part of doctoral investigation conducted by the author at the University of Amsterdam within the framework of European Marie Skłodowska-Curie Innovative Training Network *New Approaches in the Conservation of Contemporary Art* (*NACCA*) between 2016 and 2020; see Wielocha (2021).

A. Wielocha (✉)
Bern Academy of the Arts, Bern University of Applied Sciences, Bern, Switzerland
e-mail: aga.wielocha@hkb.bfh.ch

R. van de Vall, V. van Saaze (eds.), *Conservation of Contemporary Art*, Studies in Art, Heritage, Law and the Market 9, https://doi.org/10.1007/978-3-031-42357-4_14

1 Introduction

Contemporary art presents a challenge to the preservation of artworks, a task considered to be one of the principal duties of the museum as a collecting institution. This issue is not new and has been addressed multiple times by academics and museum practitioners from different disciplines, such as art history and theory (e.g., Buskirk 2003; Dekker 2018), curatorial studies (e.g., Altshuler 2005; Graham 2014), cultural anthropology (e.g., Domínguez Rubio 2014) and conservation (Wharton 2005; Scholte and Wharton 2011). Building on this body of work, this essay proposes that this challenge originates in the object-based nature of art museums, and offers an approach that may help museums to adapt to the needs of contemporary art.

In contemporary art the boundary between artworks and documents is increasingly blurry, a development stimulated by a dynamic coming from both sides. On the one hand, a great deal of performance and conceptual art documentation that has entered museums in various ways, whether as photographs or videotapes, has taken on the status of belonging to "the work" itself over time (Westerman and Giannachi 2017). On the other hand, the physical art objects acquired by museums often deteriorate or cease to function, leaving behind documentation that can substitute or represent the artwork or be used for the artwork recreation (Gordon 2015; Hölling 2015). Furthermore, many contemporary artworks when not installed "exist" only in the form of instructions and documentation (Laurenson 2004; Phillips 2015). Many consider documentation a primary tool for conservation of contemporary artworks, such a sin relation to, for example, time-based media art (Laurenson 2006; van Saaze 2015). And finally, the appreciation, comprehension and use of many contemporary artworks rely on the documents produced around it.

Unlike other memory institutions like libraries and archives, museums have been designed as collectors of objects from the outset. Whereas over the last decades the concept of "heritage" changed significantly and now also includes intangible forms of expression and art has become more conceptual, processual, relational and less focussed on physical finished products, the organisation and practices of art museums have remained by and large object-based. Even though the documentation of a contemporary work of art carries a large part of its identity and often renders the physical object readable as an artwork, museums do not tend to consider art objects and documents as equally important categories. While art objects enter the collection, as part of the museum's core activity, more or less related documents are distributed between various, often unstable micro-archives (Wharton 2015; Hölling 2013) which traditionally fulfil an auxiliary function. The practices related to collecting and collection care are prioritised accordingly. Upon acquisition, art objects need to be crated, insured, shipped, registered, catalogued, checked and stored in appropriate conditions. In comparison, the effort and resources allocated in the production and care of documentation are usually significantly smaller.

In this chapter I argue that to secure the continued cultural relevance of contemporary art, museums need to address this ambiguity involved in the role of artworks versus the role of documentation. Museums need to revise the corresponding practices by considering artwork-related documents as objects of conservation that are as important as the art objects collected. To do so without revolutionising the traditional concept of the museum as built around a collection of objects, documents need to be included in the museum collection and be accessible on the same terms as art objects. Departing from the notion of artwork as an archive introduced by conservation theorist Hanna Hölling, this chapter outlines a theoretical proposal that could potentially facilitate incorporating this change.

My argument in this contribution develops in four steps. First, I focus on the content and structure of artwork-related documentation in art museums, touching on rising importance of documentation as a conservation tool and the challenges related to documenting contemporary art within the museum setting. Next, building on the approach of French documentalist Susan Briet and her concept of "the dynamism of living documentation," I propose a conceptual framework for documentation of an artwork within the context of an institutional collection. Thirdly, I provide a description of practices employed by two museums together with the context in which those practices were developed. Both institutions have approached the challenge of bridging the categories of artworks and documents for different purposes, but following similar conceptual underpinnings. The case studies demonstrate that it is possible to rethink the traditional museum structure and adjust it to the needs of contemporary art and that the effort to question and challenge their own specific systems allow to shed new light on artworks, the process of their musealisation and their institutional lives and futures. Finally, I introduce the theoretical model of artwork-as-(an)-archive, as a reflection on the challenges regarding the implementation of this model, while also indicating several potential directions of further research.

Before proceeding to this chapter's main body, three additional remarks are relevant. While the first remark pertains to clarifying how I conceive of contemporary art in the context of this chapter, the second remark explains how I approach the difference between artwork and art object here, and the third one sheds light on the specific notion of conservation employed. The way the term "contemporary art" is used in this study is related less to a particular moment in time or an art-historical period than to art that exemplifies particular features. As such this approach follows the definition by sociologist Natalie Heinich, who proposes that contemporary art should be considered as a new paradigm of artistic practice, an aesthetic category within the arts. Within this framework she contends that "the artwork is no longer exclusively the actual object proposed by the artist, but rather the whole set of operations, actions, interpretations, etc., brought about by this proposition" (Heinich 2014, p. 35). Following this particular understanding of "contemporary art," this chapter will distinguish between "artworks" and "art objects." Both terms commonly circulate in the fields to which this study relates—art history and conservation—and are often used interchangeably. Nevertheless, as I argue, in the case of contemporary art the substance and identity of the artwork lies beyond its physical embodiment, which, in the context of a museum collection, I will call an "art object."[1] Starting from the assumption that the traditional notion of conservation needs to be expanded in order to ensure the future of contemporary works of art, this chapter uses the term "conservation" in a specific way. Conservation is understood here as an approach that includes all activities that stem from the methodological recognition of an artwork's identity, is aimed at safeguarding the artwork's continuation, and is performed in an informed, structured and documented manner (Wielocha and Markevicius 2019). This expanded notion of conservation, crafted for the purpose of addressing contemporary art with a primary focus on a museum framework, is understood as a set of scientific, technical and social activities that are performed by various individuals and groups, including conservation professionals (Avrami et al. 2000). Moreover, conservation is regarded here as a comprehensive effort of the entire collecting institution that acts on behalf of the communities which it represents.

2 Documentation in a Museum Collection Context and Challenges Related to Documenting Contemporary Art

Conventionally, artwork-related documentation—seen from an institutional perspective—encompasses the description of the physical characteristics of an artwork, contextual or interpretive writings relating to it and information required to manage it (Seren 2001). It may consist of various types of documents of different provenance (Haylett 2019). The first type is information supplied by an artist, artist's studio, former owner or a gallery that facilitates artwork's purchase or acquisition, and this category covers drawings, sketches, certificates, installation manuals, artist's statements etc. The second one is the information on an artwork's biography and the context of its creation gathered by an institution, including artwork's provenance, exhibition history, information about the artist and the description of similar artworks by the artist held in other collections. The third category includes documents coproduced by the artist (studio, estate, gallery) and the institution, such as contracts, pre-acquisition questionnaires, communication with artists, interviews. The fourth type comprises documents produced by a museum during the institutional life of an artwork, for example descriptions, visual documentation, technical manuals, equipment lists, display requirements, condition reports, loan agreements, treatment reports, iteration reports etc. The last type consists of documents produced by the

[1] A similar consideration was presented by philosopher and conservation theorist Renée van de Vall while addressing the issue of change: "we need to distinguish between changes which have an impact on the work as an artwork, and thereby on the range of appropriate interpretations, and changes which only affect the work as an object, leaving its possible interpretations unchanged" (van de Vall 2015, p. 296).

artwork itself, such as records of interaction with the public for participatory works (see Haylett 2019). This category often includes physical objects, such as props produced for a particular iteration of a performance piece, or obsolete functional equipment that bears witness to the artwork's technological history. If all abovementioned categories might overlap and intermingle, one will always run into documents that fit neither of them. The way the documentation of a musealium can be outlined and organized within an art museum varies from one institution to the next and depends on a museum's history, subject, scale and structure. Still, there are various common approaches, procedures, workflows and standards (Wythe 2004). In most institutions the operational core and the main reference in structuring the information about collected artworks is the Collection Management System (CMS), software that offers a database for tracking information related to particular objects. Usually, the record of a musealium in the CMS includes all the basic factual data about an artwork, as well as references to other sources of information. However, the CMS often does not allow for storing and managing multiple graphic and textual documents (Barok et al. 2019), which are therefore frequently placed in various micro-archives, both analogue and digital (Hölling 2018).[2] The way the documents are dispersed among these archives varies depending on an institution's departmental structure. For instance, correspondence with the artist about the artwork collected may be kept in the acquiring curator's private archive, while information on how an artwork should be displayed may be found in the records of an exhibition in which it was presented. Numerous institutions work with so-called "object files" that compile essential information related to artworks, and allow this information to be shared between departments and with the public, mostly by appointment. Still, the content of "object files" and the way information is organised and gathered changes from museum to museum, to the extent that in some institution different departments run their own "object files," e.g., Curatorial Object Files or Conservation Object Files (Hölling 2018; Wielocha 2021; Wythe 2004).

Traditionally, the goal of documentation as a conservation tool focused on describing the art object "in the best objective way possible" (Dekker et al. 2012, p. 22), mainly by means of text, numbers and images. Most of the conventional documentation methods consisted—and in many museums still consist—of different kinds of imaging techniques and measurements and are akin to natural science research. Yet, with the shift in artistic practices in visual arts, the scope and the role of documentation has changed significantly. To ensure the future comprehensibility of the art created in the last decades, documentation has to cover multiple dimensions of the artwork's nature. This may pertain to documenting its physical appearance such as the space, acoustics, light levels, tactility and olfactory effects, as well as the way one enters and leaves the installation (Laurenson 2004; Trevisan

[2] It is important to note that collection management systems are mostly created by private companies and are undergoing constant development. Consequently, a lot of deficiencies described in the literature in the last decade has been addressed and fixed progressively. This does not mean, however, that all new features are implemented in museums immediately; such implementation often depends on the scale and resources of an institution.

2013), but also relate to conceptual characteristics such as function, interactivity, variability and meanings, which are hardly representable by images and numbers. Moreover, as the identity of a contemporary artwork is defined in the introduction, which renders it less a physical object and more a set of operations, actions and interpretations to a certain extent conveyed through its intangible aspects, the importance of documentation as a conservation method for contemporary art forms has shifted significantly (Almeida Matos et al. 2015; Heydenreich 2011; Hummelen and Scholte 2004, 2006). As Pip Laurenson once claimed, in reference to time-based media art: "conservation is no longer focused on intervening to repair an art object; it is now concerned with documentation and determining what change is acceptable and managing those changes" (Laurenson 2004, para. 5).

In parallel to changes in the role of documentation in contemporary art conservation practice, both theoretical and technical approaches to documentation have evolved as well. In the first place, the field has, by and large, come to acknowledge the subjectivity of the documentation process as being dependent on the selection criteria of documentalists, as well as other factors (Stigter 2015; van Saaze 2015). This, in turn, coincided with the accessibility of new technologies for document management, storage and retrieval systems, and later on with the large-scale digitalization of information. As a consequence of these changes, new ways of thinking about the practice of documentation have emerged, resulting in numerous local and international research projects focussed on developing new documentation models for contemporary art.[3] Although in most cases these models have not been implemented directly in the museum context, they have often served as a basis or inspiration for building institutional strategies for documentation.[4]

Despite numerous initiatives undertaken during the last two decades, the notion and organisation of artwork-related documentation in museums that collect contemporary art remains neither standardised nor fixed, and, moreover, it is currently facing major challenges. The investigation of documentation practices by various museums with contemporary art in their collections conducted between 2016 and 2019 (Wielocha 2021) led to the conclusion that these challenges are often related to the traditional structure of the art museum as oriented towards a unique, relatively stable object—a condition incompatible with the processual, relational and changeable nature of contemporary art.

Contemporary artworks are often complex entities and their rigorous documentation might be a complicated and time-consuming enterprise. Objects are settled at the core of art museums' identity and, consequently, institutions allocate an

[3] Examples of models developed for contemporary art documentation, registration and condition reporting: the Model for Data Registration and the Model for Condition Registration (Hummelen and Sillé 2005); Variable Media Questionnaire (Depocas et al. 2003); the Matters in Media Art model (Matters in Media Art|Tate 2015); the DOCAM Documentation model (DOCAM/Documentation and Conservation of Media Art Heritage 2005); 2IDM (Scholte and Wharton 2011); the Documentation Model for Time-Based Media Art (Phillips 2015).

[4] The Matters in Media Art model has been applied at Tate, while the Documentation Model for Time-Based Media Art has been adopted by the Guggenheim.

important part of their resources to their maintenance and care. Thanks to developments in science, refined preventive methods of care are likely to ensure their longevity for hundreds of years. In the meantime, the gathering, production, management and preservation of artwork-related documentation is usually undervalued within the hierarchy of museum priorities and in consequence receives less attention, time and resources. Despite the recognition of the importance of the intangible characteristics of contemporary artworks and their potential to change, institutional conservation-oriented documentation is still mainly geared to objects. At the same time, intangible features of contemporary artworks are usually recorded in documents produced and/or collected outside the conservation domain, for instance in the curatorial department. In many cases, these documents were conceived for purposes other than conservation, and as such they are frequently not taken into consideration when evaluating an artwork's possible futures. As a consequence, one of the major problems with documenting and therefore preserving contemporary art lies in the lack of interaction between documentation produced expressly for conservation purposes and other kinds of documents that might be essential for an artwork's longevity.

3 The Art Object as Document and Documented: Shifting Our Perspective on the Notion of Contemporary Artwork Documentation

Adopting the perspective applied in the field of performance art studies (Giannachi 2016, 2018; Gordon 2015; Macdonald 2009), this section offers a theoretical reflection on the ontological dimension of documentation. It considers the nature of documentation from the point of view of information sciences and introduces the notion of the art object as a document, and of documentation as a matrix or network of signs. The latter concept will allow for a reflection on documentation's internal hierarchy, and for re-defining the documentation of contemporary artwork within the museum context.

Although traditionally, documents are considered as text and visual records, this perspective started to shift in France when in the late 1920s museum objects too were included by some documentalists within the definitions of "document" (Buckland 1997). In the mid-twentieth century, the work of European pioneers of information science such as Paul Otlet and Suzanne Briet brought other physical forms of "information" to the discussion over the nature of documents. Otlet is known for his observation that documents could be three-dimensional, which enabled the inclusion of sculpture (Buckland 1997). His view on what a document is, comprised objects originally not intended for communication, for instance traces of human activity such as archaeological finds. Briet in her seminal book *What is Documentation?* developed even further the idea of the possible forms a document could take, stating that "the forms that the documentary work assumes are as numerous as the needs from which they are born" (Briet 2006, p. 36).

Briet's theoretical approach deserves a closer look, because besides allowing objects to be included in the definition of a document, it also provides a vision of documentation as a dynamic network of interrelations and a crucial aspect of knowledge production. Briet challenges the traditional, positivist vision of the document "as a proof [*evidence*] in support of a fact" and expands it to "any concrete or symbolic indexical sign [*indice*], preserved or recorded toward the ends of representing, of reconstituting, or of proving a physical or intellectual phenomenon" (Briet 2006, p. 10). According to Briet, a star is not a document, but a photograph of a star is; a stone is not a document, but a stone in a mineralogical collection is; an animal in the wild is not a document, but an animal in a zoo is (Briet 2006, p. 11). The implication of this categorisation is that documentation should not be viewed as only related to a textual record, but needs to be understood within a broader notion of access to evidence and context.

Is an art object in the museum collection also a document? Following Briet's definition, it might be seen as such. If so, an art object included in the institutional collection would be evidence of the artistic practice of a particular artist, a document of particular tendencies in visual arts of the time, of the institutional collection policy, curatorial choices, and finally of the artwork as such. In this light, inclusion of an artwork into the museum collection, or, in other terms, its musealisation, might therefore constitute a shift in an artwork's nature from artwork to artwork/document.

Furthermore, Briet classifies documents as primary, secondary and auxiliary. The second category refers to those documents that are created from the initial documents and the third to those which are created from the interrelation of documents (Giannachi 2018). These categories should not be regarded as hierarchical in terms of value, as they merely illustrate ways in which a document can be produced. Briet notes that instances of documentation are contextual, and, rather than delivering the remains of an isolated phenomenon, they form a matrix or a network of signs. Through the juxtaposition, selection and comparison of documents, a process that for Briet is genuinely creative, the content of documentation becomes "inter-documentary" (Briet 2006). Briet referred to this shift away from a traditional static documentary model as "the dynamism of living documentation" (Briet 2006, p. 41; Macdonald 2009). The assumption that an art object is a document situated within networks of other primary, secondary and auxiliary documents may allow for a new understanding of documentation of contemporary artworks.

The concept of documentation as built upon Briet's approach comprises documents/signs that represent the artwork or some aspect of it. It allows for the inclusion of an art object as a document that is equally important as the other elements comprising the artwork. Documentation understood in this way is a dynamic system of interrelated documents that create knowledge by interacting with each other. To complete the conceptual construct, the issue of internal hierarchy should be addressed. For this purpose, the Deleuzean trope of the "rhizome" might prove useful. The term, borrowed from botany, was developed by Gilles Deleuze and Félix Guattari to characterize networks. Unlike a tree, whose branches all grow from a single trunk, the rhizome does not develop out of a single source; rather, it is heterogeneous and multiple, with no beginning, no end and no centre. It has many different entry points, all of which connect to each other (Deleuze and Guattari 1987). Accordingly, rhizomatic documentation is open-ended, decentralized and has non-hierarchical multiple entry and exit points.

The notion of documentation based on the above-described terms comes with certain features that may harbour solutions that move beyond the incompatibility between the object-based organisation of museums and the character of contemporary artistic production, and, as a consequence, facilitate the task of safeguarding the continuation of contemporary artworks. Conceptualised following Briet's approach, artwork-related documentation challenges the traditional classification principles of museums in two ways: first, by implicitly diminishing the privileged position of art objects within the museum's ecosystem and placing them on equal terms with documents, and, secondly, by elevating the importance of documents in relation to artworks.

Applying Briet's perspective on the nature of documents I argue that upon musealisation a contemporary artwork transforms into the documents that represent it. Because this transformation is de facto and automatic, my proposal is ultimately not to treat art as documents, but to recognise that this conversion already took place, and to adjust institutional practices accordingly. Therefore, the musealised contemporary artwork is a set of documents of the same provenance, and as such resembles an archive.

4 Merging Collection and Archive, Artworks and Documents: Radical Institutional Practices

Over the last decades, several collecting institutions have addressed the discrepancy between the traditional object-centred structure of the museum and the character of contemporary artistic production. Some of them have responded to this challenge by revising the traditional separation of artworks and documents or collection and archive, and the interrelated classification principles. This section features two examples of institutional practices that meet these characteristics—that of the Museu d'Art Contemporani de Barcelona (MACBA) and the Van Abbemuseum in Eindhoven. Although the purposes behind this institutional, critical self-reconsideration differ from those that motivated this chapter, which is oriented towards preservation, its practical results might clarify, illustrate and expand my argument. Moreover, the purpose of emphasising similarities between innovative approaches to institutional contemporary-art collecting, as discussed in the curatorial and conservation fields, seeks to bring them into closer connection and encourage future collaboration.

In Europe, critical thinking about the structure of the art museum, and its possible obsolescence in relation to new art forms and experimental artistic practices, developed within the framework of New Institutionalism. In the arts, New Institutionalism relates to a series of curatorial, administrative and educational practices that emerged at the end of the 1990s mostly in medium-sized, publicly funded contemporary art institutions, and involved the reorganisation of their structures and a re-definition of activities (Kolb and Flückiger 2013). As a term, "New Institutionalism" was introduced by the curator and critic Jonas Ekeberg, for whom the main aim of this development, at least on a discursive level, involved catching up with contemporary art and the changing working methods of artists. Novel practices aimed at de-emphasising the role of the exhibition in favour of fostering the production of artworks, promoting the participation of artists in institutional programmes, designing new approaches to mediation and education, and transforming institutions into discursive platforms for socio-political, economic and cultural issues oriented towards micro-publics (Preston 2014, p. 183). New Institutionalism was a temporary phenomenon related to a certain discursive context within contemporary art institutions identified by particular curators, rather than a fixed alliance or movement. Although its historical phase ended in the mid-2000s (Deiana 2017), its influence still resonates in many contemporary art institutions, and the concepts and practices presented in this section are rooted within this tradition.

The urge to critically reinvent contemporary art institutions as fostered within the framework of New Institutionalism found its continuation in the activities undertaken by the confederation *L'Internationale*. This consortium of six public and semi-public European modern and contemporary art museums has defined itself as a "transinstitutional organisation," which, among other pursuits, promotes the shared use of collections and museum archives across its network. As indicated by the consortium, art and its institutions have the power to question and challenge their own specific systems, such as the bureaucratic and self-referential structure, by experimenting with new protocols and developing more decentralised models (Gül Durukan and Tezcan Akmehmet 2020; "L'Internationale," n.d.). The internal experiments around the idea of connecting the collection and the archive were carried out mainly by two members of the organisation—MACBA and Van Abbemuseum. While the first works towards reinventing the registration and cataloguing system, the second uses display as its testing ground.

At the turn of the millennium, MACBA decided to address the growing interest in documentation in contemporary art and the need to embrace research within the scope of institutional activities by launching the Centre for Study and Documentation (CED).[5] Opened in 2007, the CED hosts and cares for the documentary material that constitutes the Archive and Library, and it is in charge of disseminating and activating the content of both. The Archive and Library, which constitute the CED's core, act within the structure of the museum as a continuation of the MACBA

[5] On the English version of the MACBA website, as well as in the other English-language sources, this unit is called the Study Center. However, for the purpose of this chapter I decided to employ a direct translation of its original name (in Catalan: Centre d'Estudis i Documentació) because in my view it reflects more precisely the actual scope of its activities.

Collection, and these three branches—Archive, Library and Collection—are conceptualised as "Patrimonio MACBA" (MACBA heritage), formed by materials in a wide range of formats and supports. In the words of Mela Dávila Freire, the former director of MACBA Public Activities, the CED's collections "are not seen as subsidiary or secondary to the art collection; rather, they complement, expand and strengthen it, establishing ties, not of dependency, but of mutual bonding" (Dávila Freire 2012, p. 200). According to Fereire, this approach derives from the need to respond to the reduced importance of the end-products of artistic activity, namely art objects, and the need to shift the focus to relations between different actors involved in the creative process, as well as the creative process as such (Dávila Freire 2012). This line of thinking led the museum to reject the conventional categories of "artwork" and "document," a separation that MACBA considers outdated (Dávila Freire 2011). To overcome this distinction in practice, the museum employed a cataloguing structure that no longer differentiated between "the artistic" and "the archival," creating a single cataloguing method and system for both collection and archive.[6]

To understand what this radical gesture entails from the perspective of this chapter, it is important to introduce the CED Archive and its holdings. The Archive is divided into three categories: Documentary Collection, Personal Fonds and MACBA's Historical Fonds.[7] The first one consists of artists' publications, publicity material, posters and other such materials. The second one contains documentary material generated by activities of actors linked to contemporary artistic practice, who could be artists and artistic collectives, collectors, curators, etc. The third one, MACBA's Historical Fonds, holds the documentation generated by the museum in the course of its activities.[8] The common cataloguing method makes it possible to link information that is usually dispersed all over the institution in a common platform.[9] In practical terms this means that a search performed in MACBA's collection management system by the title or inventory number of a particular artwork from the collection will yield all related items (records), such as the main

[6]Dávila Freire commented on additional, practical advantages of implementing a common system for collection and archive in the following way: "amongst other things, this fluid relationship avoids the need for endless, futile discussion aimed at ascertaining whether certain research collections are 'works' or 'documents.' Rather, it emphasises their hybrid nature, their combination of the two categories" (Dávila Freire 2012, p. 199).

[7]The use of the word "fonds" stems from one of the basic principles of archival science called *Respect des fonds*. It means "to group, without mixing them with others, the archives (documents of every kind) created by or coming from an administration, establishment, person, or corporate body. This grouping is called the *fonds* of the archives of that administration, establishment or person" (Duchein 1983, pp. 1–2).

[8]The museum designed procedures and workflows that facilitate the gathering of the documents produced by museum departments at the end of each institutional activity. These documents feed the category "MACBA's Historical Fonds."

[9]The common collection management system for collection and archive employed by MACBA is the MuseumPlus. In consequence, the archival material was catalogued according to standards for musealia, which is different than those used for the archives.

entry of the artwork, documentation of exhibitions organised by the museum where the artwork was presented, all public activities related to the artwork including talks and conferences, articles, books, videos showing the installation process, interviews with artists in the form of transcripts and/or video recordings, and much more.[10] These records, which represent analogue or digital documents that are physically stored in various locations, create a virtual archive of the artwork. Simultaneously, the CED is the infrastructure for the systematic care and reservation of the archive, which stewards, replenishes and activates it by fostering research and providing accessibility.

How does the structure introduced by MACBA differ from the traditional cataloguing systems used in museums? The difference lies in the way the information is structured and the scope of interaction between the documents. In most of the Collection Management Systems used in museums today, documents related to the artworks, such as certificates of authenticity, instructions provided by the artist, lists of equipment necessary for displaying the piece, exhibition publications or conservation reports can be attached to the artwork's record. The structure of information about the artwork in the CMS is thus fixed and linear: the entry for a particular artwork contains limited information that has been assigned to it. Documents that define the artwork are predetermined—one can add new ones or delete the existing ones, but the scope of the information that defines the artwork is constrained. By contrast, the system implemented by MACBA makes it possible to access documents that, although only indirectly related to the artwork, nevertheless provide data that are significant for its comprehension. Let me take as an example a list of fifty artworks featured in one exhibition. In a traditionally structured CMS this list would need to be attached to the record of every artwork separately. In MACBA's system this list is catalogued independently and appears in the search related to each of the listed artworks. An example of a document that defines the artwork is the recording of a public talk by artist at one of the museum events, which, despite being created for reasons other than documenting the artwork collected by the museum, includes key information for a proper understanding of the work. In the traditional system this document, produced by employees responsible for public events who are not involved in collection care, would not be attached or linked to the CMS record of the artwork. At MACBA this kind of documents are separate archival entities represented in the database by a record that appear while searching by the name of the artist, title of the artwork or inventory number of the latter. Thanks to the cataloguing structure which treats artworks and archival material equally, MACBA's system allows for a deeper contextualisation of artworks and increases the possibility of constructing alternative narratives.

From the perspective of this research, the structure built by MACBA so far presents several weak points, the most notable of which is related to the scope of

[10]The complexities of the system employed by MACBA were explained to me by CED employees Noemí Mases Blanch, Paloma Gueilburt and Elisabet Rodríguez in a series of personal conversations during my research residency at MACBA in October/November 2018.

the information comprised. The CED Archive does not encompass all the documentary material generated and kept within the museum. The archive of the collection department (or "area" in MACBA's terms), which includes for instance artists' installation instructions and the majority of conservation-related documents, remains separate, and access to the information it contains is restricted. Furthermore, as there is not a system for archiving correspondence, the museum does not collect emails exchanged between stakeholders involved in the acquisition and/or presentation of an artwork, another aspect identified in the field of contemporary art conservation as important for understanding processes behind the shaping of the musealium. Nevertheless, the MACBA team has acknowledged these gaps as important to address within a series of challenges to take on in the long-term process of reinventing the institution. More experience and the potential of existing infrastructure built through the years will offer room to address these challenges methodologically.

Another member of *L'internationale* that experiments with the traditional museal classification systems and bridging the taxonomic separation of artworks and documents is the Van Abbemuseum. In 2004 this museum started to test new ways to work with institutional resources—not only the collection, but also the archive and the library (Bishop 2013). In line with the theoretical underpinnings of MACBA's practices, the idea behind the novel approaches of Van Abbemuseum was to look at and use the museum's collection as a whole without making distinctions between the artwork and the "paperwork around the artwork" (Esche et al. 2012, p. 5). As argued by museum research curator Steven ten Thije, this shift was necessary because art changed following the logic of the ready-made and was now produced by installing things without as much attention to the quality of the "thing itself" (ten Thije et al. 2013, p. 11). This is why the strong similarity between "the artwork itself and a sort of collection or archive" (ten Thije et al. 2013) serves to blur the boundaries between traditional categories of collection and archive. However, while at MACBA the merging of categories was tested "behind the scenes," at Van Abbemuseum the main space of experimentation involved the display. The Van Abbemuseum was not the only or the first art institution to bring archival materials into the exhibition space, but they did it in an unorthodox way by elevating documents to the same level of importance as the artworks from the collection (Gül Durukan and Tezcan Akmehmet 2020).[11] In the series of research exhibitions called *Living Archive*, copies of the archival material were shown on the walls together with the artworks. Contracts and letters exchanged between artists and successive directors told stories about the circumstances of the acquisition, whereas other sources, such as reports or press clippings, contextualised the artwork within broader discourses.[12] This approach

[11] For more details related to the novel approaches of Van Abbemuseum, see Franssen, D. (February 2018). The Archival Turn in Van Abbemuseum. Presented at the seminar *The Boundary Condition: About the Archive and its Limits*, Museu d'Art Contemporani de Barcelona (MACBA). Retrieved from: https://www.macba.cat/en/the-boundary-condition-discussion-with-mela-davila-and-diana-franssen.

[12] The series of exhibitions *Living Archive* curated by Diana Franssen was organised at Van Abbemuseum between 2005 and 2009. The most interesting episode of the series from the

shifted the emphasis away from artists, their oeuvre and their place in the canon, to the biography of the artwork and the context in which it was created and functioned, or, in other words, to change from one universal, linear art historical narrative to various site-specific and context-specific micro-stories (Esche 2017; Esche et al. 2012).

5 The Museum Collection as a Collection of (An)archives

As argued above, upon crossing the threshold of a museum a contemporary artwork transforms into documents that represent it. Following this line of thought, the artwork-related documentation is a set of documents of the same provenance and as such can be conceptualised as an archive. To facilitate the shift of importance of artwork-related documents within a museum, regarded here as a prerequisite for perpetuation of contemporary artworks, this chapter adapts and expands on the notion of "artwork-as-an-archive," introduced by conservation theorist Hanna Hölling (2013, 2015, 2018). Hölling's concept encompasses both a physical and a virtual sphere of an artwork, where the former contains "all documents, leftovers and tangible materials produced by the artwork" while the latter "entails tacit knowledge, skills, and memory of everyone involved in the process of shaping the work" (Hölling 2015, p. 86). This combining of the physical and the conceptual under one umbrella concept is similar to the notion of "artwork-related documentation," as discussed above. Given that subsequent manifestations of an artwork produced on the basis of the archive in turn enter the archive and transform it, the archive evolves as a dynamic entity directed towards the future shape of the artwork (Hölling 2015). This theoretical construct embraces the artwork's possibility for and the inevitability of change. Although Hölling's concept was proposed principally in the context of media art, in my view it is also relevant to contemporary art as defined in the introduction to this chapter. Conceiving an artwork as an archive might lead to a re-conceptualisation of the museum collection as a collection of archives.

Expanding the notion of "artwork-related documentation" to "artwork-as-an-archive" requires a critical reflexion on the notion of the archive, which has been at the centre of discourses of cultural theorists, observers and practitioners over the last fifty years (Giannachi 2016). In the modern era the archive stands for the means by which historical knowledge and forms of remembrance are accumulated, stored and recovered, created both by institutions and individuals (Merewether 2006). The archive entails some form of organisation of storage media for purposes extrinsic to the archive itself, and connotes origin and order (Derrida and Prenowitz 1995). It is a

perspective of this chapter is *Mixed messages* (14/04/2008–14/09/2008), in which pieces from the museum collection were displayed alongside documentation. This combination permitted a reassessment of the artworks' significance as the outcome of social, political and economic factors. "Mixed messages can be considered a reconstruction, disassociating itself from the autonomy of art as something quite separate from the existing order" (Fletcher et al. 2009, p. 99).

powerful institution whose purpose is to maintain and expand the power of those who established and control it (Zielinski et al. 2014). That implies classification, categorisation and authority—terms rarely compatible with the liberal and experimental character of contemporary artistic practice. The contradiction between the traditional principles of the archive and the character of today's art led media theorist Siegfried Zielinski to coin the concept of "anarchives." Zielinski states that adding "an" as a prefix liberates the archive from "the obsessive sense of order and the detailed claim to leadership" (Zielinski et al. 2014, p. 22). The concept of "anarchives" emerged from the logic of multiplicity and variety, which makes them particularly suited to deal with time-based experiences, processes and events (Zielinski et al. 2014). They do not appropriate the truth about the origin of things, and most importantly, about their possible futures. They do not pursue a fixed design, and instead of promoting "the one and only story" they organise micro-narratives. Zielinski illustrates the idea of anarchives with the disorder of personal archives of, for instance, artists, scholars or curators. For him, an example of the transformation of an anarchive into an archive is the deconstruction of the archive and library of influential curator Harald Szeemann for the purposes of the Getty Research Institute. The "individual methodology" applied by Szeemann to develop his exhibitions and artistic objects was significantly altered by its adaptation to the "universal order of a hygienically organized, representative cultural research archive" on the Getty Institute's immaculate white shelves (Zielinski 2015, p. 116; Zielinski et al. 2014). The concept of anarchives might strengthen the potential of the theoretical model of artwork-as-an-archive by offering the freedom to adjust its organisation according to the needs of a particular artwork.

To suggest, as this chapter does, that a museologised contemporary artwork might be conceptualised as an (an)archive is to view it as an open-ended set with a rhizomatic structure and a dynamic system containing interrelated documents (tokens) that represent an artwork. Particular elements of the archive create knowledge by interacting with each other, and this interaction is activated by means of research.

Why then might the model of artwork-as-(an)archive facilitate conservation and decision-making regarding the artwork's future shape? On a conceptual level, the artwork-as-(an)archive grants the possibility of collecting and caring for contemporary artworks beyond their material embodiment. Gathering together the evidence of an artwork's conception, as well as the knowledge produced around it during its "life," makes it possible to represent its multi-levelled, complex nature. Although the archive's own limitations prevent it from fully representing the artwork, the accumulation of documentation allows gaps to be identified and addressed, and, more importantly, makes it possible to foster relations between individual elements of the set. The artwork-as-(an)archive is a common source of information about the artwork that facilitates equal access to and distribution of information, and prevents the exercise of authority based on the appropriation of knowledge. This non-hierarchical (un)structure offers space for flexibility and (some) creativity in shaping the artwork-as-(an)archive on a case-by-case basis.

Yet, there are still questions that need to be answered regarding the practical implications of the model of the artwork-as-(an)archive and why its application might help institutions to safeguard the continuation of contemporary artworks from their collections. First, the artwork-as-(an)archive offers the possibility of switching from a single governing narrative of what the artwork is and does, to various micro-stories that foster alternative interpretations and broaden possibilities concerning the artwork's future shape. Secondly, it helps shift the concept of conservation within the museum from a set of object-oriented actions to a collaborative effort encompassing the whole institution. In the framework of the artwork-as-(an)archive, a musealised artwork ceases to consist only of art objects in order to embrace documents gathered and produced by the artwork's stakeholders. In turn, the artwork's continuation relies not only on conservators but also, and explicitly, on other institutional actors. The artwork-as-an-(an)archive emphasises the contribution to and responsibility for the perpetuation of an artwork as the common task of a long list of figures: curators and educators who collect, produce and promote interpretations; archivists and registrars who gather and organise knowledge produced within the institution; librarians who take care of information produced outside the museum walls; photographers and audio-visual technicians who document and install artworks in galleries; event coordinators responsible for producing and staging the artworks, etc. The emphasis on conservation as a common task might help to overcome the divisions between different organisational domains, thereby making it a more attainable reality. Moreover, the artwork seen as an (an)archive can become a space for collaboration that encourages all stakeholders to take an active part in conserving the artworks collected. Thirdly, the model pushes museums to reconsider the act of acquisition as more than just purchasing art objects, and extending it to the production and gathering of documentation within the process, and consequently, to having this reflected in the acquisition budget. From this perspective, without collecting the documents that carry the artwork's identity, the acquisition would not be considered complete. Fourthly, it fosters a need to build an infrastructure to facilitate collecting understood as documenting, and to create a space for documents to interact with each other as a network. And finally, it helps to embrace the complementation and activation of the archive through research within the framework of collection care and locates it at the same level of priorities as the-state-of-art high-tech storage that hosts the art objects. In other words, it supports the recognition of research as a full-fledged conservation tool for safeguarding the artwork's continued presence and importance while respecting its changeability.

Despite having different raisons d'être, the experiments of MACBA and Van Abbemuseum and the model of artwork-as-an-(an)archive featured in this essay overlap in several ways. Concepts and practices rooted in New Institutionalism developed as a response to the artistic strategies of contemporary art, changing relations between museums and society at large, and coming to understand art not as a "thing in itself," but as existing in dialogue with the social sphere (Aikens et al. 2016). As such, they invite users to think critically and allow them to construct their own narratives around the artworks collected. Although the concept of artwork-as-(an)archive was introduced not as a means to reinvent art institutions but as a strategy for securing artworks' sustained life, it shares conceptual underpinnings with practices introduced here. Similar to the cataloguing and display practices of MACBA and Van Abbemuseum, the reconceptualization of the artwork as an (an)archive allows us to reconsider traditional museum classification principles and work towards the accessibility, transparency and activation of museum holdings. It opens up the institutional space to a multiplicity of perspectives and dialogue by rejecting a single governing narrative.

The concept of artwork seen as an archive is akin to the "object file," since both gather documents taking the artwork as a classification principle, provide a space for assembling these documents together, and make them interact with each other. One of the major challenges in applying the model of artwork-as-(an)archive in a museum is the issue of accessibility and the scope of the institution's willingness to disclose documents. In today's museums the accessibility of "object files" depends on institutional policies, legal regulations, existing unspoken rules, social agreements and, most importantly, on the will, motivation and interest of the museums themselves. However, granting access to institutional documentation and sharing it with others means relinquishing power and giving up some authority over the collected artwork. The model of artwork-as-an-(an)archive is a tool for critical inquiry that makes it possible to confront notions of exclusiveness, closure and property traditionally related to museums. Its application would eventually give rise to questions about what it means to own an artwork whose nature lies in documents that, in the digital era, are not unique but reproducible, easily accessible and can even be cloned and distributed among different institutions. The artwork/archive model enables in-depth exploration of the difference between having and holding, or possessing and safekeeping, and opens up the possibility for institutional collecting to distance itself from the regime of the art market. However, the crucial question of whether museums are ready or inclined to take on this challenge needs to be addressed in further research.

6 Conclusion

Based on the postulation that the museum's traditional division between objects and documents, and, as a result, between collections and archives is rendered obsolete by contemporary art, this essay proposes a different way of thinking about a musealised contemporary artwork. Instead of a discrete object or a set of objects to be preserved as autonomous physical entities a contemporary artwork has been conceptualised here as an archive that contains art objects and documentation produced about and generated by the artwork. The documentation of a contemporary artwork carries a large part of its identity, and acts as evidence of its potential changeability. As such, it needs to be dynamic and, in Susan Briet's terms, "inter-documentary." This implies contextual reliance and, in consequence, the formation of a network of documents that interact with each other. Applying Briet's perspective on the nature of documents, art objects, too, can be seen as documents that are equally important as other documents in the set. Therefore, the musealised contemporary artwork is a set of documents of the same provenance, and as such resembles an archive. Departing from this premise, this essay advocated the model of artwork-as-(an)-archive, aimed at adjusting traditional, object-based museum structure to the needs of contemporary art and thus securing and sustaining its unique cultural value for future generations.

Acknowledgements I would like to thank the MACBA team for hosting me in 2018, especially Noemí Mases Blanch for her support and guidance trough institutional back-stage and Christiane Berndes for participating in my research and acquainting me with Van Abbemuseum approaches to the collection and archive. Many thanks to my supervisors who provided insight and expertise that greatly assisted this investigation, as well to the NACCA cohort for being such wonderful and inspiring people. This research was funded by the European Union H2020 Programme (H2020-MSCA-ITN-2014) under Grant Agreement n°642892.

References

Aikens N, Lange T, Seijdel J, ten Thije S (2016) Editor's introduction. In: Aikens N, Lange T, Seijdel S, ten Thije S (eds) What's the use? Valiz, Amsterdam, pp 9–11

Almeida Matos L, Macedo R, Heydenreich G (eds) (2015) Performing documentation in the conservation of contemporary art. Instituto de História da Arte, Lisbon. Retrieved from http://revistaharte.fcsh.unl.pt/rhaw4/RHAw4.pdf. Accessed 29 Jan 2022

Altshuler B (2005) Collecting the new. a historical introduction. In: Altshuler B (ed) Collecting the new: museums and contemporary art. Princeton University Press, Princeton and Oxford, pp 1–9

Avrami E, Mason R, de la Torre M (eds) (2000) Values and heritage conservation. The Getty Conservation Institute, Los Angeles

Barok D, Noordegraaf J, de Vries AP (2019) From collection management to content management in art documentation: the conservator as an editor. Stud Conserv 64(8):1–18

Bishop C (2013) Radical museology or, what's "contemporary" in museums of contemporary art? Koenig Books, London

Briet S (2006) Suzanne Briet: what is documentation? Scarecrow Press, Lanham

Buckland MK (1997) What is a "document"? J Am Soc Inf Sci 48(9):804–809

Buskirk M (2003) The contingent object of contemporary art. The MIT Press, Cambridge, Mass. and London, UK

Dávila Freire M (2011) ¿Es una obra, o es un documento? El centro de estudios y documentación del MACBA. In: Picazo G (ed) IMPASSE 10. Llibres d'artista, edicions especials, revistes objectuals, projectes editorials, edicions independents, publicacions especials, edicions limitades, autoedicions, edicions d'artistes, publicacions digitals. Ajuntament de Lleida, Centre d'Art La Panera, Lleida, pp 300–308

Dávila Freire M (2012) Process vs. product: new paths for archiving in contemporary art. In: Peressut LB, Pozzi C (eds) Museums in an age of migrations: questions, challenges, perspectives. Politecnico di Milano, Milan, pp 193–207

Deiana M (2017) Handle with care: the influence of New Institutionalism on collection displays in Italian contemporary art museums. Stedelijk Studies (5):1–17. Retrieved from https://www.stedelijkstudies.com/journal/handle-care-influence-new-institutionalism-collection-displays-italian-contemporary-art-museums/. Accessed 29 Jan 2022

Dekker A, Wijers G, Van Saaze V (2012) The art of documentation. Rtrsrch 2(2):22–27. Retrieved from http://insidemovementknowledge.net/wp-content/uploads/2010/03/RTRSRCH_Notation_CoverSpread.pdf. Accessed 29 Jan 2022

Deleuze G, Guattari F (1987) A thousand plateaus: capitalism and schizophrenia. University of Minnesota Press, Minneapolis

Depocas A, Ippolito J, Jones C (eds) (2003) Permanence through change: the variable media approach. Guggenheim Museum Publications and The Daniel Langlois Foundation for Art, Science, and Technology, New York and Montreal

Dekker A (2018) Collecting and conserving net art. Routledge, Oxon & New York

Derrida J, Prenowitz E (1995) Archive fever: a Freudian impression. Diacritics 25(2):9

DOCAM/Documentation and Conservation of Media Art Heritage (2005). https://www.docam.ca/. Accessed 29 Jan 2022

Domínguez Rubio F (2014) Preserving the unpreservable: docile and unruly objects at MoMA. Theory Soc 43(6):617–645

Duchein M (1983) Theoretical principles and practical problems of respect des fonds in archival science. Archivaria 16(Summer):64–82

Esche C (2017) Absences felt and unfelt. In: Snauwaert D (ed) The abstent museum. Mercatorfonds and WIELS, Brussels, pp 6–14

Esche C, Franssen D, Aikens N (2012, December) On the Van Abbemuseum Archive. Asia Art Archive:1–21. https://aaa.org.hk/en/ideas/ideas/on-the-van-abbemuseum-archive. Accessed 29 Jan 2022

Fletcher A, ten Thije S, Franssen D, Esche C, Niemann K (eds) (2009) Plug in to play. Van Abbemuseum, Eindhoven

Giannachi G (2016) Archive everything: mapping the everyday. The MIT Press, Cambridge

Giannachi G (2018) The intention of the artist and the point of view of the audience: performance documentation revisited. In: Westerman J, Giannachi G (eds) Histories of performance documentation. Routledge, New York, pp 182–197

Gordon R (2015) Documenting performance and performing documentation. On the interplay of documentation and authenticity. Matos LA, Macedo R, Heydenreich G (eds) Revista de História Da Arte, 4. http://revistaharte.fcsh.unl.pt/rhaw4/RHAw4.pdf. Accessed 29 Jan 2022

Graham B (2014) Modes of collection. In: New collecting: exhibiting and audiences after new media art. Routledge, London

Gül Durukan SN, Tezcan Akmehmet K (2020) Uses of the archive in exhibition practices of contemporary art institutions. Archives and Records

Haylett S (2019) Archives and Record Management. https://www.tate.org.uk/research/reshaping-the-collectible/research-approach-archives-record-management. Accessed 29 Jan 2022

Heinich N (2014) Practices of contemporary art: a pragmatic approach to a new artistic paradigm. In: Zembylas T (ed) Artistic practices: social interactions and cultural dynamics. Routledge, London, pp 32–43

Heydenreich G (2011) Documentation of change - change of documentation. In: Scholte T, Wharton G (eds) Inside installations: theory and practice in the care of complex artworks, vol 7. Amsterdam University Press, Amsterdam, pp 155–171

Hölling HB (2013) Re: Paik. On time, changeability and identity in the conservation of Nam June Paik's multimedia installations. University of Amsterdam

Hölling HB (2015) Archival turn. Towards new ways of conceptualising changeble artworks. In: Acoustic Space, vol 14, pp 73–88

Hölling HB (2018) Archive and documentation. Art Doc 17:19–28

Hummelen Y, Scholte T (2004) Sharing knowledge for the conservation of contemporary art: changing roles in a museum without walls? In: Roy A, Smith P (eds) Modern art, new museums: contributions to the Bilbao Congress, 13-17 September 2004. International Institute for Conservation of Historic and Artistic Works, London, pp 208–212

Hummelen Y, Scholte T (2006) Capturing the ephemeral and unfinished: archiving and documentation as conservation strategies of transient (as transfinite) contemporary art. Technè: La Science Au Service de l'histoire de l'art et Des Civilisations (24):5–11

Hummelen Y, Sillé D (eds) (2005) Modern art: who cares? An interdisciplinary research project and an international symposium on the conservation of modern and contemporary art (Second). Archetype Publications, London

Kolb L, Flückiger G (2013) New institutionalism revisited. Oncurating.Org (21):6–17. http://www.on-curating.org/issue-21-reader/new-institutionalism-revisited.html#.XBj-UWj0mUk. Accessed 29 Jan 2022

L'Internationale (n.d.). https://www.internationaleonline.org/about/. Accessed 29 Jan 2022

Laurenson P (2004) Developing strategies for the conservation of installations incorporating time-based media: Gary Hill's between cinema and a hard place. Tate Papers 1(1). https://www.tate.org.uk/research/publications/tate-papers/01/developing-strategies-for-the-conservation-of-installations-incorporating-time-based-media-gary-hills-between-cinema-and-a-hard-place. Accessed 29 Jan 2022

Laurenson P (2006) Authenticity, change and loss in the conservation of time-based media installations. Tate Papers 6(6). http://www.tate.org.uk/research/publications/tate-papers/06/authenticity-change-and-loss-conservation-of-time-based-media-installations. Accessed 29 Jan 2022

Macdonald C (2009) Scoring the work: documenting practice and performance in variable media art. Leonardo 42(1):59–63

Matters in Media Art|Tate (2015). http://www.tate.org.uk/about/projects/matters-media-art. Accessed 29 Jan 2022

Merewether C (2006) Introduction: art and the archive. In: Merewether C (ed) The Archive. Whitechapel Gallery, London

Phillips J (2015) Reporting iterations: a documentation model for time-based media art. Matos LA, Macedo R, Heydenreich G (eds) Revista de História Da Arte 4:168–179. http://revistaharte.fcsh.unl.pt/rhaw4/RHAw4.pdf. Accessed 29 Jan 2022

Preston V (2014) From outside to inside: changing strategies and practices of institutional critique 1960-2014. University of London. http://bbktheses.da.ulcc.ac.uk/103/. Accessed 29 Jan 2022

Scholte T, Wharton G (eds) (2011) Inside installations: theory and practice in the care of complex artworks. Amsterdam University Press, Amsterdam. www.oapen.org/download?type=document&docid=467012. Accessed 29 Jan 2022

Seren T (2001) Integrated art documentation: the Guggenheim perspective. Art Doc: J Art Libr Soc N Am 20(1):31–35

Stigter S (2015) Co-producing conceptual art: a conservator's testimony. Matos LA, Macedo R, Heydenreich G (eds) Revista de História Da Arte 4:103–114. http://revistaharte.fcsh.unl.pt/rhaw4/RHAw4.pdf

ten Thije S, Andrews M, Cánepa Luna M (2013) From one history to a plurality of histories. Sightlines: Walker Art Reader, January. https://walkerart.org/magazine/steven-ten-thije-van-abbemuseum-opencurating. Accessed 29 Jan 2022

Trevisan R (2013) Documentation techniques. In: Ferriani B, Pugliese M (eds) Ephemeral monuments: history and conservation of installation art

van de Vall R (2015) The devil and the details: the ontology of contemporary art in conservation theory and practice. Br J Aesthet 55(3):285–302

van Saaze V (2015) In the absence of documentation: remembering Tino Sehgal's constructed situations. Matos LA, Macedo R, Heydenreich G (eds) Revista de História Da Arte 4:55–64. http://revistaharte.fcsh.unl.pt/rhaw4/RHAw4.pdf

Westerman J, Giannachi G (eds) (2017) Histories of performance documentation. Routledge, New York. https://doi.org/10.4324/9781315645384. Accessed 29 Jan 2022

Wharton G (2005) The challenges of conserving contemporary art. In: Altshuler B (ed) Collecting the new: museums and contemporary art. Princeton University Press, pp 164–178

Wharton G (2015) Public access in the age of documented art. Revista de História Da Arte 4:180–191

Wielocha A (2021) Collecting archives of objects and stories: on the lives and futures of contemporary art at the museum. University of Amsterdam. https://hdl.handle.net/11245.1/9916bb82-e5f9-4a78-9266-d47ff292104a. Accessed 29 Jan 2022

Wielocha A, Markevicius T (2019) Conservation. In: Giebeler J, Heydenreich G, Sartorius A (eds) The decision-making model for contemporary art conservation and presentation. Cologne Institute of Conservation Sciences/TH Köln, Cologne. https://www.th-koeln.de/mam/downloads/deutsch/hochschule/fakultaeten/kulturwissenschaften/f02_cics_gsm_fp__dmmcrmac_190407a.pdf. Accessed 29 Jan 2022

Wythe D (ed) (2004) Museum archives: an introduction. Society of American Archivists, Chicago

Zielinski S (2015) AnArcheology for AnArchives: why do we need—especially for the arts—a complementary concept to the archive? J Contemp Archaeol 2(1):116–125

Zielinski S, Giannetti C, Fürlus E (eds) (2014) AnArchive(s): a minimal encyclopedia on archeology and variantology of the arts and media. Oldenburg, Edith Russ Haus für Medienkunst

Aga Wielocha is a researcher, conservator and collection care professional specializing in contemporary art. She holds a PhD from the University of Amsterdam. Her doctoral research, situated at the crossroads of art history and theory, conservation, museology and heritage studies, investigated the lives and futures of contemporary art within institutional collections. Her research interests lie in processes of institutional collecting with the focus on processual, contemporary art formats, such as art projects, participatory art and performance-based art.

Decision-Making for the Conservation and Presentation of *Thermoelectronic Chewing Gum* (1970), a Political Environment by Wolf Vostell

Julia Giebeler, Gunnar Heydenreich, and Andrea Sartorius

Abstract The Decision-Making Model for Contemporary Art Conservation and Presentation (CICS 2019) was used for a case study on Wolf Vostell's interactive electroacoustic environment from 1970, *Thermoelectronic Chewing Gum* (*Thermo-Elektronischer Kaugummi, T.E.K.*), to establish to what extent it can assist in complex situations to weigh and structure arguments, to identify and clarify dilemmas and conflicts, as well as to document and justify decisions so that they are comprehensible for future generations. The process records how external factors and the personal viewpoints of the various stakeholders can influence the form, function and impact of an artwork and shape its identity. This study analyses how as a political environment *T.E.K.* was variously interpreted during the last fifty years, displaying it at times in an altered or reduced form. The application of the decision-making model illustrates this complex biography as well as selected considerations and decision-making processes aimed at the long-term preservation of this work and its future display in 2022 in the Museum Ostwall in the Dortmunder U.

Keywords Decision-making model · Biography · Subjectivity · Interactivity · Wolf Vostell · Migration · Emulation · Obsolescence

1 Introduction

Decision-making processes for the conservation and presentation of modern and contemporary art can be very complex and may constitute a crucial turning point that significantly influences an artwork's biography. Artistic concepts, the significance of materials, media, techniques and changes in condition, as well as attributed values, are frequently interpreted differently by the various stakeholders. In contemporary forms of expression like installations, new media art or performance art, the decision-making process for conservation and presentation is complicated by

J. Giebeler · G. Heydenreich (✉) · A. Sartorius
Cologne Institute of Conservation Sciences/TH Köln, Cologne, Germany
e-mail: post@juliagiebeler.de; gunnar.heydenreich@th-koeln.de; post@andreasartorius.de

R. van de Vall, V. van Saaze (eds.), *Conservation of Contemporary Art*, Studies in Art, Heritage, Law and the Market 9, https://doi.org/10.1007/978-3-031-42357-4_15

Fig. 1 Wolf Vostell: *Thermoelectronic Chewing Gum (T.E.K.)*, iteration in the Museum am Ostwall, 2010 (Photo: Jürgen Spiler © VG Bild-Kunst, Bonn 2021)

iterative, process-related, performative and participatory aspects which may be perceived differently by individuals with different cultural or professional backgrounds. With this in mind the Decision-Making Model (SBMK 1999) was recently expanded by a multidisciplinary group of experts (CICS 2019), taking into account the concept and material diversity of new artworks as well as current discourses in conservation theory (Castriota 2019; Celma 2021; Quabeck 2019).[1]

By applying the enhanced decision-making model to a specific artwork, this study explores the question of whether the framework reflects these discourses and helps to structure and weigh arguments, to identify and clarify dilemmas and conflicts, as well as to justify decisions and to make documentation more comprehensible for future generations. As a case study we selected Wolf Vostell's interactive electroacoustic environment from 1970, *Thermoelectronic Chewing Gum* (*Thermo-Elektronischer Kaugummi*, *T.E.K.*) (Fig. 1). The deceased artist's complex installation has been in the collection of Museum Ostwall in Dortmund since 1971 and poses numerous questions regarding documentation, conservation and presentation. This case study highlights how external circumstances and the personal opinion of different stakeholders can influence the form, function and impact of the work and how its identity is shaped by a series of complex considerations and negotiation processes with a far-reaching spectrum of options.

[1] Cf. also the chapter by Brian Castriota in this book.

2 Two Decision-Making Models in Conservation

The Decision-Making Model for the Conservation and Restoration of Modern and Contemporary Art was developed by a group of multi-disciplinary researchers in 1999 (SBMK 1999). It builds on Ernst van de Wetering's earlier model for decision-making in art conservation that was first presented at the 8th ICOM-CC Triennial Meeting in Sydney (Van de Wetering and Van Wegen 1987). Aiming for further professionalisation and refinement in conservation decisions, the model not only considers technical aspects but also other issues that relate to the artwork's authenticity, historicity, functionality, aesthetic and perception, as well as economical and technical feasibility, legal aspects and conservation ethics. Van de Wetering's model takes into account the fact that complex conservation decisions require a balance between various considerations that at times may conflict and involve compromises (SBMK 1999).

Van de Wetering generated his model with more "traditional" art in mind, while a need for expansion was identified in the mid-1990s, so that it could also be applied to "non-traditional" objects of modern and contemporary artworks, where the relationship between material and meaning is usually ambiguous. The expanded version of the model identifies two instances when the relationship between the material properties and the meaning of the artwork requires investigation and benefits from being graphically visualized (by circles): first, when addressing the question of whether a discrepancy between the physical condition and the meaning of the artwork exists, and secondly, when the conservation options and their consequences are considered (SBMK 1999).

The 1999 model consisted of a flowchart and seven focussing steps, each with instructions and a checklist. The first three steps concentrate on the artwork's metadata, its condition and meaning. In Step 4 the central question of the decision-making process in art conservation is addressed: whether the discrepancy between the work's present state and the artistic intention warrants a conservation intervention and what are the risks involved. Step 5 expands on the selected options, and in Step 6 their implications for the artwork are explored and compared, before a decision is made and documented in Step 7. The model is defined by a simple, flexible structure that prompts questions rather than supplying rigid answers. In an ideal scenario a wide spectrum of stakeholders would increase the variety of answers.

3 Reasons for Further Revision

Since the 1990s the diversity of new art forms and the accompanying discourse in conservation theory has begun to challenge the traditional concept of the "original" or "ideal" state of an artwork. Concept-based or kinetic art demands that the association of authenticity with the material properties of an artwork be reassessed.

Other art forms like installations or media and performance art may be reiterated in different locations that influence their meaning and identity. Their sustained life as artworks frequently depends on their re-enactment, but the decisions about their presentation may have repercussions for their conservation.

Both the artwork's material and intangible properties need to be considered when making complex conservation and presentation decisions. Taken from different perspectives, aspects like the artist's intention, sanctions, and installation instructions as well as the artwork's trajectory can be variously interpreted, and their meaning may change over time. Furthermore, different dynamics are introduced by the shifting roles of those involved and the non-linear process of decision-making. Finally, the terminology and definition of terms will require constant updating (Fischer et al. 2015; Giebeler et al. 2021).

Revision of the model was required:

- to take account of the complex trajectory and evolving character of many contemporary artworks.
- to identify which forms of presentation might affect the conservation of the artwork.
- to include important intangible properties in the decision-making process.
- to allow for subjectivity and dynamics in decision-making.
- to accommodate the evolution of terminology.

4 The Revised Model and the Concept of Perspectivism

The revised Decision-Making Model for Contemporary Art Conservation and Presentation was developed within the *NACCA* project (CICS 2019) by an interdisciplinary working group and differs in structure only marginally from its predecessor: it now comprises nine steps. The additional two steps are 1. the Point of Departure and 9. Implementation and Assessment (Fig. 2). A short text explains the aim of each step and provides a set of instructions, an example and a checklist. Relevant terminology is included in a glossary at the end.

Step 1 considers the specific point of departure, describing circumstances, initial aim(s), stakeholders and their individual interests. Data pertaining to the artwork is generated and registered in step 2. Step 3 and 4 aim to develop a profound understanding of the current and desired state(s) of the artwork. Step 5 addresses a possible discrepancy between the current and desired state(s) of the artwork. Should this be the case, in Step 6 the goals, e.g., to reduce the discrepancy, are specified and options for conservation and/or presentation are detailed. In Step 7 these are compared and weighted, after which a decision is documented in Step 8. Finally, Step 9 not only monitors the effects, but also aims at an overall assessment. A glossary in the annex of the model, authored by numerous researchers, reflects the current understanding of pivotal terms and underlying theoretical concepts in contemporary art conservation and presentation and builds a basis for future revisions of the model.

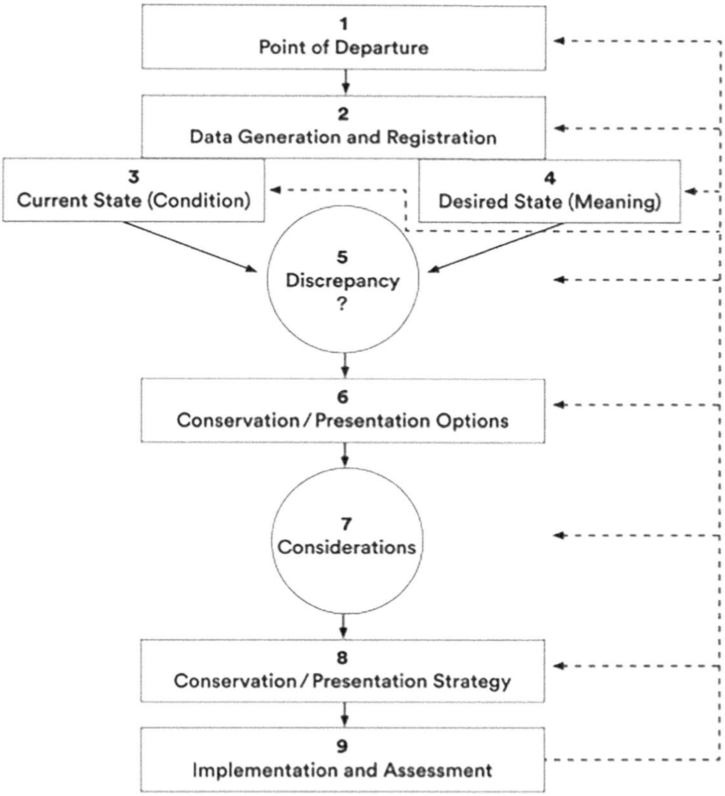

Fig. 2 The Decision-Making Model for Contemporary Art Conservation and Presentation, 2019

This new model is intended to enable a more dynamic process, permitting easy modification of earlier steps to facilitate a more nuanced reflection throughout the process.

The new Step 1, the point of departure, reflects the concept of perspectivism.[2] This concept suggests that all perception of the object of study, here the artwork, and the related decision-making regarding its conservation and presentation depend on the perspectives or interpretation of the stakeholders and their knowledge (Massimi and McCoy 2019). The principle is that in this context, aesthetics, functionality or changes of condition of an artwork are perceived differently from different perspectives, according to professional or cultural backgrounds, personal views and experiences. Considering the model of perspectivism in the decision-making process implies accepting limitations to achieve truly objective and neutral knowledge.

[2]The perspectival conception of objectivity is expressed in the writings by Friedrich Nietzsche (1844–1900).

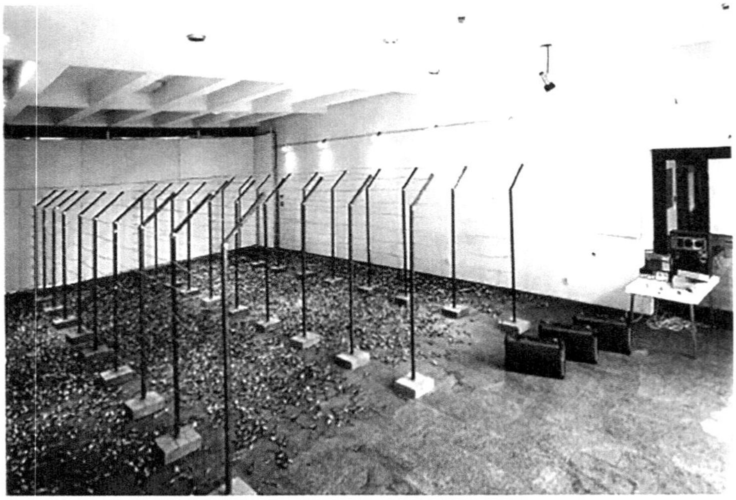

Fig. 3 Wolf Vostell: *Thermoelectronic Chewing Gum (T.E.K.)*, iteration in the Kunsthalle Cologne, 1970 (Photo: Thomas Tilly © VG Bild-Kunst, Bonn 2021)

While perspectivism does not regard all perspectives and interpretations as equally valid, it also assumes that no stakeholder has a complete view. A combination of multiple theoretical and practical views, including various methods of analysis, may provide a more comprehensive understanding of a complex object of study and thus a more holistic foundation for the decision-making. This chapter aims to illustrate how the expanded model can be applied to structure the process. It provides an overview of the complex process, while also highlighting selected aspects when discourses and different perspectives of the stakeholders become apparent and influential. A complete report will be made accessible elsewhere.

5 The Case Study: *Thermoelectronic Chewing Gum*

Wolf Vostell (1932–1998) first realized the interactive electroacoustic environment *Thermoelectronic Chewing Gum* in 1970 for the Kunsthalle, Cologne, by using barbed wire to divide the exhibition space into narrow aisles and spreading out a large quantity of cutlery on the floor (Fig. 3). Visitors were invited to put a piece of chewing gum in their mouths, to attach a transmitter microphone to their cheeks and to carry a suitcase through the fenced off aisles. Chewing noises were amplified and played back through loudspeakers and from time-to-time radio programmes or piercing whistling sounds emanated from the suitcases.

Through a direct physical and psychological experience of this exceptional situation, this political work allows the visitor to become part of the artwork.[3] By the act of walking over the cutlery and the amplified chewing of gum the visitor produces the noise and as such actively influences the artistic manifestation, perceived by many as excruciating. Due to the interactive art experience Wolf Vostell's environment offers a unique access to important subjects such as the Holocaust or political internment camps. Visitors report that they felt particularly moved by this work and encouraged to reflect, which led to discussions about both historical crimes and contemporary political events.[4] After a period of fifty years during which *T.E.K.* was presumably displayed in a greatly reduced form, and without the chewing gum component referred to in the title, the museum decided to tackle its poor condition and develop an appropriate conservation and presentation strategy.

5.1 Step 1: Point of Departure

The first step of the model builds on the idea that a decision-making process arises from a particular question, an interest or a specific situation (Fischer and Funke 2016). Thus, the circumstances and the initial aim are described as well as the stakeholders, their intentions and their overarching goal.

5.1.1 Circumstances

The *Thermoelectronic Chewing Gum* environment was acquired in 1971 by the Museum Ostwall in Dortmund directly from the artist, and since then it has been displayed in different locations. In 2018 Lisa Schiller, conservator at Museum Ostwall, recognised the need to develop a conservation and presentation strategy and contacted the Cologne Institute of Conservation Sciences (CICS). An opportunity arose to record the condition of the work within the context of a collaborative research project with the TH Köln when it was deinstalled in 2019.

5.1.2 Initial Aim

The museum conservator and the curator expressed an initial aim to develop and implement an appropriate conservation and presentation strategy so that the environment could be included as one of the main works in the planned new display of the collection in 2022.

---

[3] Nicole Grothe, personal communication, April 2019.

[4] Regina Selter, personal communication, September 2019.

5.1.3 Stakeholders, Intentions and Overarching Goal

The case study involved the museum conservator and external conservators, the curator and the museum's management as well as specialists in electromechanics, electricians, an artist and the artist's son Rafael Vostell as basic stakeholders.[5] The group was partly expanded by consultation of witnesses.[6] Thus, taking into account the variety of different professional backgrounds and views listed at the beginning of the process. Decisions were prepared in numerous discussions within the core project team and subsequently in meetings with all stakeholders, partly in front of the objects. Finally, decisions were made following the recommendation of the museum's conservator in cooperation and consensus with the curator, the director and the artist's son Rafael Vostell. In the forthcoming display of the collection, the idea is to position the environment opposite of a group of Fluxus works that can only be shown as relics in a display case. Both museum employees and external conservators from the CICS placed great importance, in the sense of an overarching goal, on the functionality of the work and the interactive experience, while at the same time valuing the historical materials and conservation ethics. In addition, the museum required that maintenance be kept to a minimum.

5.2 Step 2: Data Generation and Registration

The objective of the second step is to find and register relevant data to provide the foundation for a comprehensive understanding of the artwork, paving the way to a well-argued decision process. Within the context of this study, we conducted research in a variety of archives including museums, municipal archives and newspaper archives, as well as special collections like the Wolf Vostell archive in Malpartida in Spain. Important photographs and descriptions of the environment were discovered that give information about past iterations and the interactive experiences involved. A further source was contemporary witness interviews. Examination of the work's component parts provided key information.

[5] Lisa Schiller (Head of Conservation), Julia Giebeler and Gunnar Heydenreich (external conservators), Nicole Grothe (Head of Collections), Regina Selter (Deputy Director), Günter Thorn (artist), Hans-Ulrich Faust and Maximilian von Blohn (specialists in electromechanics), Robin Lockhart (museum technician).

[6] Former museum staff members: Kurt Wettengl (Director), Marie Luise Körber (secretary), Ulrich Lueg (technician), Anke Klusmeier (Head of Conservation), as well as Thomas Tilly (photographer and friend of Vostell) and Winfried Reckermann (gallerist).

Fig. 4 Wolf Vostell (left) and the art dealer Helmut Rywelski (right), Kunsthalle Cologne, 1970; Rywelski has a microphone taped to his cheek (Photo: Wolf P. Prange © VG Bild-Kunst, Bonn 2021)

5.2.1 Description(s) of the Artwork

The space is partitioned into several narrow aisles, created by barbed wire attached to border posts, and more than 10,000 forks and spoons are spread out on the floor. At Vostell's request the visitors should put a piece of chewing gum in their mouth, attach a transmitter microphone to their cheek and walk through one or more of the dimly lit aisles of the environment, carrying a suitcase (Fig. 4). The chewing noises are sent to a radio receiver and played back in the room amplified over a loudspeaker. During the walk-through single ceiling spotlights activate the sound technology built into the suitcases via infrared sensors, causing a radio programme or a whistling noise to resonate.[7] The catalogues accompanying the first presentation of *T.E.K.* in the Kunsthalle, Cologne (1970), and its first iteration in Museum Ostwall (1972) differ considerably in their description of the work (Table 1). Notable is that 20 sacks of flour mentioned in 1970 are no longer listed two years later. The cutlery on the floor is clearly visible in the photograph from 1970 but is omitted from that list. Vostell may have planned to cover the floor with flour but could not implement this idea and spread out the cutlery instead. Furthermore, there are also discrepancies in the date and description of the room, as well as the dimensions, the number of spots and the instructions (Leppien 1970; Museum am Ostwall 1972; Figs. 3 and 6).

[7] Nicole Grothe, personal communication, April 2019. Cf. the following publications for further interpretations of the work: Museum am Ostwall (1972), Merkert and Vostell (1975) and Vostell (2012).

Table 1 Identity of the object *Thermoelectronic Chewing Gum* at Kunsthalle Cologne (1970) and when it was acquired by the Museum Ostwall (1972)

	The first manifestation of *T.E.K.*, 1970 (Leppien 1970)	The first iteration of *T.E.K.* in the Museum Ostwall, 1972 (Museum am Ostwall 1972)
Owner:	Wolf Vostell	Museum Ostwall im Dortmunder U
Inventory number:	–	A3/71
Artist:	Wolf Vostell	Wolf Vostell
Title:	Der thermo-elektronische Kaugummi [Thermoelectronic Chewing Gum]	Thermo-Elektronischer Kaugummi [Thermoelectronic Chewing Gum]
Date:	1969/70	1970
Genre:	A Happening-Room	Environment
Technician:	Peter Saage	B. Eng. Peter Saage
Spatial dimensions:	10 × 6 × 4 m (length × width × height)	13.48 × 5.36 × 4.37 m
Material:	• 5 microphone capsules with transmitters • 5000 pieces of chewing gum • 10 radiant heaters • 2 loudspeakers • 1 amplifier, 100 watts • 1 transducer • 20 sacks of flour • 30 metal posts • 150 m barbed wire • 5 suitcases with content • Transistor radios and heat sensitive microphones • 3 washbowls	• 5 microphone capsules with transmitters • 5000 pieces of chewing gum • 5 spotlights • 2 loudspeakers • 1 amplifier, 25 watts • 1 Super-Radio • 30 metal posts with barbed wire • 5 suitcases with radios and heat sensitive microphones • 13,000 spoons and forks
Instructions:	Take a transmitter capsule and put a Juici Fruit chewing gum in your mouth. Chew and walk with the electronic suitcase back and forth through the fences. Your chewing noises will be transmitted and amplified—heat sensitive microphones activate radio stations in the suitcase. After use put your transmitter capsule in a bowl where it will be sterilized for the next user. Thank you.	Chew gum—walk on the spoons—tape the transmitter capsule to your cheek—take a suitcase and carry it around the T.E.K. room In doing so chew gum Listen to amplified chewing noises Activate radio signals in the suitcase by exposure to light

5.2.2 History of the Work

After the environment was installed for the first time in 1970 in the Kunsthalle, Cologne (Fig. 3), three further iterations followed in Karlsruhe, Aachen and

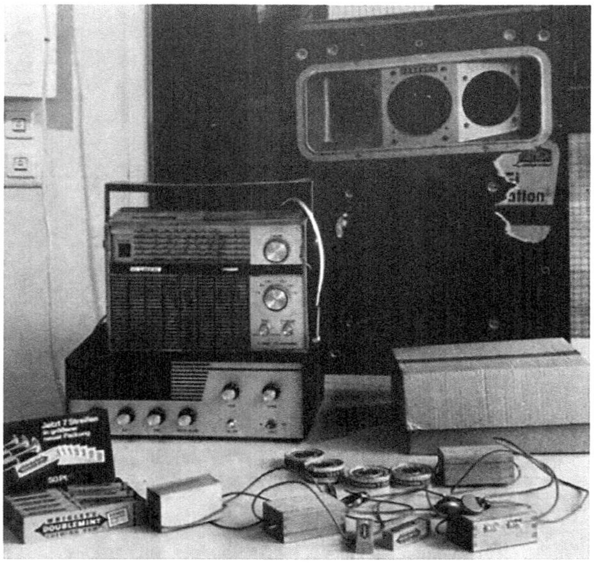

Fig. 5 Audio technology from *T.E.K*'s first iteration, Kunsthalle Cologne, 1970 (Photo: Thomas Tilly © VG Bild-Kunst, Bonn 2021)

Frankfurt. We were able to trace illustrations only from the first presentation in Cologne.[8] The technical equipment was visibly displayed on a table (Fig. 5). Before Museum Ostwall acquired the environment in 1971 it was adapted by Vostell and his assistant Peter Saage († 2013). They fitted the equipment necessary for the playback of the chewing noises into a cabinet. In contrast to the first presentation in 1970, Museum Ostwall allowed the public access only to the central aisle (Fig. 6). Whereas, in the first three weeks, the media reported frequently about the chewing gum, this was soon no longer mentioned. It can be assumed that only a few weeks after the opening the playback of the chewing noises no longer functioned.[9]

In 1974/75 the environment was shown in Paris and in 1975 in Berlin (Vostell 1974; Merkert and Vostell 1975) (Fig. 7). Between 1975 and approximately 1995, the environment was displayed in various rooms of the museum, and most likely without the chewing gum component and the cabinet required for the playback and amplification of the chewing noises.[10] In 2007 the inoperable cabinet was rediscovered in the museum storage, Peter Saage was commissioned to rework the sound technology and from 2010 until 2019 the environment continued to be displayed in a reduced form (Fig. 8).

---

[8]The first presentation: Kunsthalle, Cologne: *Jetzt. Künste in Deutschland heute*, 14 February–18 May 1970; the second presentation: Badischer Kunstverein Karlsruhe: *Kunst und Politik*, 31 May–16 August 1970; the third presentation: Neuen Galerie im Alten Kurhaus, Aachen, 15 October–27 November 1970; the fourth presentation: Frankfurter Kunstverein: *Kunst und Politik*, January 1971.

[9]*Westfälische Rundschau* (23 February 1972), *Kirchlicher Anzeiger* (27 February 1972).

[10]Regina Selter, personal communication, February 2021.

Fig. 6 Wolf Vostell: *Thermoelectronic Chewing Gum (T.E.K.)*, iteration in the Museum am Ostwall, probably 1972 (Photo: unknown © VG Bild-Kunst, Bonn 2021)

5.3 Step 3: Current State (Condition)

The aim of this step is to develop a profound understanding of the artwork's current state by interpreting the results gained in the previous step and taking into account the artwork's biography, environmental conditions, and other information concerning the properties of the artwork that may be considered significant (Fig. 8).

5.3.1 Space and Interaction

In the past, depending on the available space, *T.E.K.* was installed in an area with variables of *c.* 55–72 m^2. Between 2010 and 2019 it was displayed in a dimly lit connecting room painted grey with a suspended ceiling and dimensions of

Fig. 7 Wolf Vostell: *Thermoelectronic Chewing Gum (T.E.K.)*, iteration in Paris, 1975, Vostell walking through the environment (Photo: © VG Bild-Kunst, Bonn 2021)

6.5 × 8.5 m (Fig. 1). Here three rows of barbed wire, each with eight metal posts of 237 cm in height, formed two aisles. For the duration of the installation two suitcases were made available to the visitors to carry as they walked through both aisles over the cutlery. At this point three spots mounted on the ceiling temporarily triggered the radios or the sound module in the suitcases. In accordance with the artist instructions, the suitcases were switched on and off by a museum guard. Chewing gum and microphones were not handed out, contravening Vostell's concept.

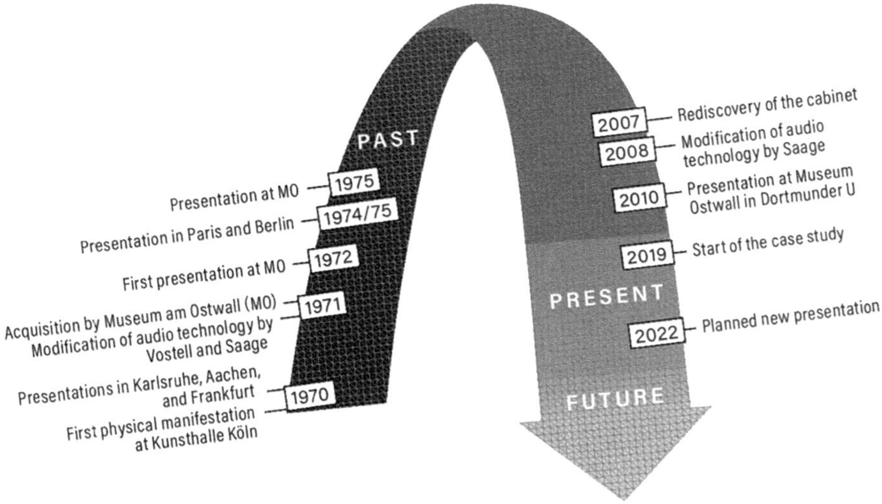

Fig. 8 A short biography of *Thermoelectronic Chewing Gum*

5.3.2 The Suitcases

According to the catalogue accompanying the first presentation of *T.E.K.* (1970), five suitcases with contents are part of the environment (Leppien 1970). Now there are four suitcases in the museum. The whereabouts of suitcase no. 1 is unknown. While there is a radio, a loudspeaker, batteries and an electronic control device in three of the suitcases, the suitcase marked 5 contains a sound module instead of a radio. All suitcases are activated by a side-mounted switch. Infrared sensors are fitted into circular openings on top of the suitcase. Infrared radiation from radiant heaters or spotlights activates the sensors and thus the built-in radios or sound module. Through this means sound is produced via an amplifier and a loudspeaker (Figs. 9 and 10).

Suitcase 5 comes with a microphone, rather than a radio, and it is mounted in a circular opening in the shell next to the loudspeaker, which currently does not work (Fig. 11). Originally the loudspeaker would have produced a sinusoidal whistling noise via audio feedback. As the microphone broke down in 2008, Peter Saage attempted to imitate the whistling noise—presumably associated in his memory with that of a train—by installing the sound module. In addition to the whistling noise, this module generates three other noises played in succession: the arrival of a steam train, that of points being changed and an acoustic warning signal at a level crossing, none of which are mentioned in previous work descriptions (Fig. 12). The suitcases are in fact temporarily operable, but the present component parts are subject to wear and time-consuming to maintain.

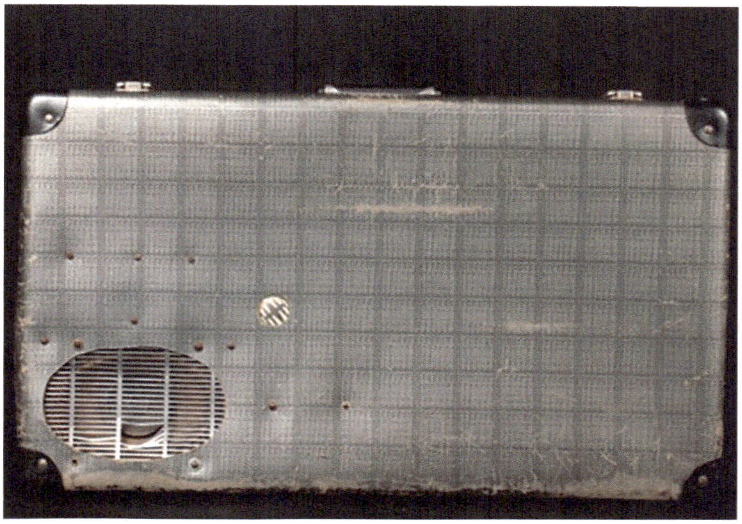

Fig. 9 Suitcase 5, closed, condition in 2019 (Photo: © VG Bild-Kunst, Bonn 2021)

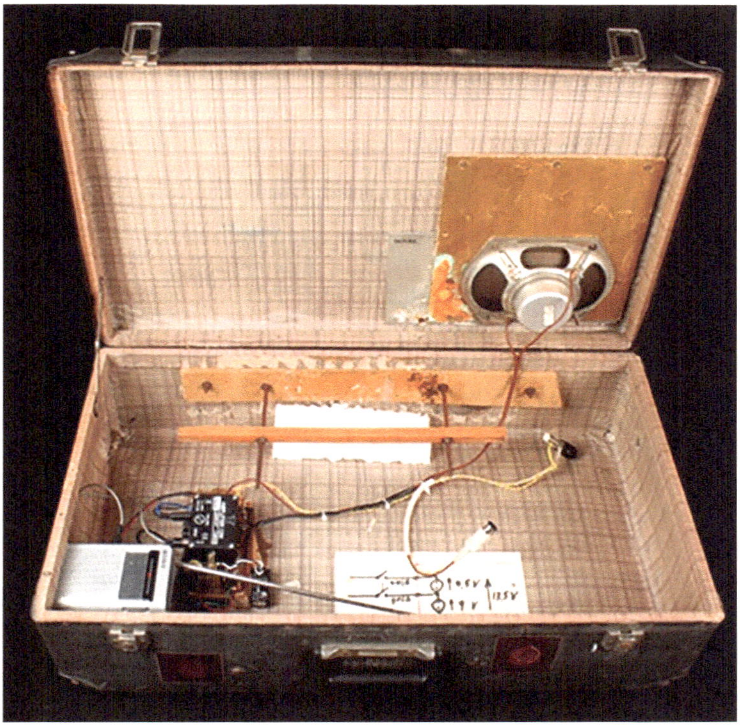

Fig. 10 Suitcase 2, open, condition in 2019 (Photo: © VG Bild-Kunst, Bonn 2021)

Fig. 11 Suitcase 5, detail of the audio technology, condition in 2019 (Photo: © VG Bild-Kunst, Bonn 2021)

5.3.3 Transmitter Microphone, Receiver and Playback System

The five transmitter microphones used to register and transmit the noise of the gum-chewing have not been preserved. In old photographs the microphones are not clearly identifiable. They probably originally came from the mouthpiece of a telephone and transmitted the chewing noise with the help of a home-made VHF transmitter to the receiving radio (Figs. 4 and 5). Before the acquisition by Museum Ostwall, Vostell and Saage fitted the technical equipment necessary for the reception, amplification, and the loud playback of the sound into a cabinet (Fig. 13). During storage in the museum this cabinet suffered damage due to moisture. In 2008 Saage renewed the external construction and replaced the loudspeaker enclosure with a new visually different model (Fig. 14). The reworked cabinet was placed in the exhibition space, but due to the missing microphone capsules it was not in operation.

Fig. 12 Suitcase 5, detail of the audio technology, condition in 2019 (Photo: © VG Bild-Kunst, Bonn 2021)

A significant challenge when determining the condition is caused by the lack of documentation pertaining to the acquisition, iterations and early alterations. Information about the use of microphones and transmission technology can only be narrowed down by comparing the available photographs with components available on the market at the time. It is not known precisely how accessibility to the public, the lighting and the volume were regulated, whether suitcase no. 1 ever arrived in Museum Ostwall and whether Vostell's instructions were ever implemented again after 1975.

5.4 *Step 4: Desired State (Meaning)*

The objective of this step is to deepen the understanding of the artwork and to reach a consensus about its identities and the states in which the artwork is considered

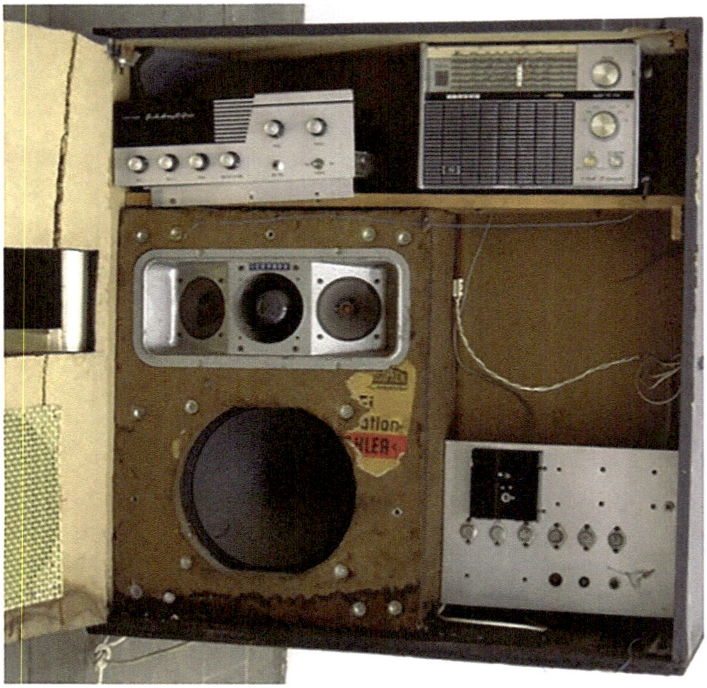

Fig. 13 Cabinet containing the audio technology shown open, condition in 2007 (Photo: A. Klusmeier © VG Bild-Kunst, Bonn 2021)

authentic. Therefore, this step is used to interpret which of the artwork's properties are essential to its identity. Different values may be appreciated that might have been attributed to the work in the past and that have changed over the years and which affect the current and future interpretation of the artwork.

In interviews, Wolf Vostell emphasised that with the deliberate integration of everyday objects like spoons and forks, or habits, like chewing gum, he wanted to trigger associations between concentration and prison camps in the past and the present that would continue to influence the visitor's daily life (Vostell 1970). In this way Vostell wanted to "embed barbed hooks in the conscious mind, so that they could assess the chaotic situation more acutely and accordingly act against it" (Vostell 1970).[11] He wanted "to allow the electronic phenomenon [. . .] to perform and thereby to facilitate awareness" (Vostell 1970).[12] As he added: "I have made efforts to have the electronics not only coming out of the loudspeaker, but to allow

[11]"Ich möchte durch meine Arbeit bei Ihnen [den Menschen] Widerhaken im Bewusstsein hinterlassen, so dass sie die chaotischen Zustände schärfer beurteilen und sich entsprechend gegen sie verhalten" (Vostell 1970, p. 2).

[12]"Ja, ich möchte das Phänomen Elektronik [. . .] praktizieren lassen und dadurch Erkenntnisse vermitteln" (Vostell 1970, p. 5).

Fig. 14 Cabinet containing the audio technology shown after adaption in 2008, condition in 2019 (Photo: © VG Bild-Kunst, Bonn 2021)

them to be directly influenced by people's behaviour. In other words, the people are responsible for the generated sound: a system or composition has not been imposed upon them, instead everything can be electronic, the chewing of gum is electronically amplified, as is also the sound of 10,000 spoons and forks; in addition, the public can choose whether to create sinus tones by walking past the photoelectric sensor; they can experience each element separately, or all the element simultaneously. As regards the composition it is left to the visitor's own initiative, as ít is usually only practised in Happenings and no other art form today" (Vostell 1970).[13]

[13] "Ich habe angestrebt, eben nicht Elektronik nur aus Lautsprechern kommen zu lassen, sondern sie direkt durch Verhalten der Leute beeinflussbar zu machen. Das heißt: die Leute sind selbst verantwortlich für die Klangerzeugung, es wird ihnen kein System, kein Kompositionsschema aufoktroyiert, sondern alles kann Elektronik sein, das Kauen eines Kaugummis wird elektronisch verstärkt, dazu der Klang von 10.000 Löffeln und Gabeln, dazu ist dem Publikum überlassen, Sinustöne herzustellen, in dem es durch Fotokontakte läuft, es kann also jedes Element einzeln erfahren oder erleben, es kann aber auch alle Elemente gleichzeitig erleben. Von der Komposition her ist dem Betrachter wirklich eine Eigeninitiative überlassen, wie sie eigentlich nur im Happening praktiziert wird und in keiner anderen Kunstform heute" (Vostell 1970, p. 5f).

By inviting the visitor to walk through the environment Vostell allows him/her to be a part of the artwork: "Memories of the concentration camp in Auschwitz, but also of prison camps of the present are evoked. He allows the visitor to experience fear, stress, confinement and noise, and prompts reflection: How does it feel to be at the mercy of others? At the same time the visitors generate the noise themselves by walking and thus contribute to this unbearable situation. In this manner Vostell addresses the question of individual responsibility for death and pain."[14]

All stakeholders agreed that the environment can only be fully experienced if accessibility is guaranteed, and all component parts are in operation. The threatening barbed wire border-fencing, the visitor's uncertain step over the erratically spread-out cutlery and the bearing of the weighty historical suitcases support the intended association with prison camps, suppression and flight. Previous iterations of *T.E.K.* differ with regard to the dimensions of the space, the number of metal posts as well as the number of aisles enclosed by barbed wire (Figs. 1, 3, 6 and 7). Specifications by Vostell are not known. Whereas in Cologne, Paris and Berlin the work was displayed in rooms with white walls, Museum Ostwall chose to exhibit in a room with grey painted walls, which were familiar to Vostell.

Both the material and the inherent aesthetics of the suitcases, as well as the guarantee of their functionality, seem essential for an authentic experience of the artwork. As the sound technology in the suitcases is not visible, it is attributed a functional role. However, the situation is different for the visible historical loudspeakers and switches on the suitcases, because in addition to a functional value, they also have an aesthetic and a historical relevance. The temporary playback of radio sequences or the generation of sinus-like noise interference in the suitcases, so far activated by three to ten spots is also assigned fundamental relevance. The microphone and the transmission technology necessary for the transmission of the chewing noises, as well as the receiver and the playback equipment concealed from view in the cabinet have primarily a functional relevance. The noises generated by this process were particularly loud, according to witnesses.[15] The acoustic quality was determined by the historical transmission technology that sent signals to a radio, after which they were increased by a tube amplifier attached to an external loudspeaker.

It is not known whether Vostell intended more than one visitor at a time to enter the environment. As five suitcases and five transmitter microphones originally belonged to the work, the stakeholders assumed that at any one time up to five visitors could enter the environment with chewing gum, a microphone and a suitcase. However, subsequent examination of the technical equipment in the cabinet revealed that with the existing construction it is technically impossible to simultaneously transmit multiple chewing noises to one radio receiver. This ranged from disturbance to overlap and interference, which disrupted, weakened or obliterated

[14]Nicole Grothe, personal communication, April 2019.

[15]Winfried Reckermann, personal communication, August 2019.

the chewing noise. Nevertheless, it cannot be ruled out that more than one person was permitted to enter the environment at any one time.

Wolf Vostell visited all the described iterations except the last one in the Dortmunder U from 2010 to 2019. It is not known whether he disassociated himself from any of these presentations. The stakeholders therefore assumed that for *T.E.K.* there are different desirable states that correspond to the meaning attributed to the artwork and that transmit its significant properties. All the well-known press and archival photographs of the various iterations (1970, 1971, 1974 and 1975) show Vostell with the transmitter microphone against his cheek, suggesting that he considered the chewing gum component to be a significant property. As Peter Saage fitted the sound module with the train noises into suitcase 5 only after Wolf Vostell's death, he could not have authorized this change.

Based on the research results, the project participants assume that the following parameters are required for the authentic experience of Wolf Vostell's environment:

1. The work should be installed in a defined rectangular space, measuring *c*. 60–70 m^2 and dimly lit. Narrow aisles should be created by the parallel arrangement of several barbed wire fences with *c*. 30 posts, at least one of these barbed wire fenced-in aisles should be accessible to the public. A large amount of cutlery should be spread out irregularly across the floor (c. 10,000–13,000 pieces).[16]
2. Chewing gum as well as functioning transmitter microphones and suitcases will be made available to the visitors, so that they can enter the environment as prescribed by the artist instructions.
3. The chewing noises generated by the visitors will be played back loudly in the room. In addition, a radio programme or audio feedback whistling noise will be activated in the suitcase by several sensors when being carried through the environment.

5.5 *Step 5: Discrepancy?*

Step 5 determines whether there is a discrepancy between the artwork's current and desired state, thus addressing the issue of conservation and presentation. During the process different values are considered, such as authenticity, aesthetic and artistic values, historicity, functionality, the artist's intent and potential future changes.

According to Vostell's statements and in the opinion of the stakeholders, there is a significant discrepancy between the desired and the work's latest state of presentation (2019). The intention articulated by Vostell to offer the visitors different possibilities of interaction and to actively explore and experience the environment

[16]In the exhibition catalogues (Leppien 1970; Museum am Ostwall 1972; Merkert and Vostell 1975; Weibel 2016) the specifications regarding the amount of cutlery varies from 10,000 to 12,000 and 13,000 pieces.

is significantly reduced. The discrepancy appears to be evident in the following aspects:

5.5.1 The Suitcases

Only four of the five suitcases conceived by Vostell have been preserved and are partially functional. Their impact is limited due to a change in their functionality, their worn appearance, and visible interventions. The sound module fitted into suitcase 5 in 2008 generates noises of trains and a level crossing, while Vostell's instructions and earlier reports describe sinus noises. The train noises and the warning signals, in combination with the historical suitcases and the barbed wire fencing, emphasise associations with deportation during National Socialism's reign in Germany, so that the change can be viewed as a distortion of the interpretation of the work. The noises of the sound module affect both the identity of the work and its impact on the visitor. In other words, all stakeholders agreed that here is a considerable discrepancy between the intended state and the current state.

5.5.2 The Chewing Gum Component

No chewing gum was provided nor was a transmitter microphone available to send chewing noises to a receiver radio that played back the noise out loud in the room via an amplifier and a loudspeaker. Vostell's instructions were not made accessible, so that the intended function and the corresponding spectrum of interaction were neither made possible nor explained. This component was, as indicated by the title, of great importance to Vostell, and without it the artwork is considered incomplete and precludes an authentic experience.

5.6 Step 6: Conservation and Presentation Options

The following options were suggested for the conservation and presentation with the aim of reducing the discrepancy between the current and the desired state and of realising a presentation of the work in 2022. A decision for or against one of these options will require further tests, including a trial installation. The options suggested by the stakeholders range between two extremes, whereby either material integrity and the age of the work are given priority, locating *T.E.K.* in the year of its creation 1970, or variables, updates and references to the present are emphasised (Stigter 2017). Many other options oscillate between these two poles that allow changes up to a certain degree. Below we summarise a selection of these options as discussed by the participating stakeholders.

5.6.1 Space and Interaction

Earlier presentations of *T.E.K.* with one accessible aisle (1972), two accessible aisles and an ambulatory (2010–19) or four singly accessible aisles (1970) could be drawn on again. Individual preferences were articulated by the stakeholders. Accordingly, a large rectangle of *c*. 60–70 m^2 defined by the museum building or a temporary space could be arranged with at least two rows of fencing, each with about 13–15 posts, or three rows with about 8–10 posts parallel to the long sides of the room. Access to an aisle fenced in on both sides must be made available to the visitor from one or both ends of the room. Stakeholders also considered that the spoons and forks should irregularly cover the entire floor. In past iterations different proposals were made regarding the character of the walls and their colour, either white or grey reflecting their presence and the lighting in the environment. The lighting should be dimmed. Safety aspects and emergency exits, including the relevant signs are to be accounted for according to current guidelines.

In order to make it possible for the visitor to explore the environment in accordance with Vostell's intention it was proposed to display the artist instructions from 1970, for example on a wall panel or reproduced as a leaflet. The exploration of the environment could be: (a) at the visitor's own initiative. That would entail switching the suitcase and the microphone on and off, attaching, removing, and cleaning the microphone, the distribution of the chewing gum as well as access; or (b) in accordance with the artist instructions assisted by a museum guard, who would hand out the suitcases and microphones, collect and clean them and ensure that the visitors enter the aisles separately.

5.6.2 The Suitcases

Conservation of the Suitcase Shells and the Sound Technology With the aim of showing the suitcases as close to their original state and of making them operable using the original technology, this option gives priority to the conservation and reuse of the original suitcase shells. Defective historical elements of the sound technology could, if possible, be repaired or replaced by almost identical components.

Conservation of the Suitcase Shells and Migration/Emulation of the Sound Technology With a view to show the suitcases as close to their condition in 1970, to guarantee functionality, while keeping costs and maintenance low, the historical suitcase shells could be reused, but for functional purposes they would require the addition of a modern electronic control box and a new radio. The original sound technology would remain in the suitcase as a historical reference.

Preparation of a Display Copy of the Suitcases and Emulation of the Sound Technology Exhibition copies could be produced with a view to guarantee a sustainable functionality and exclude the risk of further damage to the historical suitcases from usage. The sound technology which is not visible could also be replaced by modern elements. Moreover, activation of the sound elements could be optimized by using modern infrared emitters (installed next to the light bulbs), which would allow a smooth operation regardless of the light source and general light levels in the room.

The original suitcases could be: (a) exhibited as inoperative relics and where appropriate accompanied by information about their history and original construction or (b) kept in the storage room. The following options were suggested for suitcase 5: (a) to reinstate the original operating function (audio feedback), and (b) emulation of the original operating function by attaching a new sound module that plays back the audio feedback noises.

The choice of radio station influences the temporal context in which the visitor locates the work. Here several options are also available that give *T.E.K* a more or less pronounced relevance for the present: (a) a contemporary radio station that plays pop music, (b) one that plays classical music, (c) a contemporary news station or (d) a recording of historical news broadcasts from the 1970s.

5.6.3 Transmitter Microphone, Receiver and Playback Technology

Transmitter (a) Reconstruction: due to the missing microphone capsules, the amplifier and the receiver, as well as their documentation, it would be possible to realise a reconstruction of the unit used in the 1970s only on the basis of a general history of technological knowledge and the availability of the historical electronic component parts. (b) Migration: this option aims at upgrading the transmission technology and the application of common and safer technologies, like for example headsets, their appearance identifying them as modern additions. (c) Emulation: with a view to locating the sound technology aesthetically in the 1970s, the microphone capsules could be reconstructed and fitted with modern microphones and transmitters.

Receiver and Playback Technology (a) Conservation: with a view to preserving the optical and acoustic quality of the historical receiver and playback technology, the equipment inside—even though it was prone to failure—could continue to be used, if regularly maintained. Furthermore, the visual appearance of the cabinet could be adjusted to approximate the condition in 1970 or remain in the condition from 2008 after it was adapted by the assistant. (b) Migration: this option pursues a transmission and amplification of the chewing noises with as little disturbance as possible using receiver and playback technology that is synchronized with a modern transmitter microphone. The tube amplifier and the loudspeaker could be enhanced by fitting new low maintenance and user-friendly units. (c) Partial-Migration: this option also aims for a steady transmission of the chewing noises using a selected transmitter microphone and synchronized receiver and amplifier. However, unlike option (b), this option seeks to reuse single components, like for example the original loudspeakers. We also discussed further options, such as exhibiting the environment as a relic or preserving the current functionality (including the sound module added by

Peter Saage); but as they do not contribute to the reduction of the discrepancy between the current and the desired state, they will not be specified here.

5.7 Step 7: Considerations

Step 7 pertains to weighing the elaborated options—anticipating possible implications and potential risks. Therefore, several assessment criteria are taken into account that weigh differently from case to case, depending not least on the specific point of departure. The disclosure of the valuation process aims to help decision-makers, peers and future custodians to understand its outcomes, especially as these often result in some form of compromise. The challenge of weighing the specified options for the conservation and presentation of *T.E.K.* lies particularly in the consideration of the multiple parts of the interactive components. While several elements were adapted in the past or updated, other components have been missing for decades. A readaptation or an attempt to reconstruct the missing components involves the risk of increased estrangement and with that a growing discord regarding the authentic effect and experience. Below we present and explain various selected aspects of the consideration process.

5.7.1 Space and Interaction

All stakeholders give preference to the installation of *T.E.K.* in a separate room, measuring at least 6.5 × 8.5 m. Different preferences were expressed with regard to the exact arrangement, but it was agreed that there should be two accessible aisles, fenced in on both sides, consisting of 3 rows of fences, each with about 8 to 10 posts. Furthermore, it was decided that there should be a circular access allowing the visitors to enter one aisle and return through the other, providing a longer and more intense experience. This will be tested in a trial installation.

All stakeholders consider it essential to communicate Vostell's instructions. Moreover, the curator formulated the idea of conveying Wolf Vostell's intended chains of association in the form of quotations. The participants all supported the idea of a museum employee overseeing the use to ensure both the safety of the visitor and an authentic experience of the work, as well as to protect the component parts from improper handling and wear. Depending on access possibilities and safety requirements the employee should make sure that not too many visitors enter the environment at any one time, hand out the suitcases and microphones, collect and clean them and dispose of the used chewing gum. Select information about the history of the work should also be made available to the visitor, possibly in the form of special tours.

5.7.2 The Suitcases

Conservation or Preparation of an Exhibition Copy? The suggestion to replace the original suitcases with exhibition copies to protect them from further wear aroused controversy among the stakeholders, provoking long discussions: the manufacture of copies seemed technically feasible, as they were commercial suitcases which had only been partially adapted by Vostell with the addition of openings, a grille, a protective film and switches. By using copies, the originals could be maintained in their current state, it would not be necessary to equip them with new components and their wear would be considerably less. At the same time, conservators expressed the concern that the original suitcases may be forgotten once the copies were installed. The curator suggested exhibiting the original suitcases in an anteroom as a relic, conveying their historical functionality, but other stakeholders thought that working merely with "copies" could give visitors the sense that their experience of the environment was compromised. The visible display of the suitcases fitted with technical equipment could also take away the element of surprise associated with activating the sound. The stakeholders finally agreed that the option of displaying the inoperable original suitcases in the environment and using the copies offered a possibility to preserve the original cases unchanged, while at the same time guaranteeing an experience of the environment that is both low maintenance and economic.

This suggestion led to a debate about the parameters to be considered by the manufacture of the copies. Should the copies correspond with the original suitcases in size, construction, shape and colour or could modern cases fulfil the function? Whereas from the curatorial perspective the necessity for a close match between the original and the copy was emphasized, conservators discussed how close the approximation needs to be, considering that the room would only be dimly lit, and also considering technical limitations and financial constraints. It was assumed that Vostell probably acquired five new suitcases for the environment in 1969. At the time, however, they were hardly the latest models. It is not known whether Vostell acquired the older models deliberately or for financial reasons. Today these historical suitcases may kindle associations with concentration camps, deportation or flight. Modern or contemporary suitcases (trolleys) would abruptly transfer the work to the present day. Finally, then, it was unanimously decided to acquire or rebuild cases of a similar design to avoid this obvious contemporization. This included all other visible elements, like the loudspeaker enclosure, the grille and the switches. All participants agreed that a trial installation was necessary to finally decide whether the work could be presented with such copies of the suitcases. For this purpose, a single suitcase was manufactured, tested and evaluated. Design and size of the copy, including the scanned and reprinted surface pattern in colour and gloss came very close to the original suitcases. The stakeholders were not able to distinguish them on first sight. All decision-makers, including Rafael Vostell who initially suggested to enclose the original suitcases in acrylic cases to protect them from further wear as a result of the test, strongly supported the production of five exhibition copies.

Reconstruction or Migration of the Sound Technology? To fulfil the initial aim of a low maintenance functionality, the stakeholders agreed that, taking previous operative parameters into consideration, the audio technology should be replaced by modern technology using rechargeable batteries. As it is not known which radio stations were played back from the suitcases, participants suggested different possibilities. Broadcasting a modern pop radio station and locating it in the present is supported by Vostell's wish to "embed barbed hooks" in the visitor's conscious mind. At the same time, by introducing a contemporary radio station there is a risk of negating the age of the environment. The choice of a station with classical music or news like Deutschlandfunk Kultur was viewed as a compromising solution, whereby political and cultural programmes, but also music and radio plays, would be broadcast without commercial breaks. The suggestion to play back recordings of broadcasts from the 1970s via the suitcases was also a subject of controversial discussion due to a feared temporal emphasis on the past. Playing back historical broadcasts fosters the location of the work in the time of its creation, the time of the Vietnam War, but at the same time it hinders the localization that Vostell wished to establish in the present. Therefore, as no agreement was achieved in the extended discussion, it was decided to compare several contemporary radio stations and historical recordings within a trial installation, and possibly to follow Rafael Vostell's suggestion of playing back different radio stations in the suitcases.

The realisation that the train noises were not the original noises generated by suitcase 5 surprised all the participants. In the last ten years these train noises (introduced by Peter Saage) had become integrated in the narrative of the environment and were interpreted and relayed as a reminder of the deportation to concentration camps. The most urgent desire for the exhibition copy of suitcase 5 was that the audio feedback be reconstructed to reproduce the sinus-like whistle. Whether this whistling sound can be produced live in the future or should be recorded and played back will be considered within the context of a trial installation.

The option of activating the sound elements with modern infrared emitters (IR-LEDs) instead of traditional incandescent light bulbs initiated another discussion. Whereas the artist, some conservators and some technicians initially considered this optimization as inappropriate, curators and other conservators emphasized the resulting positive aspects such as the operability of the suitcases, considering the more subdued illumination of the environment, the different entrance positions as well as the possibility of switching to LED lighting in the future. As a result, it was decided to use IR-LEDs, as well as continued employment of IR-sensors with a wider spectral response to enable the implementation of an earlier operation mode if requested.

5.7.3 Transmitter Microphone, Receiver and Playback Technology

As the transmitter microphones did not survive, the challenge is to develop a sustainable solution for recording, transmitting, amplifying, and playing back the chewing noises that will be acceptable to the visitors while observing the attributed aesthetic and historical values.

Migration or Emulation of the Transmitter Microphone? If *T.E.K.* were to be localized in the 1970s the reconstruction of the transmitter microphones used at the time would be desirable. Their approximate form could be reconstructed on the basis of historical photographs, but not the technical elements as the transmission technology used is not adequately documented. From the aesthetic point of view emphasized by conservators, it would be preferable to work with microphone capsules with a decidedly historical look, rather than use, for example, a modern, commercial headset. However, all the stakeholders gave priority to the function, or, in other words, that the playback of loud chewing noises is guaranteed. Common headsets or contact microphones (migration) would clearly localize the recording and transmission of the chewing noises generated by the visitors in the present and in addition guarantee a hygienic, interference-free and sustainable transmission. Considering that by 1970 the first headsets and Lavallier clip-on microphones by the company Sennheiser were already available on the market, it would seem reasonable to optimize the technology. Alternatively, the option was discussed of using modern microphones in reconstructed microphone capsules, which visitors would then, according to Vostell's instructions, attach to the side of their cheeks with a plaster (emulation). This option would guarantee both an aesthetic localization in the 1970s and functionality. The question of whether visitors would in fact attach the microphone capsules to their cheeks in accordance with Vostell's instructions remains unanswered. In the case of the two options using modern transmission technology, the previous noise interference would be eliminated. It was therefore discussed whether the interference should be simulated. Various new transmitter microphones will be tested in a trial installation.

Reconstruction or Migration of the Receiver Technology? All the decision-makers agreed that the cabinet built in 1971 to contain the audio technology, which had since been adapted, should remain part of the environment. In alignment with the modern transmission technology the original radio receiver should be replaced by a modern receiver device, but not removed. It was also insisted by the museum technicians and the conservators that the tube amplifiers be disabled for fire safety reasons and an additional modern amplifier be fitted in the cabinet. As the inherent characteristic noise of the tube amplifier would then be lost, this prompted a discussion to address the possibility of simulation. Aesthetic considerations remain regarding the different shape of the loudspeaker enclosures introduced by Saage in 2008 and whether they should be dismantled (Figs. 13 and 14). The grey painted cabinet casing, positioned at the edge of the dimly lit room on the other hand, is barely perceptible to the visitor and therefore reversing the intervention made after the water damage was not contemplated. However, an additional plan is to place a charging unit next to the cabinet for the batteries in the suitcases and the microphones.

5.8 Step 8: Conservation and Presentation Strategy

In the strategy for the conservation and presentation of *T.E.K.*, while considering the numerous changes and uncertainties neither the age, the material integrity nor the variability and contemporization are given undue priority. After extensive discussions, the stakeholders agreed that in consideration of the historical, aesthetic and functional value of the suitcases, the idea of deactivating them and manufacturing exhibition copies as well as their activation with IR-LEDs was appropriate. This also ensured that the original suitcases could be preserved unchanged as a reference for future interventions. This approach would also allow the decision to be reviewed in the future. Likewise, the sound module, which can be interpreted as part of the work's biography, ought to be deactivated and fitted with new technology to represent the audio feedback loop produced by the original control system. Playing a contemporary and yet moderate radio station complies with Vostell's intention of locating the environment in the present, and by upgrading to modern headsets to transmit the chewing noises, it might even be given visual expression. However, emulation of the original transmitter microphones also seemed plausible to several stakeholders. Everyone considered that the chewing noises, which had not been heard for fifty years, should be transmitted using new technology, because they are an integral part of the title. With this approach the participants seek to give equal significance to both the materiality and the history of the work, taking aesthetic, functional and economic aspects into account, as well as sustainability. Ultimately this plan requires a compromise that concludes with the proposal of different solutions for each component. The final strategy for conservation and presentation can only be determined after further tests and trial installations. As none of the participants ever experienced the environment in its original functionality and as no reports, installation instructions, film footage or floor plans are known, a trial installation may significantly enrich the stakeholder's understanding of the artwork. Experiencing the artwork's performative aspects offers the prospect of establishing parameters for the floor covering, the width of the aisles, the lighting, while also helping to further specify the optical, acoustic, tactile and interactive parameters, as well as to test and evaluate the technical viability of different options.

6 Conclusions

The case study shows that the revised model serves to structure complex decision-making processes with multiple sub-aspects, to document the various opinions held by the stakeholders and to contextualise and give transparency to interpretation. With the new Step 1 (point of departure) a stronger focus is given to the involved stakeholders, their different professional and cultural backgrounds as well as the varying viewpoints. This reflects the concept of perspectivism as well as dynamic processes within a group which may influence decisions and could therefore significantly affect the biography of the artwork. In addition, the model's glossary mirrors current discourses and thus serves communication and understanding considering the different backgrounds of the stakeholders. Through detailed research and examination of the preserved elements, it proved possible to ascertain various influencing factors that informed the biography of *T.E.K.* and directly affected its identity. The study illustrates that Vostell, beginning with the work's conception through the first presentation in Cologne and to its acquisition by the museum in Dortmund, adapted the work several times, seeking to optimise it in collaboration with his assistant. In the decades after the work's inception, an increasing discrepancy emerged between the original idea and the different iterations. For one thing, the chewing gum component in the title was almost forgotten, whereas the sound-module with train noises introduced after Vostell's death by his assistant became incorporated into the narrative of the work and was soon viewed by curators as an integral part of it. *T.E.K.'s* current state could only be determined from the results achieved by combining detailed biographical research with a technical examination of its component parts.

With a view to reduce the discrepancy between Vostell's intention and the current state, different options for conservation and presentation of *T.E.K.* are available. The participating stakeholders are all of the opinion that the political work even fifty years after its creation can be orchestrated, in accordance with Vostell's ideas, "only in Happening" (Vostell 1970). At the same time the dilemma was recognized that due to a lack of information, e. g., about the original audio components, the interaction and experience would be altered and optimized in a new way. Here the individual perspectives and interpretations of the stakeholders brought about a more comprehensive understanding, resulting in a discussion of more options and thus shaping the decisions, while some were delayed to a trial installation. In consideration of economic factors, the migration of defective, obsolete (and not visible) component parts was accepted to allow for low maintenance functionality, even though the original technology probably never functioned reliably, and the inherent characteristic interference noises might disappear. Since it is not consistently possible to draw on familiar technical procedures for the conservation of single components, while some of the proposed options can only be implemented after an installation to assess their functionality and effect, the revised decision-making model encourages users to return to earlier steps to suggest new possible solutions and to re-test and re-assess them in a dynamic decision-making process. The application of the enhanced model in this case study demonstrated that the framework may serve to structure decisions in conservation and presentation with a series of complex considerations and a rich spectrum of options. It may help to structure and weigh up arguments, to justify decisions and to make the documentation more comprehensible. There is no doubt that with new artistic forms of expression and future discourses in conservation the model needs to be re-examined and, where appropriate, further developed.

Acknowledgments We would like to thank the Museum Ostwall im Dortmunder U and in particular Dr Nicole Grothe (Head of Collections), Regina Selter (Deputy Director), Lisa Schiller

(Head of Conservation), Lisa-Maria Schaaf (Conservator) for the trusting collaboration and support. The project was made possible through the generous financial support of the Wüstenrot Stiftung.

References

Badischer Kunstverein Karlsruhe (eds) (1970) Kunst und Politik, 31 May–16 August. Karlsruhe

Castriota B (2019) Mapping critical mass: authenticity in remanifestations of contemporary art. PhD thesis, University of Glasgow

Celma MG (2021) Reproduction and the attribution of authenticity in the conservation of contemporary photography: Thomas Ruff's Portrait Pia Stadbäumer at Museum für Moderne Kunst, Frankfurt. In: Hermens E, Ricciardi P, Hall-Aquitania M (eds) Art Matters, International Journal for Technical Art History, Special Issue #1. Archetype Publications, London, pp 23–29

Cologne Institute of Conservation Sciences/TH (2019, updated version 1.2/April 2021) The decision-making model for contemporary art conservation and presentation. https://www.th-koeln.de/mam/downloads/deutsch/hochschule/fakultaeten/kulturwissenschaften/f02_cics_gsm_fp__dmmcacp_190613-1.pdf. Accessed 2 Sept 2021

Fischer A, Funke J (2016) Entscheiden und Entscheidungen: Die Sicht der Psychologie. In: Kirste S (ed) Interdisziplinarität in den Rechtswissenschaften. Ein interdisziplinärer und internationaler Dialog. Duncker & Humblot, Berlin, pp 217–229

Fischer A, Holt D, Funke J (2015) Promoting the growing field of dynamic decision-making. In: Schoppek W (editor in chief). J Dyn Decis Mak 1(1):1–3

Frankfurter Kunstverein (ed) (1969) Kunst und Politik, Frankfurter Kunstverein, 28. Nov. bis 10. Jan. 1971. Frankfurt

Giebeler J, Sartorius A, Heydenreich G, Fischer A (2021) A revised model for decision-making in contemporary art conservation and presentation. In: Hoyo-Meléndez J, Bonnie N (eds) Journal of the American Institute for Conservation. Taylor & Francis, London, pp 1–11. https://doi.org/10.1080/01971360.2020.1858619

Kirchlicher Anzeiger (1972) Small note about the reception of Wolf Vostells *T.E.K.*, Dortmund, 27 February 1972

Leppien HR (ed) (1970) Jetzt. Künste in Deutschland heute. 14 February–18 May 1970. Kunsthalle, Köln

Massimi M, McCoy CD (eds) (2019) Understanding perspectivism: scientific challenges and methodological prospects. Taylor & Francis, New York

Merkert J, Vostell W (1975) Vostell Retrospektive 1958-1974. Neuer Berliner Kunstverein e.V. in cooperation with Nationalgalerie Berlin, Staatliche Museen Preußischer Kulturbesitz. Selbstverlag/Hentrich Verlag, Berlin

Museum am Ostwall (eds) (1972) Vostell, Thermo-Elektronischer Kaugummi. Brochure in occasion of the first presentation at the museum, Dortmund

Neue Galerie im Alten Kurhaus (eds) (1970) Wolf Vostell Elektronisch. Verlag, Aachen

Quabeck N (2019) The artist's intent in contemporary art: matter and process in transition. PhD thesis, University of Glasgow

SBMK (1999) Decision-making model for the conservation and restoration of modern and contemporary art. https://sbmk.nl/source/documents/decision-making-model.pdf. Accessed 10 Nov 2020

Stigter S (2017) A behaviour index for complex artworks: a conceptual tool for contemporary art conservation. In: Bridgland J (ed) ICOM-CC 18th Triennial Conference Preprints, Copenhagen, 4–8 September 2017, art. 0910. International Council of Museums, Paris

van de Wetering E, van Wegen DH (1987) Roaming the stairs of the Tower of Babel: efforts to expand interdisciplinary involvement in the theory of restoration. In: Getty Conservation Institute (eds) ICOM-CC 8th Triennial Conference Preprints, Sydney, Australia

Vostell W (1970) Wolf Vostell in interview with Wolfgang Becker. In: Neue Galerie im Alten Kurhaus (eds) Wolf Vostell Elektronisch. Verlag, Aachen
Vostell W (1974) Environments/Happenings 1958-1974. Editions du Chene, Paris
Vostell M (ed) (2012) Vostell. Ein Leben lang. Eine Werkbiografie. Verlag, Berlin/Kassel
Weibel P (ed) (2016) Beuys, Brock, Vostell. Aktion. Partizipation. Performance. Hatje Cantz Verlag, Karlsruhe
Westfälische Rundschau (1972) Das Museumskaugummi ist schon zerkaut. In: Hammer G (ed) Westfälische Rundschau. Essen, 23 February 1972

Julia Giebeler is a freelance conservator for modern and contemporary art. She also has a half-time position at the *Moontower Foundation*, where she works with Rebecca Horn and her long-time team to prepare her estate. In 2009 Julia graduated from the Cologne Institute of Conservation Sciences (CICS), her diploma thesis being on the preservation and reinstallation of an interactive video installation. In 2012 she earned an MA from the same institute; her master thesis deals with the preservation of Heinz Mack's early light kinetics as a case study in conservation theory. From 2013 to 2021, in addition to her work as a freelance conservator, she was a research associate at CICS, where she focused on ethics, theory and decision-making in contemporary art conservation.

Gunnar Heydenreich is Professor for Conservation of Modern and Contemporary Art at the Cologne Institute of Conservation Sciences (CICS)/Technische Hochschule Köln. He studied conservation of paintings at the Hochschule für Bildende Künste in Dresden and he gained a PhD from the Courtauld Institute of Art, London. From 1995 to 2009 he was head of paintings and contemporary art conservation at the Restaurierungszentrum in Düsseldorf. He was a founding member of the International Network for the Conservation of Contemporary Art (INCCA) and co-organiser and participant of several European research projects on the conservation of contemporary art: *Inside Installations*, *PRACTICs*, *NeCCAR*, and *NACCA*. He is head of the Cranach Digital Archive (lucascranach.org) at the Kunstpalast in Düsseldorf.

Andrea Sartorius is a conservator of contemporary art at Nationalgalerie im Hamburger Bahnhof, Museum für Gegenwart, Berlin. Previously, she was the conservator at Kunstmuseum Wolfsburg (2009 – 2020). She holds an MA in conservation of paintings from the Hochschule für Bildende Künste, Dresden, Germany. She completed post-graduate internships at the Hamilton Kerr Institute (Cambridge UK) and The J. Paul Getty Museum (Los Angeles), and she won a fellowship in media art conservation at Bek & Frohnert LLC (New York). From 2017 – 2021, she worked as a research associate for the Cologne Institute of Conservation Science (CICS), focussing on decision-making in contemporary art conservation.

Part V
The Role of Research in the Art Museum

The Living Process of Conserving Performance: Theory and Practice in the Conservation of Performance-Based Artworks at Tate

Louise Lawson, Duncan Harvey, Ana Ribeiro, and Hélia Marçal

Abstract The development of the documentation and conservation of performance-based artworks has been a key priority for Tate's Conservation department. The rise in complexity of the relationship between the institution and the artworks entering the collection prompted the development of current practices relating to the documentation and conservation of performance within the time-based media conservation team. This chapter explores the development of the current documentation strategies for the conservation of performance at Tate, by highlighting not only the impact of collecting practices in the development of knowledge, but also how the process results on the creation of both theoretical and practical forms of practice. The chapter will focus on the development of core documentation tools and theoretical models for understanding performance art and how it relates to the museum.

Keywords Performance · Conservation strategy · Theory · Practice · Knowledge production

1 Introduction

Historically, performance art has predominantly existed outside of the museum, with performances only finding their way into museum permanent collections in the form of documents, props, film, video and other material remains (Wheeler 2013; Calonje 2015). However, since 2005, it became increasingly common to see performance being collected *as performance* within institutions. Tate began collecting performance in 2005, and now has over thirty performance artworks. These works have different degrees of complexity depending on aspects of display, execution, or

L. Lawson (✉) · D. Harvey · A. Ribeiro
Tate, London, UK
e-mail: louise.lawson@tate.org.uk; duncan.harvey@tate.org.uk; ana.ribeiro@tate.org.uk

H. Marçal
University College London, London, UK
e-mail: h.marcal@ucl.ac.uk

R. van de Vall, V. van Saaze (eds.), *Conservation of Contemporary Art*, Studies in Art, Heritage, Law and the Market 9, https://doi.org/10.1007/978-3-031-42357-4_16

collection care activities (Lawson et al. 2019). Given the varying complexity, it can be difficult to pin down how such complexities affect the artworks' current and future needs. Conservation, now arguably more than ever, needs to find ways to acknowledge various forms and sources of knowledge in its practice.

This chapter will explore the ways in which Tate has developed its *Strategy for the Documentation and Conservation of Performance Art* (henceforth *Strategy*). We will explore (1) how the development of the *Strategy* brought together what is commonly defined as theory and practice, considering how the relationship of these separate forms coalesce as knowledge-making activities, and (2) how the collecting and display practices intertwined with conservation, such as the acquisition and display of complex objects, triggers revision, readjustment, and the creation and development of conservation processes and procedures.

In framing the chapter, we start with a review of relevant literature on the conservation of performance. Although the exploration takes place within Tate, the chapter will discuss how and where Tate is situated within the wider museum ecology. Efforts to delimit the boundaries of the performance art object and how it behaves in the museum have been pioneered by researchers across the field, based in many institutions[1] and theoretical geographies.[2] This review will consider the ways in which the field of conservation has responded to the acquisition of performance artworks that ought to be activated *as performance*. Following on from the literature review, we will reflect on the development of theoretical frameworks and tools for the conservation of performance at Tate. We will draw on various examples from Tate's collection to examine how the key-tool of our *Strategy*—called *Performance Specification*—has developed since 2016. In this sense, we will demonstrate not only how changes in collection practices have impacted the characteristics of such a tool, but also how forms of experimentation with similar artworks have consolidated the knowledge about conservation risks, or how to capture and create documentation for various types of performance practice. Through this exploration, we argue that the development of the *Strategy* demanded a model of working based on collective effort, built on accumulated interactions with people, structures and objects. Those interactions are at the core of our knowledge-making activities, which are as live as performance artworks are meant to be. The living process of conserving live performance we will be exploring here is, therefore, recognisably made of moments of revision, of disconnect between hypothesis and experimentation, of performative

[1] The number of museums that started to collect performance artwork has steadily increased since 2010 (Lawson et al. 2019).

[2] Theoretical geographies that are part of the constellation of perspectives concerned with the material continuation of performance-based art encompass, among other disciplines, performance studies, media studies or archival sciences. Conservation has started to consistently explore this topic around 2012, with the various perspectives aligning with the understanding that performance is necessarily conservable. These draw in efforts (particularly) from continental philosophy to conceptualise the idea of conservation of performance. For more on the ontology of performance within the conservation field (in particular, viewed through new materialism), see van den Hengel (2017), or Marçal (2019, 2021).

engagements of technique and knowledge, that in the end create the conditions to look at the conservation of performance as a step in the process of their own making.

2 A Brief Look into the Conservation of Performance[3]

Performance art can be (and has been) considered one of the most volatile, intangible, precarious, and (de)materialised art genres (cf. Phelan 1993). This is due to its gestural embodiment, its resistance to categories, or its activation through forms of action. Performance art's traditional resistance to commodification (cf. Goldberg 2011 [1979]) led many to be left to wonder if performance would find its way into the museum.[4] Looking back at the history of how performance art has been displayed in museums, however, the first thing we notice is that performance artworks were never not part of the museum. Museums have been linked to performance art practice since the 1960s, when the genre was consolidated (Jones 2012). The first live art event held at Tate, for example, took place in 1968.[5] When entering museum collections performance artworks, however, initially lost some of their so-called *liveness*, being acquired as photography, moving image, or installation. The transformation of performance artworks into these indexes became part of current practice, deeply influencing most debates in the field of Performance Studies (in relation to visual and media studies) and Museum Studies (at least the ones concerning with the places occupied by performance art) in the 1990s. Particularly in the case of Performance Art, studies stemming from these debates were mostly focused on performance art ontology; specifically on how the nature of performance was rehearsed in its alignment with,[6] or opposition to,[7] practices of mediation (cf. Marçal 2022a, 2022b).

---

[3]This literature review is drawn from the article co-authored by Louise Lawson, Acatia Finbow and Hélia Marçal in 2019 (Lawson et al. 2019). Marçal's contribution to both literature reviews was partially derived from her unpublished PhD dissertation *From intangibility to materiality and back again* (2018).

[4]See, for example, the webpage of the research project *Collecting the Performative* (2012–2014), https://www.tate.org.uk/about-us/projects/collecting-performative. Accessed 10 June 2020.

[5]This event was saw Stuart Brisley and Peter Sedgley making a polyurethane sculpture in the gallery. This proto history of performance art at Tate was developed as part of the research project *Performance at Tate: Into the Space of Art*. The dates referred in this chapter were drawn from the 2016 online publication of the project: https://www.tate.org.uk/research/publications/performance-at-tate. This project included a timeline, see https://www.tate.org.uk/research/publications/performance-at-tate/timeline; for the project page see https://www.tate.org.uk/about-us/projects/performance-tate-collecting-archiving-and-sharing-performance-and-performative, all accessed 24 Oct 2018.

[6]In *Liveness: Performance in a Mediatized Culture* (2nd edn, London: Routledge, 2008 [1998]), the media theorist Philip Auslander contests the idea of live as being unmediated, asserting, on the contrary, and all live existence is inherently mediated. Several scholars influenced by poststructuralism, have aligned themselves with Auslander's proposal, in more nuanced ways.

[7]This is the view shared by Performance Studies theorists drawing on psychoanalysis and feminist epistemologies. Influenced by Lacan, Peggy Phelan suggested in *Unmarked: The Politics of Performance* (London: Routledge, 1993) that performance becomes itself through its disappearance, resisting any form of representation and mediation.

Institutions started to collect performance artworks *as performances*, beyond their previous representational indexes in 2005. This was despite performance artworks being considered unruly,[8] non-conforming to the museum's long-standing principles and structures. This shift is partly related to the development of certain approaches to the documentation of performance, largely stemming from media theorist Philip Auslander's attitude to documentation (Auslander 1998), or artistic developments that are akin to what art historian Claire Bishop has called "delegated performances" (Bishop 2012).[9] These and other efforts made clear that documentation, instead being ontologically opposed to performance art, may, in fact, be crucial for performance artworks' survival as plural and ever-changing manifestations.[10] Or, in other words, to their conservation.[11]

The conservation of performance art has been developed in the context of the conservation of time-based media art.[12] Despite being a relatively recent undertaking in conservation, several dedicated studies have emerged in the last decade. These have been mostly developed by researchers and museum conservation teams.[13] One of the main research efforts from this decade was the research network *Collecting the Performative*, launched in April 2012.[14] A key output from this pioneering effort was *The Live List: What to consider when collecting live works* (2014), which details

[8]The term "unruly" was coined in the field of sociology of art in the seminal essay by Fernando Domínguez Rubio 'Unruly Objects' (Domínguez Rubio 2014). In this essay, Domínguez Rubio characterises objects as either docile or unruly depending on the ways in which they interact with the museum structure. According to this characterisation, oil paintings, for their movability, durability or long-standing categorisation, could be considered as docile, while time-based media artworks—inherently variable, hardly portable and quite fragile—can be seen as unruly.

[9]The art historian Claire Bishop calls "delegated performances" to performance works that are executed by others than the artist following a set of instructions, or, in Bishop's words, "the act of hiring non-professionals or specialists in other fields to undertake the job of being present and performing at a particular time and a particular place on behalf of the artist, and following his/her instructions" (Bishop 2012, p. 219).

[10]The approach we are exploring in this article stems from discussions that propose that performance has a "viral" nature and that becomes itself through forms of activation (and not disappearance or loss). This perspective echoes discussions by theorists such as Philip Auslander (2008 [1988]) or Christopher Bedford (2012).

[11]Marçal (2022b) argues that performance exists within a spectrum of collectability, and, within that spectrum, delegated performances are somewhat akin to "docile" artworks, to use the terminology coined by Domínguez Rubio (2014).

[12]In the context of this chapter, we will be using the term "performance art" instead of "live art". For more on this distinction and why we use "performance art" see Lawson et al. (2019).

[13]For a description of these projects, see Lawson et al. (2019) and Marçal (2019).

[14]Tate, Collecting the Performative: A Research Network Examining Emerging Practice for Collecting and Conserving Performance-based Art, https://www.tate.org.uk/about-us/projects/collecting-performative. Accessed 3 April 2019.

some questions at the time of acquisition.[15] These were collected in a meeting that analysed the project's results and brought many people from diverse backgrounds together to discuss and agree the basic parameters of a performance work and how it can live in the museum. The results of this project offer pioneering perspectives on the challenges and possibilities of collecting and conserving performance. As identified by Pip Laurenson and Vivian van Saaze, the challenges are: (1) performance art is typically connected to a moment in time, called the original event, and is, many times, linked to the presence of particular performer (usually, the artist), (2) museum processes tend to be oriented towards material-based practices, and (3) performance artworks are part of a network of dependencies, and those relations are hard to maintain. (Laurenson and van Saaze 2014).[16]

Among the conservation strategies that have been suggested to tackle the challenges offered by performance artworks, documentation appears to have become the most prominently used by conservators inside and outside institutions. Annet Dekker and Vivian van Saaze, for example, shared the documentation process Extra Dry at NIMk (Nederlands Instituut voor Mediakunst, The Netherlands) in 2013, proposing a model that considers how documentation and artworks co-constitute each other (van Saaze and Dekker 2013).[17] Hélia Marçal has been contributing for this discussion, particularly by reflecting on the relationality of this process (e.g., Marçal 2017, 2019, 2021; Marçal and Macedo 2017). Additionally, in the context of the UK's Arts and Humanities Research Council (AHRC) funded research project *Performance at Tate: Collecting, Archiving and Sharing Performance and the Performative* (partnered by the University of Exeter), Acatia Finbow has identified documentation models stemming from museum structures (Finbow 2018). Based at the Tate, this Collaborative Doctoral Award was particularly relevant in the development of the Strategy, as it interrogated the role of documentation in the intersection of performance art and the museum, while confirmed the need for a conservation strategy specifically tailored to performance art (Finbow 2018, see also Lawson et al. 2019).

Albeit still concerned with this topic, studies on the conservation of performance art have expanded beyond documentation.[18] Three recent collaborative research projects—*Reshaping the Collectible: When Artworks Live in the Museum* (Tate, 2018–2022, led by Pip Laurenson), *Performance: Conservation, Materiality,*

[15] Based at the Tate, this research network was a cross disciplinary, cross-institutional, collaborative project that brought together museum practitioners, scholars, and artists. The Live List was developed in the final network meeting. For more on this see Laurenson et al. (2014).

[16] The idea of social network in the care of performance artworks has been further explored by the project *Reshaping the Collectible: When Artworks Live in the Museum*, through the conservation of the artwork *Ten Years Alive on the Infinite Plain*, created by the artist Tony Conrad in 1972. See Lawson et al. (2022), Marçal et al. (2022), Marçal (2022b), and Lawson and Marçal (2022) to access the results stemming from this case-study. For more information on the project see https://www.tate.org.uk/research/reshaping-the-collectible. Accessed 25 May 2020.

[17] For more on this documentation model see http://www.nimk.nl/eng/inside-movement-knowledge. Accessed 28 March 2019.

[18] For a review of bibliography and projects see Marçal (2022a).

Knowledge (Bern Academy of the Arts, 2020–2024, led by Hanna Hölling; a book resulting from this project was published in 2023 - see Hölling 2023), and *Precarious Movements: Choreography & the Museum* (University New South Wales, 2021–2024, led by Erin Brannigan, with an edited volume pending Spring 2024)—are worth mentioning, as they aim at devising novel ways to understand the relationship between performance and the museum, with some of these efforts engaging with one of the most crucial knowledge gaps from the field: how to document forms of knowledge that are not so easily described, called implicit, tacit and embodied knowledge,[19] or, to use a term coined by the performance studies theorist Diana Taylor, that are part of a "repertoire" of practices (Taylor 2013). This chapter—and the work developed by the time-based team at the Tate—also seeks to bridge (part of) such gap.

As this chapter will demonstrate, capturing such forms of practice was not an initial concern to Tate, as most of the artworks acquired until 2016 were so-called instruction-based artworks—i.e., were easily activated by following a set of clear instructions that were either provided by the artist or developed as part of the documentation process undertaken by conservators (Marçal 2022b). These instruction-based artworks allowed for the creation of conservation strategies that were akin to the processes already undertaken in the care of other time-based media artworks. But, as we will see, the acquisition of artworks with growing complexity, dependent on knowledges[20] that were not so easily conveyed or understood, led us to reflect on our process of documentation through a different lens. Specifically, it led us to analyse the ways in which we produce documentation: what and how we were recording information and what ought to be documented and through which methods. It also led us to discuss how we were engaging with theory and practice when producing knowledge about those artworks. On the one hand, we were asking ourselves what is the relationship between theory and practice in the work we do every day. On the other hand, we were keen to see if understanding the relationship between the two could lead us to reframe our assumptions and revise our tools to acknowledge and document the various types of knowledge that emerge in the conservation of performance.

[19] All of these denominations respond to different sets of practices and disciplines. In the context of this chapter, these terms will be used interchangeably with Taylor's understanding of the "repertoire."

[20] The use of the word "knowledges" here is derived from the seminal paper by Donna Haraway, called 'Situated Knowledges: The Science Question in Feminism and the Privilege of Partial Perspective' (Haraway 1988). This article puts forward the idea of "situated knowledges" as a departure from male- and Western-centred perspectives on science and knowledge production, which often convey the need for objectivity (which, objectively, according to feminist scholars, does not exist in absolute terms) and an ideal of an universal truth. Haraway states situated knowledges provide "a more adequate, richer, better account of a world, in order to live in it well and in critical, reflexive relation to our own as well as others' practices of domination and the unequal parts of privilege and oppression that make up all positions" (Haraway 1988, p. 579).

3 A Dialogue Between Theory and Practice

Discourses about the difference between theory and practice have been rehearsed in various scientific fields, including conservation (e.g., Sully 2015; Muñoz Viñas 2014).[21] Many are the instances where we hear how much theory could learn from practice and vice versa, or how theory can indeed be considered a technique (Verbeeck 2016). The continuous assertions of what makes theory and practice distinct resonates with what the physician and Nobel laureate Richard Feynman articulated as the difference between mathematics and physics, stating that "mathematicians prepare abstract reasoning that's ready 'to be used' even though they don't know what it's being used for," while physicists have "meaning to all the phrases," developing the understanding of how the abstract connects with "the real world" (Veisdal 2020, n.p.n.).[22] Feynman explains that "the greatest discoveries, it always turns out, abstract away from the model" (Veisdal 2020, n.p.n.). In other words, the abstract world and the real world are not the same and yet, as Feynman explains, mathematics would lose applicability without physics, and physics would very likely be much poorer without mathematical thinking.[23] We can think about theory and practice as a similar dichotomy, where theory would lose its applicability without the translation into practice and *vice versa* in terms of practice informing theory. However, we can see how the distinction between technique (from "techné," also translated as "craft") and knowledge expands way beyond the remit of mathematics (theory-driven) and physics (mostly experiment-driven). We can associate other dualisms to this type of binary: the one of the mind and the body, or humans and nonhumans. For the purposes of this chapter, these dualisms are worth exploring.

Firstly, the Cartesian mind-body dualism seems, at the first glance, to be self-evident if we think about the activity of solving a mathematical problem versus learning how to perform a choreography. One could say that it doesn't matter how

[21] Curiously enough, Salvador Muñoz Viñas, while suggesting that theory "is usually defined by contrasting it with practice", provides an understanding of conservation theory as being related to ethics: "When a conservation teacher explains, for instance, the effect of a solvent's surface tension on its dissolving capabilities when applied to a paint layer, he or she is dealing with a theoretical topic within the conservation field; however, no one would consider it to be 'conservation theory.' 'Conservation theory' is most often related to 'conservation ethics,' although these notions are not synonyms. This is a convention which, even though it is very widespread, is still a convention" (Muñoz Viñas 2014, p. xii).

[22] The Feyman lectures are available in many places on the Internet, having also been widely published. Veisdal (2020) provides some excerpts specifically relevant to discuss the differences between mathematics and physics.

[23] Many are the theoretical understandings between the real-world and its representations, and mathematics and physics are, evidently, not the only disciplines that aim to create theoretical models for describing the world and the universe. In this case, the chapter is informed by feminist perspectives that are intrinsically linked to modern theoretical physics, and this relationship to the description of the uses of mathematics and physics by Richard Feynman seemed appropriate to the authors.

much you read about performing, for example, Trisha Brown's *Set and Reset*, or Tchaikovsky's *The Nutcracker*—that is something you only learn and practice by doing. Similarly, it is quite common to hear that, no matter how much you practice, you either are able to develop abstract concepts or you are not. What we see by looking closer, however, is that the body and mind are profoundly associated, intertwined. This is, of course, a political and theoretical stance[24] but, as much of the theories and models that are brought into the "real world," this one also has practical ramifications. Going back to performing a series of specific movements, somewhere during the twentieth century (Borgdorff et al. 2020), research came to acknowledge the methodological affordances of dance and movement in the constitution of knowledge that, although often implicit and untranslatable, can be essential in performing tasks related to performing movements and beyond—this is specifically the case with the development of studies around "tacit" or "embodied" knowledge (Borgdorff et al. 2020). And in producing artistic research looking for so-called practical or technical outcomes, it is clear that dancers, artists, researchers engage in experimentation and develop their own interpretations (or theory) about their own practice (cf. Borgdorff et al. 2020). To use the words of Henk Borgdorff, Peter Peters and Trevor Pinch in the introduction to the edited volume *Dialogues Between Artistic Research and Science and Technology Studies*, the shift in the past century in recognising the ways in which implicit and explicit knowledge are co-constitutive "corrected the focus in epistemology on propositional forms of knowing and understanding: a correction correlating to phenomenology, that would eventually also be taken up by contemporary non-reductive cognitive science" (Borgdorff et al. 2020, p. 11).

It could almost be said the same type of co-constitution also happens in the interaction between humans and the so-called nonhumans, such as technology, nature or, for example, artworks.[25] Although intuitively humans associate knowledge-making activities as a one-way street, studies in material culture (e.g., Ingold 2013), or new materialisms (e.g., Barad 2007 or Haraway 1988), have unveiled how much of the knowledge we, as humans, develop is dependent on the object or material being studied. The agency of these objects can be seen in various knowledge-making activities, including conservation: as an example, the types of

[24]This theoretical and political stance is also related to feminist perspectives derived from Donna Haraway, and explored, among others, by Karen Barad. The need to assert the inseparability of body and mind has political ramification particularly in what pertains to the idea of "situatedness," and to the impact of biases in the production of knowledge. To use Haraway's words: "[B]odies as objects of knowledge are material-semiotic nodes. Their boundaries materialize in social interaction. Boundaries are drawn by mapping practices; 'objects' do not pre-exist as such. Objects are boundary projects. But boundaries shift from within; boundaries are very tricky. What boundaries provisionally contain remains generative, productive of meanings and bodies. Siting (sighting) boundaries is a risky practice" (Haraway 1988, p. 595).

[25]The study of humans and nonhumans has been particularly prominent in philosophy of science and science and technology studies. Of course, one can mention here the work of Callon, Latour and Law and the development of ANT. This terminology is also widely used within the field of new materialisms.

knowledge one can produce from conserving a relatively stable artwork on paper are expectedly quite different from the ones emerging from the interaction with a degraded polyurethane sculpture (see e.g., Marçal 2019, 2021). It is through our interaction with different types of objects that we develop our own theoretical models. Those models can, in turn, be refuted in each interaction with a new type of object or, even, when we get to see an object that we have known for many years through a different lens.

Through this exploration it is clear that exchange of theory and practice is critical within conservation. Knowledge-production for conservation is driven by interaction with people, structures, and objects, being characterised by the melting pot that happens, to use the words by the scholar and conservator Hanna Hölling, "at the crossroads of theory and practice" (2017, p. 7). Theory has been defined by the philosopher and conservator Muriel Verbeeck as a way "to distance ourselves from the profusion of specific cases and formulate principles; not rules, but guidelines," with theory working as an instrument that "clarifies our decision-making choices, prior to any intervention" (Verbeeck 2016, p. 238). In the context of our work in the conservation of performance, we can define theory as the development of a series of ideas and hypotheses that are built on what we observe through thought-experiments and practice. That is the case, for example, when we categorise forms of performance practice depending on their characteristics—such as defining them as instruction-based artworks—and then make assumptions about their behaviour with time. The empirical data collected by engaging with artworks is, therefore, synthesised in developing further experiments, tools or concepts that might be relevant for our ongoing practice. From these descriptions and the above discussion, it becomes evident how much of the process of knowledge production in conservation, usually defined and described as consisting of separate phases of theory and practice (hence discussions about the divide between them), actually seems to be inevitably intertwined. When considering the conservation of performance, this discussion on theory-practice further leads us to two questions:[26] (1) What are the affordances of conservation, collecting, and display practices in the creation of theoretical models? And (2) In which ways can the development of theoretical models respond to the needs of the "real world," and to the call to capture and translate knowledges that resist forms of abstraction? Although answering these questions in full goes beyond the scope of this chapter, in drawing on the process of developing our *Strategy for the Documentation and Conservation of Performance Art*[27] we can begin to explore some of the answers.

---

[26] Here we are using "theory-practice" to highlight the intraconnectedness of these processes.

[27] For more information see https://www.tate.org.uk/about-us/projects/documentation-conservation-performance/strategy-and-glossary. Accessed 10 June 2020.

4 Conservation of Performance Art at Tate: Bridging Practice and Theory

The development of the *Strategy* started in 2016, drawing on an infrastructure of practice that had been created since the appointment of the first Curator of International Art (Performance) in 2003, and the acquisition of the first live performance artwork into the Tate permanent collection two years later in 2005: Roman Ondak's *Good Feeling in Good Times* (2003). It is impossible not to recognise the impact of this curatorial trend in the shift that was observed in the conservation department. The somewhat unruly (after Domínguez Rubio 2014) behaviour of these works led to the development of strategies and procedures, in movements that resemble—in the words of Vivian van Saaze and her co-authors—"processes of adaptive change" (van Saaze et al. 2018). Similar to what is described by van Saaze et al., there were key moments that indeed triggered change and, yet, the consolidation of practice and the reframing of institutional processes are both developed through the accumulation of such moments. One of those key-moments came with the opening of the Blavatnik building and the simultaneous development of the curatorial programme *BMW Tate Live*, which led to the activation of five key performances from Tate's collection in one single weekend in June 2016. In response to the announcement of the displays, the, at the time, Time-based Media Conservation Manager Louise Lawson and Collaborative Doctorate Award student Acatia Finbow began to research the five proposed artworks with the goal not only to understand the ways in which they would be activated in the gallery and the conservation documentation's role in such process, but also to probe the ways in which the processes for documenting and conserving performance could be systematised and formalised. This process prompted a review of the applied documentation models, leading also to a reassessment of our existing conservation strategies.

The approach to the conservation of performance was further developed in the years following the first acquisitions of performance artworks into the collection, mostly by applying and adapting existing procedures. This process of adaptation took into consideration the short to long-term needs of each work, negotiated through ongoing collaboration with artists and their representatives. At this early stage, the time-based media conservation team used existing documentation strategies and templates to answer the needs of time-based media artworks like video and film installations. The template "display specification,"[28] is one of these documents, and is typically used to gather the display characteristics of installations.

The adaptation of existing strategies was first clearly seen in 2014 with the acquisition of *A Tax Haven Run By Women* by the artist Monster Chetwynd (created

[28] A display specification is a document used by time-based media conservation at Tate to capture information on an artwork specifically related to the requirements for the works display, such as description, exhibition media format details, gallery, equipment and power requirements, details on spares, consumables or other items relevant for the installation or display, wiring diagrams, technological, as well as costs.

in 2010–11). The work has multiple sculptural components, including a large bus in the form of a cat and several costumes, which can be exhibited alongside a digital video of the performance. Working in close collaboration with the artist, curatorial and conservation, a display specification for the video element of the work was written.[29] The use of this template, however, shifted in both form and narrative style, with the conservator adding specific fields, such as performance instructions and casting and make up guidelines. These fields were added as the display specification in its standard template form did not have existing sections that could be utilised. The narrative style changed to become more fluid, with the incorporation of hand drawings from the artist, which, besides the extensive research on audiovisual materials from previous activations, were used to capture the movement of the performance at different moments across its duration. This change in a working practice of the team highlighted that the operative models of understanding and interpretation were not immediately sufficient to capture the contingencies offered by performance artworks. The knowledge production process undertaken by conservators, and triggered by the characteristics of this work, prompted a change in established paradigms, namely the ones that were allowing us to define the boundaries of performance artworks as with any other time-based artwork in collection.

The issue witnessed with *Tax Haven Run By Women* was also prevalent with other artworks in the collection, and the *BMW Tate Live* programme in 2016 prompted an analysis of the information we had specifically for the five artworks that were going to be activated. *The Live List: What to Consider When Collecting Live Works*, which was an output from the research project *Collecting the Performative*, was used to analyse the existing documentation held by conservation on each artwork. This analysis identified gaps in the existing documentation. The *Live List* proved to be a robust tool to facilitate such an analysis, but it also identified themes that would be useful to group together, such as space, time and documentation and to situate existing questions and develop new questions that would further probe that specific theme. It also became clear through the analysis that the information was separate and could benefit from being pulled together in one main documentation tool, moving the live list from a tool to prompt at the point of collecting to a tool that could also be used for the ongoing care of the performance. Discussions between the conservation and curatorial departments allowed for testing the assumptions that were underpinning this first model.[30] These discussions determined the expectations we had regarding documentation process—from contextual information to the development of material histories and a clear understanding of technical information—looking towards the integration of these in future development efforts.

Through their interaction with the artworks in their activated state, and knowledge transfer with other internal Tate teams, Lawson and Finbow worked to ultimately create what is now called the *Performance Specification*. This document has

[29] Documentation created by time-based media conservator, Esther Harris across 2014–2016.

[30] Internal workshop on the development of model for performance conservation. Led by Louise Lawson and Acatia Finbow in March 2017.

multiple incarnations and names, initially when created it was called the *Tate Live List*, a proto-documentation model that captured the parameters that were essential for each of the five artworks as a series of questions and answers. This then developed to become a blank template that had ten themes; space, time, condition, performers, physical components, logistics, audience, documentation, previous and future performances. Each theme has a series of promoting questions. This was called *Display Specification – Performance-based Artworks*. This was later refined to seven themes (space, time, condition, physical components, performers, audience, logistics) with two themes (previous and future activations) becoming separate supporting documents (Lawson et al. 2019). This document was ultimately renamed *Performance Specification*, to reflect more accurately its applicability and use, later on becoming the key-tool to apply to artworks entering the collection. However, the development of this work would need to be further stretched in both the possibilities afforded by this tool and the horizons of the operative concepts on which it was based.

5 Redefining Boundaries, Rehearsing New Models

In exploring the affordances of the *Performance Specification*, it was important to continue examining how this tool would be stretched with the acquisition of more complex performances. Working to consider how, with Tate's ambition to collect more significant and complex performance, the characteristics of a tool would develop, require revision or adjustment and where and how new processes would be needed. The opportunity to further test and stretch the performance specification continued across 2016, which was a critical year with the proposal to acquire both *The Reverse Collection*, by the artist Tarek Atoui, and *Your Face Is/Is Not Enough*, by the artist Kevin Beasley. *The Reverse Collection* would highlight the need for creation of a comprehensive strategy that would have to include the formalisation of theoretical models, such as terminology and overall assumptions about the role and purpose of the documentation produced by the time-based media conservation team. *Your Face Is/Is Not Enough* would, on the other hand, highlight the importance of creating additional moments where conservation would engage with the artwork, such as the rehearsals and different moments of activation, leading to the development of new tools.

5.1 *The Reverse Collection, Tarek Atoui, 2016*

In 2016, Tate invited Tarek Atoui to activate *The Reverse Collection,* the third stage of an ongoing performance project informed by an interest in the "oral tradition" in music, and the effect that the standardisation of musical notation and instrumentation had on this.[31] The artist characterises the work as an exploration of the "transformation of form through sound and orality"; its digital sound files, instruments and performances are a "result or consequence" of this exploration.[32]

The project began as part of the 2014 Berlin Biennale, the artist, with six percussion, six wind and six string musicians, was granted access to play and record over 50 instruments held within the collection of the Ethnological Museum of Berlin, Dahlem. Pivoting on the idea of oral tradition, the instruments were chosen on the basis that they lacked significant information regarding "their sociocultural provenance, or, crucially, any instructions on how to play them" (Sawa 2016). From the audio recording of the Dahlem performance, the artist created seven edited sound files which were presented to instrument makers and a ceramicist who were to create new instruments that would somehow reflect their response to the file. This "reverse engineering" was the process behind the creation of ten instruments that served as the focal point of the second and third stages of the project, *The Reverse Sessions*, performed in the Kurimanzutto Gallery in Mexico in 2014, and *The Reverse Collection*, as it was seen at Tate in 2016.

The Reverse Collection was collected by Tate as both a performance and a multimedia installation. As an installation it comprises six instruments and two installed sound recordings, one from *The Dahlem Sessions* and one from its display at Tate Modern in 2016. The performance version can be activated in one of two "modes," "Happening Mode" and "Concert Mode." "Happening Mode" refers to open-ended, purely improvisational musician-led performances to take place during the opening hours of the exhibiting institution; it is to be seen in contrast to "Concert Mode." "Concert Mode" refers to a specific concert-style performance of a given duration with a distinct beginning and end led by a composer or ensemble of musicians presenting a pre-conceived improvisational composition.[33] These performances centre around the notion of musical experimentation based on collaborative improvisation between the players. The approach was guided by a conscious desire to subvert typical methods of ethnomusicological preservation, a point further emphasised when one considers the subjects of his experimentation were instruments that had become static museum objects.

The central issues that were encountered with *The Reverse Collection* occurred primarily during the acquisition of the work. These focused on the complexities of attempting to articulate the critical aspects of the work in its two display modes, the sculptural elements, the requirement to identify and support the networks for the performance that existed beyond the institution and the need to articulate our theoretical models differently to address the contingencies brought to the fore by the work. The theoretical models developed until the acquisition of this work relied on an understanding of performance artworks as a series of events and movements that could be conveyed as instructions. As it will become clear, *The Reverse*

---

[31] Artist Interview (2016, p. 2). Unpublished Tate internal documentation.

[32] Ibid., 30.

[33] 03 Activations Atoui (2016, p. 1). Unpublished Tate internal documentation.

Collection contradicted that model both in the ways that it defined the boundaries of performance artworks and how it led us to describe and conserve them through the *Performance Specification*.

The differences in the two display modes of the work led to a clear need to articulate what we called the "condition" of the work in ways we had not experienced before. The ways in which the *Performance Specification* template was made, namely its structure, did not allow for flexibility in making clear the two display modes, which led the team to undertake the first revision of the template, moving "condition" to the first page of the document. The inherent variability of the artwork also made evident that the word "condition" did not suffice the complexity of what we were trying to describe—i.e., the material conditions needed to display the artwork and how they could change with time. We, then, decided to change the name of this section from "condition" to "artwork requirements," as we thought this term was more truthful to the practice we were trying to rehearse with this document. This change, however, led to many other reflections about what "requirements" could mean, and, ultimately, on what we were trying to achieve.

One of the main aspects that were particularly hard to grasp was how much a "requirement" would continue to be a "requirement." Also, in recognising how much the will to respond to the word "requirements" could impair forms of change that were not only acceptable, but desired in the case of *The Reverse Collection*, the time-based media conservation team were determined to find a way to relay to lending institutions the features that were flexible. The possibilities afforded by this artwork—from its display modes to the sheer fact that it had the possibility of having the instruments remade in each iteration—made us think less about fixed properties, which could be deemed essential to the work, and more about how the artwork could change in each materialisation, repeating patterns and performing behaviours in each activation. This led us, once again, to revise the theoretical models we had rehearsed with instruction-based artworks, making visible that there the various elements that constituted the artwork were less static, and instead developing with the artwork itself. We began to consider what would be "constant" or "in flux" in each iteration of *The Reverse Collection*. We would define "constant" as material conditions that must exist for the work to be activated, while "in flux" would describe what would, could and should change every time the artwork was to be shown. The use of these terms highlighted a shift from a more essentialist (cf. Castriota 2019 as well as Castriota's contribution in this volume (Chapter 4) - Castriota 2023), or somewhat formulaic, way of looking at performance art, towards an understanding of the identity of these works as existing in a flux and being manifested through their "ongoing historicity," to use a term coined by the new materialist scholar Karen Barad (2007). Identifying the materiality of a performance artwork as a fluid process, or a balanced act between constant features and materialities in flux, highlighted the need to reflect on what remains after the event is over. In the case of *The Reverse Collection*, such reflection took the sculptural elements that are made and remade as part of the performance as a starting point.

Understanding the possibilities of *The Reverse Collection* and how much of the process of conservation was based on the recognition of the *ongoing historicity* of artwork, led to the identification of two forms of performative existence, afforded by the sculptural elements that form part of the artwork. Besides discussions on the status of these objects, which were undertaken with the artist, the curator and registrars, there were other explorations offered by these objects. As the work had sculptural elements that would be stored, questions around what does a stored performance look like and mean began to surface. Some components of the work (such as sculptural or media elements) may be preserved or even stored, but the physical manifestation of performances is always in flux, appearing and disappearing in its multiple forms. This reflection was the first moment that led us to refute one of the axioms of the theoretical models we had previously applied to performance artworks in the collection that were considered to be instruction-based: that of the performance artworks disappearing when not being displayed in the gallery. How much of this model could be performed when considering the artwork as unfolding?

The musical instruments kept by Tate are testimonies of a process, which has many other witnesses, namely the people who made the instruments: the knowledge- and instrument-makers. Not only were the instruments a way of storing part of the performance artwork, but the act of making such instruments existed way beyond the gallery walls.[34] As a matter of fact, the practices sustaining the creation of instruments, which were at the core of the artwork's formulation since its inception, continue to vibrate outside the museum, even as the artwork in its fullest stays invisible in the gallery space. The recognition of the hidden ways in which performance artworks remained in the gallery even after their physical manifestation in the galleries led us to reframe our understanding of artworks in the collection—instruction-based or not, moving from trying to contain the "disappearance" of the work, and rather changing our theoretical models to reflect shifts in its visibility and accessibility. We felt the need to articulate this shift in our interpretation of artworks in the collection by identifying states of existence as "dormant," used to describe a performance work in storage, or "active," indicating the period from the moment the artwork is selected for display until the last second of activation is over.

The recognition of these two states has also allowed the time-based media conservation team to rehearse and formalise the purpose of conserving performance art in the institution, as that of maintaining the conditions for artworks to move from a dormant to an active state. Articulating the purpose of conserving a performance artwork in the museum as a process of ensuring its activation and change across time not only reflects the ideal of keeping artworks live, but also promotes the expectation of keeping them alive. Assuming this expectation at the forefront of the overarching goals for our practice, it became clear that the documentation tool that was created for the preservation of performance—the *Performance Specification*—did not go far enough in writing the material history of these artworks, defining the ways in which they change over time, or mapping the people, networks, objects and technology that

[34] Pip Laurenson discussed this issue further in a talk called 'Can Artworks Live in a Museums Collection?', September 19, 2016, at the MoMA, New York. For more information see https://vimeo.com/184868009. Accessed 10 June 2020.

contribute to the ways they are made. This prompted an awareness of the criticality of articulating an overall *Strategy* that would approach the many issues raised by performance artworks not conforming to an instruction-based model, to provide context for the conservators now working with performance. The terms that emerged from our work with *The Reverse Collection* were put forward as a Glossary, which had the purpose of serving as an overarching framework for the *Strategy*, clarifying both its goals and its operative concepts. The development of the *Strategy* continued and, similarly to what happened in 2016 with the acquisition of *The Reverse Collection*, it was, once again, the acquisition and display of a complex performance artwork that propelled this effort, highlighting, in the process, aspects that were not visible with any other work in the collection. That artwork is called *Your Face Is/Is Not Enough*, and was created by the artist Kevin Beasley in 2016, the year it was also acquired by Tate.

5.2 *Your Face Is/Is Not Enough, Kevin Beasley, 2016*

First commissioned for the group exhibition *Ticks of the Watch* at the Renaissance Society in Chicago in 2016,[35] *Your Face Is/Is Not Enough* consists of twelve NATO-issued gas masks with megaphones sculpted by the artist into unique objects using several materials such as polyurethane foam, baseball caps and umbrellas, as well as eleven microphone stands and the participation of twelve hired performers. The hybrids of gas masks and megaphones are described as "poised both to defend against and to facilitate expressions of power."[36] In addition, they can be seen as "transforming symbols of control,"[37] which "evoke gestures of empowerment and agency within individual and collective acts of protest, power and protection."[38]

It is required that the performance must occur at least once, on the opening of an exhibition. Prior to the performance, eleven microphone stands should be installed in the space. When the performance takes place the twelve performers wear the gas masks and carry the megaphones. Each enters the gallery space, stops beside a microphone stand, attaches the hand-held voice-receiver of the megaphone to the nozzle of the gas masks using Velcro, and begins a series of three deep and audible breaths followed by a loud "AAH" sound. This sequence is repeated thirty times over a period of approximately 25–30 min. At the end the receiver is detached from the gas mask and is re-attached to the megaphone. The megaphone is rested on the

[35] *Your face is/is not enough* performance video recorded at the Renaissance Society, 2016: https://renaissancesociety.org/publishing/703/performance-kevin-beasley-your-face-is-is-not-enough/.

[36] The Renaissance Society at the University of Chicago. Apr 24–Jun 26, 2016 BETWEEN THE TICKS OF THE WATCH, Kevin Beasley, Peter Downsbrough, Goutam Ghosh, Falke Pisano, Martha Wilson.

[37] See Liverpool Biennial's website at: https://www.biennial.com/2018/exhibition/artists/kevin-beasley. Accessed 9 Aug 2019.

[38] Ibid.

floor, and the mask is placed on top of the stand except for one, which does not have a microphone stand and is installed directly on the floor. The performers bow and leave the space. With the masks placed onto the stands, the end of the activation means that the work can be experienced as a sculptural installation. While visitors are not allowed to physically interact with the sculptures, they are invited to walk around them as no barriers are permitted in the space.

Your Face Is/Is Not Enough was first activated at Tate in 2018, as part of the Liverpool Biennial.[39] For this activation, the performance was instantiated once over two different days during the opening of the exhibition weekend, following a period of rehearsals conducted by the artist. Activating the work requires the involvement with either the artist or one of their representatives to direct the rehearsals with the performers and other aspects of the preparation for the display. In the days prior to the performance, hired performers are required to attend two three-hour rehearsals, where the artist or their representative transmits the work. Given this was the first activation of the work within Tate, it meant it was the first time conservators could not just experience it but also test documentation already gathered, logistics involved and understand what else should be considered beyond the documentation supplied to us as part of its acquisition.

The reliance on the artist or one of their representatives to activate the performance made us aware that probably there were forms of knowledge at play that perhaps were not conveyed as part of a set of guidelines, including those provided by the artist's studio. Building on the practice that had been developed in the last two years, and on the theoretical models that had been first rehearsed and revised with the work undertaken around *The Reverse Collection*, the time-based media conservation team designed a protocol to interact with this artwork. This protocol was divided in three phases: (1) preparation of documentation and fieldwork, (2) fieldwork including interview with the artist and capture of the performance during activation at Tate Liverpool, and (3) completion and reflection of documentation tools post-activation.

In preparing for the fieldwork, we developed a detailed schedule around the performers rota and the scheduled activities with the artist, not only to determine the different roles of the time-based media conservation team members involved but also to ascertain what instances of the fieldwork were to be captured. Developing this schedule allowed us to be prepared to observe pivotal moments of both the performances and the rehearsals, alongside any other moments when decisions-making could take place. To avoid ending up with too many unedited hours of footage it was decided at the time that only the performances would be video- and audio recorded.

The fieldwork in Liverpool revealed aspects of the work that were unknown to us. The first aspect that became clear is that our plan to document the performances alone would not fulfil the intention of recording key moments of this activation. Although we were planning to observe the rehearsals, it became clear that these moments, which they called "workshops," were actually an integral part of the

[39] Ibid.

work.[40] The inseparability between the rehearsals and the performance, once again spoke to our understanding of performance as a set of practices which are "in flux." This relationship led us to capture the second rehearsal and to reflect on the possible need to document not only performance but also the process of their activation, which includes rehearsals.

The rehearsals highlighted the need for a close interaction between the artist and the hired performers. During the two scheduled rehearsals, but also in the times in-between, the artist transmitted more than a set of instructions and guidelines, indeed performing a practice alongside the performers. To use Diana Taylor's words, the transmission of "repertoire" (Taylor 2013) complemented what is barely (or not at all) conveyed in words and descriptions. The intimate environment created between the artist and the hired performers was essential in creating the atmosphere where the artwork materialises. Transmitting the "repertoire" of practices for this work included embodied gestures and vocalisations, instructions on how to use and care for each mask, and also conversations around how the institution engages with the public and local groups from a diverse range of backgrounds are represented.[41] The importance of experiencing this first activation of the work within Tate made us acknowledge the need to further reflect on how these moments could find their way into our documentation, as well as on the role of "workshops" in shaping the artwork's documentation.

Additionally, a discussion about the role of the masks and their continued use raised further queries about the role of documentation. The use of the masks raised some questions, particularly regarding how dependent the performance is on their ongoing use. The material of the masks, however, makes their long-term conservation challenging, particularly if they are to be worn as part of the performance. The reliance on these particular masks for activating the work does raise some issues not only on the care needed, but also on the possible uses of documentation for the artwork's future materialisation. Alongside our experience with the forms of embodied knowledge that transpired through the interaction between the hired performers and artist, it was crucial to understand the possible future role of the documentation we are capturing.

The experience of activating this work led us not only to revise the templates in use—specifically the *Performance Specification*—but also to further reflect on the possibilities of the *Strategy for the Documentation and Conservation of Performance*. The *Strategy* was being developed in tandem with the process of documenting *Your Face Is/Is Not Enough* (Lawson et al. 2019), with Kevin Beasley's work being the first complex artwork in which one of the *Strategy*'s main tools—the *Activation Report*—was used.[42] The *Activation Report* records decision-making, with the indication of the stakeholders involved. These reports

[40] *Performance Specification* (2019, p. 6). Unpublished Tate internal documentation.

[41] Ibid., 6.

[42] The *Activation Report* was developed by Louise Lawson, Hélia Marçal and Acatia Finbow in 2018.

allow us to track changes and the ways an artwork evolves within the collection, and understand the risks involved in their ongoing transmission and its internal and external dependencies; in that sense, creating a record of the artwork's material history. Testing out the tools that had emerged from the revision of our theoretical models led us to further explore the potential of our documentation tools, creating new techniques for capturing forms of embodied knowledge, and expand on the theoretical models themselves.

Reflecting on the *Performance Specification*, it was important with our new understanding of the importance of documenting both the rehearsals and the performance, to make revisions to its content and to add an additional field to capture "requirements for documentation." This field captures the artist specified requirements alongside the key moments identified further, such as the rehearsals. Our experience dealing with lending performance works led us to understand that such an important feature of the artwork's ongoing care should be placed right at the beginning of the specification so that the borrowing institution can see the requirements for documentation alongside the requisites for activating the artwork. The *Performance Specification*, however, did not allow for capturing aspects of the performance that directly relate to the "repertoire" of practices that was brought to the rehearsals and performance by the artist. We were particularly concerned with making visible the relative importance of documentation processes in our workflows, while also understanding how this work can be sustained by distributed forms of knowledge and developed through and with its documentation.

Aiming at fostering a transparent way of recording a distributed memory of the artwork, the time-based media conservation team set itself to design additional tools that were then applied to the documentation of the work, which were called *activation and production diagrams*.[43] These diagrams map the live archive of the artwork and how it evolves, identifying different activations of the performance and linking them to the different documentation objects captured or developed for each one of them. Each activation of the work will produce its own documentation: video and audio materials, activation reports as well as other documents developed by the time-based media conservation team at Tate and other teams in lending institutions. These can all be tracked in one single document which helps visualise how the documentation is evolving and also moments of change in our approach to documenting this work. Although this map does not surface the intent of capturing instances of embodied knowledge, it does allow for a visualisation of the distributed nature of the "repertoire" of practice of the performance, making evident how much of conservation is a shared activity. Identifying the key stakeholders in making this performance what it is also allows for further investigation to be undertaken on how we can foster the development of knowledges outside the institution, and how we

[43]The development of these diagrams was inspired by the production diagrams already in use in the conservation department to track the media generation of time-based media (mostly audiovisual) artworks. The production and activation diagram was developed by Ana Ribeiro in 2018.

can interpret the theoretical models developed so far, specifically for artworks that depart from the instruction-based model and are dependent of a social environment.

With the need of mapping and characterising the networks of people, objects and technology that contribute to the ways performance is materialised in the gallery, or, in other words, answering to the need to adapt our theory-practice to the social needs of performance works, we have introduced and developed a new tool called the *Map of Interactions* as part of our *Strategy*.

The *Map of Interactions* is designed to map out the dependencies of artworks. These dependencies might be internal or external, and they are often critical in defining the means of production needed to activate artworks in the collection. Within the map the networks that support the artwork are identified, so those involved in the care of these artworks can understand and assess areas of possible vulnerability. Recognising the agency of people outside the institution in the making of knowledges in conservation practice also promotes creative ways to preserve and document these networks. This further allows conservation of performance to move beyond the transmission of a set of instructions and to extend it to the transmission of a "repertoire" of practice that is collaboratively shaped and is situated in as many places as the artwork is materialised, in its multiplicity.

6 Between Theory and Practice

The development of the *Strategy for the Documentation and Conservation of Performance Art* did not follow a linear route from identifying the needs of the collection and creating theoretical models and associated tools that serve to inform our practice; instead, it was developed through interactions with individual artworks. The production of knowledge is sometimes messy, characterised by revisions of assumptions as new data is collected, and as new experiences create layers of collective knowledge. The process of developing the key-tool for the *Strategy* was driven by our wish to create a practical outcome that could be used to effectively respond to the growing needs of the performance artworks in Tate's collection. Theoretical models played a key role in formulating and testing various configurations of the *Performance Specification*, making clear the influence of the collected artworks—and hence, collecting practices—in the ways in which we redefined our assumptions, interpretations and how they were conveyed into the tools we now use.

The bridging of theory and practice was seen not only in the ways in which the *Strategy* was developed, but also in how it was informed by theories on documentation and performance art and its permanence, in the first instance, and, then, changed by the multiple encounters with artworks and contexts. The co-constitution of the artworks and the institution becomes visible with the process of understanding how, on the one hand, theory led to the development of the *Strategy* (and how this operative tool also works as a theoretical model itself), and, on the other hand, how the continuous relationship with artworks promoted the expansion and revision of this framework. While the co-constitution of the *Strategy*, the institution and its collection, and these artworks is particularly evident during moments of acquisition, we see how artworks, such as Tarek Atoui and Kevin Beasley's works, participate in the development of the *Strategy* and the ways in which their impact as agents of change expands the network of their influence beyond specific case studies and moments in time.

The relationality inherent to this process also raises further questions about the unruly nature of these artworks. Critical within the development of the *Strategy* is to support the performance artworks unruliness and develop practices and processes that facilitate retaining this intention. At first glance, if we accept that these artworks are unruly because they do not fit the museum structures, one could argue that the process of entering a collection and the exchanges prompted by this process could promote some degree of domestication. However, assuming that each new connection among artworks, people and institutions comes with (big or small) transformations, we would hope instead that engaging reflexively with those processes of co-constitution can also lead to a continuous inquiry on the conditions of the museum structures, the relationship of these structures with the artworks and their wider networks. Thus, ensuring our "repertoire" of practices can support the artworks, coupled with an ongoing critique and reflection of our own work and knowledge production activities.

7 Conclusion

The process of knowledge production described here reveals some of the reasons why the dichotomy between theory and practice neither reflects the ways in which knowledge is created nor is useful in analysing the outcomes of such processes. It is not the case that gaps in our knowledge do not exist, but focusing on the lack of translation between practice and theory and vice versa, two processes that are mutually and recursively constituted, seems to be narrowing the scope of what we can learn and how. In other words, dismantling the duality between practice and theory is needed not just as a way to make evident implicit knowledges, but also to identify opportunities for documenting such knowledges in the development of our theory-practice.

Each new performance artwork creates moments of reflection and understanding. Married with the development of theory, either prompted by our own investigations or those more broadly emerging in the field, our work continues. The future development of the *Strategy* is focused on honing our approach and developing practical processes in the acquisition and display moments of a performance artwork. Our future work will look at how we can capture instances of embodied knowledge while also fostering the creation and sustainability of "repertoires" of practices outside of Tate. As we describe our work with performance artworks, as a living process, so will our strategies transform, mutate, and so does the symbiotic relationship between theory and practice continues.

Acknowledgements The authors would like to acknowledge and thank the following people who have been involved with the development of time-based media conservation approach to the conservation of performance and each artwork. Firstly to those who have been part of the Performance Conservation Team at Tate: Acatia Finbow for her work to analyse and develop tools for documentation performance—namely the *Performance Specification*, *Activation Report*, and *Map of Interactions*, Lia Kramer for her work on performance, supporting the development of the glossary and work on the documentation of *Your face is/is not enough* by Kevin Beasley, and Deborah Potter, Director, Collection Care, who supports this area of conservation. Esther Harris for her work on the acquisition of Monster Chetwynd's *A Tax Haven for Women* and Tarek Atoui's *The Reverse Collection.* Pip Laurenson for reviewing and commenting on the chapter. And to the whole time-based media conservation team for their ongoing support. Hélia Marçal's participation in this study was supported by the Andrew W. Mellon Foundation through the project *Reshaping the Collectible: When Artworks Live in the Museum.*

Authors' Contributions

Leading on from the presentation at MACCH Conference 2019: *Bridging the Gap. Theory and Practice in the Conservation of Contemporary Art* 24–27 March 2019 (co-authored by LL, HM and Acatia Finbow), LL and HM, engaged with AR and DH to write a collaborative chapter highlighting the work of the time-based media conservation team engaged with performance and its documentation and conservation. LL is directly leading the development of the strategy for the documentation and conservation of performance. LL and HM (alongside Acatia Finbow) developed the following tools: Performance Specification, Activation Report, and Map of Interactions. LL and HM worked directly on the development of the theoretical apparatus, the literature review and the development of the strategy. DH wrote directly on the artwork Tarek Atoui based on their experience of acquiring this artwork into Tate's collection. AR developed the activation and production diagrams tool. AR wrote directly on the artwork by Kevin Beasley, based on their experience of acquiring this artwork into Tate's collection and its first activation at Tate Liverpool. This also includes support from DH, HM and LL on aspects of this artworks acquisition and activation. All authors contributed text in different areas of the chapter. LL and HM fully reviewed and edited the chapter. LL edited the chapter prior to submission. All authors read and approved the final chapter.

References

Auslander P (2008 [1998]) Liveness: performance in a mediatized culture. Routledge, London

Barad K (2007) Meeting the universe halfway: quantum physics and the entanglement of matter and meaning. Duke University Press, Durham

Bedford C (2012) The viral ontology of performance. In: Jones A, Heathfield A (eds) Perform, repeat, record: live art in history. Intellect in collaboration with the Live Art Development Agency, London, pp 77–88

Bishop C (2012) Artificial hells. Participatory art and the politics of spectatorship. Verso, London

Borgdorff H, Peters P, Pinch T (2020) Dialogues between artistic research and Science and Technology Studies: an introduction. In: Borgdorff H, Peters P, Pinch T (eds) Dialogues between artistic research and Science and Technology Studies. Routledge, London and New York, pp 1–15

Calonje T (2015) Introduction. In: Calonje T (ed) Live forever: collecting live art. Koenig Books, London, pp 11–26

Castriota B (2019) Authenticity, identity, and essentialism: reframing conservation practice. In: Mairesse F, Peters R (eds) What is the essence of conservation? Papers from the ICOM-CC and ICOFOM Session at the 25th General Conference Held in Kyoto, 4 September 2019. ICOFOM, Paris, pp 39–48

Domínguez Rubio F (2014) Preserving the unpreservable: docile and unruly objects at MoMA. Theory Soc 43(6):617–645

Finbow A (2018) The value of performance documentation in the contemporary art museum: a case study of Tate. PhD dissertation, University of Exeter

Goldberg R (2011 [1979]) Performance art: from futurism to the present. Thames & Hudson, London and New York

Haraway D (1988) Situated knowledges: the science question in feminism and the privilege of partial perspective. Fem Stud 14(3):575–599

Hölling HB (2017) The technique of conservation: on realms of theory and cultures of practice. J Inst Conserv 40(2):87–96. https://doi.org/10.1080/19455224.2017.1322114

Hölling HB, Feldman JP, Magnin E (eds) (2023) Performance: The Ethics and the Politics of Conservation and Care, Volume I, Routledge, London.

Ingold T (2013) Making: anthropology, archaeology, art and architecture. Routledge, London and New York

Jones A (2012) Timeline of Ideas: Live Art in (Art) History, A Primarily European-US-based Trajectory of Debates and Exhibitions Relating to Performance Documentation and Re-enactments. In: Heathfield A, Jones, A (eds). Perform, Repeat, Record: Live Art in History. Intellect, Bristol pp 425–432.

Laurenson P, van Saaze V (2014) Collecting performance-based art: new challenges and shifting perspectives. In: Remes O, MacCulloch L, Leino M (eds) Performativity in the gallery: staging interactive encounters. Peter Lang, Oxford, pp 27–41

Laurenson P, Berndes C, Folkerts H, Franssen D, Glew A, de Haan P, Hummelen Y, Lissoni A, Maidment I, Matyssek A, Parsons K, Perrot C, van Saaze V, Scholte T, Smithen P, Stigter S, 't Hoen P, van de Vall R, Wijers G (2014) The Live List: what to consider when collecting live works, Collecting the Performative Network, 24 January 2014. http://www.tate.org.uk/about-us/projects/collecting-performative/live-list. Accessed 19 June 2020

Lawson L, Marçal H (2022) Method for assessing conservation documentation for complex performance artworks. In: Reshaping the collectible: Tony Conrad, Tate Research Publication. https://www.tate.org.uk/research/reshaping-the-collectible/method-assessing-conservation-documentation-complex-performance-artworks. Accessed 21 July 2022

Lawson L, Finbow A, Marçal H (2019) Developing a strategy for the conservation of performance-based artworks at Tate. J Inst Conserv 42(2):114–134. https://doi.org/10.1080/19455224.2019.1604396

Lawson L, Huyton S, Marçal H, Ribeiro A. Institutional practices: collecting performance art at Tate. In: Reshaping the collectible: Tony Conrad, Tate Research Publication, 2022. https://www.tate.org.uk/research/reshaping-the-collectible/institutional-practices-collecting-performance-art-at-tate. Accessed 21 July 2022

Marçal H (2017) Conservation in the era of participation. J Inst Conserv 40(2):97–104

Marçal H (2019) Contemporary art conservation. Published as part of the research project Reshaping the collectible: when artworks live in the museum, Tate. https://www.tate.org.uk/research/reshaping-the-collectible/research-approach-conservation. Accessed 31 May 2020

Marçal H (2021) Towards a relational ontology of conservation. In: Bridgland J (2021) Transcending boundaries: integrated approaches to conservation. ICOM-CC 19th Triennial Conference Preprints, Beijing. International Council of Museums, Paris

Marçal H (2022a) A word about performance art. In: Engel D, Philips J (eds) Conservation of time-based media art. Routledge/Taylor & Francis, London and New York, 9 pp. https://doi-org.libproxy.ucl.ac.uk/10.4324/9781003034865

Marçal H (2022b) Ecologies of memory in the conservation of *Ten Years Alive on the Infinite Plain*. In: Reshaping the collectible: Tony Conrad, *Ten Years Alive on the Infinite Plain*, Tate Research Publication. https://www.tate.org.uk/research/reshaping-the-collectible/conrad-ecologies-memory. Accessed 21 July 2022

Marçal H, Macedo R (2017) The aim of documentation: micro-decisions of the documentation process of performance-based artworks. In: Bridgland J (2017) ICOM-CC 18th Triennial Conference Preprints, 4–8 September 2017. International Council of Museums, Paris
Marçal H, Lawson L, Ribeiro A (2022) Experimenting with transmission. In: Reshaping the collectible: Tony Conrad, Tate Research Publication. https://www.tate.org.uk/research/reshaping-the-collectible/tony-conrad-experimenting-transmission. Accessed 21 July 2022
Muñoz Viñas S (2014) Contemporary theory of conservation. Routledge, London
Phelan P (1993) Unmarked: the politics of performance. Routledge, London and New York
Sawa DB (2016) Why Tate Modern's new collection of musical instruments is striking an unfamiliar chord. The Guardian, September 6. https://www.theguardian.com/music/2016/sep/02/why-tate-moderns-reverse-collection-of-musical-instruments-is-striking-an-unfamiliar-chord. Accessed 10 June 2020
Sully D (2015) Conservation theory and practice: materials, values, and people in heritage conservation. In: Coombes AE, Henning M, Leahy HR, Macdonald S, McCarthy C, Message K, Phillips RB, Witcomb A (eds) The international handbooks of museum studies. John Wiley & Sons, Ltd, New Jersey. https://doi.org/10.1002/9781118829059.wbihms988
Taylor D (2013) The archive and the repertoire. Performing cultural memory in the Americas. Duke University Press, Durham
van den Hengel L (2017) Archives of affect: performance, reenactment, and the becoming of memory. In: Munteán L, Plate L, Smelik A (eds) Materializing memory in art and popular culture. Routledge/Taylor & Francis, London and New York, pp 125–142
van Saaze V, Dekker A (2013) Surprising uses of a documentation model: on the notion of boundary objects and beyond. Int J Perform Arts Digit Media 9(1):99–113
van Saaze V, Wharton G, Reisman L (2018) Adaptive institutional change: managing digital works at the Museum of Modern Art. Mus Soc 16(2):220–239. https://doi.org/10.29311/mas.v16i2.2774
Veisdal J (2020) Richard Feynman on the differences between mathematics and physics, Medium Magazine. https://medium.com/cantors-paradise/richard-feynman-on-the-differences-between-mathematics-and-physics-c0847e8a3d75. Accessed 10 June 2020
Verbeeck M (2016) 'There is nothing more practical than a good theory': conceptual tools for conservation practice. Stud Conserv 61(2):233–240. https://doi.org/10.1080/00393630.2016.1188647
Wheeler BB (2013) The institutionalization of an American avant-garde: performance art as democratic culture, 1970-2000. Sociol Perspect 46(4):491–512

Louise Lawson is the Head of Conservation at Tate. Prior to this she was the Conservation Manager, Time-based Media. In this role she was responsible for the strategic direction, development and delivery of all aspects relating to time-based media conservation at Tate. Her work has focused on developing how performance artworks in Tate's permanent collection are documented and conserved, through the project *Documentation and Conservation of Performance at Tate (2016–2021)*. Louise has shared the knowledge developed through this project via lectures, presentations and academic publications. She has also been part of the project team for *Reshaping the Collectible: When Artworks Live in the Museum (2018–2021)*, and her current focus is leading on the conservation of chorography and dance as part of *Precarious Movements: Choreography and the Museum (2021–2024)* for Tate which is a research project hosted by the University of New South Wales and involving partner organisations Tate, the Art Gallery of New South Wales, the National Gallery of Victoria, and the Monash University Museum of Art.

Duncan Harvey is a time-based media conservator at Tate focusing on loans-out, acquisitions programmes and Tate's High-Value Digital Asset (HVDA) storage project. In his time at Tate, he has worked as a Conservation Technician working on displays and acquisitions. He holds an MA in Politics from the University of Glasgow.

Ana Ribeiro is a time-based media conservator at Tate. She has studied Conservation and Restoration in Lisbon (FCT-UNL), and subsequently trained in media art conservation at the S. M.A.K., Ghent, NiMK, Amsterdam and at Tate, London. At Tate Ana has worked on loans out program area and part of her current role she focuses on all aspects of bringing new time-based media works to the collection. Ana's main areas of interest are documentation practices, collection care sustainability and degrowth, digital video and performance preservation. Ana was part of the project *Documentation and Conservation of Performance at Tate (2016–2021)* and she worked on the acquisition of Tony Conrad's *Ten Years Alive on the Infinite Plain,* part of the *Reshaping the Collectible: When Artworks Live in the Museum* research project. Ana's current focus is on the preservation of dance and choreographic works in the museum through the *Precarious Movements: Choreography and the Museum (2021–2024)* research project hosted by the University of New South Wales and involving partner organisations Tate, the Art Gallery of New South Wales, the National Gallery of Victoria, and the Monash University Museum of Art.

Hélia Marçal is Lecturer (Assistant Professor) in History of Art, Materials, and Technology at the Department of History of Art, University College London. Before this appointment, she was the Fellow in Contemporary Art Conservation and Research of the research project *Reshaping the Collectible: When Artworks Live in the Museum*, at Tate, London (2018–20). In addition, she was the coordinator of the Working Group on Theory, History, and Ethics of Conservation of the Committee for Conservation of the International Council of Museums (ICOM-CC 2016-2023).

Integrating Front-of-House with Behind-the-Scenes Practice in Contemporary Art Conservation

Caitlin Spangler-Bickell

Abstract The "biographical approach to contemporary art conservation" has highlighted the efforts required by professionals to maintain the identity of complex artworks, given the changes that occur when they move between biographical stages such as creation, acquisition, installation and storage. Although this model indicates that *every* life phase should be a locus of professional attention, conservation practice is concentrated more on the transitional phases before and after exhibitions than on the exhibition period itself. Because conservators must turn their skills and energy to preparations for the next exhibition soon after an installation is complete, the exhibition period is an underrepresented biographical phase in conservation—an especially urgent deficiency for works that are only fully "activated" when on display. To remedy that, this chapter argues for expanding the collections care remit to integrate the "front-of-house" with behind-the-scenes conservation practice by making use of "ethnography *for* conservation" during the exhibition life phase. A participant observation study in the gallery space of the interactive exhibition *Take Me (I'm Yours)* at Pirelli HangarBicocca illustrates how this methodology, as well as an amplified role for invigilators, can help understand and assess risks, generate mitigation tactics and improve collections care.

Keywords Conservation · Contemporary art · Exhibition space · Guards · Invigilators · Museum ethnography · Object biography · Participant observation

1 Introduction

Museum and gallery professionals tasked with caring for artworks have long observed that mechanical damage to objects is among the most common and destructive hazards to collections. It is noted also that the moments at which such damage is at highest risk of occurring are in those transitional phases when works are physically moved or handled: packing, crating and shipping for domestic or

C. Spangler-Bickell (✉)
Maastricht University, Maastricht, Netherlands

R. van de Vall, V. van Saaze (eds.), *Conservation of Contemporary Art*, Studies in Art, Heritage, Law and the Market 9, https://doi.org/10.1007/978-3-031-42357-4_17

international transit as loans, movement to and from conservation studios for interventive treatment, transfers during storage reorganizations or renovations, and exhibition installation and deinstallation.

However, recent developments in contemporary art conservation theory have drawn attention to the unstable nature of many artworks even when they are not physically moving from one location to another. The "biographical approach to contemporary art conservation" (van de Vall et al. 2011) has highlighted how the dormant life phase of a work in storage can often engender risks like dissociation, technological obsolescence and loss of the knowledge required to assemble, install or activate the work.

Contemporary art conservation researchers have also investigated other museum-based biographical phases such as acquisition and installation, demonstrating the critical role of collections care professionals in shaping how artworks are presented and documented. In order to write biographies of works that "alter in appearance and require some kind of intervention by the museum to enable their continued display" (van Saaze 2013, pp. 15–16) these scholars must "take us to the backstage of the art museum, a space that has been conveniently left out from the grand narratives of art history, but without which such narratives would be simply impossible" (Domínguez Rubio 2016, p. 65).

Theories on artwork biographies have thus prompted greater investigation into how institutions affect artworks behind-the-scenes; but although these theories imply that *every* life phase should be a crucial locus of observation and action for conservators, the majority of conservation and collections care[1] activity still takes place in the transitional phases before and after exhibitions—not during. This chapter suggests that the exhibition period is an underrepresented life phase in conservation practice and argues for the integration of behind-the-scenes work with new activities that focus on the front-of-house[2] areas where visitors encounter the art.

[1] My use of the terms "conservation" and "collections care" in this chapter reflect, to a certain extent, definitions from the Australian Institute for the Conservation of Cultural Material (AICCM). In this understanding, "conservation is about preventing damage and loss to our cultural heritage" (https://aiccm.org.au/conservation/), while "collection care refers to the methods of storage and display of collections items as well as basic approaches to condition reporting, environmental monitoring and control of pests" (https://aiccm.org.au/conservation/collection-care/). Setting aside the fact that the meaning of what constitutes "damage" and "loss" can be critically debated, the AICCM terminology is useful as it highlights how the more focussed practices of conservation fall within the overarching field of collections care, the latter of which also includes activities related to how works are exhibited.

[2] I use the terms "behind-the-scenes" and "backstage" interchangeably in this chapter; however, I do not make use of the term "frontstage" as their counterpoint, and instead refer to "front-of-house." Both "behind-the-scenes" and "backstage" denote the perspective of those constructing and producing a performance to be experienced by others, while remaining unseen. The term "frontstage," while implying a visibility to others, nevertheless remains "onstage" and retains the perspective of those producing and performing. In contrast, the term "front-of-house" refers to all the areas of a performance venue that are open to the public and denotes the perspective of visitors experiencing the event.

Divided into three main sections, this chapter begins with a discussion of the theory of a biographical approach to contemporary art conservation (Sect. 2) and examines why engagement in the front-of-house domain is an especially urgent undertaking for ephemeral artworks with interactive elements. Interviews with staff at the Fowler Museum at UCLA highlight the opportunities for a professional protocol that more closely examines the exhibition life phase of works that only fully unfold within a display space, as opposed to in an artist's studio or a fabricator's workshop.

The next section (Sect. 3) details the methodology which I believe is best suited to address the biographical approach to conservation in practice. The field of Museum Ethnography can inspire a holistic approach to the front-of-house arena through the use of participant observation, and literature is presented that demonstrates the burgeoning use of ethnographic methods in conservation research. I make a distinction between the reflexive ethnographies *of* conservation represented in that literature, and the notion that collections carers can also directly apply ethnographic methods *for* conservation in practice.

The following section (Sect. 4) presents the results from an exploratory case study into the potential of utilizing ethnography *for* conservation during the exhibition phase. I discuss the findings from participant observation during the preparation and opening hours of the 2017–2018 exhibition *Take Me (I'm Yours)* at Milan's contemporary art space Pirelli HangarBicocca, and I address how some simple actions by collections care professionals to engage in the front-of-house space can help to better understand and assess risks, generate mitigation tactics in response to those risks, and forge new documentation methods for contemporary artworks.

Finally, in Sect. 5 I suggest expanding the conservation knowledge and engagement of gallery invigilators to round out a campaign of continuous collections care (Sect. 6). A summary of the argument serves as conclusion of this chapter in Sect. 7.

2 The Biographical Approach to Conservation and the Exhibition Life Phase of an Artwork

Instead of the traditional conservation aim of preserving physical matter, the goal of the "biographical approach to conservation" is to record the variability of artworks through significant life stages while preserving their artistic integrity over time. The authors who introduced this concept into conservation—Renée van de Vall, Hanna Hölling, Tatja Scholte and Sanneke Stigter—were inspired by anthropological theories on material culture to examine the museum context in which contemporary artworks are embedded and the ways those contexts inscribe meaning (intentionally or unintentionally) in artworks. Rather than relying only on artist interviews for information, it is now common for conservators to document the artistic processes of creating and installing or transmitting works (Matos et al. 2015; Scholte and Wharton 2011), and to critically reflect on how museological practices themselves affect the identity and interpretation of artworks (Davies and Heuman 2004; Irvin 2006; Marçal 2021; Stigter 2015).

The biographical approach has thus been widely embraced for the care of contemporary artworks.[3] Recent research has concentrated on capturing vital information during many of the biographical stages of artworks that are relevant to museums, such as collection and acquisition of works (Laurenson and van Saaze 2014; Moomaw 2016; Ryan 2016), artwork creation, fabrication or installation (Fiske 2009; Hummelen and Scholte 2004; Phillips 2015), and the storage stage mentioned by van de Vall et al. (Depocas et al. 2003). However, the discipline has largely ignored one of the most crucial biographical phases that contemporary artworks undergo: exhibition.

Collections care remains principally a backstage operation, and rarely, if ever, is there an attempt by collections care professionals to systematically study how artworks live while on display during the opening hours of a museum or gallery. In museums of all types, the majority of conservation activity (e.g., condition checking and reporting, testing and treatment, documentation, preparation, packing and crating, mountmaking, installation and deinstallation) takes place in the transitional phases before and after exhibitions—not during—as the skills and energy of conservators turn back behind-the-scenes to prepare for upcoming exhibitions soon after the previous installation is complete. This blind spot in conservation is a particularly urgent deficiency in the practical care of works that are only fully active or activated when on display in an exhibition space, such as performance art,[4] relational art or interactive installations.

There is a behind-the-scenes/front-of-house disconnect in current museum and gallery working methods that must be overcome in order to bridge the gap between theoretical developments regarding artwork biographies and the ways those biographies are accounted for in daily collections care practice. This disconnect is acknowledged by professionals from various museum and gallery disciplines whose schedules seldom permit them to experience and explore their institution's front-of-house areas, restricting their knowledge of many artworks on display. The way in which many museum professionals currently consider the front-of-house arena is typified in the words of the Head of Public and Educational Programs (HPEP) at a contemporary art institution:

> "There's a sense of guilt, just spending 30 minutes in the exhibition space" (personal communication, 2017-11-20).

---

[3]The biographical approach to conservation has also been applied beyond contemporary art, from interactive altars in museums (Spangler-Bickell 2021) to medieval European polychrome sculpture (Ebert 2018, 2019; Spaarschuh 2018).

[4]The "exhibition life phase" of performance art has long been a focus of documentation as a matter of course, but performance pieces that have a longer and more frequent presence in exhibitions will generally be observed or documented only a small number of times for archival records. This ignores a large percentage of a work's exhibition experience during which valuable insights into the piece could otherwise be gleaned. Recent initiatives such as Tate's *Documentation and Conservation of Performance* (2016–2021) and the Andrew W. Mellon-funded project *Reshaping the Collectible: When Artworks Live in the Museum* (2018–2021) have pursued a fuller investigation of works with performative elements (see Lawson and Marçal 2021).

It is the job of this professional to create public content centred around exhibitions; and yet, the HPEP lamented, there is a feeling that taking time to really absorb the works on display from the visitor's perspective would be shirking the urgent duties waiting to be addressed back in the office. There is often an understanding, whether self-imposed or explicitly ordained, that the work to be done—and a professional's proper place—is backstage.[5]

The HPEP further explained that this feeling has consequences in the form of missed opportunities when workflow and protocol do not provide professionals with the time to examine what happens in the front-of-house, or provide a platform to process and address those activities amongst staff members. A good illustration of how current collections care practice, with its lack of emphasis on the exhibition life phase, affects the ability to care for and document interactive works can be drawn from the Fowler Museum at UCLA's history of exhibiting interactive contemporary altars and artworks.

The Fowler Museum, which "explores global arts and cultures with an emphasis on Africa, Asia, the Pacific, and the Indigenous Americas—past and present," has included (inter)active altars and shrines—some of which were also contemporary artworks—in many of their exhibitions for over twenty years (Fowler Museum at UCLA n.d.). Created in collaboration with communities of believers, spiritual practitioners, and artists, these altars have provided context to exhibitions such as: *Sacred Arts of Haitian Vodou* (1995), *Botánica Los Angeles: Latino Popular Religious Art in the City of Angels* (2004–2005), *Mami Wata: Arts for Water Spirits in Africa and Its Diasporas* (2008), *Transcultural Pilgrim: Three Decades Of Work By José Bedia* (2011–2012), *In Extremis: Death And Life In 21st-Century Haitian Art* (2012–2013) and *Sinful Saints and Saintly Sinners at the Margins of the Americas* (2014).

Research into these altars[6] revealed that the production and installation phases of the assemblages do not suffer from a lack of attention. Interviews with staff members yielded detailed accounts about the production and development of altars; from the names and locations of the stores where objects were bought to construct them, to the names of the Vodou or Santería practitioners who consecrated them.[7] Curatorial and conservation records contained step-by-step textual and visual instructions for altar installation and packing processes. Complete "walk-through" photographic

[5]Even conservation projects undertaken in public gallery spaces, rather than in a laboratory, carry the perception of providing visitors with a glimpse "behind-the-scenes" of the museum and maintain a distinct separation between the roles and activities of professional versus visitor.

[6]Undertaken by the author during my period as a conservation intern at the Fowler Museum and as a Visiting Graduate Researcher with the UCLA/Getty Conservation Institute Master's Program in the Conservation of Archaeological and Ethnographic Materials (February–August 2017).

[7]Although immaterial, emotional or spiritual information regarding these altars were accessible through interviews with museum staff, there was not always a comprehensive protocol for documenting these events for future consultation in institutional archives. For more on the challenges of documenting these ephemeral altar assemblages, see Spangler-Bickell (2019).

documentation depicted the entire exhibition space, providing the spatial context for each altar installation.

Once the exhibition phase began, however, standard professional protocol no longer required such painstaking attention. Memories about how these ephemeral accumulations lived while on exhibition do remain with staff members today; but these memories are unevenly distributed and recalled with varying levels of certainty. When asked about the kinds of visitor interactions that took place during the exhibitions, staff members from conservation, registration, collections management and exhibitions, as well as curators, did not respond with the kinds of specific details they provided for the creation and installation stages. Instead, there were a number of responses that included phrases such as: "I don't know," "I don't believe so," "That might have been...," "I'm not sure if...," "I think we would have..." and "I'm trying to remember..." interspersed with more vivid memories.

The absence of information about the exhibition phase is in no way evidence of these professionals not doing their job. On the contrary, the paucity of information about the works while on display is precisely *because* these practitioners had dutifully turned to their subsequent tasks and were hard at work preparing for the next exhibition. The museum's Head of Conservation (HoC) considers this an issue of resources and time, explaining that:

> when the show goes up, we're on to the next thing. There are some times when I never step into a show again; the whole time it's been on display. If something happens, then I'll go down there and check it out, and usually a guard will alert me or someone's walked in and seen something. But I think [more systematic visits] should happen [...] You put everything into this show to open it, and then once it happens, you just kind of forget about it almost; which is a shame. I guess it's not so much maybe on the education end, if they're doing public programs. But certainly on my end. And I know on exhibitions' end. And, I'm pretty sure, registration and collections; we don't have time to examine and review the exhibition until deinstall. (Personal communication, 2017-08-09)

The HoC's statement highlights how conservators do of course enter the display areas to address any issues that arise regarding the condition or safety of objects; but they may rely on initial reporting by others whose professional commitments already include the front-of-house arena, such as guards. It also draws attention to the fact that some museum staff members do consistently spend time investigating the front-of-house activities during the exhibition life phase; however, the work conducted by Education and Public Programs staff is focussed on the benefit and well-being of *visitors*. In this chapter I make the case that collections care professionals should consider how front-of-house activities during the exhibition life phase can be made to work for the benefit and well-being of the *artworks*.

The argument that the exhibition space provides new opportunities for conservation finds confirmation in a further statement by the Fowler's Head of Conservation. He recalled a contemporary artwork where visitors were invited to participate by writing messages and attaching these to the installation. Although the artist did *not* request any monitoring or reporting on the condition or development of the installation and was well aware of changes in condition over time from similar installations, the HoC now feels that observing the work during opening hours would have been beneficial,

> just to see where those elements are being attached, if there's some kind of damage occurring to the original structure of that substrate that it's being pinned to... Are visitors grabbing on to things? Handling things poorly? To see visitors' contact with it, how that would affect the work. (Personal communication, 2017-08-09)

Just as contemporary artworks may undergo active processes of change while they are unobserved by conservators in storage, they may also undergo important changes while they are unobserved by conservators on exhibition—especially if, as in the examples listed above, they are participatory, interactive and ephemeral. If the theoretical paradigm of the biographical approach to contemporary art conservation is to be implemented in practice, this blank spot in the biographies of artworks can no longer be ignored.

In order to develop collections care methods that are capable of apprehending what knowledge can be gained during the exhibition life phase of artworks, I now turn to literature on Museum Ethnography and the increasing body of texts in which ethnographic methods are used in conservation research.

3 Opportunities of Participant Observation and Ethnography for Museum Research and Practice

Although a review of literature on museum visitor studies, visitor research, or audience studies shows that observation has long been used amongst visitors in display galleries, these have predominantly been undertaken not to focus on artworks, but to "focus on the experiences, attitudes, and opinions of people in and about museums of all sorts" (Hooper-Greenhill 2006, p. 363). While some visitor studies have indeed instrumentalized field research in the museum space to gain insight into presentation strategies of artworks as well as visitor behaviour,[8] most publications in the visitor studies field have sought to learn about visitor demographics (Golding and Modest 2013), learning styles and attention patterns (Bitgood 2013; Falk and Dierking 2000, 2013; Hein 1998; Hooper-Greenhill 1994) and visitor pleasure or satisfaction (Kirchberg and Tröndle 2012, p. 442). Useful methods from this field such as surveys, interviews and observation are all also present in the methodology used by anthropologists; but "ethnographic" research perspectives are more holistic in scope and maintain an emphasis on the subjective personal participation of the researcher in the subject matter under investigation.

---

[8] A notable example is Luise Reitstätter's book *Die Ausstellung verhandeln. Von Interaktionen im musealen Raum* (*Negotiate the exhibition. Of interactions in museum space*), which explores the dynamic relationship between people and things in exhibition spaces (Reitstätter 2016). I am grateful to the peer reviewer who introduced me to this book.

3.1 What Is Ethnography?

The word "ethnography" refers both to the research methodology used by anthropologists and to the textual (or audio-visual) presentation of the results of that social scientific fieldwork.[9] Although it encompasses the use of statistical data, surveys, and formal and informal interviews, paramount within this eclectic method of inquiry is anthropology's signature concept of "participant observation." Participant observation is built on principles of phenomenology (the study of structures of consciousness and experience) and cultural relativism (the idea that every culture should be studied in terms of its own internal logic), and it follows the assertion that in order to truly understand a practice, an event, an object or a ritual, one must experience it first-hand using all the senses instead of just sight and/or sound (Hammersley and Atkinson 2007).

Since the end goal of ethnography is to better understand the learned and shared ideas and patterns of behaviour that constitute a certain culture—as well as the means by which they are learned and shared amongst cultural members—ethnographers constantly shift focus between immersing themselves in intimate, personal everyday experiences, and discerning larger configurations of social norms and comportment. This combination of participating oneself and actively observing others, I argue, makes ethnography particularly well-suited to the conservation of art that is interactive. However, I am by no means the first to explore this methodology in conservation research, or the museum world in general.

3.2 Museum Ethnography and the Rise of Ethnographic Methods in Conservation

The field of Museum Ethnography provides many examples of how ethnographic research methods have been used in cultural heritage institutions.[10] Ethnographic studies have been carried out in various types of museums to interrogate the professional working cultures in ethnographic museums (Durand 2010; Herle 2008), science museums (Macdonald 2001, 2002), art museums (Bunzl 2014) as well as the art worlds that comprise artist studios, galleries, art fairs and auction

---

[9] The adjective "ethnographic" can refer to anything related to ethnography as a research method or product (e.g., ethnographic fieldwork, ethnographic data, ethnographic research approach). It has also often been used to describe material culture that is not considered part of western Fine Arts traditions, and to describe the museums that collect and display that material. The term is problematic because of its historical application to objects of non-European origin, leading to the "othering" of the cultures which produced those objects as well as the false implication that European material culture—including Fine, Modern and Contemporary art—are not also shaped by cultural constructs and embedded in cultural systems.

[10] The UK-based Museum Ethnographers Group hosts annual conferences and publishes the *Journal of Museum Ethnography* (http://www.museumethnographersgroup.org.uk/en/).

houses (Rothenberg and Fine 2008; Thornton 2008). Other ethnographic studies in arts organisations have not sought purely to analyse and explain the social processes that govern the art world and its institutions, but have also taken a critical approach to find out what effects those processes have on the artworks themselves.

Albena Yaneva used the technique of "following" an object (a bus) as it was transformed into *Mückenbus*, an artwork by Carsten Höller and Rosemarie Trockel, at the Musée d'art moderne de la ville de Paris in 1999. Yaneva states in her article that the museum as such is only visible "in the ordinary operations, everyday attitudes and gestures [where] the artistic work is related to the manual work of different collectivities of actors"; a world which can best be uncovered through ethnographic methods developed precisely to capture "everyday attitudes and gestures" (Yaneva 2003, p. 126). Conducting participant observation as a museum intern allowed Yaneva to contrast the simple and clear-cut image of installation artworks held by museum visitors with the "unstable state of art" revealed behind-the-scenes during her research.

In a similar effort to make backstage museum processes visible, Vivian van Saaze's book *Installation Art and the Museum. Presentation and Conservation of Changing Artworks* (2013) describes the process of conducting research in van Saaze's own professional milieu of art museums by stepping out of her role as practitioner and into the more unstable position of ethnographer.[11] Van Saaze called her work "an empirical investigation into the working practices of contemporary art museums involved in the presentation and conservation of installation artworks," taking the staging, or the "doing," of three artworks by museum professionals as case studies to openly examine the typically invisible practices that exist behind-the-scenes in museums (van Saaze 2013, p. 16).

This is indicative of a trend within the larger field of Museum Ethnography that centres research explicitly around the discipline of conservation. Another example can be found in the work of Fernando Domínguez Rubio, whose participant observation was based in the conservation lab of New York's Museum of Modern Art. Like Yaneva, Domínguez Rubio followed the material components of artworks and used an object-based approach to demonstrate the agency of those objects in the museum setting. He cites examples of what he calls "unruly" objects to show how "artworks organize museums as much as museums organize artworks" (Domínguez Rubio 2014, p. 641). The contrast of conservation's historical efforts of stabilisation, control and neutrality, juxtaposed with the ethnographic data he collected, allows for an explicit case to be made that artworks are forcing a change in conservation and collections care practice. This echoes what van Saaze's "empirical research into several case studies" proved: that "much of conservation theory and ethics is distant from the day-to-day practices of contemporary art conservators. A theory of

[11] This work was part of the research initiative *Inside Installations: preservation and presentation of installation art* (2004–2007). The findings of that project were published in the volume *Inside Installations - Theory and Practice in the Care of Complex Artworks* (Scholte and Wharton 2011).

contemporary art conservation," van Saaze concluded, "should therefore be more in tune with its practices" (van Saaze 2013, p. 183).

The work produced by Yaneva, van Saaze and Domínguez Rubio have provided captivating evidence of the misalignment of traditional conservation theory and current practice; but though they have brilliantly raised the necessary questions to prompt professional evolution, they do not attempt to provide answers in the form of practical day-to-day professional techniques to be adopted. They have produced incredibly valuable examples of ethnographies *of*, instead of strictly *for*, conservation.

3.3 A Distinction: Ethnography *of* and *for* Conservation

I make a distinction between the two main ways that anthropological methods can be applied in the conservation field: by conducting an ethnography *of* conservation, and by employing ethnography *for* conservation.[12]

Ethnographies *of* conservation are reflexive studies of the ethics and philosophies of professional cultures of conservation as they are manifested in practice. Such studies can be carried out either by researchers or by practicing conservators in order to shape the future of the discipline in a broad, long-term sense by influencing evolved ethical standards, setting new best-practice guidelines, and providing precedents for future conservators who face similar challenges. Such research entails an ethnographic study of museum and conservation professional practices in order to generate theoretical analyses that will serve future and/or other conservators, and only by extension serve the artworks in their care.

Ethnography *for* conservation is not about interrogating the nature of conservation itself; it is rather the use of ethnography-inspired research methods for the express purpose of completing imminent conservation duties such as ensuring proper display of, creating adequate documentation for, or treating works of art and cultural expression. An example of using ethnography specifically to further conservation efforts for an artwork can be found in Nina Quabeck's use of the ethnographic approach of "messy text" to interrogate the Kunstsammlung Nordrhein-Westfalen's acquisition of Wolfgang Tillmans' large-scale work *Life is*

[12] I previously outlined the concepts of ethnography *of* and *for* conservation in a presentation "Exploring Ethnography in Conservation Research" at the Marie Skłodowska-Curie Innovative Training Network *NACCA* (*New Approaches in Contemporary Art Conservation*) public event at Tate Modern's Tate Exchange, 16 Jan. 2017 (poster PDF can be found at https://doi.org/10.6084/m9.figshare.4558138). In a 2018 collective presentation by my fellow *NACCA* doctoral candidates and myself entitled "Beyond the Artist Interview: Notes from the Field," we made the related categorical distinction of "research/fieldwork of, for, and through conservation" at the *SBMK (Dutch Foundation for the Conservation of Contemporary Art) Summit on (Inter)National Collaboration: Acting in Contemporary Art Conservation*, 15 Nov 2018 (presentation slides and script can be found at https://uvaauas.figshare.com/s/7dac0c019b7f136aaea4).

Astronomical Installation (2001–2012) (Quabeck 2021). Ethnographic methods have also gained traction in the conservation of performance art, which often revolves around the role of embodied knowledge in performer transmission, as collections professionals begin to engage more deeply with artworks by learning and performing them (see Hélia Marçal's writing on the conservator's body-archive (Marçal 2017), Athena Christa Holbrook's reflections on learning Simone Forti's *Dance Constructions* at MoMA (Holbrook 2018), and Robert Lane and Jessye Wdowin-McGregor's consideration of the work of Tino Sehgal alongside oral and bodily transmission strategies from cultures like Australian Aboriginal communities (Lane and Wdowin-McGregor 2016)).

The data for these two types of methodological engagements—ethnography *of* and *for* conservation—inevitably overlap, and the findings from each of them can and should inform each other; but the first remains a scholarly pursuit that academic researchers will more likely be able to perform, while the second has more practical elements that can be utilised by professionals working in museums and galleries.[13] Rather than meeting requirements of academic ethnography, such as the deep immersion in a culture through participant observation over long periods of time and the complete analysis of that data, ethnography *for* conservation is closer in nature to the "Rapid Assessment Procedures" used in the field of Applied Anthropology. Applied Anthropology has sought to find ways that balance reliable and rigorous data collection with realistic research constraints and the goal of putting what is learnt through ethnographic study into immediate and effective use. Rapid Assessment Procedures (RAP) "are ethnographic methods for quickly gathering social, cultural, and behavioral information relevant to specific [...] problems and prevention programs" (Harris et al. 1997, p. 375). With RAP, "the task is not to solve theoretical puzzles or generate theory but to reach more rational decision-making processes in real-life circumstances" (Taplin et al. 2002, p. 81).

By performing a rapid ethnographic assessment of the front-of-house environment in which artworks are exhibited, collections care professionals can gather information in real time about specific problems that may endanger the artworks, to inform improved decision-making for the means to prevent or remedy those dangers. The following section presents results of such an assessment study, outlining some examples that showcase the potential benefits of adopting ethnography *for* contemporary art conservation.

[13] Conservator Sanneke Stigter has explored the reflexive technique of "autoethnography" as a new approach that conservators can employ to make "a critical assessment of the conservator's own role in the conservation process and consequence [of her actions] for the object's biography" (Stigter 2016, p. 227). She does this by retrospectively recording her thought process while performing a physical conservation intervention and by drafting an annotation to a past artist interview. Such auto-ethnography both provides information regarding conservation practice (ethnography of conservation) as well as important biographical information for the specific artwork being studied (ethnography for conservation). This technique could also be thought of as ethnography *through* conservation: the collection of reflexive information through conservation activities and practices.

4 Case Study Application: *Take Me (I'm Yours)* at Pirelli HangarBicocca

4.1 Behind-the-Scenes

In an exploration of how to integrate behind-the-scenes with front-of-house collections care, I conducted an ethnographic study during the exhibition *Take Me (I'm Yours)* (TMIY) at the contemporary art space Pirelli HangarBicocca (PHB) in Milan, Italy. Originally conceived by Hans Ulrich Obrist and Christian Boltanski in 1995 for London's Serpentine Gallery and resurrected twenty years later in various cities, *Take Me* aims to break all the rules of exhibiting art. It interrogates the "myth of the unique artwork and question[s] its methods of production" by creating an exhibition of interactions amongst artists and visitors "characterised by its open form which evolves in time" (Monnaie de Paris 2015). The Milan edition of the show, curated by Obrist and Boltanski in collaboration with Chiara Parisi and Roberta Tenconi, ran from November 2017-January 2018 and featured an exhibition booklet that explained to visitors that they were meant to actively take, create, participate in, exchange or buy the artworks.

Many of the artists and artworks included in *TMIY* can be categorized as Relational Art, a school which considers "the work of art as social interstice" (Bourriaud 2006 [1998], p. 160). This genre was first theorised for the 1996 exhibition *Traffic* by curator Nicholas Bourriaud, who later published a treatise on what he called "Relational Aesthetics," in which he described how the artists working in this field "create and stage life-structures that include working methods and ways of life, rather than the concrete objects that once defined the field of art. They use time as a raw material. Form takes priority over things, and flows over categories: the production of gestures is more important than the production of material things" (Bourriaud 2006 [1998], p. 170). My study aimed to integrate the more oft-studied backstage biographical phases of preparation and installation with the exhibition-phase where those "social interstices" and "life-structures" manifest themselves in the front-of-house arena.

Participant observation in the exhibition space cannot replace the invaluable knowledge gained through the traditional professional pursuits of research, interaction with artists, and exhibition preproduction; but it recalibrates those experiences with new perspectives. Before conducting the front-of-house study for *TMIY*, I participated in the preparation of Pirelli HangarBicocca's show by researching the exhibition's history—online, in materials from previous exhibition venues, and with PHB's curatorial resources—and by writing the exhibition label text for a number of artworks.[14] During this period of research, I became familiar with how the works had

[14]Instead of one single panel next to the work, these labels were printed on small sheets of paper that could also be collected and taken home by visitors. The exhibition booklet and artwork captions can be downloaded from the Pirelli HangarBicocca website at https://pirellihangarbicocca.org/en/exhibition/take-me-im-yours/#.

been interpreted, documented and described by different institutions in the past; perceptions which could then be measured against my personal experiences during the exhibition phase. I then encountered the physical media of the works for the first time as I joined the PHB production team for four days to install the exhibition, during which time I was also able to speak with many of the artists about their vision for the work.

It cannot be overstated how drastic the shift in mentality was from the role of professional to that of visitor; and how different were the kinds of knowledge about each work gained from either side of that divide. Many works I felt I "knew" or "got"—a belief buoyed by my research, artist interviews, caption drafting and installation—radically transformed once I encountered them in the front-of-house as a visitor.

4.2 Front-of-House

Once *Take Me (I'm Yours)* opened to the public, I began participant observation in the exhibition space,[15] which was open Wednesday-Sunday. To gain a representative understanding of the front-of-house domain, I conducted this work twice a week—one weekday and one weekend day—making sure to evenly cover opening, midday, and closing hours. This amounted to 75 hours of observations over the two-and-a-half-month run. The mobile phone was chosen as a research tool for taking notes and photographs rather than a large professional camera and paper notebook, which allowed me to conduct fieldwork that was not disruptive for visitors, was easy and efficient, and aligned my own experience with that of fellow exhibition-goers who were also snapping photographs and reading or typing on their smartphones. These methods allowed me to build up a holistic picture of the patterns of behaviour seen in others, while also "captur[ing] the versatility of tacit knowledge and non-tangible aspects" of artworks that can only be gained from first-hand, subjective experience (Hummelen and Scholte 2004, p. 212).

Scholars of contemporary art conservation, and particularly of performance art, have written about the difference between seeing and speaking about a work cognitively, and the bodily knowledge that comes from physically experiencing it (Holbrook 2018; Lane and Wdowin-McGregor 2016; Marçal 2017). My study of *TMIY* confirmed this as I engaged in works like Francesco Vezzoli's *Take My Tears* (2017). For this piece, another artist acts as Vezzoli's alter ego in the exhibition space, as he sits at a table for two and draws street-style portraits of visitors one at a time while making conversation with them. As a bystander watching someone else

[15] A notice was posted at the entrance desk in the foyer in Italian and English, notifying visitors that the exhibition was being observed as part of doctoral research. Information was included on the themes and goals of the project, and contact information was provided for myself as well as all three of my supervisors.

in the seat, the conversation is inaudible, and there is no sense of what it feels like for the visitor to sit under spotlights being studied by Vezzoli's stand-in and being watched by a crowd of onlookers in the shadows.

Prior to participating, but having read the work's caption that described how visitors "become protagonists of a fictional imagery" and having watched others being sketched, I imagined the work aligned with the exhibition's push to invert traditional display technologies and would make the visitor feel that *the art is now looking at you*. However, once I sat in the chair across from the street artist, as I recorded in my notes,[16] "it was easy not to notice the people standing all around because I got lost in the conversation." The artist told me how "it's less about drawing an exact aesthetic image, but more about how the person's spirit appears to him. As soon as they sit down there is an immediate connection." Indeed, by experiencing the work as a visitor, I discovered that it had little to do with feeling watched or seen; the spotlights actually served to obscure the presence of the crowd around the table, making me instead feel hidden. While watching as a spectator placed emphasis on the drawing, as a participant the portrait itself became secondary to the conversation and connection with the artist. By participating myself, I thus gained a better understanding of the relationship between the lighting design and performance techniques, and the phenomenological responses they engender.

The Decision-Making Model for Contemporary Art Conservation and Presentation asks us to consider whether a work "evoke[s] associations or reactions that are important for its identity/meaning" (Giebeler et al. 2019, p. 11). There are many artworks for which associations and reactions are evoked simply by experiencing the works through non-contact senses such as sight, sound and smell: paintings, sculpture and performances can all provoke emotional responses even when spectators are only passively engaged. But how is it possible to truly know what associations or reactions are evoked for a portrait sitter in *Take My Tears* until one sits for a portrait? That experience *is* the work; and without having participated personally, any understanding of the work will be missing a vital element of its biography.

However, it was not only the emotional insight gained through participation that was significant; understanding the connections between the physical and material conditions in the front-of-house exhibition arena (like lighting design) and the associations or reactions evoked by these (like the intimacy of the encounter with Vezzoli's artist/performer) is one of the most substantial benefits of this methodology. The Decision-Making Model prompts practitioners to determine if there is a discrepancy between the "current state" and "desired state" of an artwork in order to shape "conservation/presentation options and strategies" (Giebeler et al. 2019, p. 3). This ethnographic study produced a number of examples in which personal participation uncovered conditions in the front-of-house that distanced a work's current state from its desired state and indicated possible practical measures to expediently minimize that discrepancy.

[16]Personal TMIY Field Notes taken 8 December 2017.

For Dominique Gonzalez-Foerster's work entitled *Or Not* (2017), four chairs were set up as a locus for visitors to sit and give or receive advice. The seats were often occupied by people just taking a rest from standing in the exhibition space, and conversations did not always happen. When I sat down to try it as a visitor, leaning way out over my knees and straining to hear the other person, I realised that the chairs were too far apart for any meaningful conversation to occur. Adjusting the markings on the ground that designated the placement of these chairs was an easy, immediate intervention that the institution could take to more fruitfully support Gonzalez-Foerster's intentions for the work. The visitor should have a choice to converse, *or not*; but if it is physically too difficult to converse, they have no such choice.

Regarding time-based works, the Decision-Making Model checklist asks: "Can the work be faithfully displayed/continued/perpetuated also when the time-based components are not functioning/performing anymore?" (Giebeler et al. 2019, p. 12). For a work like *Or Not*, the work's time-based components are people, conversation and advice; and there is no way to know whether those components are "functioning" without observing and experiencing the work first-hand in the front-of-house.

Professor of Modern and Contemporary Art Julia Bryan-Wilson said after many years of teaching art history courses that included Yvonne Rainer's iconic dance piece *Trio A*:

> Having studied many photographs, screened the film numerous times for my students, and read incisive written accounts of it, I thought I had a pretty good sense of what it entailed. I was wrong. I now approach the question of the medium of *Trio A* differently, because in the fall of 2008, over the space of about six months, I took a class from Rainer at the University of California, Irvine and learned *Trio A*. (Bryan-Wilson 2012, p. 58)

This same kind of bodily learning, or learning through doing, occurred for me with Yona Friedman's *Street Museum* (2017). One of the works for which I wrote the *TMIY* exhibition caption, *Street Museum* was installed as piles of hula hoops with posted diagrams sketched by the artist for visitors to collectively build their own structure and then transform it into a "museum" by attaching personal objects that became its "collection." Like Bryan-Wilson, I too came to approach the medium of *Street Museum* differently after engaging with the work physically. An incredible amount of material knowledge was gained from participating: how deceivingly difficult it actually was and how long it took to make just one small structure; how frustratingly often the masking tape provided by PHB would break; just how much tape was required to secure each hoop; and the fact that the one roll of tape originally set out meant that only one group at a time could participate—something which hadn't occurred to me until I began my observations, though in hindsight seems glaringly obvious. When I only *observed* the behaviour of others, I had noticed bits of tape strewn around the floor and felt that visitors were being slightly hasty or careless; it was only upon attempting the work myself, when I stood there with my own fists full of broken tape, that I realised... there was nowhere else to put it.

With these material conditions, the hula hoop structures often remained weak or were abandoned by visitors before completion, and few people left items on the structures. The current state of the work lacked one half of its desired nature:

although construction of the "museum" occurred, there was hardly any deposition of "collection" objects. Luckily, these observations from having participated could be turned into actions: another roll of tape was added, a larger instructional sign was placed next to the work, a rubbish bin was added nearby, staff began leaving their own objects to kickstart the work's desired deposition facet, and they began posting on the PHB website and social media pages encouraging people to prepare for their visit by bringing items to add to *Street Museum* and other works that invited visitor contributions. These interventions made a direct impact, and this ailing work was brought back to life.

Vivian van Saaze has pointed out the diminished role of materials in the way Relational Aesthetics are usually considered and discussed:

> Although Bourriaud is the first to deny that relational artworks celebrate immateriality per se, many of the examples he describes seem to have discarded the physical object as the dominant form of expression and take on more immaterial, temporary and interactive forms such as events or services. An interesting question, though not addressed by Bourriaud, is what role is there for physical objects and the museum in relational art? (van Saaze 2013, p. 158)

This case study into the potential use of ethnography for conservation has brought the material conditions of relational works into focus and helps to answer van Saaze's question: physical objects and the museum clearly play an active role in relational art insofar as they must create and maintain the material configurations necessary for relational artworks to live as intended.

5 An Expanded Role for Guards, Invigilators and Cultural Mediators

It is significant that the problems outlined above by staff from the Fowler Museum at UCLA were reflected identically by staff at Pirelli HangarBicocca, a very different kind of institution. The Fowler is both a collecting and exhibiting museum which displays a wide range of objects from the past and present; it is based on campus at a public American university, with permanent conservation staff and a steady stream of conservation interns working in an onsite conservation lab. In contrast, PHB is a private Italian contemporary art space with no permanent collection, no conservation professionals on staff, and without dedicated in-house conservation facilities. Yet despite their many differences in resources, infrastructure and audience type, both cases present a lack of—but desire for—detailed information about the exhibition life phase of the works they host, particularly ones with visitor participation.

I was told by multiple Pirelli HangarBicocca staff members how important they felt my case study was, because they themselves were not currently able to spend a significant amount of time in the front-of-house observing and participating. Next to my own research, they underlined the importance of the role played by their highly trained "cultural mediators" who act as guards to protect artworks and who offer deeper explanations and interpretation regarding the works. Recalling once again the

Fowler Museum's Head of Conservation who pointed to the role of invigilators in communicating information from the galleries to the collections care staff, these cultural mediators reported back on their experiences with *Take Me (I'm Yours)* during weekly meetings with PHB staff.

Many more mediators than usual were hired for *TMIY* because, the PHB curatorial team explained, "they really had to reinstall, restage, replace objects every single day... During the opening [hours], of course, but also when the show was closed—before and after."[17] This confirms that the responsibilities to care for these works do indeed cut across the boundaries dividing afterhours from opening hours and backstage from the front-of-house. The PHB curators continued, saying that visitors needed more explanation than usual in order to even begin engaging with the works—something my observations confirmed as I heard parents preventing children from engaging with works while they searched for a sign outlining "the rules." The curatorial team considered this mediation by the invigilators a vital part of conservation:

> regarding the conservation of the pieces, it's this parallel between the way you can activate the work and the way you take care of the work. There was this *tangenza* between these two aspects that usually are more disconnected [...] This kind of relation is what made it really interesting; the idea of conservation *within* cultural mediation. (Personal communication, 2018-04-19)

Although I do strongly advocate for institutions to reorganize professional priorities to allow conservators and collections care professionals the time to engage with artworks personally, this statement presents an additional tool or alternative route for institutions in which that cannot (yet) happen. Many institutions already have workflows in place that allow conservation and exhibition departments to liaise with team members from security and gallery services for reporting on the condition of works and to adapt and adjust presentation strategies. These structures can be further utilised in addition to—or, if necessary, in lieu of—an expanded presence of collections care staff in the exhibition space.

A deeper relationship with invigilators who are already posted in the front-of-house can become an important conservation strategy; but it will have to be carefully crafted. Regular meetings between collections care staff and invigilators could provide consistent opportunities for what happens in the front-of-house during exhibition to be written into artwork biographies. Often invigilators are already given comprehensive information regarding curatorial communication about artworks, but I suggest that further training specifically on practical conservation issues and general conservation principles must be communicated to heighten their sense of which observations should be reported and with what degree of urgency. Guards will need to be counselled not only on what is meant to occur in the front-of-house, but also looped into the behind-the-scenes conservation plans so that they can fully contextualize *how* they protect artworks on exhibition with *why* they are ultimately asked to do so.

[17] Interview with the Pirelli HangarBicocca curatorial team conducted 19 April 2018.

6 Continuous Collections Care

That contextualisation of the *why* and *how* behind collections care practice should be an evolving, iterative process; especially for Relational Art or any kind of art that is itself meant to evolve and iterate. A few months after *Take Me (I'm Yours)* closed I interviewed the curatorial team, who reflected on how, with *TMIY*,

> you learn over time how to approach the care of the works; because it has so much to do with the interaction of the public, and that's not something you can always foresee. For certain things that maybe we didn't expect, or we thought were more obvious... [after the] experience of a certain number of weeks of interaction, then we would adjust. (Personal communication, 2018-04-19)

This continuous engagement with the exhibition and how to care for the artworks was a function of the need for constant maintenance, since objects for visitors to take home had to be restocked and replenished every week. One Assistant Curator said it felt "like every week was the opening of a new show." If we think of this exhibition as suspended in that constant cycle of installation and deinstallation, then conservation and care should certainly also be ongoing. Engaging participant observation in the front-of-house space is a promising methodology to register and react—*in real time*—to the risks to and needs of ephemeral, evolving contemporary art. Furthermore, the reflections from staff at Fowler Museum at UCLA included in this chapter suggest that such a methodology would be welcome not only for contemporary art, but also for interactive altars or any cultural material on display that attracts museum visitor participation.

My presence as a researcher in pursuit of improved collections care for *Take Me (I'm Yours)* was certainly not the *only* source of information on how visitors and artworks behaved and interacted in the display space. PHB staff did visit the exhibition, but as mentioned, this was contingent on myriad other professional duties. Although cultural mediators posted in the space also had impressions and observations that they were able to share at weekly meetings, these were mentally noted and occurred only during their allocated working shift, during which time their primary professional tasks were to enhance visitor experience and intervene for security issues. I, on the other hand, was free to systematically observe and record vital information from a variety of sources, including statements from cultural mediators and curatorial staff, holistic observations of visitor and artwork behaviour, and my own subjective experiences from first-hand participation with the exhibition.

It is possible that some of the collections care interventions recounted in this chapter could have arisen from sources other than my own study—an invigilator may well have noticed visitors sitting too far apart from each other in Dominique Gonzalez-Foerster's chairs, and staff members could easily see that Yona Friedman's *Street Museum* was not receiving visitor-supplied objects for its "collection." However, an element of unstructured happenstance plagues the care of interactive and participatory works without a dedicated eye on their exhibition life phase. The systematic nature of my activities and the centralised point of contact that my presence provided were crucial elements that demonstrate the value of recalibrating conservation practice to include front-of-house activities during the exhibition phase for continuous collections care.

7 Summary

The field of contemporary art conservation is at a significant and exciting moment of professional growth and maturity. Various developments in innovative practice by professionals all over the world in the past few decades have firmly and clearly left marks on the shape of conservation philosophy, and practitioners who have encountered these pioneering theories are embracing the adoption of novel methods to align their practice with those theories.

The biographical approach to contemporary art conservation was one such theory that has been acknowledged as a fruitful paradigm with which to approach the care of contemporary artworks. While undertaking research to discern how this theoretical approach could be put into practice, it became clear that the exhibition life phase of artworks has been underexamined by conservators and collection carers due to heavy workload, but also due to the perception of collections care as a backstage activity.

In determining the best methods of addressing this blind spot in conservation practice, literature on visitor studies in museums proves only partially useful. While visitor studies can yield valuable information about the behaviour of the public (through observations) as well as the opinions and impressions of the public (through visitor books, surveys, and interviews), the motivations *behind* that behaviour and the processes *leading* to those impressions cannot be fully understood except by experiencing the exhibition oneself from the position of a visitor. For this reason, the tradition of ethnography in the museum is a more appropriate field in which to situate efforts to apply the biographical approach to conservation. While there are many recent examples of scholars conducting ethnographies *of* conservation to build and refine conservation theory, this chapter presented examples of how ethnography can be instrumentalized *for* conservation.

Reflections on past exhibitions from staff at the Fowler Museum at UCLA highlighted the need for collections care-centred engagement in the exhibition life phase for interactive works of cultural material and contemporary art. This prompted the development of a case study to test the use of participant observation during opening hours for the exhibition *Take Me (I'm Yours)* at Pirelli HangarBicocca, a dissimilar institution where staff members nonetheless divulged similar concerns and constraints. This study yielded the benefits of being able to more deeply understand the artworks, the public, and the exhibition environment. It illuminated the very different kinds of risks to each of the varied works, and it gave the exhibiting institution the chance to adapt material configurations and communication strategies in real time to mitigate those risks. These small adaptations can have an immediate impact, lessening the discrepancy between the current and desired states of the works.

The added burden on collections care professionals to commit increased time to the exhibition space can be eased—if not always by an external researcher such as myself, then more realistically by a transformed relationship with the guards, invigilators, or cultural mediators who are already positioned in the front-of-house. The care of works would greatly benefit from increased training of cultural mediators that extends their capacity beyond the normal purview of security and of curatorial insight to include essential aspects of conservation and details of the conservation strategies in place.

With the added knowledge gained from employing ethnographic methods for conservation during the exhibition life phase of contemporary artworks, the front-of-house exhibition space can become a locus of conservation intervention; not only to maintain the proper function of technology (as Time Based Media conservators already do) or to capture vital documentation (as conservators of performance art already do), but also to ensure the necessary material conditions for the artists' intended immaterial experiences to occur, and to guarantee that communication to visitors is adequate and effective.

The final point to be made is that integrating recent theory with practice will entail a shift in practitioner priorities, and ultimately in professional mentality. With this chapter I have made the case that collections carers who spend time during working hours in a gallery space—engaging with works from the perspective of a visitor and observing others around them—*are working*. This can only improve the way they care for the works on exhibition; something about which no collections carer should ever have to feel guilty.

Acknowledgements This chapter is based on doctoral research carried out at Maastricht University (UM) and MUDEC (Museo delle Culture)-Milan, and funded by the European Union H2020 Programme (H2020-MSCA-ITN-2014) under Grant Agreement n°642892. My sincere thanks go to the staff, crew and cultural mediators at Pirelli HangarBicocca for their enthusiastic support of and participation in this research, especially Roberta Tenconi, Lucia Aspesi, Fiammetta Griccioli and Giovanna Amadasi. Thanks also to the Fowler Museum and the UCLA/Getty Conservation Program for hosting me in 2017, particularly my advisors Christian de Brer and Ellen Pearlstein for their generous insights. As always, I am very grateful to my PhD supervisors Carolina Orsini (MUDEC-Milan), Iolanda Ratti (Museo del Novecento-Milan) and Renée van de Vall (Maastricht University) for their expert guidance, and to the entire *NACCA* cohort.

References

Bitgood S (2013) Attention and value: the keys to understanding museum visitors. Left Coast Press, Walnut Creek

Bourriaud N (2006) Relational aesthetics (1998). In: Bishop C (ed) Participation. Whitechapel Gallery, London; The MIT Press, Cambridge, pp 160–171

Bryan-Wilson J (2012) Practicing Trio A. October, 140:54–74. https://doi.org/10.1162/OCTO_a_00089

Bunzl M (2014) In search of a lost avant-garde. An anthropologist investigates the contemporary art museum. The University of Chicago Press, Chicago

Davies L, Heuman J (2004) Meaning matters: collaborating with contemporary artists. Stud Conserv 49(sup2):30–33. https://doi.org/10.1179/sic.2004.49.s2.007
Depocas A, Ippolito J, Jones C (eds) (2003) Permanence through change: the variable media approach. Guggenheim Museum Publications, New York
Domínguez Rubio F (2014) Preserving the unpreservable: docile and unruly objects at MoMA. Theory Soc 43(6):617–645. https://doi.org/10.1007/s11186-014-9233-4
Domínguez Rubio F (2016) On the discrepancy between objects and things: an ecological approach. J Mater Cult 21(1):59–86. https://doi.org/10.1177/1359183515624128
Durand CA (2010) Artistic practice and (museum) ethnography. Curator: Mus J 53(4):491–500. https://doi.org/10.1111/j.2151-6952.2010.00049.x
Ebert B (2018) Saintly relationships or grounds for divorce? An examination of workshop links between two medieval polychrome sculptures. J Inst Conserv 41(2):95–112. https://doi.org/10.1080/19455224.2018.1463923
Ebert B (2019) Biographies carved in wood: turning points in the lives of two medieval Virgin sculptures. J Mater Cult 24(2):144–175. https://doi.org/10.1177/1359183518811355
Falk JH, Dierking LD (2000) Learning from museums: visitor experiences and the making of meaning. Alta Mira Press/Rowman and Littlefield, Walnut Creek
Falk JH, Dierking LD (2013) The museum experience revisited. Left Coast Press, Walnut Creek
Fiske TL (2009) *White Walls*: installations, iteration and difference. In: Richmond A, Bracker A (eds) Conservation: principles, dilemmas and uncomfortable truths. Elsevier/Butterworth-Heinemann, Amsterdam, pp 229–240
Fowler Museum at UCLA (n.d.) About the Fowler Museum at UCLA. https://www.fowler.ucla.edu/about-fowler/. Accessed 11 June 2022
Giebeler J, Sartorius A, Heydenreich G (2019) The decision-making model for contemporary art conservation and presentation. https://www.th-koeln.de/mam/downloads/deutsch/hochschule/fakultaeten/kulturwissenschaften/f02_cics_gsm_fp__dmmcrmac_190407a.pdf. Accessed 11 June 2022
Golding V, Modest W (eds) (2013) Museums and communities: curators, collections and collaboration. Bloomsbury, London, New Delhi, New York and Sydney
Hammersley M, Atkinson P (2007) Ethnography. Principles in practice (Third). Routledge, New York
Harris KJ, Jerome NW, Fawcett SB (1997) Rapid assessment procedures: a review and critique. Hum Organ 56(3):375–378
Hein GE (1998) Learning in the Museum. Routledge, London and New York
Herle A (2008) Relational objects: connecting people and things through Pasifika Styles. Int J Cult Prop 15(2):159–179. https://doi.org/10.1017/S0940739108080090
Holbrook AC (2018) Second-generation huddle: a communal approach to collecting and conserving Simone Forti's Dance Constructions at The Museum of Modern Art. R-Journal Beiträge Zum Erhalt von Kunst- Und Kulturgut VD 1:118–123
Hooper-Greenhill E (1994) The educational role of the museum. Routledge Lynch, London and New York
Hooper-Greenhill E (2006) Studying visitors. In: Macdonald S (ed) A companion to museum studies. Wiley, New York, pp 362–376
Hummelen Y, Scholte T (2004) Sharing knowledge for the conservation of contemporary art: changing roles in a museum without walls? Stud Conserv 49(sup2):208–212. https://doi.org/10.1179/sic.2004.49.s2.045
Irvin S (2006) Museums and the shaping of contemporary artworks. Mus Manag Curatorship 21(2): 143–156. https://doi.org/10.1016/j.musmancur.2006.03.009
Kirchberg V, Tröndle M (2012) Experiencing exhibitions: a review of studies on visitor experiences in museums. Curator: Mus J 55(4):435–452. https://doi.org/10.1111/j.2151-6952.2012.00167.x
Lane RL, Wdowin-McGregor J (2016) This is so contemporary? Mediums of exchange and conservation. Stud Conserv: IIC 2016 LA Congress: Saving the now 61(2):104–108. https://doi.org/10.1080/00393630.2016.1204528

Laurenson P, van Saaze V (2014) Collecting performance-based art: new challenges and shifting perspectives. In: Remes O (ed) Performativity in the gallery. Staging interactive encounters. Peter Lang, Oxford, pp 27–41
Lawson L, Marçal H (2021) Unfolding interactions in the preservation of performance art at Tate. In: Bridgland J (ed) Transcending boundaries: integrated approaches to conservation. ICOM-CC 19th Triennial Conference Preprints, Beijing, 17–21 May 2021. International Council of Museums, Paris
Macdonald S (2001) Ethnography in the science museum, London. In: Gellner D, Hirsch E (eds) Inside organizations: anthropologists at work. Berg, Oxford/New York, pp 77–103. http://scholar.google.com/scholar?hl=en&btnG=Search&q=intitle:Ethnography+in+the+Science+Museum#0. Accessed 11 June 2022
Macdonald S (2002) Behind the scenes at the science museum. Berg, Oxford/New York
Marçal HP (2017) Conservation in an era of participation. J Inst Conserv 40(2). https://doi.org/10.1080/19455224.2017.1319872
Marçal HP (2021) Towards a relational ontology of conservation. ICOM-CC 19th Triennial Conference 2021 Beijing
Matos LA, Macedo R, Heydenreich G (eds) (2015) Performing documentation in the conservation of contemporary art. de História da Arte (Vol. Série W). Insituto de Historia da Arte, Lisbon. http://revistaharte.fcsh.unl.pt/rhaw4/RHAw4.pdf. Accessed 11 June 2022
Monnaie de Paris (2015) Press kit - *Take Me (I'm Yours)*. Monnaie de Paris, Paris. https://www.monnaiedeparis.fr/en/press/releases/take-me-i-m-yours. Accessed 11 June 2022
Moomaw K (2016) Collecting participatory art at the Denver Art Museum. Stud Conserv: IIC 2016 LA Congress: Saving the now 61(2):130–136. https://doi.org/10.1080/00393630.2016.1190904
Phillips J (2015) Reporting iterations. A documentation model for time-based media art. In: Matos LA, Macedo R, Heydenreich G (eds) Revista de História da Arte 4:168–179. http://revistaharte.fcsh.unl.pt/rhaw4/RHAw4.pdf
Quabeck N (2021) Messy text and the accessioning of Wolfgang Tillmans' *Life is Astronomical* installation (2001–2012). ArtMatters Int J Tech Art Hist (Special Issue #1):77–90
Reitstätter L (2016) Die Ausstellung verhandeln. Von Interaktionen im musealen Raum. Transcript, Bielefeld
Rothenberg J, Fine GA (2008) Art worlds and their ethnographers. Ethnologie Francaise 38(1): 31–37. https://doi.org/10.3917/ethn.081.0031
Ryan G (2016) Considerations in the acquisition of contemporary art: refabrication as a preservation strategy. Stud Conserv: IIC 2016 LA Congress: Saving the now 61(sup2):198–202. https://doi.org/10.1080/00393630.2016.1204517
Scholte T, Wharton G (eds) (2011) Inside installations - theory and practice in the care of complex artworks. Amsterdam University Press, Amsterdam
Spaarschuh C (2018) A holistic approach – taking into use a cultural biographic perspective for the conservation of a medieval crucifix. Paper presented at the ICOMOS International Scientific Conference Conservation Ethics Today: Are our Conservation-Restoration theories and Practice ready for the 21st Century? 1–3 March 2018, Florence, Italy
Spangler-Bickell C (2019) Collections care challenges and innovations for ephemeral altar assemblages. ICOFOM Study Ser 47:171–190. https://doi.org/10.4000/iss.1814
Spangler-Bickell C (2021) Dividuality, partibility, individuation: a paradigm for the care of expanding artworks. ArtMatters: Int J Tech Art Hist (Special Issue #1):98–105. https://www.amjournal.org/_files/ugd/14a82d_40e896cadc354b55b022abaea4236c61.pdf. Accessed 11 June 2022
Stigter S (2015) Co-producing conceptual art: a conservator's testimony. In: Matos LA, Macedo R, Heydenreich G (eds) Revista de História da Arte 4:103–114. http://revistaharte.fcsh.unl.pt/rhaw4/RHAw4.pdf. Accessed 11 June 2022
Stigter S (2016) Autoethnography as a new approach in conservation. Stud Conserv: IIC 2016 LA Congress: Saving the now 61(S2):227–232. https://doi.org/10.1080/00393630.2016.1183104

Taplin DH, Scheld S, Low SM (2002) Rapid Ethnographic Assessment in urban parks: a case study of Independence National Historical Park. Hum Organ 61(1):80–93. https://doi.org/10.17730/humo.61.1.6ayvl8t0aekf8vmy
Thornton S (2008) Seven days in the art world. Norton, New York
van de Vall R, Hölling H, Scholte T, Stigter S (2011) Reflections on a biographical approach to contemporary art conservation. In: ICOM-CC: 16th Triennial Conference, Lisbon, 19–23 September 2011: preprints [cd-rom] by J. Bridgland (ISBN 9789899752207). https://doi.org/10.1177/1745691612459060
van Saaze V (2013) Installation art and the museum. Presentation and conservation of changing artworks. Amsterdam University Press, Amsterdam. http://books.google.com/books?id=rgEXAwAAQBAJ&pgis=1. Accessed 11 June 2022
Yaneva A (2003) When a Bus Met a Museum: Following Artists, Curators and Workers in Art Installation. Museum and Society 1(3):116–31.

Caitlin Spangler-Bickell is an anthropologist whose work engages theories and practices of conservation and collections care. She is a PhD candidate at Maastricht University whose research based at MUDEC Milan was undertaken as part of the Marie Skłodowska-Curie network *NACCA (New Approaches in the Conservation of Contemporary Art)*.

Is Trust Enforceable? The Conservation of Contemporary Artworks from a Socio-legal Perspective

Zoë Miller and Anke Moerland

Abstract The conservation of works of contemporary art is a complex endeavour and involves a variety of actors. As well as the artist, museums, collectors, gallerists and conservators are involved in activities relating to conservation. It is not self-evident that all of them will have the same interests when dealing with a contemporary artwork. Conflicts can occur in relation to the conditions of ownership, access, display, and integrity of the artwork. In order to manage a divergence of expectations, it is essential for parties to trust that they will work according to shared values and beliefs. This chapter explores the relationship between artists and museums in terms of trust and control and considers the role that contracts can play to manage expectations of artists and museums, and to regulate aspects of the conservation of contemporary artwork currently not addressed by copyright law. Drawing on literature from the fields of sociology and art, we explore how trust and control influence the relationship between the artist and the museum. Legal doctrinal methods help us to explain how copyright law applies to aspects of the conservation of contemporary art, and what provisions contracts could include to address parties' expectations.

Keywords Contemporary art conservation · Ownership · Access · Copyright · Contracts · Trust

1 Introduction

The conservation of works of contemporary art is a complex endeavour and involves a variety of stakeholders, including the artist, museums, collectors, gallerists and conservators. To manage all parties' expectations, parties need to trust each other

Z. Miller
Tate, London, UK

A. Moerland (✉)
European and International Law Department, Maastricht University, Maastricht, The Netherlands
e-mail: anke.moerland@maastrichtuniversity.nl

R. van de Vall, V. van Saaze (eds.), *Conservation of Contemporary Art*, Studies in Art, Heritage, Law and the Market 9, https://doi.org/10.1007/978-3-031-42357-4_18

that they will work according to shared values and beliefs. It requires balancing theoretical, ethical, material, and aesthetic considerations. This chapter explores the relationship between artists and museums in terms of trust and control and considers the role that contracts can and do play within this relationship concerning the conservation of contemporary artworks.

We first explore the general attitudes to and practices around contracts in the art world, discussing the perceived resistance and antipathy to contracts in this field. Next, we consider the professional and institutional norms that apply to the conservation of contemporary art, focusing on the concepts of the integrity and authenticity of the work, and the artist's intent as central to the artist-museum relationship.

These ethical norms and guidelines are then located in the context of the broader discussion on the ethic of trust that shapes all human relationships (Granovetter 1985; Tyler 1990). A classic definition of trust is "the process that enables actors to deal with irreducible uncertainty and vulnerability" (Möllering 2006, p. 110). Trust is needed to facilitate cooperation and coordination of mutual benefit in situations where (1) uncertainties and risks exist, and (2) actors are interdependent on each other. Where artists depend on museums to exhibit their works, and museums on the cooperation of artists to display and conserve their works, a relationship of trust is essential. It, however, entails both parties taking a risk, a "leap of faith," that the other party will meet their expectations.

These risks and responsibilities are determined in part by social structures. We rely on literature that emphasizes the complementary relationship between social structures and trust. This helps us to understand how contracts can influence the relationship between artists and museums.

Relying on social structures as embedding of people's behaviour, we understand contracts to clarify or further specify these structures. Institutional norms and rules form part of these structures. But where they are implicit, actors may find it difficult to extend their trust in the other party, also to aspects that are not (yet) or fully addressed by the relevant norms and rules. We suggest that the value of contracts in contemporary art conservation, therefore, lies in their capacity to formalise and clarify social structures, providing the basis for the relationship of trust between the parties. We argue that the usefulness of contracts also lies in alleviating uncertainty that derives from the variation of national laws, limited case law, and the uncertain application of copyright laws to emerging artistic practices.

In a 2019 panel discussion, Marianna Houghton Mermin, a lawyer at the Solomon R. Guggenheim Museum, commented that when entering into contracts with artists, the aim of the institution was "to memorialise expectations" (Stringari et al. 2019). We adopt a similar perspective, proposing that contracts are a mechanism for articulating expectations of artists and collectors, particularly in areas which copyright law does not regulate, such as mandating consultation with the artist and defining the roles of actors involved in conservation.

We adopt a social-legal approach, which recognizes that contracts are embedded in, and influenced by, informal norms and social sanctions. Literature from sociology and the art world is used to establish norms and values that apply to conservation of contemporary art. Literature on trust and control informs the framing of the relationship between contracts on the one hand, and trust and control on the other. We use doctrinal legal methods to assess how artists use contractual arrangements to regulate the conservation of their artworks, and the role executants play in relation to the work. We draw on copyright legislation and case law to interpret relevant legal rules, which contracts can clarify.

Throughout this discussion we refer to Cuban artist Tania Bruguera's *Tatlin's Whisper #5*, 2008 and the contract that she concluded with Tate on the acquisition of the work in 2009. *Tatlin's Whisper #5* is a work of performance art grounded in political activism, which was performed on 26–27 January 2008 at Tate Modern. The work involves two police officers in uniform, who patrol the gallery space on a white and a black horse. The police officers use crowd control techniques, manipulating the visitors into a single group, encircling them to tighten that group, frontally confronting them with the horse and breaking the audience up again into two distinct groups. An important aspect of the work is that the visitors do not recognize the performance as art, as it is unannounced (Article 3.II.a, "Conditions for Showing *Tatlin's Whisper #5* 2008 by Tania Bruguera," in Westerman 2016). Bruguera wants to create an experience of "how easily a safe space can become threatening when power announces itself" (Westerman 2016).

2 Contracts, Ethical Norms and Trust in the Artworld

Before discussing the role of contracts in the relationship between artists and museums, we explore the normative framework that governs this relationship. Firstly, we survey the general practices and attitudes to contracts in the art world. This context is important as it demonstrates the (anecdotal) antipathy of the art world towards contracts and reveals the ethic of trust that underpins relations within the field. We then highlight key aspects of conservation theory and practice that provide normative structure to the relationship between the artist and the museum, before exploring literature on the broader notions of trust and control that regulate social relationships.

2.1 Resistance to Contracts

The art world is often described as reluctant to enter into contracts. Buck and McClean describe this reticence in their handbook on commissioning artworks, noting

> many elements of the art world have been highly resistant to written contracts—and to lawyers in general! Even in today's global multimillion art market, many agreements for both the sale and the purchase of the most valuable artworks are still frequently made on the basis of a handshake and the delivery of a basic invoice, rather than with the use of a proper legally binding contract. (2012, p. 218)

The perceived reticence to enter into contracts stems from the assumption that contracts undermine the ethic of trust that ought to underpin relationships between artists, dealers, and collectors. Contracts are viewed as adversarial rather than cooperative instruments. Kee notes that contracts are often understood as indicative of a compromised relationship: "in many cases, the very use of contracts implies that no one will get everything he, she, or it wants" (2017, p. 517).

Several artists are particularly resistant to limiting their artistic freedom. Jeremy Deller, for instance, describes his view on contracts as follows:

> I try not to sign any piece of paper . . . to commit myself to doing this, that or the other or to stick to an idea. I try to leave it to the last possible moment to sign anything. . . . You don't want to lock yourself into something that you are not happy with a week or a month later. . . and why should you, if the work is in progress? (Buck and McClean 2012, p. 218)

Despite the presumed reticence towards contracts, some contemporary artists have displayed interest in and engagement with the aesthetics and function of legal forms and processes, embracing what McClean calls "the legal moment" (McClean 2010). This engagement can be viewed in artistic and political rather than legal terms; in many cases the documents do not amount to binding legal agreements. The examples briefly discussed here reveal an artistic engagement with legal language and discourse that contributes to the reflexive relationship between art and law.

Artworks may incorporate or consist of valid legal instruments, rendering the law both subject matter and medium of the work. This becomes clear in particular where the work is based on a transaction of some kind, such as Tania Bruguera's *Obra nueva que no existe—todavía* (New work that does not exist—yet) (2007). Bruguera auctioned on eBay a work that "did not exist yet: not even in the mind of the artist" (Calonje and Bruguera 2014, p. 41). In these ways, legal instruments may amount to—or stand in for—artistic medium. Ima-Abasi Okon's work ^^^^^^^^^^^^^^^^^^^^^^^^^^^, 2018, exhibited at The Showroom in London as part of the group exhibition "there's something in the conversation that is more interesting than the finality of (a title)," comprises a dishwasher and a printed copy of the "General Service Agreement" between Okon and the gallery (Okon 2019). This document sets out the terms of the agreement, according to which the artist will make tablets for the dishwasher and supply them to the gallery. Okon's work shows that contracts can form an intrinsic part of the artwork itself, demonstrating artistic engagement with legal instruments, forms, and language.

Contracts also play a separate important role in artistic practice more broadly, facilitating the acquisition of works by collectors, and setting conditions for their custodianship. Okon's 'General Service Agreement', which sets out the specific terms of her labour and remuneration, also shows that the division between contracts *as* artworks and contracts *for* artworks is not clear cut. Adrian Piper, whose exhibition and sale agreement, the 'Solo Exhibition Agreement,' is adapted from Siegelaub and Projansky's contract, has stated that she does not view the document itself as an artwork, but that it forms "part of [her] conceptual work in art" (Piper and Eichhorn 2009, p. 203).

In this context, contracts may be exploited by artists as mechanisms for making political statements, as methods of neo-institutional critique, and as instruments valued as much for their communicative and declaratory properties as for their capacity to create enforceable legal obligations (McClean 2010). Piper's 'Solo Exhibition Agreement,' for instance, contains a clause requiring that the dealer or gallery representative does not under any circumstances offer a percentage discount on her work, as "it is already subject to the 50% Off Black Artists Discount and the 25% Off Women Artists Discount" (clause 5(b), reproduced in Piper and Eichhorn 2009, p. 210). The exhibition *In Deed: Certificates of Authenticity* displayed a selection of certificates of authenticity, diagrams and instructions, divided into categories, including documents deemed to be "Assertive Acts" (Hapgood and Lauf 2012, p. 81). This categorisation recognises the political instrumentality of contracts in the art world, separate to their legal function and value.

Thinking about contracts in this way reinforces an understanding of them as social and political as well as legal instruments. They are a vehicle for artists to use legal forms, methods, and rhetoric to articulate and enact a political position. The most widely known artist contract is 'The Artist's Reserved Rights Transfer and Sale Agreement,' drafted by dealer and gallerist Seth Siegelaub and lawyer Robert Projansky, published in 1971. Speaking about the contract, which was made freely available to use, Siegelaub stated: "We have done this for no recompense, for just the pleasure and challenge of the problem, feeling that should there be a question about artists' rights in reference to their work, the artist is more right than anyone else" (Siegelaub 1973, p. 144). The use of Siegelaub and Projansky's agreement demonstrates a commitment to ensuring that artists have the right to consultation and control over alterations and conservation of their works.[1]

Among other things, the agreement stipulates that in the event that the work is resold, the artist shall be paid 15% of the appreciated value (implementing, through contract, the equivalent of a *droit de suite*) (Article 2(b)), that the collector not intentionally modify, alter, or destroy the work (Article 9), that the collector must obtain the artist's consent prior to the work's exhibition (Article 7), and that the artist is to be consulted in the event that the work requires repair (Article 10). Incorporating these conditions into the contract of sale articulated a political position regarding the standing of artists in their dealing with collectors and institutions. At the same time, it gave artists rights not afforded to them by legislation.

Either working with lawyers—Daniel Buren drafted his artist's contract *Avertissement* (1968/69) with lawyer Michael Claura; Seth Siegelaub collaborated with Robert Projansky in developing 'The Artists' Reserved Rights Transfer and Sale Agreement'—or alone, some artists have embraced contracts as a means by

[1] Lauren Van Haaften Schick traces the use and adaptation of Siegelaub and Projansky's contract by various artists (van Haaften Schick 2018). Maria Eichhorn's edited volume *The Artists' Contract: Interviews with Carl Andre, Daniel Buren, Paula Cooper, Hans Haacke, Jenny Holzer, Adrian Piper, Robert Projansky, Robert Ryman, Seth Siegelaub, John Weber, Lawrence Weiner, Jackie Winsor* includes interviews with artists known to have used the contract or a version thereof (Eichhorn 2009).

which they can "make his or her own law" (Eichhorn 2009, p. 15). For them, contracts provide a mechanism by which they can exercise control over their works after they have been sold, and this has significant implications for the conservation of contemporary art.

The use of contracts, however, does not negate the importance of a relationship of trust; contracts are an instrument and artefact of the relationship between the parties and their meaning, and should be interpreted as such. This is illustrated by the final provision in artist Ima-Abasi Okon's 'General Service Agreement':

> Although this agreement is informed by employment law regulations, it is not a binding contract as understood in English and Welsh contract law. It is rather governed and bound by mutual respect and a sincere commitment to each other as human beings. It is based on the recognition that both parties agree to fully pursue the agreement both in spirit and in practice. (2018, Article 8)

2.2 *Norms and Guidelines for the Conservation of Contemporary Art*

While a full account of the norms and guidelines for the conservation of contemporary art is beyond the scope of this chapter, some key concepts inform this discussion of the relationship between artists and museums, namely the integrity and authenticity of the work, and artist's intent. These concepts are deeply intertwined, related to understandings of the status of the artist (van Saaze 2013, p. 48).

Respect for a work's integrity is enshrined in professional codes of ethics as a central concern of conservation. Sease describes integrity broadly, as "an unmarred, unimpaired or uncorrupted condition" (1998, p. 102). This definition encompasses both tangible and intangible aspects of the work. Conservation literature and professional codes propose an understanding of integrity as multiple: physical, aesthetic, historic, cultural, and conceptual (Clavir 1998; Muñoz Viñas 2005; ECCO Art. 5; AICCM Art 2).

For works of contemporary art, ensuring physical integrity does not guarantee conceptual integrity. This is reflected in evolving ideas of authenticity that have shifted from ensuring the persistence of a work's material form to reliance on the artist's ongoing approval of the work's manifestation/s. The ethical commitment to integrity is thus linked to both notions of authenticity and the artist's intent. Conservation literature has placed artistic intent as a central concern and wrestled with the ethical dilemmas posed when an artist's intent is unarticulated, ambiguous, or conflicts with established professional standards (Irvin 2005; Sommermeyer 2007; Gordon and Hermens 2013; Quabeck 2019).

These theoretical positions inform standard institutional practices of care for contemporary artworks, which involve gathering extensive information and knowledge about the work from the artist, through documentation, interviews and ongoing dialogue and consultation (INCCA 2002; Mancusi-Ungaro 2005; Beerkens et al. 2012). The artist's participation—through interviews, consultation, and ongoing dialogue—is crucial to developing and implementing conservation strategies for their work. Caring for works of contemporary art, therefore, often depends on a relationship of trust and goodwill between the artist and the institution.

Contracts, therefore, have an important place in contemporary art conservation theory and practice. They may be framed as part of what Irvin describes as "the artist's sanction," the body of an artist's explicit and implicit communications about the work (Irvin 2005). Contracts for artworks may also be viewed as forming part of the work's "score" (Laurenson 2006; Rinehart 2003; Phillips 2015; Burke 2018).[2] Contracts occupy a position of authority among other types of documentation that conservators routinely draw to build an understanding of a work and develop conservation strategies.

2.3 *Trust and Control*

In this chapter, we ask how the ethical guidelines applicable to the art world can be reconciled with contractual commitments. In particular, we consider whether relationships between artists and museums are governed mainly by trust, control in the form of regulation or rules, or a combination of the two. For that purpose, we explore the concepts of trust and control, and how they may apply to the relationship between the artist and museums.

Mayer, Davis and Schoorman distinguish trust from the ability to monitor or control. According to them, trust entails:

> the willingness of a party to be vulnerable to the actions of another party based on the expectation that the other will perform a particular action important to the trustor, irrespective of the ability to monitor or control that other party. (1995, p. 712)[3]

Control is defined here as the level of constraint imposed on the other (Möllering 2005, p. 286). Coleman characterizes monitoring, controlling and sanctioning as mechanisms of distrust, the opposite of trust (1990, p. 100).

While this perspective was dominant in the 1990s, later research has presented a more nuanced position towards trust and control. It supports that the two can complement and strengthen each other (Six 2013, p. 165), emphasising the possibility of a positive relationship between trust and control (Möllering 2005, p. 285). Möllering speaks in this context of a duality of the two concepts rather than a dualism. Such a duality perspective assumes "the existence of the other" (Möllering 2005, p. 284). We follow this perspective on trust and control, as it takes the reflexive nature of modern social relations into account and is developed on the basis of contract negotiations, a case similar to the subject of this article.

---

[2] For a discussion of understandings of artist's contracts as sanction and/or score, see Miller (2021).

[3] Later, similar definitions were adopted, among others, by Rousseau et al. (1998).

Following notions of embedded agency, actors are constrained by social structure but also exercise agency, through contingent and purposeful action (Garud and Karnøe 2001, pp. 9–11). This analytical framework helps us to understand how actors form positive expectations of the behaviour of other actors to whom they are vulnerable (Möllering 2005, p. 286). Since social interaction depends on both embeddedness and agency, actors will form their expectations of the behaviour of others on the basis of both variables. Relating this back to trust and control, the reliance on structural influences on the embedded person represent control, whereas assumptions of benevolent agency by the person represent trust (Möllering 2005, pp. 287–288).

Trust assumes the existence of control because when relying on the benevolence of a person, one also assumes the particular social structures in which this benevolence can occur. At the same time, where one relies on the controlling influence of social structures on persons, one also assumes that these structures leave a certain degree of freedom to act, and that that freedom is not malevolently exploited. Therefore, Möllering argues, "control alone is not enough, if it is not supported by trust" (2005, p. 290). Translating this to the art world and contracts, Stephen Snoddy, Director of the New Art Gallery in Walsall (United Kingdom), reflected this idea in his own words:

> It is very helpful to have a simple and straightforward agreement at the outset, so that the artist knows exactly where he or she is. This is not so much within a legal framework; it is done on the basis of trust. I have learnt that if you don't have something that lays out the parameters, then that trust can quickly go. (Buck and McClean 2012, p. 217)

Social structures consist of various factors. In professional relationships, the general rules of the trade as well as past mutual experiences play an important role (Möllering 2005, p. 290). General rules of the trade can be unwritten rules for negotiations, ethical norms etc. Social structures in this sense provide a certain level of control. However, actors will still need to trust that within these structures, the other will not exploit his agency in a malevolent way, by possibly even going against social structures. According to Daniel McClean, contracts should best be understood as providing a promise that is contingent upon trust rather than certainty: it is the personal relations founded upon trust between the artist and collector that count more than the law (McClean 2012, p. 94).

How much trust is needed depends on the level of social structures that control the possible actions by actors. The room for agency depends on the room left by social structures. For this reason, there is a reflexive relationship between the two (Möllering 2005, p. 291). Applying this to the relationship between contemporary artists and museums, one can identify several social structures that apply to this field: the legal rules that determine the rights of the artist, the ethical and professional norms of conservation, established practices for acquiring works of art, the relationship of goodwill between the artist and the institution, and the past experiences of both the artist and the museum.

In this context, written contracts between artists and museums that specify certain treatment, ownership or display of the artwork could be viewed as having two effects. Where contracts stipulate rules that are not yet defined or specified in previous social structures, they increase the level of social structures by regulating more than previously accepted norms, and hence leave less room for individual agency. Parties will then only have to trust that the other will use that reduced space of action benevolently.

In other situations, where contractual provisions formalize norms that are underlying previous social structures, a contract does not add new rules but merely makes these rules explicit and adds a stronger control mechanism. Arguably the same level of trust is then required that the trustee will act benevolently. Importantly, no matter whether more social structures or stronger structures are created, trust is still required for positive expectations of each other and a fruitful cooperation after all.

3 Contractual Arrangements as a Mechanism to Manage Expectations

Starting from the presumption that social structures are inherent to relationships between artists and museums, we perceive contractual arrangements as a means to provide more clarity about these social structures. In particular, where the law does not regulate aspects of importance to artists and museums, contracts may help to manage expectations between the parties. Works of performance and political art, such as *Tatlin's Whisper #5*, represent a particularly volatile and contingent medium; an explicit agreement setting out the terms of performance can help to preserve the very idea of the artwork. We suggest the option of contractual arrangements because parties in the art market already turn to the law when disputes arise, in particular for conflicts among artists and collectors for the high end of the global art market (McClean 2018, pp. 13–14). Using legal means like contracts upfront to prevent disputes from arising could offer more legal certainty and, in the end, reinforce the relationship built on trust. As Mark Stephens, partner at the London law firm Finers Stephens Innocent, put it:

> It is essential with commissioned artworks, in the interests of both artist and commissioner that a written, clear and detailed commissioning contract is in place from the outset. This paves the way for artistic freedom and better creative outcomes. The commissioning contract should help to create certainty and foster trust between the parties in a spirit of partnership rather than lead to distrust and mutual suspicion. (Stephens cited in Buck and McClean 2012, p. 223)

Many areas of law establish rules that are applicable to the art market, such as the broader field of property law, tort law, law of obligations, law protecting cultural heritage, etc. However, where questions of treatment of contemporary artworks are concerned, relevant rules are established in copyright law. In this chapter, we therefore look at current copyright rules in a few jurisdictions, and how contracts could help to clarify and provide legal certainty on how contemporary artworks should be treated. In particular, we consider two aspects of copyright law that differ between jurisdictions and often are not regulated in statutes or by case law. First, the protection of a work's integrity; second, the role of executants as (co-) authors in the realisation or installation a conceptual artwork.

We are aware that contracts cannot deviate from the principles of reasonableness, or equivalent concepts of national contract law. While the present chapter does not provide a detailed account thereof, we acknowledge that contracts that pertain to regulate aspects of copyright law that have been left unregulated, cannot be overly restrictive on the rights of buyers or commissioners, as it would produce unjust outcomes that then may be unenforceable (van Haaften Schick 2018, p. 17).[4] In addition, contracts regarding the treatment of works will inherently be limited to the parties that have consented to them. If future owners or inheritors do not wish to accept the contract's terms, they will not be bound by the rules set out (van Haaften Schick 2018, p. 18).

3.1 *Safeguarding a Work's Integrity*

The conservation of contemporary artworks often raises questions about authority—whether the artist or the owner of the artwork can determine how it is conserved or displayed. Examples concern the question as to whether artists must be consulted before each installation of their work, or about the context in which the work should be displayed. In 2021, for instance, the estate of Cy Twombly objected to the renovation of the Salle de Bronzes, a gallery in the Louvre, in which the artist created a 350 square metre ceiling painting. The estate claims the recent renovation of the gallery—which includes painting the walls dark red instead of white and changing the works displayed from antique bronzes to Etruscan artefacts—has altered the work without prior consultation or authorisation (Noce 2021).

When an artwork is acquired by a museum, this is generally accompanied with a license of some of the economic rights associated with the work. As such, the museum may have the right to display the work to the public, to reproduce it in catalogues, and to document the work. In addition to these economic rights, copyright grants artists moral rights over their work which cannot be licensed or transferred. Where two parties share rights to the same object, drawing the line between where the rights of one and the other stop can create conflicts. This is particularly so for moral rights, which among other things concern the integrity of a work—a rather open norm.

Moral rights constitute a set of rights recognized under copyright law that are meant to specifically protect the relationship between the author and her work. These rights differ substantially between jurisdictions, especially between common law

[4] A statutory limitation in UK copyright law pertains to the prohibition to override the exceptions for librarians, curators or archivists of a museum to make a copy of an artwork under the conditions specified in CDPA s42(7).

countries, such as the UK, the US, and Canada and civil law jurisdictions such as the Netherlands, France, and Germany. Civil law countries generally confer strong protection to authors; their systems are known as "authors' rights systems" (*Auteurswet*, *droit d'auteur*, *Urheberrecht*). On the other hand, common law countries tend to protect moral rights to a more limited extent, as the reason for protecting copyright in their system lies more in the utilitarian idea of benefit to society rather than protecting the personality rights of the author.

A common definition of moral rights can be found in Article 6*bis* of the Berne Convention, the primary international treaty on copyright, which stipulates two moral rights: the right to be attributed as the author, and the right of integrity. The latter is what is most important to our assessment of the treatment of contemporary artworks. It entails the right:

> to object to any distortion, mutilation or other modification of, or other derogatory action in relation to, the said work, which would be prejudicial to his honor or reputation. (Berne Convention, Article 6*bis*(1))

In other words, where a certain treatment such as modification or distortion, or any other derogatory action is prejudicial to the honour or reputation of the author, she can object to such treatment. The emphasis lies on prejudice to the author's honour or reputation—only in the case of such effect on an author's honour or reputation can the right be invoked. This is markedly different from the meaning of integrity in the field of conservation discussed above, which views integrity as a combination of physical, aesthetic, historical and conceptual integrity, with the artist's intent at its core (Clavir 1998, p. 2).

The national transpositions of the integrity right and case law that interprets this right are leading when an artist wants to rely on such a right in a particular conflict with a collector, conservator or exhibitor. This scope for national variation is illustrated by the different positions of courts in the UK and the Netherlands on the relevance of the context of a work to the work's integrity.

For example, in the UK as a typical common law country, the right of integrity is expressed as the right of authors to not have their work subjected to "derogatory treatment" (CDPA s80(1)). The term 'treatment' in the Act is limited to "any addition to, deletion from, or alteration to or adaptation of the work." The "treatment" of a work is considered derogatory only if it "amounts to distortion or mutilation of the work or is otherwise prejudicial to the honour or reputation of the author" (CDPA s80(2)(b)). Courts have confirmed that the clause "prejudicial to the honour or reputation of the author" applied to "distortion or mutilation" as well as other treatments. This notably excludes situations where a work is placed in an inappropriate and damaging context, the physical relocation of a work, or the destruction of a work. This interpretation of integrity focusses on the persistence of the work as a contained material object, rather than the work's conceptual, historical, or aesthetic qualities. As a consequence, the scope of the integrity right in the UK is significantly limited (*Confetti Records v. Warner).*

The integrity right is interpreted more broadly under Dutch law. Pursuant to Article 25(1)(c) of the DCA, the author of a work has the right to oppose any alteration to the work, unless the nature of the alteration is such that opposition would be unreasonable. In fact, any adaptation of or alteration to the work is covered. In addition, under Article 25(1)(d) of the DCA, the author has the right to oppose any distortion, mutilation or other impairment of the work that could be prejudicial to the honour or reputation of the author or to her dignity as an author. Significantly for works of contemporary art, interfering with conceptual elements of an artwork has been held to infringe the Dutch integrity right if the objection is not unreasonable (*Devens v Eijsden, Chiffrun v Foundation Rotary Projects Veendam*). An artist's objection to the alteration of the height at which his painting was installed, was found to be reasonable, on the basis that it had a material impact on the way it was viewed (*Van Soest v De Meerpal).* In determining reasonableness, contractual agreements to the placement of the work have been taken into consideration.

In view of the difficulty of ascertaining the exact scope of moral rights protection in the relevant country, and in order to provide more clarity about the intentions of the parties involved, contracts provide a tool that can specify conditions for the work's conservation and display. This can be especially valuable for safeguarding crucial conceptual or contextual aspects of a work's identity. For example, the contract used by Bruguera for *Tatlin's Whisper #5* includes the following stipulation of the right to integrity:

> The artist has the right to the integrity of the work. The work cannot be modified or changed without the authorization from the artist. (Certificate of Authenticity and Ownership Conditions)

This is an expansive articulation of the right to integrity; it extends to any modification of or change to the work and requires authorization for such modification. There is no requirement of prejudice or harm to the honour or reputation of the artist, unlike in Article 6*bis*(1) of the Berne Convention. The range of situations covered is therefore considerably broader. It should be noted, however, that it is not clear whether such a provision might be deemed to impose an unreasonable burden on the purchaser of the work. This would be a matter for a national court to determine.

As well as this statement of the artist's right to the work's integrity, Article 3.1a) of Bruguera's contract further specifies:

> The work is shown in places where abrupt social and political events have happened, either in recent history of the place or at the moment when such events are overwhelming presence in the media. (Conditions for Showing *Tatlin's Whisper #5* 2008 by Tania Bruguera)

This requirement speaks to the complexity and importance of political context for *Tatlin's Whisper #5*, which depends on the decontextualization of familiar images from the news into the space of the museum. According to Bruguera, the contracts she enters into with museums are not only about listing a set of conditions, but they are also designed to be a provocation and invitation to the institution to ensure her works retain their political potency. Discussing Tatlin's Whisper #5 in an interview with art historian Claire Bishop, she explains that while the contract requires the work only be shown in certain social and political contexts, it is up to the museum to decide when those contextual requirements are met (2020, p. 74).

Bruguera's focus on the social and political context of the work, rather than its material form, reveals an understanding of the artist's right of integrity that is quite different to its enactment in law. This demonstrates the capacity of contracts to clarify the existing expectations of the parties—that the museum will work alongside the artist to safeguard the conceptual and contextual integrity of the work.

3.2 *The Role of Executants as (Co-)Authors in the Realisation or Installation of a Conceptual Artwork*

Philosopher Sherri Irvin observes that "[in] the museum context, conservators and curators often play a role in the shaping of works of contemporary art" (2006, p. 143). This idea has been explored by various scholars, including Albena Yaneva, discussing the collective work underpinning installations (2003), by Vivian van Saaze, through the concept of "doing" artworks (2013), and by Sanneke Stigter, in applying the notion of autoethnography to contemporary art conservation practice (2015).

In the field of copyright law, there is a considerable grey area when it comes to authorship of a conceptual artwork that is installed by executants or participants. This is due to the primacy of the idea in conceptual art, as well as the delegated realisation often entailed by these works. LeWitt's well-known writing on conceptual art sets out the role of the idea in relation to the work:

> In conceptual art the idea or concept is the most important aspect of the work. When an artist uses a conceptual form of art, it means that all of the planning and decisions are made beforehand and the execution is a perfunctory affair. (LeWitt 1967)

In other words, the idea or concept behind a work is more important than the actual artwork. This very notion already poses a challenge to copyright law because the subject of copyright protection is the expression of a creative idea, rather than the idea itself (Article 2, WIPO Copyright Treaty). If the value of the artwork lies in the idea, however, it becomes difficult to protect it under copyright (Clarida 2016; Said 2016; Burke 2017). Only when the artwork is expressed in either a set of written instructions, diagrams or the execution or instantiation itself, it will be protected.

Copyright protection is contingent upon the expressed form of the artwork. This prompts the question of who should be acknowledged as the author of the artwork when the execution is left to others. Is the artist who conceptualised the work the single legal author, or are the executants in the museum or gallery who install the artwork according to the guidelines of the artist considered single authors or co-authors together with the artist?

The legal answer to these questions is not straightforward, and, as Bently and Biron explain, it may significantly diverge from social understandings and practices of authorship. When looking at copyright law in various jurisdictions, three elements seem to be important for determining co-authorship: (1) the relationship between the artist and participants, (2) the level and kind of participation, and (3) the degree of integration of the different contributions (Bently and Biron 2014, pp. 237–238).

In the UK, joint authorship requires "the collaboration of two or more authors in which the contribution of each author is not distinct from that of the other author or authors" (Copyright Designs and Patents Act, s10). Collaboration in this sense requires coordination or cooperation in the realisation of a common plan or design. The Dutch rules on joint authorship similarly require that the contributions of each author are not distinct (Spoor et al. 2005, p. 32).

A key factor that determines whether executants of the artwork should be attributed co-authorship or even sole authorship over the artwork, is the level of detail of the instructions given by the artist, and the level of involvement in the execution thereof. When looking at the input of the artist on a continuum, a strong involvement is reflected by a high degree of detail in the instruction and close control and supervision over the expression of the ideas.

An example of detailed instructions is contained in the contract regarding the acquisition of Tania Bruguera's *Tatlin's Whisper #5*. The detailed instructions stipulated in Article 3.1 discussed above, as well as her involvement in the performance at Tate Modern in 2008, suggest a strong engagement of the artist. This is further underscored by the inclusion in the same provision, of the right to veto the work's performance:

> The artist has the right to veto in case she considers that the (political, social and artistic) context and conditions of the project where the performance would be included contradicts or devaluates the original intention of the work. (Conditions for Showing *Tatlin's Whisper #5* 2008 by Tania Bruguera, Article 3.1)

A looser involvement can be found where only general guidelines are provided by the artist, and it is left up to the gallerist, exhibitor, collector, assistants or other participants to execute the work. This is the case for works by the American artist Sol LeWitt, who in some cases only provided general guidelines in the form of diagrams, instructions and/or a sketch for how the work is to be executed by his assistants (Bently and Biron 2014, p. 245; van Haaften Schick 2018, p. 9). Similarly, conceptual artist Lawrence Weiner was not always closely involved in the exhibition of his work, leaving it up to the collector or exhibitor to follow his aesthetic specifications (van Haaften Schick 2018, p. 9).

In light of the rather uncertain assessment as to whether a participant in the execution of the artwork will be considered as author or co-author in copyright law, contracts can help to agree upon the role of the artist and executants, in order to determine authorship of the work. The contract can set out detailed instructions on how the artwork is to be installed and under which conditions. It could include pictures, diagrams or other documentation that clearly illustrate the idea behind the artwork.

In addition, the role of the artist in the execution of the artwork can be specified in the contract. Artists could reserve for themselves a leading role in the execution of the artwork, similar to Bruguera's contract for *Tatlin's Whisper #5* cited above.

Another example is the agreement used by Daniel Buren, which specified in Article 7 that he has a right to be notified in a timely manner when his work is displayed by the collector. The artist furthermore reserved a right to advise and veto the exhibition of the work (Eichhorn 2009, p. 14; van Haaften Schick 2018, p. 15). As an alternative to Bruguera's and Buren's right to veto, a right to be consulted on the exhibition of the work could be agreed upon, with a best effort intention on behalf of the collector to respect the advice of the artist.

Contracts between the artist and the museum or gallery that will install the artwork could also stipulate that the artist should be declared as author, while the collaborators who participate in the installation and execution of the artwork should be attributed as "contributors." An attribution right for contributors, as an alternative of trying to establish co-authorship, is not foreseen in copyright law but has been suggested by Bently and Biron (2014, p. 267). Moral rights protection already recognizes the right of attribution for authors, but not yet for other participants. Such rights—independent of authors' rights—could help to acknowledge and correctly represent the actual collaboration in the creation of conceptual artworks. Contracts present an opportunity for providing this acknowledgement and making these contributions visible, even though copyright law does not yet require it.

4 Conclusions

This chapter has explored the role of contracts in conservation, and in particular in relation to the work's integrity and the role of executants. Relying on a socio-legal perspective, we acknowledge that contracts cannot be seen outside of the social structures inherent to the art world. They are defined by the legal and ethical guidelines, and customary norms that actors share and abide by. How much actors will rely on trust depends on the extent of their shared social structures. Strong social structures will require less trust, as more options, such as ethical and professional norms of conservation and acquisition of works of art, are already pre-defined; conversely, weak social structures require more trust that the other will act benevolently within the defined structures.

The art world has been traditionally resistant to using contracts, based on the perception that contracts are limiting for artists and indicate a compromised relationship. In this chapter, we approach contracts as a way of making social structures more explicit and as a tool for clarifying shared norms and expectations. At the same time, the relationship still requires an amount of trust that actors will act benevolently towards each other within these structures. We therefore argue that contracts are no substitute for trust, but a way to manage expectations better.

The field of copyright law opens up several options for clarifications through contracts. We relied on the limited number of contracts publicly available, legal and sociological literature, focusing in particular on the practice of Cuban artist Tania

Bruguera. We discussed how the role of participants in the execution of a conceptual artwork could be specified in contracts, and whether any rights can be attributed to them. This would create legal certainty and reduce the need to rely on different approaches to co-authorship in various jurisdictions.

The differences are even more substantial regarding moral rights protection, which is relevant in relation to the treatment of an artwork, and its possible impact on the integrity of the work. Defining the exact boundaries of what the right of integrity entails is complex and difficult. Based on examples from several contracts between artists and institutions, we discussed possible ways of defining the right of the artist to be consulted or to veto a modification or repair to her work. We also showed that principles like reasonableness or equivalent limit the burden that contracts can place on the buyer. If such a burden is unproportionable, the contractual provision can become unenforceable.

While this chapter provides a first discussion of how contracts can be used to formalize the role of actors involved in the exhibition and conservation of a contemporary artwork, it does not do so extensively in the context of national contract law. Actors interested in exploring the option of clarifying expectations through contracts should seek legal advice from a professional in copyright and contract law.

Acknowledgements Zoë Miller's contribution to this research was realised as part of the Marie Skłodowska-Curie Innovative Training Network *New Approaches in the Conservation of Contemporary Art (NACCA)*, funded by the European Union H2020 Programme (H2020-MSCA-ITN-2014) under Grant Agreement no 642892.

Treaties

Berne Convention for the Protection of Literary and Artistic works of 9 September 1886 (latest version, Paris 1971)
WIPO Copyright Treaty (WCT), adopted in Geneva on December 20, 1996

Professional Ethical Codes

European Confederation of Conservator-Restorers' Organisations Professional Guidelines
Australian Institute for the Conservation of Cultural Material Code of Ethics and Code of Practice

Cases

Confetti Records v Warner [2003] EWHC 1274 [UK]
President of the District Court of Groningen 20 October 1993, Chiffrun v Foundation Rotary Projects Veendam [Netherlands]
Court of Appeal of Den Bosch 24 February 1993, Devens v Eijsden, *NJ* 1993, 440 [Netherlands]
President of the District Court Zwolle 14 April 1989, Van Soest v De Meerpal [Netherlands]

References

Beerkens L, ’t Hoen P, Scholte T et al (eds) (2012) The artist interview. For conservation and presentation of contemporary art. Guidelines and practice. Jap Sam Books, Heijningen
Bently L, Biron L (2014) Discontinuities between legal conceptions of authorship and social practices. In: Bently L, Biron L (eds) The work of authorship. Amsterdam University Press, Amsterdam
Bruguera T, Bishop C (2020) Tania Bruguera in conversation with Claire Bishop. Fundación Cisneros, New York
Buck L, McClean D (2012) Commissioning contemporary art: a handbook for curators, collectors and artists. Thames & Hudson, London
Burke S (2017) Copyright and conceptual art. In: Bonadio E, Lucchi N (eds) Non-conventional copyright: do new and atypical works deserve protection? Edward Elgar, Cheltenham and Northampton, pp 44–61
Burke S (2018) Score, performance and the posthumous conductor. In: McClean D (ed) Artist, authorship & legacy. A reader. Ridinghouse, London
Calonje T, Bruguera T (2014) In conversation with Tania Bruguera. In: Live forever: collecting live art. Koenig Books, London
Clarida B (2016) Copyrightability of conceptual art: an idea whose time hasn’t come. Columbia J Law Arts 39(3):365–371
Clavir M (1998) The social and historic construction of professional values in conservation. Stud Conserv 43(1):1–8. Available at: http://www.jstor.org
Coleman J (1990) Foundations of social theory. The Belknap Press of Harvard University Press, Cambridge
Eichhorn M (2009) The artist’s contract. In: Fietzik G (ed) Interviews with Carl Andre, Michael Asher, Daniel Buren, Paula Cooper, Hans Haacke, Jenny Holzer, Adrian Piper, Robert Projansky, Robert Ryman, Seth Siegelaub, John Weber, Lawrence Wiener, Jackie Winsor. Walther König, Köln
Garud R, Karnøe P (2001) Path creation as a process of mindful deviation. In: Garud R, Karnøe P (eds) Path dependence and creation. Lawrence Erlbaum, Mahwah, pp 1–38
Gordon R, Hermens E (2013) The artist’s intent in flux, CeROArt. Available at: http://journals.openedition.org/ceroart/3527
Granovetter M (1985) Economic action and social structure: the problem of embeddedness. Am J Sociol 91(3):481–510
Hapgood S, Lauf C (eds) (2012) In deed: certificates of authenticity in art. Roma Publications; in Coproduction with SBKM/De Vleeshal, Amsterdam

International Network for the Conservation of Contemporary Art (INCCA) (2002) Guide to good practice: artists' interviews. Available at: https://incca.org/incca-guide-good-practice-artists-interviews-2002
Irvin S (2005) The artist's sanction in contemporary art. J Aesthet Art Crit 63(4):315–326
Irvin S (2006) Museums and the shaping of contemporary artworks. Mus Manag Curatorship 21(2): 143–156
Kee J (2017) Félix González-Torres on contracts. Cornell J Law Public Policy 26:517–531
Laurenson P (2006) Authenticity, change and loss in the conservation of time-based media installations: a conceptual framework for traditional fine art conservation. Tate Papers 6 (Autumn). https://www.tate.org.uk/research/publications/tate-papers/06/authenticity-change-and-loss-conservation-of-time-based-media-installations
LeWitt S (1967) Paragraphs on conceptual art. Artforum 80
Mancusi-Ungaro C (2005) Material and method in modern art: a collaborative challenge. In: Scientific examination of art: modern techniques in conservation and analysis. National Academy of Sciences, Washington, DC, pp 152–161. Available at www.nap.edu/catalog/11413.html
Mayer RC, Davis JH, Schoorman FD (1995) An integrative model of organizational trust. Acad Manag Rev 23(3):709–734
McClean D (2010) The artist's Contract / from the Contract of Aesthetics to the Aesthetics of the Contract. Mousse (1 September 2010). Available at: https://www.moussemagazine.it/magazine/daniel-mcclean-the-artists-contract-2010/
McClean D (2012) Authenticity in art and law: a question of attribution or authorization? In: Hapgood S, Lauf C (eds) In Deed: certificates of authenticity in art. Roma Publications, Amsterdam, pp 87–95
McClean D (2018) Introduction. In: McClean D (ed) Artist, authorship & legacy. A reader. Ridinghouse, London
Miller Z (2021) Enacting artistic authorship in contemporary art conservation: contracts, incompleteness, and the possibility of making. ArtMatters Special Issue 1:63–69
Möllering G (2005) The trust/control duality: an integrative perspective on positive expectations of others. Int Sociol 20(3):283–305
Möllering G (2006) Trust: reason, routine, reflexivity. Elsevier, Oxford
Muñoz Viñas S (2005) Contemporary theory of conservation. Elsevier Butterworth-Heinemann, Oxford/Burlington, MA
Noce V (2021) Cy Twombly foundation "absolutely prepared to take legal action" after Louvre "destroys" artist's ceiling painting in renovation works. The Art Newspaper 18 February
Okon I-A (ed) (2019) ^^^^^^^^^^^^^^^^^^^^^^^^. PSS, London
Phillips J (2015) Reporting iterations: a documentation model for time-based media art. Matos LA, Macedo R, Heydenreich G (eds) Revista de História da Arte 4:168–179. http://revistaharte.fcsh.unl.pt/rhaw4/RHAw4.pdf
Piper A, Eichhorn M (2009) Interview with Adrian Piper. In: Eichhorn M (ed) The Artist's Contract. Walther König
Quabeck N (2019) Intent in the making: the life of Zoe Leonard's *Strange Fruit*. Burlington Contemporary (May). Available at: http://burlingtoncontemporary.org.uk/journal/journal/intent-in-the-making-the-life-of-zoe-leonards-strange-fruit
Rinehart R (2003) Perspectives Berkeley Art Museum/Pacific Film Archive. Permanence through change: the Variable Media Approach. Guggenheim Museum Publications and The Daniel Langlois Foundation for Art, Science, and Technology, New York
Rousseau DM et al (1998) Not so different after all: a cross-discipline view of trust. Acad Manag Rev 23(3):393–404
Said ZK (2016) Copyright's illogical exclusion of conceptual art. Columbia J Law Arts 39:335–354
Siegelaub S (1973) Introduction to the The Artist's Reserved Rights Transfer and Sale Agreement (1971), vol 6. Leonardo. Available at: https://primaryinformation.org/the-artists-reserved-rights-transfer-and-sale-agreement-1971/

Six F (2013) Trust in regulatory relations: how new insights from trust research improve regulation theory. Public Manag Rev 15(2):163–185

Sommermeyer B (2007) Who's right? The artist or the conservator? In: Scholte T, Wharton G (eds) Inside installations. Theory and practice in the care of complex artworks. Amsterdam University Press, Amsterdam

Spoor JH, Verkade DWF, Visser DJG (2005) Auteursrecht – Auteursrecht, naburige rechten en databankenrecht. Kluwer, Deventer

Stigter S (2015) Co-producing conceptual art: a conservator's testimony. Matos LA, Macedo R, Heydenreich G (eds) Revista de História da Arte 4:103–114. http://revistaharte.fcsh.unl.pt/rhaw4/RHAw4.pdf

Stringari L et al (2019) Decommission: rights, responsibility, and the status of the work. In: Object lessons: The Panza Collection Initiative Symposium. New York

Tyler TR (1990) Why people obey the law. Yale University Press, New Haven

van Haaften Schick L (2018) Conceptualizing artists' rights: circulations of the Siegelaub-Projansky Agreement through art and law. Oxford Handbooks Online

van Saaze V (2013) Installation art and the museum. Presentation and conservation of changing artworks. Amsterdam University Press, Amsterdam

Westerman J (2016) Tania Bruguera, *Tatlin's Whisper #5* 2008. In Performance at Tate: Into the space of art. Tate Research Publication. Available at: https://www.tate.org.uk/research/publications/performance-at-tate/perspectives/tania-bruguera

Yaneva A (2003) When a bus met a museum: following artists, curators and workers in art installation. Mus Soc 1(3):116–131

Zoë Miller is a doctoral researcher in the New Approaches in the Conservation of Contemporary Art (NACCA) programme. She holds degrees in arts and law, and a MA in Museum Studies. Her research focuses on the intersection between art and law, particularly around issues of authorship and ownership in contemporary artistic practice and conservation.

Anke Moerland (LL.M.) is Associate Professor of Intellectual Property Law in the European and International Law Department, Maastricht University. She holds a PhD in Intellectual property protection in EU bilateral trade agreements from Maastricht University. Her educational background is in political science (International Relations) and law. Anke has published widely on IP law and policy, with a particular focus on IP law between new technologies and tradition. In that light, she is at the forefront of discussing how copyright rules foster the preservation and digitization of cultural heritage.

Making Time

Pip Laurenson

Abstract This chapter considers the different temporalities within the contemporary art museum and explores how externally funded research affords thicker care time to enable an engagement with works that challenge the structures, systems and temporalities of the museum. Drawing on the idea of a "timescape" introduced by the sociologist Barbara Adam, it considers the "timescapes" of conservation practice and thinking, of the museum and of artworks, and how these different and sometimes conflicting temporalities impact our practices of care.

Keywords Time · Timescapes · Temporalities · Productivism · Care · Contemporary art museum · Research grant funding · Conservation practice

1 Introduction

In 2022 the three-year research project *Reshaping the Collectible: When Artworks Live in the Museum* drew to a close.[1] The project had been funded by the Mellon Foundation and had spanned two epoch defining events, the global Covid 19 pandemic and the mobilisation against racism following the death of George Floyd in 2020.

During the years that spanned the life of the project, we conducted two rounds of formative evaluation where we considered the value of the research to the museum, the participants and the field. Some achievements were easy to quantify: papers given, publications produced, videos made, displays hosted, new procedures and

[1] *Reshaping the Collectible: When Artworks Live in the Museum* is a three-year project funded by the Mellon Foundation. The project involved researchers from across conservation, collection management, archives and records and curatorial within Tate as well as benefiting from four Senior Academic Research Fellows and two doctoral students. For more information, see Tate (2019). The project was coordinated by the author of this chapter, Pip Laurenson, then Head of Collection Care Research at Tate.

P. Laurenson (✉)
Department of History of Art, University College London, London, UK
e-mail: p.laurenson@ucl.ac.uk

R. van de Vall, V. van Saaze (eds.), *Conservation of Contemporary Art*, Studies in Art, Heritage, Law and the Market 9, https://doi.org/10.1007/978-3-031-42357-4_19

protocols developed and adopted, complex issues with specific artworks or groups of artworks resolved. Other impacts were harder to pin down, such as learning, the transformation of our thinking and approaches to our practice, and how we as individuals had been changed during this time. However, in conversations with staff the value they most commonly identified was that the project bought time, allowing for a different temporality to enter into the "timescapes" of their work in the museum.

I will explore this idea of "buying" or "making time" through the lens of the work of Maria Puig de la Bellacasa, in particular her thoughts on soil time in her book *Matters of Care: Speculative Ethics in More than Human Worlds* (2017) and the concept of a "timescape" as developed by Barbara Adam (1998, 2008).

2 Timescapes

Barbara Adam has identified seven features of timescapes: timeframes, temporality, timing, tempo, duration, sequence and the temporal modalities of past, present and future (Adam 2008). In her 1998 book *Timescapes of Modernity*, Adams writes: the concept of a timescape "stresses the temporal features of living. Thinking with timescapes, contextual temporal practices become tangible. Timescapes are thus the embodiment of practiced approaches to time" (Adam 1998, p. 10).

During the pandemic the normal rhythms of our lives changed. For those not involved in frontline work, the day was no longer punctuated by a commute, the normal markers of milestones in our lives and the lives of our friends, colleagues and family disappeared, our worlds both shrunk and expanded through online communication, and people wrote songs to be shared on the internet called things like 'The Keep Going on Song' (Bengsons 2020) expressing a common experience for many white-collar workers and families who were locked down. Before the pandemic the project *Reshaping the Collectible* had explored ideas of care, in particular in relation to the social networks surrounding and sustaining particular artworks we were studying (Geismar 2022; Laurenson 2022). During the pandemic, as making relationships visible and mapping the social took on a different meaning, our work had a very particular quality that highlighted and questioned the idea of "care time" as the temporal dimension of care understood as "the fostering of the endurance of objects through time" (Puig de la Bellacasa 2017, p. 171). The experience of working together through the pandemic caused us to reflect on what care time had meant before the pandemic and what it might mean now.[2]

The aim of *Reshaping the Collectible* was to look at works that did not fit easily into the museum and to learn from them. During the course of the project, I came to

[2] It is important to acknowledge that there is a sense that the concept of care itself has been worn out by recent global events and become exhausted by a rhetoric of care that has repeatedly failed to meaningfully translate into action.

see that a common feature of the works of art we focussed on within the project were that they, in different ways, resisted and refused the timescapes of the museum and served to expose these assumed temporalities. Understanding more about the temporalities at play more generally within the project therefore took on a new importance.

How can Maria Puig de la Bellacasa's work on time help inform our understanding of these multiple temporalities in the museum? In her discussion on time in her study of "soil time", Puig de la Bellacasa identifies three different temporal scales within the dominant timescapes of society that are deeply entangled: the epoch frame, embedded time and embodied time. She sees epoch time as marked by the linear imperative of progress that harbours a fear of regression. Embedded time is understood as time that is embedded in practice and that is paced to a productionist ethos. Embodied time is our everyday experience of time which Bellacasa argues is focussed on an uncertain future but calls us to act now. Embodied time is characterised by what Puig de la Bellacasa calls "restless futurity" (Puig de la Bellacasa 2017, p. 175).

The author also argues that care time entails "making time" and in getting involved in the diversity of timescapes that make up the web of more than human agencies. This idea of "making time" points to different experiences of time such as the feeling of "timeless time" or "thick time", both of which convey a sense of time which does not have any of the highly structured constraints of embedded time and productionist timescapes, and open up different possibilities for attention and care. It acts as a disruptive intervention within the dominant temporal landscape. "Making time", I will argue, echoes what was made possible through the grant funding of a research project, and by the acts of resistance or refusal performed by some artists and their artworks.

3 The Timescapes of the Contemporary Art Museum

What are the features of the timescapes of the contemporary art museum, the context in which the research project performed its magic of "making time"?

In any visit to a conservation lab, you will encounter close, painstaking work taking place in the service of objects. Most commonly for museum objects this takes the form of slow cleaning, stabilisation or repair, often under magnification. For time-based media conservation this might be careful monitoring of video signals, or checking the grading of a film, or the significance of a section of source code, adjusting the mechanics of a film projector, or recalibrating the sound to a specific display space. This type of concentrated work is also sometimes encountered despite and within the hustle and bustle of a very different tempo, for example while a display or exhibition is being installed and can feel at odds with the other paces and schedules encountered in the museum.

The contemporary art museum holds within it an inherent tension between its different timescapes that often feel at odds with each other. We encounter the timescapes associated with acts of care and repair, sitting alongside a more frantic world of spreadsheets, targets, art fairs, openings and deadlines and also the timescape of the museum as an institution that transcends current time to be able to carry its collections into the future.

In her 2009 paper 'Contemporary Museums of Contemporary Art', conservator Jill Sterrett provides an account of the "brisk tempo" of the timescapes of the contemporary art museum. Anticipating Bellacasa's idea of embodied time, she writes "Contemporary art is about now and, as such, museums of contemporary art are called upon to keep pace. To operate in the present means to value agility; keeping current is, after all, key to being about whom we are today" (Sterrett 2009, p. 223). She notes that museums are in competition with other aspects of the leisure industry and dark galleries are frowned upon and installation times are compressed. However, she also notes that trust in the museum is based on a longer view. "In the museum, it is the notion of temporality that situates art within a context; approaches it and describes it as part of a larger, discursive continuum." Sterrett goes on to advocate for variable speeds "rapid cycles of engagement paired with sustained follow-through, in-the-moment presence coupled with reflection, breakneck speeds that work in tandem with strategic pauses" (Sterrett 2009, p. 227). This acknowledgement of alternative and multiple temporalities characterises what it means to effectively care. To take time to observe and respond effectively, it is one of the competencies of care (Puig de la Bellacasa 2017, pp. 195–203).

The rhythm of museum activity, for those who focus on the collection, is dictated by programmes of display changes, exhibition, loan and acquisition. Each activity has a timeframe structured through meetings that follow a pre-determined schedule within the year—pushing decision making through a structure until they reach the committee that ratifies the decisions. These structures determine the tempo of the work of the museum, the insistence of set lead times for a loan, the petitioning about workload and clashes of major activities across sites, resulting in the co-ordinating of complex timing of a range of different events. Some of the decisions made during these meetings, such as whether to display, loan or acquire a work, will impact the life of a work and its care very directly. All works of art entering the collection at Tate go through an acquisition process preparing the work for its life in the museum. This is often the time when for some objects they will receive the most attention in their new museum life.

There are pressures associated with this workload. For example, works must be ready for shipping, exhibitions must open on time, acquisition work must be completed so artworks can be paid for in a timely manner. Reputations, relationships and money are at stake. During the 1990s the museum sector in the United Kingdom went through a moment defined by managerialism which sought to make public sector activities more aligned to commercial practices. Managerialism argued that management was context independent and was a set of skills that would improve organisational performance regardless of the context (Palmer 1998). In response to this belief and under pressure to demonstrate that its government grant was well spent, Tate launched a programme called *Effective Tate* and employed a firm of consultants who questioned staff in the Collection Care Division about their standards of care. Their approach challenged cultures of care within conservation, a department that had previously confidently articulated its ambitions in terms of providing the highest standards of care. It was during this time that the conservation department introduced timesheets for its staff.

This type of productionism reduces what counts as care to a managerial set of tasks to follow. In this environment there is a risk that care time is devalued as "unproductive" (Adam 2004, p. 127 cited in Puig de la Bellacasa 2017, p. 208). Deeply engaged and transformative acts of care can be understood as acts of resistance to managerialism (Singleton and Law 2013). Conservators working in this context often feel guilty about exploring "thicker"[3] care time in their work. This is in part because working in a culture of scarcity, caring for one artwork means the potential neglect for another, but also because the more open and responsive nature of that encounter is hard to contain within the way in which time is allocated for specific tasks to be completed.

Sitting alongside this parcelled and productionist idea of present time, is the idea that the museum is an institution designed to transcend the timescale of a human life and support the survival of objects into the future in the form of a "permanent collection". This ability to transcend time is linked to the structures of the museum which present a sense of what Ariella Azoulay has identified as a timelessness which renders invisible the fact that the structures of the museum and the archive have been created by human beings. The effect of this sense that they have always been there is to make it hard to imagine changing such structures (Azoulay 2019, p. 190). Azoulay links these elements of the museum and the archive to "imperial and colonial practices and imaginaries that promoted detachment, standardisation, perpetual movement, external and superior goals, and investment in the future, the parcelling out of time and mastering of time's fictive unity" (Azoulay 2019, p. 193). Again, the responsiveness of care time to the specifics of a work of art can act as a point of resistance to these imperial and colonial practices.

Many of the strategies for protecting collections operate on a scarcity model where a work is seen to have a limited life span, such as the number of hours it can be exposed to a certain light level, before it is in effect "used up". Reversing this logic and making visible the value brought about by bringing an artwork into dialogue

[3] I use the idea of "thicker" care time here both in the sense used within moral philosophy and also the philosophy of science (Efstathiou 2016). Within moral philosophy it has been used by Williams (1985) to indicate concepts that are both descriptive and evaluative, so that the idea of "care time" carries with it a call to act in a certain way. I also use "thick" here in the way in which it is used by philosophers of science, meaning that as a concept "care time" is descriptively rich and specific. This also speaks to Donna Haraway's notion of the layering of knowledge, where she advocates for knowledge production as an additive process (Puig de la Bellacasa 2017, p. 75; Haraway and Goodeve 2000, p. 108). Building an understanding, through practice, about what care time might mean for a specific artwork in a specific situation becomes part of an ethics of care and also is suggested as an addition to our conservation ethics. For both the moral philosophers and the philosophers of science "thick" concepts are guided and rooted in the world and express situated knowledge that acknowledges multiple entanglements.

with people, other artworks, and practices of care through attention in the present, helps us to examine and question their underpinning logic.

In her 2020 paper the focus on preservation for future generations was questioned by the conservator Jane Henderson. In her paper 'Beyond Lifetimes: Who do we exclude when we keep things for the future' (Henderson 2020) she challenged a foundational idea in conservation thinking, which privileges a future generation, who, as Henderson points out, will probably be from a very similar demographic to our current museum visiting audiences, over drivers to widen participation within current generations by providing greater access now. To challenge this idea is to challenge the "restless futurity" of conservation's framing as a professional responsibility to focus on protecting things in the present to ensure they have a future—a future that promises to be better and more important and valuable than the present.

So, although this notion of the future is fundamental to the idea of the museum and its purpose, it raises interesting questions as to what care time is excluded in its future focus that has traditionally placed care for current generations and their access to collections at odds with care for the collection.

4 Timescape of Works of Art

It their book *Anachronic Renaissance* Alexander Nagel and Christopher Wood (2010) write:

> The work of art is a strange kind of event whose relation to time is plural. The artwork is made or designed by an individual or by a group of individuals at some moment, but it also points away from that moment, backward to a remote ancestral origin, perhaps or to a prior artefact, or to an origin outside time, in divinity. At the same time it points forward to all its future recipients who will activate and reactivate it as a meaningful event. (p. 9)

The art historian Martha Buskirk has picked up this theme in her book *The Contingent Object of Contemporary Art* writing that "the transition of a work of art's initial appearance to its extended life as an object to be preserved, collected, and contextualised as part of a historical narrative involves a complex process of negotiation" (Buskirk 2003, p. 12).[4] This constant negotiation requires a different relationship to time for many art objects, one that acknowledges their unfolding and becoming and resists the idea of fixity.

The relationship of the temporal modalities of past, present and future as described by Nagel and Wood does not however acknowledge the challenge of any material object to fit within the timeframe envisaged by a museum and its "permanent collection". In his paper 'On the discrepancy between objects and things. An ecological approach' (Dominguez Rubio 2016), Fernando Domínguez Rubio highlights this expectation of the temporality of a museum object which is at odds with their materiality. In his account of the biography of the painting known as

[4] This passage from Martha Buskirk is also quoted in Sterrett (2009), p. 226.

the *Mona Lisa* painted by Leonardo da Vinci c. 1503, Domínguez Rubio illustrates the struggle and labour involved in the maintenance of the "object place" of works of art—labour that enables them to remain art objects rather than becoming simply a "thing". Care in this context is seen as the fostering of endurance of art objects through time, defying their material temporalities and the inevitability of change.

Some objects are even more at odds with the temporalities of the museum than Leonardo's *Mona Lisa*. Fernando Domínguez Rubio carried out extensive ethnographic work at the Museum of Modern Art (MoMA) in New York and in his account of his time at MoMA he identifies a group of artworks as "unruly objects" which do not docilely comply to the temporalities and regimes of care within the art museum (Dominguez Rubio 2014, 2020). Such works can act as points of resistance or at least friction within the dominant timescapes of the museum.

Time-based media works of art (works of art for which the primary artistic medium includes video, audio, film, slides, software or performance) are inherently unruly, challenging the timelines assumed by the regimes of care within the art museum. Time-based media works are impacted by dependencies on technologies which are subject to rapid technological change and obsolescence dictated by industries whose operating logic is unconcerned with preservation but conform to an industry driven temporality related to innovation and profit. Performance artworks often depend on complex memory ecologies and networks of care outside the museum to sustain them. Careful storage as a preservation strategy is not an option for these works whose demise cannot be slowed by common museum technologies such as the control of temperature and humidity, light, pests and carbon scavengers. Instead, they require ongoing maintenance and care, for, for example, the migration of electronic signals, the timely emulation of obsolete platforms, conversations with the artist as to possible modes of intervention that might enable a work to continue to be displayed. These works do not do well with attention being portioned out according to the standard rhythms of display which are unlikely to be frequent enough to respond to their needs.

Urgency is created around these works in the risk of loss, uncertainty about the use of unproven materials for making art, obsolescence of skills, materials and technologies on which these works futures rely, and the disintegration of networks of care on which they might depend outside the museum. Within contemporary art there is also urgency related to the transition of a work beyond the death of the artist.

To ground these thoughts, in the following I want to touch upon three different works that challenge and resist the timescapes of the museum which were studied as part of the research project *Reshaping the Collectible: When artworks live in the museum*. Within the project a group of works which very directly resisted the structures and temporalities of the museum were a group of 15 net based artworks which were commissioned by Tate between 2000 and 2011. These works had been commissioned but not acquired by Tate and sat disconnected from the main site (Bayley 2021; Haylett 2021).

One of these works is Shilpa Gupta's *Blessed Bandwidth* which is a work that addresses issues related to state control and religion. Blessed-Bandwidth.net, 2003 is a multi-part net art work that has been described by the artist as a "space which

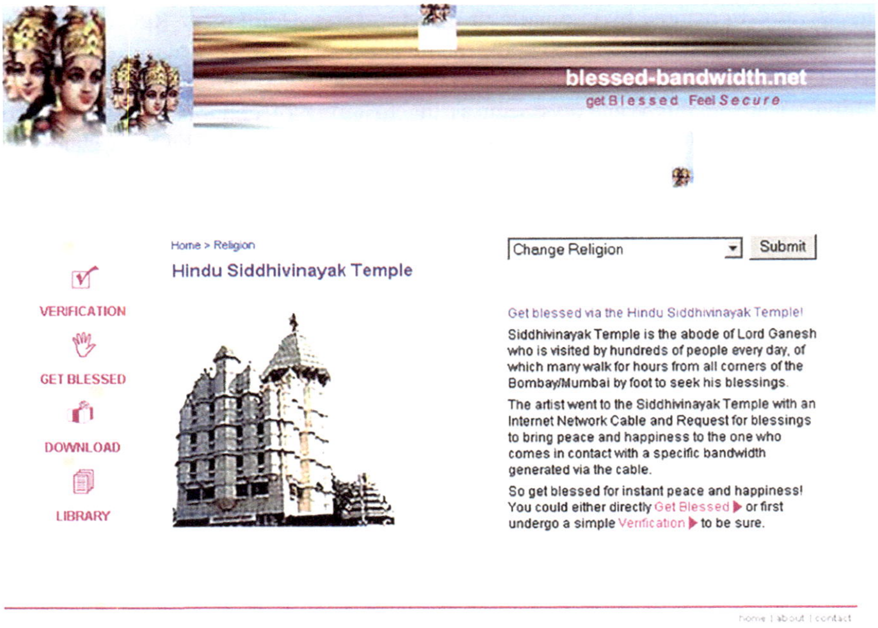

Fig. 1 Screenshot of *Blessed Bandwidth* provided via the artist's website, accessed 29 Jan 2023 (© Shilpa Gupta. Courtesy the artist)

considers what it indeed 'real' against the background of growing up in a place torn apart by riots on the basis of which god you worship", it consists of a website with interactive elements and downloadable content. The website provided users with the chance to receive a "blessing", via a network cable which the artist had taken to religious leaders and places of worship to be blessed. It also provides an opportunity to outsource the time involved in religious worship, by having someone else do it for you.[5] In engaging with this work, the visitor chooses their religion and place of worship. The visitor can download a god onto their computer who will pop up during the day asking for attention "Feed me, Thrill me, Love me. I am your God.exe and I will love you back." The visitor to the site can also contribute a diary of their sins. The technologies on which this work depends include Flash for which Microsoft ended support on 30 December 2020 (Bayley et al. 2023) (Figs. 1 and 2).

Websites have an advantage over other works which depend on schedules of display as a means to ensure they receive the care and attention they need, as they could potentially be permanently on display online. To remain fully operational this website would require a routine of maintenance and upgrades common to the work of those who maintain websites. Often this care work remains with the artist and their

[5] A point made by Sarah Cook in her conclusion to Bayley et al. (2023).

Fig. 2 Screenshot of *Blessed Bandwidth* provided via the artist's website, accessed 29 Jan 2023 (© Shilpa Gupta. Courtesy the artist)

network as they carry it into the future through a regime of regular small or large adjustments.

However, this work was conceived by Shilpa Gupta as a time bound project, disrupting the idea of an art object as a thing that persists over time, confounding the museum and its mission. How might we respond to this very different timescape? Does this work persist as a fragment, an incomplete record of its former self? Or might a desire emerge to develop a different form of the work that might conform more closely to the temporal logic of the museum?

In their work with the artist Ima Abasi Okon, which has been so powerfully written about by the conservators Libby Ireland and Jack McConchie (Ireland 2022; McConchie 2022), Okon challenged the conservators to slow down, to work to a different timescale so they might better understand the work and so Okon might better understand the museum.[6] This included a resistance to technologies of the

[6]For a discussion of slowness in relation to Okon's works and their conservation, please see Ireland (2022).

recorded artist interview which Okon perceived as a tool to separate her from the work, and one that also brought about a delay. Instead of storing an interview as a record for future interpretation, because the artist had asked the conservators not to record the interview, they would meet after each conversation and work together to agree what they had heard, immediately working to agree their understanding and interpretation of the conversation. The inability to rely on a recording created this moment of shared reflective practice and the need to engage in the present with what had been said. This served to change the tempo and the temporality of their work.

The selection of works by Okon that came to Tate also came with a reading list from the Chisenhale Gallery where they were first shown,[7] which provided its own pace, as those involved formed a weekly book group to work through the list in a structured and scheduled way. This created a very particular rhythm to the week for those who participated, as the texts were challenging, the task time consuming and the deadline of having read the alloted text in time important (Figs. 3 and 4).

Similarly, instead of carrying out a test install in an attempt to identify the possible future configurations of the sound and sculptural elements, learning was carried out over the days of the install, less compressed than usual due to the conditions of the pandemic. In this process the possible configurations were not closed down but instead it was agreed that those decisions would be made over time during the life and lives of the works as they unfolded, allowing for indeterminacy, ceding control and acknowledging uncertainty (McConchie 2022) These experiences disrupted the standard logic behind the processes of acquisition and display but led to a richer relationship to the care of the work.[8]

In the case of Tony Conrad's *Ten Years Alive on the Infinite Plain* (1972), the work to understand the parameters of this experimental sound and film performance when it came into Tate's collection involved understanding its fifty-year history, tracking its biography since it was first performed in 1972 and gathering memories from those involved as performers, curators and engineers in the production of performances of this experimental work. The time afforded by the research project allowed an expansive range of encounters with different moments in the history of the work, including transmitting the embodied knowledge of past performers to new performers, the acknowledgement of the limits of documentation in this task and the importance of this body-to-body transmission. This involved a recursive time of returning and looping back on memories and experiences that resisted short cuts (Figs. 5, 6, 7 and 8).

[7] For all the shows at the Chisenhale staff and the artist work together to produce a reading list. I have not experienced a situation, however, where as part of an acquisition process a reading list associated with a work was studied. For the reading list associated with this selection of works by Ima Abasi Okon, see Chisenhale (2019).

[8] For more detail, please see McConchie (2022) and Ireland (2022).

Fig. 3 Installation view Ima-Abasi Okon's display at Tate Britain, London, 2021. Images 3 and 4 show two ends of the same room, facing east (above) and west (to the right) © Ima-Abasi Okon. All rights reserved 2023. Courtesy the artist. Photo: Seraphina Neville, Tate

5 Conservation, Maintenance and Repair

As we have seen in the short descriptions of these practices of care in relation to these examples, care for these works of art involved patterns of maintenance and care that are at odds with a scientific discourse of breakthrough, where progress is made by breakthroughs that have the potential to change everything. The work of conservation described in this chapter is not heroic but reflects practices of care that require continuity in everyday acts of attention and negotiation. The evolution of conservation practice is not linear, and we learn from older forms of care and from forms of care from non-western traditions that have been overlooked by western conservation practices. It is a practice that chimes with the words of Stephen Jackson who calls for practices of maintenance and repair that are more than functional and instead

Fig. 4 Installation view Ima-Abasi Okon's display at Tate Britain, London, 2021. Images 4 and 5 show two ends of the same room, facing east (above) and west (to the right) © Ima-Abasi Okon. All rights reserved 2023. Courtesy the artist. Photo: Seraphina Neville, Tate

moral—and evoke "a very old but routinely forgotten relationship of humans to the things in the world; namely an ethics of mutual care and responsibility" (Jackson 2014, p. 231).

6 Conclusion

Conservation has scope to develop or champion different relations of care: the social, aesthetic and spiritual value in our practices of care. It is possible to change the timescapes within which we work. What I am advocating here are multiple approaches that allow for different timescapes to operate alongside each other. Museums are ambivalent about how to include, value and cultivate thicker care time, they struggle with how to value this within the management of time that is dominated by an official productionist discourse, and it feels a little subversive but mainly naïve to champion what is seen as a luxury within this culture. However, in the public imagination this is what is expected of museums.

As Puig de la Bellacasa writes, "Care time suspends the future and distends the present, thickening it with myriad multilateral demands" (Puig de la Bellacasa 2017, p. 207). She calls for a rearrangement and rebalancing of relations between a diversity of co-existing temporalities. To simply begin to notice the different

Fig. 5 Photograph taken from the performance of Tony Conrad, *Fifty-One Years on the Infinite Plain* 1972–201336, Live Arts Week II, Bologna 16 April 2013. The image shows a clock, a diagram with notes and timings and a Persian rug (Photo: Francesca Liccardi)

temporalities at work within the museum and around artworks starts to bring them into focus and adjust our modes of care. What I like about this recalibration that comes with paying attention to different temporalities, and this desire to allow for and create different possible timescapes through our practices, is that it speaks to something important to many of those who work closely with the conservation and care of artworks within the contemporary art museum. It suggests that there is an ethical demand to acknowledge, value, champion and allow space for different temporalities to emerge and be acknowledged in a world at risk of only being validated by productionist ideas of time.

Fig. 6 Feedback session after the new performers had played for the transmitters, Tate Liverpool, May 2019. Left to right violin transmitter Angharad Davies, long string drone transmitter Rhys Chatham, curator Xavier Garcia Bardon, in the background registrar Stephen Huyton and research manager Kit Webb (© Tate, Roger Sinek)

Fig. 7 Catherine Landen, George Maund and Emily Lansley performing *Ten Years Alive on the Infinite Plain* by Tony Conrad, Tate Liverpool 2019

Whilst these moments can be found in other places within the museum, when time is made, and different and slower timescapes of care time are able to emerge, *Reshaping the Collectible* created this space within the project, and this was acknowledged as perhaps the most significant contribution of the project by those who were touched by it. I would like to pay tribute to the funders and all of those